MARIOLOGY

Contributors

CYRIL VOLLERT, S.J., S.T.D.

AIDAN CARR, O.F.M.Conv., S.T.D.

GERMAIN WILLIAMS, O.F.M.Conv., S.T.D.

SALVATORE BONANO, C.M.F.

JOHN F. BONNEFOY, O.F.M., S.T.D.

GERALS VAN ACKEREN, S.J., S.T.D.

PHILIP J. DONNELLY, S.J., S.T.D.

FRANK P. CALKINS, O.S.M., S.T.D.

VERY REV. FRANCIS J. CONNEL, C.SS.R., S.T.D., LL.D

WENCESLAUS SEBASTIAN, O.F.M., S.T.D.

JUNIPER B. CAROL, O.F.M., S.T.D.

ARMAND J. ROBICHAUD, S.M.

LAWRENCE P. EVERETT, C.SS.R., S.T.D.

FIRMIN M. SCHMIDT, O.F.M., S.T.D.

Mariology

VOLUME 2

Edited by
Juniper B. Carol, OFM

MEDIATRIX PRESS
MMXIX

NIHIL OBSTAT:
Bede Babo, O.S.B. Censor librorum

IMPRIMATUR:
✠ James . McNulty Bishop of Paterson
January 2, 1957

The nihil obstat and imprimatur are official declarations that a book or pamphlet is free of doctrinal or moral error. No implication is contained therein that those who have granted the nihil obstat and imprimatur agree with the contents, opinions or statements expressed.

ISBN: 978-1-953746-23-8

©Mediatrix Press, 2018

Mariology, volume 2 is in the public domain. The typesetting and editorial changes made in this volume ©Mediatrix Press. No part of this work may be reproduced in print or electronically except for quotation in articles, blogs, and educational works.

Cover art: *Visitação*,
by Jerónimo Ezquerra, 1737.

Cover design: ©Ryan Grant.

Table of Contents

By Way of Introduction xi

The Scientific Structure of Mariology
    By CYRIL VOLLERT, S.J., S.T.D. 1

    I. Is Mariology a Science? 2
    II. Internal Structure of the Treatise 14
    III. Relation of Mariology to the Rest of Theology 25

The Fundamental Principle of Mariology
    By CYRIL VOLLERT, S.J., S.T.D. 32

    I. Nature of a Theological Principle 32
    II. What Is the Fundamental Principle of Mariology? 39

The Predestination of Our Blessed Lady
    By JOHN F. BONNEFOY, O.F.M., S.T.D. 94

    I. Principal Theological Systems on the
        Divine Plan of Creation 95
    II. The Order of Predestinations 99
    III. Conclusions 111

Mary's Immaculate Conception
    By AIDAN CARR, O.F.M.Conv., S.T.D., and
    GERMAIN WILLIAMS, O.F.M.Conv., S.T.D. 119

    Certitude of the Privilege 123
    Adversaries of the Doctrine 125
    Tenor of the Bull "Ineffabilis Deus" 125
    Argument from Scripture 127
    Argument from Tradition 136
    The Theological Argument 165
    The Position of the Blessed Virgin Relative To the Law of Original
        Sin 175
    The Immunity of Mary from Concupiscence 183

The Relation of Mary to the State Of original Justice 188

MARY'S IMMUNITY FROM ACTUAL SIN
  By SALVATORE BONANO, C.M.F. 192

  Definition of Terms 192
  Scripture Proofs 197
  Theological Proof 207
  Freedom from Imperfection 208

MARY'S DIVINE MOTHERHOOD
  By GERALD VAN ACKEREN, S.J., S.T.D. 209

  I. The Fact of Divine Motherhood 210
  II. The Essence of the Divine Motherhood 233
  III. Mary's Motherhood and Her Other Privileges 260

THE PERPETUAL VIRGINITY OF THE MOTHER OF GOD
  By PHILIP J. DONNELLY, S.J., S.T.D. 263

  I. The Witness of Scripture to the Virginity of Mary 264
  II. The Patristic Tradition Concerning Mary's Virginity 301

MARY'S FULLNESS OF GRACE
  By FRANK P. CALKINS, O.S.M., S.T.D. 337

  I. Initial Fullness 338
  II. Mary's Growth in Grace 343
  III. Final Fullness of Grace in Mary 352

OUR LADY'S KNOWLEDGE
  By VERY REV. FRANCIS J. CONNELL, C.SS.R., S.T.D., LL.D. . . . 355

  I. Beatific Knowledge 356
  II. Infused Knowledge 360

MARY'S SPIRITUAL MATERNITY
    by WENCESLAUS SEBASTIAN, .O.F.M., S.T.D. 367

    I. the Nature of Mary's Spiritual Maternity 367
    II. Theological Evidence 384

OUR LADY'S COREDEMPTION
    by JUNIPER B. CAROL, O.F.M., S.T.D. 423

    I. the Ordinary Magisterium on Mary's Coredemption.... 428
    II. The Argument from Sacred Scripture. 433
    III. The Teaching of Tradition 439
    IV. Nature and Modalities of Mary's Coredemption 458
    V. Difficulties and Solutions........................... 465
    Conclusion 473

MARY, DISPENSATRIX OF ALL GRACES
    By ARMAND J. ROBICHAUD, S.M. 476

    I. the Fact of Mary's Role as Dispensatrix of All Graces 478
    II. The Nature of Mary's Role as Dispensatrix of All Graces 505
    Conclusion 510

MARY'S DEATH AND BODILY ASSUMPTION
    by LAWRENCE P. EVERETT, C.SS.R., S.T.D. 514

    Meaning and Scope of the Definition 514
    I. the Assumptionistic Movement 523
    II. The Teaching of the Ordinary Anduniversal Magisterium 526
    III. Indications of Our Present Belief Found in Remote Testimonies 529

THE UNIVERSAL QUEENSHIP OF MARY
    By FIRMIN M. SCHMIDT, O.F.M.Cap., S.T.D............. 548

    The Notion of "King" and "Queen" 549
    Christ the King....................................... 550
    The Kingdom of Christ and Mary 552
    I. The Magisterium and the Queenship.................. 556

II. Sacred Scripture and Mary's Queenship............... 577
III. Tradition and Mary's Queenship 582
IV. The Nature and Extent of Mary's Queenship.......... 599
Conclusion... 604
Appendix 605

MARY AND THE CHURCH
by CYRIL VOLLERT, S.J., S.T.D........................ 609

I. Foundation of the Analogy 613
II. The Analogy Presented............................. 618

By Way of Introduction

HE presentation of this rather ambitious work to the learned American public fairly assumes that the reader is already familiar with the genesis, primary purpose, and general outline of our Marian trilogy, as briefly set forth in the introduction to the first volume of the set.

In harmony with the plan originally envisaged by the Editor, the present symposium undertakes to elaborate a coherent exposition of Mariology as such. We say, *as such;* for Mariology is not a composite of unrelated doctrinal data bearing on Our Blessed Lady, such as might be found scattered through biblical, patristic, liturgical, and papal documents.

Mariology being an integral part of the sacred science of theology, it must, of necessity, embody the classical pattern of theological procedure. It must, in other words, gather the manifold phases of Christian teaching relative to Our Lady's sublime mission and unique prerogatives, establish their theological justification, explore their reciprocal relationships, draw further conclusions from already acquired truths, and arrange all into a systematic and organic whole. This is precisely what the authors of the present symposium have endeavored to produce, in line with the methodology proper to the sacred discipline.

Subsequent to the period of history which inaugurated the treatment of Mariology as a distinct theological tract, countless efforts have been made, more or less successfully, toward the logically ordered presentation of the various Mariological questions. Indeed, one of the salient characteristics of the vigorous Mariological movement within recent decades has been the publication of numerous Marian treatises which evidence the specific trend of which we speak. Admittedly, such works stand as eloquent proof of the considerable progress realized in this respect. Nevertheless, it is equally obvious that the language in which they are almost invariably written renders their excellent contents somewhat inaccessible to the average English-speaking reader.

As to the few Mariological treatises already available in our own language, while we fully recognize their many merits, we feel that they were conceived and elaborated with a less ambitious scope in mind. The present symposium, on the contrary, commends itself principally for the unusual comprehensiveness of the treatment and for the impressive erudition displayed in its bibliographical apparatus. These features alone, reflecting amplitude of perspective and painstaking scholarship, sufficiently justify its publication.

Introducing a work of this nature to the public normally calls for a few preliminary observations by the Editor on such pointed questions as the right of Mariology to constitute a distinct treatise within the theological system, the exact place it ought to occupy within the series of dogmatic tracts, its internal structure grounded upon and issuing from the basic principle which gives it logical and organic coherence. These opening remarks, *de rigueur* in similar projects, serve to orient the reader through the immense field explored in subsequent dissertations, and to set forth the various sections and details of the complex Mariological fresco in their proper perspective.

Fortunately for all concerned, and very especially for the Editor, these and several other related questions have already been elucidated in masterly fashion by the distinguished Jesuit theologian, Father Cyril Vollert, in the first two chapters of this symposium. Utilizing the vast resources of his remarkable theological knowledge, Father Vollert has not only said everything that could possibly be said on these matters, but has said it with penetrating insight and incomparable brilliance. Any duplication here would — besides being redundant — only mar the lucidity of his exposition.

INTRODUCTION xiii

On the appearance of this second volume the Editor again takes occasion to acknowledge his profound indebtedness to all who have in any way aided him in the preparation and publication of this humble tribute to Our Blessed Lady. He is particularly grateful to his own religious superiors for enabling him to continue his Mariological enterprises; to the various collaborators for their learned and scholarly contributions; and to the publishers for their generous assistance and many gracious gestures.

Rev. Dr. J. B. Carol, O.F.M.
Editor

Editor's Introduction

MEDIATRIX PRESS is pleased to offer this second volume of *Mariology*, published 60 years ago. We have undertaken the work to completely reproduce this volume because it fills a vacuum in contemporary Mariology. Since the 1960s, there has been a great deal of ambiguity in the works of theologians, and at times denials of what the Church has always believed. The lack of precision in the writings of some theologians as well as the increasingly poor understanding of the faithful has largely been due to the divorce from the tradition caused by the fall in scholarship and linguistic abilities that has only increased since the 1960s. There are few books that give clarity in doctrinal teaching, let alone tracing the development from the Fathers of the Church, the Medieval Theologians, the Baroque Theologians, and these teachings and doctrines as understood and refined by the magisterium not only in those times, but comparatively recently. *Mariology* is just that book, written by theologians but accessible to the laity by its clarity of thought and organization. We hope that the republication of these volumes, especially this second volume which comprises the very heart of Mariological teaching, will fill the gap of modern knowledge with the clear teaching of the universal tradition.

We would like to especially acknowledge Fr. Michael Cunningham, FSSP, who both suggested the project and provided the original volumes. We would also to thank Jeffrey Medlock, who generously assisted with the funding of the republication. Above all, we wish to thank Ben Douglass who edited the OCR of the original, which was a herculean task given the vast amount of text and footnotes. The accuracy to the original you will find here is a fruit of his attention to detail.

Laslty, we offer this work for the Universal Church, that it may enlighten the hearts of many and provide a basis for recovering clarity in the doctrines of Our Blessed Lady, the incomparable Virgin Mary.

Post Falls, ID
2019

To His Excellency
The Most Reverend John J. Wright, D.D.
Bishop of Worcester
Episcopal Chairman of
The Mariological Society of America
Outstanding Promoter of Marian Studies
This Mariology Set Is Dedicated
With Sentiments of Profound Gratitude

Mariology

Bacteriology

The Scientific Structure of Mariology

By CYRIL VOLLERT, S.J., S.T.D.

HEOLOGY may be described as discursive wisdom about God and all other things in their relations to God, acquired under the light of divine revelation as proposed by the Church.

The subject of theology, the reality that is investigated by theologians, is God Himself. It is He, and in the last analysis He alone, as He is known to Himself and can be known to others only through supernatural revelation, who is studied in sacred theology. Yet theologians devote a great part of their scholarly energies to creatures: the Church, the sacraments, the angels, man and his moral life, the Blessed Virgin, and many other things. However, as St. Thomas points out, theology treats of such realities "under the aspect of God ... because they are related to God as to their beginning and end."[1] Theology is by no means a composite of angelology, anthropology, ecclesiology, soteriology, eschatology, etc., as pursued for their own sakes. It is a study of God as God, *sub ratione Dei*. Since the entire world proceeds from God as its efficient and exemplary cause, and is meant to return to God as its final cause, theology considers all things from the viewpoint of their reference to God.

In harmony with this truth, the general pattern of theological procedure has been permanently settled. Because the theologian's chief aim is the acquisition and exposition of knowledge about God, not only as He is in Himself, but also as He is the first cause and the ultimate end of things, particularly of rational creatures, he will treat, first, of God; second, of the rational creature's progress toward God; and third, of Christ who as man is our way to God.[2]

The mystery and the career of Christ are inconceivable without Mary, for the Incarnation took place through her. The theologian cannot reflect on the Word of God or elaborate his science without including

---

[1] S. Th., *I*, q. 1, a. 7; cf. II-II, q. 1, a. 1.
[2] *Ibid.*, I, q. 2, Introd.

the Blessed Virgin. Among the countless beings that have issued from God's creative hand, revelation places her on an eminence not to be attained by other creatures, and theology signalizes her with a title never before or since accorded to any member of the human race. Around the person of God's Mother and her unique function in the economy of salvation, many truths and thoughts of Christian tradition converge. These elements, scientifically explored and organized, combine to form Mariology, a part of theology which must be inserted and articulated into the queen of sciences and which, in turn, is called on to further the progress of theological labor by contributing to the realization of theology's high aim: the clearer, the more certain, the more abundant knowledge of God through a study of His words, His actions, and His works. Therefore, theology is about Mary.

Around the time of the fiftieth anniversary of the definition of the Immaculate Conception, that is, toward the beginning of the twentieth century, a renewed advance in Marian theology was gathering momentum. By the year 1930 the movement had become truly impressive and in many respects, particularly in precision and fruitfulness of discussion, surpassed all previous endeavors. The goal of this new movement, which shows no sign of abating but on the contrary is steadily accelerating, is no less than the achieving of a thoroughly scientific Mariology.

I. Is Mariology a Science?

The theologian's objective is *intellectus fidei*, an understanding of the faith. Quite naturally, Christ and the mystery of His person were the first truths that had to be clarified; theology started as Christology. Pressing hard in the steps of St. Paul and St. John, the two apostles who were also great theologians, the early Fathers triumphantly vindicated the divinity of Jesus Christ.

Soon thereafter the Fathers turned to Mary; for, when the fullness of time had come, the Saviour, begotten of God before the world began, was born of a woman. The foundation stone of all Mariology was laid: Mary is the Mother of God. Other stones were set in place on the foundation. One had been prepared by St. Paul, who drew out the antithesis between Christ and Adam; extension of this parallel led to the perception that Mary is the new Eve. Furthermore, although Mary was literally the Mother of God, she conceived and gave birth to Jesus without hurt to her virginity, a perfection she never lost. Again the angel had proclaimed that she was full of grace, and that God was with her in a special way. The profound implications of Gabriel's announcement slowly came to be understood. In contemplating Mary's holiness, theologians saw more and more clearly that she was free from original sin, and that at the close of her earthly life the Mother of God was gloriously assumed, body and soul, into heaven.

Theological reflection continued, and, as the centuries rolled on, a voluminous teaching about the Blessed Virgin was progressively accumulated. Like other theological disciplines, an organized Mariology could not appear except at the end of long ages of investigation, formulation, inference, and speculation. At the culmination of such a process, the need for systematic organization becomes imperative. Has this culmination been reached in Mariology? Is Mariology a scientific treatise in theology?

When the alert Christian mind applies the resources of human reason to the data of revelation about God and creatures in their relationship to God, theology begins. Since the earliest eras of the Church, an intense effort to penetrate into revealed truth has marked Catholic thought. During many hundreds of years, powerful intellects have concentrated on the enterprise. The vast mass of knowledge painstakingly gathered has been put in order by the great Christian scholars and is grouped around certain cardinal doctrines that are like centers of attraction. In this way logical parts or divisions have been devised for the convenient study and teaching of theology. By now they are traditional and even classical; they are known as theological treatises. Such a treatise is not a mere segment arbitrarily isolated and cut out of the organic whole, but is an integral part of the whole that has a special aptness for manifesting the value which a particular class of revealed truths possesses in God's design for man's salvation. The complete series of treatises, carefully worked out and harmoniously arranged, makes up the great corpus of theological teaching and embraces, so far as is possible at any stage of doctrinal progress, the entire subject matter of theological knowledge.

The scientific form of this Christian teaching is what we call theology. Since the beginning of our century theologians have engaged in prolonged reflection on the nature of theology, its object, its methods, and its scientific quality. They have tested anew the foundations of their theological syntheses and are coming back to a true understanding of St. Thomas, whose doctrine had been somewhat distorted by theories mistakenly attributed to him.

When St. Thomas replies affirmatively to the question whether Christian teaching verifies the notion of science, he understands science in the Aristotelian sense, to the extent that this concept is applicable to theology. According to Aristotle, science is knowledge of one reality in another that accounts for it; science is knowledge of a thing in its cause or principle. Such knowledge is discursive, not intuitive; we do not see consequences in their principles or properties in an essence, but have to draw them out of their source and attach them again to their source by reasoning; science is knowledge in principles and from principles. The purpose of science, thus conceived, is to reconstruct by reasoning procedures the ontological connections whereby that which is derived or subsequent in things is based on and accounted for by that which is primary.

St. Thomas did not think that he had to change the concept of science radically when he transferred it to the domain of supernatural cognition. In that order, too, science is knowledge through causes that explain why things are as they are and cannot be otherwise.[3] The great difficulty that, in spite of the infused light of faith, the principles of theology or articles of faith are not evident to us, was satisfactorily solved by the observation that theology is a subalternate science which accepts its principles from a superior science. Since theology is a science that is subalternate to the science of God and the blessed in heaven, it receives its principles from this higher science in which the principles are intrinsically evident.[4]

Rightly, then, St. Thomas does not simply identify theology with science as described by Aristotle. His question is this: Does Christian teaching verify the notion and function of science? He finds that

---

[3] Cf. *Posteriora Analytica*, lib. I, lect. 4.
[4] Cf. *S. Th.*, I, q. 1, a. 2; *In Boetium de Trinitate*, q. 2, a. 2 et ad 5.

theology meets the two requirements of any science. First, Christian teaching furnishes us with truths, intrinsically evident to God and the beatified, that are the sources of other truths. Faith adheres unquestioningly to both kinds of truths. But when we discover the values and relations among the truths of Christian teaching, we find that these truths fall into place according to an intelligible pattern in which those that express secondary and derived realities are joined, as conclusions to principles or as effects to causes or as properties to essences, to truths that express primary and principal realties.[5] And thus the second requisite of a science is fulfilled.

Accordingly, we have a science when, starting with known truths in any area open to our cognition, we advance to a knowledge of things we had not understood before. Our grasp of Christian teaching likewise takes on the form of science when, beginning with the primary truths we know by faith in consequence of our assent to the First Truth, we come to a knowledge of other truths in our customary fashion, by proceeding from principles to conclusions.[6] This knowledge is discursive; on the basis of the truths revealed to us by God, truths to which we adhere by faith, we endeavor to relate what is less clearly perceived to what is more clearly perceived, and ultimately to attach all truths in hierarchic order to the First Truth, God. Hence theological study is an effort, made by the believer, to arrive at a knowledge of all reality as God knows it, not on the level of the simple assent of faith, but on the level of our discursive reason, utilizing all the resources and procedures of scientific investigation.[7]

Theology starts out with a knowledge of a whole new world of facts and occurrences, the existence of which is attested by revelation. Contemplating these new things and events, it seeks to understand them by discovering the causes that elucidate them and link them together. The theologian studies the divine nature as revelation manifests it to him, in order to know the reason for God's teaching about Himself and His works. He desires to perceive why the realities taught by God are what they are, and why, in the designs of providence, they cannot be

---

[5] Cf. M. J. Congar, *Théologie*, in *D.T.C.*, Vol. 15, col. 459 f.
[6] St. Thomas, *In Boetium de Trinitate*, q. 2, a. 2.
[7] Congar, *art. cit.*, col. 460.

other than they are. He endeavors to find the explanation of all that the sources of revelation attribute to God, considered in Himself and in His relations with creatures.[8] He tries to apprehend the subordination and gradation among all the realities made known to him, for the purpose of building up an organic body of doctrine and of bringing into the open all the factors it actually contains. No truth he ponders has its full value apart from the whole of which it is an element, or outside the chain of causes of which it is a link and which connects all supernatural realities with the ultimate principle of their intelligibility, the divine essence itself in its infinite perfection.[9]

Since the theologian's procedure is scientific, he necessarily employs syllogistic reasoning that leads to conclusions. Yet, since his goal is an understanding of the faith, a grasp of the revealed mysteries in their relations with one another and with man's last end,[10] his main purpose in drawing conclusions is not the uncovering of remote implications of revealed truths, but an intelligent apprehension of the revealed truths themselves. The notion of a theology that strays from the truths of faith deeper and deeper into alien regions the farther it advances, has given way again to the Thomistic conception of a theology that leads to an understanding of God.[11]

Deduction is, of course, an indispensable operation in theology, and theologians rightly infer conclusions that have not been revealed. Yet the chief function of deduction in theology is not the derivation of new truths, but an ascent to a more perfect intelligence of truths that are already possessed with the certitude of faith. The theologian reasons and he understands; and his very reasoning is understanding, for he moves from principles to conclusions in order to embrace both principles and

---

[8] Cf. M. R. Gagnebet, O.P., *Nature de la théologie spéculative. II. La théologie de saint Thomas*, in *Revue Thomiste*, Vol. 44, 1938, p. 220 f.

[9] Cf. E. Marcotte, O.M.I., *De saint Thomas à nos manuels*, in *Revue de l'Université d'Ottawa*, Vol. 16, 1946, p. 166*.

[10] Cf. Vatican Council, *Const. de fide catholica*, cap. 4; D.B., 1796.

[11] See B. Lonergan, S.J., *Theology and Understanding*, in *Gregorianum*, Vol. 35, 1954, pp. 630-648. This article is a sympathetic critique of J. Beumer, *Theologie als Glaubensverständnis* (Würzburg, 1953), with a needed corrective to Beumer's exposition of theology according to the mind of St. Thomas.

conclusions in one comprehensive view.[12]

To the mind of St. Thomas, at any rate, the scientific character of theology is not gauged by the deduction of new, unrevealed truths; theology as science is the rational organization of Christian teaching, effected by joining truths that are conclusions to truths that are principles.[13] From the argument of appropriateness to the derivation of consequences, St. Thomas engages in the contemplation of revealed truth, and his aim is to know and elaborate, through the complicated processes of discursive reasoning, what God knows in the absolute simplicity of intuition.[14] The final objective of theological study is not the knowledge of conclusions, but the knowledge of God such as He has revealed Himself to us.

Accordingly, theology, so far as it can within the limits of human, rational activity, imitates and tries to reproduce the knowledge God has of Himself. As St. Thomas says, it is a sort of impress of God's own knowledge, *impressio divinae scientiae*, which is one and simple, yet reaches out to everything.[15]

The general effort at self-examination made by theology is particularly significant when applied to Mariology. The twentieth century is active in perfecting a special treatise on the Blessed Virgin; Marian Theology is in full course of progress. Although the content of revelation about Mary is restricted to a few sentences in the Bible and to brief passages in the ancient Fathers concerning the woman who is the Mother of God and the new Eve, under the guidance of the Holy Spirit immense wealth has been mined from these sources. Indeed, what is knowable about Mary and her redemptive office is so abundant that countless works have been written on the subject. However, in spite of the advance that has been made, Mariology has not yet acquired its full development. Theological endeavor has ample opportunity to exert itself in order to construct by research, reflection, and discursive reasoning, an ordered and coherent corpus of Marian doctrine which is capable and worthy of occupying a distinctive place among the treatises of

---

[12] *Ibid.* See also St. Thomas, *S. Th.*, I, q. 14, a. 7; q. 79, a. 8; II-II, q. 8, a. 1 ad 2.
[13] M. J. Congar, in *Bulletin Thomiste*, Vol. 5, 1938, p. 500.
[14] M. D. Chenu, O.P., *La théologie comme science au XIIIe siècle* (2nd ed., 1943), p. 98.
[15] *S. Th.*, I, q. 1, a. 3 ad 2.

theological science, and which, thus articulated as a part in the whole, may in turn contribute to the end of theological study, the more certain and perfect knowledge of God in Himself, in His actions, and in His effects.

When theologians ask whether Mariology may rightfully be regarded as a special treatise in theology, their inquiry is theoretical and methodological. Practically considered, the question has long been answered in the affirmative. Theologians coming after Suárez have actually constructed such a treatise, as their predecessors had erected treatises on the Trinity, Christology, and the sacraments. They had every right to proceed as they did, for they had copious materials to classify and principles that permitted a synthesis.

Yet the methodological question has been repeated. Do we have good reasons and sufficient means for achieving, on the basis of Catholic teaching about the Blessed Virgin, a discipline that will be truly theological and that will constitute a special part of the sacred doctrine?[16] Is Mariology rightly a distinct treatise in dogmatic theology? Can or ought the study of what revelation discloses on the subject of the Blessed Virgin result in a series of questions organically connected so as to form a doctrinal whole that exposes the value of a vital element of our faith, irreducible to any other class of revealed truths?[17]

The response to such queries depends on the place and function that are to be assigned to Mary, according to God's plan, in the economy of salvation. The reason for a distinct treatise on Mariology as an integral part of theology can be discerned only in this perspective, in which Mary is the Saviour's Mother who takes her stand at the side of her Son with a personal role in the accomplishment of our salvation. Although a perception of the details of Mary's cooperation is the fruit of centuries of contemplation and has not yet been completely elucidated, a substratum of doctrine was possessed by the Fathers in common with later theologians. The Fathers beheld in Mary, not only the Mother of Christ, but an associate who shared in the redemptive activity of the

---

[16] J. Lebon, *L'élaboration d'un traité théologique de mariologie est-elle possible?*, in Journées Sacerdotales Mariales (Dinant, 1952), p. 15.

[17] E. Druwé, S.J., *Position et structure du traité mariale*, in Bulletin de la Societé Française d'Études Mariales, Vol. 2, 1936, p. 11.

Saviour. From early times Mary was recognized, though not with the clearer insight of contemporary theologians, as mediatrix of salvation. In this general sense, at least, her mediatory office is a truth taught by the Church. Inheriting that much, theologians have enough to assert the right of Mariology to be a theological treatise.

Not every exposition of Marian doctrine is a treatise in Mariology. In some manuals written a generation ago, we are likely to find a number of pages about the Blessed Virgin, complementing a discussion of Christology and soteriology. But Mariology is not a mere appendix to the Incarnation or a collection of scattered truths about Mary in conjunction with the birth of Christ. Other textbooks reveal a situation that is still less satisfactory. In various parts of the courses on dogmatic theology and even in different volumes, truths about the Blessed Virgin are introduced as exceptions to the common designs of divine providence. The Immaculate Conception is viewed as an exemption from the universal law of original sin, the Assumption is taken to be an anticipation of the general resurrection, and so on. Even if such dispersed theses were brought together in one book bearing a distinctive title, they would not constitute a true treatise of Mariology, because they would not be a systematic exposition of questions organically linked and stressing a vital factor in the economy of salvation.

A treatise is not a simple series of chapters or theses referring to a single subject. To be a treatise, all the truths knowable about the subject must be reduced to unity through a consolidating principle that will dominate the entire development and will enable us to appreciate, in due perspective, the importance of every aspect that has a bearing on the intelligibility of the whole. The deepest foundation on which the structure stands must be reached, and it must support the complete edifice as a unit and in all its parts. Briefly, the treatise must be scientific. For a treatise in theology is an integral part of theology, which has the function and verifies the notion of science.

No one would maintain that every book written about the Blessed Virgin is scientific; far from it. To be scientific, all the truths that integrate Mariology must be arranged in a coherent system of principles and conclusions, governed by one fundamental principle. The documents on which it is based must be investigated, their authenticity must be critically established, texts must be interpreted according to rigorous exegetical norms. But these labors of positive theology are not enough; the entire discipline must be organized under the unity of a single principle that will sustain, link together, and illuminate all the realities ascertained by the study of documents, so as to foster a clear and comprehensive vision of Mary's function in the mystery of salvation.

That Mariology is, or can be, scientific is the conviction of all theologians. It is undoubtedly capable of being formed into an organic system of truths logically articulated in the light of principles received from God. It is a part of the science of theology and, like all theology, is originally taught by God through revelation. It also teaches about God, as all theology does; no creature can equal the Blessed Virgin, Mother of God, in making God known to us. Finally, it leads to God, for Mary, in association with her Son from whom she is inseparable, is the way to God for us all.

Repeated pronouncements by the Holy See in recent times and intensified study by theologians have opened up vast areas of knowledge about the Mother of God. Her unique mission in the economy of redemption is being more clearly perceived. Grave questions remain to be solved; various aspects of Mary's association with the Saviour clamor for clarification; the need of the mind for understanding has to be satisfied. The task of theology is to supply answers that will enable us to know better the perfection of God through the work He accomplishes in the greatest of His creatures. Subject matter for a special treatise in Mariology is at hand in rich abundance. Moreover, the many truths relative to the Blessed Virgin are known by God, and are knowable by us, not in isolation or without connection, but unified in a logically ordered synthesis. Therefore, the special treatise can be scientific.

Fully to realize the potentialities of his science, the Mariologist has to meet certain requirements.[18] Remarkable progress has been made. Yet theology has never entertained the thought that further improvement is impossible. Mariology must continue to interrogate itself, verify its bases, examine its sources, test the quality of the arguments it uses to develop these sources, and explore the avenues of future advance. The

---

[18] Cf. A. Mouraux, *Quelles sont les conditions de la valeur d'un traité théologique de mariologie?*, in *Journées Sacerdotales Mariales* (Dinant, 1952), pp. 31-76.

Mariologist may never lose sight of the fact that his profession is closely linked with the mission he has received from the magisterium and involves responsibilities to the Christian populace.

However, the theologian's main task is not the guidance of Christian piety. His constructive work is in the domain of knowledge, not of edification or conversion. After he has discharged his proper office, he may adopt another attitude that is more apostolic. But his primary concern is the investigation of the deposit of revelation.[19]

This revelation has been confided to the magisterium of the Church, from which the theologian receives it, guaranteed by the stamp of God's own authority. Theology without the magisterium is no more possible than is Christianity without the Church. Since Christ has delivered to the Church the whole deposit of revelation, that is, Sacred Scripture and tradition, to preserve, defend, and interpret, the magisterium is the proximate and universal norm of truth in matters of faith and morals for every theologian.[20] Possessing this rule and fortified by all the resources of reason illuminated by faith, the theologian is equipped for work.

Once he has searched out and explained the present teaching of the magisterium, the theologian is ready for his next step, study of the remote sources. The magisterium possesses these sources, for it has received them from God; the magisterium, in turn, gives them over to the theologian, and supplies him with an authentic interpretation of them. To theology is entrusted the noble task of showing how the truths taught by the living magisterium are contained, explicitly or implicitly, in Sacred Scripture and tradition.[21] That is the work of positive theology, which undertakes its scrutiny according to the mind of the Church, not in pursuit of the possibly magnificent phantoms of the investigator's own creative imagination.

Reason naturally desires to plumb the content of revelation communicated by faith, and it is here that scientific theology, in the Scholastic sense of science, has its opportunity. Speculation achieves its objective by exploiting all the powers of reason, to arrive at some

---

[19] Pius XII, Encycl. *Humani generis*, in *A.A.S.*, Vol. 42, 1950, p. 568.

[20] *Ibid.*, p. 567; see also pp. 563, 569, 576.

[21] *Ibid.*, p. 568 f.

intelligence of revealed reality. In the light of the living faith, the theologian must interrogate the ancient witnesses and draw on their insights to vitalize his own speculations.

The same requirements must be met by the Mariologist, for Mariology is true theology. Its task is the scientific study of revelation concerning the Blessed Virgin. God has disclosed to us the necessary mystery of His trinitarian life and the free mystery of man's salvation that is effected through the redemptive Incarnation. The main quest in Mariology is the discovery of Mary's place and function in the divine program of redemption, an undertaking that safeguards for Mariology its theological character, that is, its constant reference to God. The theologian's proper business is the investigation of facts, not of possibilities; and in the domain of Mariology these facts originate in God's wise and freely devised plan, which is not known to man except by divine revelation. Consequently, this plan cannot be fabricated by us through a process of rigorous deduction, as in the science of geometry.[22]

Therefore, the Mariologist "must always go back to the sources of divine revelation," and these sources "contain treasures of truth so numerous and rich that they will never be exhausted."[23] Scripture and tradition are the remote sources, for the teaching Church is the proximate source. Hence the Mariologist must first interrogate the magisterium, with the purpose of making a methodical inventory of its teachings, properly evaluating their sense and their degree of certitude. As the liturgy is one of the organs of the magisterium, it can furnish testimonies and proofs that are valuable to Mariology.[24]

The teaching of the magisterium is the point of departure and the guide for further researches into Scripture and tradition. Even after a doctrine has been defined, such researches are necessary to contribute precision and enhance understanding. They are strongly encouraged by the Church, which assigns to theology the duty of showing how the defined dogma is contained in the deposit of revelation.[25] Pope Pius XII sets an example in the Apostolic Constitution on the Assumption; after

---

[22] A. Mouraux, *art. cit.*, p. 45.
[23] Pius XII, *Humani generis*, A.A.S., Vol. 42, 1950, p. 568.
[24] Pius XII, *Munificentissimus Deus*, in A.A.S., Vol. 42, 1950, p, 758 ff.
[25] Pius XII, *Humani generis*, loc. cit.

affirming that the actual unanimity of the teaching Church is a sufficient criterion, he summons the witnesses of tradition to give their deposition. Their testimonies occupy an important part in the document.

The speculation that takes up where positive theology leaves off must proceed *sedulo,* with care and incisive acumen, yet at the same time *sobrie,* with due measure and prudence. The speculative theologian must maintain contact with the sources. His work may not anticipate the research of the positive theologian but must follow it and find support in it; revealed truth regulates every phase of theological activity. The procedures to be employed by speculative theology have been indicated by the Vatican Council.[26] To arrive at a more perfect understanding of revelation, reason should seek clarity from similarities it apprehends between naturally known things and the supernatural world. Knowledge of relations among human beings, such as the relations existing between a son and his mother, between a mediator and the people he is trying to reconcile, can direct the mind to a better grasp of relations in the supernatural order. Ideas gained from a consideration of secular royalty can aid toward a description of the regal dignity of Christ and Mary. Other comparisons brought out by positive theology or presented by the liturgy yield illuminating insights. The parallel between Eve and Mary is particularly fruitful; as Eve contributed to our fall, so Mary has cooperated in our redemption. The striking points of likeness between Mary and the Church are being intensively studied by Mariologists of our time.

The Vatican Council further directs the theologian to promote understanding by searching out the connections that exist among the mysteries of revelation, particularly the connection with man's last end. Such bonds are real, for God's plan is unified. They are epspecially important in Mariology, as *Munificentissimus Deus* points out, in passages that stress the harmony which, by God's will, prevails among Mary's privileges and functions.[27]

A Mariology that is constructed in accord with these ideals is truly scientific. It is a subalternate science which receives its principles, the articles of faith, from the higher science of God. It fulfills the two

---

[26] *Const. de fide catholica,* cap. 4; *D.B.,* 1796.

[27] *A.A.S.,* Vol. 42, 1950, pp. 754, 758-761.

requisites of science, for it possesses truths that are sources of other truths, and joins derived truths or conclusions to primary truths or principles, relating what is less clearly perceived to what is more clearly perceived, and eventually to God, the First Truth. It is knowledge of realities in other realities that account for them, grasping both principles and conclusions in a unified, comprehensive view. Its final end is the reproduction in ourselves of God's own knowledge of Himself and of His works, faint though that reflection may be, for it is but discursive science as compared with God's infinitely perfect intuition.

Accordingly Mariology may be defined as a distinct, though by no means separate or isolated, part of the science of theology, which treats of the Blessed Virgin Mary, Mother of God, from the viewpoint of her position and function in the divine economy of salvation.

II. Internal Structure of the Treatise

Contemporary Mariologists are devoting much thought to the problem of the structure of their science. Progress has been realized and will continue; yet a thoroughly satisfactory treatise has still to be written. Two tendencies are current, and have been succinctly described by M. J. Congar. Of the two ways of constructing a theological treatise about the Blessed Virgin, the one that has been too often adopted proceeds according to the following scheme. Having learned once for all that Mary is the Mother of the Incarnate Word and that on this score she enjoys exceptional privileges, theologians of the first persuasion consider her as she is in herself, elaborate a sort of metaphysics concerning her by deducing a series of timeless attributes, and unroll more and more consequences of these privileges. Their procedure is like that of the philosopher or theologian who, in the treatise on God, deduces His attributes from the principle of His absolute perfection. Use is made of principles that are disputable, such as the axiom: "Mary has by grace all that God has by nature and that is compatible with the condition of a creature." Congar thinks that this is a poor method of working out a theology on the subject of Mary, and he does not see how Mariologists who limit themselves to it can reconcile their procedure with the principle, inscribed on every page of Sacred Scripture, of the liberty with which God dispenses grace, and of the free and positive nature of all that depends on His election.

Fortunately, this tendency is on the wane. Other theologians are much more intent on investigating biblical sources and on developing a theology that is more solidly rooted in tradition. Mariologists of this second kind, whose number is likely to increase, view Mariology in the light of the economy of salvation, of the free designs of God's grace, as made known by the witness of Scripture interpreted according to the tradition of the Church.[28] A sign of the shift in attitude is the favorable reception accorded to R. Laurentin's aphorism: "Everything can be connected with the mystery of the Blessed Virgin's maternity; practically nothing can be deduced from it."[29] This is perhaps an exaggeration, but it points in the right direction.

In any case, the necessity of erecting Mariology on the rock of faith must be emphasized; theology has to rest on revelation. Speculative theology may not be separated from positive theology. A theology that does not constantly revert to its foundations, that does not ever seek to vitalize itself at the sources of revelation, is ready to sign its death warrant. That is true of all theology, and it is true of Mariology. The passages of the New Testament that formally teach us about Mary must be thoroughly exploited by all the resources of exegesis. Other biblical texts in which Mary is not expressly named, from the third chapter of Genesis, through the Psalms, the sapiential books, the prophets, and up to the Apocalypse with its vision of the woman clothed with the sun, must be probed, sifted, interpreted, and applied. Tradition is likewise indispensable. It is needed as a guide toward an understanding of Scripture and as a witness to the unceasing growth of comprehension in the mind of the Church concerning the Blessed Virgin's place in the economy of salvation.[30] Studies of the sources must be conducted in the full light of the teachings of the magisterium. If that is done, the

---

[28] M. J. Congar, *Notes théologiques à propos de l'Assomption*, in *Dieu Vivant*, Vol. 18, 1951, p. 109 f.

[29] *Le movement mariologique à travers le monde*, in *La Vie Spirituelle*, Vol. 86, 1952, p. 183.

[30] Cf. E. Druwé, S.J., *Position et structure du traité mariale*, in *Bulletin de la Société Française d'Études Mariales*, Vol. 2, 1936, p. 33.

fecundity of theological speculation is assured.[31] Piloted by the magisterium, the theologian can decide what ought to be kept or abandoned in the Mariological efforts of the past, and can prepare the way for Mariological progress in the future.

Such progress will be fostered if the Mariologist constantly keeps before his eyes several norms that ought to regulate the structure of the treatise. In the first place, unity is essential. The basic principle of the treatise must control its entire development, provide the standard for an accurate appreciation of the relative importance of its various parts, and direct the organization of all the truths about Mary into a well-integrated science. Furthermore, Mariology must be closely linked to Christology. Mary exists for Christ. Christology and Mariology must be joined in our knowledge because Christ and Mary are joined in reality. Lastly, the true place of Mariology in the whole of theology must be clearly discerned and correctly assigned. Its due prominence must be recognized and its full value must be safeguarded. It may not be omitted from the theological synthesis or allotted the status of a poor relation.

Some authors, perceiving the necessity of associating Mary with Christ in the enterprise that is common to both of them, wish to develop Christology and Mariology in parallel lines and to model the latter on the former. The Abbé Bonnichon goes so far as to suggest a "reform" that consists in breaking up the course *De Beata Maria Virgine* and distributing its theses among the other treatises of theology. Since the mystery of Jesus and the mystery of Mary illuminate each other, why not join them step by step throughout? The thesis on the Immaculate Conception is inserted into the treatise *De peccato*. Study of the divine maternity forms part of *De Verbo incarnato* and is followed by the thesis on Mary's perpetual virginity. Consideration of Christ's grace is followed by the corresponding thesis on Mary's sanctity. Our Lady's spiritual motherhood complements the theses on Christ's capital grace. The section on Mary as Coredemptrix is attached to the treatise *De Christo Redemptore*, and the Assumption is added at this point. Room is found in the treatise *De Ecclesia* for Mary's queenship; the course *De*

---

[31] Cf. Pius XII, *Humani generis*, in *A.A.S.*, Vol. 42, 1950, p. 568.

gratia is the place for her universal mediation.[32]

The author thinks that this scheme has the advantage of displaying the close union between the mystery of Jesus and that of Mary; it sets forth the divine plan in all its sweetness, of which the Blessed Virgin's constant collaboration is not the least cause. He sees only one real disadvantage: the unity of Mariology would be destroyed and the strong coherence of the treatise would be weakened. In reply to this objection, he asserts that his proposal of integrating most of Mariology into Christology assures rather than imperils its unity.

In the discussion that followed the reading of Bonnichon's paper at the 1936 meeting of the French Mariological Society, the Abbé Petit mentioned that over the years he had taught Mariology ten times. He had employed both methods, that of fusing Mariology with other treatises, and that of presenting it as a distinct discipline. His experimentation had convinced him that the advantages of the second method were far superior.[33] Agreement with this criticism is expressed by F. J. Connell. Presentation of the theology of Our Lady as a separate treatise stresses the importance of Mariology and brings out the momentous fact that Mary's part in the divine plan of salvation was far greater than merely providing the Incarnate Word with a body in which He was to endure suffering.[34]

Notwithstanding Bonnichon's assurances, J. Thomas perceives the threat to the very existence of Mariology that is inherent in the suggested "reform." He admits that, since Jesus and Mary, constituting a single principle of life for humanity, are joined to the point of being but one, the ideal would be that the two sciences, Christology and Mariology, should also be but one. However, their fusion would be fatal to clarity of ideas. In his view, the best structure of a treatise in Mariology would be a plan that groups all the truths about the Blessed Virgin together, but at the same time connects them with Christ. He likens his own formula to a great Christological fresco exhibiting the

---

[32] Bonnichon, *Rapport sur la pratique de l'enseignement de la théologie mariale*, in *Bulletin de la Société Française d'Études Mariales*, Vol. 2, 1936, p. 61 f.

[33] *Ibid.*, p. 82.

[34] *Toward a Systematic Treatment of Mariology*, in *Marian Studies*, Vol. 1, 1950, p. 57; cf. p. 58 ff.

realization of God's design for salvation and devised as a diptych, in which Christ occupies the primary place and Mary takes her subordinate place. Such a fresco would show forth the unity of mediation in the duality of the mediators.[35]

To secure this unity in duality, a preliminary chapter on the predestination of Christ and Mary is set at the head of the two divisions of the single treatise. Such a chapter will show that Mary is willed by God along with Christ to be comediatrix with the Mediator. The treatise itself will unfold in a sort of diptych in which Christ and Mary are studied in parallel fashion. There will be three parts to the treatise and each will include two sections. The first part treats of the person of the Mediator, and is followed by a study of the person of the mediatrix. The second part takes up the work of the Mediator, and then the work of the mediatrix. Finally, the third part considers the glory of the Mediator, and is completed by a consideration of the glory of the mediatrix.[36]

This contrivance preserves Mariology as a distinct division of theology, but one that is not studied for itself alone. The difficulties are solved by treating Christ and Mary *per modum unius* in the preliminary chapter and by subsequently developing Christology and Mariology in a fresco with two panels. Thomas believes that his proposal discloses the true sense of Mary's mediation, which, though subordinate, is essential and is modeled on that of Christ because in reality the two are one. There is a single mediation, but it is carried out by two agents who are associated by God's eternal will.[37]

A previous attempt to match Christology and Mariology had been made by R. Bernard, O.P., who wished to derive an entire theology of the Blessed Virgin from the theology of the Incarnate Word, in such a way as to pattern the former exactly, step by step, on the former.[38] The idea did not arouse enthusiasm. M. Becqué, C.SS.R., thought that the endeavor to harmonize the two treatises in every detail would turn out

---

[35] J. Thomas, *Quelle est la meilleure structure interne d'un traité théologique de Mariologie?*, in *Journées Sacerdotales Mariales* (Dinant, 1952), p. 108 f.

[36] *Ibid.*, pp. 109-118.

[37] *Ibid.*, p. 124.

[38] *La maternité spirituelle de Marie et la pensée de Saint Thomas*, in *Bulletin de la Société Française d'Études Mariales*, Vol. 1, 1935, pp. 105-114.

quite defective.[39] In all such projects, the treatise on the Incarnate Word, which is usually divided into two parts, Christology and soteriology, is followed by a bad copy, Mariology and Marian soteriology. The chapters written about Christ, His mediatorial work, and His glorification are re-edited under a Marian label. The clarity produced by such iteration is illusory. We have not been redeemed twice, first by Christ and then by Mary, mediatrix of all graces. No one thinks that we have, but even the appearance of caricature ought to be shunned.[40] The truth is that Mary is not a simple replica of Christ. The respective missions of both would be falsified if they were forcibly compressed into a single scheme. A rigid system may not be substituted for the living reality of the mystery.[41]

The light of experience gained from teaching Mariology guides M. M. Philipon in drawing up the broad outlines of the plan he prefers. In Mariological science the divine motherhood has the same pivotal role as the hypostatic union in Christology. The treatise is divided into major parts, following the distinction between the order of being and the order of operation, as in the treatise on the mystery of Christ.

The first part is a scientific study based on causes. Mary's divine motherhood, viewed against the background of the redemptive Incarnation, is the constantly recurring theme. The essential nature of the divine maternity and its connection with the hypostatic order must be determined. Then the consequences of the divine motherhood are to be drawn out. These are: (*a*) in regard to God, special relationships with the Blessed Trinity; (*b*) in regard to Christ, Mary's association with Christ as the new Eve, coredemptrix of the world; (*c*) in regard to mankind, the spiritual motherhood; (*d*) in itself, Mary's fullness of grace and all her personal privileges. The first part is concluded by a study of Mary as universal mediatrix, which sums up the whole mystery as the name "Mediator" sums up the whole mystery of Christ.

In the second part, the great acts of mediation in Mary's life are investigated. Mention of the prophecies of the Old Testament bearing on

---

[39] *Que penser des essais modernes de réalization d'un traité de mariologie*, in *Journées Sacerdotales Mariales* (Dinant, 1952), p. 102.

[40] Cf. G. Philips, *Lugar de la mariología en la teología católica*, in *Estudios Marianos*, Vol. 10, 1950, p. 9.

[41] Cf. R. Laurentin, *Marie et l'Église*, in *La Vie Spirituelle*, Vol. 86, 1952, p. 304.

Mary is followed by a consideration of the acts of God's Mother on behalf of mankind: her cooperation at the Incarnation, her coredemptive compassion at the foot of the cross, and her mediatory activity in heaven. By way of general conclusion the cult of Mary is studied; it comprises the cult of hyperdulia and the Marian devotions practiced in the Church.[42]

Construction of a truly organic treatise of Mariology requires a thorough analysis of the Blessed Virgin's divine maternity and its illustration by the analogy of human maternity, considered in all the wealth of its spiritual elements.[43] The divine motherhood, root of all the supernatural prerogatives of Mary, perfectly explains her collaboration in the work of our redemption on earth and our sanctification in heaven, as well as her own glorification. Analysis of the divine maternity suffices to account for all her gifts, which are the principles enabling her to perform her mission.[44]

The disruptive effects of Bonnichon's suggestion, which proposes a fusion of Christology and Mariology, and the element of artificiality discerned in the "fresco" designed by Thomas, which envisions Mariology as a parallel to Christology or its minor counterpart, can be avoided without in any way impairing the structure of Marian theology. In fact, the integrity of both treatises requires the preservation of the unity of each as a distinct part of theology.

The divine maternity is the bond forever uniting Mary with Christ, and therefore Mariology with Christology.[45] Likewise the divine maternity, not as viewed by us "in the abstract" but as viewed by God in His infinite wisdom, is the basis of Mary's enduring union with her Son in life, mediatorial activity on earth and in heaven, and eternal glorification. At the head of all Catholic beliefs about Mary stands the

---

[42] M. M. Philipon, O.P., *The Mother of God* (Westminster, Md., 1953), p. 132 ff.

[43] This has been done with remarkable competence by M. J. Nicolas, O.P., *Le concept intégral de maternité divine*, in *Revue Thomiste*, Vol. 42, 1937, pp. 58-93, 230-272. See also the article by G. Van Ackeren, S.J., *Mary's Divine Motherhood*, in the present volume.

[44] F. M. R. Gagnebet, O.P., *Questions mariales*, in *Angelicum*, Vol. 22, 1945, p. 167.

[45] From all eternity the Mother of God is united with the Incarnate Word *uno eodem decreto*, in one and the same mysterious decree of predestination. Cf. Pius XII, *Munificentissimus Deus*, in *A.A.S.*, Vol. 42, 1950, p. 768.

truth that she is the Mother of Jesus, and therefore the Mother of God. Her motherhood engages her in the mystery of the Incarnation; therefore, she is associated with Christ in His mission and His work.

To understand the divine maternity, we must recall that the universe of creatures is divided into three great orders, according to their relationship with God.[46] If creatures are simply effects of God, made to His image and gathered together in an orderly world the better to resemble Him, we have the order of nature. If they are, in addition, united to God by supernatural knowledge and love, we have the order of grace, which all spiritual creatures are invited to enter. If a created nature is taken into a personal union with God, we have the hypostatic order, which the Incarnate Word occupies and which draws to itself the orders of nature and of grace. Mary belongs to this hypostatic order because she is the Mother of God. She is not substantially united to God, but has a unique relation of real affinity[47] with the Second Person of the Trinity. Her divine motherhood elevates her above every creature; inseparable from her Son, she is in the hypostatic order, along with the human nature of the Word, above the entire universe and the world of grace.[48]

Since the order of grace is wholly orientated to the hypostatic order, which is its foundation, exemplary cause, and end, it must find its summit and fullness in those who occupy the hypostatic order, that is, in the human soul of Christ and in the soul of His Mother. The person who stands closest to Christ, the source of grace, receives grace in plenitude from that source. This person is His Mother, for from her He received His human nature. Therefore, the Blessed Virgin is the "one full

---

[46] Cf. M. J. Nicolas, O.P., *Essai de synthèse mariale*, in *Maria. Études sur la Sainte Vierge*, ed. H. du Manoir, S.J., Vol. 1 (Paris, 1949), pp. 707-741. The sketch of the internal structure of Mariology attempted in the following pages utilizes some of the ideas expressed in this excellent article, which in turn capitalizes on the Dominican theologian's previous study, mentioned in note 43 above.

[47] Cf. St. Thomas, *S. Th.*, III, q. 27, a. 4.

[48] This does not imply that Mary is "thereby snatched away from us," as A. Müller objects in *Divus Thomas* (Freiburg), Vol. 29, 1951, p. 398. On the contrary, it is the very reason why she is so close to us in the order of grace, and especially why she is our Mother, as will appear later.

of grace."[49] Mary's fullness of grace involves, in turn, her Immaculate Conception, her freedom from personal sin throughout her life, and her complete consecration to God without reserve. These great gifts are all revealed, and are entirely intelligible in the light of the divine motherhood.

The same is true of Mary's perpetual virginity. Her maternity, regarded "in the abstract," can be thought of without this prerogative.

In the physical order, indeed, a certain repugnance between maternity and virginity is encountered.[50] Yet, with revelation before us, we can readily comprehend why the womb of God's Mother, made fruitful by the action of the Holy Spirit, should preserve an intact virginity at the birth of Christ and ever afterward.[51]

Our Lady's mediatorial office is likewise intelligible. Her divine motherhood locates her in the hypostatic order, in closest proximity to God, who employs the most perfect beings, the ones nearest to Him, as intermediaries between Him and less perfect beings. Consequently, the Mother of God, along with the man Christ and in total dependence on Him, is called on to share in the works of divine mercy. Furthermore, Mary accomplished a true work of mediation by the very fact that she became the Mother of God, because by her personal action she rejoined two extremes that had been sundered. Ever thereafter, filled with the same love and desire to serve that had animated her soul at the Incarnation, she could not cease to promote the union of God and man. Her continued mediation is but a prolongation of her divine maternity.

The mediatorial character of Mary's motherhood is traditionally manifested in the ancient theme of the new Eve. By her obedience, her freely yielded *fiat,* she welcomed in herself the incarnation of Him who is the source of life, and thus has given life to the world. Christ is the new Adam, the new first man, in whom man receives a new origin and a new life. The obedience of Christ saves us, as the disobedience of Adam devastated us. Mary is the new Eve, the new first woman, in this resumption of the creative plan, this regeneration of the human race. She is the mother of the newly living through intimate association with Him

---

[49] St. Thomas, *S. Th.*, III, q. 27, a. 5; cf. q. 7, aa. 1, 9, 13.
[50] Cf. Elias de la Dolorosa, in *Estudios Marianos,* Vol. 3, 1944, p. 48.
[51] Cf. J. Lebon, in *Journées Sacerdotales Mariales, p.* 23.

who is their head.

Woman was created to be the companion of man, his associate in life and particularly in the transmission of life. That is true of the original creation, and is true of God's regenerative plan. God becomes man and is the new prototype of the human race. By her motherhood, the woman is associated with Him in closest community of life. The man is God, the woman is Mother of God. To call her the new Eve is to call her His companion. She is associated with Him in the divine life of grace and in the propagation of the same divine life of grace.

Her association with Christ is a consequence of her divine maternity. To tell the truth, an ordinary mother is not the lifelong associate of her child. In fact she becomes more and more separated from him as time goes on and he matures. He has his own work and life, and finds the complement of his being in another woman. But the divine motherhood is not an ordinary motherhood. The Word existed eternally before Mary was born. He chose her as His Mother, and by becoming incarnate in her contracted with her a bond that has no equivalent in ordinary motherhood and that recalls, while it incomparably transcends, the bond that exists between spouses. Thus Mary's association with Christ stems from the Incarnation of the Word in her womb, from her divine maternity.

An exercise of this association is Mary's cooperation in our Redemption. Christ's mediation is wrought in three phases: in the Incarnation, in the Redemption by which the God-Man performed the sacrificial act that reunited man with God, and in eternal life whereby the risen Christ communicates to men from heaven, one by one, the graces He merited for them by His passion and death. How could the new Eve, associated with the new Adam in the first and third phases of His mediation, be deprived of a part in the second? This would imply a misunderstanding of the organic linking of these three phases; Mary would have no share in the dispensing of grace if she had no part in its acquisition. And she would have no such function if she were not the consecrated *Socia Christi* by her maternity. To give the Incarnate Word to us was not enough for her; in order to have her proper part in the causality of the new life which her Son desires to live in the soul of every man, she had to consent to His death and offer Him to God in sacrifice.

What else should we expect? Mary is the perfect Mother, entirely Mother, with all her energies centered in her only Son and His life's work, for He is her life and apart from Him she has none of her own. Perfect Mother, she exists wholly for Him. She is the only Mother in the world who can exist exclusively for her Son, for He is the only Son in all the universe who is God — her Son and her very end, the end of her person and her activity. His will is hers, and therefore she cooperates with Him in every detail of His life and death. If He suffers, she joins Him in suffering. If He wills to die, she also wills Him to die. If He desires to sacrifice Himself on the cross for man's salvation, she desires the same and with all her heart offers Him to the Father for the Redemption of the world.[52]

Thus associated with her Son in the redemptive act of sacrifice, Mary is further associated with Him in heaven for distributing the graces of salvation and sanctification that were merited on Calvary. As always, Christ has the main action; but in complete accord with Him and dependence on Him, the Mother contributes to the birth of the children of God and to their growth in the life of grace.

Christ's total victory over sin entails His total victory over death, the wages of sin, by His glorious resurrection. Mary's maternal contribution to the victory over sin makes intelligible her anticipated glorification in body and soul by her Assumption into heaven. The connection between the Assumption and the divine maternity is even more direct. The sacred body of the Incarnate Word could not be suffered to undergo the corruption of the grave; how could He allow the body from which He issued and with which, in His human nature, He eternally preserves a relation of origin and dependence, to crumble into dust?

Lastly, Mary is the universal Mother. Her whole finality is to be the Mother of God, the God-man Jesus Christ. But Jesus Christ is the head to which are to be joined many members, who make up His mystical body, the Church, the two forming a single mystical person, the Whole Christ. Therefore, she who has given birth to the head cannot fail to give birth to the members. Mother of the historical Christ, her motherhood

---

[52] These considerations, succinctly expressed, are the fruit of several discussions with my colleague, G. Van Ackeren, S.J.

embraces the Whole Christ.

At the Incarnation she conceived us spiritually, for her maternal action inaugurated the generation of the mystical Christ. On Calvary she bore us spiritually, for there she cooperated maternally to bring about our rebirth in Christ, by gaining for us, in subordination to Him, the graces of our incorporation into His body. And her mediatory action in heaven is maternal, not only by the love that animates it, but by its proper effect, which is the supernatural birth of men and their growth in divine life. This maternity is the exemplar and the end of all maternity on earth, for nature is for the supernatural, and all men are born to be reborn by being incorporated into the body of Mary's Son.

A Mariological synthesis constructed along these lines indicates the hierarchic relations existing among all the truths knowable about the Mother of God. Revelation is the beginning and must be the guiding light throughout. Logic is here in plenty; but it is not the logic of "theodicy," for the simple reason that theology is not philosophy. It is the logic of revelation, the logic of God's plan as it unfolds in the ordering of His infinite wisdom. Discovery of this design, perception of all the connections among the truths communicated to man, is the theologian's proper task. His objective is the reproduction in the human mind of the knowledge in God's mind — the effort to determine the order of facts as known and willed and revealed or revealable by God, with all the implications of those facts the intellect is able to ascertain.

In consequence of these considerations, the place Mariology ought to occupy in the whole of theology is easily indicated.

III. RELATION OF MARIOLOGY TO THE REST OF THEOLOGY

Theology has never neglected study of the relations existing among the mysteries of revelation and of their bearing on man's last end. Yet the strong doctrine of the Vatican Council about such procedures has stimulated theological investigation and steered it in the right direction. Reflection on the relations of the mysteries with one another has engendered insights into all phases of revealed truth, and consideration of the connection which each mystery has with man's final destiny has enabled theologians to arrive at a better appreciation of the place of all the mysteries in the economy of salvation.

No part of theology may be erected on its own independent foundation; such isolation would distort perspectives in every part. Scientific labor and didactic method require division of work, but any spirit of divisiveness that results in a closed system is evil and has to be exorcised. The Mariological synthesis may not take on even the appearance of autonomy; every chapter must exhibit the vital relations which the treatise has with the whole of theology. Fidelity to the vast, harmonious design of God's wisdom demands the integration of Mariology into the entire Christian mystery.

A tendency in the direction of autonomy appeared in the evolution of Mariology during the very centuries that witnessed the decay of all theology, when scholasticism suffered an eclipse. St. Thomas had introduced the Blessed Virgin into his *Summa* in connection with the Incarnation of her Son. He raised and solved a number of important questions about Mary, without giving them the full development they subsequently received. The synthesis composed with masterly skill by Aquinas was a whole, not a congeries of treatises. During the period of transition to such treatises, the followers of St. Thomas were careful to relate them to the various parts of the *Summa*, of which their own works were commentaries. They regarded Mariology as a function of Christology, and insisted on keeping together the Mother and Son whom God Himself had joined. For St. Thomas, the theology of Mary was a sort of chapter in his theology of Christ; for his disciples, the section *De Beata Maria Virgine* became rather an addition appended to the larger division, *De Christo*.[53]

Mariology in the narrower sense is a product of the revival of scholasticism in the sixteenth century. The great theologians of that era were the first to compose distinct treatises about the Blessed Virgin and her part in the Redemption. Beginning with the seventeenth century a cleavage gradually opened up between Mariology and the rest of theology. Mariologists were dominated by the desire to add new jewels to the crown of Our Lady, and tended at times to exalt her without reference to the framework of theology as a whole. Scheeben did much to block that movement, although his initial influence was slight. By the

---

[53] Cf. M. Becqu, C.SS.R., *Que penser des essais modernes de réalization d'un traité de mariologie?*, in *Journées Sacerdotales Mariales* (Dinant, 1952), p. 80 f.

end of the nineteenth century the treatise on Mariology had acquired its definite position, situated immediately after the treatise on the Incarnation and Redemption. The decade prior to World War II inaugurated a new impetus that has not lost momentum. Contemporary Marian endeavor, with its program of a thoroughly scientific Mariology, is surpassing all previous efforts and shows many signs of wholesome progress. Most heartening of all is the firm determination to integrate Mariology into the general theological synthesis, to bring out all its relations with every facet of theological truth. The idea of an "independent" Mariology is happily receding.

Mariology occupies so necessary a place in the divine plan of salvation that without it theology is incomplete and therefore defective. The mystery of Christ is inseparable from the Blessed Virgin through whom the Incarnation was effected. If we wish to know Jesus, we must know who His Father is; but we must also know who His Mother is. We do not sufficiently understand the work of Redemption unless we are aware of the special way Mary was redeemed, and the special activity allotted to her in the Redemption of the rest of us. We do not perceive the extent of the Saviour's love for us unless we appreciate the exquisite kindness that induced Him to give His own Mother to us as our Mother. We do not apprehend the deifying power of Christ's grace until we look at her who is full of grace.

Indeed, knowledge of Mary leads to knowledge of God Himself. And that is the very purpose of theological study: to know God as fully and deeply as possible, by contemplating what He has revealed about Himself and about His works in creation, particularly in the creatures He has raised to the supernatural order. The more noble a creature is in this order as a result of God's special love and action, the more such a creature reflects the divine perfections. But among all pure creatures none has been so favored with God's most lavish gifts, none has been entrusted with so important a mission for the execution of God's designs as Mary. She is unique by reason of her supernatural endowments and hence of her power to make known to us the perfections of the Creator. She is the *Virgo singularis,* never equaled in the past and never to be equaled in the future. She is the only one who is Mother of God, the only one conceived immaculate, the only one who is Coredemptrix and universal comediatrix with Christ, the only one who is already wholly glorified in body and soul by her Assumption into heaven.[54] Consequently, knowledge about Mary is knowledge about God, because she is the greatest and most beautiful of His works, next to the Saviour's sacred humanity. She is the Queen of the universe, the ideal woman as Christ is the ideal man, the fullest realization of God's own idea of a perfect human being. The very Trinity of divine Persons is revealed in her, inasmuch as she is the Bride of the Holy Spirit, the Mother of the Son, and the Daughter of the Father by adoption and by true affinity.

Any lingering danger that Mariology, as cultivated by specialists, may tend to become an "independent" treatise, isolated from the rest of theology, can easily be obviated. In our own day it is being offset particularly by the study of Mariology in the perspectives of ecclesiology.[55] The two great theological treatises of modern times, Mariology and ecclesiology, are being scrutinized in their reciprocal relations, compared in detail, and drawn together. Mary and the Church are both mothers of men. The Mother of Christ is the Mother of Christ's mystical body.[56] Christ and Mary and the Church are all for our salvation; as Mariology cannot be independent of Christology, so neither can it be walled off from ecclesiology.

Another theological discipline that gains valuable insights from Mariology is the treatise on the Last Things. The Blessed Virgin's Assumption into heaven bears powerful witness to the truths of eschatology. The coming of the Messias inaugurated the latter times in the history of the world. Many centuries, perhaps hundreds and thousands of them, may yet have to unroll; for all we know, we may still be in the early stages of the Christian era. But the kingdom of heaven is near. The last terrestrial phase has been opened by the bodily exaltation of the Mother of God; with her, the ascent of the human race into heaven has begun.

The importance of Mariology in the organism of theology, indicated

---

[54] Cf. J. Lebon, in *Journées Sacerdotales Mariales*, p. 25.

[55] See the article on Mary and the Church in the present volume. Literature on this phase of Mariology and ecclesiology is already enormous, and is rapidly increasing.

[56] Cf. C. Vollert, S.J., *The Place of Our Lady in the Mystical Body*, in *Marian Studies*, Vol. 3, 1952, pp. 174-196.

SCIENTIFIC STRUCTURE OF MARIOLOGY

by these few samplings, is gauged mainly by the place which the Blessed Virgin's person and cooperation with Christ have in the economy of salvation. She stands close to the Church, but closer to Christ, for the mystery of Mary finds its explanation in Christ Himself, the Incarnate Word, rather than in the Church, Christ's mystical body. Her maternal relation to the Church is derivative from her maternal relation to Christ, and her collaboration in the genesis and building up of the Church is a consequence of her collaboration with Christ in the Redemption of mankind. Therefore, C. Journet proposes an unacceptable theory when he writes: "Mariology is a part of ecclesiology, that part of ecclesiology which studies the Church at its most excellent point."[57] Mariology is not a part of ecclesiology, but a distinct part of theology in its own right. Moreover, although Mariology is, indeed, connected with ecclesiology, it is far more closely connected with the theology of the Incarnate Word.

Theologians have not been entrusted with the responsibility of creating the place Mariology occupies in theology. Their task is to scrutinize what God has made known. As theology is the science of revelation, the position of Mariology in theology is the same as the position of Mary in revelation. The place of Mary, and therefore of Mariology, is in the heart of the mystery of God who gives Himself to us in Christ and in the continuation of Christ which is the Church; she is in the very depths of Christology, which has its prolongation in ecclesiology.[58]

Since the fundamental principle of Mariology is the divine maternity[59] and since the rights of Mariology as a distinct part of theology are based on the Blessed Virgin's cooperation in the work of Redemption, the treatise on Mariology ought to be located as close as possible to the treatise on the Incarnation and Redemption. This arrangement has the advantage of bringing out the force of the truth that God, who could have saved man by the direct causality of His omnipotence, has actually willed to employ mankind itself as the instrument of His saving work. Mankind itself, plunged into sin by the

---

[57] *L'Église du Verbe Incarné*, Vol. 2 (Bruges, 1951), p. 393.
[58] Cf. G. Philips, *Lugar de la mariología en la teología católica*, in *Estudios Marianos*, Vol. 10, 1950, p. 8.
[59] See the article on *The Fundamental Principle of Mariology* in this volume.

disastrous decision of its first parents, was to be the instrument of its own restoration. In pursuance of His plan, God drew from Mary the conjoined instrument of our Redemption, and required her to consent to the Incarnation in the name of the human race that issued from Adam.[60] The initiative of our salvation belongs to the Father. But the Father carries out His work through the God-man with His assumed humanity as conjoined instrument and with Mary as subordinate instrument closely linked with the principal instrument.[61] The place thus attributed to Mary in the work of Redemption is in full harmony with the teaching of Benedict XV: "Mary suffered so grievously with her suffering and dying Son, and, almost at the point of death herself, so generously renounced her maternal rights over Him for the salvation of man and immolated Him, so far as lay in her power, to placate divine justice, that she may correctly be said to have redeemed the human race along with Christ."[62]

Mary, Mother of God and of men, inseparably linked with Christ and His redemptive work, is situated at the very summit of the Church, mystical body of Christ. Theologians are coming more and more to the perception that Mariology will not achieve its full development unless its relations with the redemptive Incarnation and ecclesiology are clearly apprehended and thoroughly exploited, in causal interactions yet to be worked out. Accordingly, the best place for Mariology is between the treatise on the Redemption and the theological or dogmatic treatise on the Church.

Theologians of our time are eager to elaborate a scientific Mariology that will have its true importance and rightful function in theology. They vigorously oppose any deviation toward isolation that would leave Mariology dangling on the fringes of the sacred doctrine. Much work remains to be done; but the progress that has been made is an earnest of progress yet to be achieved.

Mary is the perfect model of the children of God, the ideal of redeemed mankind. Redemption has been completely victorious in her

---

[60] St. Thomas, *S. Th.*, III, q. 30, a. 1.

[61] Cf. E. Druwé, *Position et structure du traité mariale*, in *Bulletin de la Société Française d'Études Mariales*, Vol. 2, 1936, p. 30 f.

[62] Litt. Apost., *Inter sodalicia*, in *A.A.S.*, Vol. 10, 1918, p. 182.

alone, for in her alone the blood of the Saviour was able to exert all its power. She is the masterpiece of the Redeemer, the supreme triumph of Christ over the hostile forces of evil. She is our triumph, too, for the victorious Virgin, Mother of God, is also the Mother of men.

The Fundamental Principle of Mariology

By CYRIL VOLLERT, S.J., S.T.D.

F MARIOLOGY is a part of the science of theology, it must possess a trait that is characteristic of all science. It must marshal all the factors of its material object according to a principle of order. In other words, it must rest on a fundamental principle that will be an immovable base supporting the whole of Mariology in unity and assuring coherence to all its elements. Furthermore, if Mariology is not a mere appendix to some other branch of theology but is a distinct theological discipline in its own right, it must have its own fundamental principle that will formally distinguish it from other parts of theology and that will serve as a source of unity promoting the organization of all the truths knowable about the Mother of God.

Although theologians agree that Mariology is scientific theology, they are far from accord when they consider the question of its fundamental principle. The clash of opinions emphasizes a problem that has to be faced. What is the basic principle of Mariology? Before this question can be answered, another must be asked. What is the nature of a primary principle in theology?

I. Nature of a Theological Principle

The primary principle of a science is governed by the nature of the science; as sciences vary, their principles must vary. Sacred theology is a science unique in kind; alone of all the sciences, it receives its principles from a higher science that is beyond the reach of the intellect's natural resources. The principles of theology can be known only through divine revelation.

God, the infinite Being, knows Himself intuitively and all other beings in Himself, as participations of Himself. Since God has created the universe, He knows the order and intelligibility of all that He has made. The knowledge God has of Himself and of all being has been communicated to men, perfectly in the beatific vision, imperfectly in supernatural faith. Yet faith yearns and strives for a knowledge that is less imperfect.

This tendency toward a better understanding of revealed truth operates through an activity of the believer in response to God's initiative. The believer joins his activity to the gift of faith he has received. Thus there arises a new kind of knowledge that starts with faith and engages in an elaboration of the content of faith. The activity is rational and discursive, unfolding according to all the laws, procedures, and powers of reason. Such intellectual contemplation of the teachings of faith is theology; and, as illuminated and developed in man's reason, it takes the form and obeys the exigencies of all human knowledge. Two such exigencies are particularly imperative in theology: a need of order and a need of unity among the objects of knowledge.

God has made all things with order. This order, product of God's creative knowledge, passes from God to all His works and also to His Word, who communicates some of His knowledge to us. Since reason cannot renounce its need of order, it has to discover order among the objects of the new knowledge which faith inaugurates. The truths given to us for our salvation have to be organized into an orderly body of knowledge, in which what is first in intelligibility is sought as the basis of all the rest, so as to reproduce the order of God's creative knowledge.

The second exigency, likewise shared by faith and reason, is the need of unity among the objects of knowledge. Reason seeks unity between the knowledge it gains from observation and demonstration, and the new truths it receives from faith. The teaching of revelation is developed and illuminated by all the procedures at the disposal of human reason, and tends to take a rational form, discursive and scientific, which is theology.

The most important activity of reason in this domain is the organization of the revealed mysteries into a coherent corpus of doctrine; for the revealed mysteries *are* coherent, both with one another and with all truths that are naturally knowable. Theology draws its very life from the contemplation of such connections and relations.

Among these mysteries, some have been revealed directly for their own sake, because of the surpassing importance of their content; they are the articles of faith which are also the principles of theology.

Others have been revealed for the sake of the main mysteries, which they serve to bring out and illuminate. The truths that constitute the primary object of faith are summed up in the twofold mystery or economy: the necessary mystery of the last end, comprising all that is beheld by the blessed in the beatific vision, and the free mystery of the means by which men are brought to eternal life.[1]

In the work of penetration and intellectual organization of the revealed mysteries, carried on by the study of analogies which natural knowledge furnishes and by the contemplation of the relations which the mysteries have with one another as well as with man's last end, the activity of reason may take different forms, reducible to three: the explanation of revealed truth, the *rationes convenientiae* or perceptions of appropriateness, and deductive theological reasoning.[2] What is most important, however, is not the deducing of new theological conclusions, but rather the explanation of the realities of faith, the gaining of a deeper insight into them, the discerning of their hierarchical relationships, and the understanding of them in their proper function in the whole of revelation. The conclusions themselves are sought, not precisely for their own sake, but to aid us in arriving at a more perfect intelligence of the truths of our faith, whose richness and power they bring out. The entire activity is directed to the goal clearly set forth by the Vatican Council: that reason, enlightened by faith, may by God's gift acquire a fruitful understanding of revealed mysteries.[3]

That the theologian may perform his task, he must discover a general principle that will dominate the whole of theology or any of its parts, such as Mariology, and that will permit its organization. The mind is avid for unity; theology's proper business and its work of predilection is the reduction of the multiple to unity so that each factor in the science may be comprehended. Revelation is not an accumulation of disparate

---

[1] Cf. St. Thomas, *S. Th.*, II-II, q. 1, a. 6 ad 1; a. 8; q. 2, a. 5; a. 7. *Compendium theologiae*, I, cap. 2.

[2] Cf. M. J. Congar, O.P., *Théologie*, in *D.T.C.*, Vol. 15, col. 454-456. According to R. Garrigou-Lagrange, *Thomisme*, in *D.T.C.*, Vol. 15, col. 849-851, St. Thomas, and with him theologians generally, whatever their theories about the nature of theology may be, employ eight different procedures, of which only the last and least important is concerned with the inferring of new conclusions that are not revealed.

[3] *Constitutio de fide catholica*, cap. 4; *D.B.*, 1796.

truths, but God's communication to us of the Word that will save us. Attentive study of each revealed truth will enable us to grasp more clearly the internal unity of the one great mystery. Such investigation requires a basic principle that will regulate the structure of the science.

In general, a principle is a primary truth with which other truths are logically connected in a relationship of subordination and dependence. The principle of a science is not a comprehensive formula englobing all the truths that integrate it, a cameo that condenses the whole science into a miniature, but a truth that is situated at the point of departure. The initial truth sought by the theologian is a principle of intelligibility that will shed light over all the teachings presented by tradition and will empower us to apprehend their basic unity. Theological thought does not proceed exclusively from the one to the many; it also endeavors to gather together many partial visions and reduce them to the original unity of God's knowledge. The movement does not lose itself over the horizon, but with each of its discoveries turns back enriched toward the center.[4]

To serve as primary or fundamental principle of a treatise in theology, a truth must fulfill certain conditions. It must be revealed, for in theology the principles are articles of faith. Since it is revealed, it is absolutely certain, as the principle of any science must be, and therefore can impart its own firmness and consistency to all the elements of the science. Further, it must be theologically rich and fecund, permitting the deduction of theological conclusions and the arrangement of all the factors of the science in logical organization. As the very term denotes, the principle must possess priority that is ontological as well as logical; it must be a supreme, primary reality expressing the basic order of God's knowledge and of His plans for the universe. Finally, the principle must be one. If several principles are put forward, one will have to be the principle of the other, which will then be subordinate and cannot be primary; or else they will be coordinate and independent, with distinct sciences corresponding to the independent principles.

The problem of the primary principle of a theological treatise cannot be settled *a priori*, in accord with the demands of a preconceived system,

---

[4] Cf. G. Philips, *Perspectives mariologiques: Marie et l'Église*, in *Marianum*, Vol. 15, 1953, p. 440.

but must be solved *a posteriori*, after thorough examination of the data of revelation as delivered to us by the magisterium with its interpretations and directives. The task is to investigate what God has ordained; only when we are in possession of the facts can we proceed to work out the harmonies of the divine plan so as to discover what is primary and what is consequent. Who are we to dictate the actions of God by our syllogisms? The theologian must indeed exploit syllogisms; the illative syllogism for drawing conclusions, but mainly the explanatory syllogism as an indispensable instrument for developing understanding. Faith is the principle of this science. Yet even faith is only the proximate principle, for the ultimate principle is the intellect of God, which stamps its imprint on theology.[5]

This problem is basic in Mariology. The primary principle dominates the entire structure of Mariology, gives it consistency, confers order on its various parts, and expedites the unified organization of the whole treatise.[6] Without it, Mariology cannot be a true science, but only a series of questions or theses succeeding one another without logical coherence.

The primary principle cannot be established independently of revelation. Few treatises are so conditioned by the sources as Mariology. What we know about Mary is not what we may esteem to be most fitting for her, but what God in His wisdom has actually ordained and made known to us. Revelation, it is true, does not directly deliver such a principle to us; we should waste our time if we undertook to scrutinize Scripture and the Fathers for a solution of the problem as formulated by later theologians. Yet the sources do specify the various offices and functions of the Blessed Virgin, and also indicate the order and subordination among them. God has assigned to her a definite activity in the economy of salvation, and has richly endowed her with all the graces and aptitudes needed to discharge it.

The material object of Mariology is made up of the aggregate of

---

[5] Cf. St. Thomas, *In Boetium de Trinitate*, q. 2, a. 2 ad 7: "Huius scientiae principium proximum est fides, sed primum est intellectus divinus." *S. Th.*, I, q. 1, a. 3 ad 2: sacred doctrine is "quaedam impressio divinae scientiae."

[6] Cf. G. M. Roschini, O.S.M., *La Madonna secondo la Fede e la Teologia,* Vol. 1 (Roma, 1953), p. 97.

graces, offices, and privileges with which Mary was invested. The supreme principle that has to illuminate and explain all these elements, thus imparting the unity and consistency that will elevate Mariology to the plane of science, must express the primary and fundamental mission of Mary in the world, her essence and the very reason for her existence, as well as the precise place she occupies in the program of divine providence. Mariology deals with many facts freely ordained by God and involving Mary's free cooperation.

Consequently, God's plan as realized in these facts must be studied by examining revelation. Discovery of this plan requires discovery of the supreme truth that organizes the chain of events, unifies all its links, and arranges them systematically. Once the intellect knows this order which all the facts have in God's mind, it is satisfied; it has achieved science: *cognitio rei in causis.*

Yet, even when we have found the primary principle, we cannot deduce from it alone all that is knowable about Mary in the shape of certain conclusions which may henceforth dispense with the sources. The tendency of a purely inferential theology is to plumb the depths of revelation in the hope of laying bare a hidden axiom from which all the truths about the Blessed Virgin may be derived by strictly rational procedures, as though dogmas such as the Immaculate Conception or the Assumption had to be demonstrated by sheer logic. In that case, a few well-constructed syllogisms would suffice to draw out a string of neatly formulated propositions. If one key concept does not yield the desired result, theologians of this frame of mind come forward with a second, by supplementing the divine maternity, for instance, with the idea of Coredemption. They then surround these two basic notions with a number of subsidiary norms that will direct the process of exploitation, such as principles of fittingness, transcendence, eminence, and the like. Having recast two or three Scripture texts into the form of geometrical theorems, they laboriously go on to deduce an endless series of Mariological conclusions. If this method were carried to the extreme, all further investigation of Scripture and tradition and even of the declarations of the magisterium could be bypassed.

Perhaps no Mariologist goes that far. Certainly no theologian would be so rash as to think that he could deduce the entire treatise on the

Incarnate Word from the prologue of St. John's Gospel, or infer all the implications of original sin from a few verses in the Epistle to the Romans. The situation is not different in Mariology. What God has told us about His Mother is too stupendous to he impressed into one or two principles or to be enclosed in an axiom as in a nutshell. Theology is more than pious metaphysics, and Mariology is more than holy logic.

The Mariologist must carefully harvest all the data revelation proposes about the Blessed Virgin. Under the constant guidance of the magisterium he must search the Scriptures, the Fathers, and all tradition. With his intellect attuned to the mind of the Church, he can then contemplate the rich treasures spread out before his eyes. Gradually he will perceive order among his facts; he will begin to glimpse something of God's eternal design, and will discern one great truth that sheds light over all the rest, a supreme principle of clarity and harmony, a key to all facts and events that themselves are revealed or, products of discursive reasoning in the unfolding consciousness of many minds, are new gains to be added to the original fund which they both illuminate and reflect.

Exaggerations of the role of deduction in Mariology seem to stem from a defective notion of theology. Some authors compare Mariology with theodicy and seek a principle that is the counterpart of the *esse subsistens* from which to derive their whole science by rigorous rational methods. Such a procedure is possible in natural theology because the attributes of God are essential properties that flow necessarily from the principal source, the necessary divine *esse*. But Mariology is quite different in nature from such a metaphysical science which can be developed by reason alone. Metaphysics is concerned with necessary consequences; much of theology, especially in the domain of the economy of salvation, is concerned with free consequences. All the truths of Mariology are indeed necessary; not, however, by antecedent, metaphysical necessity, but by the necessity that issues from the free will of God who in His wisdom has disposed matters as He has freely chosen yet could have disposed them otherwise. We can know what God has freely willed only if He tells us; at every step in our science we have to be enlightened by His revelations.

Mariology is a theological discipline still in formation. Its progress requires that every proposal made for its elaboration should be subjected to wholesome criticism. That is particularly true of its fundamental principle, which is the clue to the mystery of Mary.

II. WHAT IS THE FUNDAMENTAL PRINCIPLE OF MARIOLOGY?

Concerning this question theologians are far from agreement, and the major differences among them are by no means affairs of mere verbal refinements. Three tendencies are observable in the discussions. Some Mariologists propose a single simple principle, some favor a single composite principle, and others, unable to see how the whole of Mariology can be deduced from one principle, frankly acknowledge that there are two. The main reason accounting for the divergence of opinions is the notion authors have about the function of the primary principle in a theological treatise.

Theologians who liken theology to theodicy seek in Mariology a supreme principle that will emulate the virtualities of *ipsum esse* or aseity, a principle from which all conclusions can be deduced with strict logic. If the divine maternity does not meet the requirements, they turn to Mary's association with Christ. If neither of these principles is such that all the privileges and functions of Mary are linked to them with metaphysical necessity, they try to combine these ideas in a higher synthesis or, judging that the key ideas are distinct and irreducible, contend that the whole of Mariological science rests on two independent principles as on two gigantic pillars.[7]

On the other hand, authors who perceive that all revelation, all faith, and hence all theology are referred to the twofold mystery of God, that is, the necessary mystery of God's trinitarian life and the free mystery of our salvation through the redemptive Incarnation, and who likewise note that all the other articles of faith are but applications or explanations of these two essential articles,[8] place Mariology under the second, the free mystery. Therefore they seek, not a connection of metaphysical necessity between the conclusions and the primary principle of Mariology, but the necessity that is consequent on God's free decrees about Mary's position in the economy of Redemption,

---

[7] Thus A. Luis, C.Ss.R., *Principio fundamental o primario ¿cómo enunciarlo si se da ese único principio?* in *Estudios Marianos*, Vol. 3, 1944, p. 188 f.

[8] Cf. St. Thomas, *De veritate*, q. 14, a. 11.

involving Mary's free cooperation as eternally known and willed by God. Mariology, like all theology, is a science subalternate to the science of God, and has as its own necessity the necessity of the divine science.[9] Accordingly, the theologian's aim is not to proceed in the fashion of the geometrist or philosopher, but to discover from the data of revelation the order existing in God's freely designed plan. He will at once discard any suggestion of several supreme, independent principles of Mariology, and will find in a single basic truth of revelation the principle of intelligibility that imparts unity, clarity, and cohesion to Mariology.

A complete classification of all the opinions need not be repeated; Mariologists are generally content to accept the list compiled by G. M. Roschini.[10] The main proposals of recent Mariologists will be discussed, including several omitted by Roschini or added since his latest book.

A. OPINIONS AND CRITICISMS

1. The Divine Maternity

Under various aspects, the Blessed Virgin's divine maternity is regarded by the majority of Mariologists as the primary principle of their science. One point of view was ably presented by the Abbé Blondiau in 1921.[11] At the base of the entire edifice of Mariology, veritable cornerstone on which it rests and which assures its cohesion and solidity, is this truth, clearly contained in Scripture, affirmed by tradition, and defined at Ephesus: Mary is the Mother of God. The whole of Christianity reposes on this foundation; can we desire for Mariology a base more solid than that on which the whole of Christianity logically rests? To this first truth there is attached another, likewise contained in

---

[9] Such is the necessity that is proper to all theology which depends on the supreme principle of the free mystery of salvation. Thus St. Thomas shows that Christ's resurrection is necessarily the cause of our resurrection; yet, even if the Word had never become incarnate, God could have ordained our resurrection in some other way, if He had so willed. Cf. *In primam epistolam ad Corinthios,* cap. 15, lect. 2.

[10] *Mariologia,* 2nd ed., Vol. 1 (Romae, 1947), pp. 324-337; *Compendium Mariologiae* (Romae, 1946), pp. 4-12; *La Madonna secondo la Fede e la Teologia,* Vol. 1 (Roma, 1953), pp. 97-115.

[11] L. Blondiau, *Les fondements théologiques de la marialogie,* in *Mémoires et rapports du Congrès Marial tenu à Bruxelles,* 8-11 Septembre 1921, Vol. 1 (Bruxelles, 1921), pp. 122-125.

revelation: Mary is the new Eve, the mother of men, associated with the new Adam, Christ, in the order of reparation, as Eve was associated with Adam in the disorder of ruin. The whole of Mariology flows from these two truths; its assertions are corollaries drawn from them and all its questions are related to what is implicitly comprised in them. Yet the divine maternity is the source of the new Eve relationship, since Mary's spiritual motherhood which is involved in her title of new Eve is dependent on her physical motherhood.

The aspect of the divine maternity concretely considered that is implicit in Blondiau's presentation was insisted on repeatedly by J. M. Bover. He argues that, since Mary's primary reason for existence is her maternity, the germinal idea from which the truths of Mariology issue is the fact that she is the Mother of the Redeemer. However, to serve as fundamental principle, the divine maternity must be taken, not in an abstract sense, but in the concrete and historical sense exhibited in Scripture and tradition. Thus understood, the divine maternity implies another element, namely, the principle of association with Christ's redemptive work. This principle of association invests the divine maternity with its historical or concrete significance, and makes it the supreme axiom of all Mariology.[12]

Bover's insistence on the divine maternity in its concrete and historical sense is taken up by other authors, among them J. A. de Aldama, who endeavors to clarify the connection between Mary's motherhood of Christ and her motherhood of men. In the present order the divine maternity essentially implies the spiritual maternity. The supreme principle of Mariology is the divine maternity or, if another formula is preferred, Mary's motherhood over the Redeemer. The Blessed Virgin was chosen to be the Mother of the Redeemer. Her maternity as decreed by God must be understood concretely and historically, in relation to the actual Redeemer. Hence her election to this exalted dignity includes: (*a*) her election to be Mother of God, for the Redeemer is God; (*b*) her election to maternal union with the Redeemer as such; therefore, the Mother of God must be associated with the

---

[12] Cf. J. M. Bover, S.J., *Síntesis orgánica de la Mariología en función de la asociación de María a la obra redentora de Jesucristo* (Madrid, 1929); idem, Los principios mariológicos, in *Estudios Marianos*, Vol. 3, 1944, pp. 11-33.

Redeemer in a maternal way, for the very work of Redemption; (c) her election to spiritual motherhood over men, for Redemption is a new communication of divine life brought about by the fact that men, incorporated into Christ as true members, receive from God an adoptive sonship that flows to them from the natural sonship of Christ. Thus Mary's maternal function by which a human nature is given to the Son of God, involves our incorporation into Christ. Therefore, Mary, who was made Mother of God for our Redemption, is by that very fact Mother of the Whole Christ, head and members.[13]

As thus compressed, the reasoning is not wholly clear; other authors have contributed further light. Elias de la Dolorosa contends that all the secondary principles and conclusions of Mariology can be reduced to the divine maternity, regarded fully and adequately, especially if the *terminus ad quem* is recognized as the main aspect.

From this point of view Mary, considered physically and physiologically, is Mother of Jesus-man; considered theologically, she is Mother of Jesus-God; considered morally, she is Mother of Jesus-Redeemer. The moral maternity may be called soteriological, because it is wholly directed to the salvation of men and, in its integral concept, embraces both Christ the Redeemer and redeemed men who by their solidarity form the mystical body in union with Christ the head. The point of connection between Mary and Jesus as God and Jesus as Redeemer is the physical maternity. The adequate maternity includes all three modalities.[14]

The necessity of a single primary principle of Mariology is illustrated by M. R. Gagnebet. He recalls that St. Thomas, when developing his doctrine on the Incarnate Word, employs the single principle of the redemptive Incarnation. In this formula the qualification adds, not a new principle, but a determination needed to express the concrete form according to which the mystery of the hypostatic union is realized. Throughout the treatise on the Incarnation, whether there is question of perfections, of coassumed defects, of consequences of the hypostatic

---

[13] J. A. de Aldama, S.J., *Mariologia*, in *Sacrae Theologiae Summa*, 2nd ed., Vol. 3 (Matriti, 1953), pp. 337, 340.

[14] Elias de la Dolorosa, C.P., *La maternidad de María, principio supremo de la Mariología*, in *Estudios Marianos*, Vol. 3, 1944, p. 40 f.

union, or of the mysteries of Christ's life, the principle of explanation is always this integral concept of the redemptive Incarnation. In the same way, if the divine maternity is envisaged in its integral concept of motherhood over the Incarnate Word Redeemer, it is seen to be the single first principle of Mariology, to which Mary's association in the work of Redemption is linked as a consequence. The Mother loves her Son with a love which grace has elevated and adapted to the divine personality of her Son, in order to equip her for her part in the supernatural work of Redemption. This love makes her experience in her heart all His joys and sorrows, and associates her inseparably with all the actions of His life. Above all, it gives her the power to share in the climactic action toward which every one of His desires and efforts tended. This close union of Mary with Christ makes her the intimate associate of the Redeemer.[15]

A similar parallel between the redemptive Incarnation as principle of Christology and the coredemptive divine maternity as principle of Mariology is stressed by M. M. Philipon. In both cases the principle is but one. Throughout his Christology, St. Thomas relies in his reasonings on the principles of the hypostatic union and capital grace. But if we look closely, we see that the second flows from the first, after the fashion of a property; the first alone is the fundamental principle. All the Christological conclusions, even those derived from Christ's capital grace, are resolved in the last analysis in the light of the hypostatic union that is essentially redemptive, according to the actual plan of Providence; and St. Thomas expressly attaches the second principle to the first in the *Summa*, IIIa, q. 7, a. 13. The situation is the same in Mariology. The divine maternity is the basic principle, but other, secondary principles must be appended to the primary principle for the deducing of Mariological conclusions.[16]

A formulation of the primary principle proposed by J. Lebon in earlier works is resumed in a recent study. Once we admit that, by God's will, the Blessed Virgin is the worthy Mother of the Redeemer as such, Mariology becomes clear, falls into order, and is perfectly unified. All its

---

[15] M. R. Gagnebet, O.P., *Questiones mariales*, in *Angelicum*, Vol. 22, 1945, p. 165 f.

[16] M. M. Philipon, O.P., in *Bulletin de la Société Française d'Études Mariales*, Vol. 2, 1936, p. 41 f.; *idem, The Mother of God* (Westminster, Md., 1953), pp. 130-136.

propositions find a center toward which they converge and from which they radiate to make intelligible the execution, the culmination, and the results of the divine plan.

The formula thus stated is regarded, not as a premise from which conclusions are deduced, but as a principle of intelligibility. In its light we are able to understand Mary's unique predestination, her Immaculate Conception and perfect holiness, her perpetual virginity, and her Assumption into heaven. We understand, too, her coredemptive mission that was accomplished in association with and subordination to Jesus. For her maternity conferred on her real rights over the human life of her Son, and these rights she voluntarily renounced to offer Him in sacrifice for the salvation of mankind. Finally, we can comprehend that, in consequence of her redeeming merit, she is associated with the Redeemer forever in the distribution of the graces of salvation.[17]

Many other contemporary theologians advocate the divine maternity as the basic principle of Mariology.[18] Yet the opinion, especially as proposed by some of its champions, is not without difficulties, and objections have been raised against it.

Appeal is made to authority to dislodge the principle of the divine maternity. The first speculations in the field of Mariology turned around the Eve-Mary parallel. As Adam is the principle of natural life for all men, including Christ, so Christ is the principle of supernatural life for all men, including Adam. The same law of parallelism invites us to consider by what title Eve appeared at the side of Adam; she was not his mother, but his companion and aid. Because of this comparison, we ought to conclude that Mary was primarily predestined as associate; she was to be an aid to Christ, an aid similar to Him. This is the reason that

---

[17] J. Lebon, *L'élaboration d'un traité théologique de mariologie est-elle possible?*, in *Journées Sacerdotales Mariales* (Dinant, 1952), pp. 22-24.

[18] For example, F. M. Braun, O.P., *La Mère des fidèles* (Paris, 1953), pp. 99, 115, 181; E. M. Burke, C.S.P., *The Beginnings of a Scientific Mariology*, in Marian *Studies*, Vol. 1, 1950, p. 121; H. Lennerz, S.J., *Maria-Ecclesia*, in *Gregorianum*, Vol. 35, 1954, p. 93; M. Llamera, O.P., *La maternidad espiritual de María*, in *Estudios Marianos*, Vol. 3, 1944, p. 162; H. Rondet, S.J., *Introduction à l'étude de la théologie mariale* (Paris, 1950), p. 44.

accounts for her existence.[19]

Furthermore, the divine maternity seems to provide no norm enabling us to decide which graces and privileges are required by the dignity of God's Mother. Do we merely say that a particular privilege appears to us as suitable for the Mother of God and that another one is not suitable?[20] Indeed, even though we regard the divine maternity in the concrete, as historically realized, so that both the divine maternity of Mary and her association with the Redeemer are recognized in her, these two ideas are formally distinct and do not integrate a single principle that could be the foundation of Mariology.[21] The divine maternity as such does not include Mary's share in the work of Redemption, for there is no intrinsic connection between it and participation in that work.[22] Therefore, it has to be considered in the concrete, as coredemptive; but then it becomes a composite or complex principle, equivalent to a double principle, and we can no longer speak of a simple primary principle.[23]

Prescinding from this complication, the principle that Mary is the Mother of the Redeemer is not sufficient to contain in germ her entire mission. It indicates her initial association in the work of salvation, in the sense that she brought forth the Redeemer, but does not express the continuation of such association as extending to the objective Redemption or to the distribution of all graces.[24] At most, the principle thus formulated suggests that Mary *de facto* cooperated with the Redeemer; but no reason is given; we lack an explanation why the Mother is associated with Christ's work.[25]

---

[19] J.-Fr. Bonnefoy, O.F.M., *La primauté absolue et universelle de N. S. Jésus-Christ et de la Très-sainte Vierge*, in *Bulletin de la Société Française d'Études Mariales*, Vol. 4, 1939, p. 90 f.

[20] E. Druwé, S.J., *Position et structure du traité mariale*, in *Bulletin de la Société Française d'Études Mariales*, Vol. 2, 1936, p. 22.

[21] *Ibid.*, p. 23; Roschini, *Compendium Mariologiae* (Rome, 1946), p. 8.

[22] F. J. Connell, C.SS.R., *Toward a Systematic Treatment of Mariology*, in *Marian Studies*, Vol. 1, 1950, p. 60.

[23] Roschini, *La Madonna secondo la Fede e la Teologia*, Vol. 1 (Roma, 1953), p. 112 f.

[24] Roschini, *loc. cit.*; *Compendium Mariologiae*, p. 8, Connell, *loc. cit.*

[25] J. Bittremieux, in *Ephemerides Theologicae Lovanienses*, Vol. 12, 1935, p. 608.

The main objection against the divine maternity as primary principle of Mariology seems to be that it is not a source of necessary conclusions. According to Bonnefoy, maternity pertains to the natural order, even for Mary. Therefore, it does not require grace, for grace cannot be demanded or merited by what is natural.[26] L. P. Everett admits that Mary had a right to the state of grace at the moment of the Incarnation and a right never to lose that grace. But he adds that no necessary connection can be found between her other prerogatives and the fact that she was the Mother of God. The Immaculate Conception, the perpetual virginity, and the office of Coredemptrix were merely fitting, not necessary.[27] Since all the conclusions of Mariology cannot be deduced from the divine maternity, such as the idea of the new Eve, and since other conclusions are only congruous but not necessary, it cannot be the supreme principle.[28] The doctrine of the divine maternity is not rich enough to comprehend all the perfections and prerogatives of Mary, in such a way that they can be derived from it as logical, necessary, definitive conclusions. Therefore the divine maternity cannot serve as the foundation of Mariology.[29]

The attitude of theologians who draw up such objections is quite apparent. They seek an axiom that will contain all Mariology in germ, a principle from which all the conclusions of the science may be deduced with the metaphysical necessity of a rigorous logical demonstration. Their procedure is like that of the philosopher who undertakes to develop the whole of natural theology from the *ipsum esse* or the aseity of God.

2. *The Mission of Coredemption*

Recent proponents of the opinion that the basic principle of Mariology is Mary's coredemptive mission or her function of new Eve, build up a strong case. Among them, S. Alameda searches into the

---

[26] *Art. cit.*, p. 93.

[27] L. P. Everett, C.SS.R., *The Nexus Between Mary's Co-redemptive Role and her Other Prerogatives*, in *Marian Studies*, Vol. 2, 1951, pp. 140-152.

[28] Roschini, *Compendium Mariologiae*, p. 6.

[29] A. Luis, C.SS.R., *Principio fundamental o primario*, in *Estudios Marianos*, Vol. 3, 1944, pp. 197-199.

Fathers for light on the problem.[30] He acknowledges that the Fathers do not speak expressly of a primary principle in the way that the question is phrased by later theologians, but contends that in their discussions of the relations among the various offices of the Blessed Virgin they sufficiently manifest their minds.

An examination of passages culled from the works of St. Justin, St. Irenaeus, Tertullian, St. Ephraem, and some other ecclesiastical writers up to St. Bernard leads Alameda to the conviction that enough evidence is at hand to show that Mary's mission as Coredemptrix is the basic idea of Mariology. The Blessed Virgin intervened in our Redemption in the way that Eve intervened in our ruin.[31]

The principle thus expressed is not identical with the principle of Mary's general association with Christ. Alameda does not deny the fact of such association, but is opposed only to its errors and inexactitudes. The main reason why he rejects Mary's universal association with all the mysteries and works of Christ as primary principle, is that it is not revealed. The view seems to stem from the desire of creating a facile system of Mariology: the system of applying to the Blessed Virgin the entire Christological soteriology, with certain attenuations. What Christ did, Mary likewise did, although with grace received from Him; the graces which Christ had, Mary also had, although in less eminent degree. The system is easy but dangerous; we must remember that Mary is the *ancilla Domini*, far inferior to Christ.[32]

As more correctly stated, the principle derived from the Fathers is the Blessed Virgin's office of coreparation, which in ecclesiastical parlance finds adequate expression in the formula: Mary, the second Eve. This principle is true; the Fathers have employed it since apostolic times to assert that Mary intervened in the work of reparation as Eve intervened in our fall. It is also most firm, since it is formally revealed, as the Fathers insinuate when they comment on the Proto-gospel. Further, it is supreme, for it expresses the ruling idea in God's plan, the end to which all the graces, offices, and privileges of Mary are ordained.

---

[30] S. Alameda, O.S.B., *El primer principio mariológico segun los Padres*, in Estudios Marianos, Vol. 3, 1944, pp. 163-186.

[31] *Ibid.*, pp. 168-177.

[32] *Ibid.*, p. 180 f.

In consequence of this office of second Eve, Mary was made the Saviour's Mother. Other consequences follow. Among them is Mary's virginity, for only as a virgin, with a vow of virginity, could she merit to be chosen Mother of the Saviour. Another consequence is her sanctity, enabling her to conquer the serpent, and also her immunity from all sin, original and personal. Mary's title of mother of men, her office of universal mediatrix of graces, her Assumption, her queenship, and the cult of hyperdulia owing to her are all consequences of her coredemptive mission.

Finally, the principle of the Blessed Virgin's function as coreparatrix expresses a single idea, a single fact, that of her intervention in the work of our reparation. At the same time it is so rich that it alone involves all Mariological truths, and has the added advantage of being a formula consecrated by the Fathers and the whole Church from the beginnings of Christianity.[33] Accordingly, in Alameda's judgment, the coredemptive mission ought to be regarded as the primary principle of Mariology. It guarantees the unity and consistency of Mariology as well as, or better than, the principles favored by modern theologians.

L. P. Everett, perhaps the ablest exponent of the view that Mary's office of coredemption is the fundamental principle of Mariology,[34] acknowledges that revelation does not teach a single, simple fundamental principle of Mariology, since the Gospels show the Blessed Virgin fulfilling both the office of God's Mother and that of Coredemptrix, while the Fathers did not treat the question explicitly. However, he adds that, in developing the science of Mariology, theologians have a right to put forward a simple, basic principle that will give scientific order and coherence to the discipline.[35]

Mary was chosen to fulfill a twofold office: to bring forth the Saviour and to cooperate with her Son in the work of salvation. Of these two offices, which was the more basic? The correct answer will yield the fundamental principle. The divine maternity may, indeed, be called a principle, yet the nexus between it and most of the prerogatives of body

---

[33] *Ibid.*, p. 183 f.

[34] L. P. Everett, C.SS.R., *The Nexus Between Mary's Co-redemptive Role and her Other Prerogatives*, in *Marian Studies*, Vol. 2, 1951, pp. 129-152.

[35] *Ibid.* p. 151.

and soul possessed by Mary is one of fittingness only.[36] An examination of the other alternative results in a perception of absolutely necessary connections. Since God chose Mary to be Coredemptrix of the human race, He had to confer on her the prerogatives required to fulfill this office. Since her victory over Satan was to be complete, she had to be conceived immaculate and to be preserved from the slightest taint of personal sin. Moreover, because of her association with Christ the Mediator in the work of Redemption, she had to be preserved from the consequences of sin; hence she overcame concupiscence and death. Her victory over concupiscence was shown in her virginal maternity, and her victory over death by her accelerated resurrection. Finally, by reason of her association with Christ in the acquisition of grace, she merited for herself a strict right to the title of Queen of all men and Dispensatrix of all graces.[37]

On the grounds of this necessary, causal connection between the Coredemption and the other prerogatives, the office of Coredemption ought to be accepted as the fundamental principle of Mariology. If any of Mary's singular prerogatives should be removed, she would cease to be the Coredemptrix of the human race. Although the divine maternity is the reason why this particular woman, Mary, possessed such great prerogatives, yet the cause of the prerogatives is not the divine maternity but the Coredemption.[38]

In an essay on the structure of Mariology, J. Thomas asserts his belief that a study of Mary's predestination leads to the discovery of the true principle that should eventually supersede the principle ordinarily proposed (the divine maternity, understood in the sense that Mary is the Mother of God the Redeemer as such). He regards the principle of the Blessed Virgin's necessary union with Christ the Mediator as more essential than the divine maternity.[39]

Mary's mediatorial association with Christ, her *consortium mediativum*, is the principle that unifies the treatise. She is the

---

[36] *Ibid.*, p. 142.

[37] *Ibid.*, pp. 143-149.

[38] *Ibid.*, p. 151.

[39] J. Thomas, *Quelle est la meilleure structure interne d'un traité théologique de mariologie?*, in *Journées Sacerdotale Mariales* (Dinant, 1952), p. 113.

Comediatrix with Christ because she is the Mother of the Mediator as such. She is associated with Christ in all that He is and does, because she was thus willed by God. As the man Christ Jesus is the Mediator between God and men, she is the Mediatrix with the Mediator. This principle governs the whole internal structure of Mariology, causing its unity and determining its development.[40]

In spite of the patristic evidence adduced by Father Alameda and the argumentation worked out by Father Everett, the theory that the basic principle of Mariology is found in the doctrine that Mary is the new Eve, associated with the new Adam in redeeming the world, has not commanded much support among theologians. J. Bittremieux dismisses it on the ground that it is excluded by tradition, which considers the divine maternity as the foundation of Mariology.[41] In the judgment of A. Luis, no argument of weight can be urged in its favor. Although the idea of the new Eve is the earliest form under which Mary's intervention in salvation appears in tradition, and may have been the first of her prerogatives that presented itself chronologically to the Fathers, that does not mean that ontologically it had to precede the idea of the divine maternity.[42] According to G. Roschini, the Fathers did indeed emphasize the idea of Mary as second Eve. But we go beyond their thought and their words if we say that in their minds the divine maternity was a consequence of the office of second Eve or a means to realize that office. The Fathers do not say this and they cannot say it. Alameda makes the Fathers assert much more than they actually do assert.[43] Although the Fathers are aware of a relationship between Eve and Mary, the new Eve in patristic tradition is the Church rather than Mary.[44]

Moreover, as Luis observes, in treating of the supreme principle of Mariology we may not prescind from the divine maternity, Mary's most sublime prerogative; and the divine maternity cannot be deduced from the principle of association. Reasons of fittingness may be urged in favor of uniting both privileges in the same person; but such reasons are not

---

[40] *Ibid.*, p. 124.

[41] Cf. *Ephemerides Theologicae Lovanienses*, Vol. 12, 1935, p. 608.

[42] *Principio fundamental o primario*, in *Estudios Marianos*, Vol. 3, 1944, p. 200 f.

[43] *La Madonna secondo la Fede e la Teologia*, Vol. 1, p. 113.

[44] C. Moeller, in *Lumen Vitae*, Vol. 8, 1953, p. 249.

enough to found a scientific system.⁴⁵ The same difficulty occurs to F. J. Connell, who asks: "How does this doctrine include the divine maternity?" Even though some connection could be shown, the subordination of the divine motherhood is highly incongruous.⁴⁶ Roschini agrees that it is wrong to degrade the divine maternity to a secondary place. Besides, the divine maternity cannot be deduced from the principle of *consortium*, for God could have conferred on Mary the quality of new Eve without elevating her to the dignity of being His Mother.⁴⁷ If the association is understood concretely, in the sense that it presupposes the divine maternity on the ground that Mary is Christ's *socia* because she is the Mother of God, then the divine maternity itself and not the idea of new Eve is prior and ought to be recognized as the fundamental principle.⁴⁸ By what right does anyone make the divine maternity depend on the office of second Eve? The contrary is true: the office of second Eve depends on the divine maternity.⁴⁹

3. Twofold Principle: Mother and Associate

Dissatisfied with the principles thus described, and in despair of finding a single principle from which the whole of Mariology may be deduced, some theologians contend that two primary principles must be acknowledged. Others, who are generally of the same mind, verbally deny the existence of two such principles, but propose theories that actually assert two distinct principles.

With complete candor, J. Bittremieux prefers to speak of two principles: the Blessed Virgin is the Mother of God and she is the associate of her Son the Redeemer. A theoretical reason favors this preference: divine maternity and association in the office of the Redeemer are distinct. They are, indeed, connected; association presupposes the divine maternity as its foundation, and the maternity is ordered by God to the association. Yet to be mother is one thing and to

---

[45] A. Luis, *art. cit.*, p. 200.
[46] *Toward a Systematic Treatment of Mariology*, in *Marian Studies*, Vol. 1, 1950, p. 60.
[47] *La Madonna secondo la Fede e la Teologia*, p. 113.
[48] Roschini, *Compendium Mariologiae*, p. 7.
[49] Roschini, *La Madonna secondo la Fede e la Teologia*, loc. cit.

be associate is another. A practical reason supports the same view: Mariology can thus be constructed on the model of Christology. Theologians generally divide this treatise into two parts, of which one treats of the Incarnate Word, the person of Christ, and the hypostatic union with all its consequences, while the second treats of the office of Christ the Redeemer. Accordingly we have a parallel: as Christ is God and Redeemer, Mary is Mother of God and associate of the Redeemer.[50]

This duality cannot be denied. Mary's maternity and her association in Christ's work do not coalesce into a single concept. Yet the duality is coherent. It is fitting that the new Eve should stand at the side of the new Adam and that men should have a mother and Coredemptrix at the side of Christ the Redeemer.[51] Although these two offices are realized in the same person, they are not necessarily connected, for the association cannot be reduced to the divine maternity. Therefore, they are two formally distinct principles.

In his work on the Mariology of St. Alphonsus de Liguori, C. Dillenschneider presents these two principles: Mary is the worthy Mother of God, and Mary is the worthy associate of Christ the Mediator.[52] He himself embraces this doctrine wholeheartedly. Yet these two primary principles are not simply parallel; there is a close bond between them. Our Lady's divine maternity and her mediation, or her divine maternity and her maternity of grace, are inseparable and imply each other. The first is ordered to the second, and the second finds its ontological foundation in the first. However, they are not reducible to a single concept; the active role of Mediatrix or of new Eve cannot be strictly inferred from the title, Mother of God. The two ideas ought to remain formally distinct and may not be mingled in theological reasoning.[53]

During a discussion of this question at a later date, Father

---

[50] J. Bittremieux, *De principio supremo mariologiae*, in *Ephemerides Theologicae Lovanienses*, Vol. 8, 1931, p. 250 f.

[51] J. Bittremieux, in *Ephemerides Theologicae Lovanienses*, Vol. 12, 1935, p. 609.

[52] *La Mariologie de St. Alphonse de Liguori* (Fribourg, 1934), p. 56.

[53] *Ibid.*, pp. 58-61. The same theory is shared by J. Keuppens, *Mariologiae Compendium* (Antverpiae, 1938), p. 12, and by G. Alastruey, *Mariologia* (Vallisoleti, 1934), Vol. 1, p. 3 f.; and others.

Fundamental Principle of Mariology

Dillenschneider remarked that he preferred to speak of a single concrete reality (the Blessed Virgin Mary) with two different formal principles. The original unity has to be guarded, but for reasoning the two principles are required.[54]

After observing that any science is more solid and harmonious in proportion as the truths integrating it are more perfectly contained in its generating principle, A. Luis asserts that Mariology, to be a genuine theological treatise, must combine the traits of true science. In addition to ordering its material object systematically, it must be founded on a principle from which its theses are derived with impeccable logic and to which all its truths converge. As in theodicy, all authors admit *actus purus* or aseity as a basic principle, so in Mariology it is necessary to assign a note, quality, or perfection that is the fundamental principle from which all the other excellences and prerogatives of the Mother of God are deduced, a principle that accounts for their unity.[55]

But none of the activities of the Blessed Virgin as Mother of God and men may be omitted from the formulation of the supreme principle. Mary's mission is twofold: to invest the Word with human nature and to cooperate with Him in restoring the human race.[56] The Mother of God is the spiritual mother of men because she supplies them with the life of grace, aids them in developing it, and preserves them in it. This spiritual maternity is so important for a grasp of Mary's saving mission that it may well replace the principle of association to designate her activity as Coredemptrix of mankind.[57]

Thus the principle must include the divine maternity and the spiritual maternity in the full sense of its soteriological functions. Is this

---

[54] Cf. *Bulletin de la Société Française d'Études Mariales*, Vol. 2, 1936, p. 41. This renowned Mariologist subsequently modified his views in favor of the proposal that the basic principle of an organic Mariology is Mary's divine, messianic maternity in its personal, soteriological, and ecumenical dimensions. Cf. his book *Le principe premier d'une Théologie Mariale organique* (Paris, 1956), esp. p. 172. This work, a notable addition to the literature on the subject, was received after the present chapter had already been set up in type.

[55] A. Luis, C.SS.R., *Principio fundamental o primario*, in *Estudios Marianos*, Vol. 3, 1944, p. 188.

[56] *Ibid.*, p. 189.

[57] *Ibid.*, p. 212.

principle single or double? Luis feels impelled toward a single principle because of his conviction that Mariology is *one* science, and to be *one* it cannot be better governed than by a single principle. Yet he is unable to see how the entire coredemptive mission of Mary can be derived from the concept of divine maternity. He perceives that Mary, by giving birth to Christ, head of the mystical body, concurred in the initial phase of our regeneration and so is mother of men in an inceptive way. But he does not perceive how that first cooperation in the redemptive work includes her association in the whole of Redemption.[58] Until further clarification of the union between the two maternities is forthcoming, in such a way that the maternity of grace is shown to be formally included in the divine maternity, he reluctantly gives his adherence to the theory of a double basic principle.

Reflection on the problem has led Roschini to relinquish his former position in favor of a new theory. However, the earlier point of view had exerted considerable influence, and hence is included in this survey. According to the opinion he subsequently abandoned, neither the divine maternity nor association with the Redeemer can constitute the supreme principle of Mariology; therefore the mind has to turn elsewhere.[59] Although the idea of the divine motherhood is quite distinct from the idea of association, the two can be combined into a single supreme principle which is not simple but complex. In other words, the two distinct ideas are closely linked and hence enable us to speak of one principle; for coordination and connection imply unity, which is like a middle term between duality and simplicity. The primary (single though complex) principle of Mariology should be thus formulated: "Mary is the Mother of God and associate of the Mediator." From these two truths, aptly combined in this fashion yet equivalent to two irreducible principles, all the conclusions of Mariology can be inferred.[60] This "conciliatory opinion" is substantially identical with Bittremieux's teaching, as Roschini himself avows.[61]

---

[58] *Ibid.*, p. 216 f.

[59] G. M. Roschini, O.S.M., *Mariologia*, 1st ed., Vol. 1 (Mediolani, 1941), p. 433; *Compendium Mariologiae* (Romae, 1946), p. 7.

[60] *Compendium Mariologiae*, p. 11 f.

[61] *Mariologia*, 1st ed., Vol. 1, p. 443.

FUNDAMENTAL PRINCIPLE OF MARIOLOGY 55

Support for this view is given by A. Mouraux,[62] who turns to the texts of the New Testament that describe the place and role of Mary in the economy of salvation. These passages disclose the principle of Mariology, and are summed up by Pius XII in *Munificentissimus Deus*: "Sacred Scripture proposes to us, as before our eyes, the gracious Mother of God in closest union with her divine Son and always sharing His lot."[63] The Holy Father's words indicate the very principle of Mariology, which contains two ideas that are connected though distinct: the maternity of Mary regarding the Redeemer as such, and the close association between Jesus and Mary.[64]

The formulation of this double principle is declared by E. Druwé to represent true progress in the scientific elaboration of Mariology. The authors who hold it bring out the fecundity of each of these principles, but also insist on the intimate connection of Mary's two missions. However, they have to concede that the two ideas remain formally distinct and that no process of strict reasoning permits passage from one to the other. Yet who does not sense that in the divine mind the idea realized in Mary must imply a higher unity in which both of these aspects are synthesized and fused?[65] The desired "higher synthesis" has been disclosed by M. J. Scheeben, who may well have discovered the true principle of Mariology.[66]

Working in his own personal and original way, Scheeben had unearthed a vein of patristic tradition that led him to the concept of bridal maternity (*braütliche Gottesmutterschaft*), meaning that Mary was at once the Mother and the spouse of Christ, as Eve had been given to Adam as his wife and aid. The divine maternity itself is the main, basic, and central privilege to which all the privileges are joined as

---

[62] *Quelles sont les conditions de la valeur d'un traité theologique de mariologie?*, in *Journées Sacerdotales Mariales* (Dinant, 1952), pp. 31-76.

[63] *A.A.S.*, Vol. 42, 1950, p. 768.

[64] Mouraux, *art. cit.*, p. 62.

[65] E. Druwé, S.J., *Position et structure du traité mariale*, in *Bulletin de la Société Française d'Études Mariales*, Vol. 2, 1936, p. 23.

[66] *Ibid.*, p. 29.

subordinate, derived attributes.[67] But the factor that distinguishes Mary's motherhood from all others and constitutes her personal character[68] is a special, supernatural union with the person of her divine Son which cannot be better designated than as a divine matrimony in the strictest sense of the word. "Mary, as united with the Logos, is taken up by Him in complete possession; the Logos, on His part, as infused and implanted in her, gives Himself to her and takes her to Himself as partner and helper in the closest, fullest, and most lasting community of life."[69]

Scheeben makes this personal, materno-sponsal character of the Blessed Virgin the keystone of his entire Mariology. Mary is the Mother of Christ because she gave birth to Him; she is the Bride of Christ because she is joined to Him in a union like that of husband and wife. The motherhood itself is bridal because of Mary's freely given consent to be God's Mother. All the truths of Mariology are derived either from Mary's motherhood or from her consortship with Christ, yet neither concept can be logically deduced from the other. That is why Scheeben bent all his efforts to the discovery of a higher synthesis that would include both the motherhood and the consortship. Ultimately he found this higher synthesis in the formula, Mary's "bridal motherhood."[70]

The ideas put forward by Scheeben have been further reworked by C. Feckes,[71] who shows that according to tradition the fundamental principle of Mariology must include the divine maternity; yet the divine maternity alone is not enough. Even the so-called "adequate maternity"

---

[67] M. J. Scheeben, *Handbuch der katholischen Dogmatik*, Vol. 3 (Freiburg im Breisgau, 1882), p. 489.

[68] On Scheeben's views concerning Mary's "personal character," see H. Mühlen, *Der "Personalcharakter" Mariens nach J. M. Scheeben: Zur Frage nach dem Grundprinzip der Mariologie*, in *Wissenschaft und Weisheit*, Vol. 17, 1954, pp. 191-213. In dependence on Scheeben, the author inquires whether Mariology ought to be erected on the principle of the distinction between nature and person, which is essential to the dogmas of the Trinity and Incarnation. He inclines toward an affirmative answer.

[69] Scheeben, *ibid.*, p. 490 f.

[70] Perhaps the best exposition of Scheeben's doctrine on the primary principle is found in C. Feckes, *M. J. Scheeben, théologien de la mariologie moderne*, in *Maria. Études sur la Sainte Vierge*, ed. H. du Manoir, S.J., Vol. 3 (Paris, 1954), pp. 564-568.

[71] *Das Fundamentalprinzip der Mariologie*, in *Scientia Sacra* (Köln-Düsseldorf, 1935), pp. 252-276.

is not a sufficient basis for Mary's role as associate. If the title, "New Eve," is taken as principle, the way to the maternity would be unsafe. The solution consists in combining both concepts into the bridal motherhood of God, in which "the two apparently disparate ideas are joined in Mary because they are connected in the one divine idea."[72] The divine maternity requires Mary's assent; since the assent is free, the concepts of Mother of God and of associate appear united, and Mary is at once Mother and Spouse of God. The bridal motherhood is a single idea; Mary is Mother because her first service as associate was her maternal contribution; and she is Bride because her maternal service had a bridal character through her *fiat*.[73]

Although E. Druwé regards the proposal of a double principle as a sign of progress in Mariology, he prefers Scheeben's formula, which involves more than a mere juxtaposition of two distinct concepts that are united only *de facto* in the actual realization of the redemptive economy. The "bridal motherhood" is a single concept in which the formal aspects of spouse and mother are intrinsically united, so as to integrate a reality that is perfectly one.[74]

Criticism of the double principle has been far more widespread than acceptance. Few Mariologists would agree with the encomium pronounced by J. Coppens on the occasion of a review of the theological career of Bittremieux: "There is question here of the keystone of the whole system. ... If it is well cut and placed, the entire edifice holds solidly together. ... Bittremieux has followed an impeccable logic so as to assure to each of the parts the needed firmness."[75]

In fact the theory of two principles, consisting in the divine maternity combined with the principle of association or with that of coredemption or with that of spiritual maternity, is judged inadmissible. Since there are two principles, the unity of Mariology is shattered. The device of joining the principles into a complex formula fails to save the

---

[72] *Ibid.*, p. 268.

[73] *Ibid.*, p. 269.

[74] E. Druwé, S.J., *Position et structure du traité mariale*, in *Bulletin de la Société Française d'Études Mariales*, Vol. 2, 1936, p. 26. On pp. 27-29 Druwé shows how various truths about Mary flow from this principle.

[75] J. Coppens, in *Ephemerides Theologicae Lovanienses*, Vol. 23, 1947, p. 348.

situation; the artificial formula does not change the reality.[76]

The basic reason advanced in favor of this dualism is rejected by Elias de la Dolorosa. Authors who affirm two fundamental principles in Mariology are misled by the comparison they make between Mariology and theodicy. They seek a principle from which all the conclusions of the science can be deduced with metaphysical necessity. They analyze the concept of maternity and are unable to find the coredemption included in it; the ideas of maternity and coredemption are ontologically distinct and independent. Therefore the coredemption does not flow from the divine maternity; hence the latter is not by itself the supreme principle of Mariology, and requires the principle of coredemption as its companion principle. The false reasoning consists in the misguided notion that the two sciences are identical in structure, whereas they are wholly diverse. We must focus the powerful light of Scripture and tradition on Mary's maternity. If the divine maternity, thus illuminated by the light of revelation, is found to include the coredemption, we easily perceive that it is the supreme principle of Mariology. The source of the connection is not the nature of the relation between the abstract concepts of maternity and coredemption, but the will of God who intends His Mother to be His associate in the work of salvation. Accordingly, those who assert that the divine maternity and Mary's association in Redemption are irreducible principles, have been seduced by their erroneous notion of the nature of theology.[77]

Like every branch of theology, Mariology must have one simple principle; otherwise it would not be a single treatise. Roschini's composite principle does not elude the difficulty. For if one of its members is not reducible to the other, we have two principles; if it is thus reducible, there is only one simple principle.[78]

Although in his earlier writings Roschini had no quarrel with the twofold principle, he objected to the doctrine taught by Terrien in *La Mère de Dieu et la Mère des hommes* and later resumed by Luis, that the

---

[76] S. Alameda, *El primer principio mariólogico según los Padres*, in *Estudios Marianos*, Vol. 3, 1944, p. 181.

[77] Elias de la Dolorosa, C.P., *La maternidad de María, principio supremo de la mariología*, in *Estudios Marianos*, Vol. 3, 1944, pp. 38-44.

[78] M. R. Gagnebet, O.P., *Questions mariales*, in *Angelicum*, Vol. 22, 1945, p. 165.

supreme principle is composed of Mary's divine maternity and her spiritual maternity. Against this, he argued that the concept of association is wider than that of spiritual maternity and is to be preferred, since the basic principle ought to be most universal. The concept of association is not limited to Mary's association in the supernatural regeneration of men (spiritual maternity), but includes her association in the reconciliation of men (objective Redemption) and in the distribution of graces (subjective Redemption).[79]

Roschini finds little to commend in Scheeben's theory of "bridal maternity." The idea seems to him to smack of novelty; it is unknown to the Fathers and was apparently personal with Scheeben. Actually, it means nothing else than coredemptive maternity. Therefore it should be called coredemptive maternity, which is a more precise theological term.[80] Even so, Mary's association in the work of the Redeemer is not sufficiently expressed. The initial association is indeed expressed, in the sense that Mary truly gave birth to the Redeemer, but the continuation of such association is not brought out. Therefore, we must come back to the complex principle: "Mary is Mother and associate of God the Redeemer."[81]

But in that case the theory is exposed to all the ruinous attacks launched against the views of Bittremieux and Dillenschneider. Scheeben's notion does not go beyond a mere verbal junction,[82] and so does not represent any substantial advance toward a solution of the problem.[83] To understand Mary's intimate and loving association with the work of her Son, we need not have recourse to the confused concept of bridal maternity that is so dear to Scheeben's disciples, for such cooperation is a manifest consequence of her maternal relationship with Jesus Christ, the Redeemer.[84]

The assertion that Mary is not only Mother but also spouse of Christ has no foundation in revelation. Nowhere in Scripture do we read that

---

[79] Roschini, *Compendium Mariologiae*, p. 11.

[80] *Ibid.*, p. 9 f.

[81] *Ibid.*, p. 8.

[82] Charles Moeller, *Doctrinal Aspects of Mariology*, in *Lumen Vitae*, Vol. 8, 1953, p. 248.

[83] Luis, in *Estudios Marianos*, Vol. 3, 1944, p. 206.

[84] Gagnebet, *Questions mariales*, in *Angelicum*, Vol. 22, 1945, p. 166.

Mary is spouse of the Word; she is exclusively His Mother. This union between Mother and Son surpasses the union of husband and wife. The Blessed Virgin is, indeed, associated with Christ in His Redemption; not, however, as His spouse, but as His Mother. Her motherhood includes eminently all that the biblical image of spouse suggests.[85] Nor do the Fathers lend support to Scheeben's view. They do not, as is sometimes averred, teach that Mary is related to Christ as Eve is related to Adam. They established a certain relation between Eve and Mary, and then resumed the relation between Adam and Christ that is brought out by St. Paul. For the Fathers, the new Eve as spouse of the new Adam is not Mary, but the Church.[86]

Thus the Mother of God is not identified with the spouse of God either by Scripture or by the Fathers. The combination, "bridal motherhood," is the invention of Scheeben, who mingles the flowery and figurative language of the Fathers with the formal and abstract vocabulary of the Scholastics, and tries to include the disparate qualities of mother and spouse in a single, unthinkable concept.[87]

4. Mother of the Whole Christ or Universal Mother

A frame of mind common to Mariologists who eventually come to two principles is the persuasion that all the prerogatives and offices of Mary cannot be strictly deduced either from the formal concept of divine maternity or from her position as second Eve. García Garcés shares this attitude. However, he prefers a formula that in appearance, at least, is simple, even though it may contain two virtualities which are actually reduced to two principles. Moreover, he desires to supplant the idea of Mary's association with Christ by her spiritual maternity, which enjoys greater favor in ecclesiastical usage and is more easily grasped.[88] Combining the divine maternity and the spiritual maternity in a single

---

[85] F. M. Braun, O.P., *Marie et l'Église, d'après l'Écriture*, in *Bulletin de la Société Française d'Études Mariales*, Vol. 10, 1952, p. 15 f.

[86] Y. M. J. Congar, O.P., in *Revue des Sciences Philosophiques et Théologiques*, Vol. 34, 1951, p. 625, note; idem, *Marie et l'Église dans la pensée patristique, ibid.*, Vol. 38, 1954, pp. 3-38.

[87] G. Philips, in *Marianum*, Vol. 15, 1953, p. 443.

[88] N. García Garcés, C.M.F., *Mater Coredemptrix* (Taurini-Romae, 1940), p. 121 f.

principle is not difficult; to express Mary's motherhood over Christ and over us, we have the apt formula: "The Blessed Virgin is the Mother of the Whole Christ." This principle discloses God's will of associating Mary's physical motherhood regarding Christ, head of the mystical body, with her spiritual motherhood over men, Christ's mystical members. It also emphasizes Mary's special characteristic: she is always and completely Mother. With the aid of this principle we can deduce all conclusions pertaining to the nature, properties, and exercise of her spiritual maternity.[89]

In his earlier works, Roschini had slight esteem for this opinion. He held that the concept of *consortium* was wider than that of spiritual maternity, as it included, besides Mary's cooperation in the spiritual regeneration of men, her association with Christ in the reconciliation of mankind with God and in the distribution of graces.[90] Moreover, two ideas or two really distinct principles, that of divine maternity and that of universal mediation, are discerned in this proposition, with the added inconvenience that the two diverse ideas are joined in a vague and obscure formula which has merely an illusive appearance of a single principle.[91]

Nevertheless, the views of García Garcés influenced Roschini's subsequent thinking and led him to take a similar position. Roschini confesses that he had formerly held substantially with Bittremieux, as he thought that two supreme principles had to be admitted, the divine maternity and association with the Mediator, because the divine maternity is quite distinct from the idea of association in the work of mediation, so that one could not be reduced to the other.[92] By the time the second edition of his *Mariologia* appeared, in 1947, he had abandoned this position, and was in quest of a formulation of the primary principle that would express Mary's august mission in a simpler and more universal way. After long reflection he felt that he had at length found the desired principle: the universal maternity of Mary: Mary is the Mother of Christ and of His mystical body, of the Creator and of

---

[89] *Ibid.*, p. 123 f.
[90] *Compendium Mariologiae*, p. 11.
[91] *Ibid.*, p. 10.
[92] Roschini, *La Madonna secondo la Fede e la Teologia*, Vol. 1, p. 114.

creatures; briefly, Mary is universal Mother. This principle is formally one and virtually complex, since the universal motherhood comprises all beings, the Creator as well as His creatures.[93]

The concept of universal motherhood dissolves all the seeming antinomies found in the theory of two principles. This universal maternity is a most simple concept: the concept of maternity. Hence it is a single, simple principle, and accounts for all of Mary's prerogatives, which God conferred on her either in preparation for, or as a result of, her divine maternity with relation to Christ and her spiritual maternity with relation to men. Even Mary's mediation is a consequence, not a source, of the universal maternity. Mary is mediatrix because she is Mother, not Mother because she is mediatrix. Thus the idea of universal mediation, which is diverse from the idea of Mother of the Creator, is not diverse from the general idea of universal Mother, that is, Mother of the Creator and of creatures. Hence the idea of mediatrix of creatures coincides with the idea of mother of creatures. Consequently, the supreme and simple principle of all Mariology is found in the idea of universal Mother.[94]

Patrons of such theories try to join the divine maternity and the spiritual maternity in a single principle, and they think they succeed because the formula, Mother of the Whole Christ, or similar variants, possess a specious unity. Yet, as Alameda observes, formulas of this kind involve the acquisition of two ends, the exercise of two offices, the discharging of two missions: the giving of physical life to the Saviour and of spiritual life to men. Since the ends and missions are different, not all can aspire to the honor of being the first. The illusive unity of the formula is the result of a desire to reduce the principles of Mariology to one and thus to safeguard its integrity.[95] But all the objections lodged against the double principle retain their validity.

Furthermore, the substitution of Mary's spiritual maternity for the coredemption is a step backward. The spiritual maternity implies the coredemption; Mary is our spiritual mother because she bore us spiritually by coredeeming us. Roschini's conversion to his new opinion

---

[93] *Ibid.*
[94] *Ibid.*, p. 115.
[95] Alameda, in *Estudios Marianos*, Vol. 3, 1944, p. 181 f.

was unfortunate. He now holds that Mary's universal mediation and queenship flow from the universal maternity. But the truth is that the universal queenship and the spiritual maternity are consequences of the universal mediation.[96]

Roschini's aim has been the discovery of a formula that would join the two essential ideas, mother and associate, into one basic principle. At first he found his solution in the complex proposition, "Mary is the Mother of God and associate of the Mediator." This was a mere makeshift. The two ideas are correct, but lack coherence. Later he adopted the simple formula, "Mary is the Universal Mother," that is, Mother of God and mother of men. The new solution has the aspect of greater unity, but, like the old one, is wanting in strict logical coherence.[97]

The most penetrating criticism is that of A. Luis. He is ready to admit that the formula, "Mary is Mother of the Whole Christ," has a fair appearance. But it labors under the heavy disadvantage that the term "mother" has a tremendously different value as applied to the head and to the members of the Whole Christ. The term has two senses, which vary as it is applied to the diverse parts making up the Whole Christ. Mary is Mother of Christ according to nature, and mother of men according to grace. The principle revolves around a twofold maternity, and so is reducible to two distinct principles.[98] This theory does not bring us a single step closer to a satisfactory solution of the problem.

5. Mary, Prototype of the Church

Most of the difficulties inherent in the question of the fundamental principle of Mariology vacillate between two poles: Mary is Mother of Christ, Mary is associate of Christ. Some authors try, without notable success, to surmount the dichotomy by reducing the first term to the second or the second to the first. Others resign themselves to the embarrassing duality. Otto Semmelroth proposes a new way out. The two principles are merely two aspects of a third that is more basic. The

---

[96] L. P. Everett, in *Marian Studies*, Vol. 2, 1951, p. 135 f.

[97] A. Müller, Um die Grundlagen der Mariologie, in Divus Thomas (Freiburg), Vol. 29, 1951, pp. 387, 390.

[98] Luis, in *Estudios Marianos*, Vol. 3, 1944, p. 211.

true fundamental principle is Mary regarded as the archetype or prototype of the Church.

The divine maternity, even when qualified as bridal, can be traced back to a more fundamental Mariological principle. We can find this principle if we compare the mysteries involving Mary, in an endeavor to perceive how one of them results from another until we come to one that cannot be reduced any farther. This principle is Mary, as prototype of the Church. Even the divine maternity has its basis in this idea. Mary was called by God to be His Mother in order that she might be the archetype of the Church.[99]

If we go on to ask, which of all the Marian mysteries most closely links the Blessed Virgin with the economy of salvation, we again come to Mary as prototype of the Church. The basic principle of Mariology must be that mystery which, while conferring unity on the science, is also the point at which it is inserted into the whole of theology. Mariology is theologically significant only because of Mary's vital relationship with the work of Redemption. The center of the economy of salvation is not the physical, historical Christ, but the whole Christ, that is, Christ with His Church, which as His bride appropriates His work by receiving from Him its fruits and distributing them to the various members. Therefore, the basic mystery of Mariology is the one which brings Mary into closest proximity with the Church; and that is the mystery of Mary as prototype of the Church. This mystery places Mary in the very center of the economy of salvation, the Church in its essential function as intermediary of Redemption. As prototype of the Church, Mary is the Church in germ; hence she possesses the fullness of the grace of the Church, and this grace she imparts to the Church as it develops in space and time.[100]

The main interest in this point of view is the new conception it offers of Mary's association with the mystery of Redemption. The principle of Mary as prototype of the Church enables us to attribute to her a coredemptive function, not like that of Christ, but like that of the Church. The role of mankind, represented and typified in the Blessed Virgin, is not an active, causal, productive cooperation in the work of

---

[99] O. Semmelroth, S.J., *Urbild der Kirche* (Würzburg, 1950), p. 37 f.
[100] *Ibid.*, p. 39 f.

FUNDAMENTAL PRINCIPLE OF MARIOLOGY

Redemption, but exclusively a free receptiveness, under the influence of grace, of saving union with God.[101] The acceptance of Redemption was made by the Church, in the person of Mary, at the time Jesus was accomplishing His work on Calvary. Thus Mary had a real office in the order of objective Redemption; but this was entirely an office of receiving, with a causality that was purely receptive.[102]

Commentators tend to take a dim view of Semmelroth's thesis. The idea of Mary as prototype of the Church is an illuminating aspect of Mariology, but can hardly be its foundation. To be such, it would have to be derived directly from Scripture and the patristic writings of the earliest centuries. On this capital point, the author's interpretations of the passages he adduces are far from being decisive.[103] The view that Mary is a type of the Church is undoubtedly found in some witnesses of tradition; but the contention that his notion is the basis of Mariology cannot derive support from them.

A notable weakness of this solution is that it reduces the divine maternity, which is more fundamental, to the Church, which is a consequence of Mary's motherhood.[104] The theory errs in subordinating the divine maternity, which is revealed in Scripture, to the Church, which presupposes the dogma that Mary is Mother of Christ.[105] The difficulty is compounded by the fact that in the Christian consciousness the parallelism between Mary and the Church is much less clearly perceived than the divine maternity. How, then, can it serve as principle?[106]

At the beginning of his study, Semmelroth shows that Mariology has suffered grievously from being based on a double principle, such as

---

[101] *Ibid.*, p. 83.

[102] Further consideration of these views about Mary's part in our Redemption is reserved for another paper in this volume, on Mary and the Church. An interesting question arises: is Semmelroth's primary principle the source of his coredemptive theory, or did the latter inspire his quest for a primary principle? In any case, they are likely to stand or fall together.

[103] J. Bésineau, S.J., in *Sciences Ecclésiastiques*, Vol. 6, 1954, p. 283; cf. Congar, in *Revue des Sciences Philosophiques et Théologiques*, Vol. 34, 1951, p. 627.

[104] R. Laurentin, *Marie et l'Église*, in *La Vie Spirituelle*, Vol. 86, 1952, p. 299.

[105] C. Moeller, in *Lumen Vitae*, Vol. 8, 1953, p. 248.

[106] G. Philips, in *Marianum*, Vol. 15, 1953, p. 453.

"Mother of God and new Eve," "Mother of God and spouse of the Word," and the like. But the new principle he advocates does not dissipate this ambiguity. Mary's relation to the Church supposes a term that is common to both of them, and what is this if not the divine maternity? Thus his principle expresses a double enunciation: "Mother of God and type of the Church."[107] The theory is a sort of appendix to Scheeben's thought.[108] And Semmelroth admits that Scheeben's "bridal maternity" expresses more or less the mystery he himself has in mind when he speaks of Mary as prototype of the Church.[109] Hence the objections brought against Scheeben's thesis can be effectively turned against Semmelroth's essay.

With regard to the consequence drawn from the principle of prototype, that Mary's role in the Redemption is one of mere receptivity, we may well ask whether Semmelroth's presentation of the concept of Coredemption does not destroy the concept itself. This distorted idea of Mary's coredemptive function hardly does justice to the declarations of the Popes, especially of St. Pius X and Benedict XV.[110]

6. Fullness of Grace

Like Semmelroth, Alois Müller derives inspiration from Scheeben. The theory he advances is the fruit of his book, *Ecclesia-Maria: die Einheit Marias und die Kirche* (Freiburg in der Schweiz, 1951), a patristic inquiry into the nature of Mary and the Church. Müller himself summarizes the main points brought out in his book:

Mary's decisive act with regard to salvation was her motherhood of Christ; on this the Fathers are unanimous. Mary's contribution was her faith and obedience to God. By faith her virginal womb conceived the Word of God.

From the beginning the Church, too, was designated as "Mother of God." The two scriptural truths, that Eve is fulfilled in the Church and that she is likewise fulfilled in Mary, prepared the way for recognizing

---

[107] Bésineau, *loc. cit.*

[108] Moeller, *loc. cit.*

[109] Urbild der Kirche, p. 40.

[110] J. Brinktrine, in *Theologie und Glaube*, Vol. 44, 1954, p. 473.

first the Church, and then Mary, not only as Mother of God but also as bride of God. The Church is the virgin that conceived of the Holy Spirit and thus became Mother of God.

Christ is conceived in the hearts of His followers by the fact that they hearken to the word with faith, and is born in them through baptism and the grace of sanctification. This birth of Christ in the hearts of the faithful and in the Church is the accomplishment of the work of Redemption, a divinization and sanctification of mankind in Christ, a union with God as Christ's human nature was united with the Logos.

Therefore, the chief mystery of Mary and the essential mystery of the Church coincide: it is the bridal union with God through grace, which leads to divine maternity. This mystery was accomplished in Mary and in Christians under the same conditions: by opening the soul for the Word of God by faith; and the union is based on the real union of Christ with His mystical body. Hence the mystery of the divine motherhood in the Church is not a special mystery, but is simply the general mystery of grace, of man's salvation.[111]

The final conclusion of the patristic investigation is that "Mary is the perfect (realization of the) Church — the essential mystery of the Church is the mystery of Mary."[112] And the mystery of Mary is the mystery of man's salvation, of the union with God granted by God and received by the creature.

This doctrine which, in Müller's interpretation, is taught by the Fathers, gives rise to a problem. At the bottom of the problem two truths are found. The first truth is the identity of Christ with His mystical body. The second truth is that men or the Church form members of Christ, become mothers of Christ, by the act of faith, that is, by conceiving the word of God. Mary also conceived Christ by faith in the word of God. Consequently, Mary's divine maternity and reception of grace in the Church are one and the same thing. Hence, the mystery of the Church and the mystery of Mary are one and the same mystery, that is, the mystery of human salvation, the mystery of the union between God and

---

[111] A. Müller, *Um die Grundlagen der Mariologie*, in *Divus Thomas* (Freiburg), Vol. 29, 1951, p. 389. A summary of this article in English, under the title *The Basic Principles of Mariology*, appears in *Theology Digest*, Vol. 1, 1953, pp. 139-144.

[112] *Ecclesia-Maria*, p. 232.

the creature, a union in which the creature has the function of spouse and mother. Thus Mary is the absolute, universal, and perfect realization of the Church, that is, of God's salvific plan.[113]

At this point a question arises: Is a new fundamental principle of Mariology required by this teaching of the Fathers? Up to now the divine maternity has been put forward as the basic principle. But according to Müller's discoveries, this principle is simply and purely grace which, however, has always been regarded as subordinate to the divine maternity and as coming to Mary in consequence of that dignity. How are sanctification through grace and the divine maternity related?[114]

In undertaking a reply to this question, Müller insists that Mary's divine, bridal motherhood is identical with the bridal motherhood of the Church; the former is the perfect realization of the latter.

Hence we can take as fundamental principle of Mariology: Mary is (the archetype of the Church or) the perfect Church. Here the Church is regarded in its most general and primary aspect of bridal reception of grace in Christ. And so there emerges the fundamental principle of Mariology which was first heard from the angel's lips: Mary is the one who is full of grace. Here we stand at the foundation and beginning of the whole theology of salvation. All we know of grace and the Church has its perfect form in Mary, and all we know of Mary has a counterpart in the Church and in the life of grace.[115]

Now the question can be answered. If Mary and the Church are equal in divine motherhood, and if this motherhood rests on reception of grace, we are forced to the conclusion that Mary's physical motherhood of Christ is the immediate consequence, a kind of formal effect, of her perfect sanctification through grace. Müller is quite aware that this contention will be rejected by all theologians, who have always represented Mary's fullness of grace as the first necessary consequence of her predestination to the divine maternity, as Christ's created grace is the consequence of the hypostatic union.[116]

---

[113] A. Müller, *L'unité de l'Église et de la Sainte Vierge chez les Pères des IVe et Ve siècles*, in *Bulletin de la Société Française d'Études Mariales*, Vol. 9, 1951, p. 36.

[114] *Um die Grundlagen der Mariologie*, in *Divus Thomas* (Freiburg), Vol. 29, 1951 p. 386.

[115] *Ibid.*, p. 390.

[116] *Ibid.*, p. 393.

Fundamental Principle of Mariology

Nevertheless, Müller thinks that his position is correct, for there is only one plan of salvation: to unite human nature to God in the Son and to divinize mankind by participation in Christ. This participation is brought about by the free decision of man, who surrenders himself to God as bride to her husband through faith and by the sacrament of baptism. By this receptive act, which is like that of a wife, man conceives and gives birth to a member of Christ, and so is rightly called a mother of Christ. But Mary conceived and gave birth to the physical body of Christ by the same act. Therefore, her act is compared by the Fathers to the act of faith made by every Christian, and the birth of the natural body of Christ is compared to the birth of the mystical Christ. Since sanctifying grace, in conjunction with the baptismal character, makes the Christian a mother of Christ, sanctifying grace also causes the divine maternity in Mary. Straightway a new question emerges: Is Mary's divine maternity, caused by grace, different only in degree and not in kind from the maternal dignity of every Christian? Would any Christian, on condition that he had as much grace as Mary, also become literally Mother of God?[117]

With the admission that a definitive solution of this difficulty is not at present available, Müller advances several proposals which he thinks are in the right direction. He lays down the principle that all habitual grace is a maternal and sponsal participation in the Incarnation. For by receiving grace the Christian becomes mother of Christ, in a partial, limited sense, with reference to the mystical body of Christ. Therefore, perfect grace is the most perfect possible materno-sponsal participation in the Incarnation, namely, physical maternity over the physical body of Christ.[118]

This principle is then applied to the case of Mary. The grace which the Blessed Virgin received is the perfect grace of the Church carried to its culmination; it is the universe of grace which God has wished to give to mankind. This grace has made Mary the Mother of God, for it caused her to give supreme feminine, materno-sponsal collaboration to the

---

[117] *Ibid.*, p. 395.

[118] In connection with this inference, H. Lennerz, *Maria-Ecclesia*, in *Gregorianum*, Vol. 35, 1954, p. 92, is tempted to ask: "Is the same to be said of the perfect grace in the soul of Christ? If so, a marvelous conclusion follows" — Christ would be His own mother!

work of redeeming mankind. Every grace is given by God and produces its proper effect when it is accepted by man. Therefore, every man who receives grace gives, partially, a maternal, feminine collaboration to the Redemption. Mary has done so universally.

Mary's unique, incomparable privilege consists in the fact that she alone has received the universal grace of the Church; all other persons receive it only in part. This difference between the perfect and the imperfect does not change the species, but it is more than a difference of degree. For difference of degree exists among different grades of the imperfect, whereas the perfect stands above such gradations. Accordingly, the entire Church has received the grace to be the mother of the Whole Christ, head and body, but this supreme grace has not been realized except in one individual, Mary, who alone, therefore, is literally Mother of God.[119]

Müller holds that his hypothesis is tenable and that it is supported by the most ancient tradition: God has only one plan of salvation and has established only one order of grace. This grace is essentially ordained to the divine maternity, which is realized where grace is perfect, in Mary. Therefore "Mother of God" means simply "full of grace." The idea, "fully endowed with grace," is at the very basis of Mary's existence; the divine maternity is its interior fruit, its formal effect.[120] Thus the fundamental principle of Mariology is the Blessed Virgin's fullness of grace.

The praise awarded by scholars to Müller's patristic exposition in his book, *Ecclesia-Maria*, has been withheld from the two articles in which he ventures into the realms of theological speculation. Of the critiques that have appeared, one of the fairest is the appraisal made by H. Lennerz.

Basic to Müller's theory is the identity he perceives between habitual grace and the divine maternity. The assertion of such identity begets a great difficulty. Habitual grace is a created gift that is infused in justification, whereby man becomes a sharer in the divine nature and is made an adopted child of God. And this same grace is said to be a

---

[119] *Art. cit.* in *Bulletin de la Société Française d'Études Mariales*, Vol. 9, 1951, p. 36 f.; cf. *art. cit.* in *Divus Thomas*, Vol. 29, 1951, p. 396 f.

[120] *Art. cit.* in *Divus Thomas*, Vol. 29, 1951, p. 398 f.

participation in the Incarnation, by which the divine Word is conceived according to human nature. Therefore, the generation by which man "becomes God" is a participation in the generation by which God becomes man. This is hard to grasp. True, in both the Incarnation of God and the justification of man, there is union between God and man. But these two unions are essentially diverse. In fact, they are opposed to each other: in the Incarnation man does not become God, but God becomes man; in justification the exact opposite occurs: man "becomes God."[121]

The reason why habitual grace is said to be a participation in the Incarnation is that, when the Christian receives grace, he becomes, in some limited sense, mother of Christ with reference to the mystical body. This can have a good meaning, and similar things are found in the Fathers. But it has nothing to do with a participation in the Incarnation. Members of Christ's mystical body are generated in the Church, but the Incarnate Word of God is not generated in the Church. Certainly the Church is the mystical body of Christ, but the Church is not Christ, and Christ is not the Church. The Church, mystical body of Christ, is a visible society founded by Christ; but Christ is not a visible society founded by Christ, and so the Church is not the Incarnate Word. The Church is the mother of Christians but is not the mother of Christ. Therefore, the maternity of the Church regarding the members of Christ's mystical body is utterly diverse from the Blessed Virgin's maternity regarding Christ; and Müller's thesis collapses.

Do the Fathers really teach what Müller asserts they do? The very first "truth" he thinks he finds in the Fathers arouses doubt. Christ is the divine Word Incarnate, Son of the Virgin Mary. The mystical body is the Church, a visible society instituted by Christ. Identity between them means that the divine, Incarnate Word is the Church, a visible society. The Fathers did not teach that. Hence the "identity" cannot be understood in a strict sense; therefore, in some wider sense, leaving intact the difference between Christ and the Church.

The second "truth" is this: as men form members of Christ and consequently become mothers of Christ by an act of faith, so Mary conceived Christ by faith in God's word. Müller concludes from this that

---

[121] H. Lennerz, S.J., *Maria-Ecclesia*, in *Gregorianum*, Vol. 35, 1954, p. 92.

Mary's divine maternity and reception of grace in the Church are one and the same thing. If to "form members of Christ, to become mothers of Christ" is understood of the grace of regeneration, it is not true that this is accomplished by the act of faith. An act of faith is indeed required of adults, along with other acts, as a disposition for justification; but man is not justified or regenerated by the act of faith. The Blessed Virgin believed what the angel said, but she did not conceive Christ by an act of faith. In the generation of Christ, God was made man; in the regeneration of a Christian, man is made an adopted son of God. Far from being identical, the generation of Christ and the regeneration of the Christian are diametrically opposed.[122]

Finally, the Church guards the firm conviction that the Blessed Virgin was adorned with her matchless privileges of grace precisely because she was to be the Mother of God. To perceive this, we have only to read the beginning of the Bull *Ineffabilis Deus*, or the prayers of the liturgy; no theologian of note teaches otherwise. Müller's inversion, that Mary's divine maternity was the effect of her fullness of grace, is completely inadmissible.[123]

7. Mary as the New Paradise

In a survey of Mariological literature written several years ago, Congar recalls that Thomist tradition has clung to the formal notion of divine maternity as the primary principle of Mariology.

However, he believes that the developments of piety have led us to pass beyond this point of view which, confined within its proper limits, does not account for Mary's recognized role in the economy of salvation. Efforts are made to explain Mary's coredemptive office by applying the theme of the new Eve and that of prototype of the Church. But the difficulty is that the Fathers recognized, not the Blessed Virgin, but the Church, as the new Eve who is spouse of the new Adam. According to the Fathers, Mary is rather the new Paradise.[124]

This hint was taken up and developed by Charles Moeller in an

---

[122] *Ibid.*, p. 92 f.

[123] *Ibid.*, p. 93.

[124] Congar, in *Revue des Sciences Philosophiques et Théologiques*, Vol. 34, 1951, p. 624 f. and note 79.

article that is somewhat lacking in theological precision. The author was engaged in tracing two lines of thought, Mother of God and spouse of the Word, that stem from positive data. Could these two be referred to a third that would contain them? Or must we place one in front and attempt to lead the other to it? This third thing cannot be Scheeben's "bridal maternity" or Semmelroth's *Urbild* or the "new Eve." These aspects of Mary are interesting speculative elements of Mariology, but the entire science cannot be erected on any of them. A fourth idea includes the three preceding ones but does not exhibit their disadvantages; it is the idea of Mary as the "New Paradise" suggested by Congar.[125]

This idea unifies Mariology. By the Immaculate Conception, Mary is the new Paradise of God, the new creation. By the Assumption, Mary represents the eschatological Paradise, anticipated in her. By the divine and virginal maternity, she appears as the Paradise in which God is wholeheartedly received, the enclosed garden in which the betrothal of God and mankind is accomplished in the incarnate Christ. Paradise itself is a creature, but a creature that is transparent to the divinity dwelling within it. Mary, the new Paradise, remains in the order of creation; as a perfect creature, the Paradise of God, she verifies the perfect notion of creation, cooperating with the grace of God in the work of God.[126]

The idea of the new Paradise integrates Mariology into theology: into Christology, for Christ is the new Adam of this Paradise regained; into ecclesiology, for the Church is also a Paradise, the new Eve of the new Garden of Eden, the Jerusalem adorned as bride for her husband; into "pneumatology" for, as the Spirit of God moved over the waters of the abyss at the first creation, He later operated mysteriously in the virginal maternity for the sanctification of Mary and the Church; into eschatology, for the horizon of the history of salvation, from Genesis to the Apocalypse, is dominated by the Kingdom that will be realized in the Paradise of God.[127]

Such is the idea which Moeller prefers, because it keeps Mary's motherhood and betrothal in the same line, without subordinating one

---

[125] C. Moeller, *Doctrinal Aspects of Mariology*, in *Lumen Vitae*, Vol. 8, 1953, p. 248 f.
[126] *Ibid.*, p. 249 f.
[127] *Ibid.*, p. 250.

to the other; it is also patristic.

Reaction to this suggestion has been negligible. Philips acknowledges that it avoids amalgamating the qualities of mother and spouse in a single unthinkable concept, such as Scheeben's "bridal motherhood." And it is, indeed, patristic. However, Moeller's "idea" is not an idea at all, but only an image.[128] As such, it cannot be seriously regarded as the basic principle of Mariology.

8. Perfect Redemption of Mary

Essential to an understanding of one of the most recent theories, proposed by Karl Rahner, is the presupposition that Mary did not actively cooperate in the objective Redemption wrought on Calvary. Mary's cooperation is limited to her consent that made the Redemption possible by permitting it to be accomplished in her and through her, for the salvation of all. The concept and term *Coredemptrix* ought to be avoided, because it evokes the idea that Mary cooperated in the Redemption on the level and in the function reserved for the one Mediator.[129]

At the time of the Incarnation, Mary wholly accepted, in soul (by faith) and in body, the Word of God who was made flesh for the Redemption of mankind. By doing this, she also accepted God's mercy for herself, in the order of her own subjective Redemption. Thereby she took her stand entirely on the side of the redeemed. By her faith she surrendered herself unreservedly, in soul and body, to the gift of the incarnate Grace of the Father. Accordingly, she is the perfect model of Redemption, the perfect type and representative of the Church.

Clear affirmations of Scripture (mainly Genesis 3:15, the *fiat* and fullness of grace reported in Luke, and Mary's position at the foot of the cross as described in John) convey a knowledge of the Blessed Virgin's person and place in the history of salvation. This makes possible the formulation of the fundamental principle of Mariology: Mary is she who,

---

[128] G. Philips, in *Marianum*, Vol. 15, 1953, p. 443.

[129] K. Rahner, S.J., *Le principe fondamental de la théologie mariale*, in *Recherches de Science Religieuse*, Vol. 42, 1954, p. 494 f. In footnote 23, the author states that he associates himself with the criticisms made by Goossens, Lennerz, Köster, and Semmelroth against the theological teaching, widespread today, about Mary's coredemptive function.

by grace, has been perfectly redeemed, the one who realizes and represents most perfectly what the grace of God achieves in mankind and the Church.[130]

The various theories proposed about the basic principle from which are derived all the properties and functions of the Blessed Virgin come more or less to the same thing: Mary, by her divine maternity, occupies a unique and decisive position in the history of salvation. The formula here advocated, "Mary is the one who has been redeemed in the most perfect way," is not opposed to the other theories. For Redemption is a reception of salvation, bestowed by God in the flesh of Christ, a reception that cooperates in this salvation; consequently, the most perfect redemption is reception of the Incarnate Word in a perfect cooperation of both soul and body, and is, moreover, cooperation in the salvation of all.[131] Because of such considerations, Rahner holds that his formula implies all the elements stressed in other enunciations of the fundamental principle or principles of Marian theology.

This formula has several advantages. It results more directly from Scripture. More clearly than others, it traces the line connecting Mary's perfections with the fundamental principle. Thus the Immaculate Conception is the effect of preservative Redemption; exemption from all sin is its perfect grace; Mary's holiness is the most eminent found among creatures; and the Assumption is a consequence of her place in the history of salvation. We cannot deduce absolutely everything from it, for we must know from other sources what is possible in the case of a redemption that is brought about in the most perfect manner.[132]

A confirmation of the solidity of this principle is at hand: some truths cannot be known except in the hypothesis of this basic principle. Certain Mariological truths which are the object of the teaching and the faith of the Church were not always, from the beginning, expressly and clearly attested in the direct sources of the faith. Among them are the Immaculate Conception, the permanent freedom from all sin, and the perpetual virginity. Some principle is needed in these cases, since the truth that is deduced or deducible has not always been explicitly taught.

---

[130] *Ibid.*, pp. 503, 505.
[131] *Ibid.*, pp. 508-510.
[132] *Ibid.*, p. 510 f.

This does not mean that the fundamental principle must always have been present in the reflective consciousness of the faith of the Church, for it may have existed in a general and obscure way, without explicit formulation. Take, for example, the Immaculate Conception, as implicitly contained in patristic affirmations about Mary's absolute freedom from sin. We cannot include freedom from original sin in these affirmations unless we suppose that a redemption realized in the most perfect manner (hence a preservative redemption) was present in the minds of the Fathers. So also, as regards Mary's eminent holiness and exemption from all personal sin, the Church possessed in this fundamental idea the point of departure for further clarification.[133]

The author thinks that, after the reflections and indications he has mentioned, it is not necessary to show that the great central truths of Mariology, the divine motherhood and Mary's unique place in the history of salvation, are contained in his principle.[134] However, the importance of the principle is not so momentous with regard to these truths of faith, because they are immediately knowable in the sources of revelation, and hence are more independent of the principle.[135]

Whatever may be the best formula (which is variable according to numerous points of view possible), behind all the affirmations of the teaching of the Church about the Blessed Virgin is found a fundamental, global, non-reflective, but clear conviction: the Redemption, definitively taking hold of the world in the person of Mary, body and soul, has been realized in her in the most perfect manner.[136]

At the time of present writing, no criticisms of Father Rahner's article have come to my notice. Yet a few observations are in order. That Mary was perfectly redeemed is certain and we all gladly believe that she was. The question is, whether her perfect Redemption can be taken

---

[133] *Ibid.*, pp. 512-515. The author has his troubles when he endeavors to derive Mary's perpetual virginity from his fundamental principle, and requires four or five pages to make his point (which is not very convincing).

[134] With regard to the divine maternity, one of the pertinent "indications" seems to be that perfect reception of redemption in body implies reception of Christ, through whom alone salvation comes, in one's body by a literal maternal conception. In that case a male could not be redeemed "in the most perfect way."

[135] *Op. cit.*, p. 513.

[136] *Ibid.*, p. 521 f.

as the ultimate, basic principle of Mariology.

In this connection we may consider the author's final summing up: behind all the particular affirmations of the teaching of the Church about Mary is the conviction that the Redemption, taking hold of the world in the person of Mary, body and soul, has been realized in her in the most perfect manner. Is this really behind all the particular affirmations? Certainly not in the conviction of the Church; for the Church has a conviction that behind Mary's perfect redemption is the basic reason underlying it: she is the Mother of God, and therefore was so perfectly redeemed and had so marked a place in the history of salvation. Thus in general, concerning Rahner's whole thesis, the question always persists: *why* was the Blessed Virgin redeemed so perfectly? And the answer is no less persistent: because she was to be, and actually was, Mother of God. This is behind the perfect redemption, and therefore is the reason and the principle of all the rest.

A good example is the author's point about the Immaculate Conception, which is well and strikingly made. It is quite true that we cannot regard freedom from original sin as implied in patristic affirmations about Mary's absolute freedom from sin, unless we suppose that a redemption realized in the most perfect way, and consequently a preservative redemption, was present in the minds of the Fathers. But what is the source of their conviction concerning Mary's perfect redemption if not their appreciation of the supreme dignity of the divine maternity? The same holds for their teaching about Mary's eminent holiness and permament freedom from personal sin.

Furthermore, going far beyond the author, we can show (and I shall endeavor to do so later) that Mary could be, and was, Coredemptrix because she was God's Mother. Rahner does not admit this. He is not even willing to allow the concept or the term *Coredemptrix.* His scruples are surprising, as the concept and the term have for many years been fully sanctioned by ecclesiastical usage. If the term *Coredemptrix,* or its abstract counterpart, Coredemption, is to be avoided, it ought to be avoided by the Popes, who teach us apt terminology as well as correct doctrine. But the Popes, far from avoiding it, have employed it repeatedly and designedly. Therefore, it is not to be avoided but ought to be used.[137] In back of Father Rahner's attitude, and seemingly at the bottom of his entire thesis, is the view that the Blessed Virgin's part in the Redemption, aside from her consent which made salvation possible, is purely receptive.

The whole question eventually comes to this: Is Mary the Mother of God because she is perfectly redeemed, or is she perfectly redeemed because she is the Mother of God? Which of the two is the reason accounting for, underlying the other? In other words, which is the fundamental principle of Mariology: the perfect redemption or the divine maternity? Consultation of the official teaching authority of the Church leaves no doubt concerning this choice of alternatives.

B. MIND OF THE MAGISTERIUM

Strange neglect of directives furnished by the teaching authority of the Church has attended discussions of the primary principle of Mariology.[138] The more important the question, the graver is the theologian's duty of consulting the teaching of the magisterium. In the science of Mariology, the problem of the primary principle is supremely important, since the primary principle dominates the structure of the science, imparts consistency to it, confers order on all its parts, and makes possible the unified organization of the treatise.

Thorough investigation of the doctrine of the magisterium on this subject would be too lengthy a procedure to be considered here. Perhaps, too, it is not necessary. The mind of the Church is abundantly clear from indications found in a number of documents issued by the Popes during the past century.

A good place to begin is the Bull that defines the Immaculate

---

[137] No need to belabor this point; see summary of evidence presented by J. B. Carol, O.F.M., *De Corredemptione Beatae Virginis Mariae* (Civitas Vaticana, 1950), pp. 509-582. The recent Popes, from Pius IX to Pius XII, and many bishops describe the coredemptive office of the Blessed Virgin with such words as *reparatrix, coredemptrix,* and the like. For a more detailed answer to the various objections raised against the Coredemption, cf. the last section of Fr. Carol's chapter, *Our Lady's Coredemption,* in this volume.

[138] The necessity of heeding the guidance of the magisterium is clearly set forth by Pius XII, Encycl. *Humani generis,* in *A.A.S.,* Vol. 42, 1950, p. 567; also pp. 563, 569, 576. On the function of encyclicals as instruments of the Supreme Pontiff's exercise of his ordinary magisterium, cf. *ibid.,* p. 568.

Conception. Pius IX tells us that God had eternally foreseen the fall of the human race which would result from Adam's disobedience, and had decided to bring the first work of His love to a successful completion through the Incarnation of the Word. Therefore, from the beginning and before all time, God selected for His Son a Mother of whom He would be born, and upon her He lavished a profusion of divine gifts such as no other creature would ever receive. In addition to everything else, she was forever to be free from all sin; wholly beautiful and perfect, she was endowed with a fullness of innocence and holiness unexcelled under God and incomprehensible except to God. "It was altogether fitting that this Mother should always be radiant with the splendor of most perfect holiness and that, completely unsullied even by the stain of original sin, she should win a triumphant victory over the ancient serpent. For on her the Father had bestowed the gift of His only Son."[139] Here the reason assigned for Mary's perpetual sinlessness, incomparable fullness of grace and holiness, Immaculate Conception, and triumph over the devil is her divine maternity. God Himself, in His infinite wisdom, judged that the Mother of His Son should be thus enriched with all the treasures of divine goodness, for the reason that she was the Mother of God. The notion that her fullness of grace or perfect redemption is the source of her divine motherhood is an inversion of the order of divine providence.

Faithful to the same line of thought, Leo XIII wrote in one of his Rosary encyclicals: "The Virgin who had no part in original sin, having been chosen to be the Mother of God, because of that very fact was given a share in the work of saving the human race, and so she possesses such grace and power with her Son that no human or angelic nature has ever received or can receive greater."[140] Here again the reason why God has endowed the Blessed Virgin with such incomparable gifts, including her association in the work of Redemption, is her divine maternity.

The derivation of Mary's spiritual motherhood from her divine motherhood is brought out by St. Pius X in words of great beauty:

> Is not Mary the Mother of Christ? Therefore, she is our mother also. ... As the God-man, Christ acquired a material body as all men do; but as the Savior of our race He acquired a kind of spiritual and mystical body,

---

[139] Bull *Ineffabilis Deus*, in *Collectio Lacensis*, Vol. 6, col. 836.
[140] Leo XIII, Encycl. *Supremi Apostolatus*, in *A.A.S.*, Vol. 16, 1883-1884, p. 114.

which is the society of those who believe in Christ. ... In one and the same womb of His most chaste Mother, Christ took to Himself human flesh and at the same time added to it a spiritual body made up of all those who were to believe in Him. Therefore, Mary, while carrying the Savior in her womb, may be said to have carried likewise all those whose life was contained in the Savior's life. All of us, consequently, who are united to Christ and are, as the Apostle says, "members of His body, of His flesh, and of His bones" (Eph. 5:30), have come forth from Mary's womb, like a body attached to its head. That is why, in a spiritual and mystical sense, we are called Mary's children, and she is the Mother of us all.[141]

Accordingly, formulas such as: "Mary is the Mother of the Whole Christ" or "Mary is the Universal Mother," cannot be accepted as the primary principle of Mariology. Of the two elements comprised in these formulas, the divine maternity and the spiritual maternity, the second is dependent on the first; therefore, the first is the principle of the second. Moreover, as the Pope goes on to say, Mary distributes the treasures of Christ's merits by title of her divine motherhood, which invests her with a kind of right.[142] Finally, the special reason why the Blessed Virgin was preserved from original sin is the fact that she was to be the Mother of God.[143]

In an encyclical written to commemorate the fifteen-hundredth anniversary of the Council of Ephesus, Pius XI affirms: "From the dogma of the divine maternity emanate, as from a deep and hidden spring, Mary's unparalleled grace and her eminent rank, the highest under God." The Pope proceeds to quote two great authors, with complete approval:

As Aquinas so aptly writes, "The Blessed Virgin, because she is the Mother of God, possesses a certain infinite dignity resulting from the infinite good which is God" (*Summa*, Ia, q. 25, a. 6 ad 4). The same truth is stated and explained in greater detail by Cornelius a Lapide: "The Blessed Virgin is the Mother of God; therefore, she far excels all the angels, even the seraphim and cherubim. She is the Mother of God; that

---

[141] St. Pius X, Encycl. *Ad diem illum*, in *A.S.S.*, Vol. 36, 1903-1904, p. 452 f.

[142] *Ibid.*, p. 455: "materno veluti iure."

[143] *Ibid.*, p. 458.

is why she is all pure and all holy; that is why, under God, greater purity than hers cannot be conceived" (*In Matthaeum*, I, 6).[144]

In this passage the Pope teaches that the divine maternity is the most basic source of Mary's greatness. Her position at the summit of creation, her exaltation above all the angels, her fullness of grace, and her supreme purity and holiness are all consequences of the fact that she is Mother of God.

Before coming to the definition of the Blessed Virgin's assumption into heaven, Pope Pius XII summarizes the historical development of the doctrine. Discussion of the evidence gathered from the patristic period is followed by an examination of scholastic theologians. The Holy Father points out that their first argument was always that Jesus Christ willed the Assumption because of His filial love for His Mother. "The strength of their arguments rests on the incomparable dignity of her divine motherhood and all the other prerogatives that flow from it. These include her exalted holiness that surpasses the holiness of all men and all angels, the intimate union of Mary with her Son, and the ardor of that special love which the Son has for His most worthy Mother."[145] This line of reasoning has the wholehearted support of His Holiness; speaking later in his own name, the Pope continues:

All these proofs and considerations of the holy Fathers and theologians are ultimately based on the Sacred Writings, which set the loving Mother of God before our eyes as most closely associated with her divine Son and ever sharing His lot. Consequently, it seems impossible to think that she who conceived and gave birth to Christ, nursed Him with her milk, held Him in her arms and clasped Him to her breast, should, at the close of her earthly life, be separated from him in body, even though not in soul. ... Since He had the power to grant this great honor to His Mother, to preserve her from the corruption of the grave, we must believe that He actually did so.[146]

In these excerpts the Holy Father teaches that Mary's sublime holiness and loving union with her Son, her association with Him throughout His career, and her glorious Assumption into heaven, are all

---

[144] Pius XI, Encycl. *Lux veritatis*, in *A.A.S.*, Vol. 23, 1931, p. 513.
[145] Pius XII, Const. Apost. *Munificentissimus Deus*, in *A.A.S.*, Vol. 42, 1950, p. 762.
[146] *Ibid.*, p. 767 f.

consequences of her divine maternity.

Proclamation of the Marian Year was the occasion for an encyclical which conveys, in unmistakable terms, the doctrine that the divine maternity is the basic reason underlying the extraordinary greatness of the Blessed Virgin.

Among all the holy men and women who have ever lived, there is only one about whom we can say that the question of sin does not even arise. It is likewise clear that this unique privilege, never granted to anyone else, was given to Mary by God because she was raised to the dignity of Mother of God. ... A higher office than this does not seem possible; since it requires the greatest dignity and sanctity after Christ, it demands the fullest perfection of divine grace and a soul free from every sin. Indeed, all the privileges and graces with which her soul and her life were endowed in so extraordinary a manner and measure, seem to flow from this sublime vocation of Mother of God, as from a pure and hidden source.[147]

The divine maternity is the basic reason for many of Mary's greatest graces and functions, which are specified here and elsewhere in papal documents. This is altogether certain. Moreover, the Holy Father believes that it is the source of all her privileges and graces, although he does not here choose to teach this as certain. Hence he contents himself with saying that it "seems" to be the universal source.

That the divine maternity is the source of Mary's queenship is asserted by the Pope with all the firmness that may be desired, in the document in which he decrees the Feast of Mary as Queen. "The basic principle on which Mary's royal dignity rests is beyond doubt her divine maternity. ... She is Queen because she brought forth a Son who, at the very moment He was conceived, was King and Lord of all creation even as man, by reason of the hypostatic union of His human nature with the Word."[148]

This truth stands unassailable. However, as the Holy Father adds:

> The most Blessed Virgin is to be called Queen, not only on account of her divine maternity, but also because by the will of God she had an

---

[147] Pius XII, Encycl. *Fulgens corona*, in *A.A.S.*, Vol. 45, 1953, p. 580.
[148] Pius XII, Encycl. *Ad Caeli Reginam*, in *A.A.S.*, Vol. 46, 1954, p. 633.

exceedingly important part in the work of our eternal salvation.[149] ...By God's will, Mary was associated with Jesus Christ, the principle of salvation, in procuring spiritual salvation, in a way similar to the way Eve was associated with Adam, the principle of death... Hence we may draw the sure conclusion that just as Christ, the new Adam, must be called King not only because He is the Son of God, but also because He is our Redeemer, so, by a kind of analogy, the Blessed Virgin is Queen not only because she is the Mother of God, but also because, as the new Eve, she was associated with the new Adam.[150]

Yet the divine maternity is the ultimate principle of Mary's royal rank, and therefore of the lifelong association with Christ and His work that is summed up and has its crowning culmination in her queenship.

As is clear from this brief examination of a few pontifical documents, of all the proposals that have been made about the fundamental principle of Mariology, only one is consonant with papal teaching; and that is Mary's divine maternity.

C. Theological Vindication

Many theologians, especially among those who advocate a double principle, would admit that the divine maternity is the basic principle of Mariology, were it not for their fear that the divine maternity does not offer a secure way to Mary's association with Christ in the work of Redemption. Such theologians maintain that the notion of divine maternity does not necessarily contain the notion of Mary's cooperation in the Redemption. Analysis of the first does not yield the second; therefore, the second cannot be deduced from the first. Consequently, if our Mariology is to safeguard the Blessed Virgin's coredemptive activity, some other principle is needed.

To solve this difficulty we need but distinguish, with St. Thomas, between the necessary mystery of God's trinitarian life and the free

---

[149] This teaching lends powerful support to the contention that Mary cooperated immediately in the objective Redemption. The "important part in the work of our eternal salvation" that is here attributed to the Blessed Virgin cannot refer either to her divine maternity, from which it is distinguished, or to her activity in dispensing graces from heaven, for the latter is an exercise of her queenship, not a principle of it.

[150] *Op. cit.,* pp. 633-635.

mystery of our salvation through the redemptive Incarnation.[151] All the other articles of faith, and with them all theology, are reduced to these two supreme articles. The main task of Mariology is to discover the place and the function of the Blessed Virgin in the divine plan; consequently, Mariology belongs to the free mystery of salvation that is achieved through the redemptive Incarnation.

In the stratosphere of abstract ideas, cooperation in the Redemption cannot be deduced with metaphysical necessity from the notion of divine maternity. Prescinding from the free design of God's infinite wisdom, we cannot know that the Mother of God is associated with Christ in the enterprise of salvation. Yet there is a connection, and it is necessary, because God has eternally planned to associate His Mother with Himself in redeeming us, and He wills the execution of His plan. The nexus between Mary's divine maternity and her association with the Redeemer is not *ex natura rei* but *ex ordinatione divina*.[152] And that is the clear teaching of Pius XII: "By God's will Mary was associated [*ex Dei placito* — God's free will — *sociata fuit*] with Jesus Christ ... as the new Eve, she was associated with the new Adam."[153]

This parallel between Eve and Mary is the most ancient form found in tradition to describe the Blessed Virgin's cooperation in the Redemption.[154] It is also the most basic theme in Mariology after the principle of the divine maternity. The parallel implies a contrast: as Eve was associated with Adam in the disorder of ruin, so Mary, the new Eve, is associated with Christ, the new Adam, in the order of reparation. It also involves a comparison: as Eve, on the natural plane, is mother of all the living, so Mary, on the supernatural plane, is likewise mother of all the living. Yet the relationship is not the same in each case. Eve is the mother of all who have natural life because she is the wife of Adam, whereas Mary is the mother of all who have supernatural life because she is the Mother of Christ. Mary is a maternal, not a bridal associate of

---

[151] Cf. *De veritate*, q. 14, a. 11.

[152] Cf. Elias de la Dolorosa, *La maternidad de María, principio supremo de la Mariología,* in *Estudios Marianos*, Vol. 3, 1944, p. 42.

[153] Encycl. *Ad Caeli Reginam,* in *A.A.S.,* Vol. 46, 1954, p. 634.

[154] Cf. W. J. Burghardt, S.J., *Mary in Western Patristic Thought,* in J. B. Carol, ed., *Mariology,* Vol. 1 (Milwaukee, 1955), pp. 122-130.

her Son.

Sacred Scripture never refers to Mary as the spouse of the Word. She is exclusively His Mother. But she is His Mother in the full force of the term; not only because she brought Him into the world, but because she sustained Him in His vocation up to the supreme sacrifice. That is the lesson scriptural scholars are perceiving more and more clearly from her presence at the foot of the cross.[155] The union between the Blessed Virgin and her Son far surpasses the union of husband and wife. The idea of spouse cannot accurately represent the relationship. Mary is the Mother of Jesus, closely associated with Him in His career; but always as Mother. Any element of pertinent truth connoted by the figure of spouse is eminently included in Mary's motherhood, but in a way that incomparably transcends the image. Rightly did SS. Justin and Irenaeus find in the recital of the Annunciation a reason for contrasting Mary's obedience with Eve's disobedience; yet they fell far short of St. John in penetrating the mystery. For the Evangelist, Mary did not merely obey the angel's proposals by consenting to be the Saviour's Mother; she went much farther and acquiesced in His immolation and thus shared in His victory over mankind's ancient enemy. As Mother of the Saviour, inseparably united to her Son, she verifies the promise of Genesis: "I will put enmities between thee and the woman, and thy seed and her seed; she shall crush thy head." She is the new Eve because she is the Mother of the new Adam.

By the very fact that Mary is the Saviour's Mother she cooperated in our Redemption, at least in its initial stage. There is no metaphysically necessary reason why her intervention should not have terminated at this stage; if the Father had so willed, Christ could have carried on and achieved His redemptive work without any associate at all. Yet such a cessation would hardly be consonant with the exercise of divine providence as it is ordinarily manifested; God does not assign offices by halves. We should rather expect that the association begun should have a further cooperation as its complement.

This expectation is readily justified. Mary's maternity elevates her to the hypostatic order, in the sense that the hypostatic union between

---

[155] Cf. F. M. Braun, O.P., *Marie et l'Église, d'après l'Écriture*, in *Bulletin de la Société Française d'Études Mariales*, Vol. 10, 1952, p. 15.

Christ's assumed human nature and the Person of the Word was accomplished through her and in her; her Son is a divine Person. In the actual economy of salvation the hypostatic order is for the Redemption of the human race. Consequently, anyone who belongs to this order has a redemptive function. Therefore, the divine maternity, which introduces Mary into the hypostatic order, is also the cause of her redemptive mission. "The Virgin who had no part in original sin, having been chosen to be the Mother of God, because of that very fact was given a share in the work of saving the human race."[156]

Nevertheless, a doubt remains. To cooperate actively in the objective Redemption, Mary had to have some significant part in the very sacrifice of the cross, the climax of Christ's redemptive life. To have such an office, she had to know about it, consent to it, and effectively discharge it. All that has to be shown, and in such a way as to make clear that her coredemptive activity is an exercise of her divine maternity.

To what extent did this woman, who had been chosen by God to be the Mother and associate of the Redeemer, understand the part she was to play in the history of salvation? She was a Jewish girl, a daughter of Israel, the race that lived on the "promises" (*Rom.* 9:4), and she shared the hopes and longings of her people. The first promise of the Redemption had been made to the original parents of mankind (*Gen.* 3:15) and was progressively clarified in the course of the long centuries. Abraham received from God the promise that all nations would be blessed in the people of which he was to be the father. David was given the assurance that one of his descendants would be the Saviour, who would wield divine power and would possess sacerdotal dignity. Yet this Saviour would be a man of sorrows, as foretold by the prophet Isaias, who also announced that He would be born of a virgin.

Throughout the Old Testament, individual after individual, as well as a whole nation, the "chosen people," were called by God for a definite purpose, with each new revelation inaugurating a new period in the economy of Redemption that marked an advance over the preceding epoch. The vocation of an individual is never a private affair, but always betokens a communal call: Abraham, Moses, David, and the prophets were summoned forth by God for the salvation of mankind. Among the

---

[156] Leo XIII, Encycl. *Supremi Apostolatus*, in *A.S.S.*, Vol. 16, 1883-1884, p. 114.

individuals thus chosen is Mary, whose election is the crowning point in the general election of the people of God. The Annunciation is the fulfillment of all the earlier annunciations.

The Jewish maiden, well acquainted with the great Books and traditions of her race, was aware of all this when the angel Gabriel, carrying out the prophecy of Isaias, brought her the message from God: "Thou shalt conceive in thy womb and shall bring forth a Son." Prior to any response on her part, he told her that the time had come for establishing the everlasting Messianic Kingdom, the new empire of salvation. Her cousin Elizabeth, filled with the Holy Spirit, perceived that Mary was the Mother of the divine Saviour, and bore witness to the Virgin's association with Jesus: "Blessed art thou among women, and blessed is the fruit of thy womb." Even the shepherds were informed, shortly after Christ's birth, that Mary was the Mother of the Redeemer: "This day is born to you a Savior, who is Christ the Lord." In the temple Simeon told Mary: "This child is set for the fall and for the resurrection of many," and announced that she would share in her Son's future conflict: "Thy own soul a sword shall pierce."

How could Mary's knowledge fail to measure up to her vocation? All her life she cherished the memory of every word that was spoken about her Son or by Him, and she would ponder on all these utterances in her heart. How could God neglect to enlighten her more and more fully, as time went on, about all the implications of her calling? "We may not doubt that the Blessed Virgin received most excellently the gift of wisdom."[157] Illuminated by this gift of wisdom which, like all the infused virtues and gifts of the Holy Spirit, were proportionate to her fullness of grace, she penetrated more and more deeply into the abyss of the mystery of Jesus. "Those who were nearest to Christ, whether coming before Him, like John the Baptist, or coming after Him, like the apostles, had a fuller knowledge of the mysteries of faith."[158] But who ever stood so close to Christ as His own Mother? St. Pius X perceived this very clearly:

She was the only one who enjoyed the intimate association of family life with Jesus for thirty years, as is right for mother and son. Who

---

[157] St. Thomas, *S. Th.*, III, q. 27, a. 5 ad 3.
[158] *Ibid.*, II-II, q. 1, a. 7 ad 4.

understood better than His Mother the stupendous mysteries of Christ's birth, of His boyhood, and especially of His incarnation, the very beginning and foundation of our faith? She kept and pondered in her heart all that happened at Bethlehem and in the temple of the Lord in Jerusalem. Beyond that, she shared in the thoughts and the hidden plans of Christ; indeed, we must say that she lived the very life of her Son. ... From the home at Nazareth to the hill of Calvary, Mary was the constant associate of Jesus; she understood the secrets of His heart better than anyone ever did.[159]

However, the question whether Mary grasped, to the last detail, all the implications of her consent to the Incarnation, is basically unimportant. Full consent to God is abandonment of one's life to consequences that cannot be completely foreseen, because the person who surrenders himself to God without condition or reserve loses himself in God's immensity. Some obscurity is inevitable in such a consent, and does not lessen its value, for the surrender is made to God who is incomprehensible, to Him whose ways are unpredictable and whose decision is sovereign. Mary knew enough; she knew that she was saying "Yes" to Him whom the angel called the Son of God, come to accomplish our Redemption.[160]

Mary's free consent to the Incarnation is explicit: "Behold the handmaid of the Lord; be it done to me according to thy word." The consent itself stems from her faith for which she is declared blessed: "Blessed art thou that hast believed," and is the effect of grace, which makes it an event in the history of salvation, supposing both a call from God and her own personal response. Thereupon the Virgin, through the action of the Holy Spirit, became the Mother of the Saviour of the world.

The initiative is God's. He alone decides who is to have a commission and power in the economy of salvation. His was the will to save the fallen race through the God-man. For Him God chose a human

---

[159] Encycl. *Ad diem illum,* in *A.A.S.,* Vol. 36, 1903-1904, pp. 452, 454.

[160] Cf. K. Rahner, S.J., *Le principe fondamental de la théologie mariale,* in *Recherches de Science Religieuse,* Vol. 42, 1954, p. 492. The first part of this article expresses some beautiful truths which will be further applied in this study. Unfortunately, Father Rahner does not draw out the full consequences of the premises he himself so convincingly establishes.

mother, and out of all the women of the earth, from Eve to the last girl that would ever be born, He selected Mary, who thereby received from God a charge affecting the eternal lot of all mankind. In response to God's call, Mary gave her consent to be the Mother of the Redeemer; she understood clearly from the angel's message that her Son was the promised Messias for whose coming she, a pious Jewish girl drenched in the spirit of her people and favored with God's special graces, ardently longed.

Because of her consent Mary suddenly found herself at the decisive point in the history of salvation; through her the central act of God in the world was accomplished. All previous history led in a straight line to this act, and here also the future of mankind was decided, although Redemption still had to receive its definitive consummation in the death of the Incarnate Word.

Can we go farther and say that Mary, who consented to be the Redeemer's Mother, continued her consent to God's redemptive plan to the very end as she stood under the cross of her Son? The answer must unquestionably be affirmative, if we can show that such was God's will.

Christ Himself is the Redeemer not only by His own will, but because the Father sent Him for the purpose of redeeming us on the cross by the sacrifice of His life. Likewise the presence of the Mother under the cross was willed by God; in God's plan Mary was to have part in the passion of her Son. Otherwise God would certainly have spared her this excruciating pain. If she was not to share in the passion, why was she there at this dreadful hour? Surely not merely to care for the lifeless body after the crucifixion; another could have done that. She knew what Christ was really achieving on the cross. All His intimate associates knew that, or should have known it; He had spoken of it often enough those last months. And knowing God's will, she acceded to it completely; we simply cannot think that her will was in the slightest degree at variance with the will of God.

Accordingly, Mary was the associate of the Redeemer at His very act of Redemption, because God had predestined her to be the *Mater dolorosa* and because she fully cooperated with God's program. She was drawn into the redemptive suffering of her Son precisely because she was His Mother. She, the Immaculate who was preredeemed, the one who is full of grace and blessed among all women, did not have to suffer anything for her own Redemption, and therefore was engaged exclusively in the work of her Son for the Redemption of all mankind. The whole of her hard life, from the moment of the Annunciation to the hour of the cross, with all the periods of suffering in between, has to be understood in this way, if it is to have any meaning at all.[161]

Mary's suffering under the cross cannot be thought of merely as the Mother's sympathy with her Son. He who suffers there owes His human life to her. He is her Son, and she is His Mother; and since she is His Mother, He belongs to her; He is hers. Thus she has Something to offer to God in sacrifice; and she does offer Him, for her will is perfectly attuned to His, and His will is to do the will of His Father, to offer Himself as sacrificial victim for the salvation of the world.

How could a mother do such a thing? This Mother could, because of her perfect motherhood. The natural consequence of maternity is loving union between mother and child. Mary's motherhood was perfected by grace. God elevated it to the hypostatic order and adapted the maternal heart of Mary to the divine person of her Son, thus fitting her for her part in the supernatural work of our Redemption. This maternal union of Mary with her Son, supernaturalized beyond understanding, is what made her the intimate associate of the Redeemer. Those whom God chooses for an office, He likewise equips for the successful performance of that office.[162] God gives to everyone the grace to carry out the task for which he was elected; the Blessed Virgin received so much grace that she is closest of all creatures to the Author of grace.[163] Essentially progressive, this grace led her to the state of perfect Mother of God and associate of Christ. She was always the true Mother of the Saviour, not only by reason of her virginal conceiving, but also because of the spiritual growth of her maternity, which raised her to the summit of Calvary where she shared in the sacrifice of her immolated Son.

At the hour of the Incarnation Mary believed; at the foot of the cross she still believed. Then she had uttered her *fiat* to Him who would save His people; on Calvary she maintained, by the continuity of faith, her

---

[161] Cf. J. Auer, *Salve Maria, Regina Mundi*, in *Geist und Leben*, Vol. 27, 1954, p. 343.
[162] St. Thomas, *S. Th.*, III, q. 27, a. 4.
[163] *Ibid.*, a. 5 ad 1; cf. ad 2.

consent to the same total event, the redemptive Incarnation of the Son of God that implied His death from the outset. She had surrendered herself to God, to be disposed of without any reserve on her part; the implications of that acquiescence, dimly perceived then, were more clearly discerned at the end. But both consents form a unity; together they constitute a single act that made up the whole life of the Blessed Virgin. There is no cause to distinguish two roles for Mary, an initial one at the Incarnation and a different one at the crucifixion. She simply persevered in her prior faith and perfect abandonment to God. The Incarnation contained the death of Christ as its inevitable consequence; the effect of Mary's acquiescence is both the Incarnation and the Cross. Together they are the indivisible object of her *fiat,* which is a consent efficacious for salvation, a cooperation in the order of objective Redemption.[164]

This cooperation was given. Mary's maternity conferred on her real rights over the human life of her Son. God required the sacrifice of this life for the Redemption of man. The sacrifice entailed Christ's voluntary renunciation of His personal rights and Mary's renunciation of her maternal rights over a life that, in different ways, belonged to both. Mary made that renunciation. Instead of willing to save her Son from death, she offered Him, as He offered Himself, because she knew that it was the Father's will that the Son should redeem the world by the cross. Accordingly, as He is the Redeemer, she is the Coredemptrix.

That Mary's cooperation extended to the sacrifice on Calvary is clearly taught by some of the more recent Popes. In addition to giving birth to the victim for man's salvation, "she was commissioned to watch over the same victim, to nourish Him, and even, when the appointed time came, to place Him on the altar."[165] Her lifelong association with her Son's career included the last hours.

In the Garden of Gethsemane, where Jesus suffers the agony of fear and sadness to the point of death, and in the pretorium where he is scourged, crowned with thorns, and sentenced to death, Mary is not present. But she had long known about these things and had gone through them in imagination. For when she consented as the faithful

---

[164] Cf. K. Rahner, *art. cit.,* in *Recherches de Science Religieuse,* Vol. 42, 1954, p. 492 ff.

[165] St. Pius X, *Ad diem illum,* in *A.A.S.,* Vol. 36, 1903-1904, p. 453.

handmaid to become the Mother of God and when she offered herself wholeheartedly with her Son in the temple, even then she took her stand at His side to be His associate in the grievous work of making expiation for the human race. Nor can we doubt that she suffered intensely with her Son in her heart throughout the bitter torment of His passion. At length that divine sacrifice was to be accomplished before her very eyes; she had borne Him and brought Him up to be its victim. Out of her immense love for us ... she willingly offered her own Son to divine justice, and died with Him in her heart, pierced through with the sword of sorrow.[166]

The scope of Mary's maternal cooperation is clearly set forth by Pius XII: it reaches as far as the sacrifice of Christ and embraces all the descendants of Adam. "Free from all sin, personal as well as original, and always most closely united with her Son, as another Eve she offered Him on Golgotha, along with the holocaust of her maternal rights and her motherly love, to the Eternal Father for all the children of Adam."[167] Thus Mary's coredemptive activity is a function of her motherhood.

Since Mary is the Mother of Christ, she is also the Mother of His mystical body. "She who corporally was the Mother of our Head, by the added title of suffering and glory became spiritually the Mother of all His members."[168] It could not be otherwise. "The unbroken tradition of the Fathers from the earliest times teaches that the divine Redeemer and the society which is His body form a single mystical person, that is, as Augustine says, the Whole Christ."[169] Being Mother of the Head, she was able to be Mother of the members. When she conceived the Head, she conceived the members. In due time she gave birth to the Head, who did not as yet actually have His members. On Calvary, cooperating as Coredemptrix, offering her Son in sacrifice, she gave birth to the members *in actu primo,* who become members *in actu secundo* as they are successively joined to the Head by being incorporated into Him at their baptism. Truly she is the new Eve, mother of all the living; but

---

[166] Leo XIII, *Iucunda semper,* in *A.A.S.,* Vol. 27, 1894-1895, p. 178.

[167] Encycl. *Mystici Corporis Christi,* in *A.A.S.,* Vol. 35, 1943, p. 247.

[168] *Ibid.*

[169] *Ibid.,* p. 226. Cf. St. Thomas, *S. Th.,* III, q. 48, a. 2 ad 1: "Caput et membra sunt quasi una persona mystica."

because she is the Mother of Him who is our life.

Thus from the basic truth that Mary is the Mother of God, everything else follows. By reason of her divine maternity she is the new Eve, the associate of the Redeemer, the Coredemptrix and Mediatrix of all grace, Mother of the mystical body, universal Mother, the archetype of the Church, the new Paradise, the one full of grace, the one who is perfectly redeemed, the Queen of heaven and earth, and everything else that is true of her. None of these consequences, revealed or deduced by us with our inferential procedures, can be the primary principle of Mariology; they all proceed, by the ordering of God's wisdom, from the Blessed Virgin's predestination to be the Redeemer's Mother, inextricably united with her Son in the one eternal decree. The divine maternity is the basis of Mary's relationship to Christ; hence it is the basis of her relationship to the work of Christ, to the Whole Christ, to all theology and Christianity. Therefore it is the fundamental principle of Mariology.

The Predestination of Our Blessed Lady

By JOHN F. BONNEFOY, O.F.M., S.T.D.

HE term "predestination" has received many definitions in the course of centuries. All through this paper we shall, with the great Scholastics, understand it to mean that act whereby God from all eternity destines an elect to glory, and provides him with the means that will infallibly lead him to glory.[1]

The predestination of the Blessed Virgin raises problems which are common to all predestinations — for instance, how it is that Mary's predestination is infallible without infringing on her human liberty, etc. We have no intention of touching on such problems here. Our purpose is not so pretentious. We shall merely attempt to determine *Mary's place in the order of divine predestinations;* or, to put it differently, her place in the divine plan of creation. Yet, even this limited aspect of the question is not without its serious complexities.

To begin with, we must observe that the place and role of a part cannot be understood without an exact knowledge of the whole itself and of the order or plan that governs it. Since theologians have not reached a complete agreement as regards the divine plan of the universe, it is fitting that we expound briefly the principal systems on the matter, and that we draw the reader's attention to the flaws inherent to each system, and define the present trends in theology.

As a sequel to this historical part of our paper we shall then append a speculative section in which we shall attempt to give an objective answer to the question under discussion. We shall expound and substantiate an order of predestination which has its starting point in

---

[1] St. Bonaventure, *In I Sent.*, d. 46, q. 1, arg. 3; *op. omn.,* Vol. 1, (Ad Claras Aquas, 1882), p. 819b: "Dum enim [Deus] proponit dare gratiam et gloriam praeparare, praedestinare dicitur." St. Thomas, *Summa Theol.*, I, q. 23, a. 2, ad 4: "Praedestinatio dicitur esse praeparatio gratiae in praesenti, et gloriae in futuro." J. Duns Scotus, *Oxon.*, I, d. 40, q. 1; *op. omn.*, Vol. 10 (ed. Vivès, Parisiis, 1895), p. 180: "Praedestinatio proprie sumpta dicit actum voluntatis divinae, videlicet ordinem electionis per voluntatem divinam alicujus creaturae intellectualis vel rationalis ad gratiam et gloriam."

the primacy of Christ and of the Blessed Virgin in the ontological order, which is also the order of final causality. From this primacy is derived logically, according to our human way of thinking and understanding, the priority in the order of predestination.

So much by way of preliminary remarks. We must now attempt to remove a number of further difficulties that stand in the way of an adequate solution.

I. PRINCIPAL THEOLOGICAL SYSTEMS ON THE DIVINE PLAN OF CREATION

Thinkers who make synthesis their chief preoccupation are rarely found. Still more rare are those who have been able to present a plan of creation which satisfies all the exigencies of revelation and of reason. It is an undeniable fact that the graveyard of theological essays on the divine plan of the universe is very large; and, of those systems which are still in vogue, none have been able to rally a unanimous consent of theologians. The reason is simply this, that they all contain flaws and shortcomings which only the prejudices of the different schools of thought have been able to hide from their followers.

We can omit the system of the apocatastasis advocated by Origen and Papini; and also the theory of numerous Greek Fathers who taught that God would not have created women, had He not permitted and foreseen original sin. The teaching that God created mankind to replace the fallen angels was a little more widespread. Despite the illustrious names of its advocates (St. Augustine, perhaps St. Anselm, certainly St. Gregory, St. Isidore, Peter Lombard, St. Bonaventure, St. Thomas, etc.), this theory has today been universally abandoned. It can neither be proved by Revelation nor deduced from it.[2]

However, brief mention must be made presently of the representatives of the Thomistic system, of the Scotistic system, and of the various theories which we shall designate as "middle-course" opinions.

---

[2] Since we are unable to indicate here all the source material pertinent to this part of our paper, we refer the reader once and for all to our article: *La place du Christ dans le plan divin de la création*, in *Mélanges de Science Religieuse*, Vol. 4, 1947, pp. 237-284; Vol. 5, 1948, pp. 39-62.

1. THE THOMISTIC SYSTEMS

The common starting point of the various Thomistic systems is the following: "If Adam had not sinned, the Word would not have become Incarnate." With a conditional formula the authors of these opinions affirm a positive fact: the dependence of the Incarnation on the sin of Adam. Since the nature of this dependence was not clearly defined, the Thomists have considered original sin either as the *occasion*, or the *condition*, or the *final cause* of the Incarnation. Some authors use several of these formulae indifferently, as though they were synonymous, thus giving evidence of the chaotic state of their thinking.

Indeed, none of these three interpretations is acceptable. One need merely recall that what is made to depend on the sin of Adam is not a human happening but a divine decree, the decree of the Incarnation willed in the first place, according to our legitimate way of speaking, and therefore independently of all the rest.

Let us examine the Thomistic theories individually.

To affirm that original sin was a *motive* for God, would be tantamount to saying that God was moved by something. This would be metaphysically impossible.[3]

The absolute and universal primacy of Christ, based on the formal testimony of Holy Scripture and on theological reasoning, is today admitted by all schools of theology. As a corollary one must accept the threefold extrinsic and secondary causality of Christ: the efficient causality per *modum meriti*, as well as the exemplary and final causality as regards everything which is inferior to Christ. It is erroneous on these conditions to say that Adam was the *final cause* of Christ, for causes cannot be causes *ad invicem* in the same order.[4] It would be a still greater error to attribute the role of final causality to the rebellion of our first parent.

---

[3] Cf. J.-F. Bonnefoy, *La primauté absolue et universelle de N.S. Jésus-Christ et de la Très-Sainte Vierge*, in *Bulletin de la Société Française d'Études Mariales*, 1938, pp. 41-100, esp. p. 43; *id., La place du Christ ...*, p. 247, quoting Father De Régnon, S.J., *La métaphysique des causes*, 2nd ed. (Paris, 1906), pp. 559-563, who proves philosophically that "the divine Will is the First Efficient Cause; it cannot, therefore, be impelled, moved or incited; it cannot have motives in the proper sense of the word."

[4] Aristotle, *Metaph.*, 1, 5, c. 2: "Causae ad invicem sunt causae in diverso genere."

As regards the theories which make original sin the *occasion* or the *condition* of the Incarnation, suffice it to remark with St. Thomas that the order of the universe does not result from conditions or occasions, but from relations of cause and effect.[5]

2. THE SCOTISTIC SYSTEMS

The Scotists all admit the absolute and universal primacy of Christ as well as the immediate corollary of this thesis, namely, the threefold extrinsic and secondary causality of Christ as regards everything that is inferior to Him.

Basing themselves on the axiom of the *philosophia perennis*: *"quanto aliquid est melius in effectibus, tanto est prius in intentione agentis,"*[6] they attribute to Christ an absolute priority in the order of divine predestinations, thus expressing in terms of theological reasoning the formal teaching of the Sapiential Books and of the Epistles of St. Paul.

In virtue of the same principle they place the predestination of Mary immediately after that of Christ. Indeed Our Lady's predestination is so close to Christ's that some authors have affirmed that Our Lord and His Mother were willed *uno eodemque decreto*. It is a known fact that this teaching and formula have been adopted by the Bull *Ineffabilis Deus*.[7]

Not daring to assert that Christ was predestined to the death of the cross before God foresaw Adam and his sin, the majority affirm that God had at first decreed the Incarnation in an impassible flesh, and that He decided, after the prevision of Adam's sin, that Christ should assume a passible flesh.

The Thomists accuse the Scotists, and rightly so, of attributing mutability to God. In reply, the latter assert that the Thomistic systems sin even more gravely against the attributes of God, and their rejoinder is also justifiable. In the final analysis both the Thomistic distinction of *gratia Dei* and *gratia Christi* and the Scotistic distinction of *caro passibilis* and *caro impassibilis* in their respective systems play the role of a *deus ex machina*. These distinctions may hide the element of mutation which

---

[5] St. Thomas, *Summa Theol.* I, q. 48, a. 1, ad 5.
[6] St. Thomas, *Contra Gent.*, 2, c. 44, 1.
[7] Pius IX, *Ineffabilis Deus;* in A. Tondini, *Le Encicliche Mariane*, 2nd ed. (Roma, 1954), p. 32.

they indirectly attribute to God, but they do not remove it.

3. MIDDLE-COURSE OPINIONS

As could be expected, some theologians have tried to avoid the pitfalls of the theories just described by opening a new way. Most of them would like to maintain the absolute primacy of Christ, as the Scotists do, and at the same time join the Thomists in upholding the dependence of Christ's passion and death on the sin of Adam. The attempts to achieve this twofold objective are very numerous.

For many of them, conditional decrees fulfill the easy role of a *deus ex machina*, for the possibilities in this line of thinking are endless.

Others try to appease both Thomists and Scotists by declaring that the motives of the Incarnation in both theories are of equal value. "The true motive of the Incarnation," writes Father Galtier, "is both the excellence of Christ and the salvation of men."[8] A hopeless solution, if there ever was one. First of all because there is not, and there cannot be, a motive for the Incarnation. And second because it is nonsense to think that one can, at one and the same time, follow a road in two opposite directions. Final causality and the order of intention which it implies belong together by their very nature.

Others, finally, thought that they could eliminate all the difficulties by simply doing away with the well-known divine decrees advocated by the Thomistic and Scotistic schools. They tried to cure the sickness by ridding themselves of the patient. To put it concretely, these theologians deprive themselves of the possibility of thinking and of describing the order of divine intentions, as I have shown elsewhere.[9]

Nevertheless, if one takes the primacy of Christ as a starting point, there is a way of delineating the divine plan of creation without the gaps, the retouching and the amendments of which Thomists and

---

[8] P. Galtier, S.J., *Le vrai motif de l'Incarnation*, in *Nouvelle Revue Théologique*, Vol. 43, 1911, pp. 44-57, 104-124; cf. p. 46.

[9] Cf. Bonnefoy, La *Place du Christ ...*, p. 58; id., *L'Assomption de la T.S. Vierge et sa prédestination*, in *Vers le dogme de l'Assomption* (Montréal, 1948), pp. 293-335; cf. p. 296; id., *Le mérite social de Marie et sa prédestination*, in *Alma Socia Christi*, Vol. 2: *De cooperatione B. V. Mariae in acquisitione et distributione gratiarum* (Romae, 1952.), pp. 21-48; cf. pp. 23-25.

II. THE ORDER OF PREDESTINATIONS

All the predestinations, inasmuch as they are divine acts are identical with the divine nature and as eternal of God Himself.[10] In this sense there is and there can be only one divine decree concerning the world.

But the order of the world itself would not exist if God had not conceived of it and willed it: *Necesse est quod ratio ordinis rerum in finem in mente divina praeexistat,* writes St. Thomas.[11] We are authorized, therefore, to inquire into the order of divine intentions and to express that order (as is done, incidentally, by the inspired authors themselves) in terms of chronological and spatial analogies, indispensable to our intelligence.

So as not to go astray, let us first of all recall a few principles of methodology.

The order of the universe is not the result of conditions, or of occasions, but of causal subordination, as we have just seen with St. Thomas. We shall, therefore, abstain from attributing to God conditional decrees, incompatible with the divine Wisdom and Omnipotence. Recourse to this expedient has made valueless a good half of the essays written on the divine plan.

Since in reality God willed everything at once, and since He is immutable, we must at all costs avoid attributing to Him any amendment or annihilation of an anterior decree. Otherwise, we shall let ourselves be caught in the illusion of chronological analogies, and feel compelled to admit that God at one and the same time said "yes" and "no," and was not essentially immutable: *Rerum Deus tenax vigor, Immotus in te permanens...*

Recourse to chronological analogies is legitimate *only in the measure in which we can establish, by means of Revelation or the analogy of Faith,*

---

[10] Cf. St. Bonaventure, *In I Sent.*, d. 40, a. 1, q. 1; *op. omn.*, Vol. 1, p. 703a: "In praedestinatione non sunt nisi duo: scilicet principale significatum et connotatum. Principale significatum est divina essentia; connotatum vero est creatura, ut gratia et gloria et persona salvanda."

[11] *Summa Theol.*, I, q. 22, a. 1.

a relationship of cause and effect, or a relationship of substance and mode. Such analogies are convenient and even indispensable instruments, but we must be on our guard against taking them for realities, as so many authors have unconsciously done. They have a meaning only as images or as helps to the mind in its analysis of the one divine decree. As for the content of the decree, we can know it only from what Revelation says explicitly about it, or from what we can reasonably deduce from the revealed word.

As the order of intention and that of final causality are one, the various beings which compose the universe will appear in the thought of God in a decreasing hierarchical order, according to the axiom of St. Thomas: *"Quanto aliquid est melius in effectibus, tanto est prius in intentione agentis."*[12]

The concrete basis of an essay like ours must, therefore, be sought, in the last analysis, in the ontological order. Fortunately, the general outline of such an order is not unknown to us.

At the very summit we find the Word Incarnate. Christ is God and, as such, "He is seated at the right hand of God" ... "that in all things He may hold the primacy."[13]

The eminence of the grace of Mary, described by the Fathers and Doctors of the Church, is attested to by the Bull *Ineffabilis Deus:* Mary "possesses such a fulness of innocence and sanctity that outside of God no greater can be conceived, and no one but God can understand it."[14] By her plentitude of grace, Mary, therefore, comes immediately after Christ.

As for the angels and men, we have no absolute data. Hence, in conformity with the advice given by *The Following of Christ*, we shall abstain from discussing the merits of the saints. We shall likewise refrain from theories of substitution, for which there is no sound basis. It is sufficient for us to know that in the order of grace both angels and men rank *after* Christ and Mary.

---

[12] St. Thomas, *Contra Gent.*, 2, c. 44, 1.
[13] *Col.* 1:18.
[14] Tondini, *op. cit.*, p. 30.

1. THE PREDESTINATION OF CHRIST AND MARY AS KING AND QUEEN

By creation God in some sort exteriorized Himself. That is an undeniable fact. Without trying to know the "motive" of the creative act or of the decree of the Incarnation, we shall nevertheless attempt to find in Tradition the reason for the divine works *ad extra*, since God never acts without reason.

The Vatican Council (1870), referring to and completing a constitution of the Lateran Council (1215), declared that God created through His own goodness, *bonitate sua*, "not to increase His happiness, nor to acquire a greater beatitude, but to manifest His perfection through the qualities He imparted to creatures."[15] We could quote numerous texts to prove that God's goodness is the explanation and ultimate reason, not only of creation in general, but also and especially of the Incarnation.

In virtue of the axiom *Principium essendi est principium intelligendi*,[16] an *a priori* synthesis of the divine works *ad extra* should have its starting point in the principle: God is good. That God is good is both a rational and a revealed truth: *Deus caritas est*.[17] Now goodness by its very nature tends to communicate itself: *bonum est diffusivum sui*. It was, therefore, fitting that God should call into existence creatures who could in some way receive Him by sharing in His life.

The Predestination of Christ, Willed for His Own Sake

Since God is the sovereign Good, it was fitting that He communicate Himself fully and in a sovereign degree. This He decided to do through the Incarnation.[18] He would bring into existence a creature which would, as it were, be grafted onto the divinity by its hypostatic union to the

---

[15] Conc. Vat., sessio 3, *de fide*, c. 1; *D.B.*, 1783. Other pertinent texts may be found in Bonnefoy, *Le mérite social de Marie* ..., p. 29 and footnotes.

[16] St. Bonaventure, *In Hexaëmeron*, col. 1, n. 13; *op. omn.*, Vol. 5, p. 221b. Cf. St. Thomas, *In Post Anal.*, I, lect. 4, n. 5: "Eadem enim sunt principia esse rei et veritatis ipsius." Cf. Bonnefoy, *De synthesi operum Dei ad extra ad mentem Sancti Bonaventurae*, in *Antonianum*, Vol. 18, 1943, pp. 17-28.

[17] *1 Jn*. 4:8.

[18] St. Thomas, *Summa Theol.*, 3, q. 1, a. 1.

Person of the Word.[19]

We affirm that, according to our human way of thinking, Christ was willed first; and we base our statement on Pauline and sapiential texts which proclaim Him "the firstborn of every creature,"[20] or "the beginning of his [God's] ways";[21] and on the axiom of right reasoning: "the best effect is willed first." Furthermore, since we know that Christ is the secondary end of all creation other than Himself, we may lawfully assume that the Creator would verify the maxim, *"Omnis ordinate volens prius vult finem quam media."*

The Predestination of Mary as Full of Grace

In virtue of its hypostatic union with the Word the humanity of Christ would share in the very happiness of God. This happiness would certainly suffice for its eternal felicity. But from another point of view Christ's human nature would be lacking the properly divine joy of giving itself and of making others happy. Jesus Himself said that "it is more blessed to give than to receive."[22] However a creature cannot properly speaking give anything to the Creator, since everything that it is, every good deed that it does is a gift of God. "While crowning our merits it is His gifts that He will crown" (St. Augustine). "If thou do justly, what shalt thou give Him, or what shall He receive from thy hand," said one of the friends of Job.[23] He spoke so truthfully that for once the Lord approved of his words: "Who hath given me before that I should repay him?"[24] St. Paul quotes the substance of this text when he writes: "Who has first given to him, that recompense should be made him?"[25]

The conclusion is obvious. God was in no way bound to grant His future Christ the sovereign joy of manifesting His liberality and of

---

[19] St. Francis de Sales, *Traité de l'amour de Dieu*, l. 2, c. 2 and 3 (Annecy, 1892), pp. 90-96.
[20] Col. 1:15.
[21] Prov. 8:22, in Heb.
[22] Acts 20:35.
[23] Job 35:7.
[24] Job 41:2.
[25] Rom. 11:35.

making others happy; but if He wished to accord Him this privilege, He must of necessity grant existence to at least one other creature.

We know from Revelation that He did actually adopt this decision. The words of the Creator spoken to Adam in Paradise: "It is not good for man to be alone; let us make him a help like unto himself," had reference, in God's eternal designs, to the Man-God as well as to Adam. The "help like unto Christ" was to be Mary. That she be like unto her Son, God decreed that she would receive from Christ the communication of divine grace which would reside in its fullness in the Word Incarnate: *plenum gratiae et veritatis*. The grace of adoption received by Mary would be such *qua major sub Deo nullatenus intelligitur, et quam praeter Deum nemo assequi cogitando potest.*[26] Furthermore, He decided that this privileged creature would possess that same human nature as the future Christ.

The Predestination of Mary as the Mother of God

By decreeing the Incarnation of Christ, did God fully satisfy the divine need of manifesting His liberality? No, not yet. Since Christ was to be God, it was fitting that He also should give as God and that He Himself should grant to Mary the superior joy of giving to others. To realize this plan, would God be bound to bring yet another creature into existence? Not necessarily. As man, Christ could not give anything to God, but nothing would hinder Him from receiving divine favors. By an admirable exchange — *O admirabile commercium!* — and by a divine gesture of infinite thoughtfulness, God then decreed that Mary would give temporal life to Him from whom she was to receive all that she is and has. God reserved the right to create the human soul of Christ, but even this creation was subordinated to the consent of the Virgin who was to be His Mother according to the flesh. Mary would give to Christ all that a mother gives her child: something of her own substance, the benefit of her motherly care, the gentleness of her affections: *cum lacte praebens oscula*.

---

[26] *Ineffabilis Deus*; Tondini, *op. cit.*, p. 30.

The Predestination of Men and Angels

It would seem that once God had predestined Christ's Mother, the cycle of predestination could be called closed. Christ and Mary would suffice to assure their mutual happiness, the joy of giving included. It is true that God had no obligation to go further, no more than He was obliged to cause the predestinations of which we have thus far made an analysis. Yet we know from Revelation and experience that He did call other creatures into existence. The reason for these added decrees must again and always be sought in God's goodness, or more exactly, in the love He bore to the future Christ, the object of His divine complacency.[27]

Considering that the reciprocal self-dedication of the future Christ and of Mary would neither exhaust "the unfathomable riches of Christ,"[28] nor the innate goodness of His future Mother, God decided to give existence to other intelligent creatures on whom Christ and Mary could, each in his own way, bestow of their plenitude of love.

Christ would therefore grant both men and angels a share in His divine life through sanctifying grace. Mankind would constitute the spiritual family of Christ and His Mother, and the angels would be their servants.

Finally, God decreed the creation of the material universe, destined to be the throne and footstool of His Son.[29] He would hand over to the children of men the earth and its riches: *terram autem dedit filiis hominum.*[30] But the nations themselves and their territories would be Christ's inheritance: *Postula a me et dabo tibi gentes in haereditatem, et in possessionem tuam terminos terrae.*[31]

Retrospect

This new explanation of the divine plan meets all the demands of faith and reason. The hierarchy and subordination of beings as enunciated by St. Paul are perfectly safeguarded: *Omnia vestra sunt, vos*

---

[27] *Mt.* 3:17; *Mk.* 1:11.
[28] *Eph.* 3:8.
[29] *Isa.* 66:1; *Acts* 7:49.
[30] *Ps.* 113:16. Cf. *Gen.* 1:29-30.
[31] *Ps.* 2:8.

*autem Christi, Christus autem Dei.*³² This subordination is not adventitious, but in some sort consubstantial with the beings themselves. The lesser creatures are called into existence for the sake of the more perfect: *semper enim imperfectum est propter perfectius.*³³ In this synthesis the hierarchy of beings, one of final causality, exercises a natural and legitimate function, for "that which is first in the order of existence is also first in the order of intellection."³⁴

Consequently, the decrees which we attribute to God are not only warranted by the data of Revelation, but they are also *linked together by the bond of causality*. This last point needs to be stressed, because very few essays on the divine plan have made an attempt to satisfy the demands of theology as a deductive science. And still fewer, if that is possible, are the writers who have taken such essays to task for their want of coherence. We shall come back to this reflection later. Meanwhile, we must continue to give our attention to the divine plan.

Everything that we have thus far treated — the Incarnation, the predestination of Mary, of angels and of men — is included in the divine plan. Yet this plan contains further elements: the Redemption and "the mystery of iniquity"; the trial of the angels, the fall of our first parents and the sins of men. All this was either willed positively by God, or permitted and foreseen by Him. The theologian's task consists in trying to understand God's design, and to discover the reason for it.

It is precisely here that the traditional Scotistic opinion falls short, for it makes no express mention of either sin or Redemption. This objection has often been raised, and some Scotists have given their adversaries easy play by seemingly reducing the drama of Calvary to "a simple tragical episode in the immense poem of the Incarnation."³⁵ God preserve us from speaking thus, or from merely explaining the problem

---

³² *1 Cor.* 3:22-23.

³³ St. Thomas, *Summa Theol.*, I, q. 105, a. 5.

³⁴ St. Bonaventure, *In Hexaëmeron*, col. 1, n. 13; *op. omn.*, Vol. 5, p. 221b. Cf. Bonnefoy, *art. cit.*, in *Antonianum*, Vol. 18, 1943, pp. 17-28.

³⁵ Sigismond de Villeneuve, O.F.M.Cap., *La royauté universelle du Sacré-Coeur et de l'Immaculée Conception d'après la doctrine du Bx. Jean Duns Scot* (Toulouse, 1925), p. 25. Cf. H.-M. Féret, O.P., *A propos de la primauté du Christ*, in *Revue des Sciences Philosophiques et Théologiques*, Vol. 27, 1938, pp. 69-72.

raised by these historical facts in the words of the poet: "Dieu fit bien ce qu'il fit, et je n'en sais pas plus."

Neither shall we have recourse to those *deus ex machina* known as conditional decrees; nor to a revamping or rearranging of the primitive plan imposed on God by extrinsic factors. Such explanations would offend against both the immutability and the omnipotence of God.

To justify the other positive or permissive decrees of God we need merely invoke the principles we have already mentioned. We shall thus establish definitely that the divine plan, as we understand it, suffers neither interruptions nor rearrangements. Thus our retrospect is nothing more than a brief halt in our reasoning. After all, not everything can be understood or said at once. Besides, this halt coincides with the transition from the mystery of the Incarnation to that of the Redemption; or, as theologians of the past express it, from the substance of the Incarnation to its economy or mode. Hence its legitimacy.

2. The Predestination of Christ and Mary as Redeemer and Co-redemptrix

A brief analysis of the concept of "gift" has shown us that there can be no gift without a beneficiary. Continuing our analysis we find that a gift implies two other conditions:

The donor must really be the proprietor of what he intends to give. One cannot make a gift of what belongs to another, not even when one is delegated to transmit or distribute the gift.

The recipient of the gift must have no right to it in any way. The salary which an employer gives to an employee belongs to the former as long as he has not yet paid it. Yet by paying it he cannot be considered as making a gift to his employee. Neither does one designate as a gift the money returned to a lawful proprietor whom one has robbed, or to a man who has lost the sum in question. Such an act would be known as restitution, not as a gift.

In the light of these principles let us now consider the case of Christ in the indeterminate state in which the dullness of our mind has forced us to leave Him.

The Predestination of Christ, as Saviour of Mary and the Angels

Had Christ not suffered, He would appear as a "distributor" rather than as a "giver" of graces. The divine bounties would pass through His hands, but He would not have acquired them, even though He could have. It is an honor and a joy to live from the work of one's hands: *labores manuum tuarum manducabis; beatus eris et bene tibi erit.*[36] How much more so is it to donate what one has himself earned.

It was, therefore, highly becoming that Christ earn at the sweat of His brow:

Whatever He could merit for Himself; namely, His exterior glory and the exaltation of His Name, in conformity with the following passage of Holy Scripture: "He humbled Himself, becoming obedient to death, even to death on a cross. Therefore God also has exalted Him and has bestowed upon Him the name that is above every name."[37]

All the graces He would be called upon to distribute to His Mother, to the angels, and to men.

The source of His merits would be all His actions, but especially His suffering and His death; for if action is in some way common to the Creator and the creature, suffering and death are possible for the latter only.

Since God willed that His future Christ should attain to the highest degree of love, and since "greater love than this no one has, that one lay down his life for his friends,"[38] the Almighty decreed that Christ would merit by His whole life, but especially by His suffering and His death, all the graces He would have to distribute.

Among these graces the very first were those He would grant His Mother, in the natural as well as in the supernatural order, from the first moment of her existence and the Immaculate Conception to the time of her divine Maternity and her glorious Assumption. Although sinless, Mary was the first beneficiary of the graces of Calvary.

The good angels also owe to the "blood of the Cross" their final perseverance and their confirmation in grace. "For it has pleased God the

---

[36] *Ps.* 128:2. Cf. *Isa.* 3:10.
[37] *Phil.* 2:8-9.
[38] *Jn.* 15:13.

Father that in Him all His fullness should dwell, and that through Him He should reconcile to Himself all things, whether on the earth, or in the heavens, making peace through the blood of His cross."[39]

We can thus understand why the good angels associate the name of Christ with that of God when they give thanks for their victory: "Now has come the salvation, and the power and the kingdom of our God, and the authority of His Christ. ..." Then, speaking of the martyrs, they add: "And they [also, just as we ourselves] overcame him [Satan] through the blood of the Lamb."[40]

The Predestination of Christ as Saviour of Men

The future Christ would know the superior happiness of giving His life for those He loved. But there is another superior way of giving which God reserved to Him. The second condition of a true gift, as we have said, is that the receiver have no right to the gift. One can conceive of various degrees in the rights a person may have to an object, from commutative justice to the different forms of gratitude. One thing, however, is certain: the less the object is due, the more it can be considered as a gift. With this principle in mind we can assert that the gift will be all the more generous if the beneficiary, far from possessing any right to it, has been guilty of demerit toward the donor.

In saying this we are not playing with paradoxes. Did not the Master say to His disciples: "For if you love those who love you, what reward shall you have? Do not even the publicans do that? And if you salute your brethren only, what are you doing more than others? Do not even the Gentiles do that?"[41] Pardon of injuries is the full blossom of charity. The very term "pardon," which is derived from the Latin languages (French: *pardon*; Italian: *perdono*; Spanish: *perdón*), expresses this truth. It is composed of derivatives from the Latin word *"donum"* and the particle *par* or *per*, which here, as in similar compounds, denotes plenitude or perfection. (Compare the Latin *perficere, peragere*, with their

---

[39] *Col.* 1:19-20.

[40] *Apoc.* 12:10-11. A commentary on this text may be found in Bonnefoy, *Le mystère de Marie selon le Protèvangile et l'Apocalypse* (Paris 1949).

[41] Mt. 5:45-47.

French equivalents *parfaire, parachever*.[42]) Pardon, therefore, meant "a perfect gift" to those anonymous Christians who so beautifully completed the Latin vocabulary. Indeed, how could the pagan originators of the Latin language conceive so lofty an idea, when vengeance was exalted by their poets and moralists?

He "who makes His sun to rise on the good and the evil, and sends rain on the just and the unjust,"[43] did not wish to deny His future Christ this superior form of giving, this joy of a perfect gift, this "pardon" of giving His very life for His enemies. Hence it is that, although He could with His grace have forestalled any lapse in His creatures without interfering with their freedom, He decided, without impelling them to evil or concurring in the least with their sin as such, to permit the fall of our first parents and our personal sins, and to include the entire offspring of Adam, with the exception of Mary, in the original degradation.

This "reason" or explanation of the permission of sin has seemed unworthy of God to certain superficial observers. I have already shown that all the theses which go into this opinion are common doctrine.[44] The permission of evil is a positive act of God, and it would be impious to say that God placed this act without a reason, without a proportional cause. Furthermore, the reason we have just mentioned has been accepted by theologians of every extraction: Irenaeus, Ambrose, Augustine, Gregory of Nyssa, Cyril of Alexandria, Theodotus of Ancyra, Athanasius, Isidore of Seville, Peter Lombard, Bonaventure, Suárez, the Salmanticenses, Molina, Gonet, Lawrence of Brindisi. And among our contemporaries one might mention Garrigou-Lagrange, Deman, Ciappi, Carmelus ab Itergoyen, and P. Galtier.[45]

These authors did not invent anything. They can base themselves on St. Paul: "For God has shut up all in unbelief, that He may have mercy

---

[42] Cf. A. Tommasini, *Dono e perdono*, in *Vita e Pensiero*, Vol. 31, 1940, pp. 227-231.

[43] *Mt.* 5:45.

[44] Bonnefoy, *A propos de la primauté du Christ*, in Verdad y Vida, Vol. 8, 1950, pp. 228-235.

[45] P. Galtier, S.J., *Les deux Adam* (Paris, 1947), pp. 69-94. The author quotes a large number of testimonies in the same sense. Further texts may be found in Bonnefoy, *Le mérite social de Marie* ..., p. 36, footnote 2.

upon all."⁴⁶ This passage, which I would call bold were it not written by an inspired author, concludes the doctrinal part of the Epistle to the Romans. It arouses the reflections of the Apostle on "the depth of the riches of the wisdom and of the knowledge of God! How incomprehensible are His judgments and how unsearchable His ways! For who has known the mind of the Lord? ..."⁴⁷ It is evident that the Apostle feels he has come face to face with a mystery.

In a word, we can repeat with the Fathers, the Doctors, and the authors we have cited: in order that Christ might know the superior joy contained in the perfect gift of pardoning, God decreed to permit sin, and foreseeing the fall of Adam, He decided to include all men in his disobedience, with the exception of Mary whose destiny was already determined, that He might have mercy upon all.⁴⁸

The Predestination of Mary as Coredemptrix

God's designs with regard to Christ were inspired by that goodness which, in some sort, constitutes the very depths of the divine nature: *Deus cujus natura bonitas*... Since the future Christ would be God, it was fitting that God, with all due proportion, include in the same decree first the Blessed Virgin, then all those to whom Christ and His Mother would be called upon to do good. God therefore decreed that the Blessed Virgin would be His associate in the work of salvation, and would merit with Christ and dependently on Him, *etsi aliter et aliter*, the graces to be distributed to angels and men.

This arrangement of Divine Providence was, incidentally, not limited to Mary. Each member of the Mystical Body of Christ is invited to collaborate in the salvation of his brethren, of his friends, and even his

---

⁴⁶ *Rom.* 11:32.

⁴⁷ *Rom.* 11:33-34.

⁴⁸ We apply here to the transmission of original sin what St. Paul said of the permission and prevision of the actual sins of the Jews and Gentiles. The law governing the transmission of original sin is not a law of nature: fortunately for us, since that would have burdened us from birth on, not only with the responsibility of the sins of Adam, but also with that of all the sins of every one of our ancestors! Nor was the transmission of original sin imperatively required by a divine attribute. It is, therefore, dependent on a free decision of God. I see no other way of explaining it than by recourse to the reason given by St. Paul in *Rom.* 11:32.

enemies, by his prayers, good works, and sufferings, filling up in his flesh what is lacking of the sufferings of Christ, for His Body which is the Church.[49]

We do not minimize the grace of Mary when we say that it is of the same nature as ours; not even when we include her in the Mystical Body of Christ, as our present Holy Father, gloriously reigning, has done recently.[50]

III. CONCLUSIONS

From the principles thus far established we could draw many other conclusions, particularly concerning the return of the creature to God. But on the one hand, the space allotted us is limited, and on the other hand, we have dealt with the essential points of the particular subject assigned to us. All that remains, by way of conclusion, is to check the theological synthesis at which we have arrived and to group the data which concern the predestination of the Blessed Virgin.

1. Technique of the Proposed Synthesis

The great Doctors of the Middle Ages agreed, despite the diversity of their conceptions and of their formulae, in considering theology as a deductive science, similar to the sciences properly so called. This fact can already be ascertained in the writings of Origen.[51] St. Bonaventure and a few other isolated Doctors tried to present the essential data of theology in the form of a deductive synthesis.

Through a regrettable spirit of exaggeration some of St. Thomas' disciples, less than a hundred years after his death, reached the point where they falsified this tradition. I have already stated that, by proclaiming theology a "science properly so-called, in the Aristotelian sense of the word," they affirmed willy-nilly that the theologian can and must *demonstrate*, in the strictest sense of the word, authentic mysteries, *exactly as the geometer demonstrates his theorems;* namely, by beginning

---

[49] *Col.* 1:24.

[50] In the encyclical *Mystici Corporis,* Pius XII himself applies to the Blessed Virgin the text of St. Paul in *Col.* 1:24; cf. *A.A.S.,* Vol. 35, 1943, pp. 247-248.

[51] Bonnefoy, *Origène, théoricien de la méthode théologique,* in *Mélanges offerts au R. P. Cavallera* (Toulouse, 1948), pp. 87-145.

with rational, self-evident principles and arriving at necessary conclusions.[52] There would consequently be no more mysteries in the Christian religion.

When my observations did not seem convincing to those concerned, I proved, with texts to substantiate my claims, that during the first fifty years after the death of St. Thomas, only one of his disciples had interpreted the thought of the Master in the sense of later commentators; and even he retracted, presumably under pressure from his confrères.[53]

In more recent times theologians have been content with stating that, in its procedure, theology is a science analogous to the sciences properly so called, thus equating the thought common to the great Scholastics. We accept and adopt as our own the program Father Gagnebet assigns to the theologian: "The task is to know God. It consists in finding in some aspect of His essence the *raison d'être* of other aspects which are intelligibly posterior to it, the *raison d'être* also of all that He does."[54]

Has this program been realized in the past?

I have perused a large number of essays on the divine plan of creation. Not one of them gave any evidence of attempts to justify the decrees they presented with more or less logical sequence by referring them to one or several previous decrees. The tenuous, but essential, link of final causality was missing in every case.

Other authors, with no direct purpose of discovering the divine plan, were intent upon grouping the essential data of theology within the framework and according to the procedure of a deductive science. They are few in number, twenty at the most. The most outstanding essay of this nature is undoubtedly St. Bonaventure's *Breviloquium*. It has the disadvantage, however, of multiplying indefinitely the principles of its

---

[52] Bonnefoy, *La nature de la théologie selon Saint Thomas d'Aquin* (Paris, 1939); or in *Ephemerides Theologicae Lovanienses*, Vol. 14, 1937, pp. 421-446, 690-631; Vol. 15, 1938, pp. 491-516.

[53] Bonnefoy, *La méthodologie théologique de Saint Thomas*, in *Revista Española de Teología*, Vol. 10, 1950, pp. 40-41.

[54] R. Gagnebet, O.P., *La théologie de Saint Thomas, type de théologie spéculative*, in *Revue Thomiste*, Vol. 44, 1938, p. 219.

deductions, unlike the sciences properly so called, which begin with a small number of axioms or postulates and thus follow a development analogous to that of the vegetable kingdom. In each chapter on a given divine attribute St. Bonaventure presents a synthesis of which the conclusions resemble the innumerable rays emanating in every direction from a single focal point. As a result, the task of reconstructing the divine plan of creation was made impossible.

At the opposite extreme A. Réginald, O.P., endeavored to extract the whole of theology from a single principle. He thus contrived to build "a monstrous sorites of 1713 syllogisms."[55]

The two efforts of reconstructing the divine plan, and of formulating a deductive synthesis of theology have seemingly been put forth independently of each other, when in reality their only chance of reaching perfection lies in blending with each other, in conformity with the demands of an axiom dear to St. Thomas and St. Bonaventure: *eadem enim sunt principia esse rei et veritatis ipsius*. In other words: every attempt at reconstructing the divine plan should follow the deductive method; and every attempt at formulating a deductive synthesis should follow and respect the progression of the divine plan, such as conceived by the discursive mind.

Our synthesis is a fulfillment of this program. We have adopted as our starting point the traditional reason of God's works *ad extra*, namely, His goodness; but we have not refrained from invoking other principles, whether revealed or self-evident, and as such belonging to the common patrimony of the *philosophia perennis*. The framework and method of our research are analogous, though not identical with those of the sciences properly so called. Arguments of expediency often replace necessary demonstrations, for reasons of adaptation to the reality under discussion, or of respect for the liberty of the Creator's decisions. Any other theological synthesis would be erroneous. Neither Creation, nor the Incarnation, nor our elevation to the supernatural life, etc., are necessary; and it would be an error even to dream of integrating these data or theses of Revelation into the rigid framework of a "science properly so called, in the Aristotelian sense of the word."

The synthesis we have tried to delineate is certainly not perfect. If it

---

[55] M.-M. Gorce, *Réginald, Antonin*, in *D.T.C.*, Vol. 13, co. 2112.

contains any weak points, it is nevertheless deserving of the reader's leniency since it is the first attempt in history at realizing the ideal of theology as a deductive science without undervaluing essential parts of Revelation, such as the mystery of the Redemption; without having recourse to expedients like conditional decrees; without sacrificing any of the divine attributes, neither God's omnipotence, nor his liberty, nor His immutability; and having the constant preoccupation of following the subtle but essential course of final causality, according to the axiom: *principium essendi est principium intelligendi*.

2. THE PREDESTINATION OF THE BLESSED VIRGIN

The doctrinal conclusions relative to the predestination of Mary which follow from the deductive synthesis we have suggested, are those taught by the ordinary Magisterium of the Church.

The efforts of the Scotistic School to justify belief in Mary's Immaculate Conception had given prominence to the exceptional riches of her grace. From then on, her predestination appeared as posterior to that of Christ, but anterior to all the other predestinations. The inseparability of the decrees concerning Christ and His Mother was such that Scotistic theologians ended by saying that Christ and Mary were chosen first by God "in one and the same decree."

The Bull *Ineffabilis Deus* confirmed this doctrine, which it considered as commonly accepted: *ubique prope recepta:* "And hence the very words with which the Sacred Scriptures speak of Uncreated Wisdom and set forth His eternal origin, the Church, both in its ecclesiastical offices and in its liturgy, has been wont to apply likewise to the origin of the Blessed Virgin, inasmuch as God, by one and the same decree, had established the origin of Mary and the Incarnation of Divine Wisdom."[56] It would be as futile to attempt to hide the Scotistic origin of this teaching as it would be to diminish its doctrinal content. His Holiness Pope Pius XII recalled this fact recently. "If the Popes expressly pass judgment on a matter which up to then was controversial, everyone understands that this matter is no longer, in the mind and will of the Sovereign Pontiffs,

---

[56] Pius IX, *Ineffabilis Deus;* in Tondini, *op. cit.,* p. 32.

to be considered among theologians as a question open to discussion."[57]

In conformity with these principles, Pope Pius XII, before his elevation to the Sovereign Pontificate, had already taken a stand in favor of the doctrine of the primacy of Christ and the Blessed Virgin, as well as of the priority of their predestination:

> The first thought which comes to our mind with regard to Mary, the Saint among all the saints, is this: eternally, *before every other creature*, God looked down upon her; He loved her, and chose her, to make her rich with His gifts, in as far as it is possible for a creature. *That is the mind of the Church*, when She applies to Mary, with the reservations that Faith demands, what the author of *Proverbs* has said of the Son of God: "The Lord possessed me in the beginning of his ways. ..."[58]
>
> Wishing, at the beginning of time, to create the world to pour forth His love and to grant existence and happiness to others besides Himself, God *first of all* (if one may speak thus, in accordance with our successive manner of understanding and acting), God *first* cast His eyes on Him who would be their Head and King. ... There is God's masterpiece, the most excellent of His works; whatever may be the date and circumstances of His manifestation in time, this was assuredly what He willed *first, and in view of which He made all the rest.*[59]
>
> But wishing that this unique object of His complacency be born of a woman, He cast on thee, O Mary, a very gentle glance and predestinated thee to be His Mother. ...[60]

In this exceptionally dense text, we have taken the liberty to underline the adverbs of time "at first" or similar expressions which His Eminence justified summarily in the best Scholastic traditions: "If one may speak thus, in accordance with our successive manner of understanding and acting."

Remarkable likewise is the very traditional interpretation the eminent Cardinal gives the application of the Sapiential Books to the Offices and Masses *de Beata:* "This is the mind of the Church." The reason of the Incarnation which the Cardinal proposes is that of Tradition and that which we have placed at the basis of our synthesis:

---

[57] Pius XII, *Humani generis;* ed. Paulist Press (New York, 1950), n. 29, p. 11.
[58] *Prov.* 8:23.
[59] *Col.* 1:15-17.
[60] Eugenio Card. Pacelli, *Discorsi e Panegirici*, 2nd ed. (Milano, 1939), pp. 633-634.

"to pour forth His love and to grant existence and happiness to others besides Himself."

Finally, he stresses in passing the first and most important corollary of the primacy of Christ: its secondary universal finality.

Once these fundamentals are established, all the rest follows logically. The Blessed Virgin is also, *sub et cum Christo*, the final and secondary cause of everything below her; the efficient cause *per modum meriti*, secondary but universal *sub et cum Christo* of all the graces distributed to men and angels. It is here that the titles of Mediatrix and Coredemptrix are to be inserted.

Everything cannot be said at once; but it would be easy, with the help of the common principles of the *philosophia perennis*, to show that Mary plays an analogous role in the order of exemplary causality, insinuated in many a passage of the Sapiential Books: *Semper enim id quod est perfectissimum, est exemplar ejus quod est minus perfectum.*[61]

The principal Marian privileges have already appeared in this deductive synthesis. First, the plenitude of grace which made of Mary the Daughter of God and prepared her for eternal glory: this is a gift of Christ to His future Mother. Then the divine Maternity, a favor which is intrinsically of the natural order, but which is enhanced proportionately to the divinity of the Son whom Mary engenders: this again is a gift of Christ, which makes it possible for Mary to thank Him.

We have not yet mentioned the Immaculate Conception, since we had to begin with principles. But this prerogative follows logically from the premises. Like all the other Marian privileges, it is consequently a grace emanating from Calvary. To explain this origin there is no necessity of positing some sort of indebtedness on the part of Mary to the law of sin — a dependence unknown to Christian antiquity and formally rejected by the ordinary Magisterium in the dogmatic Bull *Ineffabilis Deus*: "*Numquam maledicto obnoxia, et una cum Filio perpetuae benedictionis particeps.*"[62]

---

[61] St. Thomas, *Summa Theol.*, 3, q. 56, a. 1, ad 3. We have expounded the primacy of the Blessed Virgin in the framework of the threefold extrinsic causality, with patristic texts to support our position, in *Marie dans l'Église, ou la primauté de la Sainte Vierge*, in *Bulletin de la Société Française d'Études Mariales* (Paris 1954), pp. 51-73.

[62] *Ineffabilis Deus*; Tondini, *op. cit.*, p. 44.

Advocates of the *debitum peccati* have themselves acknowledged that the denial of such a debt is a logical consequence of the priority of Mary's predestination as understood by the Scotistic School. But they have not been sufficiently aware of the fact that this doctrine had been adopted by the ordinary Magisterium.[63]

As to the affirmation by these same theologians that the Scotistic doctrine of the primacy of Christ leads to the negation of Mary's redemption by Christ, it evidently is unfounded, as can easily be seen from what we have said. Not only the Blessed Virgin, but even the angels (to whom nobody, as far as I know, has ever attributed a *debitum peccati*) owe their predestination to grace and their perseverance to "the blood of the cross," to use an expression of St. Paul.

This deductive synthesis shows, moreover, and proves with facts that God's plan concerning the world can be conceived without recourse to the famous thesis: "If Adam had not sinned, the Word would not have become Incarnate."[64] In other words, the predestination of Christ does not have to be made dependent on the sin of Adam. Indeed, the contrary is preferable, if we take into account the privilege of the Immaculate Conception and of the Assumption (which is connected with the Immaculate Conception).[65] The two predestinations find a natural explanation in this perspective, without having recourse to imaginary laws which God would make and then fail to apply. *Ego Dominus, et non*

---

[63] For historical proof of these assertions cf. Bonnefoy, *La negación del "debitum peccati" en María. Síntesis histórica* (Roma: Pont. Ateneo Antoniano, 1954), reprinted from *Verdad y Vida*, Vol. 12, 1954, pp. 103-171. For the speculative proof cf. Bonnefoy *Quelques théories modernes du debitum peccati* (Rome: Pont. Ateneo Antoniano, 1954), reprinted from *Ephemerides Mariologicae*, Vol. 4, 1954, pp. 269-331. Cf. likewise Bonnefoy, *Marie préservée de toute tache du péché originel*, in *L'Immaculée Conception. VIIe Congrès Marial National* (Lyon, 1954), pp. 187-220; A. B. Wolter, O.F.M., *The Theology of the Immaculate Conception in the Light of "Ineffabilis Deus,"* in *Marian Studies*, Vol. 5, 1954, pp. 19-70, esp. 62-70; and J. B. Carol, O.F.M., *Our Lady's Immunity from the Debt of Sin*, in *Marian Studies*, Vol. 6, 1955, pp. 164-168.

[64] Cf. Bonnefoy, *La question hypothétique: Utrum si Adam non pecasset ... au XIIIe siècle*, in *Revista Española de Teología*, Vol. 14, 1954, pp. 327-368.

[65] We have expounded the privilege of the Assumption in the light of Mary's predestination in a lecture given in Montreal in 1948: *L'Assomption de la T.S. Vierge et sa prédestination*, in *Vers le dogme de l'Assomption* (Montréal, 1948), pp. 293-335.

mutor.[66]

Our essay will have fulfilled its purpose if it has contributed toward diverting from a false anthropocentric perspective so many excellent authors who have fallen into the error of creating a narrow form of theology. True theology is theocentric, *ut sic sacra doctrina sit velut quaedam impressio divinae scientiae quae est una et simplex omnium.*[67]

---

[66] Mal. 3:6.
[67] St. Thomas, *Summa Theol.*, I, q. 1, a. 3, ad 2; cf. *ibid.*, a. 6: "Sacra autem doctrina propriissime determinat de Deo *secundum quod est altissima causa.*" — "In causando, bonum est prius quam ens, sicut finis quam forma, et hac ratione inter nomina significantia causalitatem divinam, prius ponitur quam ens." *Summa Theol.*, I, q. 5, a. 5, ad 1. These three texts would be sufficient to justify the method we have followed in this essay.

Mary's Immaculate Conception

By AIDAN CARR, O.F.M.Conv., S.T.D., and GERMAIN WILLIAMS, O.F.M.Conv., S.T.D.

HE Catholic doctrine of the Immaculate Conception of the Virgin Mary was formulated with absolute precision and for all time in the Bull of Pope Pius IX, *Ineffabilis Deus*, on December 8, 1854. The essential words of the definition are these:

> The most blessed Virgin Mary, in the first instant of her conception, was by the singular grace and privilege of almighty God, in view of the merits of Jesus Christ, Savior of the human race, preserved immune from all stain of original sin. This doctrine is revealed by God and therefore must be firmly and constantly believed by all the faithful.[1]

As is evident from the terms of this proposition, there are two constitutive elements in the definition: 1. a declaration of the privilege itself of the Immaculate Conception; 2. a statement of the certitude of that privilege.

1. DECLARATION OF THE PRIVILEGE

In order the better to understand what is contained within this singular privilege of Christ's Mother, one may examine the component parts, or "causes," of the Immaculate Conception. These are:

a) Material cause, or subject. Obviously, the subject of the Immaculate Conception is the *person* of the Blessed Virgin Mary, considered in the first instant of her conception in the womb of her mother. A human begins to be, in the true sense, at the moment the soul is created by God and infused into the fetus, and this is the moment of animation. That is called Mary's "passive conception." Passive conception is the terminus of the parents' generative act, which act is, by way of contradistinction, called "active conception."[2]

---

[1] *D.B.*, No. 1641.
[2] Cf. B. H. Merkelbach, O.P., *Mariologia* (Parisiis, 1939), p. 105 ff.

Before the human fetus is informed by a rational soul, the conception is known as "inchoate," while from the instant of the animation of the fetus, the conception is "consummated."[3] It is solely when the fetus is consummately conceived that a person has come into being. At precisely what stage of fetal development the soul is created and infused by God has always provided theologians with material for subtle discussion, but modern writers commonly favor the opinion that it takes place at the very first moment of fecundation. The definition of the Immaculate Conception offers no intimation as to the official teaching of the Church on the point.

Surely it would be untenable to argue in favor of any sanctification of Mary prior to the animation of the fetus, for until the moment of the substantial union between soul and body there is not yet a person, and hence no possible subject of grace. Only a rational person can be sanctified. The privilege accordingly affects uniquely the person of the Virgin, and not merely the soul nor merely the virginal body of the Mother of God. The initial sanctity of Mary concerns exclusively her personal conception achieved in sanctifying grace. Her freedom from the stain of all sin is identified with her being and her personality.[4]

b) Formal cause, or object. This aspect of the privilege of the Immaculate Conception concerns the fact of the preservation of the Virgin from all stain of original sin. The definition directly denies that she contracted the guilt of Adam's curse, and so indirectly it affirms, because of the diametrical opposition between sin and grace, that she possessed sanctifying grace from the first instance of her personal existence. Original sin, according to the settled teaching of the Church, is the deprivation of grace inflicted upon the posterity of Adam as a consequence of his personal sin; it is a radical enmity between a sinful mankind and the Creator.[5] Therefore, directly to exempt Mary from this essential effect of original sin is indirectly to affirm that she enjoyed an original sanctity through grace, with its accompanying adoptive filiation

---

[3] For a thorough treatment of the species of conception, cf. G. Alastruey, *Mariologia* (Vallisoleti, 1934), Vol. 1, p. 180 ff.

[4] Cf. Ephrem Longpré, O.F.M., *Exposition du Dogme de l'Immaculée Conception*, in *Deuxième Congrès Marial National* (Lourdes, 1930), p. 81.

[5] *DTC*, Vol. 7, cols. 845–846.

as a child of God. She was ever on terms of perfect friendship with God.[6]

Similarly, the privilege of the Immaculate Conception is expressed negatively when it is stated that Mary was always without original sin. It is expressed positively when it is stated that she always had sanctifying grace. While in the words of the very definition of the doctrine the formula employs the negative statement, yet in other cognate sections of the Bull *Ineffabilis Deus* the positive aspect receives due emphasis. A like duality of expression of the Virgin's sanctity, two sides of the one coin, appears in the writings of the Fathers of the Church and of later theologians, wherein sometimes is emphasized the negation of all sin, while again is stressed rather the positive fullness of grace.[7]

The angels and our first parents, prior to the angelic and human falls from grace, were immune from any sin, actual or original. But their immunity is to be distinguished from that proper to the Mother of God, for she was preserved immune. As will be seen in greater detail later, the immunity attributed to her was divinely provided for in view of the merits of Christ, which were applied to her in an exceptional and unique manner. She was redeemed.[8] The grace which adorned the angelic nature, like that granted to Adam and Eve, was "owed" to them in the hypothesis that God had decreed the elevation of the angels and of our first parents to the supernatural order. Having so to speak "obligated" Himself to give the means by which alone such an elevation could be realized, God accordingly constituted the angels and the first man and woman in a state of sanctifying grace.[9] But in the case of Mary, although in fact she was, in virtue of the privilege of the Immaculate Conception, constituted in grace from the first moment of her existence, nevertheless as a lineal descendant of Adam's infected nature, she would have been

---

[6] Cf. Charles Gonthier, *Marie et le Dogme* (Paris, 1920), pp. 26-33.

[7] Cf. C. Passaglia, S.J., *De Immaculato Deiparae semper Virginis conceptu* (Romae, 1855), Sec. 1, 2, 3. Cf. also Sedulius, *In Carmina Paschalia*, lib. 2, v. 28, PL, 19, 596; *Opera Augustini*, appendix, PL, 8, 1101; *Opera Augustini, sermo* 123, PL, 5, 1990; Ivo, *In serm. de Nativit. Domini*, PL, 162, 570. For Eastern thought on this, cf. S. M. Le Bachelet, *L'Immacolata Concezione* (Roma, 1904), *Parte I: L'Oriente*. Specifically for Spain, cf. I. M. Oller, *España y la Inmaculada Concepción* (Madrid, 1905), passim.

[8] Cf. *DTC*, Vol. 7, col. 847.

[9] Cf. S. Thomas Aquinas, *S. Th.*, I, q. 95, a. 1.

conceived in sin, had not God intervened to preserve her.[10] This miraculous preservation will be considered at length in a subsequent part of this article.

Finally, the immunity of the Blessed Virgin Mary from the stain of man's primal sin is specifically different from the freedom possessed by her divine Son.[11] He had no human father according to the flesh, for the active principle of His carnal generation was the overshadowing action of the Holy Spirit, in virtue of which His Mother conceived Him.[12] Since no seed of Adam begot Christ, there can be no question of tainted human nature in any way infecting Him. Surely the Redeemer of mankind needed no redemption!

c) Efficient cause of the privilege of the Immaculate Conception is God, or rather His great love for the woman destined to be the Mother of the Incarnate Word. This divine benevolent love motivated God to preserve Mary from the stain of all sin, in view of her sacred Maternity and through the merits of Christ her Son. This wondrous immunity effected by God's love and special providence still numbered Mary among the redeemed, but with the unique modality of redemption that might better be called "preredemption" or "redemption in a more sublime manner" than that accorded to all other children of Adam. While in the case of the rest of mankind the merits of the Saviour are applied in suchwise as to free them from the guilt of original sin already contracted at their conception; in Mary's case, on the contrary, the fruit of Christ's redeeming life and death was applied in suchwise as to preserve her from ever contracting Adam's guilt. Accordingly, this gratuitous concession on the part of God did not infringe at all on the formality of the Saviour's redemptive role.[13]

While the redemption obtained by other humans is properly described as "restorative" or "liberative," that of Mary is simply known as "preservative," and is incomparably of a nobler kind.

In this light it is evident that the doctrine of the Immaculate

---

[10] Cf. Martin Jugie, A.A., *L'Immaculée Conception dans L'Écriture sainte et dans la tradition orientale* (Rome, 1952), p. 11.

[11] Cf. S. Thomas Aquinas, *S. Th.*, III, q. 31, a. 7.

[12] *Lk.* 1:35.

[13] Cf. B. H. Merkelbach, O.P., *Mariologia*, p. 108.

Conception does not derogate from the universality of Christ's Redemption, for Mary, although immaculately conceived, was still redeemed by her Son, whose theandric life and piacular death contain the meritorious cause of His Mother's singular grace. It was the difficulty of a seeming derogation from the universality of Christ's redemption which had prevented theologians prior to the Franciscan, Duns Scotus († 1308), from affirming the truth of Mary's Immaculate Conception. It is the particular glory of Scotus, in regard to the entire doctrine of the Immaculate Conception, that he demonstrated not only the nonrepugnance of the dogma in the context of mankind's original sin, but its nonrepugnance as well in the context of Christ's universal Redemption. Other theologians denied that Mary was conceived in grace because they were persuaded that to admit it would be to detract from the honor due Christ. It remained for Scotus, on the contrary, to show that by denying the Immaculate Conception one indeed would derogate from the excellence of Christ insofar as He is a perfect Redeemer.[14]

d) Final cause, in the sense of the ultimate reason for the Immaculate Conception, was that Mary might be a fully worthy instrument for the accomplishment of the Incarnation.[15] As to the dogmatic definition itself, its ultimate reason was, as the Bull declares, "the honor of the most holy and undivided Trinity, the adornment and dignity of the Virgin Mother of God, and the exaltation of the Catholic Faith and Christian religion."[16]

2. CERTITUDE OF THE PRIVILEGE

The Bull *Ineffabilis Deus* defines that the doctrine of the Immaculate Conception is "revealed by God and therefore must be firmly and constantly believed by all the faithful."[17] Since this truth is, according to

---

[14] Cf. Carolus Balić, O.F.M., *De debito peccati originalis in B. Virgine Maria* (Romae, 1941), p. 88.

[15] Cf. the cogent argument of Scotus on this point in Sebastianus Dupasquier, O.F.M.Conv., *Summa Theologiae Scotisticae*, Vol. 3 (Patavii, 1706), p. 244. Cf. also Vincent Mayer, O.F.M.Conv., *The Teaching of the Ven. John Duns Scotus* (on the Immaculate Conception), in *Franciscan Studies*, Vol. 4 (New York, 1926), pp. 39-46.

[16] *D.B.*, No. 1641.

[17] *D.B.*, No. 1641. Cf. Ludovicus Lercher, S.J., *Institutiones Theologiae Dogmaticae*, Vol. 3 (Oeniponte, 1934), p. 338.

the words of the Sovereign Pontiff, a revealed one, it follows that it must be formally contained in the deposit of divine revelation, and not merely contained virtually therein as a theological conclusion the minor premise of which is human reason. While Pope Pius IX seems to indicate that the doctrine is formally revealed, still he does not specify whether that revelation has been made to us in an explicit manner by God, that is to say, in an express and direct manner, or whether it has been revealed only implicitly, that is to say, indirectly and obscurely. That question the Pontiff left to the deliberations of theologians,[18] restricting himself to declaring that the Immaculate Conception is a truth revealed by God. That something is in fact contained in the deposit of revelation is one thing: the way in which it is contained is another thing. Since God can reveal a truth explicitly or implicitly, it follows accordingly that this truth itself can likewise be included in revelation either explicidy or implicitly.[19]

According to the principles of the Catholic Faith, all revealed truth is enveloped in Scripture and Tradition, and one must accept, "with like pious affection and reverence" the two sources of revelation.[20] Hence the doctrine of the Immaculate Conception is not merely deduced from revelation without actually being revealed; nor is it some dogmatic fact in some way only connected with a revealed dogma to which it stands related; nor is it a new doctrine. The truth of Mary's Immaculate Conception is undeniably one given by God to the Apostles in revelation, and delivered by them to the Church.[21] The certitude of the doctrine is rooted not merely in the authoritative teaching office of the Catholic Church, making use of Scripture and Apostolic Tradition, but the writings of the Fathers and later theologians, together with the common consent of the vast body of the faithful, all offer irrefragable testimony to that certitude.

---

[18] Cf. Martin Jugie, A.A., *op. cit.*, p. VIII.
[19] Cf. *DTC*, Vol. 7, col. 847.
[20] *D.B.*, No. 1787.
[21] Cf. B. H. Merkelbach, O.P., *op. cit.*, p. 109.

ADVERSARIES OF THE DOCTRINE

Only non-Catholics stand opposed to the Immaculate Conception of the Virgin Mary. Among them must be numbered the schismatic Greek "Orthodox" Church, the "Old Catholics" founded by Dollinger late in the nineteenth century, Protestants of all sects, Rationalists, and divers other groupings. All these object to the doctrine itself, maintaining that it is no part of the Christian religion, and so reject the definition as contrary to revealed truth. As grounds for refusal to accept the Immaculate Conception, spokesmen for the objectors allege the same difficulties offered by adversaries prior to the solemn definition in 1854. This contrary position is expressed succinctly in the question of the Protestant theologian Harnack: "If this truth is a revealed one, when was it revealed and to whom?"[22]

TENOR OF THE BULL "INEFFABILIS DEUS"

In his solemn pontifical document, Pope Pius IX defined the doctrine of the Immaculate Conception to be of faith for Catholics in virtue of his supreme power as Vicar of Christ, but at the same time he acknowledged that the definition reflected the universal mind of the Church's hierarchy and of the Catholic faithful, for their opinion had been asked for and found favorable. The Sovereign Pontiff, by way of preamble to the definition proper, stated that God from all eternity chose a Mother for His Son, and because He loved her more than He loved any other creature He, therefore, endowed her with the gift of freedom from all stain of sin, a gift most becoming to the Blessed Virgin Mary.

The Pope reminded the Catholic world of the enduring attention which the Church down through the centuries had devoted to the development of the doctrine, even to the extent of having instituted a feast of the Conception and in other ways encouraging the piety of the faithful toward a cult of the unique privilege of Mary. The doctrine was favored by popes prior to Pius IX, and Alexander VII explicitly declared that the Immaculate Conception might safely be defended as Catholic

---

[22] Cf. Gabriel M. Roschini, O.S.M., *Mariologia*, ed. 2, Vol. 2 (Romae, 1948), p. 23.

truth.[23] A similar opinion was consistently held by various religious communities and eminent theologians, as well as by many synods throughout the world. The Pope further mentioned in the Bull *Ineffabilis Deus* that the cogency of the favorable testimony of the most ancient sources in the Oriental Church contributed in no small measure to the advance in the way toward definition.

Pius IX singled out the force of the argument derived from the writings of the Fathers of the Church who so greatly exalted the sanctity and dignity of the Mother of God, referring to her immunity from sin and applying to her apposite sections of Scripture, especially the references to "the woman" in Gen. 3:15, and the salutation of the angel to Mary narrated in the Gospel of St. Luke 1:28. The traditional writings of the most renowned Fathers described Mary's plenitude of grace as a kind of climax of all God's miracles in the order of grace. This conviction of Mary's high holiness and immunity from the stain of sin was shared by the generations of simple faithful as well as by the Catholic clergy of the ages, all of whom found pious consolation in venerating the Immaculate Mother of God. Countless petitions were addressed to the Holy See requesting a formal definition of the doctrine of the Immaculate Conception.

In concluding his Bull, Pius IX spoke of his own efforts with regard to the doctrine, pointing out that once elevated to the Chair of Peter he longed most ardently to promote the honor of Mary in every way possible and to enhance her cult by making her singular prerogatives more widely known. To the achievement of this end the Pontiff added that he had instituted a special commission of cardinals to examine the questions connected with the doctrine of the Immaculate Conception, and had dispatched letters to the bishops of the world in this connection in February, 1849. In reply to these Papal inquiries, the bishops confirmed the universal piety of their people toward this privilege of the Blessed Virgin, annexing their own petitions that the Immaculate Conception be defined by the Roman Pontiff. The special commission of cardinals had returned a like decision.

Accordingly, being unwilling further to delay a solemn

---

[23] Cf. Armand Robichaud, S.M., *The Immaculate Conception in the Magisterium of the Church*, in *Marian Studies*, Vol. 5 (Washington, D. C., 1954), pp. 118-120.

pronouncement, and after consultation with a consistory of the cardinals, together with much private and public prayer imploring the guidance of the Holy Spirit, the Pope determined to declare and define that the doctrine of Mary's Immaculate Conception is one of faith.

Finally, the Supreme Pontiff affirmed his joy and gratitude that it was granted to him to offer this honor to the Mother of Christ, trusting that she would continue by her patronage to aid the Church yet more in its divine work. He exhorted the faithful to increase their veneration and piety toward "the Virgin conceived without sin."[24]

ARGUMENT FROM SCRIPTURE

Support for the dogma of the Immaculate Conception as found in the sacred writings of the Old and the New Testament is neither abundant nor coercive.[25] Although this truth is contained implicitly rather than explicitly in Scripture, yet when the indications therein comprised are carefully examined in the lucid context of Tradition and authority, it becomes manifest how intimately Mary's immunity from all sin is joined to the inspired account of God's plan for man's redemption. As the sharp lines of a valley below may become apparent only when the climber stands upon a summit, similarly the profound content of God's word awaited the clarification of the passing centuries.[26]

Pertinent texts both in the Old and the New Testament are classically considered either as principal or as ancillary. The former are clearer and more forceful and so lead more immediately to a support of the doctrine; the latter are less cogent. The characteristic of the Old Testament: foreshadowing the brightness of the New Testament and representing subsequent figures through types and prefigures, is quite evident with

---

[24] Cf. Paul F. Palmer, S.J., *Mary in the Documents of the Church* (Westminster, Md., 1952), pp. 81-89.

[25] Cf. Narcisco García Garcés, C.M.F., *Titulos y Grandezas de Maria* (Madrid, 1952), p. 384 ff.; Scoti-Guarrae-Aureoli, *Quaestiones Disputatae de Immaculata Conceptione B. V. M.* (Ad Claras Aquas, 1904), p. VII.

[26] Cf. Jean-François Bonnefoy, O.F.M., *Le Mystère de Marie selon le Protévangile et l'Apocalypse* (Paris, 1949), passim; F. Ceuppens, O.P., *Theologia Biblica*, Vol. 4: *De Mariologia Biblica* (Romae, 1948), pp. 70, 208.

regard to the doctrine of the Immaculate Conception.[27] The eminent Martin Jugie has observed that there are some twenty-four places in Scripture which have been cited as favoring the dogma, and that these various allusions have perhaps been subjected to the least critical analysis of all proofs of the doctrine.[28]

I. PRINCIPAL SCRIPTURAL PROOFS

A. *In the Old Testament*

The abiding enmity between the serpent, the devil, and the woman, Mary, as developed in the exegesis of the text of Gen. 3:15: "I will put enmities between thee and the woman, and thy seed and her seed: she shall crush thy head, and thou shalt lie in wait for her heel," is commonly offered in support of the Immaculate Conception. Whatever differences may exist among Scripture scholars as to the correct interpretation of this important passage, there can be no serious doubt but that the Blessed Virgin is "the woman" mentioned.[29] Nor can any construction placed upon the famous ipsa pronoun used by the Vulgate, derogate from the force of this text, since the essential notion of Mary's utter freedom from any diabolical dominion is sufficiently indicated in the phrase, "I will put enmities ..."[30] The Blessed Virgin is the woman whose radical opposition to all that Satan stands for demands a perfect immunity from sin, specifically from original sin, and the reference to her is in a literal sense.[31] The enmity described requires that Mary be

---

[27] Cf. G. Alastruey, *op. cit.*, p. 182.

[28] Cf. Martin Jugie, *op. cit.*, p. 41.

[29] Cf. Francis X. Peirce, S.J., *Mary Alone is "the Woman" of Genesis 3, 15*, in *The Catholic Biblical Quarterly*, Vol. 2 (Washington, D. C., 1940), No. 3, pp. 245-252; Antonine De Guglielmo, O.F.M., *Mary in the Protoevangelium*, in *The Catholic Biblical Quarterly*, Vol. 14, 1952, No. 2, pp. 104-115; J. Coppens, *Le Protévangile*, in *Ephemerides Theologicae Lovanienses*, Vol. 26 (Louvain, 1950), p. 35.

[30] *DTC*, Vol. 7, col. 859. Cf. Francis J. Connell, C.SS.R., *Historical Development of the Dogma of the Immaculate Conception*, in *Studies in Praise of Our Blessed Mother*, ed. Fenton-Benard (Washington, D. C., 1952), p. 94.

[31] Cf. P. F. Ceuppens, O.P., *De Mariologia Biblica*, ed. 2 (Romae, 1951), pp. 16-17; Tiburtius Gallus, S.J., *Interpretatio Mariologica Protoevangelii* (Romae, 1949), passim; G. Arendt, S.J., *De Protoevangelii habitudine ad Immaculatam Deiparae Conceptionem* (Romae, 1904). See

finally a complete victor over the devil and his snares, and this she would not have been if for one instant she had been subjected to Satan through the slavery of sin. The crushing of the serpent's head can mean nothing else than a perfect immunity from his evil stain.[32]

The New Eve, the Mother of the Messias, and Lucifer, the author of sin, are in every way enemies, with the conquest divinely assured to be Mary's. At no time were these hostile forces as allies; at no time was the Virgin Mother a vanquished satellite of God's proud rival. Sanctifying grace alone establishes man in God's friendship and, by the same token, constitutes him Satan's bitter foe. The absence of that grace from the soul, effected by sin, ranges one in the ranks of the Prince of darkness by removing one from a share in the divine nature, the essential function of God's grace. Had there been an instant, however brief, when Mary's soul was stripped of grace, then Scripture could not properly refer to Mary as one who vanquished the very personification of evil. Whether Eve be considered as a type of the Blessed Virgin, or whether the woman described is Mary in a more literal acceptation, there is had a clear antithesis between good and evil, as between the state of God's Mother and Eve after the Fall; as between Christ the New Adam, and the old Adam, enmeshed in sin.[33]

The conjoint victory of the Redeemer and His Mother over the devil is the divine reply to the common defeat of the first parents through the wiles of the serpent and their own malice. It is a perfect parallelism and one that has traditionally been invoked to prove the Immaculate

---

Father E. May's paper in this volume.

[32] Cf. Sebastianus Dupasquier, O.F.M.Conv., *op. cit.*, p. 237; Raymundo Martínez y Ferrer, *De utilitate et ratione sufficienti ad dogmaticam definitionem* (Interamnae, 1853), p. 61; Vasco Bertelli, *L'interpretazione mariologica del Protoevangelo (Gen. 3, 15) negli esegeti e teologi dopo la Bolla "Ineffabilis Deus" di Pio IX* (Romae, 1951), passim.

[33] Cf. B. H. Merkelbach, O.P., *op. cit.*, p. 113; P. Hitz, C.SS.R., *Le sens Marial de Protévangile*, in *Études Mariales* (Paris, 1947), passim.

Conception.[34] Mary's triumph was in virtue of her Son's.[35] The most solid support of Mary's unique prerogative is thus based on one and the same divine decree, establishing her predestination to a singular grace together with the absolute and universal primacy of her Son.[36]

Neither Christ, the Seed of the woman, nor the woman herself, could for even a moment be overcome by evil, for then the victory would not be entire. The probative force of this argument in support of the Immaculate Conception is, when thus understood, considered as strongly suasive in the conclusions presented by the Pontifical Commission for the definition of the dogma of the Immaculate Conception, constituted by Pius IX, and reporting its findings on July 10, 1852.[37]

B. In the New Testament

When the angelic messenger Gabriel greeted the Virgin who was divinely destined to be the Mother of the Saviour, he spoke words manifestive of a tremendous miracle and mystery in the order of grace. "And the angel being come in, said unto her: 'Hail, full of grace, the Lord is with thee: Blessed art thou among women.'"[38]

While of itself this salutation, considered in text and context, is not a complete and explicit proof from Scripture of the immunity of Mary from original sin, yet it is undeniably an implicit or equivalent statement of the doctrine of the Immaculate Conception.[39] "Full of grace" can mean nothing other than "entirely replenished with God's love" — "in nowise deficient." And the phrase "the Lord is with thee" must similarly mean that Mary was never without Him and that the devil was never with her,

---

[34] Cf. A. H. M. Lépicier, O.S.M., *Tractatus de Beatissima Virgine Maria*, ed. 5 (Romae, 1926), p. 137, footnote; for the sense of Coredemption cf. J. B. Carol, O.F.M., *Romanorum Pontificum doctrina de B. V. Corredemptrice*, in *Marianum*, Vol. 9 (Roma, 1947), p. 165; V. G. Bertelli, *Il senso mariologico pieno e il senso letterale de Protoevangelo (Gen. 3, 15) dalla "Ineffabilis Deus" al 1948*, in *Marianum*, Vol. 13, pp. 369-395.

[35] Cf. C. Crosta, *Theologia Dogmatica*, Vol. 3 (Varese, 1932), p. 176.

[36] Cf. Jean-François Bonnefoy, O.F.M., *op. cit.*, p. 140.

[37] Cf. J. B. Carol, O.F.M., in *Marianum*, Vol. 1, 1939, pp. 314-316.

[38] *Lk.* 1:28.

[39] Cf. Sebastianus Dupasquier, O.F.M.Conv., *op. cit.*, p. 238; *DTC*, Vol. 7, col. 859.

as he indeed would have been had she been conceived in sin.[40]

When subjected to philological analysis the sense of this important text adds immensely to the general force of the scriptural argument, for how could Mary have been *filled* with God's grace in the strict rigor implied in plenitude, and yet have been without that grace at some moment of her existence? The message of the Annunciation can mean only that the Virgin possessed as perfect a degree of grace as would be possible for a mere creature, and that this unparalleled sanctity is complete both as to its proper intensity and as to its extension in time. The English rendering "Hail, full of grace" is from the Greek original χαῖρε κεχαριτωμένη and the past participle κεχαριτωμένη correctly signifies not merely the preterit quality of what is modified by it, but implies as well unvarying continuity.

A paraphrase of the first four words of the angelic salutation might well be: "Greetings to you who are so adorned with divine gifts and supernal goods, so replete with God's love and friendship that its very fullness is contained in you." In other words, such an immensity of grace was infused into the soul of the Mother of God that no other human can be compared to her by reason of this holiness, and this unique privilege has always been hers. It is also noteworthy that Gabriel is not described as exclaiming, "Hail, Mary, full of grace," but simply as saying, "Hail, full of grace." Thus the "full of grace" is used in a substantive manner, as a title peculiarly her own, her God-given name, somewhat the same as she spoke of herself to Bernadette at Lourdes, "I am the Immaculate Conception." As proper to her alone, this appellation "full of grace" is not some extrinsic designation; rather it is her property in a radical and intrinsic sense at all moments of her existence. There was no period of time, however so brief, in which she was not "full of grace."[41]

To this initial greeting the archangel added "the Lord is with thee" — ὁ κύριος μετα σου. Correlated with what has immediately preceded, these words indicate an unqualified and simple union of Mary, the

---

[40] Cf. Sebastianus Dupasquier, O.F.M.Conv., *op. cit.*, p. 239.

[41] Card. Alimonda, *Il Dogma dell'Immacolata* (Torino, 1886), p. 118: "... giacchè ivi appunto si recita e se narra a svelare la virtù divina, per la quale quei segni o miracoli si operavano; laddove a Maria sola s'indirizza autonomasticamente il celeste saluto, che altri mai non sortì."

beloved one of God, with the Lord. No reference is contained either in the text itself or in the context to any temporal limitation; rather the sense is entirely a general one: whenever Mary was, then God was with her and she with Him in His grace.[42] Had she, on the contrary, been even for the most infinitesimal period of time under the domination of sin, there would have been some interruption of this communion with God, and accordingly the archangel's universal declaration of her grace would have been itself faulty. Either the words contain an affirmation of the Immaculate Conception or else they are meaningless.

The final phrase of the salutation regarding the sanctity of the Mother of the Messias — "Blessed art thou among women" — means that she is not only blessed in herself, but blessed in comparison with all other women. This Hebraism bears the connotation of a superlative degree of blessedness, so that, by antonomasia she is the blessed one of all women as a consequence of the divine Maternity and its concomitant grace.[43] This utterly unique office carries with it a correspondingly unique infusion of grace, a blessing that is an essential link in the chain of causality that will reach its culmination in the Redemption, blotting out the curse visited upon mankind by the sin of the first parents. This scriptural reference manifests how fitting it is that she whose own gracious life was the divinely chosen instrument for the Incarnation, should herself be totally free from the very fault her Son came to remove. As will be seen elsewhere in this article, this divine Maternity is always the point of reference in treating the reasonableness of the Immaculate Conception.[44]

The basic antithesis between the blessing of God and His curse, with reference to the immunity from original sin, appears frequently in Scripture. It is a familiar note.[45] This curse, a fundamental alienation from God's friendship, is the consequence of the primal sin and as such is its chief penalty. As the one sin of Adam is the unique and ultimate cause of the blight visited upon all men descended from Adam by carnal generation, and is on that account called by antonomasia "the sin,"

---

[42] Cf. B. H. Merkelbach, O.P., *op. cit.*, pp. 112–113.

[43] Cf. Henry Bolo, *Pleine de grâce* (Paris, 1895), passim.

[44] Cf. A. H. M. Lépicier, O.S.M., *op. cit.*, p. 219.

[45] Mt. 5:44; Lk. 6:28; Rom. 12:14; James 3:10.

similarly its concomitant punishment is called "the curse." Conversely, Mary, who is by antonomasia called "blessed," must be herself immune from that sin which caused that curse. She cannot be both so completely blessed and yet be, at any moment, subject to the very opposite of blessing: God's curse.

Additional support for this antithetical parallelism is found in the words of God addressed to the serpent: "Because thou hast done this thing, thou art cursed..."[46] As this malediction falling upon the devil was the outcome of his sinful deceit, so the blessing bestowed upon Mary was the reward of an immunity from all sin. As the author of sin was cursed, contrariwise she who co-operated so intimately in the divine plan of salvation is crowned with divine blessing.

The same inference is readily deduced from the greeting of Elizabeth to Mary at the Visitation: "Blessed art thou among women, and blessed is the fruit of thy womb."[47] The Virgin is called "blessed" in somewhat the same way as her Son, observing, of course, a due analogy of proportion between the relative plenitude of grace in each case. The implication is therefore clear that Mary was always entirely free from the baneful curse identified with original sin.

The probative force of these cited passages of the New Testament, while affording a highly effective argument of convenience in favor of the doctrine of the Immaculate Conception, is rather suasive than apodictic. According to some very competent scholars, the argument taken from these chief texts in favor of the doctrine is not as strong as that of the *Protoevangelium*.[48] Be that as it may, the clearest proof from the inspired books would seem to be derived from understanding the Old Testament as the type and foreshadowing of the New Testament; the latter is the perfection of the former, just as Mary is the new and sinless Eve.[49] What is said of "the woman" in Gen. 3:15 finds its fulfillment only

---

[46] Gen. 3:14.

[47] Lk. 1:42.

[48] Cf. V. Sardi, *La solenne definizione del dogma dell'Immacolato Concepimento di Maria Santissima*, Vol. 1 (Roma, 1905), p. 796 ff.

[49] Cf. Jules Souben, *Nouvelle Théologie Dogmatique* (Paris, 1902), Vol. 4, pp. 135-137.

in Mary.[50]

II. Ancillary Scriptural Proofs

A. In the Old Testment

There are a number of texts in the Old Testament traditionally cited, with varying degrees of appositeness, as supporting the freedom of the Mother of God from the stain of Adam's sin. They are of minor moment as compared with the principal passage of Genesis. Among the more notable examples of these might be mentioned: "Thou art all fair, O my love, and there is not a spot in thee"[51] — "Open to me, my sister, my love, my dove, my undefiled"[52] — "the Highest himself hath founded her"[53] — "For wisdom will not enter into a malicious soul, nor dwell in a body subject to sins."[54] Perhaps the best cognate text is "the most High hath sanctified his own tabernacle."[55]

These and other like texts are employed in an accommodated sense by the Church's liturgy when the Blessed Virgin is the subject of the prayer, and specifically for the feast of the Immaculate Conception in the Roman Missal and the Breviary. Since the manner in which the Church prays is a criterion of its belief, it follows that the use of these various sections of Scripture is a forcible argument in favor of their actually referring to Mary's privilege in the order of grace. Because these excerpts from the Old Testament, although in themselves of minor significance, do not place temporal limits to her sanctity, and indeed because several of them intimate that her holiness was established already from the beginning, it may legitimately be concluded that the tenor of the texts is fully consonant with the precise sense of the Immaculate Conception. The application of them to Mary's immunity is in accordance with the secondary and indirect literal sense of the

---

[50] Cf. J. de Aldama, *Mariologia, in Sacrae Theologiae Summa* (ed. a Patribus Soc. Jesu), Vol. 3 (Madrid, 1950), p. 303, No. 28. Cf. also Eric May's paper in this volume.

[51] Cant. 4:7.

[52] Cant. 5:2.

[53] 53 Ps. 86:5.

[54] Wisd. 1:4.

[55] Ps. 45:5.

passages.[56]

B. In the New Testament

The best example of a subsidiary text in the New Testament used to strengthen the general argument in support of the revealed quality of the Immaculate Conception, is that of *Apoc.* 12: the vision of the woman clothed with the sun, and of the great dragon who is her persecutor. Authors are not agreed as to whether the woman mentioned is the Church, or Mary, or perhaps both.[57]

Accepting the opinion, sufficiently probable, that sees the woman as the Virgin, it can be said that her being "clothed with the sun" is an affirmation of her soul's grace, since grace is often compared to the light of justice and she is enveloped in radiant light. The stain of sin, on the other hand, is a certain deprivation of splendor marring a soul that is enslaved to anything contrary to the brilliance offered by the light of faith and reason.[58] Sin is a work of darkness because sin results in a stain; sin is found in an act not illumined by the light of reason informed by grace. Such a want of splendor cannot exist in one who is "clothed with the sun." Moreover, the struggle between the woman and the serpent, destined to end in his defeat, would not have been an unbroken combat if she had, for a time however so brief, been conquered by him.

The devil originally made his effort to overcome Mary when he seduced the first parents, from whom the infection of sin passed down to their posterity, and would indeed have engulfed Mary except for her special preservation through the causality of the Incarnate Word. His humanity taken from Mary and from the earth, became the instrument that turned aside the tide of sin lest it sweep His Mother into the bitter waters flowing from a poisoned source. This is the interpretation of verses 15 and 16 of chapter 12 of *Apocalypse*:

> And the serpent cast out of his mouth after the woman, water as it were a river; that he might cause her to be carried away by the river. And the earth helped the woman, and the earth opened her mouth, and swallowed

---

[56] Cf. B. H. Merkelbach, *op. cit.*, p. 113.

[57] See the various opinions referred to in Father M. Gruenthaner's paper in this same volume.

[58] Cf. St. Thomas Aquinas, *S. Th.*, Ia-IIae, q. 86, a. 1.

up the river, which the dragon cast out of his mouth.

The total context of chapter 12 is, more than anything else, an exaltation of Mary's spiritual Maternity, but it furnishes a confirmation as well as an interpretation of the enmity between the woman and the serpent narrated in the *Protoevangelium* contained in Genesis.[59] Mary was protected from falling under the serpent's influence through the redemptive act of Christ, becoming a satisfying victim for mankind in accordance with the prophecy of Isa. 53:6. The piacular death of the Saviour had a special efficacy for the Mother of the Messias, and this is why the serpent, the dragon, in the words of Apoc. 12:17: "... was angry against the woman: and went to make war with the rest of her seed..."

This passage in the last of the inspired books thus is a classical argument, of perhaps a lesser weight, to confirm Mary's immunity from original sin. It is the fulfillment of the promise contained in the first of the inspired books, for this promised relief on behalf of a suffering human race is accomplished, according to St. John, in the Mother of Christ and in her seed: the sacred humanity, and each person, the Virgin and her Son, enjoyed freedom from all sin. This conjoint sinlessness, Christ's natural to His divinity, Mary's special to her humanity, was a requisite to their conjoint victory over Satan by their sufferings. The doctrine of the Coredemption thus becomes a valuable asset in a proper understanding of the meaning of the Immaculate Conception. "She joined her own heroic sufferings to those of her beloved Son for the salvation of mankind, and the eternal Father was pleased to accept them for that purpose in subordination to those of the unique Redeemer."[60]

ARGUMENT FROM TRADITION

I. Force of This Argument

The question as to whether or not a particular truth is actually contained in the deposit of divine revelation, while obviously related to

---

[59] Cf. *DTC*, Vol. 7, col. 869; Jean-François Bonnefoy, O.F.M., *op. cit.*, passim.

[60] J. B. Carol, O.F.M., *Our Lady's Coredemption in the Marian Literature of Nineteenth Century America*, in *Marianum*, Vol. 14, 1952, p. 61. There is a growing emphasis in Mariology on Mary's relation to the work of her Son, the Redeemer. Cf. E. Ledvorowski, *Maternitas divina fundamentum Mariologiae*, in *Marianum*, Vol. 15, 1953, pp. 176-194.

the question of the profession of that truth by the Church, is nevertheless of a different order. The former is of the objective order: it is (or is not) a truth irrespective of what steps have been taken by the *magisterium* of the Church to render an authoritative statement on the point at issue. The latter is of a subjective order, for a public acceptance of a doctrine by the Church makes explicit and personal what was hitherto implicit and impersonal. While it is undoubtedly true that often these two orders do in fact parallel each other, and tend more and more to do so in the measure that the implicit content of revelation is made consciously explicit, still it is not necessary that such parallelism be always realized. One need not suppose that he will find in the subjective order all the content of the objective order.[61]

In keeping with this preliminary principle, and by way of application of it to the special question of the doctrine of the Immaculate Conception, it is well to remark that whether there was or was not an explicit belief in the doctrine from the earliest days of the Church is not something that can be resolved a priori. Rather it is a question of historical fact to be determined by a perusal of the sources, wherein alone can be discovered such evidence as will afford a reply to a factual question. In this connection we may fittingly invoke the philosophical axiom which affirms that objective evidence is the ultimate criterion of truth, joined to the judgment of the Church as to what truth is divinely revealed.

The word "dogma" has the meaning of something fixed and determined in doctrine, and to merit this title a proposition must be indeed revealed by God, and as such proposed by the Church to the faithful as a truth to be believed. Once so pronounced, it becomes immutably established. The transition of a truth from the objective order to the subjective: from implicit to explicit levels of knowledge, does not mean that any new thing has been revealed, for revelation terminated for all time with the passing of the last of the Apostles. To the Church has been committed this deposit of total truth, and the office of Christ's Church is to guard and to interpret it. While there can, therefore, be no increase in what is contained in that treasury, yet there can surely be an elucidation of obscure truths with the passing of the centuries. The seed

---

[61] Cf. *DTC*, Vol. 7, col. 848.

can, in a propitious climate, produce its fruit, and this climate is sometimes created by the rise of heresies which can alone be refuted by a firm declaration by the Church; sometimes it is created by controversies among theologians; or again by a development of a special piety on the part of the Church's faithful. In all these instances it must be held that the Holy Spirit is at work, guiding and enlightening the teaching function of the Church. There is never a change in doctrine. There are advances in the same line of truth.

In applying this central notion to the doctrine of the Immaculate Conception, it becomes evident in the light of investigation that this dogma was not at first expressed in technical and precise terms, but was universally believed as a part of her great purity and holiness, and that with the unfolding of the centuries, it became more distinctly Mary's prerogative. A careful and recent study on the problem of the evolution of this doctrine has stressed that in the case of the Immaculate Conception the growth of explicit belief is to be attributed rather to the inherent power of the doctrine than to exterior forces at work. The truth of the Virgin's immunity from the stain of original sin was "endowed with a victorious vitality which was nurtured by divine solicitude."[62]

Whatever may have been the inherent tendency of the doctrine, it cannot be gainsaid that immense impetus was given the development of its explicit modality by the forces of controversy, particularly in the stages prior to the final definition. In the first ages of the Church there were no doubts raised, since the reality of the Immaculate Conception formed, together with the divine Maternity and its necessary sanctity, one complex mosaic. It was not until the twelfth and thirteenth centuries that the question was thrown into issue in the schools of theology, and by about the middle of the sixteenth century scarcely anyone any longer called the Immaculate Conception into doubt.[63]

The value of the argument from tradition, based on the writings of the most distinguished ecclesiastical writers, together with the emphasis placed on the sanctity of Mary in the liturgy of the Church, affords a

---

[62] J. Duhr, S.J., *L'évolution du dogme de l'Immaculée Conception,* in *Nouvelle Revue Théologique* (Louvain, 1951), Vol. 73, p. 1032.

[63] Bernard A. McKenna, *The Dogma of the Immaculate Conception* (Washington, D. C., 1929), p. 89.

very precious adjunct to the scriptural evidence in favor of the Immaculate Conception. Indeed, independently of the interpretation and comment of the Fathers, the inspired texts remain of limited force in this respect.[64] For this reason, the current of tradition must be painstakingly examined in order to discover in what way and with what degree of unanimity the various streams of Catholic thought formed the universal conviction that Mary was conceived in grace. Founded ultimately upon revelation, written and oral, and coupled with the public prayer of the Church, these sources prepared the way for the formal definition of the Immaculate Conception. The historical and liturgical development of the doctrine is conveniently divided into chronological periods.

II. PERIOD OF IMPLICIT FAITH — UP TO THE COUNCIL OF EPHESUS (431)

a) Parallelism between Eve and Mary

This oft-repeated comparison between the first woman, the sinful Eve, who was seduced by the serpent, and the Second Eve, the blessed Mary, whose vital role in man's redemption made her the "Socia" of the Saviour, is rooted in a similar antithesis between Adam and Christ. Thus St. Paul declares, "For as by the disobedience of one man, many were made sinners; so also by the obedience of one, many shall be made just."[65] The juxtaposition of the two women, one vanquished by Satan, the other victorious over him, flows as a natural corollary to the disobedience of the old Adam and the perfect submission of the New Adam, the just Redeemer.

Perhaps the first to invoke this beautiful antithesis was St. Justin (100-167):

> While still a virgin and without corruption, Eve received into her heart the word of the serpent and thereby conceived disobedience and death. Mary the Virgin, her soul full of faith and joy, replied to the angel Gabriel who brought her glad tidings: "Be it done to me according to thy word." To her was born He of whom so many things are said in the Scriptures.[66]

---

[64] Cf. Martin Jugie, A.A., *op. cit.*, p. 473; *DTC*, Vol. 7, col. 871.
[65] Rom. 5:19.
[66] *Dialogus cum Tryphone Judaeo*, No. 100, *PL*, 6, 710 D.

Similar passages appear in the writings of St. Irenaeus (130-202)[67] and Tertullian (160-240).[68]

The contrast between the two women implies a double comparison, one of likeness; one of unlikeness. Eve and Mary are indeed similar insofar as both were stainless as they came from the hand of God, each was integral, each without corruption, each a virgin.[69] They are unlike insofar as Eve, by her disobedience and pride, became an instrument for the downfall of the human race, while Mary, humble and obedient, was found worthy to assist in the salvation of the world through her office as Mother of Jesus. If taken in an unqualified sense (and the general tenor of the antithesis warrants it), then Mary's utter freedom from corruption argues a corresponding freedom from original sin. St. Irenaeus would seem to interpret the high holiness of the Virgin as contrasted to Eve's betrayal into the snares of the serpent: the complete conformity of the all-pure Mary to the will of God effectively untied the knot of sin introduced by Eve.[70] This contrast would be imperfect and its chief characters would be inadequately in opposition if Mary had herself been stained by the sin of the first parents. From a broader view there would be a distortion of perspective if the Mother of the Messias were held to have fallen under the primitive curse, since together with her Son she forms a team that is destined to achieve a conquest over the evil resulting from the transgression of its counterpart: Adam and Eve.

b) The Sanctity of Mary in a General Sense

Among the Fathers the theme of Mary's exalted holiness appears very frequently and with considerable elaboration, and nearly always with the purpose of thereby enhancing the dignity of the Son, and defending the reality of His earthly life, suffering, and death. Many of these truths of the Saviour had been called into doubt by the early heresiarchs, and one mode, and a forceful one, to combat errors concerning the Son was to emphasize truths about the Mother.[71] The

---

[67] *Contra haereses*, lib. 5, cap. 1, No. 2, *PG*, 7, 1122.
[68] *De carne Christi*, cap. 17, PL, 2, 781-782.
[69] Cf. Ed. Hugon, *Tractatus Dogmatici*, Vol. 2 (Paris, 1935), p. 718.
[70] *Contra haereses*, lib. 3, cap. 22, *PG*, 7, 959 b-c.
[71] Cf. *DTC*, Vol. 7, col. 873.

conviction of the writers relative to her holiness is founded, necessarily, in revealed truth which became more explicit with the passing of time.[72] In denying that she herself had ever sinned, the Fathers placed her merit in a distinct class above the rest of humankind, and no eulogy was too great to describe her, nor were any words adequate to convey the measure of her holiness. She was "most pure"; "inviolate"; "unstained"; "unspotted"; "blameless"; "entirely immune from sin"; "blessed above all"; "most innocent."[73] If she was free from sin without qualification, then why not also from original sin? Assuredly, this freedom excluded deliberate venial sin, and hence with greater reason it should exclude the deprivation of grace implied in original sin, for while venial sin is more voluntary, nevertheless, simply as sin and with its conjoined ignominy, the consequences of original sin are more serious and more unbecoming to the Mother of Christ since it would put her at odds with God.[74] As St. Anselm stated (and he reflects the common mind of the writers on this point): "It was fitting that the Virgin should be radiant with such purity that under God no other can be greater."[75]

The argument for the immaculate quality of the soul of Mary receives a rather strange support from a species of the doctrine of traducianism, prevalent in some quarters in the early centuries. This taught that human souls were generated by the parents along with the body, and thus in some way the offspring received their souls from the parents. Corporeal traducianism taught that the soul derived from the material element of the parents, and Tertullian, while a Montanist, proposed this heretical theory to explain the origin of the soul.[76] Spiritual traducianism taught the origin of the human soul to be from the soul of the parents. Even St. Augustine seems to defend this doctrine, but he admits that his opinion is obscure. In either case, if Mary herself had been stained by sin, her Son would, in some way, have been affected in

---

[72] Cf. G. Jouassard, *Le problème de la sainteté de Marie chez les Pères*, in *Études Mariales* (Paris, 1947), pp. 13-28.

[73] Cf. Dominicus Palmieri, S.J., *Tractatus de peccato originali et de Immaculato Beatae Virginis Deiparae Conceptu*, ed. altera (Romae, 1904), p. 244.

[74] *Ibid.*, p. 263.

[75] Cf. *De conc. virg.*, c. 18; PL, 158, 451.

[76] *D.B.*, No. 170.

His own soul by the taint that marred His Mother's person. In this connection St. Hippolytus institutes a comparison between Christ and His Mother, developing, with considerable complexity, the need for perfect innocence on the part of Mary because of the supreme sanctity of Him whom she begot. He compares the Messias to an ark of incorruptible wood, formed from the stainless stock of Mary who gave to Him His humanity and who knew no corruption herself. This writer's use of the same phrase to describe the sinlessness of Mother and Son is a bold parallelism, and contains a forceful implicit affirmation in Mary's complete freedom from the stain of all sin. Since the "incorruptibility" of Jesus must include, of course, immunity from original sin, and since His soul (in the opinion of Hippolytus) was derived from hers, she too, must have been immaculate.[77]

One of the most direct and unqualified testimonies for the Immaculate Conception to be found among the early ecclesiastical writers is that of St. Ephrem of Syria (†373). In his Carmina Nisibena he categorically declared, in his poem addressed to Christ, "Thou and Thy Mother are alone in this: you are wholly beautiful in every respect. There is in Thee, Lord, no stain, nor any spot in Thy Mother."[78] This use of the accommodated sense of Cant. 6:7, affords a clear affirmation of the exemption of Mary from all sin, rooted in the fact of the divine Maternity. Further to single out the exclusiveness of this prerogative of the Blessed Virgin, in the context of this phrase of her freedom from spot or stain, St. Ephrem emphasizes that she alone, of all mankind, possesses such a privilege. Thus exalted above all mere creatures in the order of grace, her pure soul came immaculate from the hand of God, "like Eve before the fall, endowed with the fullness of grace, by reason of her anticipated motherhood of the Son of God."[79]

The firm stand of the Syrian Church regarding the utter sinlessness of the Blessed Virgin, as evinced in the writings of such renowned figures as St. James of Sarug (452-519), who denied that there was the slightest defect or stain upon the soul of Mary, reiterated substantially the teaching of St. Ambrose (333-397) who has Christ to say of His

---

[77] *Apud Theodoretum*, in *dialogo Eranistes*, PG, 10, 610.
[78] *Carmina Nisibena*, ed. Bickell (Leipzig, 1866), p. 40.
[79] Cf. *The American Ecclesiastical Review*, Vol. 9 (Philadelphia, Pa., 1893), pp. 406-407.

Mother: "Come ... receive Me in that flesh which fell in Adam. Receive Me not from Sara, but from Mary, a virgin incorrupt; a virgin by grace; entirely free from every stain of sin."[80]

In a celebrated passage of St. Augustine (354-430) the Doctor of Grace appears to enunciate a principle upon which might be predicated an argument that Augustine taught, in an implicit fashion, Mary's Immaculate Conception. He states: "(Concerning the Virgin) I wish to raise no question when it touches the subject of sin, out of honor to the Lord, for from Him we know what abundance of grace to overcome sin in every way was conferred upon her who undoubtedly had no sin."[81] Logically, the idea of the Immaculate Conception is contained herein, but for reasons of prudence relative to the Pelagian polemic on the transmission of original sin, Augustine evidently did not consider it prudent to place the doctrine of the Immaculate Conception in a precise formula.[82]

It cannot, of course, be successfully maintained that the truth of Mary's immunity from all stain of Adam's sin was at all explicitly taught by these and many other similar early writers of the Church. For closeness to the doctrine and for clarity of expression, implicit affirmation of the Immaculate Conception is perhaps found most vividly stated in Augustine. Surely the continuity of unqualified endorsements of Mary's holiness in general provides a very solid and entirely legitimate conclusion that the writers intended, in some way, to make the Immaculate Conception an integral part of their teaching.[83]

*c)*The Divine Maternity

The early Church Fathers are strong in their defense of the motherhood of Mary and of the incomparable sanctity which accompanied it. By her God-given grace she merited to be the Mother of

---

[80] *In Ps. 118 Expositio, PL*, 2, 782.

[81] *De natura et gratia,* cap. 36, No. 42, PL, 44, 267.

[82] Cf. Phillipp Friedrich, *Die Mariologia des Hl. Augustinus* (Köln, 1907), pp. 183-238. Also B. Capelle, O.S.B., *La pensée de saint Augustin concernant l'Immaculée Conception,* in *Recherches de Théologie ancienne et médiévale,* Vol. 4, 1932, pp. 361-370.

[83] Cf. A. Dufourcq, *Comment s'éveilla la foi à l'Immaculée-Conception et à l'Assomption aux Ve et VIe siècles* (Paris, 1946).

the Saviour, an unique honor that would never have been realized had there not been, on her part, an intimate union with her Son through the grace and charity in her soul. The Virgin perfectly pure in body and soul, she first bore Him in her heart before she conceived Him in her womb: "She alone is called 'full of grace' since she alone obtained a grace none other can claim: to be filled with the very Author of grace"[84] — "Consider the holy Mary, who was of such great purity that she merited to be the Lord's Mother."[85] Such statements are typical, for it is only to be supposed that the fact of Mary's being the exalted Mother of the Redeemer would be acknowledged by even the earliest writers, and with unanimity, as the center, the key of all the admirable privileges of nature, of grace, and of glory possessed by her. Considered in itself, the Maternity could be, absolutely speaking, without the personal holiness of the mother, since the divine Maternity is mainly a grace given for others (gratia gratis data). As such it is not directly sanctifying (according to some) and does not necessarily demand utter sinlessness on the Mother's part. But the dignity of her office in the light of the sublime dignity of the Son of God, could scarcely allow that she who bore the Incarnate Word would be other than completely stainless herself.[86] This awareness formed a basic theme in the profound stress placed by the writers on the Virgin's exceptional sanctity. It is a further reason to see the Immaculate Conception woven into the warp and woof of the pristine Mariology of the Fathers and lesser apologists.

III. Period of Incipient Explicit Faith — From the Council of Ephesus (431) to Eleventh Century

During the period of time covered by the middle of the fifth century up into the eleventh century, the belief in the total sinlessness of the Virgin among the great body of the faithful, by the writers of this era and by the teaching Church, became considerably more explicit. Nevertheless, due to the denial of original sin by the Pelagians, a heresy condemned in 418 at the Council of Carthage, the writers who opposed

---

[84] S. Ambrose, *In Expositionem Evangelii secundum Lucam* 1:29, No. 9, PL, 15, 1556 A.

[85] Pseudo-Jerome, Epist. 22 *Ad Eustochium*, No. 38, PL, 22, 422.

[86] J. Mahieu, *Sainte Mère de Dieu* (Bruges, 1940), p. 45.

Pelagius, Celestius and Julian, Bishop of Eclana, seem in some fashion to have denied Mary's immunity from Adam's sin. This denial stems, perhaps, from an overly literal interpretation of these early writings, and a failure to weigh duly the polemical exigencies of the epoch. It was held that Christ alone was free from original sin and that all other children of Adam inherited it.[87] This insistence on the universality of the taint is attributable to the tendency to attach the disorder inherent in the generative act to the transmission of original sin. The element of inordinate concupiscence characteristic of active generation was believed to carry over necessarily into passive generation. Post-Augustinian Western writers were measurably influenced by this doctrine, and it rather effectively prevented what might well have been the logical conclusion to their general teaching on Mary's exalted sanctity: that she received from God a special dispensation that exempted her from the consequence of Adam's sin.[88] The well-established "all-holy" quality of the Mother of Christ, formulated and developed with such amplitude in earlier times, and assuredly emphasized between the Council of Nicaea (325) and the Council of Ephesus (431),[89] offered abundant material for the conclusion that Mary was conceived in grace.

The Church in the Orient appears to have escaped largely from the stream of post-Augustinian thought that checked the writers in the West from a willingness to concede Mary's utter freedom from all sin. While prior to the Council of Ephesus, before the divine Maternity was unequivocally defined, many of the Eastern theologians appear to have spoken of imperfections in the Virgin, and even of positive faults. Such assertions can hardly be reconciled with a support of the dogma of the Immaculate Conception, and are probably the direct result of the authority of Origen (c. 185-254). This apologist interpreted the words of the prophet Simeon, "And thy own soul a sword shall pierce ..."[90] as indicating that Mary was under some sin, and had to be in order to be herself redeemed. This unfortunate (or perhaps fortunate) error had a

---

[87] Dominicus Palmieri, S.J., *op. cit.*, p. 225.
[88] Cf. *The American Ecclesiastical Review*, Vol. 114, (Washington, D. C., 1946), p. 346.
[89] Cf. *DTC*, Vol. 7, col. 893 ff.
[90] Lk. 2:35.

profound influence on subsequent Oriental writers, and only St. Ephrem (c. 310-378) and St. Epiphanius († 403) seem to have escaped succumbing to the renowned authority of Origen.[91] After the Council of Ephesus, reflection on the consequences of the divine Maternity led to definite conclusions concerning the entire purity of the Mother of God. The dissenting voices of certain of the Eastern writers who held that the Virgin did contract original sin and was delivered of its stain only at the moment of the Annunciation, never gained any measure of wide acceptance among the better authors.[92] The latter, in the course of time, formulated the Catholic doctrine of the Immaculate Conception in surprisingly clear terms, although these often took the form of statements in the positive sense of her unrivaled sanctity, rather than in the negative sense of a simple rejection of original sin from her.[93]

A. The Immaculate Conception in the Doctrine of the Eastern Church

1. Theological Argument

a) Fifth Century

The Third Ecumenical Council, that of Ephesus (431), declared Our Lady to be the Mother of God (*Dei genitrix*) and thereby served as an important stimulus to the development of the doctrine of her singular sanctity and unique prerogatives, both from the theological and the liturgical aspects. The condemnation of Nestorianism, the heresy that denied the genuine sense of the Incarnation, set the stage for an ever more explicit belief in the Immaculate Conception. While references to Mary's immunity from original sin are not wanting even earlier,[94] few of them equal in clarity of expression the teaching of Theodotus, Bishop of Ancyra in Galatia († 430): "In place of Eve, an instrument of death, is chosen a Virgin, most pleasing to God and full of His grace, as an instrument of life. A Virgin included in woman's sex, but without a share in woman's fault. A Virgin innocent; immaculate; free from all

---

[91] Cf. Martin Jugie, A.A., *op. cit.*, p. 474.

[92] *Ibid.*, p. 475.

[93] Cf. *DTC*, Vol. 7, col. 935.

[94] Cf. Dominicus Cerri, *Enchiridion ex quibus exurgit triumphus B. Mariae Virginis Matris Dei in originale peccatum* (Taurini, 1851), passim.

guilt; spotless; undefiled; holy in spirit and body; a lily among thorns."[95] In a similar vein of praise of the Saviour's Mother, St. Proclus, Patriarch of Constantinople († 446), compares the action of God in preparing a dwelling place for the Word to the work of a potter who would not fashion for himself a vessel of tainted clay. Hence, whatever might stain the purity of the Incarnate Word must first be removed from her who was destined to bear Him. "He came forth from her without any flaw, who made her for Himself without any stain," wrote St. Proclus.[96] And again: "Mary is the heavenly orb of a new creation, in whom the Sun of justice, ever shining, has vanished from her entire soul all the night of sin."[97]

Similarly, Hesychius of Jerusalem († c. 450) extolled the incorruptibility, immortality, immunity from concupiscence, impeccability, triumph over Satan, and the coredemptive mission of the Mother of God.[98] These qualities of Mary, in relation to the Immaculate Conception certainly appear as causes in relation to an effect; as parts in a whole of sanctity connoted in immunity from original sin. Other Eastern writers, such as Basil of Seleucia († 458)[99] and Antipater of Bostra, a near contemporary,[100] reflect this same theme of unparalleled holiness.

b) Sixth Century

As in the preceding century, the writers of the Orient repeat in the sixth century the special care God manifested in preparing the soul of Mary as a becoming instrument of the Incarnation and Redemption: perhaps no author of this period is more explicit than St. Anastasius I († 598), a stanch defender of the dignity of the Blessed Virgin, and whose writings declare, in equivalent terms, the privilege of the Immaculate Conception.[101]

---

[95] *Homil. 6 in S. Deiparam*, No. 11, *PG*, 77, 1427 A.

[96] *Oratio 1 de Laudibus S. Mariae*, *PG*, 65, 683 B.

[97] *Ibid.*, Oratio 6, *PG*, 68, 758 A.

[98] *Sermo 5, PG*, 93, 1463: 1466.

[99] Cf. *Oratio 39 in Sanctissimae Deiparae Annuntiationem*, *PG*, 85, 426.

[100] Cf. *In Sanctissimae Deiparae Annuntiationem*, Homil. 2, *PG*, 85, 1778; 1783.

[101] Cf. *Oratio 3 de Incarnatione*, No. 6, *PG*, 89, 1338.

c) Seventh Century

By the seventh century the doctrine of Mary's freedom from original sin had become well elaborated, and while the future would hold a yet more explicit statement of it, nevertheless, it may be fairly concluded that from this century on there was in reality no controversy on the substance of the teaching.[102] St. Sophronius († 637), Patriarch of Jerusalem, devoted much attention to the fullness of Mary's grace, writing of its incomparably illustrious quality; of its perpetuity; of its uniqueness since no one else received like it for no one else was "prepurified."[103] In his "Synodal Epistle," approved by the Sixth Ecumenical Council, he described Mary as "holy, immaculate in soul and body, entirely free from every contagion."[104] Similar praise of the Virgin's entire holiness can be found in other authors of this period, for example, in the work of St. Modestus († 634), another patriarch of Jerusalem.[105]

d) Eighth Century

The outstanding figure of this epoch may properly be considered St. John Damascene (c. 675-749), whose writings on the prerogatives of Mary mark him as a vigorous exponent of her Immaculate Conception. If he did not expressly teach the doctrine, nevertheless his whole treatment of Mariology points the way to it, and indeed presupposes it as an essential element in the composite of her graces.[106] This Doctor's exposition of the nature and consequences of original sin is thoroughly in keeping with the Catholic tradition and the definitions of the Church. Adam, by his transgression of the divine precept, brought harm both upon himself and upon all humans carnally generated from his infected line. In our first parent we are all sinners since he was the head of the human race, and the consequences of that sin are visited upon the children as well as the state of sin itself. Not only was there a loss of

---

[102] Cf. Dominicus Palmieri, S J., *op. cit.*, p. 284.

[103] *Oratio 2 in Sanctissimae Deiparae Annuntiationem*, PG, 87 (3), 3247.

[104] *Epistola Synodica ad Sergium*, PG, 87 (3), 3159; 3162.

[105] Cf. *Encomium in Beatam Virginem*, PG, 86 (2), 3279; 3282; 3283; 3302; 3306.

[106] Cf. Valentine A. Mitchel, S.M., *The Mariology of Saint John Damascene* (Kirkwood, Mo., 1930), p. 125.

sanctifying grace, but together with its forfeiture were lost those gifts which depended upon grace as effects depend upon their cause: freedom from death and ills of soul and body; freedom from concupiscence, from malice, from ignorance. Averted from God, mankind inclined in disorder to material and sensible goods.

When the Blessed Virgin is contrasted with this dreary portrait of fallen human nature, conceived in sin and engulfed with the dire results of the fall, St. John Damascene delineates her figure as far removed from everything connected with the primal sin. She alone is full of grace; free from all concupiscence; never for a moment was her face turned from a steady gaze upon the Creator; she submitted to death only in order to resemble her Son. In no place is original sin attributed to her, and although evidently the phrase "Immaculate Conception" is not employed, yet the exemption implied in it must be included in the absolute purity and sinlessness and grace associated in every way with her who was destined to be the Mother of the God of infinite holiness.[107]

This predestination of Mary was a special decree of Divine Providence: from all eternity God had loved her and chosen her as the Mother of the Son, and because of this sublime office she was promised a life more excellent in the order of grace than human nature itself warranted. Should she, who was thus a most special object of God's loving solicitude, have ever for a moment been displeasing to him?[108]

This position is further stressed when we see an intimate connection between Mary's conception in the womb of St. Anne and her initial grace therein. St. John Damascene writes of the Virgin as "the earth's most divine bud";[109] "the germ of justice";[110] "the divine grace in her whom St. Anne was privileged to bear."[111] He explains, in effect, that a person is conceived without stain only if, under God's grace, a stainless seed has been the instrumentality for that conception. This was the case, and uniquely so, in the daughter of Anne and Joachim.[112] In a parallel

---

[107] Cf. *De Fide Orthodoxa*, lib. 4, cap. 14, *PG*, 94, 1159 A.
[108] Cf. *ibid.*, *PG*, 96, 675.
[109] *Homilia 3 in Dormitionem Beatae Virginis Mariae*, No. 5, *PG*, 96, 762 A.
[110] *Homilia 1 in Nativitatem Beatae Virginis Mariae*, No. 9, *PG*, 96, 674 C.
[111] *Ibid.*, Homilia 1, No. 2, 663.
[112] Cf. *Ibid.*

passage the Doctor calls Mary "the most holy daughter of Joachim and Anne, hidden from the fiery dart of Satan, dwelling in a bridal chamber of the spirit, preserved without stain as the Spouse and Mother of God."[113] From what stain other than original sin could Mary have been preserved? And why would Satan have sought, through fear, to harm her, except because she was his enemy through the perfect abundance of her grace?

Just as she was immune from original sin, so she was not subject to the disorders of its guilt in the matter of carnal concupiscence: utterly pure in mind[114] and body.[115] As Adam was in his innocence, with the whole intent of his intellect devoted to contemplation of things divine,[116] similarly Mary repelled any movement toward any vice.[117] The penalty of death, so directly the consequence of Adam's fall, is exacted of every offspring of the first parent who inherits his fault. Christ the Redeemer could not be subject to death since He was sinless and death comes through sin.[118] In the case of the Blessed Virgin, St. John Damascene declares, she also was not subject to the universal law of death, but submitted to it out of loving conformity to the chosen lot of her Son, "the Lord of nature who did not refuse to experience death."[119] Thus her death indeed resembled that of sinful man, but was not associated with the humiliation of punishment for sin, for "in her," the Saint exclaims, "the sting of death, sin, has been extinguished."[120] The evidence is forceful that Damascene taught substantially the doctrine of the Immaculate Conception.[121]

e) Ninth Century

---

[113] *Homilia 1 in Nativitatem Beatae Virginis Mariae*, No. 3, *PG*, 96, 675.
[114] *Homilia 2 in Dormitionem Beatae Virginis Mariae*, No. 2, *PG*, 96, 726 B.
[115] *Homilia 1 in Nativitatem Beatae Virginis Mariae*, No. 8, *PG*, 96, 674 B.
[116] *De Fide Orthodoxa*, lib. 2, PG, 94, 978 C.
[117] *Homilia 2 in Dormitionem Beatae Virginis Mariae*, No. 3, *PG*, 96, 727 A.
[118] *De Fide Orthodoxa*, lib. 3, cap. 27, *PG*, 94, 1095 B-C.
[119] *Homilia 1 in Dormitionem Beatae Virginis Mariae*, No. 10, PG, 96, 714 D.
[120] *Homilia 2 in Dormitionem Beatae Virginis Mariae*, No. 3, PG, 96, 727 C.
[121] Cf. Stephen C. Gulovich, *The Immaculate Conception in the Eastern Churches*, in *Marian Studies*, Vol. 5 (Washington, D. C., 1954), p. 160.

Witnesses in the Eastern Church at this period are numerous in support of what must be considered a very widespread, if indeed not universal, acceptance of Mary's immunity from original sin in the Orient.[122] St. Tarasius († 806), Patriarch of Constantinople, speaks of Mary as "predestined from the creation of the world; chosen from among all generations that she might be the immaculate domicile of the Word ... the immaculate oblation of human nature." "This Virgin," the author adds in the same context, "is immaculate by her excellence."[123]

Epiphanius, in his sermon on the life of the Blessed Virgin, affirms her entire immunity from concupiscence, a freedom joined to original justice.[124] Joseph Hymnographus († 833) describes Mary as immune from all sin; wholly pure and immaculate; entirely without stain.[125] Georgius Nicomediensis whose theological opinions parallel in most matters those of his friend and contemporary Photius, the father of the Greek schism, exempts the Mother of Christ from all stain of sin and from the consequences of the fall of Adam.[126]

f) Tenth Century

The continuity of belief in the immunity of Mary from the hereditary stain is manifest during this century among authors of perhaps less renown than those of the preceding century, but whose statements in the sources are equally uncompromising where the Mother of God is under consideration. Euthymius († 917), a patriarch of Constantinople, held, together with Petrus († c. 920), Bishop of Argo, that Mary was liberated from the infection of original sin from her conception in the womb of St. Anne.[127] A contemporary, Joannes Geometra, wrote that the Mother of the Saviour "was conceived in joy," and "joy" he understood,

---

[122] Cf. C. Octavius Valerius, *De superstitiosa timiditate vitanda* (Tridenti, 1751), p. 28: "Oriente sacrum hunc statumque Conceptionis diem omnes summo concordique pietatis studio amplexati sunt nemine disentiente aut reclamante, quod ego quidem noverim aut usquam legerim."

[123] *In SS. Deiparae Praesentationem, PG*, 98, 1498; 1482; 1490.

[124] Cf. *Sermo de vita Sanctissimae Deiparae, PG*, 120, 194, 198.

[125] Cf. *Mariale, PG*, 105, 983 ff.

[126] Cf. *Oratio 7 in Sanctissimae Deiparae ingressum in templum, PG*, 100, 1454; 1443.

[127] Cf. *Oratio in conceptionem S. Annae, PG*, 104, 1351; 1359.

as the context shows, as synonymous with sanctifying grace.[128] In his celebrated hymns he yet more clearly affirmed that Mary had no sin as other men do,[129] but rather that she came into the world in the state of original justice, a "new creation" who was the supreme work of God and the personification of ideal beauty.[130]

These and like expressions among these writers convey a very distinct idea of the Immaculate Conception, often enclosing it in positive formulas by insisting on the fullness of her grace; its unbroken continuity; its resemblance to the condition of Adam prior to sin; its entirely unique character. She needed no reconciliation to God since He had already intervened in a singular fashion in order to sanctify His Mother in her very conception. Such is the tenor of these pertinent texts.

2. Argument From Liturgy

a) Relation of Liturgy to Faith

The value of liturgical worship as an index to the beliefs of the Church and the faithful is founded in the axiom "the law of prayer is the law of faith" — *lex orandi est lex credendi*. This liturgical worship consists in the public performance of an act of worship of God in forms laid down by the Church, in the name and on behalf of the whole Christian people. It is thus the social exercise of the virtue of religion, and manifests in a very definite fashion the religious creed of those who participate in it. The liturgy expresses itself in the forms of prayer and various ceremonies of the Church, particularly in the Sacrifice of the Mass and in the recitation of the Divine Office, and the liturgical books such as the Missal, the Breviary, the Ritual, among others, contain a rich fund of Catholic doctrine. Whatever names may be attached to these sources (as in the Eastern Church the *Euchologion* does the work of the Missal, the Pontifical, and the Ritual of the Latin rite), the basic idea is the same: the people pray as they believe and as the Church teaches them. It may very well happen, as it seems to have happened in the case of the Immaculate Conception, that the great body of the faithful tend

---

[128] Cf. *Sermo in Sanctissimae Deiparae Annuntiationem, PG*, 106, 819; 846.

[129] Cf. *Hymnus 3 in Beatissimam Dei Genetricem, PG*, 106, 862.

[130] Cf. *Hymnus 2 (and) 3 in Beatissimam Dei Genetricem, PG*, 106, 858; 862.

to develop in their devotions an awareness of a truth not yet universally agreed upon by theologians.[131] But such a devotional development, while important in assaying a trend in the *sensus communis fidelium*, is not strictly speaking a part of the Church's official prayer.

b) Liturgical Development in Eastern Church

The liturgical celebration of the feast of the Nativity of the Blessed Virgin preceded, as might be reasonably expected, the feast of her Conception, although in the order of time the latter mystery would naturally be prior. The evidence is convincing that Mary's Nativity merited a special day in the liturgy of the Orient already by the middle of the sixth century, or certainly by the seventh, and shortly afterward there is testimony of the celebration of the feast of St. Anne's Conception. By this was meant Anne's active conception of her daughter Mary.[132] A homily on this feast was composed by John of Euboea, a contemporary of St. John Damascene.[133] By the time of Photius the feast was observed universally in the Greek Church, a conclusion easy to reach by a perusal of the widely read homilies of George of Nicomedia († 917) and the import of the Menologium compiled in 984 by the edict of Emperor Basil II, acknowledging the feast of the Conception as celebrated on December 9.[134]

As analyzed by Jugie, the object of this feast includes the heavenly message that Mary would be conceived, through a miracle in the natural order, in the sterile womb of Anne, as well as the recognition of the exceptional graces that accompanied the Virgin's passive conception. The most noteworthy element of this liturgical celebration is the emphasis placed upon the passive conception by the hymnographers and orators who referred to the significance of the feast. Among the Greeks and the Slavs, especially in the Middle Ages, this day of "the Conception of the Mother of God" was one of solemn observance, providing occasion for panegyrics on the sanctity of Our Lady, extolling her immunity from

---

[131] Cf. H. du Colombier, S.J., *A la Gloire de Marie* (Paris, 1936), p. 24.

[132] Cf. *Canones Praecipui et Triodia, Conceptio Sanctae ac Dei Aviae Annae*, PG, 97, 1306-1318.

[133] Cf. *Sermo in Conceptionem Sanctae Deiparae*, PG, 96, 1459-1499.

[134] Cf. Stephen C. Gulovich, *art. cit.*, p. 169.

all stain, even from the first instant of her existence.[135]

The firm conviction among the Catholics of the Orient that Mary was ever holy and completely so, a conviction that was consistently reflected in the theological and liturgical movements of the Greek Church, was not altered by the schism begun under Photius in 867 and consummated under Michael Cerularius in 1054. This sad estrangement from the center of Catholic truth did not retard the development of Marian theology from the eleventh to the fifteenth century, which continued certainly up to the fall of Constantinople to the Turks in 1453. Indeed, one might truthfully assert that the Byzantines were strangers to the controversy on the Immaculate Conception that raged in the West.[136] And almost all the (unedited) sources of this later period agree with the earlier edited material in formulating expressly or in equivalent terms the doctrine of Mary's total immunity from all stain of sin.[137] It is but another evidence of the dreary consequence of the East's separation from the See of Peter that the modern Orthodox Church has forfeited its allegiance to Mary's singular prerogative. The polemical and negativistic mentality which has for centuries characterized the Oriental Christians has obscured, to a large measure, the glorious past of the devotion in the East to the Mother of God.[138]

B. The Immaculate Conception in the Doctrine of the Latin Church

From the Council of Ephesus (431) until the middle of the eleventh century is the epoch of preparation for explicit belief in the doctrine of the Immaculate Conception. The dogma was during this era in a stage of incipient explicit profession.[139] In the West the development was less rapid than in the East, due perhaps to the incursions of the barbarians as an historical cause, and to an anti-Pelagian reaction as a theological cause. Many authors feared to press too eagerly the immunity of Mary from all sin, lest they seem thereby to lend credence to the errors of the

---

[135] Cf. *DTC*, Vol. 7, col. 959.

[136] Cf. Martin Jugie, A.A., *op. cit.*, p. 473.

[137] Cf. *DTC*, Vol. 7, col. 936 ff.

[138] Cf. Martin Jugie, A.A., *op. cit.*, p. 476.

[139] Cf. *DTC*, Vol. 7, col. 979; J. de Aldama, *op. cit.*, pp. 306-310.

Pelagians on grace and original sin. But cogent evidence is available to support the argument that adequate basis for the Immaculate Conception is discoverable in the writings of the noted theologians of this period, even though it be simply incipient belief that is contained therein.

a) Fifth Century

St. Peter Chrysologus taught that Mary was destined to holiness because of the divine Maternity, and that this sanctity was with her from the beginning of her existence.[140] St. Maximus of Turin († c. 470) writes of the Virgin as "a worthy dwelling of God by virtue of her original grace," and without this grace she would not have been the Mother of the Incarnate Word.[141] Sedulius, noted as a writer of hymns, institutes a comparison between Mary all pure and the tainted nature of the rest of men, for she is "as the tender rose bloom amid sharp thorns."[142] St. Fulgentius, Bishop of Ruspa († 533), contrasts the sinfulness of Eve with the perpetual sanctity of Mary.[143] And in a commentary on the angelic salutation, he explains with considerable preciseness, the significance of "full of grace," making it practically equivalent to what is now understood to be immunity from original sin.[144]

b) Sixth, Seventh, Eighth Centuries

The line of growth in the development of the teaching on the Immaculate Conception continued during these centuries with much the same impetus as in earlier times, with an augmenting insistence on the initial quality of Mary's grace. St. Venantius Fortunatus, Bishop of Poitiers († 609), called the Virgin "a new creation," the "just seed" promised by God to Jeremias the Prophet.[145] St. Ildephonse of Toledo († 666), in a (doubtfully authentic) work on the privileges of the Blessed Mother, stresses the unbroken continuity of her grace, made firm by "an

---

[140] Cf. Sermo 140, *De Annuntiatione D. Mariae Virginis*, PL, 52, 576.

[141] *Homilia 5, Incipit dictum ante Natale Domini*, PL, 57, 235 D.

[142] *Carmen Paschale*, lib. 2, PL, 19, 595-596.

[143] *Sermo 2, de duplici Nativitate Christi*, No. 6, PL, 65, 728 C.

[144] Cf. *Sermo 36, De laudibus Mariae ex partu Salvatoris*, PL, 65, 899 C.

[145] *Miscellanea*, lib. 8, cap. 7, PL, 88, 277-281.

eternal covenant" with God.[146] Pseudo-Jerome likens Mary to a cloud which never knew darkness but was ever engulfed in light.[147] Ambrose Autpertus († 778) declares that the Mother of God was "immaculate, because in nowise corrupt," and never subject to the snares of Satan.[148] Paulus Warnefridus wrote that Mary was never "spiritually deserted" by the grace of the Word.[149] These citations are illustrations, chosen from among numerous others, of the constant affirmation of such an eminent holiness in Mary as would postulate at the same time freedom from the stain of original sin and its consequences.

c) Ninth and Tenth Centuries

In these last two centuries before the commencement of the controversy in the West, there is found a continuation of the trend of theological thought developed previously. Haymon, Bishop of Alberstadt († 853), accommodated to Mary's conception the sense of the passage in Ecclus. 24:14: "From the beginning, and before the world, was I created ..." concluding that only her unbroken sanctity could render her fit to be the Mother of God.[150] Paschasius Radbertus († 860) deduces that Mary brought forth her Son without any pain or any corruption because she herself was without any guilt or corruption, but rather was fully blessed;[151] she was exempt from all contagion of man's first progenitor.[152] In the same vein St. Fulbert († 1028) wrote that God the Father chose her soul and body as the dwelling for His Son, and therefore made it perfectly pure from all that is evil and of sin.[153]

d) Eleventh to Sixteenth Century

This wide period includes the time of controversy in the West

---

[146] Cf. (Sermones dubii), *Sermo 2, De Assumptione Beatae Mariae*, PL, 96, 252 A.

[147] Cf. *Breviarium in Psalmos*, Ps. 77, PL, 26, 1049.

[148] Cf. *Ep. 9 ad Paulam et Eustochium, de Assumptione Beatae Mariae Virginis*, PL, 30, 132 A.

[149] *Homilia 2, in Evangelium: Intravit Jesus*, PL, 95, 1573 B.

[150] Cf. *Homilia 5 in solemnitate perpetuae Virginis Mariae*, PL, 118, 765 D.

[151] Cf. *De partu Virginis*, lib. 1, PL, 120, 1369 A.

[152] Cf. *ibid.*, 1375 B.

[153] Cf. *Sermo 4, de Nativitate Beatissimae Mariae Virginis*, PL, 141, 322 B.

concerning the truth of Mary's Immaculate Conception, and its effective termination with the general acceptance of the Scotistic position. The influence of St. Anselm (1033-1109) on his contemporaries and upon the writers posterior to his era would be difficult to exaggerate, and the inference is strong that Anselm did not lean toward acceptance of Mary's Immaculate Conception for the simple reason that he could not see how Mary's conception in grace could be properly reconciled with the universality of the Redemption wrought by Christ.[154] And yet there was celebrated, certainly contemporaneously with Anselm, the feast entitled The Conception of Mary, the purpose of which was to honor the perfect purity of the Mother of God.[155] This feast was observed on the eighth or ninth of December, and, according to Baronius, it began in England about the end of the tenth century.[156] The simple piety of the faithful readily accepted it, and certain revelations and miracles were commonly associated with the feast, widely celebrated by about the middle of the eleventh century, or somewhat later.[157]

Theological backing for the feast, based upon the vast deposit of Mariological literature of the preceding centuries, was not by any means wanting, even at about the time the question of the propriety of the feast was being agitated. Eadmerus, a friend of St. Anselm, defended the orthodoxy of the feast of Mary's Conception, declaring that the Mother of God was indeed removed from the common law of inheritance of the first sin, otherwise God's wisdom would be inoperative.[158] This exclusion of Mary from the law of sin was, according to Eadmerus, from the "very

---

[154] Cf. Rogerus T. Jones, *Sancti Anselmi Mariologia* (Mundelein, Ill., 1937), p. 45; Francis M. Mildner, O.S.M., *The Immaculate Conception in England up to the Time of John Duns Scotus*, in *Marianum*, Vol. 1 (Roma, 1939), pp. 200-201.

[155] Cf. Gaetano M. Perrella, C.M., *La dottrina dell'Immacolata nella Liturgia della festa*, in *Marianum*, Vol. 4 (Roma, 1942), pp. 21-31; Andrea M. Cecchin, O.S.M., *La Concezione della Vergine nella liturgia della Chiesa occidentale anteriore al secolo XIII*, in *Marianum*, Vol. 5 (Roma, 1943), pp. 58-114.

[156] Cf. C. Octavius Valerius, *op. cit.*, p. 29.

[157] Cf. Felim O'Briain, O.F.M., *Feast of Our Lady's Conception in the Medieval Irish Church*, in *The Irish Ecclesiastical Review* (Dublin, 1948), p. 702; M. J. Scheeben, *Mariology*, Vol. 2 (St. Louis, 1947), p. 87 (footnote).

[158] Cf. Opera S. Anselmi, Appendix: *De Conceptione Beatae Mariae Virginis*, PL, 159, 304 D-305 A.

beginning of her creation."[159] This author even appears to have taught that this privilege was in the manner of a preservation, for if God prevented the good angels from personal sin, why would He not preserve His own Mother from the consequences of another's sin?[160]

e) St. Bernard

Whatever authorities may be thus invoked in favor of the celebration of a feast honoring the conception of Mary as a legitimate and sufficiently traditional liturgical observance, the historical fact is that the power and influence of St. Bernard (1091-1153) was, despite his great love for Mary, aligned with the forces that opposed such a feast. He formulated his objection in a celebrated letter to the Canons of Lyons.[161] Probably this stand of Bernard was a providential one, for it set off a controversy about the Immaculate Conception that ultimately resulted in the universal acceptance of the doctrine of Mary's immunity from original sin. It is disputed among students of Bernard's letter whether the saint intended simply to oppose the introduction of the feast as inopportune and not approved by Rome, or whether he intended to take issue with the doctrine itself of the Immaculate Conception. More probably his objection was against the doctrine as then understood.[162]

It must be remembered that at the time St. Bernard wrote, the notions concerning conception, animation, the time of the infusion of the soul, the nature of concupiscence and its relation to original sin, were neither as clear nor as well settled as they later became, especially in the course of the controversy. The feast about which the Doctor complained had for the object of its cult the seminal conception of the daughter of Anne and Joachim, and this conception, in the physiological teaching of the era (and accepted as correct by theologians), preceded

---

[159] *Ibid.*, 307 A.

[160] *Ibid.*, 305 D.

[161] Cf. *Ep. 174 Ad Canonicos Lugdunenses, PL*, 182, 332-336; but see Sebastianus Dupasquier, O.F.M.Conv., *op. cit*, p. 241: "... Bernardus non tam arguit opinionem de Immaculata Conceptione, quam institutionem illius solemnitatis inconsulta Sede Apostolica, et ex propria auctoritate."

[162] Cf. C. Octavius Valerius,. *op. cit*, p. 27; A. Raugel, *La doctrine de Saint Bernard* (Paris, 1935), p. 34 ff.; Dominicus Palmieri, S.J., *op. cit.*, p. 236.

animation. Bernard did not believe (as indeed one cannot) that something (the person of Mary) could be sanctified before it existed. And this interpretation prevailed among most of the later Scholastics.[163] The Acta of the feast under dispute emphatically indicated that the object of the feast was precisely the conception of the seed.[164] Moreover, it was believed by Bernard and other renowned theologians that in some way sin was connected with the generative act of the parents. This would disallow sanctification as concomitant with generation. Accordingly, since Mary could not be sanctified before she was conceived, nor when she was conceived, the only conclusion must be, in the mind of Bernard, that Mary was cleansed from original sin after conception but before birth.[165]

St. Bernard's position carried great weight with the writers who came after him. They followed his doctrine whenever they wrote about the question of sanctification before animation,[166] holding too that the soul was infused (animation) from forty to eighty days after seminal conception.[167] Even allowing for this difference between the opinion of the writers of those days and the opinion that subsequently prevailed, that animation is simultaneous with conception, nevertheless the Scholastics did not all admit Mary's sanctification in the instant itself of animation. Indeed, St. Bonaventure declares: "... teneamus, secundum quod communis opinio tenet, Virginis sanctificationem fuisse post originalis peccati contractionem."[168]

In substance, then, when the better known Scholastics examined the question of the Virgin's mode of conception, it was not discussed whether she was immaculately conceived, but whether her sanctification occurred before the infusion of the soul into the flesh, by some

---

[163] Cf. Antonius Ballerini, S.J., *De S. Bernardi scriptis circa Deiparae Conceptionem* (Roma, 1856), passim; Dominicus Palmieri, S.J., *op. cit.*, p. 236.

[164] Cf. M. J. Scheeben, *op. cit.*, p. 89.

[165] Cf. Pierre Aubron, S.J., *L'oeuvre Mariale de Saint Bernard* (Paris 1935), pp. 177-184.

[166] Cf. S. Bonaventura, in *III Sent.*, d. 3, a. 1, q. 1; S. Thomas Aquinas, *in III Sent.*, d. 3, q. 1, a. 1; S. Albertus Magnus, *in III Sent.*, d. 3, a. 4; Alex. Halensis, *Summa Theol.*, III, d. 3, a. 4.

[167] Cf. Dominicus Palmieri, *op. cit.*, p. 237.

[168] Cf. *in III Sent.*, d. 3, q. 2.

sanctification of the flesh itself. The freedom of the soul from the stain of original sin would be the necessary consequence, it was felt, of such a carnal sanctification. Or, further, it was discussed whether the sanctification took place after the infusion of the soul, removing from her soul that stain of sin to which union with unsanctified flesh necessarily subjected it. The first view: sanctification of the flesh before the infusion of the soul with the consequent preservation of the soul from sin, was unacceptable, both because inanimate flesh is not susceptible of sanctification, and also because such a preservation as would follow, if that sanctification were possible, would exempt Mary from the universal law of sin and the need for redemption. The accepted opinion was that not only did conception of the flesh take place in sin, but that the soul itself in its infusion into the unsanctified flesh, was contaminated by sin.

It was not yet understood that the soul could be sanctified simultaneously with its infusion.[169] Of course, St. Bernard was prepared to conform his opinion to that of the Church, should he have been required to do so.[170]

f) St. Thomas Aquinas

St. Thomas Aquinas (1225-1274) treated the question of the Immaculate Conception only incidentally, as cognate to his consideration of the sinlessness of Christ.[171] He followed the teaching of St. Bernard, and so perhaps it might he held that his unwillingness to admit Mary's immunity from sin from the first moment of her conception was due to the failure of the schools to develop an accurate notion of the moment of conception and animation. Some exponents of St. Thomas have endeavored to establish that the Angelic Doctor virtually held for the Immaculate Conception, and would certainly have

---

[169] Cf. M. J. Scheeben, *op. cit.*, p. 95.

[170] Cf. Bernard's spirit of submission, *Litt.* 174, *PL*, 182, 333.

[171] Cf. Paul F. Palmer, S.J., *Mary in the Documents of the Church* (Westminster, Md., 1952), p. 71.

taught it if "conception" had been treated completely by him.[172] But most students of St. Thomas are quite prepared to admit that the Angelic Doctor simply denied Mary's freedom from original sin.[173] The "Thomistic School" of theology has produced not a few defenders, for centuries, of the Blessed Virgin's singular prerogative. Long before the definition of the Immaculate Conception as an article of Faith, many Dominicans pledged themselves to a defense of it when taking their degrees in the schools of Europe.[174]

g) John Duns Scotus

It is one of the great glories of the Franciscan Order to have produced the Subtle Doctor, John Duns Scotus (1270-1308), whose forceful defence and brilliant clarification of the truth of the Immaculate Conception prepared the way for its ultimate definition. He showed that the reasons for sanctification of the person of Mary after animation could be possible and was fitting, and that actually "after" animation in reality means only that the sanctification followed the infusion of Mary's soul in the order of nature, but not in the order of time. That is to say, that the freeing of Mary from the stain of sin required, as a necessary precondition, the creation and infusion of her soul, but that in terms of time the sanctification and the animation were simultaneous. Scotus brought the argument to the level where alone the doctrine of the Immaculate Conception could be properly formulated and theologically

---

[172] Cf. D. Francesco Gaude, *Sullo Immacolato Concepimento della Madre di Dio* (Roma, 1856), p. 86 ff.; M. A. Bros, *Santo Tomás de Aquino y la Inmaculada Concepción de la Virgen Maria* (Barcelona, 1909), passim.

[173] Cf. G. M. Roschini, O.S.M., *La Mariologia di S. Tommaso* (Roma, 1950), pp. 236-237. It is extremely difficult to reconcile the opinion of St. Thomas in S. Th., III, q. 27, a. 2 ad 2um, with Mary's immunity from original sin: "... si nunquam anima B. Virginis fuisset contagio originalis peccati inquinata, hoc derogaret dignitati Christi, secundum quam est universalis omnium Salvator." Cf. Dominicus Palmieri, S.J., *op. cit.*, p. 291; Armandus Plessis, S.M.M., *Manuale Mariologiae Dogmaticae* (Pont-Chateau, 1942), p. 60; Emile Campana, *Marie dans le Dogme Catholique* (Montréjeau, 1913), Vol. 2, p. 200 ff.

[174] Cf. Sebastianus Dupasquier, O.F.M.Conv., op. cit., p. 236; D. J. Kennedy, O.P., *St. Thomas and the Immaculate Conception*, in *The Dogma of the Immaculate Conception*, ed. B. McKenna (Washington, D. C., 1929), p. 96.

(and philosophically) accepted by all.[175] His distinction between priority in time and priority in nature adequately took care of the objection of St. Bernard.[176]

The objection against the immunity of Mary from original sin based upon the universality of its stain, as stated by St. Paul in Rom. 5:12: "Wherefore as by one man sin entered into this world, and by sin death; and so death passed upon all men, in whom all have sinned," and the consequent universality of Christ's Redemption, had offered the greatest stumbling block to an acceptance of the Immaculate Conception.[177] The core of Scotus' answer to this classical difficulty consists in his development of the office of Christ as a perfect Mediator and a perfect Redeemer, and thus it would pertain to Him as most fitting to preserve His Mother from the stain of all sin, not merely from all actual sin, but from original sin as well. To deny this, Scotus taught, would derogate from Christ's excellence. Indeed, in virtue of the Incarnation and Redemption it was even more fitting that the merits of Christ should preserve His Mother from original sin than from actual sin, for it was to atone for the former especially that the Saviour endured His Passion.[178] Hence Christ redeemed His Mother by preservative redemption, not by restorative redemption as in the case of all the rest of mankind.[179] Moreover, Christ, not Adam, is the moral and spiritual head of the human race, for He is the source of all its grace. Because of the sin of Adam mankind became subject to the power of Satan, with the exception of Mary. She was not subject to the devil since God had already decreed, according to Scotus, that the Word should become flesh through Mary, and so, as Christ was decreed before Adam, it must follow

---

[175] Cf. Emile Campana, *op. cit.*, p. 232.
[176] Hugolinus Storff, O.F.M., *The Immaculate Conception* (San Francisco, 1925), p. 21.
[177] Cf. D. J. Kennedy, *op. cit.*, p. 90.
[178] Cf. Carolus Balić, O.F.M., *De debito peccati originalis in B. Virgine Maria* (Romae, 1941), p. 88 ff.; Joannis Duns Scotus, *Theologiae Marianae Elementa*, in *Bibliotheca Mariana*, ed. Carolus Balić, O.F.M. (Sibenici, 1933), p. 190; Scotus, *Quaestiones Disputatae de Immaculata Conceptione* (Ad Claras Aquas, 1904), pp. 12-22.
[179] Cf. Scotus (ed. Balić), p. 192: "Nobilius autem est praeservare ne offendat quis quam post offensam remittere."

that Mary was included in the same decree as her Son.[180] Although Scotus himself did not explicitly teach Mary's predestination before the prevision of Adam's sin, this doctrine would seem to follow from his theory on the absolute predestination of Christ.[181]

Of course, Duns Scotus taught that the Blessed Virgin had her origin from the carnal seed of Adam as his natural daughter, and hence she would have contracted original sin unless preserved by the foreseen merits of her divine Son.[182] And Scotus believed it to be a much greater tribute to the power, wisdom, and goodness of God that He should preserve His Mother from all sin, including original sin, rather than that He should cleanse her from it. "Either God was able to do this, and did not will to do it, or He willed to preserve her and was unable to do so. If able to and yet unwilling to perform this for her, God was miserly towards her. And if He willed to do it but was unable to accomplish it, He was weak, for no one who is able to honor his mother would fail to do so."[183] As the most perfect of all merely human creatures, the Mother of God should have received the most perfect redemption through grace: a redemption that preserved her, not one that healed her only.

Although the great Franciscan Doctors prior to Scotus, St. Bonaventure[184] and St. Anthony,[185] did not admit, at least clearly so, the doctrine of Mary's freedom from original sin, the Franciscan School after

---

[180] Cf. Hugolinus Storff, O.F.M., *op. cit.*, p. 179 ff.

[181] N. G. da S. Marcello, O.F.M., *L'Immacolata ed il Verbo Umanato* (Ad Claras Aquas, 1904), passim; Ephrem Longpré, O.F.M., *Exposition du Dogme de l'Immaculée-Conception*, in *Deuxième Congrès Marial National* (Lourdes, 1930), p. 80.

[182] Cf. Carolus Balić, O.F.M., *op. cit.*, p. 99.

[183] Cf. Sebastianus Dupasquier, *op. cit.*, pp. 243-244: "Aut Deus potuit, et noluit, aut voluit, et non potuit praeservare illam ab originali, si potuit, et noluit, ergo avarus in eam fuit, si voluit, et non potuit, infirmus fuit, certe nullus est, qui possit honorare matrem, et nolit."

[184] Cf. Emmanuel Chiettini, O.F.M., *Mariologia S. Bonaventurae*, in *Bibliotheca Mariana Medii Aevi* (Romae, 1941), p. 145 ff.

[185] Cf. Caietanus Stano, O.F.M.Conv., *De mente S. Antonii Patavini quoad Imm. Conceptionem B. V. Mariae*, in *Miscellanea Francescana*, Vol. 40 (Roma, 1940), p. 18; Candidus Romerii, O.F.M., *De Immaculata Conceptione Virginis apud S. Antonium* (Romae, 1939), p. 78; Diomede Scaramuzzi, O.F.M., *La dottrina teologica di S. Antonio di Padova* (Roma, 1933), pp. 30-39.

Scotus propounded the doctrine even more emphatically than he.[186] Up to the first half of the sixteenth century, the Dominicans continued opposed to the doctrine.[187]

h) Papal Pronouncements

In the course of the succeeding centuries the controversy continued among the various schools of thought, chiefly as between the Franciscans and the Dominicans, but after the heated sessions of the Council of Basle (1431-1438) the sovereign pontiffs declared with increasing emphasis the mind of the Church. No official affirmation of Rome's stand appeared before the Constitution *Cum praeexcelsa*[188] (1477) of Sixtus IV, wherein the Pope commended the celebration of "the wondrous Conception of this Immaculate Virgin."[189] This was followed within a few years by the Constitution *Grave nimis* (1483) of the same Pontiff, in which the Holy Father clearly distinguished the meaning of Mary's Immaculate Conception in nearly the same terms as were employed nearly four hundred years later by Pope Pius IX.[190] Although this declaration of Sixtus IV was, of course, not a definition, nevertheless in it the Pope stated that he reproved those who denied the Immaculate Conception.[191]

While the Council of Trent (1545-1563) did not define the dogma, yet it unequivocally stated in its famous decree on original sin that it did not intend to include the Blessed Virgin within the meaning of that decree: "This same Holy Synod declares that it is not its intention to include in this decree, where there is question of original sin, the blessed and Immaculate Virgin Mary, Mother of God. Rather the Constitutions of

---

[186] Cf. P. Pauwels, O.F.M., *Les Franciscains et L'Immaculée Conception* (Malines, 1904), p. 9 ff.; Jérome de Paris, O.F.M.Cap., *La doctrine mariale de Saint Laurent de Brindes* (Paris, 1933), pp. 61-74.

[187] Cf. M. J. Schceben, *op. cit.*, p. 108.

[188] Cf. C. Octavius Valerius, *op. cit.*, p. 36.

[189] D.B., No. 734.

[190] Cf. Emphrem Longpré, *op. cit.*, p. 80.

[191] Cf. Cherubinus Sericoli, O.F.M., *Immaculata B. M. Virginis Conceptio iuxta Xysti IV Constitutiones* (Romae, 1945), passim; D.B., No. 735.

Sixtus of happy memory are to be observed...".[192]

After Trent the opposition to the Immaculate Conception became greatly moderated, and even those who previously had been against it either changed their view or else discontinued any serious attacks on the complete orthodoxy of the doctrine. One of the most zealous and brilliant defenders of the doctrine during this period was the Dominican Ambrose Catarino.[193]

Pope St. Pius V (1504-1572) condemned the error of Baius wherein the latter had stated that the Mother of God was subject to original sin,[194] and in the Constitution *Quod a nobis* (1568) the Pontiff put the feast of the Immaculate Conception in the calendar of the Roman breviary.

Alexander VII in the Constitution *Sollicitudo omnium ecclesiarum* (1661) described with remarkable exactitude the sense of the doctrine of the Immaculate Conception, in words similar to those later used in *Ineffabilis Deus*.[195] Pope Clement XI, in the Constitution *Commissi Nobis* (1708), instituted the feast of the Immaculate Conception, December 8, as a holyday of obligation.[196]

The Sixth Provincial Council of Baltimore in 1846 declared Mary Immaculate to be the Patroness of the United States, and confirmation of this dedication was furnished by Pope Pius IX on February 7, 1847, less than eight years before the solemn definition of the dogma.[197]

THE THEOLOGICAL ARGUMENT

Any doctrine that contributes so richly to the spiritual, liturgical, and intellectual life of the Church as does the doctrine of Mary's Immaculate Conception, quite properly would be expected to have abundant

---

[192] *D.B.*, No. 792. Cf. M. Tognetti, *L'Immacolata al Concilio Tridentino*, in *Marianum*, Vol. 15, 1953, pp. 304-374.

[193] Cf. Giacinto Bosco, O.P., *L'Immacolata Concezione nel pensiero del Gaetano e del Caterino* (Firenze, 1950).

[194] *D.B.*, No. 1073.

[195] *Ibid.*, No. 1100.

[196] For history of the Papal acts, cf. Dominicus Palmieri, *op. cit.*, pp. 293-298. For complete treatment of acts prior to 1854, cf. J. Armand Robichaud, S.M., *art. cit.*

[197] Cf. Paul F. Palmer, S.J., *op. cit.*, p. 79.

theological reasoning in its favor.[198] Among the various arguments traditionally invoked in support of the dogma, despite the diversity of their force, all may be reduced to two general classes: (1) the possibility of the doctrine (a) on God's part; (b) on Mary's part; (c) on the part of mankind — (2) the fittingness of the doctrine (a) on God's part; (b) on Mary's part; (c) on the part of mankind.

1. The Possibility of the Doctrine

a) On God's Part

Strictly speaking, only that is impossible for God which implies a "metaphysical contradiction." Thus even God obeys the principles, for example, of sufficient reason and of identity. God can do whatever does not include some inherent repugnance, simply because He is utterly omnipotent. With regard to the Immaculate Conception, while this required a miracle in the order of grace, it is surely not impossible that God would preserve a human person from incurring the penalty of Adam's sin, if He so decreed. This was an unique exception granted to her because of her office as the Mother of the God-Man. Since the laws governing the dispensation of grace are formulated by God, He can accordingly relax the operation of such laws as He deems fit.[199]

It does not matter whether one consider the possibility on the part of any one of the three divine Persons, for all acts of God which take effect outside the divine nature are common to each of the three Persons, Father, Son, and Holy Spirit.[200] This mystery does not derogate from the dignity of the Father, who must prepare a human nature as a fit channel for the Incarnation. Nor do the prerogatives of the Incarnate Word suffer any diminution, nor is His essential sanctity affected by the great grace accorded His Mother. As the second Person of the Trinity He is substantially sanctified with the full holiness of the Godhead, and born into the world as man, He has the absolutely unparalleled distinction of being born of a woman who was without any stain of sin and a virgin. Christ's immunity from sin was by natural right as proper to the divine

---

[198] Cf. B. H. Merkelbach, O.P., *op. cit.*, p. 119 ff.
[199] Cf. St. Thomas, *S. Th.*, I, q. 105, a. 7.
[200] Cf. *ibid.*, I, q. 31, a. 1.

nature, and since He was not of Adam's seed, He can in no manner be considered as even under the law of original sin. Mary had her immunity by way of privilege. This privilege enjoyed by her did not diminish the efficacy of Christ's redemptive act, but instead exalted it, since the Immaculate Conception was in virtue of her Son's merits which preserved her in a more sublime manner than other humans enjoy.[201] Finally, the possibility on the part of the Holy Spirit cannot be impugned, for in His role of Sanctifier He is able to cleanse Mary's soul from sin in any way and at any time He so elected, just as He is fully able to preserve her entirely from contracting any stain of sin in the first place.

b) On Mary's Part

No impossibility can be alleged insofar as Mary is concerned, for as a creature she is subject to the Creator according to His will, and therefore she can be used by God to help in the achievement of His designs and thereby to manifest His power, wisdom, and goodness.[202] As seminally descended from Adam there was some relationship to sin established by this very fact, but that she did not ever actually incur this hereditary taint was indeed extraordinary and miraculous. While it was in itself extraordinary and unique that she should have been immune from original sin, yet in virtue of her office as Mother of the Messias and of her total subordination to the decrees of God in that regard, there was assuredly no impossibility on her part. And in a sense her Immaculate Conception might be termed ordinary precisely so far as she herself is concerned: merely another tremendous gift in the totality of her elevation over all the accustomed ways of God's dealings with mankind. This singular privilege remains in itself inferior to her divine Maternity, since the former was on account of the latter.[203] Exalted above all the rest of men by her preservative liberation from the law of sin, she was further exalted above all angels by the privilege of becoming the Mother of God-made-Man.

c) On the Part of Mankind

---

[201] Cf. Joannes Duns Scotus, *op. cit.*, p. 192.

[202] Cf. Pietro Parente, *Dictionary of Dogmatic Theology* (Milwaukee, 1951), p. 201.

[203] Cf. B. H. Merkelbach, O.P., *op. cit.*, p. 105 ff.

While it is a divinely revealed truth that in Adam "all men have sinned,"[204] still this "all" need not be so rigorously understood as to disallow any exception whatsoever, as is plainly evident from similar uses of the inclusive sense of certain words: "... every man is a liar ...,"[205] "... there is none that doth good."[206] Hence, while the Virgin Mary is a member of the human race and as such was in some way associated with the disabilities incumbent upon mankind, nevertheless this fact raises no insurmountable obstacle to her being exempted from the common lot of other children of Adam, if God so willed to exempt her.

2. The Fittingness of the Doctrine

a) On God's Part

If all the just are children of God in virtue of their individual share in the divine life through sanctifying grace,[207] then Mary is, to a pre-eminent degree and because of the divine Maternity,[208] God's most beloved child. The nature of her mission required that.[209] She is the first-born of all mere creatures and to her may properly be accommodated the words, "I came out of the mouth of the most High, the first-born before all creatures."[210] Chosen from all eternity for her sublime role, as Mother of the only-begotten Son of God, whatever honored her, necessarily honored Him, and whatever would lessen her dignity would, in some manner, reflect unfavorably upon her Son. Had she been affected by sin and so subject to the devil, she would scarcely have been worthy to be the Mother of God: each one is given grace according to the need of that to which God has chosen one.[211]

God the Father associated Mary to Himself in the generation of the Son in time, and the analogous relationship thereby resulting called for

---

[204] Rom. 5:12.
[205] Rom. 3:4.
[206] Rom. 3:12.
[207] Cf. St. Thomas Aquinas, *op. cit.*, I-II, q. 110, a. 3.
[208] Cf. Chan. J. Mahieu, *op. cit.*, p. 47.
[209] Cf. R. P. Poupon, O.P., *Le Poème de la Parfaite Consécration à Marie* (Lyon, 1947), p. 123.
[210] Ecclus. (Sirach) 24:5.
[211] Cf. St. Thomas Aquinas, *op. cit.*, III, q. 27, a. 5 ad 1um.

a very high share in the infinite purity and holiness of God. It is incongruous to suppose that He who from all eternity was begotten in the bosom of the heavenly Father should assume a human nature in the body of a woman who at any time had been marred by sin's guilt. The same divine Person is the Son of God and the Son of Mary, and as she was similar to God in generating the Word, so she ought to be similar to God in sanctity, in that measure possible to a mere human.[212]

If the propriety of Mary's immunity from original sin be examined in the light of Mary's relationship to the Word, an equally cogent argument is derived. Had the Son chosen to be His Mother one unworthy of that exalted dignity (and original sin would make one unworthy) then such a selection would be attributable either to a want of wisdom on the part of the Son, or to an inability to provide otherwise.

Obviously, neither of these alternatives is possible in view of the infinite knowledge and power of the Son. Therefore, Mary must have been sanctified from the first instant of her existence.[213]

The filial piety of the Son toward His Mother would assure that the amability of Mary in the eyes of God should never suffer any interruption nor be any less than possible. Had she, even for the briefest interval of time, been under original sin, she would not have been constantly lovable to the Father. Rather she would have been an object of His wrath. The Word Himself obeyed the command of God, "Honor thy mother," and this He would not have done had He, although able to preserve His Mother from the stain of sin, not done so.

Christ came to take away the sins of the world, and so He was destined to be segregated from sin[214] and from all dishonor flowing from a personal relationship with sinners: "For it was fitting that we should have such an high priest, holy, innocent, undefiled, separated from sinners ..."[215] Had His own Mother been a sinner, this revealed truth would be difficult to reconcile with her condition, for her stain would be,

---

[212] Cf. Arthur Martin, S.J., *Vida y misterios de la Bienaventurada Virgen María Madre de Dios* (Mexico City, 1950), p. 17.

[213] Cf. Bishop Ullathorne, *The Immaculate Conception of the Mother of God* (Baltimore, 1855), passim.

[214] Cf. St. Thomas Aquinas, *op. cit.*, III, q. 4, a. 6 ad 2um.

[215] Hebr. 7:26.

in some way, to His dishonor.[216]

Christ was a perfect Mediator, fulfilling to the highest degree the office of atonement and reconciliation decreed for Him by the Father: "For there is one God, and one mediator of God and men, the man Jesus Christ."[217] Physically, Christ is between the two extremes of divinity and humanity: distinguished from each and yet having something in common with each. Morally, the perfection of mediation is attributed to Christ, because the Word became Incarnate to reconcile mankind with God. As Man, the Son of Mary, Christ's suffering and death merited reparation for all, for His human actions and sufferings have a redemptive value in that they are proper to the Word, who sustains and directs the assumed nature. Christ, therefore, is Mediator according to His human nature which He received from the Virgin, without, of course, being independent of His divinity. This perfect mediatorship of Christ postulated that His Mother be preserved from sin, since He would effect in her behalf whatever was needed for the excellence of her person: she was the first fruit of His redemption.[218]

Additional support for the doctrine of the Immaculate Conception is found in Mary's own coredemptive life. As Mother of the Incarnate Word, she participates subordinately in the mediation of Christ with God, and is also Mediatrix between Christ and men. While her Mediation consists principally in praying in order to obtain for us the application of the fruits of the Redemption, yet she is not restricted to this office, because as associated with Christ, she co-operated with Him in the work of the Redemption, contributing according to the measure of God's will to the acquisition of the fruits of salvation.[219] While this function could, absolutely speaking, be carried on without freedom from the stain of original sin, it is far from fitting that it should have been so.

The prerogative of exemption from the sin of Adam placed Mary under the highest obligation to Christ the Mediator, since to be preserved from that sin is the greatest good the Redeemer could bestow.

---

[216] Cf. St. Peter Damian, *Homil. in Nativ. B. M. V.*, sermo 46, *PL*, 144, 755.

[217] 1 Tim. 2:5; cf. D.B., No. 790.

[218] Cf. Sebastianus Dupasquier, O.F.M.Conv., *op. cit.*, 243.

[219] Cf. Juniper Carol, O.F.M., *Romanorum Pontificum doctrina de B. V. Corredemptrice*, in *Marianum*, Vol. 9 (1947), p. 165 ff.

If no one had been thus perfectly redeemed, then no one would be perfectly indebted to Christ. Mary is Christ's debtor more truly than the rest of mankind because she is more perfectly innocent than any other.[220] And she is so holy because her redemption, her share in Christ's merits, is so excellent. Other humans are freed from the power of darkness; she never knew anything except the light of a supreme creatural sanctity.

The intimate union between Mary and the Holy Spirit further shows the entire fittingness of the dogma of the Immaculate Conception. It is, by analogy, like the union of spouses, for He "overshadowed" her and she conceived by Him.[221] Just as every spouse expects to find unblemished purity in his beloved, similarly the Spirit of God would take care to preserve His spouse from any spiritual detriment: from sin of any kind. How better might the great love of God be manifest than by giving Mary such singular grace as would require her having been conceived with a fullness of grace? As the daughter of God the Father, and Mother of God the Son, and as spouse of God the Holy Spirit, it is thoroughly befitting that the Virgin be endowed with the greatest purity conceivable under God.[222]

b) On Mary's Part

As Hugh of St. Victor poetically expressed it, Mary was the clay from which the Second Adam, Christ, was molded. She is the tree upon which flourished that divine fruit, and the perfection of the Saviour points unmistakably to the perfection of the source of His human life, for a tree is known by the fruit it produces.[223] Mother and Son ought to be, as nearly as possible, alike, and anything that might stand in the way of their similarity should, if possible, be removed. Original sin would be an obstacle to such a resemblance and hence fittingly it should never have stood between them.

According to the eternal decree of God, Mary was destined to be a new Eve who, together with Christ and in subordination to His

---

[220] Cf. Chan. J. Mahieu, *op. cit.*, p. 51.

[221] Lk. 1:35.

[222] Cf. St. Anselm, *De Conc. Virg.*, cap. 18, *PL*, 158, 451.

[223] Cf. Hugh of St. Victor, *De Verbo Incarnato Collationes seu Disputationes tres, collatio 3, PL*, 177, 321.

redemptive role, would repair the injury inflicted upon the human race by the first parents.[224] To accomplish her mission of opposition to Satan and his wiles and the consequences of his seduction of the first Eve, the Virgin should have been in nowise subject to the devil, and in nowise displeasing to God. Rather it was becoming that she share in the fullest degree in that divine grace which, under Christ, she would instrumentally win for and convey to other humans.[225] Arguments in favor of Mary's immunity from original sin based on her mission as the Mother of the Saviour and Coredemptrix with Him of mankind, are among the most cogent that can be adduced to support the doctrine of the Immaculate Conception. She was singularly graced because of her utterly unique place in the divine scheme.[226]

If Mary lacked the initial sanctity implied in the immunity from original sin, it would be difficult, if not indeed virtually impossible, to explain adequately her other privileges in the order of grace. Just as the divine Maternity is the radical principle of all her other gifts,[227] so too is the Immaculate Conception a cause of her fullness of grace and complete sinlessness. Considered even in a general sense, Our Lady's grace exceeds the grace of all other creatures, nearly to the extent of being inconceivably great.[228] But had she been conceived in original sin, the limits of her grace would be very manifest. Her exemption from the stain of this sin is, therefore, a necessary part of the vast ocean of grace constituting the sanctity of the Mother of God. Without her prerogative of immunity, all her other privileges assume a vague, disconnected, and unreal quality.[229]

Sanctity may be considered either from its negative aspect: moral

---

[224] Cf. Martin Jugie, A.A., *op. cit.*, p. 13.

[225] Cf. Francisco S. Ramón, *Teologia Mariana*, Vol. 1 (Guadix, 1921), pp. 290-329.

[226] Cf. J.-B. Terrien, S.J., *La Mère de Dieu et la Mère des hommes*, Vol. 1, (Paris, 1900), pp. 365-383.

[227] Cf. Dominicus Palmieri, S.J., *op. cit.*, p. 225.

[228] Cf. Alexius H. M. Lépicier, O.S.M., *op. cit.*, p. 227; Bozzola-Greppi, S.I., *Cursus Theologicus*, Vol. 3 (Neapoli, 1948), pp. 102-103; Ed. Hugon, op. cit., p. 726; C. Van Crombrugghe, *Tractatus de Beata Virgine Maria* (Gandae, 1913), p. 165.

[229] Cf. Thomas U. Mullaney, O.P., *The Nexus Between the Immaculate Conception and Mary's Other Prerogatives*, in *Marian Studies*, Vol. 5, pp. 200-218.

cleanness — absence of stain offensive to God — freedom from more or less serious deorientations from one's last end; or it may be considered from its positive aspect: the firm conjunction of the soul with God — the application of one's faculties to the love and service of God.[230] In the case of original sin there is had a privation of sanctifying grace in the soul from the moment of its very creation as it comes from the hand of God. Because it is destined to inform a body that is carnally descended from Adam by way of seminal generation, it is consequently denied the original grace that would have been present except for the sin committed by the physical head of the human race. This want of habitual grace, this denial of a share in the divine life, this refusal of heirship to the human person is called "the stain of original sin." While the essence of this sin has never been defined,[231] nevertheless it is the settled doctrine of Catholic theologians, following the teaching of St. Thomas Aquinas, that original sin is the privation of original justice,[232] and that it is in the corporal seed of man as an instrumental cause.[233] The Mother of Christ was free of this sin and its stain in virtue of sanctifying grace that enveloped her soul from the instant it was created. There is no medium between the state of sin and the state of grace: the sin is directly removed by the grace. Hence when it is stated that she was without any sin, the negative aspect of her holiness is declared.

But this includes, implicitly, the positive element of the presence of habitual grace in her soul.[234]

An additional argument for the fittingness of Mary's Immaculate Conception is found in the fact of her Queenship over the angelic world: "Queen of Angels" is a glorious title, and it applies to her in the order of

---

[230] Cf. St. Thomas Aquinas, *op. cit.*, II-II, q. 81, a. 8.

[231] Cf. Ephrem Longpré, O.F.M., *op. cit.*, p. 85.

[232] Cf. St. Thomas Aquinas, *op. cit.*, I-II, q. 81, a. 1.

[233] Cf. *ibid.*, q. 83, a. 1.

[234] Cf. Alexius H. M. Lépicier, O.S.M., *op. cit.*, p. 221. This author observes that since it is more noble to move oneself (under actual grace) to sanctification than simply to be moved (as an infant ordinarily would), therefore the Mother of God was sanctified by her own motion of will at the moment of her conception, this being due to the dignity of the divine Maternity. Since this would be simply a motion of will to God, it would be meritorious. St. Thomas Aquinas (Summa Theologica, I, q. 95, a. 1) holds a similar motion on the part of our first parents.

grace and not in the order of nature. Naturally she is inferior to them; supernaturally she is exalted above them. God preserved the good angels from the rebellion of sin. Would He not similarly, and with even greater reason, preserve His Mother from the stain of any sin? If she had not been exempted from the guilt of original sin, then she would hardly be superior to the good angels who are sinless, and would be subjected to the malign power of the chief of the fallen angels. This would be an incongruity of unthinkable proportions.[235]

Further, there were some humans other than Mary who were born without original sin, as Jeremias and John the Baptist. But Mary's excellence is of a higher order than that of either of these, and accordingly it is fitting that the mode of her sanctification be higher than cleansing in the womb, namely, a total preservation from sin by her Immaculate Conception.[236]

The freedom enjoyed by Mary from the consequences ordinarily associated with original sin, her immunity from disordered motions of the flesh;[237] from even the slightest deliberate fault; her Maternity without anguish; the noncorruption of her body upon the completion of her mortal course;[238] her virginity together with her motherhood — these wonderful privileges, presupposing first of all the divine Maternity, have their root in the privilege of the Immaculate Conception and are a complement of it. While her corporal virginity cannot be directly attributed to the Immaculate Conception, yet they are fittingly associated. Her virginity of soul finds a counterpart in her virginity of body. If God suspended, by a miracle, the operation of the natural laws of human generation so that a virgin gave birth, then with greater reason might it be inferred that He would make a special provision for her in the order of grace. Such a dispensation is both to God's and Mary's honor and glory, and it is fitting in a pre-eminent way that she

---

[235] Cf. Eadmerus, *De Conceptione B. M. V., PL*, 159, 307.

[236] Cf. *ibid.*, 305.

[237] Cf. L. Lercher, S J., *Institutiones Theologiae Dogmaticae*, Vol. 3 (Oeniponte, 1934), p. 346.

[238] The question as to whether Mary actually died or not is still an obscure question, with supporters on both sides. Cf., v.g., Gabriel M. Roschini, O.S.M., *Did Our Lady Die?* in *The Irish Ecclesiastical Record*, August, 1953, pp. 73-88.

who begot Him who is all just, should herself be totally just.[239]

c) On the Part of Mankind

The becomingness of the Immaculate Conception insofar as mankind is concerned, stems from the proposition that such a divine arrangement is a culmination of God's gifts to our race. Having determined to give His only-begotten Son as a Victim for our sins, and therefore having willed that His Son should assume our sinful nature, it would seem fitting also that He create some human who would be perpetually innocent, never a captive of the devil. Such a person would be the Immaculate Mother of the Son, co-operating with Him in the sublime work of redeeming her fallen fellow men. Such a one would serve as a perfect model of holiness although entirely human herself. She who would thus be an example for humans yet pilgrims on earth would at the same time shed luster upon the glory of the blessed in heaven, for their Queen's dignity would be enhanced by a perpetual fullness of grace. Thus her whole human family, the Church militant, and suffering, and triumphant, can truly say of this unique Mother of God: "Thou art the honored one of our people."[240]

THE POSITION OF THE BLESSED VIRGIN RELATIVE TO THE LAW OF ORIGINAL SIN

Adam, on account of his transgression of the divine precept,[241] committed a grave sin of pride and disobedience, the guilt of which has been communicated to all his posterity who form, together with their father Adam, a human solidarity. The common origin of all mankind from this infected seed makes all men to share in a common sin, even as they would have shared in a common heritage of justice, had the first parents not fallen.[242] Adam was our head, and in his sin we have all sinned[243] and accordingly have forfeited our claim to initial sanctifying

---

[239] Cf. Narcisco García Garcés, C.M.F., *op. cit.*, p. 391.
[240] Cf. St. Alphonsus de Liguori, *The Glories of Mary* (New York, 1931), pp. 287-308.
[241] Gen. 3:6.
[242] Cf. J. de Aldama, *op. cit.*, pp. 313-314.
[243] Cf. Rom. 5:12-19.

grace and the gifts which accompanied it: freedom from concupiscence, from suffering, from ignorance, from death.

With regard to Mary and her Immaculate Conception, the question presents itself under the form of her obligation to incur this stain of sin. Was she subject to this general law of inheriting sin? It is not asked, of course, whether she contracted sin, but whether she should have contracted it, and in what sense must that possible debt of contracting be understood. The solution of this problem reflects upon the dignity of Mary, and effects a logical reconciliation of the doctrine of the Immaculate Conception with the universality of Christ's Redemption.

One must distinguish on the one hand the "debt" to contract original sin, and on the other hand the actual contracting of it. It is, in other words, the distinction between what should be and what actually is, as we might say of someone who has been exposed to a particularly contagious disease, "he should be sick in consequence," but to the amazement even of doctors, he is not in reality infected by the germ in question. All are agreed, at least since the definition of the doctrine of the Immaculate Conception, and indeed well before the Bull *Ineffabilis Deus* virtually no Catholic held otherwise,[244] that Mary never actually was touched by the stain of any sin whatever. But whether or not the Blessed Virgin ought to have contracted original sin, that is, whether or not she had a debt of contracting it, has for long been a matter of controversy among theologians.[245] This discussion, never having been settled by any official statement of the Church, and being left open by the terms employed in *Ineffabilis Deus*, is properly a matter of divergent speculation among theologians. The controversy had its beginnings in the fourteenth century, and by the sixteenth century there were considerable discrepancies in the terminology relative to the debitum, and there were various schools of thought on the correct position to take concerning Our Lady's relation to such a debt. At the basis of the controversy were two distinct but related problems: the predestination of Christ and His Mother, and the exact nature of original sin.[246]

---

[244] Cf. L. Lercher, S.J., *op. cit.*, p. 344 ff.

[245] For a remarkable (older) treatment of the question, cf. Joannes Perlinus, S.J., *Apologia scholastica pro magnae Matris ab originali debito immunitate* (Lugduni, 1630).

[246] Cf. J. de Aldama, *op. cit.*, p. 311.

In its most general sense, the debt of contracting original sin is an obligation, a necessity, an exigency of a human person's being subject to an initial privation of sanctifying grace. This obligation is rooted in the universal law of solidarity existing between the common carnal head of all mankind, Adam, and each of his progeny descended from his seed. The seed of the first man thus becomes a baneful heritage for all his posterity.[247] That much is clear. But less evident is the question as to precisely how this obligation arises. Does it arise from the mere fact of carnal generation? Or does the necessity of our incurring original sin arise rather from the law of God directly operating, to the operation of which human generation is simply a *conditio sine qua non*? Stated in other words: does the law requiring our being conceived in sin operate as a cause of our incurring that sin even apart from the fact of human generation as a necessary condition? Or do the law and the fact of human generation from an infected line together constitute the cause for the transmission of original sin?

The solution to these questions has prompted most theologians to make a distinction between a "remote" and a "proximate" debt. If the law of God which places all men under the obligation to incur original sin depends upon generation merely as a *conditio sine qua non* in order for the sin to be contracted, then one would hold that the Blessed Virgin was under a remote debt to contract that sin. It would be remote in the sense that God, while excluding Mary from the law of sin, would nevertheless leave her under the conditioning obligation of incurring sin for the reason that she had a human nature derived from Adam through seminal generation.

If, on the contrary, one considers that the law and carnal generation taken together comprise a joint cause for the transmission of sin, then Mary would have a proximate debt of contracting original sin. It would be proximate in the sense that God would include her in the law of sin, but exclude her from the application of that law.

The remote debt is also termed "conditioned" debt, since under it sin would follow absolutely from the law and conditionally from seminal generation, that is to say, immediately from the law and mediately from

---

[247] Cf. Rom. 5:12-13.

human generation. It is also called a "potential" debt[248] because, even if one be excluded from the law of inheriting sin, nevertheless, because of the fact of seminal generation necessarily rendering that law operative, one would actually incur the sin unless again one were exempted by God from the operation of the law.

Proximate debt is also called "absolute" debt because of the law's being one with the fact of seminal generation, in suchwise that the act of generation is not merely a condition which enables the law to operate. Rather it is the law operating. In this notion, original sin follows absolutely upon the fact of seminal generation, unless it happen that the law is divinely prevented from the actual application of its effect.[249]

1. Opinions of Theologians Relative to the Debt of Original Sin in Mary

Some theologians hold that the distinction between the remote and proximate debt is useless because Mary was certainly a daughter of Adam, and since the law of contracting original sin is identified with the derivation of human nature from Adam, to exclude her entirely from the law would be to deny that the Virgin was a child of Adam. And this would, in effect, assert that she in no sense needed to be redeemed, even preservatively.[250]

a) Proximate Debt

According to the opinion which teaches that the Blessed Virgin had the proximate debt of contracting original sin, she was included in the law of transmission of sin in such a way that she ought to have contracted it, not only by reason of her human nature as derived from Adam, but also by reason of her person. She had, if this be held, not only a natural debt, but even a personal debt of incurring the sin of our first

---

[248] Cf. Carolus Balić, O.F.M., *De debito peccati originalis* in *B. Virgine Maria* (Romae, 1941), p. 74.

[249] Cf. Evaristo de la Virgen del Carmen, O.C.D., *Sobre el débito del pecado original* en Maria, in *Estudios Marianos*, Vol. 5 (Madrid, 1946), pp. 293-308.

[250] Cf. A. H. M. Lépicier, O.S.M., *op. cit.*, pp. 134-135; Dominicus Palmieri, S.J., *op. cit.*, p. 334; Ed. Hugon, op. cit., p. 713.

parents.[251] In the theory of the proximate debt, the divine law was decreed in such a manner that original justice was so conferred on Adam that he would either keep it or lose it for himself and his posterity, including Mary. Thus she, as all other humans, ought to have been deprived of conception in grace because of Adam's sin. But, this opinion continues, she actually did not suffer this privation because she was preserved by God: in her case the law did not apply.[252] According to this view, the preservation of the Blessed Virgin was accomplished, not by excluding her from the law of the transmission of original justice (which was a universal law without exception), but from the application of the law. The theory that Mary had a proximate debt of contracting sin is held by not a few ancient and contemporary theologians.[253]

b) Remote Debt

In the opinion favoring a remote debt in the Virgin, Mary was entirely exempted from the universal law of original sin because the law was never intended for her.[254] She had a remote debt of incurring original sin only insofar as she had a human nature derived from Adam. Therefore, this debt was only a natural one, not a personal one on her part, because she, as a person, was never subject to the law: she was preserved entirely from being subject to the law in virtue of the merits of Christ the Redeemer. In this theory, original justice was so bestowed on Adam that under the law of its transmission he would keep it for all those naturally begotten of him, and if he lost it by sin, he would lose it for himself and all his posterity except the Mother of the Saviour.[255] Hence, in consequence of this law, even under Adam's sin, Mary ought not to have been subject to the privation of grace. True enough, the opinion adds, as a natural offspring of our father Adam, she should otherwise have been included in the law, yet in fact God excluded her

---

[251] For an interpretation of Scotus' doctrine on this question of the kind of debt in Mary, cf. Sebastianus Dupasquier, O.F.M.Conv., *op. cit.*, p. 251.

[252] Cf. J. de Aldama, *op. cit.*, pp. 313-314.

[253] Cf. G. M. Roschini, *op. cit.*, Vol. 2, pars 2, p. 92; J. Keuppens, *Mariologiae Compendium* (Antverpiae, 1938), p. 65.

[254] Cf. G. M. Roschini, *op. cit.*, pp. 92-93.

[255] Cf. Ed. Hugon, *op. cit.*, p. 710 ff.

from the law of original sin in virtue of the foreseen merits of Christ.[256]

c) No Debt Whatever

The theologians who hold the opinion that there was no debt at all in the Mother of the Saviour explain their position by declaring that Mary was constituted a distinct order from the rest of mankind: she was simply outside the order of sin, either original or actual. Many distinguished Spanish scholars have supported this theory.[257]

According to this doctrine, Mary was neither included in the law of the transmission of sin from Adam, nor excluded from it. Sharing with Christ a wholly separate decree, she was above and beyond any sinful order. The divine decree concerned effected the absolute predestination of the Mother of the Messias antecedently to God's prevision of the fall of Adam, and so that decree was without any relation to the condition of the parents from whom she was generated. Authors of unimpeachable authority support this view, which seems to add to the dignity of the Virgin.[258] This school advances the argument that God both foresaw the fall of Adam and also willed that Adam represent the entire human race even in his sin, yet He did so with the single exception of Mary. Hence the Blessed Virgin was not only immune from sin itself, but even from any obligation whatsoever of incurring sin.[259]

St. Alphonse di Liguori regarded this opinion as probable, explaining that since God deigned to distinguish His Mother from the common lot of men by so many graces, that it can be correctly believed that He did

---

[256] Cf. Christianus Stamm, *Mariologia* (Paderborna, 1881), pp. 48-51; J. de Aldama, *op. cit.*, p. 313 ff.

[257] For a lucid summary of the position of leading Spanish theologians during the very important seventeenth century, cf. J. M. Delgado, O.F.M., *Exención del débito según los Mariólogos españoles de 1600 a 1650*, in *Ephemerides Mariologicae*, Vol. 1 (Madrid, October-December, 1951), pp. 501-526.

[258] In view of this, it is difficult to understand the stricture of Van Noort on those who deny any debt. Cf. his *Tractatus de Deo Redemptore* (Hilversum, 1925), p. 172 (footnote): "... omnes doceant, et docere debeant, Mariam habuisse debitum incurrendi peccatum originale. ..." Cf. also Pohle-Preuss, *Mariology* (St. Louis, 1926), p. 40.

[259] Cf. F. X. ab Abázuza, O.F.M.Cap., *Manuale Theologiae Dogmaticae*, Vol. 2 (Chile, 1949), p. 220 ff.

not include her will with Adam's in any fashion.[260]

A recent and clear defense of the position that denies any debt in Mary considers sin, as indeed it is, as a privation of something (sanctifying grace) that should be.[261] If one speaks of a debt to something negative, one must understand it differently from a debt or obligation to something positive. Considering debt from a positive aspect: that which should be present in Adam's posterity is original justice, for if Adam had remained faithful to the divine precept, all his offspring would have received grace at conception in virtue of a title as descendants of Adam. In this way, original justice is the real debitum. Mankind's loss of this title through Adam's sin is not of itself original sin, which consists rather in the privation of original justice. The title to sanctification is regained through Christ's Redemption, for He is the New Adam. The phrase "original justice" may mean either grace at the moment of origin of the soul, or it can mean justification because of one's origin. Original sin would thus involve a double negation: first, the loss of title to grace because of one's descent from Adam; second, the absence of grace at the moment of conception.

Thus, the want of grace when a human is conceived is a privation and a fault, but a fault for which the person in fault is not at fault. Rather it is Adam who is at fault, since through his infidelity the grace that should have been present in the human soul is not present. Redemption does not restore original justice in the sense of justice by reason of origin, not even in the case of Mary. Justification is not through any incorporation in Adam, but through incorporation in Christ.

Applying these notions to the Mother of Christ, it would follow that there are various different ways in which God might have preserved Mary from incurring original sin. He might have given her grace in "simple gratuity" at the moment of her conception, or else in virtue of some "title," such as because of her divine Maternity of the Redeemer. If the grace had been given in virtue of simple gratuity, Mary would not have been truly redeemed, for such a gift would not have been in view

---

[260] Cf. *op. cit.*, pp. 308-309; Clément Dillenschneider, C.SS.R., *La Mariologie de S. Alphonse de Liguori* (Fribourg, 1934), pp. 225-226.

[261] Allan B. Wolter, O.F.M., *The Theology of the Immaculate Conception in the Light of "Ineffabilis Deus,"* in *Marian Studies*, Vol 5, 1954, pp. 62-70.

of the merits of Christ.

It can be said that there was a debt in Mary if two conditions would be verified. One that she lost her title to grace in Adam's sin; the other, that God decreed not to give her grace at the moment of her conception. The title lost in Adam only made sin for her a possibility, not a necessity, and accordingly this possibility of original sin in turn makes redemption by Christ possible. But in view of the fact that God would not give grace to any child of Adam at the moment of conception except through the merits of the Redeemer, it follows that redemption would be necessary to preserve one in fact from contracting original sin. As a daughter of Adam it is true that Mary lost her title to grace at the moment of conception precisely in virtue of her origin, and therefore although sin was not necessary if God so decreed, nevertheless redemption was necessary.

Mary needed grace if sin were not to stain her soul, and to Christ is she indebted for her sanctification. But did she similarly have a necessity to incur sin by reason of a debt in Adam's sin? She was surely "indebted" to her first parent for the possibility of her contracting sin, insofar as he surrendered one title she might have had to original grace.

"Mary lost one title to the grace of an immaculate conception but she gained another. The very fact that the *Ineffabilis Deus* cites Mary's relation to Christ the Redeemer as her title to grace at the moment of conception, a title she possessed as it were from all eternity in the plan of Divine Wisdom, is it meaningful to speak of a need, a necessity, an obligation to contract sin? ... Mary never seems to have had any genuine debitum. It was grace, not sin, that she should have had."[262]

In substance, it might be pointed out in this connection, that it is in virtue of the merits of Christ that both Mary and all the redeemed have another title to grace in place of the title lost by Adam's sin. It is the title, of course, from the Saviour's Redemption. There is this vastly important difference, however, between Mary and ourselves: we have the title to be restored to grace in virtue of Christ's merits, whereas by God's special decree with regard to His Mother, she had the title in virtue of her Son's merits to be preserved, not merely from actually

---

[262] *Ibid.*, p. 69. Cf. J. B. Carol, O.F.M., *Recent Literature on Mary's Assumption*, in *The American Ecclesiastical Review*, Vol. 120, 1949, pp. 381-385.

incurring original sin, but even from the obligation or debt of incurring it.

THE IMMUNITY OF MARY FROM CONCUPISCENCE

1. Nature of Concupiscence

The consequences of original sin, in addition to the chief loss, that of sanctifying grace, include the forfeiture also of certain immunities enjoyed by our first parents, freedoms that we ourselves would have possessed had Adam not sinned. These immunities are from concupiscence (called the "fuel of sin" — fomes peccati), from death, from malice in the will, from darkness of the intellect in ignorance, from sufferings of all kinds. Man is naturally subject to inherent disabilities of this kind, and the function of the preternatural gifts which were joined with sanctifying grace and rooted in it, was to relieve man of such disagreeable impediments to a full and completely happy life. By the sin of our first parents we were made subject to the penalty of their loss. These gifts are not regained when the soul is restored to sanctifying grace through justification, the disabilities remaining in the person, with greater or less force, throughout life.[263]

The most noteworthy of these penalties is that of concupiscence, which is from Adam's sin and leads us to sin, so much so that St. Thomas describes original sin as consisting materially in concupiscence.[264] Insofar as holiness is concerned, the wound of concupiscence plays a greater part than do the other penalties, precisely because of its proclivity to make actual sin a dreadful reality in human life. It is not formally or properly in the body, but rather in the lower powers of the soul, which we call the "sensitive" faculties, having a profound influence on the body. While it is therefore materially in the body, formally it is in the soul. The entire human person is infected by concupiscence because of our deriving a corrupted nature from our first parents: "nature infects the person."[265]

---

[263] Cf. Petrus Bardus, *De Immaculata Conceptione*, in *Monumenta antiqua Immaculatae Conceptionis*, ed. Petrus de Alva et Astorga, O.F.M. (Lovanii, 1664), p. 357.

[264] Cf. St. Thomas Aquinas, *op. cit.*, I-II, q. 82, a. 3.

[265] Hugolinus Storfi, O.F.M., *op. cit.*, p. 26.

The movement of the sense appetites, which was controlled easily and connaturally by our first parents so long as they retained grace and the accompanying gifts, became so disordered in consequence of original sin that these passions are in a state of revolt against man's higher faculties. This rebellion, while not entailing a complete corruption, leads sense desires to assert their demands contrary to the dictates of man's rational appetite, the will. The immoderate tendency of the lower potencies of man to seek their adequate sensible objects in opposition to the higher faculties, results in concupiscence "in first act" (in actu primo) or "in second act" (in actu secundo). Concupiscence in actu primo is the radical state of the sense appetites, their condition of being always proximately disposed to act contrary to reason. In actu secundo, concupiscence consists in the actual motions themselves of the appetites.[266]

Man's soul was essentially rectified and oriented to God by the gift of sanctifying grace, and this supernatural elevation of the soul and its faculties was perfected in the preternatural order by the gift of integrity, which rendered sense subordinate to spirit even as spirit was, through grace, subordinated to God. The subjection of the superior part of the human composite effected by grace, once removed by sin, the loss of the gratuitous subjection of the inferior part followed as a necessary part of the punishment visited upon man by the Creator.[267] Thus in a formal sense, original justice consisted in habitual grace; in a material sense, it consisted in the hierarchy of integrity within man.

The inherent proneness of mankind toward an unreasonable satisfaction of sensible desires of whatever kind, called in actu primo by theologians, may be "released" by God simply when He permits the normal baneful effects of original sin to take their course in the human person; or it may be "bound" through the special providence of God preserving one from the inroads of concupiscence, although the "fuel of sin" is allowed to remain; or finally it may be "extinguished" by being totally removed from the subject by a special act of God. When concupiscence is thus extinguished there is realized an habitual and immovable disposition in the subject by which the inferior powers never

---

[266] Cf. J. de Aldama, *op. cit.*, pp. 314-315.
[267] Cf. St. Thomas Aquinas, *op. cit.*, I-II, q. 82, a. 3.

move against reason, their proclivity to do so being completely taken away.²⁶⁸

Concupiscence in actu secundo, the very movements of sense appetites, may be "indeliberate," when there is no question of the will's consent to the movements provoked, and therefore indeliberate motions are without any direct moral reference. These motions may be "semideliberate" when they occur with imperfect advertence or imperfect consent, and ordinarily are venial sins. Or finally, concupiscence in actu secundo may be "deliberate" if it is joined to full advertence and consent, and where grave matter is in question mortal sin results.²⁶⁹

2. Relation of Mary to Concupiscence

The fundamental principle to be borne in mind with regard to the position of Mary in relation to the wound of concupiscence is this: Our Lady was constituted in an unique state of grace, and in virtue of this most special condition she was related to all the preternatural gifts characteristic of the state of innocence.²⁷⁰ To what extent the Bull *Ineffabilis Deus* may be considered as excluding concupiscence from Mary is controverted among theologians.²⁷¹ There can scarcely be any question with regard to the Blessed Virgin's being subject to any concupiscence in actu secundo in any form, since such disordered motions are intimately associated with the stain of original sin and too immediately related to actual sin: actual concupiscence is the "motion of sin," as St. Thomas expresses it.²⁷² The suggestions of sudden movements of the flesh, springing from the violent inclination of our flesh toward sensible objects, were found among the saints, all of whom were conceived in original sin. In Mary there was no trace of such motions, even in a material sense. Thus it does not suffice to assert simply that

---

²⁶⁸ Cf. Dominicus Palmieri, S J., *op. cit.*, p. 340.

²⁶⁹ Cf. St. Thomas Aquinas, *op. cit.*, I-II, q. 73, a. 6.

²⁷⁰ Cf. Martin Jugie, A.A., *L'Immaculée Conception dans l'Écriture sainte et dans la tradition orientale* (Rome, 1952), p. VIII; L. Garriguet, *La Vierge Marie* (Paris, 1933), pp. 155-179.

²⁷¹ Cf. Martin Jugie, A.A., *op. cit.*, p. 11 (footnote).

²⁷² St. Thomas Aquinas, op. cit., III, q. 27, a. 3.

Mary never consented to disordered carnal activity; she never in fact experienced the slightest actual revolt in her lower nature.[273]

Concerning the question of Mary being subject to concupiscence in actu primo, there has not always been such complete unanimity among theologians, at least with reference to the time when even this radical form of concupiscence was removed from the Mother of God. In the doctrine of the Scholastics, whose teaching prevailed generally up to the era of the definition of the dogma in 1854, the wonderfully integral nature of the Blessed Virgin knew a "bound" concupiscence from the moment of her first sanctification (either at the moment of her conception or else subsequently while in the womb of Anna) up to the moment of her second sanctification (when the Word assumed flesh), when all concupiscence was totally extinguished.[274] This is the position of St. Thomas Aquinas, who explains that the fomes peccati remained in Mary according to its essence after her justification, but that insofar as any actual operation of concupiscence was concerned the fomes was impeded. At the instant of her conceiving the Son of God, all concupiscence was totally removed.[275]

Later theologians, at least since the date of the definition of the dogma of the Immaculate Conception, teach that there was never in Mary the slightest trace of disordered sense appetite, for the plenitude of grace possessed by her was such that her entire sense life was always perfectly in accord with the dictate of her immensely graced will.[276] This interpretation appears more generally consonant with the honor of Christ whose flesh is of the most pure flesh of Mary; with the fact that, being totally immune from all stain of original sin, she ought therefore to he similarly free from one of its chief consequences; and since this immunity was had by our first parents, then fittingly it may be claimed for her.[277] It should be remembered that Mary's freedom from concupiscence is not a result of the Immaculate Conception, at least

---

[273] Cf. Van Noort, *op. cit.*, p. 189; Ed. Hugon, *Marie pleine de grâce*, p. 127.

[274] Cf. Bozzola-Greppi, S.I., *op. cit.*, p. 103; Alexius Martinelli, O.F.M., *De primo instanti Conceptionis B. V. Mariae* (Romae, 1950), pp. 1-2.

[275] Cf. St. Thomas Aquinas, *op. cit.*, III, q. 27, a. 3.

[276] Cf. I. Keuppens, *op. cit.*, p. 65; Ephrem Longpré, O.F.M., *op. cit.*, p. 86.

[277] Cf. J. de Aldama, *op. cit.*, p. 315.

directly. It is attributable to the graces that accompanied the singular prerogative of the divine Maternity.[278] But insofar as her immunity from concupiscence is related to her being conceived in grace, modern theologians acknowledge an extirpation of all disordered sense tendencies as concomitant with Mary's initial grace. This element in her sanctification is a negative thing: the removal of the "stain" of sin effected by the infusion of grace into her soul at the instant of its union with the body, and this is sometimes called her "first perfection." Her "second perfection" became a reality at the instant of the Incarnation, by which she received consummate grace, itself capable of yet great augmentation.[279] Her first perfection, the Immaculate Conception, predisposed her to the second, serving as a means for the Word to come among men.[280] And since the Word's flesh was hers, all inordinate carnal tendencies should have been removed, and were removed even in a radical sense, at the first moment of Mary's existence as a person.[281]

In the Bull *Ineffabilis Deus* it is said that the Mother of God was free "from all stain of original sin."[282] While it is not entirely certain that it was thereby intended to declare Mary's freedom as well from concupiscence, nevertheless it may be said that concupiscence is truly part of original sin in those not yet justified, and so in Mary's case the use of "all" in the definition may have a special value.[283]

Aside from any consideration of the possible quality of

---

[278] Cf. Albert Kippes, O.M.I., *The Immaculate Conception and the Preternatural Gifts*, in *Marian Studies*, Vol. 4, p. 198; Ed. Hugon, Tractatus Dogmatici, p. 723; Gaston Démaret, *Marie de qui est né Jésus* (Paris, 1937), Vol. 2, p. 43 ff.

[279] Cf. Achille Gorrino, *Maria Santissima* (Torino, 1938), p. 42 ff.; H. Depoix, S.M., *Beata Maria Virgine* (Paris, 1866), p. 120 ff.; F. O'Neill, *The Blessed Virgin Mary and the Alleged Debt of Sin*, in *The Irish Ecclesiastical Record* (Dublin, July, 1923), p. 83.

[280] Cf. A. M. Mayer, O.S.M., *Advanced Mariology* (Portland, 1934), p. 132.

[281] Cf. Armandus Plessis, S.M.M., *op. cit.*, p. 78; Dominicus Palmieri, S.J., *op. cit.*, p. 338; A. H. M. Lépicier, O.S.M., *op. cit.*, p. 195.

[282] *D.B.*, No. 1641.

[283] X. Le Bachelet in his article on the Immaculate Conception in *DTC*, Vol. 7, cols. 845-846, attributes no special importance to the *omni* of the definition in *Ineffabilis Deus*. Martin Jugie disagrees with this position in *L'Immaculée Conception dans l'Écriture sainte et dans la tradition orientale*, p. 11 (footnote). Cf. also Dominicus Palmieri, S.J., *op. cit.*, p. 221.

concupiscence in the state of pure nature in man, a condition that has slight relevance to the actual economy of mankind's fallen and redeemed nature, it should be affirmed that where there was never original sin, there was never concupiscence. Such was Mary's prerogative.[284]

THE RELATION OF MARY TO THE STATE OF ORIGINAL JUSTICE

Our first parents were constituted by God in a state of innocence, and this condition existed more probably from the first moment of their existence, although some theologians have taught that this elevation did not take place until some time after God made man.[285] This establishment of Adam and Eve in such a perfect condition of supernatural and natural being, in which their natural powers were perfected by the preternatural gifts, is called the state of "original justice." It implies the presence in their souls of sanctifying grace by which they were children of God and sharers in the divine nature, together with infused virtues of faith, hope, and charity. They likewise possessed immunity from certain disadvantages natural to the human composite: freedom from the necessity to die, from disorder in the sense appetites, from the illness and sorrows of life, from darkness of mind and from malice of will.[286] This totality of innocence and wondrous gifts was entirely a gratuity on the part of God, in no manner owed to man.[287] God could have allowed man to remain simply in the state of pure nature, with natural means to a natural end. But He did not; in His liberality He gave human nature sanctifying grace as the formal element of original justice, and added the blessing of integrity, completing and elevating man's natural perfections. All this would have been transmitted to

---

[284] Cf. Ludovicus Lercher, S.J., op. cit., p. 347. It should be noted that, strictly considered, the deletion of original sin and the preservation from concupiscence are distinct and separable gifts. As human, Mary ought to have been subject to at least some degree of concupiscence, but because of the divine Maternity she was exempt. This is the (probable) opinion of Van Hove, De immunitate B. M. Virginis a concupiscentia, in Collectanea Mechilniensia, Vol. 14 (Malines, 1940), pp. 41-42.

[285] Cf. J. M. Hervé, *Manuale Theologiae Dogmaticae*, Vol. 2 (Paris, 1949), p. 314 ff.

[286] Cf. E. Doronzo, O.M.I., *De Baptismo et Confirmatione* (Milwaukee, 1947), p. 90.

[287] D.B., Nos. 1021, 1026.

Adam's posterity as their heritage, had he not forfeited original justice by his originating sin, communicated to us as original sin through infected human nature.[288]

The extraordinary grace accorded Mary in the divine plan of our Redemption as the Mother of the Messias presents the problem of comparing her status with that of original justice enjoyed by our protoparents. Specifically in light of her Immaculate Conception, removing as it did all stain of original sin, can it be properly affirmed that Mary was constituted in the same situation as Adam and Eve: a condition of primitive innocence? Theologians are not agreed. Some contend that the Mother of God was entirely a new Eve, endowed with all grace and privileges of first innocence, even to the extent of having a title to personal immortality. That she actually died, this opinion holds, is simply because of her role of Co-redemptrix. And had she not died, Christ would Himself have endured something that is a characteristic human experience which His Mother would not have known.[289] Still other writers deny that such was Mary's state.[290]

In substance, the determination of the Blessed Mother's position in this regard may turn on her relation to her Son as her Redeemer, who has restored her to a singular level of sanctity because she was destined to be His Mother in the Incarnation. She needed His merits in order to be the recipient of God's grace, the formal element of her holiness.[291] Consistently with the opinion supporting a debt in Mary, it would follow that the grace given the Blessed Virgin was not in virtue of the primitive elevation of man, but in virtue of a new and special elevation through Christ.[292] She was neither in the state of original justice, nor in a state of (personally) lapsed but redeemed nature. Her state was totally unique and proper to her.[293]

Even if Mary had been placed simply in the state of original justice

---

[288] Cf. St. Thomas Aquinas, *op. cit.*, I-II, q. 82, a. 4.

[289] A. H. M. Lépicier, O.S.M., *op. cit.*, p. 358, holds that the Bull *Ineffabilis Deus* states that Mary was in the state of original justice. Cf. J. de Aldama, *op. cit.*, p. 316.

[290] Cf. B. H. Merkelbach, O.P., *op. cit.*, p. 246 ff.

[291] Cf. Dominicus Palmieri, S.J., *op. cit.*, p. 222.

[292] Cf. J. de Aldama, *op. cit.*, p. 316.

[293] Cf. *ibid.*, p. 317; B. H. Merkelbach, O.P., *op. cit.*, p. 111.

through some special decree of God, it would not be necessary to conclude that she would thereby have some or all of the gifts that constitute integrity, for the possession of sanctifying grace, however so exalted in degree, does not postulate the presence of the immunities that make up integrity. The participation in divine life which is grace is quite separable from the immunities from death, suffering, and the rest.[294] The grace of the Immaculate Conception, a grace "of Christ" contrasted with the grace "of God" received by our first parents, did not constitute Mary in the condition of first innocence. Nor did she, on account of that grace, have any strict title or claim to the preternatural gifts.[295] Having been lost through the fall of Adam, they could subsequently be enjoyed by one whose role in God's plan was such that the presence of the gifts, or of some of them, would be fitting and quasi-necessary in view of some special destiny of that individual. Mary's divine Maternity meets this requirement, as well as her office of Coredemptrix.[296] Similarly, because of her propinquity to Christ, the source of grace efficiently according to His divinity and instrumentally according to His humanity, and because she gave Him that humanity, therefore Mary's grace was supreme as compared to that of any man or angel.[297] With this grace she received all the theological virtues, since she was still a pilgrim despite her office, and also the moral virtues, except penance which concerns sorrow for sin. The Gifts of the Holy Spirit were hers, of course, and actual graces beyond estimation.[298] But all these incredible manifestations of God's solicitude for the sanctity of His Mother did not remove from her such human infirmities as her Son deigned to take upon Himself.[299] As He, she was acquainted with suffering and death and the manifold trials of soul

---

[294] Cf. Albert Kippes, O.M.I., *art. cit.*, p. 197.

[295] Cf. *ibid.* But Martin Jugie, A.A., *op. cit.*, p. VIII, seems to hold otherwise, at least with regard to concupiscence.

[296] Cf. Juniper Carol, O.F.M., *De Corredemptione Beatae Virginis Mariae* (Civitas Vaticana, 1950), pp. 550, 559.

[297] Cf. St. Thomas Aquinas, *op. cit.*, III, q. 27, a. 5; A. A. Paquet, *Disputationes Theologicae* (Quebec, 1922), p. 273.

[298] Cf. Bozzola-Greppi, S.I., *op. cit.*, pp. 102-103; J. B. Petitalot, *La Vierge Mère d'après la Théologie* (Paris, 1904), pp. 85-88; Chan. J. Mahieu, *op. cit.*, p. 50.

[299] Cf. Albert Kippes, *art. cit.*, p. 199.

and body to which each human is, in this time of probation, subject. But whatever would truly be out of place in the Mother of the Saviour, whatever would lessen that dignity or be suggestive of sin, must be rigorously excluded from her. In addition, therefore, to her freedom from concupiscence, we should acknowledge her immunity from ignorance and from any debility in the irascible appetites, from all malice of will or error of intellect.[300] Mary is, under Christ, God's gracious Masterpiece. In the words of the Franciscan Doctor, St. Bonaventure:

> Mary the Virgin is the advocate of sinners
> and the glory and the crown of the just.
> She is the spouse of God, the abode of the Trinity
> and the most special resting place of the Son.[301]

---

[300] Cf. B. H. Merkelbach, O.P., *op. cit.*, p. 141.
[301] *III Sent.*, d. 3, p. 1, a. 2.

Mary's Immunity From Actual Sin

By SALVATORE BONANO, C.M.F.

ANCTITY, while implying a positive, inner transformation of the soul, presupposes as well a negative aspect, namely, the freedom from sin. Justification contains two simultaneous acts: the remission of sin and the infusion of grace. In the soul of Our Blessed Lady there was no need for the first of these two acts, for she was immaculately conceived and sinless during her whole life. Since the dogma of the Immaculate Conception has been studied in a previous article (cf. pp. 328-394), we shall concern ourselves here with the truth of her perfect sinlessness.

The thesis may be stated as follows: Our Lady, through a special privilege, avoided, during the whole course of her life, all personal sin, mortal as well as venial, and was free from every voluntary imperfection. More, she was in a unique way impeccable.

DEFINITION OF TERMS

Impeccability. By this term we understand indefectibility in the moral order, or the inability to sin. It can be either direct, deriving immediately from the absolute, essential perfection of a being; or indirect, based upon some quality of the subject to whom it is attributed, or upon a state or condition in which he finds himself. The former belongs to God alone who is subsistent sanctity and the supreme principle of all holiness. The latter, as the definition makes clear, admits of varying degrees which are determined both by the dignity of the person and the principles that account for the complete removal of the possibility of sin.[1] Thus we distinguish:

a) The impeccability that is Christ's as man because of the hypostatic union. There is only one Person in Christ, that of the Word to whom all

---

[1] Cf. J. Vosté, O.P., *De mysteriis vitae Christi* (Rome, 1940), p. 21; G. Roschini, O.S.M., *Mariologia*, Vol. 2 (Romae, 1948), p. 106; G. Alastruey, *Tratado de la Virgen Santísima* (Madrid, 1945), p. 253.

actions, both divine and human, are attributed. Were there even the slightest sin in that sacred humanity, the sinful act would have to be attributed to the Divine Word to whom that humanity belongs, an attribution that would be absurd. This we call *metaphysical impeccability*.[2]

The impeccability that is proper to the angels and the blessed, who are confirmed in good and incapable of turning away from the immediate and intuitive vision of the divine essence. This intuitive vision is made possible to the intellect of the blessed through the *light of glory*, a supernatural power infused by God. It brings about a permanent adherence to God as the highest Good and since sin, which makes man an enemy of God, consists in placing one's last end in created goods, the beatific vision confers a state of impotency in regard to sin. This is called physical impeccability.[3]

The impeccability of the Blessed Virgin. A majority of authors designate this as *moral* impeccability. That is, because of her personal title and dignity as Mother of God she could never incur the stain of sin. Mary is not intrinsically impeccable; the divine Maternity is not a physical form that intrinsically affects and transforms her soul. All theologians admit the existence in Mary of a real predicamental relation that defines her motherhood *in facto esse*, i.e., from the moment that she conceived Christ. There was, moreover, a quasi-transcendental relation of Mary to the Word in virtue of which from all eternity the entire reason for her existence is to be the Mother of God. This determines her motherhood only *in fieri*. It is a relation based on the infallible predestination of Mary to divine motherhood.[4] Thus from the first moment of her existence there is moral incompatibility with sin, for were she stained with the least sin it would reflect upon the honor due to Jesus. Suárez maintains the *possibility* of a divine motherhood in a

---

[2] Secondary causes of Christ's impeccability are the fullness of habitual grace and the beatific vision.

[3] The possession of God in the beatific vision is a state of perfect happiness, and as such excludes all sin, mortal as well as venial. Cf. P. Richard, art. Impeccabilité, in DTC, Vol. 7, col. 1275.

[4] Cf. G. Rozo, C.M.F., *Sancta Maria Mater Dei* (Mediolani, 1943), p. 66.

state of sin,[5] since between the two there is neither metaphysical nor physical opposition.

A final division is that of *antecedent* and *consequent* impeccability. The former demands in a person direct opposition to the disorder of sin through some title or added intrinsic principle of deliberate moral acts. The latter implies the infallible divine prevision that a man or an angel will *de facto* never sin. Our Blessed Lord, the angels, the blessed in glory, and the Mother of God possessed an antecedent inability to sin, not merely the inability due to divine prevision.

Sinlessness. This may be defined as actual freedom from all personal sin. As distinct from impeccability it has an aspect that relates it to the order of fact. For a person may avoid sin *de facto* through an abundance of grace, the gift of integrity, or a special assistance of Divine Providence; none of these reasons, however, can remove the power itself to sin. This sinlessness embraces freedom from all mortal sin only, whereby sanctifying grace would be lost, or from all venial sin as well.[6]

Privilege. Our Lady's absolute sinlessness is a special privilege, for it is of faith[7] that the just man is unable to avoid all venial sin during the whole course of his life. If Mary did so, we have a clear exception to the law, and therefore, a privilege. This means that neither ordinary nor special helps which are gratuitously given to those who persevere to the end, were sufficient, but that a very unique gift was required consisting in a constant assistance of Divine Providence influencing her will in the

---

[5] *De mysteriis vitae Christi*, op. omn. (Parisiis, 1860), Vol. 19, q. 38, a. 4, disput. 22, sectio 2, p. 327. It is beyond the scope of this article to enter into a study of the precise nature of the divine Maternity and whether or not it is a forma *ex se justificans*. For Scheeben, the grace of Mary's motherhood accounts for incapability of sinning on the analogy of that of Christ's humanity. *Handbuch der katholische Dogmatik*, Vol. 3 (Friburgi i. Br., 1882), nn. 1602-1603; *Mariology*, transl. by T. Geukers, Vol. 1 (St. Louis, Mo.), p. 205 f.; Vol. 2, p. 135 f. The sixteenth-century theologian S. Saavedra propounded the theory of an intrinsically supernatural form that raised Mary to the dignity of Mother of God. J. Delgado, *La maternidad divina según Silvestre de Saavedra*, in *Estudios Marianos*, Vol. 4, 1945, 521; J. Alonso, C.M.F., Gracia de María: naturaleza y fundamentos, in *Estudios Marianos*, Vol. 5, 1946, p. 104. De Rhodes holds that the divine Maternity excludes sin from Mary more efficaciously than habitual grace, but that of itself it is not a form that sanctifies. *Disputationes Theologiae Scholasticae*, Vol. 2 (Lyons, 1661), Tract. 2, q. 4.

[6] G. Roschini, *op. cit.*, p. 107.

[7] *D.B.*, No. 833.

direction of good. The fall of our first parents is clear proof that the state of innocence does not of itself confirm the soul in good. It is called a special privilege — no one else has had it as extensively nor to the same degree. After the descent of the Holy Spirit into their souls, the Apostles were so confirmed in grace[8] that they avoided all mortal, and even, in the opinion of some theologians, all deliberate venial sin. Yet they were able to experience the rebellion of the flesh and a deceptive influence on the mind. Actually, through an abundance of grace and special helps, they succeeded in repressing these inordinate movements of the sense appetite, but concupiscence itself as an effect of original sin was always present and therefore also the *possibility* of having the disordered acts arise. Regarding St. Joseph, theological debate centers on whether he was free from all actual sin and confirmed in grace during his entire life or only from the time of his *marriage* to Our Lady.[9]

ERRORS

The Lutherans and Calvinists protested against, and belittled the import of the Catholic attitude toward the idea of Mary's utter sinlessness. Erasmus[10] had already prepared the way for the Reformers with the introduction of his religious humanism and derisive attacks against devotion to Mary. The imputation of sin to Our Lady was due, among other factors, to false conceptions entertained by the Reformers on the nature of theology which they considered an illegitimate body of deductions from Scripture. For them the Bible and the Bible only was the literal expression of God's word for all men. The Scripture, they claimed, contains very little about the Blessed Virgin and certainly does not authorize the belief in the surpassing holiness and great gifts of soul and

---

[8] St. Thomas, *De Veritate*, q. 24, a. 9, ad 2; B. Merkelbach, Mariologia (Parisiis, 1939), p. 149.

[9] Garrigou-Lagrange, O.P., *The Mother of the Savior*, transl. by B. Kelly, C.S.Sp. (St. Louis, Mo., 1948), p. 326; A. Michel, art. Joseph, in *DTC*, Vol. 8, col. 1518; Lépicier, *Tractatus de Sancto Joseph* (Paris, 1908), a. 2, pp. 153-161; Alastruey, *op. cit.*, p. 254. It is commonly held that in particular virtues some saints were free from all sin, e.g., St. Thomas in chastity and humility, St. John the Baptist in speech. Cf. *Breviarium Ordinis Praedicatorum*, feast March 7, Second Nocturn, First Antiphon.

[10] Erasmus, *Oeuvres*, Vol. 1 (Basle, 1540), p. 663. Cf. also A. Noyon, S.J., art. *Mariolatrie*, in *D.A.F.C.*, Vol. 3, col. 315.

body that Catholics attribute to her.

Moreover, their views on original sin, the intrinsic corruption of nature, and justification led logically to a denial of Mary's sinlessness, Christ Himself being the only pure and perfect God-Man.

Turmel (under the pseudonym Herzog) attempted to prove that the traditional teaching of the Church prior to the thirteenth century was that Mary, like any other human being, had sinned. Sacred Scripture and the primitive Christian community, he holds, teach the same.[11]

The Jansenists, in rejecting the cult of Mary as an effect of superstition and a deterrent from a true interior piety, also taught that she stood in need of purification at the time she presented Jesus in the Temple; her Son contracted this stain from her.[12] Highly derogatory to Our Lady's moral perfection was the work of A. Widenfeld, *Monita salutaria B. Mariae ad cultores suos indiscretos*, put on the Index in 1676.[13]

Pope Pius V condemned the proposition of Baius which states that the death of the Blessed Virgin is to be attributed to the fact that she incurred the stain of original sin.[14]

MAGISTERIUM

The Council of Trent has solemnly declared that Mary, by special privilege, was preserved free from all actual sin, mortal and venial, throughout her whole life. "If anyone asserts that man, after he is once justified ... is able to avoid throughout his lifetime all, even venial sin, except by a special divine privilege, as the Church holds in regard to the Blessed Virgin, let him be anathema."[15] According to Merkelbach this decree does not define Mary's immunity from all sin because of the use

---

[11] *La Sainte Vierge dans l'hi A.A.S. stoire* (Paris, 1908). Cf. the condemnation of this work in, Vol. 1, 1910, p. 554, and Vol. 22, 1930, pp. 517-520.

[12] *D.B.*, No. 1314.

[13] *Ibid.*, No. 1316. Cf. Grenier, *Apologie des dévots de la Sainte Vierge* (Brussels, 1675), p. 3. The Monita influenced the reform of the Gallican liturgy. Outstanding opponents of Mariological Jansenism were De Montfort (1716), A. Liguori, (1787), G. Crasset, S.J., (1618-1692), Bossuet (1628-1704), Th. Raynaud (1583-1632), G. of Rhodes (1661), Contenson (1641-1674), P. Poiré (1584-1637).

[14] *D.B.*, No. 1073.

[15] Session 6, c. 23; *D.B.*, No. 833.

of the word *tenere* rather than *credere*. It is not, therefore, an article of faith but certain Catholic doctrine.[16] J. de Aldama, S.J., holds that the Council is here defining the belief of the Church in Mary's privilege: "*definitur fides Ecclesiae circa hoc privilegium.*"[17] Roschini has an excellent study on the history behind the formulation of Canon 23, and his conclusion is that Trent has defined the Marian privilege as well as the general law of which it is an exception.[18]

The soul in the state of grace can avoid any venial sin considered separately, but cannot avoid all venial sins cumulatively taken. The Council adds "throughout his life" so as not to exclude the possibility of freedom from them over a given period of time.

Pope Pius IX in the Bull *Ineffabilis Deus* declares that God filled Mary "far more than all the angelic spirits and all the saints, with an abundance of all heavenly gifts from the treasury of His divinity, in such a wonderful manner that she would always be free from absolutely every stain of sin."[19]

SCRIPTURE PROOFS

The privilege of Mary's absolute sinlessness is implicitly revealed in the Book of Genesis in the words spoken by God to the serpent (Gen. 3:15): "I will put enmities between thee and the woman, between thy seed and her seed; she shall crush thy head and thou shalt lie in wait for her heel." The enmity that is set up between the woman and the serpent

---

[16] *Op. cit.*, p. 143.

[17] *Sacrae Theologiae Summa*, Vol. 3 (Matriti, 1953), p. 363. Cf. also his *El valor dogmático de la doctrina sobre la inmunidad de pecado venial en Nuestra Señora*, in *Archivo Teológico Granadino*, Vol. 9, 1946, pp. 53-67.

[18] *Op. cit.*, pp. 110-111. Fr. de Aldama, S.J., shows conclusively that the verbs tenere and credere have equal value for the Fathers of Trent, *loc. cit.*, p. 58 f. On the meaning of "auxilium speciale," "magnum perseverantiae donum," and similar Tridentine expressions cf. Hefner, *Die Enstehungsgeschichte der Trienter Rechfertigung Dekretes* (Paderborn, 1909), p. 352. This Canon does not touch the question of Mary's impeccability, nor the cause of her absolute sinlessness.

[19] Cf. *Ineffabilis Deus*; in Col. Lac., Vol. 6, p. 836. Cf. also *Mystici Corporis* of Pius XII, A.A.S., Vol. 35, 1943, 247.

must be absolute as the text demands.[20] Now, were Mary even for a moment a slave to sin, she would not share in the complete victory of her Son over the devil. All sin, original and actual, mortal and venial, is absolutely incompatible with the state of her perfect enmity.[21]

Her sinlessness is again implicitly contained in the words of the angel to Mary: "Hail, full of grace ... blessed art thou among women" (Lk. 1:28). Traditional teaching on this point is that the words express a fullness of grace that extends to the first moment of her life, a fullness that warded off from her all contact with sin.[22] The Greek perfect participle κεχαριτωμένη signifies a state fully realized and still persevering in its effects, a state of being "endowed with grace," or with "divine good pleasure" in an extraordinary way. The Latin equivalent would be *tota gratiata*. The phrase "the Lord is with thee" is to be understood as a statement of fact, not as an indication of desire: *"Dominus est,"* not *"Dominus sit tecum."*[23]

Difficulties. Some of the Fathers, in explaining certain passages of Scripture that refer to the Blessed Virgin, implied or asserted that she sinned venially or showed some weakness.[24] The Reformers of the

---

[20] J.-B. Terrien, S.J., *La Mère de Dieu et la Mère des hommes*, Vol. 3 Paris, Bk. 1, pp. 26-49. F- Peirce, S.J., *Mary Alone is "the Woman" of Genesis 3, 15*, in *The Catholic Biblical Quarterly*, Vol. 2, 1940, p. 245.

[21] Though the pronoun "she" in the Hebrew text is masculine and stands for the posterity of the woman, there is no essential difference between it and the Vulgate ipsa, since the woman is to achieve perfect victory in association with her seed.

[22] Cf. *Ineffabilis Deus*. Hence the Church applies to her, as the sponsa Christi, this text from the Canticle of Canticles, 4:7: "Thou art all fair, O my love, and there is no stain in thee."

[23] M. Jugie, A.A., *L'Immaculée Conception dans l'Ecriture Sainte* (Rome, 1952), p. 48 f.; U. Holzmeister, S.J., *Dominus tecum*, in *Verbum Domini*, Vol. 8, 1928, p. 363.

[24] Fathers and early writers who seem to have erred: (1) Tertullian says that Mary for a short time failed to believe in Christ. "With the brethren of Jesus, Mary did not believe in Him and hence must yield to Martha and Mary Magdalen in faith," *De carni Christi*, 7; *PL*, 2, 766. (2) St. Basil: *Epistola*, 260, 9; *PG*, 32, 965. (3) St. John Chrysostom appears to have thought that there was taint of vainglorious self assertion in Our Lady's action at the marriage feast of Cana: *Homilia 44 in Mathaeum*; *PG*, 57, 463. (4) Maximus of Turin: *Homilia in Epiphania Domini*, 1; *PL*, 57. St. Cyril of Alexandria interprets the sword of sorrow as the scandal she experienced on Calvary: *In Joannem*, 19, 25; *PG*, 74, 661. Origen says that the sword of sorrow were the doubts and scandal that shook the faith of Mary during the Passion: In Lc. homilia 17; PG, 13, 1845. Cf. *Biblica*, Vol. 29, 1948, p. 226. He

sixteenth century seized on these passages to belittle the Mother of Christ in the eyes of the people. The biblical texts are the following:

1. St. Luke 1:34: "But Mary said to the angel, 'How shall this happen, since I do not know man.'" Mary shows signs of unbelief in the message of the angel.[25]

Answer: Our Lady knows, on the one hand, that her vow of virginity is God's will for her, and, on the other, that the angel's message means the Infant will have Joseph as His father. There is no conflict between her will and God's will, but between an antecedent divine will approving her virginity and the manifestation through Gabriel of a subsequent will of God revealing a plan apparently incompatible with a virginal state. She is at a loss as to how to reconcile the two, and so, not wishing to displease God, asks which course should be followed.[26]

2. St. Luke 2:35: "And thy own soul a sword shall pierce." Origen, St. Cyril of Alexandria, and others interpret the sword as meaning the uncertainty, unbelief, scandal that afflicted Mary at the foot of the cross.

Answer: There is no basis for such an interpretation either in Scripture or in the general teaching of tradition. The sword of sorrow, looked at in the light of her faithful vigil near the cross, is a revelation of her compassion and Coredemption. The Passion of Christ and the compassion of Mary form a unity that reveal her destiny of association and communion with the dying Christ. The Greek term for sword ῥομφαία is never used to mean "doubt,"[27] nor does it ever symbolize

---

influenced several writers of the time.

[25] Thus Harnack, *Zu Lc. 1*, 34-35, in *Zeitschrift für die neutestamentlich Wissenschaft und die Kunde der älteren Kirche*, Vol. 2, 1910, 55 f. He parallels Lk. 1:34 and Lk. 1:18. But there is a marked difference between the two. Zachary doubts the word of the angel and asks for a sign that he may believe. Hence the punishment that follows. Mary believes from the start and inquires only as to the way in which the fact is to be accomplished. Suárez, op. cit., q. 27, a. 6, disputatio 4, sectio 3: Zachary asks, "How shall I know this?" Mary, "How shall this be done?"

[26] Cf. P. Joüon, S.J., *Note d'Écriture Sainte*, in *Nouvelle Revue Théologique*, Vol. 66, 1939, p. 794. This question implied no positive error on her part, since she interpreted the words of the angel in their natural meaning. Her perfect conformity to the will of God is shown by the words: "Be it done to me according to thy word."

[27] G. Estius, *Annotationes in praecipua ac difficiliora S. Scripturae loca* (Antwerp, 1652), p. 349.

restlessness or vexation.[28] Its real and obvious metaphorical meaning is deep sorrow.[29]

3. St. Luke 2:44f.: In losing the Child Jesus, Mary *(a)* was negligent; *(b)* gave way to excessive sorrow; *(c)* was unduly disturbed as shown by her words to Jesus.

Answers: *a)* The parents of Jesus left Jerusalem on the third day of the Paschal solemnity with other Galilean pilgrims. The older children were free to join any of the various groups that formed. Mary and Joseph, therefore, were not anxious as to where Jesus was, "thinking that he was in the caravan," and so traveled the first day alone. In the evening, noticing that He was not among the friends and relatives, they were greatly disturbed and the next morning set out for Jerusalem to search for Him.[30]

b) It was a case of motherly concern. Mary had the tender love of a pure soul for her Son. Her sorrow cut deep, but it was not inordinate.

c) Mary's words: "Son, why hast thou done so to us?" are expressive not of impatience, but of deep love, of a mother's genuine sorrow, of maternal authority. The answer of Jesus is not a reproach, for His parents were not at fault. It is the answer of Jesus as a teacher. He is giving them to understand that His subjection to them must always be conditioned by the will of the Father in matters that have reference to His messianic mission. To this will Mary was by no means opposed. But even though aware in a general way that He must be about His Father's business, she may have been ignorant of the time, the place, and the precise manner for the accomplishment of that business.[31]

---

[28] T. Zahn, *Das Evangelium des Lucas* (Leipzig, 1813), p. 157.

[29] W. Bauer, *Wörterbuch zu N.T.* (Berlin, 1937), p. 284; Zorell, *Novi Testamenti lexicon graecum* (Paris, 1931). Note also that the text has διελεύσεται which means not merely a blow that wounds but that pierces all the way through bringing certain death, so that in relation to sorrow it means "unto death." Cf. T. Gallus, S.J., *De sensu verborum Lc. 2, 35 eorumque momento Mariologico*, in *Biblica*, Vol. 29, 1948, pp. 220-239.

[30] L. Fonck, S.J., *Duodennis inter doctores*, in *Verbum Domini*, Vol. 2, 1922, p. 21.

[31] Cf. B. Bartmann, *Christus ein Gegner des Marienkultus?* (Freiburg, 1909), pp. 47-52; *Maria im Lichte des Glaubens und der Frömmigkeit*, (Paderborn, 1922), pp. 123-126; Lagrange, *L'Évangile selon saint Luc* (Paris, 1948), p. 94. On the meaning of "my Father's business" cf. F. Fields, *Notes on the Translation of the N.T.* (Cambridge, 1889), pp. 50-56; P. Temple, *"House" or "Business" in Lk. 2, 49*, in *The Catholic Biblical Quarterly*, Vol. 1,

MARY'S IMMUNITY FROM ACTUAL SIN

4. St. John 2:4: "What wouldst thou have me do, woman? My hour has not yet come." Literally: "What to me and to thee?" The tone of the reply seems to be a rebuke and an implicit admission that the Mother's request was uncalled for.

Answer: Our Lord uses the term "woman" in six other passages and in the same meaning as that given to it in the present text. It is used in contexts where He is sympathizing, healing, consoling, affirming, praising, but never when reproving.[32] Both in Greek and Semitic the term indicates, not domestic intimacy, but an honorable address, with sentiments of filial love and piety, as shown from its use by Our Lord on the cross.[33]

The words "What to me and to thee?" have to be understood from biblical, not modern, usage. The phrase does not mean: "What concern is it of ours?" nor "What do you have against me?" In all the biblical passages where it occurs, it signifies, according to context, a greater or lesser divergence of viewpoint between the parties concerned. With Ceuppens[34] we may translate it as: "What have I in common with you?" The answer was expected to be in the negative and taken as a conditioned refusal, for immediately Our Lord adds: "My hour is not yet come." Christ's hour for His messianic work, for His public career, had not yet arrived; the time to prove by miracles that He was the Son of God was to be reserved for a later date. Mary, confident of obtaining what she has asked, tells the servants: "Do whatever he tells you." It is clear, then, that Jesus neither reproached His Mother, nor denied her petition, but rather showed that the mere mention of a need from her

---

1939, pp. 342-352; U. Holzmeister Quaestiones Biblicae de S. Joseph, in Verbum Domini, Vol. 24, 1944, p. 241.

[32] E. Power, S.J., *Quid mihi et tibi, mulier? nondum venit hora mea*, in Verbum Domini, Vol. 2, 1922, p. 129. P. Gächter, *Maria in Kana*, in Zeitschrift für Katholische Theologie, Vol. 55, 1931, pp. 351-402; E. Zolli, *Quid mihi et tibi, mulier?*, in Marianum, Vol. 8, 1946, pp. 3-15; E. di Cristo Re, *Che significa "quid mihi et tibi"?* in Scuola Cattolica, Vol. 75, 1947, pp. 137-142; P. Vanutelli, *Alle nozze di Cana*, in Marianum, Vol. 10, 1948, p. 72; G. Roschini, O.S.M., *La vita di Maria* (Roma, 1945), p. 245.

[33] Cf. *A Catholic Commentary on Holy Scripture. The Gospel according to St. John* (London, 1953), p. 983, 786 b.

[34] *De Mariologia Biblica* (Romae, 1948), p. 184. P. Joüon, *Notes philologiques sur les Évangiles*, in Recherches des sciences religieuses, Vol. 18, 1928, p. 356.

carries great weight with Him.

5. St. Matthew 12:48: "Who is my mother and who are my brethren?" Commenting on the text, St. John Chrysostom (later the Reformers) remarks that Our Lady gave in to a feeling of vanity in the presence of the crowd. The words of Our Lord are a rebuke.

Answer: This is a completely gratuitous assertion as a study of the context shows. Mary is His Mother and wants to be near Him as she was on Calvary. The meaning is that He must not neglect to fulfill the mission for which He came into the world and therefore must set forth an example of complete detachment in the interests of the Father. Recall Lk. 2:44 f. concerning His "Father's business." Spiritual affinity is superior to natural kinship — His Mother is to be numbered among those related to Him spiritually.[35] The text of St. Mark 3:21 gives no grounds for the assertion that she shared in the opinion that "He has gone mad," for it is not certain that the Greek οἱ παρ᾿ αὐτοῦ necessarily means relatives or friends,[36] or if understood in that sense, it still remains doubtful whether we are to see in the persons referred to, the "mother and brethren" of verse 31.[37] At any rate, we could very well expect His Mother to be concerned, but we see not the least indication of any desire to take advantage of her position as His Mother to receive the adulation of the crowd.

Concerning the Fathers who attribute either venial sin or imperfection to Our Blessed Lady, we note:

a) They are not speaking as witnesses of tradition, but rather presenting tentative explanations to solve an exegetical difficulty.

b) They do not interpret one and the same text.

c) They do not speak of sin in the strict sense of the term, but rather

---

[35] Cf. F. Friedel, S.M., *The Mariology of Cardinal Newman* (New York, 1928), pp. 281-282. M. Scheeben, *Mariology*, transl. by T. Geukers, Vol. 2, p. 131. J. de Aldama, S.J., *Sacrae Theologiae Summa*, pp. 365-366.

[36] *La Sainte Bible*, L. Pirot-A. Clamer, Vol. 9, *Évangile selon S. Marc*, pp. 438-439. The Greek term ἐξέστη under the influence of the Vulgate has been given the meaning of "mad," but the true meaning is "was beside himself."

[37] J. Steinmueller, *Exegetical Notes*, in *The Catholic Biblical Quarterly*, Vol. 4, 1942, pp. 354-359.

of feminine frailties.[38]

TRADITION

a) During the first four centuries we find the tradition of Mary's sinlessness in an implicit state, contained especially in the doctrine that she is the Second Eve. She is also compared to the Church and both are said to be without stain or wrinkle (Eph. 5:27), that is, completely sinless and all-holy. In the Oriental liturgy, said to have originated with St. James, and endorsed by the Sixth Ecumenical Council, Our Lady is referred to as "most pure, immaculate, irreproachable in every way."[39]

The tradition becomes explicit with St. Ephrem the Syrian. His authentic works, as well as those put out in his name, are replete with texts that extol her sinlessness: "In thee, O Lord, there is no fault, and in Thy Mother there is no stain."[40] Classical is the text of St. Augustine which is universal enough to exclude sin of any kind from the Blessed Virgin. In controversy with Pelagius, who had appealed to the saints of the Old Law as examples of sinlessness, St. Augustine states emphatically that all saints must confess with one voice that they have known the defilement of sin, "with the exception of the holy Virgin Mary in regard to whom, out of respect for the Lord, I do not propose to have a single question raised on the subject of sin."[41]

b) The second period comprises the fifth to the thirteenth centuries. This period reveals an explicit profession of faith in Mary's immunity

---

[38] C. Boyer, S.J., *Synopsis praelectionum de B. Maria Virgine* (Romae, 1946), p. 23. Friedel, S.M., op. cit., p. 283.

[39] J. D. Mansi, *Sacrorum Conciliorum nova et amplissima collectio*, Vol. 11 (Florentiae, 1775), canon 32, col. 958. The universal tradition of the Eastern Church has ascribed this liturgy to St. James in which we find many prayers and invocations to Our Lady. The Jacoban Syriac liturgy has the following: "The Father sent Me the Word ... and Gabriel, as a husbandman, sowed Me. The womb of Mary as the good soil received me ..." J. Comper, *A Handbook of Liturgies* (Edinburgh, 1898), p. 74.

[40] *Carmina Nisibena*, ed. Bickell (Leipzig, 1866), pp. 28-29. St. Ambrose describes her as endowed, through grace, with an integrity that rendered her sinless. *Expositio in Ps. 118, sermo 22*, n. 30; *PL*, 15, 1521.

[41] *De natura et gratia*, c. 36, n. 42; *PL*, 44, 267. The opinion of St. Augustine dominated the whole of tradition. Cf. Le Bachelet, art. *Marie-Immaculée Conception*, in *DTC*, Vol. 3, cols. 210-275.

from all sin during the whole course of her life. We also have a more accurate interpretation of Scripture texts which in the third and fourth centuries had offered some difficulty to this universal belief.

The sanctification or purification of Our Lady which, according to some writers, took place at the moment of the Incarnation, was not to free her from actual sin, but to completely extinguish concupiscence (*fomes peccati*) which up to then had only been restrained (*ligatus*). SS. Leo the Great and John Damascene[42] speak of the purifying action of the Holy Spirit on her soul at the moment of the Incarnation.[43] This is to be interpreted in the light of the general teaching of the writers of this period, as meaning that, prior to the conception of Christ, she was not free from inordinate concupiscence in actu primo, as a habit or tendency that of itself inclines to evil and retards from the practice of virtues. Yet this habit was bound and hindered from eliciting acts contrary to right reason. After the conception of the Saviour she was freed entirely from the very habit or essence of concupiscence.

At the beginning of the twelfth century, Eadmer and Hildebert of Mans explicitly assert that Mary was exempt from all stain both in body and soul all her life.[44] In a letter to the monks of Lyons, St. Bernard writes that Mary was granted a privilege accorded no other creature, that of being exempt from all fault during the whole of her life.[45]

c) In the period extending from the thirteenth to the sixteenth century, there is an attempt to determine the immediate principle or cause of Mary's sinlessness and impeccability. For St. Albert the Great that principle is the fullness of grace.[46] St. Thomas Aquinas holds this to

---

[42] Sermo 22, *PL*, 54, 196. *De fide orthodoxa*, 1, 3; *PG*, 94, 986; *In dormit. B. Mariae Virginis*, 1.3; *PG*, 96, 704.

[43] Thus Venerable Bede writes that through the operation of the Holy Spirit she was purified from carnal concupiscence. *Homilia, Opera paraenetica*, lib. 1, Homilia 1; *PL*, 94, 12.

[44] *De excellentia B. V. Mariae*, 3; *PL*, 159, 560. Hildebert, Sermo 69; *PL*, 171, 677.

[45] St. Bernard, *Epistola 174*, 5, *PL*, 182, 334. Richard of St. Victor, *Explicatio in Cant. Canticorum*, 26, 29; *PL*, 116, 482 and 416; *De emmanuele* libri duo, 1; *PL*, 196, 660.

[46] *Mariale*, q. 134; *Opera Omnia* (Paris, 1898), Vol. 20, p. 91. Alexander of Hales, *Summa theologiae* (Venetiis, 1575), part 3, qq. 8-9, m. 3, a. 2, p. 32. According to St. Bonaventure, Our Lady was powerless to sin from the moment of the Incarnation, the reason given being that the closer one comes to the source of grace, the greater are the supernatural

be inadequate. A special assistance of Providence is needed to keep her free from the occasion of sin and to influence her will in the direction of moral good. His reason is that the human will is not sufficiently confirmed in good prior to the beatific vision.[47] In this life the beatific vision is given to no one in a permanent manner, save the case of the privilege conferred upon the sacred humanity of Christ. The abundance of grace, he says, makes the commission of sin difficult, because of the infused virtues which give the soul a strong inclination to the act of the love of God and the state of constant contemplation which withdraws the soul from sin.[48] But previous to the Incarnation this grace, granted to the Blessed Virgin, while contributing to the suppression of inordinate acts that anticipated the act of reason, did not render impossible movements of the sensitive appetite.[49] In addition to grace, she stood in need of a special protection from God for the "binding" of concupiscence, i.e., to prevent the disordered acts from arising. After the Incarnation she received a fullness of grace that confirmed her soul in good by the complete extinction of concupiscence and by the gift of perfect perseverance through the special assistance of Divine Providence.[50]

After the declaration of the Council of Trent concerning Our Lady's perfect immunity from actual sin, theological elaboration centers mainly on providing solutions to the objections of Protestants. Prominent in this field was St. Peter Canisius who wrote the monumental *Opus Marianum*

---

gifts that one receives, and the more remote the possibility of sin. Mary, as the Mother of God, came into immediate contact with the divine Person and sacred humanity of her Son, and thus received the perfect fullness of grace that confirmed her in good while extinguishing concupiscence. *De purificatione B. M. V.*, sermo 1, (IX, 634 ab); in 3 sent., d. 3, pars 1, q. 2, quaestio 3. Cf. E. Chiettini, O.F.M., *Mariologia S. Bonaventurae* (Romae, 1941), p. 150 f. As corroborative arguments of fitness he gives the following: her absolute virginity, the impossibility of damnation, and a holiness surpassing that of the angels.

[47] *S. ?Th.*, 1, q. 100, a. 2.

[48] *De veritate*, q. 24, a. 9.

[49] *S. Th.*, 3, q. 27, a. 4 ad 1.

[50] *Contra Gentiles*, lib. 3, Chap. 155. The dogma of the Immaculate Conception makes it clear that Mary was free from concupiscence *in actu primo et secundo* from the first instant of her existence.

directed against the Centuriators of Magdeburg.[51] The first book studies the childhood and perfectly sinless life of Mary, while the fourth examines and interprets in an orthodox sense various Gospel texts, the so-called Protestant *loci communes*, such as Our Lord's words to His Mother in the Temple and at the marriage feast of Cana.[52] In defense of traditional Mariology, he also develops masterfully the Patristic antithesis of the first and Second Eve.[53]

It is the unique merit of Suarez to have been the first to study systematically and by use of the Scholastic method, the divine Maternity of Our Lady with all its eminent prerogatives. In his *Disputationes de mysteriis vitae Christi*, we have a Marian theology in the strict sense of the term, wherein not only Mary's actual sinlessness, but also her impeccability are brilliantly expounded and defended.[54] The root principle of Mary's impeccability for these theologians generally is the absence of concupiscence, the fullness of grace, a special protection of Divine Providence, and a constant flow of efficacious graces that kept her faculties free from all fault.

The Marian movement that arose during this period is still in progress. Based on a more accurate exposition of the theology of Christ and His Church, Mariology presents us with the Mother of God as stainless and perfectly holy as the Mystical Body.

---

[51] *Opus Marianum*, first put out in 1577, p. 780 under the title *De Maria Virgine incomparabili et Dei Genetrice sacrosancta libri quinque, Secundus Commentariorum de verbi Dei corruptelis* (Ingolstadt, 1583), lib. 1, c. 10, lib. 4, c. 1 f. Vol. 2, p. 73, 386 ff.

[52] In Bourassé's *Summa aurea de laudibus Beatissimae Virginis Mariae*, Vol. 8, col. 1210 ff. Cf. O. Braunsberger, *B. Petri Canisii Societatis Jesu epistulae et acta* (Friburgi i. Br., 1896-1923), 8 vols.; Vol. 7, p. 392.

[53] Scheeben, *op. cit.*, p. 488.

[54] *Opera omnia*, Vol. 19 (Parisiis, 1860). Cf. Manteau-Bonamy, O.P., *Maternité divine et Incarnation* (Paris, 1949), p. 175; J. Bover, S.J., *Suárez Mariólogo*, in *Estudios Eclesiásticos*, Vol. 22, 1948, pp. 311-337. Another noteworthy Marian theologian of this period is St. Lawrence of Brindisi. His *Mariale* develops the fundamental Mariological principles, while his *Lutheranismi Hypotyposis* (3 vols.) traces the historico-doctrinal genesis of Lutheranism. Opera omnia, 9 vols. (Patavi, 1928-1944). Cf. G. Roschini, *La Mariologia di S. Lorenzo da Brindisi* (Padua, 1951). Cf. also Roberti Bellarmini opera omnia, Vol. 3 (Parisiis, Vivès, 1870), preface, pp. 134 and 137; book 3, ch. 16, pp. 319 and 321.

THEOLOGICAL PROOF

1. St. Thomas gives the fundamental reason for this privilege when he says: "God prepares and disposes those whom He has chosen for a special purpose in such a way as to make them capable of performing that for which He selected them" (3, q. 27, a. 4). Now God had chosen Mary for the Mother of His Son. Were she at any time under sin she would have been unfit for her high office.

Hence God gave her grace sufficient to make her always a fit Mother of Jesus.

2. If she is the Mother of God, then "for the honor of the Lord" she was absolutely sinless. Dishonor in parents reflects dishonor upon the children. Aquinas remarks that the Word who is Wisdom and Light could dwell only in a womb that was sinless (3, q. 27, a. 4).

3. Mary was chosen by God to be the associate of Christ in the work of Redemption. Now sin certainly does not contribute to co-redemptive mediation, much less does it have any satisfactory value.

4. Where there has been no mortal sin there can be no venial sin, for the latter arises from a revolt of the sense appetite against reason, whereas the former is a revolt of reason against God. Now the sense appetite is perfectly subject to reason as long as reason remains subject to God. Thus the first sin of Adam and Eve had necessarily to be a grievous sin. As it is absurd to admit a grievous sin or even its possibility in the Mother of God, we conclude that she was free from all venial sin.

This immunity from all mortal sin was due more proximately to a very high degree of habitual grace and charity which gives the soul a very strong inclination to the act of the love of God, while withdrawing it from the attraction of sin. Our Lady's freedom from all sin, due to a special privilege, demanded also a special assistance of Divine Providence through actual and special supernatural helps that gave her a prompt and generous state of soul. She was in this manner confirmed in good and rendered incapable of committing any sin. Thus, though our first parents in the state of original justice were unable to sin venially, they could sin mortally, because they lacked this confirmation in grace.

There are three reasons, deriving ultimately from her dignity as the Mother of God, that show, not only her de facto sinlessness, but also her absolute inability to sin. This impeccability was caused by: (1) the extinction of concupiscence as to its very essence, (2) the abundance of grace, (3) a special assistance of Divine Providence.[55]

FREEDOM FROM IMPERFECTION

Theologians debate the question as to whether there is a real distinction between positive moral imperfection and venial sin. The more probable opinion holds the affirmative: Imperfection differs from venial sin, for the latter, being a disordered act, cannot be ordained to the end of charity, whereas an imperfection is a morally good act which can be ordained to that end, though lacking a certain amount of perfection.[56] What we have said on Mary's immunity from venial sin applies likewise to freedom from all moral imperfection. "The answer usually given to this problem," says Garrigou-Lagrange, "is that there was never any imperfection, however slightly voluntary, in the lives of Jesus and Mary, for they never failed in their prompt obedience to every divine inspiration by way of counsel."[57]

---

[55] Cf. St. Thomas, *Scriptum super sententias*, lib. 3, d. 3, q. 1, a. 2, sol. 2.

[56] Garrigou-Lagrange, *Christian Perfection and Contemplation* (St. Louis, Mo., 1944), p. 430. Cf. A. Schellinckx, *Autour du problème de l'imperfection morale*, in *Ephemerides Theologicae Lovanienses*, Vol. 4, 1927, pp. 195-207. For the negative, cf. E. Ranwez, *Péché veniel et imperfection*, ibid., Vol. 3, 1926, pp. 177-200. Hugueny, *Imperfection*, in *DTC*, Vol. 7, col. 1286. Prümmer, *Manuale Theologiae Moralis*, Vol. 1 (Friburgi i. Br., 1915), p. 81.

[57] Garrigou-Lagrange, *The Mother of the Saviour*, p. 75.

Mary's Divine Motherhood

By GERALD VAN ACKEREN, S.J., S.T.D.

"Y SOUL is glorifying the Lord and my spirit rejoicing in God my Savior" (Lk. 1:46). With this antiphon Our Blessed Mother herself began an everlasting hymn of praise to the Majesty of God for the wondrous mystery of divine motherhood which God had worked in her. Each succeeding generation has added its voice to the chorus according to Mary's prophecy, to glorify the divine goodness "whose mercy is from generation to generation" (Lk. 1:50). In making Mary His Mother, God has poured forth on her all the treasures which His loving omnipotence could confer on a person who is not God Himself. Because Mary is God's Mother, she stands next to her divine Son, at the summit of creation, above the angels and saints, having within her the very fullness of divine grace and purity and holiness. As Pius XII wrote in his encyclical *Fulgens Corona*, "A higher office than this [the divine motherhood] does not seem possible; since it requires the greatest dignity and sanctity after Christ, it demands the fullest perfection of divine grace and a soul free from every sin. Indeed, all the privileges and graces with which her soul and her life were endowed in so extraordinary a manner and measure, seem to flow from this sublime vocation of Mother of God, as from a pure and hidden source.[1]

The divine motherhood is not only Mary's greatest privilege, but it is the key to the understanding of all her other privileges, as has been shown in a previous chapter. Not only does this truth hold the primacy in Mariology, but it is so intimately connected with the whole economy of salvation in Christ that for the past 1500 years the recognition of Mary as Mother of God has been a touchstone of Christian orthodoxy. For if Mary is not truly the Mother of God, then her Son, Christ Our Redeemer, is not true God as well as true man; moreover, His salvific work for the Redemption of mankind would be nothing more than vapid imaginings of a restoration that had never taken place.

---

[1] *A.A.S.*, Vol. 45, 1953, p. 580.

In one brief chapter it is obviously impossible to treat adequately of this great privilege of Mary which seems to exploit the very omnipotence of God Himself.[2] We shall limit ourselves here to the following points: (1) the revealed fact of the divine motherhood in Scripture, Tradition, and history: (2) an attempt at delineating the essence of the divine motherhood; (3) some reflections on the relationship of Mary's motherhood to her other privileges.

I. THE FACT OF DIVINE MOTHERHOOD

For Mary to be the Mother of God, two things are necessary: first, that she be really the Mother of Jesus; and second, that this Jesus whom she bore be really God. If both these conditions are fulfilled, Mary is truly the Mother of God.

Hence we must try to understand what exactly is meant when it is said that Mary is a real mother and then why it must follow that, if Mary's child is God, Mary is truly the Mother of God.

Every man who comes into the world has a mother who has conceived him, carried him in her womb, and brought him forth. A

---

[2] The bibliography on the divine motherhood is rather extensive. The following are some of the more important modern books and articles: J. M. Alonso, C.M.F., *Hacia una Mariología trinitaria: dos escuelas*, in Estudios Marianos, Vol. 10, 1950, pp. 141-191; Vol. 12, 1952, pp. 237-267; id., *Trinidad, Encarnación, Maternidad divina*, in *Ephemerides Mariologicae*, Vol. 3, 1953, pp. 86-102; J. M. Delgado Varela, O. de M., *Fr. Silvestre de Saavedra y su concepto de maternidad divina*, in *Estudios Marianos*, Vol. 4, 1945, pp. 521-558; id., *Teoría de Saavedra sobre la divina Maternidad en su aspecto dinámico*, in *Alma Socia Christi*, Vol. 7, 1952, pp. 233-277; id., *En torno a la Maternidad de la Santísima Virgen*, in *Estudios*, Vol. 10, 1954, pp. 297-318; L. Donnelly, *Causalidad instrumental de la Maternidad divina según Saavedra*, in *Estudios*, Vol. 9, 1953, pp. 7-19; C. Koser, O.F.M., *De constitutivo formali maternitatis B. Mariae Virginis*, in *Alma Socia Christi*, Vol. 11, 1953, pp. 79-114; H. M. Manteau-Bonamy, O.P., *Maternité divine et Incarnation. Étude historique et doctrinale de Saint Thomas à nos jours* (Paris, 1949); M.-J. Nicolas, O.P., *Le concept intégral de maternité divine*, in *Revue Thomiste*, Vol. 42, 1937, pp. 58-93, 230-272; S. Ragazzini, O.F.M.Conv., *La divina maternità di Maria nel suo concetto teologico integrale* ... (Roma, 1948); G. Rozo, C.M.F., *Sancta Maria Mater Dei, seu de sanctificatione B. Mariae Virginis vi divinae maternitatis* (Milano, 1943); F. Vacas, O.P., *Maternidad divina de María* (Manila, 1952); G. de Yurre, *La teoría de la Maternidad divina formalmente santificante en Ripalda y Scheehen*, in *Estudios Marianos*, Vol. 3, 1944, pp. 255-286. See also *Estudios Marianos*, Vol. 8 (1949), and *Marian Studies*, Vol. 6 (1955), which are entirely devoted to the study of the divine motherhood.

woman is prepared for motherhood from the very beginning of her life by the feminine structure of her body. On coming to puberty she develops within herself maternal ova designed to issue in children of her womb when fertilized by the male sperm. This fertilization disposes the ovum in such a way that it calls for the creation and infusion of a rational soul on the part of God. In the very instant that the soul is infused and a new being essentially like herself is formed in her womb, a woman is said to conceive or generate a child. A tiny globular embryo at first, the child is nourished in her womb from her bloodstream and develops there in the course of nine months into a recognizable human baby. Then the mother brings him forth into the world.

No woman can be said to be a mother in the proper sense of the word unless she has generated a child. Generation requires, first of all, that the offspring be a living subsistent being.[3] For what is generated is a being existing completely in itself, not in another, as, for example, a part exists in a whole. It would be wrong, therefore, to say that a woman who conceives a child generates his body or his soul or his nature; these are only parts of her child. She generates the whole child, the being which exists completely in itself. That is why your mother is the mother of you, not the mother of your nature or your body or your soul.[4]

Second, generation requires that the offspring be of the same nature as the parent. This point is too obvious to dwell upon; for God the Father generates God the Son; human parents generate human children, doves generate doves, giraffes generate giraffes.

Third, part of the very substance of the parent must pass into the substance of the child, so that the child is really from the substance of the parent; otherwise there is no real generation, no real fatherhood or motherhood. Hence adopting a child can never bring about real parenthood. Or suppose that God should create out of nothing a child's body as well as his soul and lodge it in the womb of a woman in such a way that the child would develop there and be delivered by way of natural birth, even then the woman would not really generate the child and thus be its true mother; it would not be from her own flesh that the

---

[3] On the notion of generation see St. Thomas Aquinas, *Summa Theologica*, I, q. 27, a. 2c; q. 33, a. 2; *Summa contra Gentiles*, IV, c. 11.

[4] St. Thomas, *Sum. Theol.*, III, q. 35, a. 1.

child had originated. It may seem useless to emphasize this rather obvious point, but it has been misunderstood in the past.

Fourth, the child must originate from that part of the parent which has the specific design and function of bringing about the same kind of nature in the offspring. If God should form an infant from the heart of a woman or from any part of her body other than from her maternal ova, she could not be truly said to generate the child and to be its mother. The child must originate from the seed or ova of the parent; otherwise there is no true generation.[5] We do not say that Adam generated Eve, that he was the father of Eve; for although Eve originated from Adam's flesh, she did not come from his seed.

Unless all these elements of generation are verified in the production of her child, no woman can be properly said to be a mother.

MARY THE MOTHER OF JESUS

It is astonishing with what clarity the Scriptures speak of Mary as a genuine mother. From the beginning of God's revelation of the promised Redeemer, it was clear that He would have a real mother. He would be the "seed of a woman" (Gen. 3:15), a descendant of Abraham, Isaac, and Jacob, of the seed of David according to the flesh (Rom. 1:3; Acts 2:30), a shoot that would spring from the root of Jesse (Isa. 11:1), the fruit of a virginal womb (Isa. 7:14). By the power of the Most High and the overshadowing of the Holy Spirit (Mt. 1:18-25; Lk. 1:35), Mary would conceive Jesus as her own Son (Lk. 1:31), and bring Him forth (Lk. 2:7; Mt. 1:16). From her He was made (Gal. 4:4), the fruit of her womb (Lk. 1:42). She gave Him His name and brought Him up as her Son (Lk. 2), a man in all things like the rest of men, except sin (Hebr. 4:15).

Difficulty begins to arise only when we try to understand how the Mother of Jesus is truly the Mother of God. We know from Scripture and Tradition that Jesus, the Son of Mary, is the only-begotten Son of God. He has a human nature which He received from His Mother, and He is therefore man like ourselves. But He is not a human person. He is a divine Person who is also man, who subsists not only in the divine nature which He receives in eternity from the Eternal Father, but also in

---

[5] Cf. F. Suárez, S.J., *in III partem Divi Thomae*, q. 32, a. 4, disp. 10, sect. 1; ed. Vivès, Vol. 19, p. 167.

the human nature He has received in time from His human mother. Mary, therefore, in generating her Son, did not generate a human person. Does, then, the mere fact that she gave a human nature to the Second Person of the Blessed Trinity give us the right to say that she generated that divine Person, that she is truly the Mother of God?

We have seen that the object of generation, the being which is generated, is not just a part of the offspring, but the whole being existing completely in itself at the term of generation. If the offspring has an intellectual nature, as is the case in all human generation, then it is a person. Hence a woman's motherhood always refers to the person of her child. What she mothers, what she generates or conceives, is a person.[6]

The very way in which we speak about a mother makes this truth clear to us. We say, for example, that St. Monica was the mother of St. Augustine. St. Augustine is a person. We ask: "Who is your mother?" or "Whose mother is she?" *Who* and *Whose* refer only to persons. Thus we see that our very manner of speaking about a mother and her child indicates that the relationship of mother to child is one of person to person; in other words, what a woman mothers is a person.

It is true, however, that a mother is not the cause of the soul or the personality of her child except in so far as she provides the matter disposed in such a way that it requires the creation of the soul of her child immediately by God. But even though a mother is not the *total* cause of her child, even though what she gives him by her own proper activity is not his soul nor his personality but only the flesh of his human nature, nevertheless she is truly *his* mother, the mother of the person of her child. Although what she gives of her own is only part of her child, she is mother of the whole child.

If Mary did for Jesus everything that any human mother does for her child, then Mary is as much the mother of the person of Jesus as any other woman is the mother of her child. The fact that Jesus had no human father does not make Mary any less His mother. The essential difference between purely human motherhood and divine motherhood is not that Mary did something more or something different in the conception of her child. It is simply this: Mary's Child is a divine Person, whereas the child of an ordinary mother is a human person.

---

[6] Cf. St. Thomas, *op. cit.*, III, q. 35, a. 1.

We know that only God can create the soul of a child and make soul and body as one human nature exist completely in itself; in other words, God alone makes the human nature exist as a human person. Personality is the term of human generation as a gift from God, rather than as produced by human generation.[7] Hence human motherhood is not in the least interfered with or compromised, if God creates the soul in the flesh provided by maternal activity in such a way that the human nature produced does not exist completely in itself as a human person, but is assumed by a divine Person. If instead of giving human personality as the term of maternal activity, God gives the divine Person of His own Son to be clothed with a woman's flesh, then far from interfering with her motherhood, this action of God raises it to "an almost infinite dignity."[8] For such a mother bears the most perfect Son that can possibly be born.

The divine motherhood leads us right into the heart of the Christian mystery: the unfathomable truth that Jesus Christ is both true God and true man, in whom the human nature received from His human mother and the divine nature received from His eternal Father are united in the one Person of the Son of God. Unless Jesus is true man, Mary cannot be a true mother. Unless the Child Jesus born of Mary is a divine Person and God Himself, Mary cannot be called the Mother of God.

THE SCRIPTURES ON DIVINE MOTHERHOOD

Although the Scriptures do not explicitly call Mary the Mother of God, the angel Gabriel at the Annunciation speaks of the Child Mary is to conceive as the "Son of the Most High," "the Son of God" (Lk. 1:32, 35). Elizabeth salutes Mary as the Mother of her Lord (Lk. 1:43). Although Lord (*Kyrios*) is employed in the New Testament for man as well as for God, in the present context it seems more certain that the Holy Spirit revealed the mystery of the Incarnation to Elizabeth in full. When she asks why should "the mother of My Lord come to me"? Elizabeth speaks of the same *Lord* of whom Mary sings: "My soul

---

[7] Cf. M. J. Nicolas, O.P., *Théologie Mariale*, in *Revue Thomiste*, Vol. 54, no. 3, 1954, p. 636.
[8] Cf. Pius XI, *Lux veritatis*, in *A.A.S.*, Vol. 23, 1931, p. 513; also Pius XII, Munificentissimus Deus, in *A.A.S.*, Vol. 42, 1950, p. 762; and Fulgens Corona, in *A.A.S.*, Vol. 45, 1953, p. 580.

MARY'S DIVINE MOTHERHOOD

magnifies the Lord, and my spirit rejoices in God my Savior" (Lk. 1:47).[9] It is beyond the scope of this essay to expound the testimony of Scripture regarding the divinity of Mary's Son. Still, because this truth is at the very foundation of the divine motherhood, it may be well to recall the precious prologue of St. John's gospel in which he trumpets forth the divinity of Jesus Christ. The Word *is* God, he says (Jn. 1:1). God the Word was made flesh (1:14). God the Word-made-flesh is Jesus Christ, of whom John the Baptist gave testimony (1:15-17). Jesus Christ is Mary's Son.

In the Synoptics we read that when Jesus was on trial for His life before the Sanhedrin, He professed under oath (Mt. 26:63, 64) that He was the Christ, the Son of God, and was charged guilty of death for blasphemy (Mk. 14:64), a charge having no meaning unless His claim meant equality with God Himself. Moreover, at least three times Jesus is explicitly called God by the Apostles. Recall the profession of faith on the part of doubting Thomas, as Jesus shows him the wound in His side: "My Lord and my God" (Jn. 20:28). St. John in his first epistle is direct and explicit about the divinity of Christ:

> We know also that the Son of God is come, and has given us understanding to know Him who is true: and we are in Him who is true — in His Son Jesus Christ. *He is the true God and life eternal* (1 Jn. 5:20).

Furthermore, St. Paul not only says that "God sent His Son, born of a woman" (Gal. 4:4), that Jesus was "in the form of God" (i.e., by nature God) and regarded Himself "equal to God" (Phil. 2:6), but speaks of "Christ in the flesh, who exalted above all things is God blessed forever" (Rom. 9:5).[10]

Therefore, even though Mary is never explicitly called the Mother of God in Scripture, she is explicitly called the Mother of the Lord, the Mother of Jesus; and her Son Jesus, whom she conceived, is explicitly called God. Mary is the Mother of God.

---

[9] Cf. Bernard J. Le Frois, S.V.D., *The Theme of the Divine Maternity in the Scriptures*, in *Marian Studies*, Vol. 6, 1955, pp. 115-117.

[10] See F. Prat, S.J., *The Theology of St. Paul* (tr. from 11th ed. by J. L. Stoddard, Westminster, Md., 1946), Vol. 2, pp. 125-127.

History and Tradition

The history of the Church's teaching is to a great extent the history of her combat with error. Her infallible authority to interpret the deposit of faith and guard it from error leads the Church to define more and more precisely her own teaching. So it has been with the doctrine of Mary's divine motherhood.

In the very early ages of Christianity belief in Mary's divine motherhood found its expression in the creed attributed to the Apostles. According to the form in use at the time of Hippolytus (c. 215), the catechumens were asked:[11]

> Dost thou believe in Christ Jesus, the Son of God, who was born of the Holy Spirit and the Virgin Mary. ...

St. Ignatius of Antioch, a bishop and martyr who died shortly after the close of the first century, and who was probably a disciple of the Apostles themselves, is an eloquent witness to the early teaching of the Church. In his letter to the Ephesians he says:[12]

> *God our Lord Jesus Christ was born in the womb by Mary*, according to the dispensation of God, from the seed of David, by the power of the Holy Spirit.

As Mary can be the Mother of God only if she is truly the mother of Jesus and if her son Jesus is truly God, distorted views of the Word's Incarnation logically involve a denial of the divine motherhood. The basic errors about the Incarnation are two: (1) Jesus, the Son of God, did not really become flesh, at least not flesh of our flesh, and hence cannot be said to have had a mother in any real sense; (2) the man, Jesus, who was born of Mary was only a human person, not the second Person of the Blessed Trinity. Therefore we can trace the history of the Church's teaching on Mary's divine motherhood by studying the Church's reaction to each of these two heretical tendencies.

Gnosticism

The first great menace to the doctrine of the divine motherhood was

---

[11] *The Apostolic Tradition of St. Hippolytus*, XXI, 15 (ed. Gregory Dix, London, 1937, p. 36).
[12] *Ep. ad Ephesios*, 18, 2; *PG*, 5, 660; Rouët de Journel, *Ench. Patr.*, No. 42 (italics are my own).

Gnosticism.[13] While to the Jews it appeared blasphemous for any man to call himself the Son of God, the stumbling block for the Gnostics was rather that any god and savior of mankind should become incarnate by taking to himself real human flesh from a woman. To them the flesh was an evil thing, coming from an absolute source of all evil; the body was to be despised, abhorred, even annihilated. While the concern of true Christianity was the redemption and restoration of the flesh through the Incarnation, death, and resurrection of a divine Person, the main doctrine of Gnosticism was redemption *from* the flesh by a process of purification and deliverance from the flesh through knowledge (*gnosis*).

Basic in nearly every form of Gnosticism was a fundamental dualism between matter and spirit; it was impossible for any good god or savior of mankind to become enfleshed or to be born of the human substance of a woman. One form in which the Gnostic mind expressed itself was called Docetism — from the Greek word *dokein*, meaning "to seem," "to appear," "to make believe." These "make-believers," as Ignatius of Antioch called them, taught that Christ's body was but a phantom, that "the Savior was unborn, incorporeal and without form ... a man only in appearance."[14] Valentinus taught that although Christ had a real body, it was not a material body like our own, but a celestial body, which came down from heaven into this world by merely passing through Mary's body, as through a channel. Marcion went so far in his effort to obliterate any recollection of Christ's human descent from David through Mary, that he not only discarded the Old Testament completely but even rewrote the New Testament according to his own Gnostic views. In Marcion's gospel, Christ appears as a full-grown man without any human parents. Marcion turns the words of Christ, "Who is my mother and who are my brethren?" into a proof that Christ had no mother whatsoever.

St. Ignatius of Antioch about the year 110 is already warning the Christians of Trallia against such doctrine:[15]

> Stop your ears therefore when anyone speaks to you who stands apart

---

[13] Cf. G. Bareille, *Gnosticisme*, in *D.T.C.*, Vol. 6 (2), cols. 1434-1467; K. Algermissen, *Christian Denominations* (tr. by J. W. Grunder, St. Louis, 1946), pp. 275-282.

[14] Cf. St. Irenaeus, *Adversus Haereses*, 1, 24, 2; *PG*, 7, 674-675.

[15] *Ad Trallianos*, 9-10; *PG*, 5, 681.

from Jesus Christ, from David's scion and Mary's Son, who was really born and ate and drank, was really persecuted by Pontius Pilate, really crucified and died. ...

But if, as some atheists, that is, unbelievers say, His suffering was but a make-believe — when in reality, they themselves are make-believers — why then am I in chains? Why do I even pray that I may fight wild beasts? In vain, then, do I die! My testimony after all is but a lie about the Lord!

Justin, Irenaeus, Hippolytus, and Tertullian, all vigorous opponents of Gnosticism in the West, not only used expressions which equivalently affirm Mary's divine motherhood, but testified explicitly to the basic truths handed down in Scripture and Tradition upon which Mary's divine motherhood is founded.[16] Here we shall be content merely to present a significant text from St. Irenaeus, who abounds in statements covering the fact of the divine motherhood and founds his teaching solidly on the Scriptures and apostolic Tradition:[17]

> That He (Christ) is Himself in His own right, unlike all men who have ever lived, God and Lord, King Eternal, and Incarnate Word, proclaimed by all the prophets, apostles, and by the Spirit Himself, may be seen by all who have arrived even at a small portion of the truth. The Scriptures would not have given this testimony about him, if like others He had been a mere man. That He had in Himself, unlike all others, that pre-eminent birth which is from the Most High Father, and also underwent that pre-eminent generation which is from the Virgin, — both these facts the divine Scriptures testify about Him; also that He was a man without comeliness and subject to suffering. ...

MANICHAEANISM

Closely related to Gnosticism was the doctrine of the Manichaeans.[18] Under its founder, Mani, Manichaeanism spread rapidly in the West and even claimed for a time the great Augustine who was later to become its most vigorous opponent. According to Faustus, the protagonist of the Manichaeans against Augustine, Jesus was the "Son of God," but in no

---

[16] For a summary of these Western Christian writers on Mary's divine motherhood, see Volume I of this work, pp. 147-149.

[17] *Adversus haereses, 3, 19,* 2; *PG, 7 (1), 940; cf.* Ench. Patr., No. 222.

[18] See G. Bardy's fine article, *Manichéisme,* in *D.T.C.,* Vol. 9 (2), cols. 1841-1895.

Mary's Divine Motherhood

sense was He the child of Mary. With telling inconsistency, as Augustine pointed out, Faustus taught that the virgin overshadowed by the Holy Spirit in the conception of Christ was not Mary, but the earth itself. Under the influence of the Holy Spirit, the earth conceived and fashioned the mortal Jesus, who later became the Son of God at the time of his baptism.[19]

Although St. Augustine never used the expression "Mother of God" in his writings against the Manichaeans, he does call Mary God's Mother (*genitrici suae*) in his sermons, and sets Mary's "conception of her Creator" in sharp contrast with Elizabeth's conception of John:[20]

> It was a man Elizabeth conceived, a man that Mary conceived. Elizabeth was the mother of John, Mary the mother of Christ. But Elizabeth conceived only a man, Mary conceived one Who is both God and man. A stupendous thing it is, how a creature could conceive the Creator!

The Manichaeans won adherents in Spain in the fourth and fifth centuries, even among the clergy. The Manichaean errors associated with Priscillian, the Bishop of Avila, were condemned at the Council of Braga in Portugal. Among these we find the following:

> If anyone does not honor the birthday of Christ according to the flesh, but only pretends to do so, fasting on the very day itself and on Sunday, for the reason that, like Cerdon, Marcion, Mani and Priscillian, he does not believe that Christ was born in the nature of man, let him be anathema.[21]
>
> If anyone says that the moulding of the human body is of the devil's fashioning, and that conceptions in the wombs of mothers are brought about with the help of devils, and for this reason does not believe in the resurrection of the flesh, as Mani and Priscillian have said, he is a heretic.[22]

The abhorrence of the flesh as something evil in itself which roused the Church Fathers against the Gnostics and Manichaeans in defense of Christ's true manhood and Mary's true motherhood is an idea that has been long in dying. It appeared again in the twelfth century among the

---

[19] Compare with the doctrine of the Gnostic Cerinthus (c. A.D. 170), in Irenaeus, *Adversus haereses*, 1, 26, 1; *PG*, 7, 686.

[20] *Sermo 289*; *PL*, 38, 1308; also *Sermo 186*; *PL*, 38, 999, and *Sermo 195, 2*; *PL*, 38, 1017.

[21] D.B., No. 234.

[22] D.B., Nos. 234, 242. See Paul Palmer, S.J., *Mary and the Flesh*, in the book, *Mary and Modern Man*, ed. Thomas J. M. Burke, S.J. (New York, 1954), pp. 125-126.

Albigensians of southern France, probably transplanted there from a Manichaean sect in Asia Minor called the Paulicians. The Albigensians denied not only that Mary really conceived and gave birth to Jesus, but even that Mary herself was a woman of real flesh and blood. She had, they said, a kind of celestial body, and from her celestial flesh the Word of God was born.[23]

Again in the sixteenth century, Simon Mennon, the founder of the Mennonites, came forth with the doctrine that Jesus was not born of the flesh of Mary; he taught that the man Jesus was somehow produced from the seed of the Eternal Father. Likewise the Puritans reflected in their beliefs this abhorrence of the flesh. Even today Christian Scientists, although they verbally admit the virgin birth, regard matter as an illusion; they hold, moreover, that because evil is always associated with matter, evil too is a delusion of the human mind which can be destroyed only by spiritual understanding.[24]

ARIANS

The Gnostic-Manichaean attack on the real humanity of Christ resulted in the explicit, unequivocal affirmation of Mary's real motherhood: Mary is truly the Mother of Jesus. Moreover, Christians were all along implicitly professing their belief that Mary is the Mother of God in the recitation of the Apostles' Creed: "in Jesus Christ, His only Son our Lord, who was conceived by the Holy Sprit, and born of the Virgin Mary." The first to reject this implication were the Arians. Because they denied that the Word of God who became incarnate was the uncreated Son of the Eternal Father, equal to Him in all things, the Arians denied both Christ's divinity and Mary's divine motherhood.

It is not surprising then to find St. Athanasius (d. 373), who spearheaded the forces of orthodoxy against the Arians, explicitly calling Mary "The Mother of God" (*Theotokos*). Moreover, Athanasius does this with the full awareness of its theological implications, because in the same work against the Arians in which he calls Mary *Theotokos,* he gives theological basis for the doctrine by presenting for the first time the

---

[23] Cf. F. Vernet, *Albigeois*, in *D.T.C.,* Vol. 1, cols. 677-687.

[24] Cf. George Channing, *What is a Christian Scientist?* in *Look,* November 18, 1952, p. 54 ff.

theological explanation of the communication of idioms.[25]

Athanasius was not the first to use the term *Theotokos* of Mary. Earlier patristic writings frequently make use of the term.[26] In the early fourth century, perhaps even in the third century, the faithful themselves were calling on *Maria Theotokos* in the prayer, "We fly to Thy protection, O Holy Mother of God."[27]

NESTORIANISM

Although the doctrine of Mary's divine motherhood was generally believed in the Church for more than a half century before the rise of the Nestorian heresy, it was not defined until after this belief was seriously challenged by the Patriarch of Constantinople. Nestorius himself had been a disciple of Theodore, Bishop of Mopsuestia, who in turn had been a disciple of Diodorus, Bishop of Tarsus. All these men were representative of the Antiochian school of theological thought which found itself in opposition to the school of Alexandria on the question of the human-divine relations in Christ.

The school of Antioch tended to separate too much the human and the divine in Christ. They explained the union of divinity with humanity as a kind of indwelling of the second divine Person in the man Christ. They saw two physical persons in Christ, because He had two natures: "The Son of God is distinct from the son of David"; and this is the heart of the Nestorian heresy.

The Alexandrian school, on the other hand, tended to exaggerate the

---

[25] *Oratio III contra Arianos; PG*, 26, 385, 389, 392-393.

[26] For the use of *Theotokos* in the Eastern Church, I refer the reader to the chapter on Mary in Eastern Patristic Thought in Volume I, pp. 207 ff. One remarkable testimony to the unanimity among the Fathers and ecclesiastical writers on Mary as *Theotokos* is worth mentioning here. John, Patriarch of Antioch, in a letter to his friend Nestorius written after Nestorius had been threatened with excommunication by Pope Celestine in 430, encouraged Nestorius to give up his stubborn attack on the title *Theotokos*. "For," he says, "this title no one of the ecclesiastical doctors has ever rejected. Those who use it are found to be numerous and especially renowned; those who do not use it have never accused those who do use it of any error" (*Epistola ad Nestorium; PG*, 77, 1455).

[27] M. J. Healy, *The Divine Maternity in the Early Church*, in *Marian Studies*, Vol. 6, 1955, pp. 48-51. See also W. J. Burghardt, *Mary in Western Patristic Thought*, in the first volume of this work, p. 147, n. 108.

union of the human with the divine and in the end tried to explain this union as a fusion of two natures into one. They saw only one nature in Christ, because He was only one person; this is Monophysitism. The tendencies within both schools culminated in heresies about Christ, which are equally opposed to Mary's divine motherhood. But opposition to *Maria Theotokos* came only from within the school of Antioch.

According to Diodorus and Theodore, the Word of God dwelt in the man Christ as in a temple; Mary was not the Mother of God; the one whom Mary brought into the world was not the divine Person of the Word, who united in Himself a human nature with the divine, but only the man Christ in whom the Godhead dwelt substantially.

Nestorius' doctrine was a repetition of the teaching of Diodorus and Theodore. Pius XI sets down the teaching of Nestorius as follows: "This extremely proud man claimed that two complete hypostases in Christ, the human of Jesus and the divine of the Word, are united in one common 'person' [*prosopon*], as he termed it, and hence denied that marvelous substantial union of two natures, which we call the hypostatic union. He therefore asserted that the only-begotten Word of God did not become man, but that His presence in human flesh was by way of indwelling, by divine good pleasure, and by power of operation; and therefore He should be called, not God, but *Theophoron* or God-bearer, in much the same way that prophets and other holy men can be called God-bearers because of the divine grace given to them."[28]

---

[28] *Lux veritatis,* in *A.A.S.,* Vol. 23, 1931, pp. 496-497. In recent years there has been considerable discussion as to whether Nestorius really held the doctrine for which he was condemned. In a recent study of the question Father J. L. Shannon, O.S.A. (*Marian Studies,* Vol. 6, 1955, pp. 120-130) concludes that Nestorius was really guilty of the heresy for which he was condemned. In Nestorius' final work, the *Liber Heraclidis,* an attempted justification of his position, the heresiarch says that the title "Mother of God" could be used of Mary if properly explained, but then he proceeds to explain away the title by still denying the orthodox explanation of the hypostatic union. Jugie has this comment on the question: "It would be more than astonishing if both friends and enemies were deceived in this affair, and that having been misunderstood by all his contemporaries the unfortunate Nestorius has been appreciated only by a few choice souls several centuries after his death" (*D.T.C.,* 5, 161-162). Pius XI in his encyclical *Lux Veritatis* has this to say: "It should be clear to all, therefore, that Nestorius really preached heretical doctrines, that the Patriarch of Alexandria was a strenuous defender of the Catholic faith, and that Pope Celestine together with the Council of Ephesus guarded the ancient doctrine and the

Controversy flared to ecumenical proportions only after Nestorius began a series of sermons in Constantinople in defense of his secretary, Anastasius, and Dorotheus, the Bishop of Marcianopolis, both of whom had been preaching to the people that no one should call Mary the Mother of God. With his gift of eloquence and with all the authority to which he could swell as Patriarch of Constantinople, Nestorius did his best to discredit Mary's title as Mother of God. As was to be expected, his teaching caused considerable unrest and confusion among the people who for more than a half century had been calling upon the Mother of God.

But in the providence of God, what St. Irenaeus had been against the Gnostics, St. Athanasius against the Arians, and St. Augustine against the Manichaeans, St. Cyril of Alexandria was to be against the Nestorians. Once alerted to the dangerous doctrine, Cyril began to turn out letters, sermons, and treatises in defense of the true doctrine of the Incarnation and the divine motherhood. He pleaded with Nestorius to heed the Fathers of the Church, who "did not hesitate to call the holy Virgin the Mother of God (*Theotokos*), not as if the nature of the Word or His divinity took origin in being from the holy Virgin; but because He took from her that sacred body animated with an intellectual soul to which He was hypostatically united, the Word is said to be born according to the flesh."[29]

Nestorius could not understand what we call the communication of idioms; how what Christ did as man, e.g., to suffer and to die, could be attributed to the Word of God. He continued to maintain that the exact title of Mary was *Christotokos*, not *Theotokos*.

Cyril's explanation of why the Blessed Virgin is to be called *Theotokos* has become classic in Marian theology:[30]

Therefore the Word indeed was God, but He became also man; and because He was born according to the flesh, because of His humanity it is necessary that she who gave birth to Him should be the Mother of God. For if she did not give birth to God, certainly neither will He be called God who was begotten of her. But if the divine Scriptures call Him

---

supreme authority of the Apostolic See" (*A.A.S.*, Vol. 23, 1931, p. 505).

[29] *Epistola ad Nestorium; PG*, 77, 48-49.

[30] *Scholia de Incarnatione Verbi; PG*, 75, 1400.

God, she then gave birth to God made man, because a man could not otherwise come to be except through generation from a woman. How then is not she who bore Him the Mother of God? That He is true God who was born of her, we learn from the divine Scripture.

Nestorius first, with several letters, and then Cyril too, appealed to the Pope as judge. After a synod at Rome (430) which condemned the teaching of Nestorius, Pope Celestine commissioned Cyril to execute the sentence of excommunication and deposition against Nestorius, unless he retracted his errors within ten days. But when Cyril dispatched his famous "test letter of the anathemas"[31] to Nestorius, the delegation learned that the Emperor Theodotius II had already called a general council for Pentecost (June 7) of the following year (431). Moreover, it seems that Nestorius had meanwhile admitted in some sense the title *Theotokos*. Furthermore, when Cyril's anathemas became known at Constantinople and Antioch, they stirred up a hornet's nest of opposition against Cyril.

THE COUNCIL OF EPHESUS

In spite of considerable opposition, Cyril finally opened the Council on the twenty-second of June, even though the long-awaited papal legates and the Patriarch of Antioch with his suffragans had not yet arrived. In the very first session one of Cyril's doctrinal letters to Nestorius (καταφλυαροῦσι) was read and unanimously approved. Nestorius was declared deposed.[32]

According to historians of the day, on the night of this decree the streets of Ephesus were filled with enthusiastic crowds who waved and shouted: *"Hagia Maria Theotokos"* — "Holy Mary, Mother of God" — a cry that has never died on Catholic lips.

But four days later, John, the Patriarch of Antioch, arrived, and

---

[31] Cf. G. Jouassard, *Marie à travers la patristique*, in *Maria. Études sur la Sainte Vierge*, edited by Hubert du Manoir, S.J., Vol. 1 (Paris, 1949), p. 125 ff.

[32] The words of deposition are striking: "... Our Lord Jesus Christ, outraged by the blasphemous utterances of this man, has defined through this most holy council that the same Nestorius is deprived of the episcopal dignity and is cut off from all priestly association and gathering." Mansi, *Sacrorum Conciliorum nova et amplissima collectio*, 4, 1294-1295.

charging that the Council presided over by Cyril was illegal, organized a separate council favoring Nestorius and condemning Cyril. With the arrival of the papal legates, however, the sessions of the council headed by Cyril were resumed and the acts of the first session were formally approved.

The doctrine formally approved by the Council is contained in the doctrinal letter of Cyril which was read at the first session and unanimously accepted. The letter of the anathemas, although read at this same session, was not proposed for the approval of the Council; the anathemas have doctrinal authority, however, in view of the fact that they were referred to by the Second Council of Constantinople as part of the acts of Ephesus and highly praised.[33]

The most pertinent part of Cyril's doctrinal letter should be given here:[34]

> For we do not say that the nature of the Word became man by undergoing change; nor that it was transformed into a complete man consisting of soul and body. What we say rather, is that by uniting to Himself in His own person a body animated by a rational soul, the Word has become man in an inexpressible and incomprehensible way and has been called the Son of Man; not merely according to will or complacency, but not by merely assuming a person either. And we say that the natures that are brought together into true unity are different; still, from both there is one Christ and Son; not as though the difference between the natures were taken away by the union, but rather both divinity and humanity produce the perfection of our one Lord, Christ and Son, by their inexpressible and mysterious joining into unity. ... It was not that first an ordinary human being was born of the holy Virgin, and then the Word descended upon that man; but in virtue of the union He is said to have undergone birth according to the flesh from His mother's womb, since He claims as His own birth, the generation of His own flesh. ... Thus [the holy Fathers of the Church] have not hesitated to call the holy Virgin *Mother of*

---

[33] The first anathema reads as follows: "If anyone does not profess that Emmanuel is truly God and that the holy Virgin is, therefore, Mother of God (for she gave birth in the flesh to the Word of God made flesh): let him be anathema" (*D.B.*, No. 113). While it is probable that the doctrine of *Maria Theotokos* was not the object of *canonical definition* as such at the Council of Ephesus, the official approval of the doctrine contained in Cyril's letter was the practical equivalent of a definition (cf. G. Jouassard, *art. cit.*, pp. 131, 135).

[34] Mansi, *op. cit.*, 4, 1138; cf. *D.B.*, No. 111a.

226   MARIOLOGY

God (Theotokos).

All famous causes have their famous battle cries, which serve to rally the common mass of men, incapable of comprehending the nice distinctions of theologians and statesmen. In the fourth century good Catholics (most of whom could neither read nor write) could identify themselves by crying, *"Homoousios,"* which meant that Christ is of the same nature as God the Father. In the fifth century, the battle cry was a happy combination of sound theology with one of the most profound devotional instincts in the Church: veneration of Mary on account of her divine motherhood.

After Ephesus *Theotokos* became the hymn of the Christian heart. Sermons resounded, feasts were celebrated, and churches dedicated in honor of *Maria Theotokos*.[35] The memory of the "glorious and ever virgin Mary, Mother of God" began to be commemorated even in the Sacrifice of the Mass.

From Ephesus in 431 to the present day, *"Hagia Maria Theotokos,"* heralded by the Fathers of the fourth century, has proved to be one of the great touchstones of Christian orthodoxy. It demands faith in the true human nature of Christ; otherwise Mary would not be a real mother. It is a confession of the divinity of Mary's Son; otherwise Mary would not be truly the Mother of God. It is a declaration of belief in the hypostatic union of two distinct natures subsisting in the divine Person of the Word of God; otherwise Christ would not be both Son of God and Son of Mary. It likewise proclaims the truth that the hypostatic union took place in the first instant of Mary's conception of her Son; otherwise the Mother of the man Christ would not be truly the Mother of God.

PROTESTANTISM

For over a thousand years after Ephesus the whole Christian world (apart from a few fitful resurgences of a doomed Gnosticism) hailed Mary as God's Mother. Protestants who frequently seem offended by the honors which Catholics give to Mary may be surprised at the following tribute to the Mother of God penned by Martin Luther even after his

---

[35] Cf. M. J. Healy, *art. cit.*, pp. 60-61.

complete separation from the Catholic Church:[36]

> The great thing is none other than that she became the Mother of God; in which process so many and such great gifts are bestowed upon her that no one is able to comprehend them. Thereupon follows all honor, all blessedness, and the fact that in the whole race of men one only person is above all the rest, one to whom no one else is equal. For that reason her dignity is summed up in one phrase when we call her the Mother of God; no one can say greater things of her or to her, even if he had as many tongues as leaves and blades of grass, as stars in heaven and sands on the seashore. It should also be meditated in the heart what that means: to be the Mother of God.

However, Luther was not long out of the Church (1522) before he began to change his attitude toward the Mother of God. He objects to the special honor being paid to her, because it derogates from Christ who alone is our Saviour. Luther still calls Mary the Mother of God, but only "because we cannot all be Mothers of God; otherwise she is on the same level with us."[37]

The first of the Lutheran confessional writings, the *Augsburg Confession* (1530) clearly professes the teaching of Ephesus that "the Word, that is, the Son of God, assumed a human nature in the womb of the Virgin Mary, with the result that there are two natures, the human and divine, inseparably united in the unity of the person, one Christ, truly God and truly man, born of the virgin Mary. ..."[38]

Even in the Formula of Concord (1579), the last of the Lutheran confessional writings, the doctrine of the divine motherhood is given accurate expression: "By reason of the hypostatic union and the communion of natures, Mary the virgin most worthy of praise, brought forth not only a man, but a man who is truly the Son of the Most High God. ... Hence she is truly *Theotokos*, Mother of God, and yet remained

---

[36] Martin Luther, *Die Erklärung des Magnificat* (*Luthers Werke* [ed. Weimar], 7, 546). Cf. Paul Palmer, S.J., *Mary in Protestant Thought*, in *Theological Studies*, Vol. 15, December, 1954, pp. 519-540, esp. 523-531.

[37] *Luthers Werke*, ed. Weimar, Vol. 10, part 3, p. 316.

[38] *Die Bekenntnisschriften der evangelisch-lutherischen Kirche*, 2nd ed. (Göttingen, 1952), p. 54.

a virgin."[39]

But Luther had set the style for Protestants when he attacked the Catholic prayer "Hail Holy Queen" which he regarded as blasphemous. "Your prayers, O Christian," he says, "are as dear to me as hers. And why? Because if you believe that Christ lives in you as much as in her, you can help me as much as she." Eventually Luther was led to limit the communion of saints to the Church on earth because of his complete rejection of any intercessory power on the part of the saints in heaven.

In the course of Protestant history the lesson of Nestorianism was repeated: any derogation from the Mother inevitably leads to a rejection of the truth about the Son. "The Christ and Satan agreed in this," wrote Cardinal Newman, "that Son and Mother went together; and the experience of three centuries has confirmed their testimony, for Catholics, who have honored the Mother, still worship the Son, while Protestants who now have ceased to confess the Son, began then by scoffing at the Mother."[40]

Since the time of Newman, Protestantism has struggled through various phases of sentimentalism, rationalism, and liberalism. In some quarters today, however, there is a tendency to return to the Church of the first four centuries. But even among the "neo-orthodox," we do not find any outright affirmation of Mary's divine motherhood. Paul Tillich, for example, whose opinion about Christ is described as a kind of Nestorianism, does not regard Mary as the Mother of God, nor even as the Mother of Christ. A study of his theology is necessary to understand what he means when he says that Mary is only the Mother of Jesus of Nazareth and that it is this Jesus who is sacrificed to Jesus as the Christ. In Tillich's opinion, Mary has no significance in Protestantism.[41]

Emil Brunner, important neo-orthodox theologian, who looks upon faith not as an acceptance of revealed truth on the authority of God, but as an "encounter with the living Christ," thinks that anything beyond

---

[39] *Ibid.*, p. 1024.

[40] *The Glories of Mary for the Sake of Her Son*, recently reprinted in *The New Eve* (Westminster, Md., 1952), p. 71.

[41] Cf. *Systematic Theology* (Chicago, 1951), Vol. 1, p. 128.

the fact that the Son of God became man is useless speculation.[42] Perhaps for him Mary is the Mother of God, but never does he give her the title.

Karl Barth, who is suspected by some Protestants of "crypto-Catholicism," speaks of and unhesitatingly defends the "dogma of the Virgin Birth" and the Incarnation of the Son of God, but never speaks of Mary as Mother of God. Will he ever take the logical step and affirm the divine motherhood itself?

The phrase "Mother of God" continues to frighten most Protestants. A recent survey of the present position of Protestantism in the United States gives some indication of the variety of Protestant opinion today.[43] Of the one hundred replies which were received from a questionnaire sent out to Protestant ministers and professors of theology, only twenty-two professed belief in Mary's divine motherhood; over half of these were Episcopalians. Fifteen did not make their answer clear. Sixty-three denied Mary this privilege.

Undoubtedly one of the foremost objections to the title, Mother of God, springs from a lack of conviction about the divinity of Christ Himself. When pressed with the question, whether Christ is God in exactly the same sense that the Father is God, most Protestants in the United States today will hedge, or at least hesitate, if not give an outright negative answer. Their thinking in this matter is very much akin to Nestorianism.

Other Protestant difficulties stem from rejection or at least a misunderstanding of the nature and role of tradition and the development of dogma in the Church. To the fundamentalist, Scripture is the sole rule of faith. If he does not find a truth explicitly contained in the Scriptures, he is at least skeptical about it. As one Protestant writer says: "He (the Protestant) cannot but be impressed by the considerable disproportion which exists between the attitude of biblical writers with regard to the Virgin and the veneration sometimes tantamount to

---

[42] *The Christian Doctrine of Creation and Redemption, Dogmatics* (tr. by Olive Wyon, Philadelphia, 1952), Vol. 2, 363.

[43] Kenneth F. Dougherty, S.A., *Contemporary American Protestant Attitudes toward the Divine Maternity,* in *Marian Studies,* Vol. 6, 1955, pp. 137-163.

worship that is paid to her...."[44] A widespread misconception of Catholic teaching among Protestants today is that Catholic Mariology "divinizes" Mary; some writers who should know better continue to use the term "Mariolatry." As recently as May 25, 1955, we find 906 lay and clerical commissioners of the Presbyterian Church in the United States, gathered in assembly in Los Angeles, approving unanimously the following statement:[45]

> In the figure of the Virgin the church of Rome has created a semidivine female being who becomes virtual head of the church, the hope of all who are distressed and the sovereign overlord of all that occurs in history. The devotion to Mary now equals, and even exceeds, the devotion to Christ himself.

Although the rejection of tradition is almost invariably accompanied by an opposition to the veneration of the Mother of God, a new trend is discernible in the work of the Protestant theologian, Max Thurian, of the Reformed Church of France. Although critical of the special privileges of "the Mother of the Lord" as proclaimed in the unfolding tradition of the Church, Thurian has taken a strong stand in favor of introducing Mary into Protestant piety and worship. He asks his co-religionists to put aside their fears of the Blessed Virgin Mary, and calls them to task for not realizing in themselves Mary's prophecy, "Behold, henceforth all nations shall call me blessed." If Protestants would follow Thurian's lead, "Catholic Mariology would no longer remain 'the most agonizing problem for ecumenical thought.' "[46]

We hope that the Spirit of ecumenism (the Holy Spirit) will eventually lead the Protestant world back to the teaching of Ephesus which is recapitulated in a remarkable passage by Pius XI in his encyclical commemorating the fifteenth centenary of the Council:[47]

> ... He who was conceived in the womb of the Virgin by the action of the Holy Spirit, He who is born and is laid in the crib, who called Himself

---

[44] *Ways of Worship. A Report of a Theological Commission of Faith and Order* (London, 1951), pp. 289-291.

[45] From the text printed in the convention program.

[46] Paul Palmer, S.J., *Mary in Protestant Thought*, in *Theological Studies*, Vol. 15, 1954, p. 540.

[47] *Lux Veritatis*, in *A.A.S.*, Vol. 23, 1931, pp. 506-507, 511, 513.

the Son of Man, who suffered and died nailed to the cross, is the same identical person who is called in a wonderful and solemn manner "My Beloved Son," who with divine power forgives sin, who by His own power restores the sick to health and recalls the dead to life.

All this clearly shows that in Christ there are two natures from which proceed divine and human actions. Likewise it shows no less clearly that Christ is one, God and likewise man, through that unity of the divine person in virtue of which He is called the God-Man (Theanthropos). ...

From this principle of Catholic doctrine ... there necessarily follows the dogma of the divine motherhood which we predicate of the Blessed Virgin Mary ...

If the Son of the Blessed Virgin Mary is God, she certainly who bore Him should rightly and deservingly be called Mother of God. If in Jesus Christ there is only one person and that divine, surely Mary is not only Mother of Christ but she should be called the Mother of God, *Theotokos*. The woman who was saluted by Elizabeth, her relative, as "Mother of my Lord," who is said by the Martyr Ignatius to have brought forth God, from whom Tertullian says God was born, we can all venerate as the benign Mother of God, whom the eternal Godhead favored with fullness of grace and honored with so much dignity.

WHY GOD WISHED TO HAVE A MOTHER

In treating any theological truth, a theologian must not only establish the fact that the proposition is true and contained somehow in authentic sources of divine revelation, but he must also try to find the divine reasons why the proposition is true so that the truth revealed by God may be assimilated by the human intellect operating under the light of faith; *fides quaerit intellectum*. What, then, must have been God's reasons for wanting to have a human mother? We can best approach the answer to this question by looking into God's own plan for the Redemption of mankind.

To restore His creation which had been ruined by man's sin, God called upon the infinity of His love and the omnipotence of His divine artistry. Unlike the human artist, who can only imperfecdy represent his idea in matter, the Father of heaven and earth could put His very own Living Idea, His Eternal Word, into the very materials of His creation to remold it into His own image with infinitely greater beauty. In taking to Himself human flesh, the Eternal Word summed up within Himself the whole hierarchy of reality — matter and spirit, body and soul, the human and divine, creature and Creator — in order to restore harmony to the world in the Image of God. The mystery of the Word-made-flesh became the supreme communication of God's wisdom and love to a disintegrated world and opened up for man a vision of the goodness and beauty of every part of creation when rebuilt in the Eternal Image of God.

The flesh assumed by the Word for the Redemption of mankind was not newly created out of nothing, but taken from the stock of Adam in whose flesh sin and death entered the world. For omnipotent love had decreed that the same flesh which through sin had become subject to corruption and death would be instrumental in its own redemption and resurrection. Divine respect for the creature of His making decided that the nature which had fallen should be lifted back to God by the very same nature, so that the victory over the world, the flesh, and the devil could be the achievement of the human race.[48] Infinite justice had ruled that no other flesh than that belonging to the one human family should be fashioned for the redeeming Word of God, because no other flesh had sinned; nor would any other flesh be offered in the holocaust of sacrifice;[49] for no other flesh had to be saved.[50] In this economy of divine love it was necessary that the redeeming Image of the Father be of the same family as those who perished in Adam; the Son of God must become a son of Adam; God's own Son must be born of a human mother.

In the divine plan the process of restoration was to be an exact counterpart of the process of the fall, a counteraction paralleling and corresponding inversely to the action of the fall — somewhat like the

---

[48] Cf. St. Thomas Aquinas, *Sum. Theol.*, III, q. 4, a. 6.

[49] Cf. St. Ambrose, *De Incarnationis Dominicae sacramento liber unus*, 6, 54; *PL*, 16, 832: "From us He (Christ) received what as His very own He offered in our behalf, so that He might redeem us out of what was ours and confer upon us what was not ours out of His own possessions."

[50] Cf. St. Irenaeus, *Adversus haereses*, 3, 21, 10; *PG*, 7, 955: "... Why then did not God again take up dust [out of which to fashion His body as was the case with the first Adam] instead of bringing about His enfleshment from Mary? It was so that no other flesh should be made, nor any other flesh should be saved; but the very same flesh [as had sinned in Adam] was to be recapitulated [in Him] and the analogy preserved."

untying of a knot.[51] A virgin had co-operated in the ruin of men by heeding an angel in disobedience to God; likewise, then, a virgin should co-operate in redeeming the world by believing an angel in obedience to God.[52] As the ruin caused by Adam could not have spread to his progeny apart from the motherhood of Eve, so salvation, as it was willed by the Father, would be given to the race only through the motherhood of the New Eve.

These are but a few of the divine reasons why God wanted to have a human mother. They give us a glimpse into the riches of divine omnipotence and wisdom and justice and merciful love that have gone into an economy of salvation which required that God should have a mother. In this plan He becomes like us in all things except sin, even to a point of having a mother of His own to cherish and love; and on our part, we can more naturally approach Him since we know Him as a baby in His Mother's arms. He can and does love us with a kind of natural love for His human brothers.[53] He can give us an example of obedience to His Mother, of humility in subjection to parental authority, of divine life in a human family. What greater proof could He give that He had a real human body like our own? And what greater inspiration could be given men to respect all womankind than to see one of them elevated to the greatest dignity that God's omnipotent wisdom can confer upon a human person?

II. THE ESSENCE OF THE DIVINE MOTHERHOOD

Thus far we have only made a beginning in our study of the divine motherhood. We have seen that both Scripture (at least implicitly) and Tradition teach that Mary is truly the Mother of God, and that this doctrine has been the object of the infallible teaching authority of the Church for over 1500 years. But if we are to understand more fully why

---

[51] This aspect of the divine plan was developed to a remarkable degree already by St. Irenaeus. See Volume 1, pp. 123-126 for Fr. Burghardt's summary of the theology of "recapitulation," as it is called, in Western patristic thought.

[52] Cf. Tertullian, *De carne Christi*, 17; *PL*, 2, 728; also Irenaeus, *Adversus haereses*, 5, 19, 1; *PG*, 7, 1175-1176; also *Adversus haereses*, 3, 21, 10: *PG*, 7, 954-955.

[53] Cf. St. Thomas Aquinas, *op. cit.*, II-II, q. 26, a. 8. See also Maximus Taurinensis, *Sermo* 29, *PL*, 57, 594: "... in Christo enim caro nostra nos diligit, ..."

the divine motherhood is the greatest dignity that can be conferred on a created person, why it is Mary's greatest privilege, and the reason for all her other privileges,[54] then it is necessary to probe more deeply into the nature of the divine motherhood in order to determine its very essence.

Here we are at the very heart of Mariology. For as has been shown in a previous chapter, the divine motherhood is the basic principle of Mariology. If a principle is to be used with the precision demanded by science, its essential content must be clearly determined. But, surprising as it may seem, not all theologians agree on what constitutes the essence of the divine motherhood.

According to the common opinion, the divine motherhood consists essentially in the relationship which Mary has to the Word of God Incarnate, because she has conceived Him as her Son. This relationship is a real relation having the person of Mary as its real subject, the divine Person of Jesus as its real term, and Mary's action of generating Him as its real foundation; as is evident, the subject (Mary) and the term (the Son of God Incarnate) are really distinct. No other element is necessary for the constitution of a real relation. This relation, moreover, is intrinsically supernatural; for to have a divine Person as the term of human generation is altogether beyond the natural capacities of human nature.

The point to make note of in the common opinion is that the real foundation of Mary's relationship to her Son is located in her action of generating the Son of God.[55] For while *all* theologians agree that the divine motherhood consists essentially in a real supernatural relation of Mary to her Son, not all agree that the proper foundation of this relationship is her generative action.

The mother-child relationship in which motherhood consists, the state of being a mother, we may call (1) *actual motherhood*. It is to be distinguished from (2) *potential motherhood,* which includes all those

---

[54] Cf. Pius XI, *Lux Veritatis*, in *A.A.S.*, Vol. 23, 1931, p. 513.

[55] See especially among modern theologians: J. M. Bover, S.J., *La gracia de la Divina Maternidad*, in *Estudios Marianos*, Vol. 5, 1946, pp. 147-164; Severino M. Ragazzini, O.F.M.Conv., *La Divina Maternità di Maria* (Roma-Forlì, 1948); pp. 20-24, 74-89; Guillermo Rozo, C.M.F., *Sancta Maria Mater Dei* (Mediolani-Tridenti, 1943), pp. 24-30.

elements belonging to motherhood by way of remote or proximate preparation for motherhood; (3) *motherhood in fieri* (sometimes called the physical aspect of motherhood): the act of conception in virtue of which a woman becomes an actual mother; (4) *the operations or functions belonging to actual motherhood,* such as bringing forth the child, caring for him until he has reached manhood, and loving him always as a son.

In purely human motherhood there can be no question of a real relation or bond between mother and child before the child is constituted in existence at the term of conception; for no real relation can exist before the child exists as its term. But in divine motherhood which involves the conception of a pre-existent Person, the question arises whether the relation of motherhood cannot precede conception. For if actual motherhood is a bond between the person of the mother and the child, such a relation might exist between Mary and her Son in the very action of conception which is prior by nature to the constitution of the Child as Man. Such a relation might even exist from the first instant of Mary's life since Mary was united to her Son even from that moment in virtue of her predestination as physical Mother of God.

It is surprising to discover how many theologians have taught that Mary was somehow constituted Mother of God by a perfection infused in her which preceded in nature or even in time His constitution as Man. To mention just a few of the more prominent, we find a doctrine of this sort taught by Fathers Sylvester de Saavedra, O. de M.,[56] and M. J. Scheeben,[57] and in recent years even more emphatically by Fathers J. M. Alonso, C.M.F.,[58] and J. M. Delgado Varela, O. de M.[59] Their teaching

---

[56] Sylvester de Saavedra, O. de M., *Sacra Deipara, seu de eminentissima dignitate Deigenetricis immaculatissimae* (Lugduni, 1655).

[57] M. J. Scheeben, *Handbuch der katholischen Dogmatik,* Vol. 3 (Freiburg i. Br., 1882), esp. nn. 1588-1609.

[58] J. M. Alonso, C.M.F., *Hacia una Mariología trinitaria: dos escuelas,* in *Estudios Marianos,* Vol. 10, 1950, pp. 141-191; Vol. 12, 1952, pp. 237-267. See also his article, *Naturaleza y fundamento de la gracia de la Virgen,* in *Estudios Marianos,* Vol. 5, 1946, pp. 11-110.

[59] J. M. Delgado Varela, O. de M., *Maternidad formalmente sanctificante (origen y desenvolvimiento de la controversia),* in *Estudios Marianos,* Vol. 8, 1949, pp. 133-184. Cf. also by the same author: *En torno al sistema mariológico de Saavedra (actos "ad extra") y sobrenaturaleza de la divina maternidad* in *Estudios,* Vol. 3, 1947, pp. 25-38; *Sylvestre de Saavedra y su concepto de maternidad divina,* in *Estudios Marianos,* Vol. 4, 1945, pp. 521-

reflects the thought of St. Peter Chrysologus: "... And was she not a mother before His conception, who was a virgin mother after His birth? Or when was she not a mother who conceived the Author of the World?"[60]

1. *Saavedra.* The problem of determining more accurately the essence of the divine motherhood has come into prominence in recent discussions about the divine motherhood as a *formal* principle of Mary's holiness. In this regard many Spanish theologians have turned back to study the work of Sylvester de Saavedra, O. de M., whose work had gathered dust on their shelves for two centuries.

According to Saavedra, the most basic element, the fundamental grace of divine motherhood, is a corporeal form infused into the generative potency of the Virgin Mary, putting her in first act for the generation of the God-man. With fuller actuation of this same grace Mary conceives her Son, thus giving rise to her Mother-Son relationship.[61]

It would seem, therefore, that according to Saavedra the relationship of motherhood in Mary is founded not precisely on her generative action, but on the enduring corporeal form infused into her generative potency. However, what has especially interested present-day theologians in Saavedra is his doctrine that the divine motherhood is a formal participation in the fecundity of the Eternal Father. The development of this point will be taken up later.

2. *Scheeben.* Whereas Saavedra looked upon the divine motherhood especially from its aspect of assimilating the Virgin Mother to the Eternal Father through a formal participation in His fecundity, M. J. Scheeben, the greatest theologian of the nineteenth century, considered the divine motherhood as a relationship of union with the Word of God, a union which is the primary analogue of the hypostatic union.[62]

Scheeben describes the divine motherhood as the supernatural distinguishing mark of Mary's person. It is more than a mere privilege

---

558.

[60] *Serm. 146; PL,* 52, 592.

[61] Cf. Delgado Varela, *Maternidad formalmente santificante* ..., in *Estudios Marianos,* Vol. 8, 1949, pp. 137, n. 16; 155-159.

[62] M. J. Scheeben, *op. cit.,* nn. 1589-1590.

or office entrusted to her by God. It involves the highest service a mere creature can offer to God. For in her motherhood Mary co-operates in the birth of the most perfect Son that can be born, and touches the very confines of the divinity. In union with the Eternal Father she conceives His Son in her womb. The Son makes the perfect gift of Himself to Mary, giving Himself to be her Son, clothing Himself with her flesh in her womb.

The mutual giving of the persons of the *Word* and *Mary* to each other in mutual consent can be described only as a divine marriage. Mary possesses the Word who gives Himself to her as her Son, and "forms with her an organic oneness," in which Mary is His closest associate and helper in the most intimate and permanent community of life.[63]

Mary is Bride and Mother of the Word: Bride because she is Mother, and Mother because she is Bride. These two aspects are indissolubly associated in Mary; one element cannot be adequately conceived without the other. These two elements taken together constitute what Scheeben calls the supernatural distinguishing mark of Mary's person.[64]

Mary's state as Bride, specifically designed to achieve and complete her Motherhood, is a spiritual and personal union with the Word. This bridal union is described in terms of a "sacramental" marriage (*matrimonium ratum*) between Mary and the Word, a real objective consecration and anointing, by which the Word is already made her own Son by right. These divine nuptials do not merely prepare or place in prospect the actual divine motherhood, but already give it *virtually* and *radically*. In this form the divine motherhood is possessed by Mary from the first moment of her existence.[65]

Mary's divine brideship reaches its perfect completion, however, only with the infusion of the Word into her body to make her actually His Mother. This perfected union with the Word, described as a

---

[63] *Ibid.*, n. 1588.

[64] *Ibid.*, n. 1597; cf. Charles Feckes, *The Mystery of the Divine Motherhood* (New York, 1941), pp. 65-66; also by the same author, M. J. Scheeben, *théologien de la mariologie moderne*, in *Maria. Études sur la Sainte Vierge*, ed. by H. du Manoir, S.J., Vol. 3 (Paris, 1954), pp. 555-571; also E. Druwé, S.J., *Position et structure du Traité Marial*, in *Bulletin de la Société Française d'Études Mariales*, Vol. 2, 1936, esp. pp. 26-27.

[65] M. J. Scheeben, *op. cit.*, n. 1590.

"completed" marriage (*matrimonium consummatum*), is the most perfect image of the hypostatic union.[66] However, the spiritual union, which is intensified by the Word actually taking flesh in her body, is formal with respect to the bodily union; for in its purely physiological aspects the divine motherhood does not reveal the most proper foundation of the dignity of Mary's motherhood.[67]

The formal perfection by which Mary's Bridal Motherhood is constituted is not merely an accident or a moral relation; it is in a sense an "hypostatic, substantial or essential distinguishing mark" of Mary's person, due to her spiritual union with the Word dwelling in her with whom she is formed into one organic whole. By reason of this union the whole dignity and perfection of Mary is determined, even her substantial individuality.[68]

Thus the divine motherhood is substantial in content, mode, and time. Fundamentally it is the divine substance of her Son infused into her. His divine Person is joined with her in a substantial manner; He becomes "grown together with her" as a fruit with its root, and dwells bodily in her. Mary is endowed with this substantial grace from the beginning of her existence, making her always the bride of the Person of the Word, so that this relation to His Person conditions and determines her whole being, elevating it to the hypostatic order.[69]

Mary's motherhood then consists formally in an entirely unique union with uncreated grace, a bridal, spiritual union of Mary with her Son. The proper foundation of Mary's Mother-Son relationship to the Word is a grace given her in the first instant of her creation.

According to both Saavedra and Scheeben, although the full realization of divine motherhood is a Mother-Son relation of Mary to the

---

[66] *Ibid.*, n. 1589.

[67] *Ibid.*, n. 1609.

[68] *Ibid.*, nn. 1602, 1591.

[69] *Ibid.*, n. 1603. Scheeben's idea of a bridal union between Mary and the Word has no foundation in Scripture or patristic tradition. Hence there is a real difficulty in accepting his analysis of the divine motherhood as being essentially a bridal motherhood. See F. M. Braun, O.P., *Marie et l'Église, d'après l'Écriture*, in *Bulletin de la Société Française d'Études Mariales*, Vol. 10, 1952, pp. 7-21, esp. pp. 15-16; also Y. M.-J. Congar, O.P., *Marie et l'Église dans la pensée patristique*, in *Revue des Sciences Philosophiques et Théologiques*, Vol. 38, 1954, pp. 3-38, esp. p. 19.

Word, the root and perfection of this relationship is found in a grace infused into Mary's body (Saavedra) or soul (Scheeben) antecedent either in nature (Saavedra) or also in time (Scheeben) to Mary's action of generating her Son. While Saavedra looks upon this relationship as primarily assimilating Mary to the Eternal Father as generating principle of the only Son of God, Scheeben considers this relationship primarily as an assimilation to the Son in the closest possible union between a created and a divine person.

3. *M. J. Nicolas, O.P.* In the present century the most illuminating presentation of the notion of the divine motherhood has been given by Father M. J. Nicolas, O.P.[70] He exposes the fallacy of considering Mary's motherhood as consisting primarily in a *relationship of union* with the Word Incarnate; it is rather a relation of origin, even of opposition, as we shall see. Moreover, he presents a different explanation of the foundation for the Mother-Son relation in Mary.

According to Father Nicolas, Mary is Mother because she has conceived a man and has thus become the original principle of human flesh in a person distinct from her. She is Mother of God, because she has conceived the Son of God whom she has not called into existence, but who has drawn her to Himself, clothing Himself with her flesh in her womb. Father Nicolas distinguishes between the essential and the integral concept of the divine motherhood. Essentially the divine motherhood consists in "the assumption of her human motherhood" by the Son of God. The "assumptive action" by which the human nature of Christ is made to subsist in the Word, at the same time constitutes Mary formally and physically the Mother of God. The "assumptive action" itself is entirely incommunicable, and in no way elevates Mary's generative action itself in its intrinsic efficacy, but only in its term.[71]

The supernatural reality which is conferred on Mary by the assumption of her human motherhood is the foundation of a relation whose term is essentially separated from the person of Mary. This relation is not a relation of union, but of origin, even of opposition.[72] For

---

[70] M.-J. Nicolas, O.P., *Le concept intégral de maternité divine*, in *Revue Thomiste*, Vol. 42, 1937, pp. 58-93, 230-272.

[71] *Ibid.*, pp. 64-66.

[72] *Ibid.*, p. 241.

the person terminating a generative action is separated from the person who conceives him at the very instant the new human nature appears with personal being. The proper effect of generative action is *precisely* separation, for it terminates at the person only in giving him existence apart in a determined nature. Mary therefore is not "substantially" united to the divine Word. The instant the hypostatic union is realized, the flesh substantially sanctified is no longer Mary's flesh, although it proceeds immediately from her and preserves this *élan* of origin. Still the two substances are joined in the closest possible way.[73]

Thus the divine motherhood, considered in its essence, is not a *union* with the Word Incarnate. Rather it is a relation of origin, founded upon a supernatural reality which stands midway between two orders of union with God, namely the hypostatic union and the accidental, intentional union realized through sanctifying grace. In its very essence divine motherhood is faced toward the grace of the hypostatic union.

The divine motherhood itself, however, can be called a union with the Word only so far as it is a kind of possession by way of physical right to union with the Word in knowledge and love. This right is essential to a Mother whose Son is God. The supernatural physical reality, which is the foundation of the Mother-Son relationship, demands the union of Mary with her Son, but it does not formally realize this union.[74]

Thus, according to Father Nicolas, the divine motherhood is essentially a Mother-divine Son relationship of origin, of immediate consanguinity. Its foundation is not Mary's generative action, but the ineffaceable supernatural modification in Mary following upon the generation of a divine Person. While Mary could not be the Mother of God except through her generative activity, it is only consequent upon this activity as it terminates in a divine Person that Mary possesses the enduring supernatural reality grounding her real relationship to her divine Son. Whereas Saavedra and Scheeben conceive the foundation of the Mother-Son relationship as antecedent at least by nature to the action of generation, Nicolas understands this foundation as subsequent to the generative action.

---

[73] *Ibid.*, p. 242.
[74] *Ibid.*, p. 243.

MARY'S DIVINE MOTHERHOOD

Here we have considered just a few of the more important attempts on the part of theologians to determine more accurately the essence of the divine motherhood. All agree that the divine motherhood consists somehow in the relationship of Mary to her Son and that it necessarily involved in one way or another her generation of the God-Man. But in their analysis of the idea they arrive at different explanations as to what is the precise perfection or activity within Mary which in the most proper sense is the ground or foundation for the relationship called the divine motherhood. Here we are faced with the deepest problem in Mariology.

Is the proper foundation of Mary's divine motherhood the action itself of generating the God-Man? Or is it the grace itself which elevates and/or actuates Mary's generative power in the very conception of the God-Man? Or is it some modification of Mary's substance in the first instant of her existence, a grace radically determining her character as Mother, uniting her spiritually to the Word in a kind of vital union which achieves its fullness of expression with the infusion of the Word into her body? Or, finally, is it a supernatural reality which Mary has consequent upon her act of generating the God-Man?

First of all, it seems clear that the perfection (whatever it is) upon which the relationship of motherhood is grounded must be actually in Mary. For motherhood is something which endures. Mary is *still* really Mother of God. A relation is real and actual only if it has a real subject, a real term, and a real foundation; nobody doubts this point. But to be real, at least in this context, means to be actually existing. Certainly the term "real" means actually existing when applied to subject and term of a real relation. Why should its meaning be changed when in the same definition it is applied to the foundation? It follows, then, that a relation without an *existing* foundation is not a real relation.[75]

---

[75] Among the best modern studies of the nature of relation are: Juan B. Manyá, *Metafísica de la relación 'In Divinis,'* in *Revista Española de Teología*, Vol. 5, 1945, pp. 249-284, and A. Krempel, *La doctrine de la relation chez Saint Thomas* (Paris, 1952). That the foundation of a real relation must *actually* exist so long as the relation is said to be real seems to need comment. A foundation is what here and now *determines* the kind of relationship (after the manner of a formal cause) and gives it whatever actual perfection it has. Hence a relationship without an *existing* foundation would not be a real relationship. This point is illustrated with special force in such relationships as similarity. For if the foundation

It is not surprising, then, to see a tendency among modern theologians to place some enduring perfection in Mary which permanently grounds her motherhood by reason of which she *is* and *ever will be* Mother of God.

To place this perfection in Mary antecedent to her conception of the God-Man, as being the root and source of both her conception and her relationship of motherhood does not seem to be the answer to the problem. For Mary can be called actual Mother of God only at the term of her generative action when the Word of God is constituted as her Son. Before that, He was not her Son, regardless of what other relationship she may have had to the Word.

Even the fact that Mary was predestined from all eternity to be the Mother of God does not put anything in Mary whereby she could be called actual Mother of God before she conceived the God-Man. Predestination, as St. Thomas reminds us, is not something in the one predestined, but in the one who predestines.[76] Nor can her conception precisely as a *future* action ground any real relation in Mary because what is future has as yet no real being.[77] Mary was prepared, of course, for the dignity of divine motherhood by her Immaculate Conception; but neither does this preparation give her actual motherhood any more than the preparation preceding the reception of sanctifying grace gives us actual divine adoption.

If, then, the relationship of motherhood is one of mother to child, the Word cannot properly be called Mary's Son nor can Mary properly be called His Mother, until she has conceived Him. To say that the perfection which grounds Mary's relationship to her Son is antecedent to her conception of Him is the same as saying that it is not the proper foundation of the divine motherhood itself. Thus Scheeben is led to distinguish the bridal, spiritual union of Mary with the Word from her strictly maternal union, although he says these aspects of divine motherhood are indissolubly connected with each other. Many other

---

for the similarity of two things ceases to exist, then the two things are no longer similar. We can say that as long as the foundation existed, the two things were similar, but when the foundation ceased to exist, their similarity became a thing of the past.

[76] Cf. *Sum. Theol.*, I, q. 23, a. 2.
[77] Cf. A. Krempel, *op. cit.*, pp. 217-218.

difficulties are involved in putting the perfection which grounds the divine motherhood in something antecedent to Mary's conception of the God-Man.[78] But here we cannot consider them.

Next, is Mary's activity in generating the God-Man the proper foundation of the relationship of Mary to her Son? Theologians commonly say *yes*. But the difficulty involved in this opinion is that the generative action in question is transient and passing, therefore no longer existing in Mary as a ground for her motherhood. Of course, it will always be true of Mary that she *did* generate the God-Man. But can an action in the past be the real foundation of a relation existing in the present?[79]

In general, we can say that if the foundation of the real relation ceases to be, the relation ceases to be real. But the generative action in Mary was a transient action which ceased with the constitution of the Word as man in her womb. Hence Mary's generative action cannot be the foundation of Mary's divine motherhood, for then it would follow that Mary's relation to her Son would no longer be a real relation!

St. Thomas helps us with the difficulty. He explains that "there are some relations which do not arise from actions insofar as they are in act, but rather insofar as they have been in the past; as some one is called a father after the effect of his action (the child) is produced. *And such relations are founded upon that which remains in the agent by reason of the action*, be it a disposition or a habit or some right or power or some such other thing."[80]

Accordingly, the perfection which actually and properly grounds the enduring relationship of the divine motherhood in Mary is something which is left in Mary as a result of her act of generating the God-Man.

Among modern theologians only Father Nicolas, so far as I can ascertain, has adequately stressed this point: namely, that the actual and proper foundation of the relationship called the divine motherhood is a perfection (supernatural, of course) which is in Mary consequent upon

---

[78] Cf. G. Van Ackeren, S.J., *Does the Divine Maternity Formally Sanctify Mary's Soul*, in *Marian Studies*, Vol. 6, 1955, p. 83.

[79] Cf. A. Kremple, *op. cit.*, pp. 221-223.

[80] *In III Sent.*, d. 8, a. 5; ed. Moos, n. 59.

her conception of the God-Man.[81] This supernatural perfection is the reason why Mary actually *is* and *forever will be* Mother of God. This point is of a special importance to all the followers of both Scotus and St. Thomas. For according to these theologians a real relation considered in its formal character precisely as relation (*esse ad*) prescinds from perfection.[82] A relation derives whatever actual perfection it has from its foundation.

If this doctrine about relation is true, then the permanent foundation in Mary on which her actual motherhood is grounded is what *actually*

---

[81] M. J. Nicolas, O.P., *art. cit.*, pp. 83-90; especially the following (pp. 84-85): "That which remains between a mother and her son is a relation. But the foundation of this relation also remains, which is not the transient act of motherhood, but the real and ineffaceable modification of this woman by this act. It will be always true that she has given him birth and in the manner we have said. Sometimes we have the wrong conception of the metaphysical permanence of the past in the present; it is founded on the indefinable identity of the subject with itself in the course of its changes. We remain, in effect, affected by each of the acts in which our personality is engaged, independently of the material or psychological traces which they have been able to leave. Nothing can bring it about that a past thing has not been. When this thing is a modification of a substance nothing can bring it about that this substance has not been modified. When in the supreme unfolding of its activity, it itself is given in its effect, nothing can destroy the reality of this origin. The being depends on the second cause only in its becoming: It preserves, however, towards it a permanent relation, an inferior but real imitation of its total and necessary dependence with regard to the First Cause. The memory in higher beings is only the psychological translation of this permanence of the past, just as simple knowledge is the psychological translation of present reality. And this is why the personality is so bound up with the memory that every other reality has been denied it except to be the perception of a succession of phenomena in their connection.

"The connection of the child with its mother is then a real bond, and the relation which relates one to the other is founded on a foundation as enduring as their own substance. Their immediate consubstantiality is a reality of the metaphysical order. We are rooted in our origins. We are still living in virtue of the original vital *élan*. When a being is one of those which has not always been, it is necessary to know how to read in it beyond what it actually is."

[82] Cf. Scotus, *In I Sent.*, d. 8, 2. 4; *Quodl.*, q. 5; St. Thomas, *De potentia*, q. 7, a. 9, ad 7. For a more extensive treatment of the teaching of Scotus, see E. Longpré, O.F.M., *De B. Virginis maternitate et relatione ad Christum*, in *Antonianum*, Vol. 7, 1932, pp. 289-313; C. Koser, O.F.M., *De constitutivo formali maternitatis B. Mariae Virginis*, in *Alma Socia Christi*, Vol. 11, 1953, pp. 79-114, esp. pp. 89-114; M. Müller, O.F.M., *Das reale Sohnschaftsverhältnis Christi zu Maria*, in Wissenschaft und Weisheit, Vol. 4, 1937, pp. 264-270.

gives her her sublime perfection and dignity as Mother of God. Her action of generating the God-Man then is not intrinsic to her dignity as Mother of God, but is to be regarded rather as belonging in the order of efficient causality with respect to her motherhood.

In order to understand better the perfection which is left in Mary from her action of generating the God-Man, the perfection which is the foundation of her divine motherhood, we must consider more accurately the nature of human motherhood itself. St. Thomas tells us that such relationships as paternity and maternity, which arise from action, are founded upon what remains in the agent from the action performed. This, he says, is a disposition or a habit or right or power or some such thing.[83] To my knowledge, no one except Father Nicolas has tried to describe what sort of perfection is left in a mother by reason of generating a child.[84] To describe it in terms of a modification in her body, insofar as what was part of her body is now part of her offspring, is true but incomplete. For the operation of generation is an operation of the human composite. Its radical principle is not the body as such but the composite of body and spiritual soul. Hence the result of such an operation in the agent is something in the composite, affecting both soul and body.

Generative activity, whose most striking side is so concerned with matter and the senses, has a whole interior and spiritual side governed by laws of the spirit, laws founded upon the very nature of man's being. For this reason it is metaphysically impossible for a man to make any purely animal use of his generative power which is not inhuman. If a woman conceives a child in violation of the laws of her spiritual nature and/or in any other way than by human consent, then her action of conception is not fully human.

Unlike a substance or essence, which if it exists at all, necessarily possesses its complete substantial perfection, an action or habit can exist in varying degrees of perfection.[85] Human generation is an action; of its very nature it is an action of the spirit as well as of the flesh. It consists

---

[83] *In III Sent.*, d. 8, a. 5; ed. Moos, n. 59.

[84] *Art. cit.*, pp. 84-89.

[85] Note that even the same specific substances can exist with diverse *existential* perfection, as is the case with our human nature and the human nature of Christ.

in some activity of the spiritual forces of the soul, at least insofar as the spiritual soul is the substantial form of the physical principle of generation. But the spiritual element will be so much the more perfect as this spirituality passes more and more perfectly into act through the explicit conscious ordination of the generative function to the end inscribed in it by nature. Such ordination to an end supposes that the end be consciously known and loved, so that the spirit loves and wills precisely what the body begets.[86]

By its very nature the generative act requires the operation of the spirit and finds therein the perfection of its operation. While this role of the spirit is imperfect owing to the frailty of fallen nature, its existence is a necessity and its absence a privation. If we take the case of two women, one of whom wills what she conceives, and the other conceives contrary to her will, although both generate a child, nevertheless the action of the one is very imperfect in comparison with the action of the other. In the one case generation is truly human, in the other it is simply an action of a human being. Although both actions verify the definition of generation, nevertheless in their concrete existence, one verifies the definition in a more perfect way than the other. Moreover, the effects produced by these actions in the souls of the two mothers will differ greatly in perfection. If an act of human generation, however, is *perfect in its specific perfection*, it necessarily participates in the knowledge and love of the spirit.[87]

In Mary, as in every mother, the action of generating her Son was an action in which both her spirit and her flesh took an essential part. But spirituality of her nature alone, however, was not enough for Mary to become the Mother of God. Spirituality in act was necessary, because, as we shall see, by her conception Mary attained the divine Person of the

---

[86] Cf. M.-J. Nicolas, O.P., *art. cit.*, p. 76.

[87] Father Nicolas (*ibid.*, p. 75) regards the spiritual acts of the soul in human generation as extrinsic to the essence of the generative act. I regard this spiritual element as intrinsic to the generative action itself, if it is human action. The action itself is composite, possessing a unity not of essence but of order, in which the spiritual element is formal with respect to the material. Both elements are essential. But the perfection of the action is to be measured by the perfection of the spiritual, formal element rather than by the material element. On the unity of the human action, see G. P. Klubertanz, S.J., *The Unity of Human Activity*, in *The Modern Schoolman*, Vol. 27, January, 1950, pp. 75-103.

Word Himself. As the Word of God assumed only a nature perfect in its humanity, so too He submitted Himself only to a human generation which was perfect, informed with spiritual love. In making this human conception His own, He removed from it as from His own human nature, every shadow of imperfection. That is why He wished it not only to be chaste and virginal, but that it be conscious and voluntary, radiant with the highest spiritual love.[88] Mary's generative action was *a perfect human action*.

The part played by Mary's soul in the generation of her Son is described in Scripture in terms of belief or consent. "Be it done unto me according to thy word" (Lk. 1:38). As Augustine says, "Mary believed and what she believed was done in her."[89] As the Eternal Father conceived His divine Son from all eternity in knowing, Mary conceived the same Eternal Son in time in believing. Thus while there were two elements in Mary's generative act, the spiritual (including believing) and the material (fecundation), there were not two distinct actions; there was only one action, an action possessing a unity not of essence, but a composite unity of order.

We must recall, however, that the action itself of generation is not the proper foundation of human motherhood; the foundation for this relation is what remains in the agent from the action of conception. In a purely human mother, the perfection resulting in herself from conception can be described as a modification of her composite nature consisting in a permanent disposition (a habit) orientating her to the child of her womb as an immediately connatural object of knowledge and love. This disposition gives rise to an instinctive love in a mother for her child, a love which is natural in the strongest sense of the term; imposed as it is with the first inclinations of nature, this natural instinct cannot be violated without monstrosity.[90] As the action as well as the agent of human generation is composite in character, so too is the disposition resulting from this action in the agent; it has its spiritual as well as material element.

In Mary as Mother of the God-Man the perfection founding her

---

[88] Cf. Nicolas, *art. cit.,* p. 76.

[89] *Sermo 25* ("in redditione symboli"), *PL,* 38, 1074.

[90] Cf. Nicolas, *art. cit.,* pp. 84-89.

motherhood is a permanent disposition of her nature orientating her person to the Child of her womb as an immediately connatural object of her knowledge and love.[91] This perfection in Mary, as in any mother, is complex, having its spiritual and material elements. But its spiritual element is the reason why it could be elevated to the hypostatic order.[92] As divine adoption in men presupposes the substantial perfection which human nature has by reason of its spiritual form, so *divine* motherhood presupposes the perfection which human motherhood has by reason of its spiritual element. Human nature is elevated to the supernatural order by a participation in the divine nature. Human motherhood is elevated to the hypostatic order in Mary by a participation in the relationship of the Eternal Father to His divine Son. Because Mary has generated the Son of God, she has a relationship which is a formal image of the relationship which the Eternal Father has to the same divine Son. Moreover, owing to the maternal disposition resulting in her nature from her generative action, Mary is orientated instinctively toward the same divine Person incarnate as to an *immediately connatural* term of her knowledge and love. The Father, of His very nature, has this orientation to His Son. Mary can share in this same relationship only by participating in the perfection of the one Eternal Father.

The reason why the foundation of Mary's human motherhood must be elevated to the hypostatic order by participation in the divine paternity is that *through generating the Eternal Son* Mary has acquired a "connatural," "instinctive" regard or orientation, not to a human

---

[91] *Ibid.*, p. 261.

[92] Father Nicolas, along with many other theologians, does not hold any *intrinsic* elevation of Mary's generative action (*ibid.*, p. 64). However, it is not necessary to discuss this question here. What is important for our present purpose is that the foundation itself of Mary's motherhood be a permanent disposition resulting in her from her generative action; whether the action itself is intrinsically elevated or not, the resulting disposition must be elevated by grace to the supernatural order. To consider this foundation as a supernatural reality coming to Mary in its entirety from the Word *as term* of her generative action, as Father Nicolas seems to suggest (*op. cit.*, pp. 240-241), would rob Mary of what is natural in her motherhood instead of elevating what is natural to the supernatural order. In ordinary motherhood it is not the child as term who gives his mother the perfection founding her motherhood; it is the action of generation which accomplishes this perfection in her. In Mary, however, this foundation of her motherhood must be elevated by grace.

person, but to the divine Person of the Son of God. This orientation to the divine Son can be had only through a participation in the divine nature as it is fecund in the Father, because this relationship is exclusively proper to the Eternal Father. Thus Mary's nature needed to be elevated by a participation in the divine nature not only to love her Son, but actually *to be* His Mother.

Because Mary has generated the Son of God, she now possesses the human perfection of motherhood in a manner which makes her the most perfect possible created image of the Eternal Father. She alone is like the Father in being related by way of generation to His divine Son. Only the Eternal Father and Mary have generated the same eternal Person, He according to His divine nature, she according to His human nature. This perfect created assimilation of Mary to the Father is suggested in the writings of the Fathers of the Church when they speak of a correlation between virginal and divine motherhood. As Father Bover interprets their thought, virginal motherhood could be had only by the Mother of God; and the Mother of God would have to be a virginal mother.[93] This notion is based ultimately on a real assimilation of Mary's human motherhood to the virginal paternity of the Heavenly Father, an assimilation which can be explained only by some sort of participation of Mary's motherhood in the divine paternity of the Father.

It is upon this assimilation of Mary to the Eternal Father in generating His divine Son that St. Thomas builds his treatment of the virginity of the Blessed Virgin.[94] In the seventeenth century we find Sylvester de Saavedra speaking of this assimilation of Mary to the Father as a formal participation in the fecundity of His nature.[95] However, only in recent years has the notion of Mary's formal participation in the fecundity of the Eternal Father been given further serious consideration by theologians.[96]

---

[93] J. M. Bover, S.J., *Cómo conciben los Santos Padres el misterio de la divina maternidad. La virginidad, clave de la maternidad divina*, in *Estudios Marianos*, Vol. 8, 1949, pp. 185-256.

[94] *Sum. Theol.*, III, q. 28, aa. 1-3.

[95] Sylvester de Saavedra, *op. cit.*, vest. 1, nn. 460-475.

[96] See, for example, the following: Guillermo Rozo, C.M.F., *Sancta Maria Mater Dei, seu de sanctificatione Beatae Mariae Virginis vi Divinae Maternitatis* (Mediolani, 1943); also Joaquín M. Alonso, C.M.F., *Naturaleza y fundamento de la gracia de la Virgen*, in *Estudios*

That there is some real assimilation of Mary to the Father by reason of her divine motherhood seems unquestionably true. Moreover, there is good reason to think that Saavedra is right in calling it a formal assimilation. For to be related to the Eternal Son by way of generation is exclusively proper to the Eternal Father. Hence no one else can have this relationship to the Eternal Son except through a participation in what is proper to the Eternal Father. Such a participation of its very nature would assimilate its possessor formally to His hypostatic character. Now Mary, like the Eternal Father, is related by way of generation to the same Eternal Son. Hence she is formally assimilated to the Eternal Father. Just as sanctifying grace is a formal assimilation (although analogous) to the divine nature (even to the divine Persons), so the divine motherhood is a formal assimilation (albeit analogous) to the first divine Person.

DIFFICULTIES

Theologians in general have been slow to accept the conclusion that Mary's divine motherhood is a formal participation in the divine paternity. Many of them speak eloquently of Mary's resemblance to the Father, but refuse to affirm any formal assimilation. For example, Father Nicolas refers to Mary's generation of the God-Man as "more than a resemblance to the Eternal Generation."[97] "This woman," he says, "shares the very same Son with the Father. ..."[98] In all creation Mary's motherhood is the only thing comparable to the created humanity of Christ: "The only two created realities which include in their essence a relationship to one divine person to the exclusion of the others, are the humanity of Christ and the divine motherhood. ..."[99]

Father Nicolas quickly passes over Mary's resemblance to the Eternal Father, restricting his consideration chiefly to the relationship Mary has

---

Marianos, Vol. 5, 1946, pp. 11-110; *Hacia una Mariología trinitaria; dos escuelas*, in *Estudios Marianos*, Vol. 10, 1950, pp. 141-191; Vol. 12, 1952, pp. 237-267. Likewise J. M. Delgado Varela, O. de M., *Maternidad formalmente santificante (origen y desenvolvimiento de la controversia)*, in *Estudios Marianos*, Vol. 8, 1949, pp. 133-184.

[97] Cf. Nicolas, *art. cit.*, p. 259.

[98] *Ibid.*, p. 260.

[99] *Ibid.*, p. 257.

with her Son.

> ... We must admit that a power is more united with its own object than a mother can be with her Son simply by reason of her motherhood, which separates her from him precisely in giving him autonomous existence. This order of divine subsistence is so far beyond the reaches of a creature that it cannot be attained without the loss of its own proper personality. ...[100]

In this quotation we can perhaps see the reason why Father Nicolas backs away from the idea of the divine motherhood as a formal participation in the divine paternity: namely, the hypostatic order is so utterly above any mere creature that union with (or formal assimilation to) any one divine Person involves a loss of the creature's own personality (as happens in the hypostatic union). In other words, it seems simply outside the realm of possibility that a mere creature, preserving its own subsistence, should be united to one divine Person exclusively, no matter how great a grace God confers upon it.[101]

It is evident, of course, that if the very notion of created formal assimilation to a divine Person compromises the authentic teaching of revelation on the transcendence of the Blessed Trinity and the operation of the divine Persons in the world, the idea of Mary's formal assimilation to the Father must be abandoned. Our Holy Father Pius XII warns us against any such compromise in our attempts to explain our union with Christ in the Mystical Body. His statement must also serve as a guide in discussing Mary's union with the Father:

> ... We do not censure those who in various ways and with diverse reasonings strain every effort to understand and to clarify the mystery of this our marvelous union with Christ. But let all agree uncompromisingly on this, if they would not err from truth and from the orthodox teaching of the Church: to reject every kind of mystic union, by which the faithful would in any way pass beyond the sphere of creatures and rashly enter the divine even to the extent of predicating one single attribute of the eternal Godhead of them as their own. And besides let all hold this as certain truth,

---

[100] *Ibid.*

[101] *Art. cit.,* p. 259. "... Mais si haute et si parfaite que soit la Vision Béatifique à laquelle aboutit une telle grâce, si infiniment qu'on élargisse pour Marie et pour l'Homme-Dieu la communication intentionnelle de la Divinité, l'âme transfigurée ne saurait prendre par là la moindre part aux communications intra-Trinitaires, ni toucher à la Subsistence Divine comme telle. ..."

that all these activities are common to the most Blessed Trinity, in so far as they have God as supreme efficient cause.[102]

Moreover, in any theological explanation of one problem, the teaching which theologians present as certain must be duly respected; and philosophical principles used in the discussion must be solidly grounded in reality. Today the number of theologians is growing, who see no conflict between the doctrines to be safeguarded and formal created assimilation of Mary to the Eternal Father. But no one has yet devised a theological theory for such an assimilation which does not encounter serious objections.

Father Alonso's Theory

Among the theologians who have devoted themselves in a special way during the past ten years to the theoretical explanation of the divine motherhood as a formal participation in the fecundity of the Eternal Father are Father Joaquín María Alonso, C.M.F., and Father Delgado Varela, O. de M.[103]

Father Alonso finds in the Greek Fathers and their interpretation of the function of the divine Persons in the communication of grace the basis for his opinion regarding the trinitarian nature of all grace.[104] In the light of his patristic study he gives a somewhat novel interpretation to the dogmatic truth that all divine operations of efficient causality are

---

[102] *Mystici Corporis*, in *A.A.S.*, Vol. 35, 1943, p. 231.

[103] In his book entitled *Sancta Maria Mater Dei* (Mediolani, 1943), Father William Rozo, C.M.F., defends the divine motherhood as a formal participation in the fecundity of the Eternal Father, but treats the matter rather from a positive than speculative point of view. He has only a few pages (pp. 65-68) on the metaphysical aspect of the divine motherhood. He devotes most of his study to a consideration or the physical aspect (pp. 15-64), since he regards Mary's generative action as the proper foundation of the divine motherhood. Father Joseph Bover, S.J., also is a strong proponent of Mary's formal assimilation to the Eternal Father. Like Rozo, he centers his attention rather on the generative action of Mary, since he, too, considers this action the proper foundation of the divine motherhood. See his interesting article, *Cómo conciben los Santos Padres el misterio de la divina maternidad*, in Estudios Marianos, Vol. 8, 1949, pp. 185-256.

[104] J. M. Alonso, C.M.F., *Hacia una Mariología Trinitaria; Dos Escuelas*, in Estudios Marianos, Vol. 10, 1950, pp. 141-191; Vol. 12, 1952, pp. 237-267. See also his article, *Naturaleza y fundamento de la gracia de la Virgen*, in Estudios Marianos, Vol. 5, 1946, pp. 11-110.

common to the divine Persons, from whom such operations proceed as from one principle. Father Alonso holds that in the very order of efficient causality the three divine Persons retain their distinct personal functions *in identity of operation and (at least in the supernatural order) impress their personal characters on the effect produced.*[105]

While every grace consists in the life of the Blessed Trinity unfolding itself in the soul, the divine motherhood is an altogether singular supernatural communication of trinitarian life, giving Mary a specifically distinct kind of possession of the divine Persons in a presence which is reductively substantial. The Father gives Himself to Mary in a formal participation of His own fecundity. By reason of this communication the divine fecundity, which manifests itself within the divinity in the Word, is now manifested externally through the unique and perfect image of the divine paternity which alone could be the reason why Mary could have the same Son as the Eternal Father.[106]

This gift of the Father to Mary brings with it the gift of the Son who gives Himself formally as Son; for the only reason that the Son of God could be the Son of Mary is precisely that His personal being is to be Son.[107]

The Holy Spirit also gives Himself according to His own personal function, realizing in Mary the fecundity of the Father and the filiation of the Son; for every external actuality must be "verified in Him, who is the ultimate trinitarian actualization."[108]

The supernatural form which the presence of the divine Persons effects in Mary is called her personal maternal being, her *esse maternale,* which *receives its specification directly from the trinitarian relation of the Father.*[109]

This trinitarian presence was in Mary from the first instant of her conception and remains always specifically one identical presence before, during, and after the Incarnation.[110] Before the Incarnation it was

---

[105] Alonso, *Naturaleza y fundamento...*, in *Estudios Marianos*, Vol. 5, 1946, pp. 49-54.
[106] *Ibid.,* p. 87.
[107] *Ibid.,* p. 84.
[108] *Ibid., p. 89.*
[109] *Ibid.,* pp. 101-102.
[110] *Ibid.,* p. 82..

a dispositive preparation of Mary's whole being. In the Incarnation it is the effective realization of itself. The only thing which distinguishes the trinitarian presence before and after the Incarnation is the realization of an effect achieved in the Incarnation.[111]

By *analogy* this *esse maternale* is for Mary what the *esse personale* is for the humanity of Christ. It elevates her whole being, not merely in an accidental way, as is the case with sanctifying grace, but with a kind of hypostatic, personal elevation. Mary is vitally and organically built into the supernatural order.[112] This *esse* is absolutely and totally *the one single* supernatural form which gives to Mary her specific supernatural being. It is the only sanctifying form she possesses. It is an eminently sanctifying grace, sanctifying her in all orders of her being.[113]

Here we can only point out three difficulties in Father Alonso's explanation. First, the attempt to explain the trinitarian character of created effects, especially grace, in terms of efficient causality seems to go contrary to the truth which Pius XII says we must safeguard in these discussions: namely, "all these activities [regarding the sanctification of men] are common to the most Blessed Trinity, in so far as they have God as their supreme efficient cause." All the divine Persons, it is true, are present to their effects in the souls of men; moreover, as present, they do not lose their mutual distinctions and hypostatic characters. But hypostatic character and mode of presence are really distinct realities. Plurality of the one does not necessarily involve plurality of the other.

To say that through their efficient causality the divine Persons impress their personal characters on the effects produced seems to deny implicitly that all divine operations of efficient causality are referred to the divine Persons acting precisely as *one indistinct principle* of the effect. How, then, could Mary's grace of divine motherhood precisely as term of divine efficiency give her any formal likeness to the Father as distinct from the Son and Holy Spirit? Father Alonso's answer to this question gives one pause.

Moreover, if the presence of the Father in Mary is restricted to His presence by way of efficient causality, then it is difficult to show that

---

[111] *Ibid.*, p. 84.
[112] *Ibid.*, pp. 102-103.
[113] *Ibid.*, pp. 103-104.

such a presence in Mary or in any other sanctified soul differs essentially from God's natural presence in creatures.[114]

A second difficulty in Father Alonso's theory arises from his denial that Mary has a sanctifying grace of the same specific character as our own. For in his theory Mary does not have any grace distinct from her motherhood, *specifically* identical with ours. How, then, can she be called our Mother?

Finally, there is the difficulty involved in predicating *maternal being* of Mary from the first instant of her conception. Father Alonso, however, does emphasize a very important point in the solution of the problem: namely, that the communication of the Father to Mary necessarily involves the communication of the other divine Persons. Mary's assimilation to the Father of necessity involves the communication of the Eternal Son as *her* Son and the gift of the Holy Spirit. All three divine Persons communicate themselves to Mary, each in His own way: the gift of the Father formally assimilating Mary to Himself is, of its very nature, a sharing of His Son with Mary as her Son, and His Spirit as her Spirit. If Mary's formal assimilation to the Father were conceived as a communication to Mary of the Father only, there would be occasion for added conflict with theological teaching: namely, that outside the case of *hypostatic union,* there can be no communication of one divine Person to a creature which does not necessarily involve the communication of the others.[115]

FATHER VARELA'S SYNTHESIS

Father Delgado Varela, O. de M., intends in his work to overcome the existing differences of opinion among theologians about the divine motherhood by presenting a superior synthesis of doctrine. The philosophy which serves him as a basis for his solution is a modalistic philosophy stemming from John Vincentius, O.P., and Dominic Palmieri, S.J.

The principle used as a point of departure is the following: the fruit

---

[114] See M. J. Donnelly, S.J., The Inhabitation of the Holy Spirit; A Solution According to de la Taille, in Theological Studies, Vol. 8, 1947, pp. 455-456.

[115] Cf. Alfred Eröss, Die persönliche Verbindung mit der Dreifaltigkeit, in Scholastik, Vol. 11, 1936, pp. 381-382.

of generation is the norm and measure of the generative potency and act from which it issues; hence the Word of God Incarnate is the norm and measure of the divine motherhood.[116]

The fruit of Mary's womb is norm and measure of her motherhood in the order of *efficient causality,* insofar as Mary through the miraculous activity upon her maternal ovum causes efficiently the formation of the human body of Christ with an exigency for its soul. Thus she is constituted *transmitting principle* of her own nature to her divine Son. This element is not a characteristic proper to the Mother of God, but proper only to virginal conception, which is in its own way a reflection of the virginal fecundity of the heavenly Father.[117]

The fruit of her womb is also norm and measure of her motherhood in the order of relation, insofar as Mary is really ordered to the generation of the Son of God. Thus she is constituted *generative principle* of a divine Person in human flesh. Her motherhood in this relative order, according to Varela, is divine and cannot be called human.

This relation is explained both by the filial gift of the Son to Mary giving her the quality of Mother and by the gift of the virginal fecundity of the Father. The gift of the first two divine persons implies the gift of the Holy Spirit in order to accomplish the sanctity which the Incarnation demands.

The Father gives Himself to Mary as generating principle, not to cause the formation of the body of Christ and thus be a transmitting principle of His human nature, but to give Mary a relation to His Son as generative principle of His Person. To be a transmitting principle of nature does not constitute the differentiating element of the divine motherhood, although it is essential to the concept of motherhood.

The divine motherhood thus includes within its essence the elements of intrinsic finality, efficiency, and relation.[118] It is not *a form* inhering in Mary, but a permanent accidental mode of being, not really distinct from Mary's substance, divinely "maternalizing" her whole being. This mode is the term of the gift of the fecundity of the Eternal Father, and is realized in Mary not through the mediacy of any form, but as the

---

[116] Cf. J. M. Delgado Varela, O. de M., *Maternidad formalmente santificante...*, pp. 148-149.
[117] *Ibid.,* p. 182.
[118] *Ibid.,* p. 167.

immediate term of a positive divine decree.[119] It belongs to Mary from the first instant of her conception, and all the stages of its actuation possess a functional unity. Up to the Incarnation, it is a real potency; in the Incarnation it is a potency and an act.[120] It is this one mode which physically and substantially transforms Mary's whole being; she has no other sanctifying principle.[121]

Such, in general, is the construction of Father Varela's theory. His underlying philosophy is not Aristotelian-Thomistic in character, but a sort of ontological correlativism, in which the concepts of substance, accident, person, relation, etc., do not correspond to objective realities, but rather to "elements intertwined by an essential correlation."[122]

Father Varela's theory has met with little, if any, acceptance on the part of theologians. He is not particularly concerned, as was Father Alonso, with reconciling the communication of personal characteristics of the divine Persons with the identity of the efficient operation. Working with a modalistic philosophy, which has been quite generally rejected since Leo XIII relieved Palmieri of his chair of theology at the Gregorian University, Father Varela finds himself swimming upstream and alone in the current of Mariological discussion.

SUGGESTION FOR A SOLUTION

In the previous analysis of the divine motherhood, we have seen that the proper foundation of the divine motherhood must be something actually existing in Mary which was accomplished in her by conceiving the God-Man. This foundation is a permanent disposition, spiritual in character, as well as material, modifying Mary's nature and giving her an orientation to the fruit of her womb, a relationship of origin in regard to an immediately connatural term of knowledge and love. Because this term is the Eternal Son Incarnate, the disposition founding Mary's parental relationship to Him must be elevated to the hypostatic order through a formal participation in the fecundity of the Eternal Father.

---

[119] *Ibid.*, p. 171.
[120] *Ibid.*, p. 170.
[121] *Ibid.*, p. 171.
[122] Cf. J. A. de Aldama, S J., *El tema de la Divina Maternidad de María en la investigación de los últimos decenios*, in *Estudios Marianos*, Vol. 11, 1951, pp. 59-80; esp. pp. 79-80.

A study of the Fathers, especially the Greeks, such as that made by Fathers Alonso, Bover, and Rozo, gives reasonable grounds for this assertion. However, formal participation in a property of a divine Person encounters theological and philosophical difficulties which have not yet been satisfactorily solved by theologians. Father Alonso's theory seems to falter in his interpretation of the unity of divine efficient causality; Father Varela's theory fails especially owing to its philosophical substructure.

Most theologians who reject Mary's formal assimilation to the Father do so on metaphysical grounds. However, an approach which does not seem to violate any solidly established principles of trinitarian metaphysics is the application of De la Taille's theory of the supernatural to the divine motherhood.[123]

There is no space to give an exposition and justification of the suggested theory. A very brief description of its application to the divine motherhood will have to suffice. For Father De la Taille, that which ultimately endows a divine gift with a strictly supernatural quality is not its relation to God as an effect to an efficient cause, but rather a *relation of union* between created obediential potency and uncreated act. Union with any of the divine Persons as such involves some strictly personal communication to the creature. But since all divine efficiency must be attributed to the three Persons acting precisely as one indistinct principle of operation, any kind of strictly personal communication must

---

[123] Father De la Taille presents his theory of the supernatural in the following essays: *Actuation créée par acte incréé*, in *Recherches de Science Religieuse*, Vol. 18, 1928, pp. 253-268; *Entretien amical d'Eudoxe et de Palamède*, in *Revue Apologétique*, Vol. 48, 1929, pp. 5-26, 129-145; *The Hypostatic Union and Created Actuation by Uncreated Act* (West Baden College, Indiana, 1952). This last work includes not only translations of articles mentioned above, but also Father De la Taille's paper entitled *The Schoolman* given at the 1925 session of the Summer School of Catholic Studies held at the University of Cambridge. See also the following explanations and applications of Father De la Taille's theory: M. J. Donnelly, S.J., *The Theory of R. P. Maurice de la Taille, S.J., on the Hypostatic Union*, in *Theological Studies*, Vol. 2, 1941, pp. 510-526; *The Inhabitation of the Holy Spirit. A Solution according to De la Taille*, also in *Theological Studies*, Vol. 8, 1947, pp. 445-470. Finally, see a recent criticism of De la Taille's theory by Thomas A. Mullaney, O.P., *The Incarnation: De la Taille vs. Thomistic Tradition*, in *The Thomist*, Vol. 17, 1954, pp. 1-42. The criticism, in places somewhat rhetorical, fails, I think, to destroy the validity of De la Taille's position. This is not the place to evaluate his article.

fall into a different order of causality. Thus, Father De la Taille discovers a kind of "extrinsic formal" causality, described in the phrase "created actuation by uncreated act."

APPLICATION OF DE LA TAILLE'S THEORY

As the human nature of Christ is elevated and united to the Word in a substantial union by the communication of the *Esse Verbi* to the humanity, so *analogously in the accidental order*, the *foundation* of Mary's human motherhood is elevated and assimilated to the Father by the communication of His fecundity. Such communication is necessary, not that she be a mother, but *to be Mother of the Father's divine Son*. It gives her the Father's Son as her own Son.

The *created actuation* given to Mary's human motherhood proceeds efficiently from all the divine Persons acting as one indistinct principle, insofar as it is a *created* perfection of her nature; but the actuation comes personally from the Father by way of "extrinsic formal" causality insofar as it assimilates and unites Mary accidentally to the Father and gives her His divine Son. Divine efficiency, of course, is necessary; but the *ratio* of the efficient cause does not enter formally into her relation to the divine Persons.

This personal communication from the Father not only elevates the permanent foundation of Mary's motherhood, but also intrinsically elevates her generative action. Mary's generative action might in this respect be compared with the act of perfect charity in a sinner which brings sanctifying grace apart from actual reception of the sacrament. According to the Thomistic explanation, the act of charity in this case is caused by sanctifying grace infused into the soul, and yet is a necessary disposition for this grace.[124] Likewise Mary's generative action is brought about by the same created actuation for which it is a necessary disposition. Hence there are not two distinct actuations, one affecting the generative action and the other the resulting foundation of her motherhood; the same actuation from different points of view accomplished both. In this chapter, however, we have omitted discussion of the elevation of Mary's generative action, because within the space

---

[124] Cf. L. Billot, S.J., *De Gratia Christi*, ed. 4a (Romae, 1928), Thesis 17, pp. 211-217.

allotted it was more important to stress the permanent disposition required for Mary's actual motherhood.

This suggested application of De la Taille's principles to the divine motherhood may prove helpful in the reconciliation of Mary's assimilation to the Father with a trinitarian metaphysics. At least, it seems worthy of consideration.

III. MARY'S MOTHERHOOD AND HER OTHER PRIVILEGES

If we can establish the doctrine of Mary's formal assimilation to the Father as the most fundamental element in her dignity as Mother of God, we will gain what seems to be a deeper insight into the connection between the divine motherhood and Mary's other privileges. On the one hand, some theologians have tried to establish some metaphysical connection between them, but have frequently given themselves over to rhetoric instead of metaphysics. On the other hand, the arguments from propriety (*argumenta convenientiae*) are often given short shrift because "they do not give certitude." Father Vollert indicated earlier in this volume that the reason why arguments from propriety or suitability do not give certitude is the divine freedom.[125] God does not have to create or give any gift whatsoever, even though it be good and suitable. Everything He does, of course, is good and suitable, but not everything good or suitable need be done by Him.

The only reason which can, as it were, compel the divine action is the necessary connection of one effect with another effect which God freely chooses to produce: a hypothetical necessity. Hence, if God chooses to create man, He must give him an immortal soul.

Therefore, the famous argument in Mariology, *Decuit, potuit, ergo fecit,* has no probative value unless it is certain that God really wills to do everything which is truly appropriate and possible for His Mother. That such is actually the will of Christ seems certain from the very analysis of the revealed truth that the Word Incarnate willed to be a perfect Son, honoring His Mother with perfect filial love. For intrinsic to the very notion of a perfect son is his desire and will to do everything for his mother which is appropriate and possible. The truth of this principle

---

[125] See Chap. 2 of this volume, pp. 35-36.

is confirmed, moreover, by an inductive consideration of the privileges Christ has actually conferred on His Mother.

If this principle is established, namely that Christ willed to be a perfect Son, then it is necessary only to demonstrate a certain appropriateness as well as the possibility of any privilege, and the privilege itself is demonstrated. It is important to note, however, that the appropriateness of a privilege is not to be determined *a priori* in the abstract, nor from mere piety, but in view of the definite end for which He chose His Mother: namely, to have a perfect Mother for Himself *as* perfect Redeemer (the perfect and altogether singular assimilation of redeemed human nature to divine life).[126] The manner of this assimilation can be more fully determined by a consideration of the other privileges which were given to Mary.

In such a use of the argument from appropriateness, we achieve not only some understanding of the connection between Mary's other privileges and her divine motherhood, but actual demonstration of her privileges becomes possible, if not from any *necessary* connection with her motherhood, then from their appropriateness for the end of divine motherhood as freely intended and willed by God. For once it is certain that Christ willed to be a *perfect* Son to Mary, this necessarily includes the will to do everything He could for her, provided it was *appropriate* to the end for which He chose her to be His Mother.[127]

There is still another aspect of this argument in Mariology. We cannot strictly deduce Mary's immediate co-operation in the Redemption simply from the fact that she was Mother of the Redeemer. But if we can establish that Christ efficaciously willed to have a *perfect* Mother, with Himself the Reedemer as her only progeny, then from this efficacious will of God it follows infallibly that Mary herself, because perfect Mother, willed to do everything possible and appropriate for her Redeemer Son. If then it can be shown that her immediate co-operation was possible and appropriate, the coredemptive activity of Mary is demonstrated. Here again what is appropriate is not to be determined *a priori* in the abstract, nor from mere piety, but from the purpose for

---

[126] See Karl Rahner's enlightening article, *Le principe fondamental de la théologie mariale*, in *Recherches de Science Religieuse*, Vol. 42, 1954, pp. 508-511.

[127] Pius XII, *Munificentissimus Deus,* in *A.A.S.,* Vol. 42, 1950, p. 768.

which God chose to have a perfect Mother.

If this approach to the argument from appropriateness is observed by Mariologists, Mariology would suffer much less from the effervescence of pietistic imagination.

Moreover, if, as maintained in this essay, Mary's dignity as Mother of God consists formally in a created assimilation to the Eternal Father, then we can observe an intrinsic and necessary connection between her motherhood and some of her other privileges. For example, Mary's formal participation in the fecundity of the Eternal Father necessarily and formally sanctifies her soul. Moreover, because the perfection of motherhood cannot be lost, the sanctity which Mary has in virtue of her motherhood necessarily means impeccability. Whereas Mary was impeccable at least in an extrinsic and consequent sense before the conception of her Son, afterwards she was intrinsically and antecedently impeccable; of course, she remained free to merit, a mystery we meet primarily in Christ.

Second, this notion of the divine motherhood *seems* to involve some necessary and intrinsic connection with virginity. For if the divine motherhood is the most perfect possible created assimilation to the divine paternity, it seems that Mary's divine motherhood is necessarily a virginal motherhood; otherwise something possible would be lacking in its assimilation to the virginal divine paternity. However, a good deal of obscurity lurks here, and we may have to be content with the connection demanded by the purpose of divine motherhood as freely intended by God.

Third, there may be some intrinsic connection of divine motherhood with the Assumption, or even bodily immortality, although it seems very doubtful.

In any case, the notion of the divine motherhood as a formal participation in the divine paternity opens up many avenues for gaining new insights into the divine economy of salvation. We must humbly remember that it is one of God's great mysteries and we cannot fully understand it. If this chapter has stirred any of its readers to a greater admiration of God's loving condescension in raising one of our fallen race to the highest possible created participation in His trinitarian life, the author will be very grateful.

The Perpetual Virginity of the Mother of God

By PHILIP J. DONNELLY, S.J., S.T.D.

UR Blessed Lady's virginity is intimately connected with her sublime prerogative as Mother of God. Indeed, as St. Bernard so forcefully pointed out, Mary's motherhood is gloriously singular and unique precisely because it is virginal.[1] Since the former privilege has been treated at length in the preceding chapter, the latter now logically calls for detailed consideration.

Far from being merely a passing prerogative, Mary's virginity was and is everlasting, pervading every stage of her life, and particularly the sacred moments in which she became the Mother of God in Nazareth and brought Him forth in the cave of Bethlehem. The dogma of Mary's perpetual virginity means precisely this: (1) that she conceived the Son of God, the Second Person of the Blessed Trinity, virginally; (2) gave birth to Him virginally; (3) remained a virgin throughout her earthly life, and, consequently, now and forever reigns gloriously as the Virgin of Virgins, Queen of Heaven.

The Catholic Church, the faithful spouse of her Son, has expressed this truth in the striking formula that Mary was a virgin *"ante partum, in partu, et post partum,"* i.e., before the birth, in the birth, and after the birth of Christ. This affirmation is not a mere pious sentiment; it expresses the universal and unanimous belief of Christ's Church; it is a revealed truth; it is a solemnly defined dogma. The Lateran Council, held under Pope St. Martin I in the year 649, in its third canon, defined:

If any one does not, in accord with the Holy Fathers, acknowledge the holy and ever virgin and immaculate Mary as really and truly the Mother of God, in as much as she, in the fulness of time and without human seed, conceived by the Holy Spirit God the Word Himself, who before all time was born of God the Father, and without loss of her integrity brought Him forth, and after His birth preserved her virginity

---

[1] St. Bernard, *Sermo 4, de Assumptione*, n. 5 (ed. Mabillon), Vol. 2, col. 111.

inviolate, let him be condemned.[2]

Pope Paul IV in the Apostolic Constitution *Cum quorumdam* (1555), confirmed by Pope Clement VIII in 1603 in the Brief *Dominici Gregis*, condemned as heretical the following error, namely that "... the Blessed Virgin Mary is not true Mother of God and that she did not remain forever in her virginal integrity, before Christ's birth, in the birth itself, and perpetually after His birth."[3] The Catholic dogma, then, concerning Mary's virginity teaches: first, that she became the Mother of God solely through the omnipotent power of God, and that her divine Son had no earthly human father; second, that Jesus was not born in the ordinary normal way, that the virginal integrity of His Mother, which was not violated by His conception, was in no way injured or impaired by His birth; and finally, that Mary remained integrally and completely a virgin after Christ's birth throughout her earthly life. In this paper we shall endeavor to corrobate the Catholic dogma with the witness of Sacred Scripture and Tradition.

I. THE WITNESS OF SCRIPTURE TO THE VIRGINITY OF MARY

In this section we will consider: A) the testimony of St. Matthew; B) that of St. Luke; and C) the objection of the critics.

A. TESTIMONY OF St. MATTHEW

In the first chapter of St. Matthew's gospel (vv. 18-25) we read:

> 18 Now the origin of Christ was in this wise. When Mary his mother had been betrothed to Joseph, she was found, before they
> 19 came together, to be with child by the Holy Spirit. But Joseph her husband, being a just man, and not wishing to expose her to
> 20 reproach, was minded to put her away privately. But while he thought on these things, behold, an angel of the Lord appeared to him in a dream,

---

[2] *D.B.*, 256.

[3] *D.B.*, 993. In the first volume of this work (*Mariology*, ed. Juniper B. Carol, O.F.M., Milwaukee, 1954) Eamon R. Carroll, O.Carm., has dealt thoroughly with the documents of the Magisterium concerning Mary's perpetual virginity; cf. Section II "Ever Virgin," pp. 10-145 see also Paul Palmer, S.J., *Mary in the Documents of the Church* (Westminster, Md.: 1951).

saying, "Do not be afraid, Joseph, son of David, to take to thee Mary thy
wife, for that which is begotten
21 in her is of the Holy Spirit. And she shall bring forth a son, and thou shalt
call his name Jesus; for he shall save his people from
22 their sins." Now all this came to pass that there might be fulfilled what was
spoken by the Lord through the prophet, saying,
23 "Behold, the virgin shall be with child,
and shall bring forth a son;
and they shall call his name Emmanuel";
24 which is, interpreted, "God with us." So Joseph, arising from sleep, did
as the angel of the Lord had commanded him, and took unto
25 him his wife. And he did not know her till she had brought forth her
firstborn son. And he called his name Jesus.

In the first volume of this work, Father Michael Gruenthaner has dealt with the text, the context, and various problems concerning this passage and others in the New Testament.[4] Presupposing this background, no further commentary is needed. The angel makes clear to St. Joseph beyond the possibility of any doubt that Mary has become a mother miraculously, without any intervention of man, by the power of God. Mary's virginity *ante partum* is taught so explicitly here that it may well be considered as a clearly revealed truth from this passage alone.

Furthermore the appeal to the prophecy of Isaiah (7:14) by St. Matthew (vv. 22, 23) seems to imply also the virgin birth. As Father Eric May, O.F.M., has brought out so well in the first volume of this work,[5] despite the difficulties in interpreting this passage on a purely historico-exegetical basis, Catholic tradition and the authoritative decision of the Holy See are eminently justified in teaching that the prophecy is Messianic, and that it is devoid of meaning, even in its purely historical context, unless it foretells the virginal conception of the Messiah;[6]

---

[4] M. Gruenthaner, *Mary in the New Testament*, cf. especially "Betrothal," p. 92, "Annunciation," p. 94, and "Joseph's Ordeal," p. 100.

[5] E. May, *Mary in the Old Testament*, pp. 69-73; see also pp. 57-63.

[6] Cf. Pius VI in the brief *Divina*, in *Enchiridion Biblicum*, no. 59; M. J. Lagrange, *La Vierge et Immanuel*, in Revue Biblique, Vol. 1, 1892, p. 486; A. van Hoonacker, *Het Boek Isaias* (Brugge, 1932), p. 67; J. Coppens, *La Prophétie de la 'Almah*, in *Ephemerides Theologicae*

furthermore, traditional Catholic exegesis has always seen in this prophecy at least the probability that Isaiah taught also the virginal birth of Christ, namely that the virgin will not only conceive, but will bring forth Emmanuel, as such, i.e., with her virginal integrity remaining inviolate.

It is obvious, and accepted by all modern exegetes, that vv. 22 and 23 of Matthew are his own statement, and are not to be included in the angelic message.[7] He cites the prophecy, with the exception of two words, from the Septuagint, with its markedly Marian interpretation of the Massoretic text.[8] But this is to be noted, that Matthew already believed and accepted fully as a revealed truth the fact of the supernatural, miraculous, and virginal conception of Christ; the prophecy of Isaiah by no means inspired or suggested his belief; he rather sees his conviction as something fulfilling the prediction of Isaiah. Although St. Matthew, altogether independently of Isaiah, teaches the virginal conception of Christ, he does not elaborate explicitly on the virgin birth, nor does he state whether he understood the prophecy as including the virgin birth as well as the virginal conception of Christ. We are not then justified in appealing to St. Matthew for an apodictic testimony to Mary's virginity *in partu*, though we are completely justified in thinking that it is implied, by the very fact of his appeal to Isaiah, and by subsequent traditional exegesis of the prophecy.

Even archenemies of Mary's virginity are forced to extravagant limits to find any loophole in the text of St. Matthew against the virginal conception of Christ. Helvidius, however, followed later by numerous Protestant authors, sought indications that Matthew denied Mary's perpetual virginity after the birth of Christ. They argue from verse 18: "... she was found, before they came together, with child." Their objection is based on the supposition that the phrase "come together" refers exclusively to sexual intercourse; hence for them the text would

---

Lovanienses; Vol. 28, 1952, pp. 649-682; E. P. Arbez, *Modern Translations of the Old Testament*, in *The Catholic Biblical Quarterly*, Vol. 17, 1955, pp. 469-474.

[7] Cf. Lagrange, *Évangile selon saint Matthieu*, ed. 8 (Paris, 1948), p. 15: "v. 22) C'est un commentaire de l'évangeliste (tous les modernes sauf *Weiss*) et non une suite des paroles de l'ange (*Chrysostom*)."

[8] Cf. Lagrange, *op. cit.*, p. 17.

imply that after the conception and birth of Christ, Mary and Joseph took up the normal relations of married life. Both in his commentary on St. Matthew, and in his polemic against Helvidius,[9] St. Jerome accepts the interpretation that the phrase "to come together," when spoken of married persons, refers to sexual relations generally, but then shows, from many examples of Scriptural usage, that the word *"before* (they came together)" by no means implies, much less teaches, that Mary and Joseph "came together" after the birth of Christ.

Other Catholic exegetes have rejected the fundamental supposition of the objection; they deny any sexual connotation whatsoever to the phrase "come together"; but rather, presupposing that Mary and Joseph were only betrothed, and not yet married at the time of the Annunciation, the phrase "before they came together" refers simply to the interval before Mary's departure from her parents' home, and the beginning of her life under Joseph's roof.[10] This divergence among Catholic exegetes in the interpretation of the phrase "before they came together" is closely allied to a disagreement on a larger matter, namely whether Mary and Joseph were merely betrothed or were actually married at the time of the Annunciation; we need not enter into the technicalities of this question, except to note that the first opinion (betrothal only) is much more common;[11] Ceuppens,[12] however, who, with St. John Chrysostom,[13] St. Ambrose,[14] Theophylact,[15] and Maldonatus,[16] argues very acutely for the actual marriage of Mary and

---

[9] St. Jerome, *Commentarius in evangelium Matthaei; PL,* 26, 25; "Quod autem dicitur *antequam convenirent,* non sequitur ut postea convenerint, sed Scriptura quod factum non sit ostendit." Cf. also his *De perpetua virginitate Beatae Mariae adversus Helvidium; PL,* 23, 195 ff.

[10] Cf. Lagrange, *op. cit.,* p. 9.

[11] Cf. Lagrange, *loc. cit.:* "Ces points connus, et ils ne sont pas douteux, on voit que Mt. a voulu se placer d'abord dans la situation où Marie était accordée, mais où le mariage n'était pas encore conclu comme mariage, parce que Joseph ne l'avait pas introduite chez-lui. C'est le sens de prin e sunelthein autous."

[12] F. Ceuppens, *De Mariologia Biblica,* ed. 2 (Taurini-Romae, 1951), pp. 56-60.

[13] St. John Chrysostom, *In Matthaeum Homilia* 4, n. 6; *PG,* 57, 46; cf. *ibid.,* 42-44.

[14] St. Ambrose, *Expositiones in Lucam,* lib. 2, n. 5; *PL,* 15, 1635.

[15] Theophylact, *In Matthaeum* 1:18; *PG,* 123, 135.

[16] Maldonatus, *In Matthaeum* 1:18.

Joseph at the time of the Annunciation, feels that this opinion brings out much more sharply the fact of the virginal conception, and shows just as conclusively that St. Matthew in nowise opposes the perpetual virginity of Our Lady.

Similarly, the sentence: "And he did not know her till she brought forth her (firstborn) son" (v. 25), has been used by critics since the time of Helvidius to indicate at least that St. Matthew is opposed to Mary's perpetual virginity. We may note that "firstborn" here is not authentic, but is probably a gloss from Luke 2:7, where it is certainly authentic; the supposed difficulty, then, is in itself authentic, even though without textual foundation here. St. Jerome answered the objection thoroughly; he notes that there is no justification whatsoever in concluding from the notion "firstborn" that Mary had other children afterwards: "For it is the custom of the Scriptures to designate with the title *firstborn*, not one who subsequently has brothers or sisters, but one who is born first."[17] It was a technical legal term, since special laws were to be observed for the "redemption" of the firstborn (Exod. 34:19-20). As St. Jerome stated so trenchantly, from Scriptural usage: "Every only child is a firstborn child, but not every firstborn is an only child."[18]

Likewise, the expression "he did not know her," which is the ordinary Semitic idiom for expressing conjugal relations (cf. Lk. 1:34), "until she brought forth her (firstborn) child," by no means necessarily implies that Joseph *knew her* after the birth of Christ. Again, from Scriptural usage, the word "until" designates an event or action as not having taken place up to the time under consideration in the context, but does not in any way prejudice what may happen in the future; what may or may not happen in the future can only be known from other criteria, from further manifestations. Thus the simple statement of St. Matthew (1:25), whose obvious intent is to stress the virginal conception of Christ, by no means justifies the completely unwarranted conclusion that St. Joseph "knew her" after Christ's birth, any more than the statement (2 Kings 6:23): "No son was born to Michol, the daughter of

---

[17] St. Jerome, *In Matthaeum; PL*, 26, 26: "Cum hic sit mos Scripturarum, ut primogenitum non eum vocent, quem fratres sequuntur, sed eum qui primus natus est."

[18] St. Jerome, *De perpetua virginitate B. Mariae adversus Helvidium*, 10; PL, 23, 202: "Omnis unigenitus est primogenitus, non omnis primogenitus est unigenitus."

Saul, until her dying day" implies that Michol had a son after her death.[19]

We may summarize briefly the teaching of St. Matthew: (1) he is an unassailable witness to the virginity of Mary before the birth of Christ; (2) his use of the prophecy of Isaiah (7:14), particularly in the light of dogmatic tradition, implies, at least, the virgin birth; (3) as to Mary's perpetual virginity after the birth of Christ, he is silent; he says nothing positive to attest it, but also says nothing positive against it.

B. Testimony of St. Luke

The testimony of St. Luke is more extensive than St. Matthew's. For, not only does he teach explicitly the virginal conception, but also furnishes further elements on which to base the conclusions that Mary gave birth to Christ without the loss of her virginal integrity, and that she preserved her virginity inviolate throughout her life (Lk. 1:26-38):

The Annunciation of the Savior

26 Now in the sixth month the angel Gabriel was sent from God to a town of Galilee called Nazareth,
27 to a virgin betrothed to a man named Joseph, of the house of David, and the virgin's name was
28 Mary. And when the angel had come to her, he said, "Hail full of grace, the Lord is with thee. Blessed art thou among women."
29 When she had seen him she was troubled at his word, and kept pondering what manner of greeting this might be.
30 And the angel said to her, "Do not be afraid, Mary, for thou
31 hast found grace with God. And behold, thou shalt conceive in thy womb and shalt bring forth a son; and thou shalt call his name
32 Jesus; and the Lord God will give him the throne of David his
33 father, and he shall be king over the house of Jacob forever; and of his kingdom there shall be no end."
34 But Mary said to the angel, "How shall this happen, since I do not know man?"
35 And the angel answered and said to her, "The Holy Spirit shall come upon thee and the power of the Most High shall overshadow thee; and therefore the Holy One to be born shall be called the
36 Son of God. And behold, Elizabeth thy kinswoman also has conceived a son

---

[19] Cf. J.-B. Frey, *La signification du terme PROTOTOKOS d'après une inscription juive*, in *Biblica*, Vol. 10, 1930, pp. 373-390.

in her old age, and she who was called barren is now
37 in her sixth month; for nothing shall be impossible with God."
38 But Mary said, "Behold the handmaid of the Lord; be it done to me according to thy word." And the angel departed from her.

Because of the excellent commentary of Father Gruenthaner in the first volume of this work,[20] we shall confine ourselves exclusively to the question of Mary's virginity. Since verses 34 and 35 establish beyond all doubt the virginal conception of Christ, critics[21] have had no other means of escape in their arbitrary denial of the doctrine than to deny the genuinity and authenticity of these verses. We shall not waste time on the exposition of their arguments; this has been done ably with devastating criticism by such outstanding scholars as Bardenhewer, Lagrange, Vosté, Holzmeister, and others.[22] The genuinity of a text must not be prejudged according to falsely preconceived and baseless grounds, such as the *a priori* impossibility of the supernatural and of miracles, but solely from the testimony of documentary evidence; there is not a single codex containing the first chapter of St. Luke which omits these verses.[23] One can imagine the legitimate and horrified scandal of critics, if Catholics, in order to avoid embarrassment or to fit a document into preconceived bias, were to adopt such unscholarly procedures, by decreeing through the process of an *ipse dixit* the annihilation of a solidly established text. We can then dismiss this objection as not only frivolous, but unworthy of the consideration of serious scholars.[24] The

---

[20] M. Gruenthaner, *art. cit.*, pp. 94-98.

[21] Mainly, Johann Hillmann, *Die Kindheitsgeschichte Jesu nach Lukas kritisch untersucht*, in *Jahrbücher für protestantische Theologie*, Vol. 17, 1891, pp. 192- 261, and A. von Harnack (with many followers), *Zu Lukas I, 34, 35* in *Zeitschrift für die neutestamentliche Wissenschaft*, Vol. 1, 1901, p. 53 ff. For a fine historical summary of these views and their refutation, see J. Gresham Machen, *The Virgin Birth of Christ* (New York, 1930), Ch. 6, "The Integrity of the Lucan Narrative," pp. 119-168.

[22] Cf. A. Médebielle, art. *Annonciation, B. Authenticité des versets* 1:34, 35, in *Dictionnaire de la Bible; Supplément*, Vol. 1, coll. 271-280.

[23] Cf. O. Bardenhewer, *Mariä Verkündigung*, in *Biblische Studien*, Vol. 10, 1905, pp. 8-13.

[24] It is interesting to note that von Harnack himself, shortly before the article cited above (note 21), had proved the perfect literary conformity of the first two chapters of Luke with the rest of the gospel: *Das Magnificat der Elisabeth nebst einigen Bemerkungen zu Lukas* I *und* II, in *Sitzungsberichte der königlich-preuss. Akademie der Wissenschaften zu*

text of St. Luke has been accepted from earliest times, even by heretics and not excluding the Marcionites, who were responsible for tendentious alterations, especially of Lucan texts.[25]

Not only do these verses (34 and 35) bear irrefragable witness to the virginal conception of Christ, but Our Lady's question to the angel (v. 34) reveals her sentiments concerning virginity itself: "How shall this happen, since I do not know man?" Mary's question is totally opposed in spirit to the question of Zachary (1:18), who doubted the message of the angel, and by implication rejected the possibility of its fulfillment, and hence demanded a sign. As St. Ambrose observed, Mary believed completely the content of the angelic message and inquired solely about the way in which it would be accomplished.[26] But although she in nowise doubted the message, even less did she suppose that the promised Child would be the son of Joseph, as is clear from the phrase "since I do not know man."[27]

This expression manifestly alludes to the carnal intercourse of married persons, according to a consecrated Semitic idiom. But how could a virgin already betrothed, and soon to be married (this would be even more strange if Mary were already married) give such a reason for her question: "How shall this happen?"? We may note that Mary in no way looked to the past, as if she were to have said: "... since up to this time, I have not known man," as Cajetan proposed; for in this supposition St. Luke would have used the past tense (aorist: *ouk egnon*) instead of the present (*ou gignosko*) absolute, which includes the intention of not making use of matrimonial rights in the future.[28]

From this question and the added reason, we see that in her own mind Mary's virginity was sacred, inviolable, consecrated to God, and that she did not feel free to withdraw her consecration. If this be true,

---

Berlin, 1900, pp. 538-556.

[25] For example, Lk. 10:21, 25; 11:29-32, 42; 13:28; 16:12; 21:27, 32; 23:2, 5; 24:12. Cf. E. C. Blackman, *Marcion and His Influence* (London, 1948), p. 60.

[26] St. Ambrose, *Expositiones in Lucam*, lib. 2, n. 5; *PL*, 15, 1635: "Haec iam de negotio tractat, ille [Zachary] adhuc de nuntio dubitat."

[27] Cf. J. Vosté, *De conceptione virginali Iesu Christi* (Romae, 1933), p. 12: "At si non dubitat de nuntio, ita minime supponit promissum filium futurum esse filium Ioseph."

[28] Cf. Lagrange, *Évangile selon saint Luc*, ed. 7 (Paris, 1948), p. 32.

how could Mary have consented to her betrothal with Joseph? We answer with Loisy that this would be unintelligible unless both Mary and Joseph had at least resolved, if not vowed, to observe continence in their married life: "Luke represents Joseph and Mary as having the same dispositions as two Christian spouses who preserve their continence in marriage."[29] Nor can it be legitimately said that such a practice was unheard of among Israelites of that era; for at that very time, there was a tendency toward a more severe asceticism, including continence, as we know from the practices of the Essenes.[30] Father Lagrange states that we do not know the precise and concrete motivation of Joseph and Mary in this resolve, and that the fabrication of multiple hypotheses is useless; the simplest solution, he maintains, is to hold that marriage with a man such as Joseph removed Mary once and for all from importunate demands for her hand, and would allow her to fulfill in peace her resolve to consecrate her virginity to God.[31] Various other hypothetical reasons given by certain Fathers of the Church are exposed concisely by St. Thomas of Aquin.[32] The foregoing represents the traditional exegesis of Catholics for centuries; Our Lady's consecration of her virginity to God before the Annunciation is indissolubly bound up, in traditional thought, with the dogma of her perpetual virginity, and the basis of this dogma is found in St. Luke (1:34).

Apart from Cajetan in the sixteenth century,[33] whose views were characterized by Bishop Jansenius of Ghent as "most absurd,"[34] we do not find any Catholics who deny or doubt that Our Lady consecrated her virginity to God, either by vow or at least by a firm resolution, before the

---

[29] A. Loisy, *Les Évangiles Synoptiques*, Vol. 1 (Ceffonds, 1907), p. 291: "Luc s'est représenté Joseph et Marie dans la disposition de deux époux chrétiens gardant la continence."

[30] Cf. Médebielle, *art. cit.*, col. 289.

[31] Lagrange, *op. cit.*, p. 33.

[32] St. Thomas, *Summa Theologica*, III, q. 29, a. 1.

[33] Cajetan, *In quattuor evangelia Commentarii*, Vol. 1 (Lugduni, 1556), fol. CVII: "Non dixit, *non cognoscam* sed *non cognosco*, quia intellexerat verba angeli tunc implenda, dicendo angelo *ecce concipies*"; then follows Cajetan's interpretation of Mary's mind, *ibid.*: "Maximam affero rationem inquirendi modum quo nunc concipiam, quoniam usque in praesens viri cognitionem non habeo, hoc est, quia virgo sum."

[34] Jansenius, *Commentariorum in suam concordiam ac totam historiam evangelicam partes IV* (Lugduni, 1684), p. 27a: "... qui intellectus absurdissimus est."

Annunciation, until this century. On the other hand, although many Protestant writers have proposed views similar to Cajetan's, not a few and perhaps the most learned exegetes among Protestants hold that the text of Luke 1:34 is unintelligible unless it be understood of a resolution to preserve virginity; among these Protestant scholars may be mentioned several who have written in this century, such as E. Klostermann,[35] F. Kattenbusch,[36] K. Rengstorf.[37]

In recent years, however, some renowned Catholic scholars, while not denying the possibility of a vow under the inspiration of the Holy Spirit, nevertheless deny the fact and maintain that this denial is in no way contrary to the spirit of Catholic dogma concerning Mary's virginity. These authors are J. Landersdorfer,[38] D. Haugg,[39] P. Gächter, S.J.,[40] J. Auer,[41] Féret,[42] K. Rahner, S.J.[43] In a recent article, B. Leurent, S.J., exposes carefully the views and arguments of these authors. He then surveys convincingly and thoroughly the whole of Catholic tradition beginning with St. Augustine, deals with the influence of apocryphal literature, discusses historically the questions whether Mary made a vow

---

[35] E. Klostermann, *Das Lukasevangellum* (Tübingen, 1919), in Lk. 1:34: "Diese Stelle ist höchstverwunderliche wenn man nicht die katholische Voraussetzung macht, die Verlobte habe ein Gelübde ewiger Jungfräulichkeit abgelegt."

[36] F. Kattenbusch, *Das apostolische Symbol*, Vol. 2 (Leipzig, 1900), p. 621.

[37] K. Rengstorf, *Das Neue Testament Deutsch*, Vol. 3 (*Neues Göttinger Bibelwerk*, herausgegeben von P. Althaus und J. Behm, Göttingen, 1952), p. 27: "Die Kirche hat mit Recht in ihr Bekenntnis zu Jesus, dem eingeborenen Sohn Gottes und ihrem Herrn das 'empfangen vom hl. Geist, geboren aus Maria der Jungfrau,' aufgenommen und allen kritischen Fragen und Zweifeln gegenüber mit Recht an ihm festgehalten."

[38] J. Landersdorfer, *Bemerkungen zu Lukas 1:26-38*, in *Biblische Zeitschrift*, Vol. 7, 1909, p. 70.

[39] D. Haugg, *Das erste Marienwort: Eine exegetische Studie zu Lukas* 1:34 (Stuttgart, 1938).

[40] P. Gächter, *The Chronology from Mary's Betrothal to the Birth of Christ*, in *Theological Studies*, Vol. 2, 1941, pp. 145-170, 347-368; *id., Maria im Erdenleben* (Innsbruck, 1953), pp. 92-98.

[41] J. Auer, Maria und das Jungfräulichkeitsideal, *in* Zeitschrift für Geist und *Leben*, Vol. 23, 1950, p. 411; see however his article, *Salve Maria, Regina Mundi*, in *Geist und Leben*, Vol. 27, 1954, p. 331 f., for a slight change in his views.

[42] Féret, Messianisme de l'Annonciation, in *Prêtre et Apôtre*, Vol. 17, 1947, p. 37.

[43] K. Rahner, *Le principe fondamentale de la théologie Mariale*, in *Recherches de Sciences Religieuses*, Vol. 44, 1954, p. 517, note 73.

or only a resolution, and whether her resolution before the Annunciation was absolute or only conditional.[44] He concludes that there exists a genuine Catholic tradition that Mary consecrated her virginity to God perpetually before the Annunciation.[45]

We may quote J. Lebreton as summing up this tradition fairly: "In this verse (1:34), the entire Catholic tradition has recognized Mary's fixed resolve to remain a virgin, and this interpretation is necessary; for if she had any intention of consummating her union with Joseph, she would never have asked the question."[46] Similarly, Father Lagrange wrote: "Mary wished to say that, being a virgin as the angel already knew, she desired to remain so, or as the theologians translate her question, that she had made a vow of virginity and intended to keep it."[47] He adds in another place:[48] "To call this resolution a vow, one must add to the text theological considerations whose value is not to be denied, but which surpass a simple exegesis of the text."[49]

Immediately after its publication, Haugg's work was severely criticized by Father Spicq, O.P., as follows: "It is astonishing that this author should so strain himself to show by examples from the Old Testament and from Jewish customs, the unlikelihood of a vow of virginity on Mary's part, and that he should thus place the Mother of God psychologically and religiously, on the plane of ordinary women."[50] Equally strong criticisms came from the pens of F. X. Steinmetzer[51] and

---

[44] B. Leurent, *La consécration de Marie à Dieu,* in *Revue d'Ascétique et Mystique,* Vol. 31, 1955, pp. 226-249.

[45] *Art. cit.,* p. 244: "Le voeu de Marie est donc une vérité certaine, une conséquence et un aspect du dogme de la virginité perpétuelle. ... Cette thèse ne nous parait donc pas libre. ... En fait tous les docteurs s'accordent à voir dans la question de Marie l'affirmation de ce voeu. Cet accord constitue-t-il une interprétation authentique de ce texte dont il ne serait pas permis de s'écarter? Cela nous parait au moins très probable; nous disons: il semble, et entendons bien de respecter la liberté d'une opinion différente."

[46] J. Lebreton, *La Vie et l'enseignement de Jésus Christ,* Vol. 1 (Paris, 1938), p. 35.

[47] Lagrange, *L'Évangile de Jésus Christ* (Paris, 1928), p. 18.

[48] Lagrange, *Évangile selon saint Luc* (Paris, 1948), p. 33.

[49] Cf. J.-J. Collins, S.J., *Our Lady's Vow of Virginity,* in *The Catholic Biblical Quarterly,* Vol. 5, 1943, pp. 371-380.

[50] C. Spicq, in *Revue des Sciences Philosophiques et Théologiques,* Vol. 23, 1939, p. 144.

[51] F. X. Steinmetzer, in *Theologische Revue,* Vol. 37, 1938, p. 366 f.

K. Prümm, S.J.,[52] in reviews of Haugg's work. The editor of *Theological Studies* inserted a note in Father Gächter's article, to remind his readers of the common traditional doctrine of the Church.[53] In the recent dogmatic series published by the Spanish Jesuits, Father de Aldama writes: "One cannot say that this [the question of Mary's resolution to preserve her virginity] is a free and open question among Catholic theologians."[54] R. Laurentin, who is becoming more and more recognized as one of the most competent Mariologists of our day, has this to say about Féret's views: "This type of *a priori* reasoning minimizes the possibilities of grace in a soul as exceptional as Mary's and leads to a subtle and strange interpretation of Luke (1:34), as if Mary were to have meant to say: 'At this precise moment in which I speak to you, I do not know man, and hence am incapable of conceiving a child,' which is truly to torture the text."[55] Father S. Lyonnet, S.J., professor at the Pontifical Biblical Institute, Rome, in a public conference given at the Institute wrote: "The commonly received interpretation remains at the same time most likely and most obvious, — Mary had resolved to remain a virgin. It is objected that such a resolution, — I do not speak of a vow which would be an anachronism, — could not arise in a young Jewess of that period. Is it, however, so extraordinary that, under the influence of grace, Mary should feel herself attracted by an ideal which at that very time was very vital in certain Jewish circles, at least among men, as we now know better since the discovery of a monastery of Essenes at Qûmran, on the shores of the Dead Sea, some kilometers from the traditional location where Saint John Baptist preached?"[56]

It has further been objected that the early readers of Luke could not suspect that this text (1:34) alludes to a vow or resolution. We answer with Pope Pius XII in his recent encyclical on virginity that this virtue certainly developed and flourished in the garden of the Church from

---

[52] K. Prümm, in *Zeitschrift für katholische Theologie*, Vol. 63, 1939, p. 128 f.

[53] *Art. cit.* (*supra*, note 40), p. 160.

[54] J. A. de Aldama, *Mariologia*, in *Sacrae Theologiae Summa*, ed. 2, Vol. 3 (Madrid, 1953), p. 373.

[55] R. Laurentin, *Court traité de théologie mariale* (Paris, 1953), p. 21.

[56] S. Lyonnet, *Le récit de l'annonciation et la maternité divine de la Sainte Vierge* (Rome, 1954), p. 7.

Apostolic times; when in the Acts of the Apostles (21:9) it is written that the four daughters of the deacon Philip were virgins, the author expresses their state of life and not their youthful age.[57]

But at least it must be admitted that the ideal of virginity began only with Christ, and therefore excluded any resolution of Mary. We answer, if through the foreseen merits of Christ God could grant Mary the privilege of her Immaculate Conception, why could He not call her through the inspirations of His grace to consecrate her virginity to Him? Furthermore, the Old Testament manifested an extraordinary esteem for the virtue of continence and purity; the high priest and all the people joined together in praise of Judith because she loved purity; it was a fundamental law in the Old Testament that every intimate approach to God demanded abstention from carnal relations; when Jahweh was about to give the ten commandments to His people, Moses called upon them to sanctify themselves and to abstain from sexual intercourse; similarly, abstention was demanded of the priests during the period of their liturgical service; even for the eating of the holy bread, the priests imposed abstention on King David and his people (1 Sam. 21:4).[58]

However, since Mary was not only immaculately conceived, but also free from all concupiscence, why should she have renounced all the rights and privileges of married life? This objection passes over the fact that Mary's privileges were due solely to her preservative redemption; she was so redeemed that she might be the more closely associated with the work of Christ's Redemption; in the providential designs of God, Mary's consecration of her virginity was as it were a natural flowering of her Immaculate Conception, a remote call to the complete fulfillment of God's will by sharing in the redemptive sacrifice of her Son. Furthermore, even in the case of human beings born in original sin and subject to concupiscence, their consecration to a life of virginity is not primarily a precautionary measure against evil, but rather a response to the prevenient love and calling of God. Thus, it cannot be maintained that Mary's resolution depended solely on her free will, to such an extent that she was morally free to renounce it on hearing the Angel's

---

[57] Pius XII, *Sacra Virginitas*, A.A.S., Vol. 46, 1954, p. 162.
[58] Cf. B. Brodmann, O.F.M., *Mariens Jungfräulichkeit nach Lk 1:34 in der Auseinandersetzung von heute*, in *Antonianum*, Vol. 30, 1955, p. 41.

message. In fact, this resolution was primarily the effect of a gratuitous divine calling and only secondarily the fruit of her free consent. But the gifts of God are without repentance; how, then, could Mary admit suddenly that she could renounce freely the spiritual marriage which God Himself had inspired her to accept? Mary certainly could not take the responsibility of renouncing her resolution even after hearing the Angel announce that God willed that she should become a mother.

This, however, by no means implies, as some ancient Greek ecclesiastical writers asserted,[59] that Mary set her virginity absolutely above the incomparable privilege of her divine maternity, and that she equivalently laid down to God the following condition: "I shall become the Mother of God, only if I may remain a virgin." Such a view is not to Mary's honor; it is in reality a denigration of her sanctity; it minimizes the dignity of matrimony as a divinely instituted and holy manner of life; it leaves out of consideration the supreme dominion of God, who could command any human being to make use of matrimony without any loss of sanctity.[60] Rather, Mary was prepared to submit herself completely to the manifest will of God, even to the use of matrimony; she merely wished to be certain that the renunciation of her resolution, made initially under the inspiration of grace, would be conformed to God's will; this explains very probably why she used the present tense (*ou gignosko*, "since I do not know man") rather than the future.[61]

However, did not Mary aspire only to an ordinary life of humble self-effacement; did she not have a horror of being singular? This is true, but self-effacement and lack of singularity do not imply mediocrity. St. John Berchmans, St. Theresa of Lisieux, many other saints whose lives were hidden and retiring, and, above all, the Blessed Virgin, never confounded retirement with mediocrity. The Bull *Munificentissimus Deus* recalls the principle laid down by Suárez, that the mysteries of grace operated by

---

[59] Cf. the author of *Oratio in natalem Christi* (possibly Gregory of Nyssa); *PG*, 46, 1140; St. Sophronius; *PG*, 87, 3257; Jacobus Monachus; *PG*, 127, 648.

[60] Cf. U. Holzmeister, *Quomodo fiet istud, quoniam virum non cognosco?*, in *Verbum Domini*, Vol. 19, 1939, p. 74.

[61] Cf. Lagrange, *op. cit.*, p. 33: "L'immense majorité des exégètes catholiques a toujours entendu *ou gignosko* dans un sens absolu, excluant le futur comme le présent"; cf. also U. Holzmeister, loc. cit.

God in the Blessed Virgin are not to be measured by ordinary laws, but by the omnipotence of God, understanding always the fittingness of Mary's privileges, and their harmony with revealed truth.[62]

A final and more important objection might be drawn from the relative silence of the Magisterium of the Church, which, for example, has not established authoritatively the precise meaning of the Feast of the Presentation; even the latest encyclical of Pius XII on Mary does not mention her resolution to preserve her virginity, but merely proposes her as the model and exemplar of virginity. This discretion of the Church, however, does not in the least diminish the value of the traditional argument; for, until 1950, not even the Roman liturgy professed explicitly the corporal Assumption of Mary into heaven, and the first encyclical to allude to it was *Mystici Corporis* in 1943, and yet the doctrine itself was almost universally recognized as *proxima fidei*, a dogmatic fact, precisely because of the argument from tradition.[63]

We have dealt at some length with Our Lady's fixed resolution, before the Annunciation, to preserve her virginity perpetually, *first*, because merely from historico-exegetical grounds such a resolution alone seems to offer an intelligible explanation of Luke 1:34; an exegete, who certainly cannot be accused of any predilection for Mary or for her grandeur, felt obliged to assert: "The statement of Mary, '... because I do not know man,' is so absolute that the common consent of exegetes, who see in it the intention to preserve her virginity perpetually, cannot be called arbitrary";[64] *second*, because the historical record of agreement on this interpretation from St. Augustine until our day, with the exception of Cajetan and a few modern scholars, is so unanimous, that we have solid grounds for considering this tradition to be not merely historical, i.e., factual, but dogmatic, and founded, under the infallible guidance of the Holy Spirit, on the inspired word of St. Luke 1:34.

If this traditional doctrine be fully accepted, it magnifies immeasurably Mary's grandeur; for it means that, before the Annunciation, by a grace flowing from her initial privilege of the Immaculate Conception, she had already freely accepted and irrevocably

---

[62] Pius XII, *Munificentissimus Deus*, A.A.S., Vol. 42, 1950, p. 767.
[63] Cf. Pius XII, *Sacra Virginitas*, A.A.S., Vol. 46, 1954, p. 187.
[64] Loisy, *Les Évangiles synoptiques*, Vol. 1, p. 290.

embraced the indissoluble concomitant of her greatest prerogative — the *virginal* character of her future divine motherhood. In the infinite wisdom of God's providential plan Mary was predestined from all eternity to become the virginal mother of the Redeemer, not as a merely biological instrument and not merely with all the human warmth and selfless dedication of ordinary motherhood, but as one who would share supernaturally with her Son in the agony as well as in the love of His redemptive work, and thereby would become, much more profoundly than her prototype Eve, "the mother of all the living" (Gen. 3:20). Because of God's eternal decree, it was inconceivable that the Son of God and Redeemer should become man except from a virgin; by the same unchangeable decree, it was impossible that His virginal Mother should not accept completely, not merely the glory, but also the anguish of her virginal motherhood: "And thy own soul a sword shall pierce" (Lk. 2:35). Hence under divine predestination, Mary must accept with utmost freedom both elements of her highest dignity; unaware of her sublime destiny, she had already accepted freely the divine calling to virginity as we know from Luke 1:34; the initial message of the angel (Lk. 1:31) seemed at first to involve the renunciation of her previous wholehearted dedication; she could not accept this implication until she knew with absolute certainty that it was God's will. But God makes known to her through the angel that His gifts are given without repentance, that His summons to be the Mother of the Messiah, far from involving a renunciation of her previous sacrifice, would unite it ineffably and indissolubly with the highest gift He could possibly bestow on a mere creature — the sublime dignity of being the virginal Mother of God (Lk. 1:35).

Not only is Mary's grandeur magnified by this view if accepted as traditional, but considerable light is focused on the development of the dogma of her perpetual virginity, particularly in the virginal birth and after Christ's birth. For neither of these two aspects of Mary's virginity are stated apodictically in Scripture, at least in such a way that they are absolutely clear and removed from all doubt, if considered purely on historico-exegetical grounds. It is true that St. Matthew, after teaching explicitly the virginal conception, quotes the famous passage from Isaiah; but we have seen that St. Matthew does not elaborate explicitly concerning the virginal birth, nor does he state whether he understood the prophecy of Isaiah as including the virginal birth as well as the virginal conception. Similarly, St. Luke's statement, "And she brought forth her firstborn son and wrapped him up in swaddling clothes and laid him in a manger" (2:7), while it certainly suggests, as St. Jerome taught,[65] that Mary was not subject to the pains and travail of ordinary childbirth, and also insinuates that the birth itself was remarkable and perhaps even miraculous, nevertheless does not offer an apodictic proof of the virgin birth as understood by Catholic dogma.[66] "This very simple assertion of Luke says nothing of the circumstances of this ineffable birth. The perpetual virginity of Mary is a dogma of tradition."[67]

There are no clear grounds from Scripture for proving apodictically Mary's virginity after the birth of Christ, and there are not a few specious difficulties against this aspect of the dogma. But all doubts dissipate completely for one who accepts what seems to be a dogmatic tradition, namely Mary's fixed resolution and firm desire to remain a virgin perpetually; for, if God not only respected this resolution but was also its hidden source through His grace, if He harmonized this resolution with the reality of true motherhood in the ineffable mystery of the Incarnation, then it is inconceivable to the eyes of faith that He should not have safeguarded the complete holocaust of Mary's virginity perpetually. That this is true, that it is furthermore a revealed truth, we know ultimately and with the unshakeable conviction of faith, not from Scripture, but from the supreme rule and criterion of revealed truth, from the solemn definition of Christ's spouse and from His Vicar on earth, to whom He has entrusted the entire deposit of revelation.

Here, as in so many other instances in the development of Marian dogmas we find sharply delineated the antithesis between Catholic and Protestant thought on the place of Scripture as a rule of faith. The Church teaches that it is not necessary for every dogma to be contained in Scripture; of the solemnly defined Marian dogmas, the divine maternity and the virginal conception of Christ are certainly contained

---

[65] St. Jerome, *Adversus Helvidium*; *PL*, 23, 192; "Ipsa et mater et obstetrix fuit."

[66] Cf. Ceuppens, *op. cit.*, p. 132: "... temerarium non videtur asserere partum virginalem in animo Evangelistae fuisse."

[67] Lagrange, *op. cit.*, p. 70 f.

in Scripture. But Mary's virginity *in partu* and *post partum,* although just as truly revealed, are not made manifest in Scripture with the same unmistakable clarity; they are contained, at least implicitly, in the original deposit of revelation concluded with the death of the last Apostle and thereafter confided to the infallible teaching authority of Christ's Church, but they were not consigned explicitly to the Canonical writings of the New Testament.[68] Hence they were by no means realized or acknowledged universally as revealed truths in the early Church until the fifth century. This fact causes no difficulty for anyone who realizes that the Church is the living Body of Christ, that it is nourished by the Holy Spirit of truth of whom Christ said: "He will teach you all things, and bring all things to your mind, whatsoever I have said to you" (Jn. 15:26), and that it grows in vital awareness of revealed truths known, at least implicitly, from its birth.

Nevertheless it is important to show that there is nothing in Scripture which denies or even casts any legitimate doubt on the dogma of Mary's virginity. Critics of all eras, from the apostolic age[69] to our

---

[68] Others are of the opinion that Our Lady's virginity *in partu* is clearly contained in the passage of Isa. 7:14, when considered in its original Hebrew wording. Cf. Ceuppens, *op. cit.,* p. 23; E. May, *art. cit.,* p. 63; A. Van Hoonacker, *De maagdelijke ontvangenis en geboorte van den Messias bij Isaias VII, 14,* in *Handelingen van het vlaamsch Maria-Congres te Brussel,* Vol. 1 (Brussel, 1922), p. 158; S. J. Bonano, *Ecce Virgo concipiet et pariet filium. Isaias 7:14. Text and Context,* in *Ephemerides Mariologicae,* Vol. 4, 1954, pp. 98, 100, 106; M. Balagué, *La virginidad de María,* in *Cultura Bíblica,* Vol. 11, 1954, p. 283; J. Arendzen, *Our Lady in the Old Testament,* in the symposium *Our Blessed Lady. Cambridge Summer School Lectures for 1933* (London, 1934), p. 14; H. Pope, *The Perpetual Virginity of Our Blessed Lady, Cambridge Summer School Lectures for 1933,* p. 127; F. Feldmann, *Das Buch Isaias,* Vol. 1 (Münster i. W., 1925), p. 90; A. Kleinhans, under-secretary of the Pontifical Biblical Commission, in his mimeographed notes on Old Testament exegesis (1938). Cf. likewise in favor of the same opinion, J. B. Carol, O.F.M., *Fundamentals of Mariology* (New York, 1956), pp. 148-149.

[69] For example, Cerinthus, at the end of the first century held that Jesus was the son of Joseph and Mary, and that in His baptism, the Christ (Messiah) or the Holy Spirit descended on Him, and dwelt within Him until His passion; cf. G. Bareille, *Cérinthe,* in *DTC,* Vol. 2, coll. 2151-2155; St. Irenaeus, *Adversus Haereses,* 26, 1; *PG,* 7, 686; St. Epiphanius, *Adversus Haereses,* 18, 1; *PG,* 41, 378 f.; and J. Gresham Machen, *op. cit.,* p. 43: "The denials of the virgin birth which appear in that century ... were based upon philosophical or dogmatic presuppositions." The Ebionites, a Judaizing sect of Palestine, later followed the ideas of Cerinthus; cf. G. Bareille, *Ébionites,* in *DTC,* Vol. 4, coll. 1987-

own day, in the self-sufficiency and smugness of their all too fallible minds, have made use of every possible specious argument to prove from Scripture that Our Lady did not remain a virgin after the birth of Christ. Let us consider their stand.

C. OBJECTION OF THE CRITICS

One of their favorite arguments is derived from the biblical references to the "brethren of the Lord." It is quite true that all four Evangelists, the Acts of the Apostles, and St. Paul speak not only of the brothers but also of the sisters of Jesus.[70] Some are even named: "Is not this the carpenters son? Is not his mother called Mary, and his brethren James and Joseph and Simon and Jude? And his sisters, are they not all with us?" (Mt. 13:55.)

As we shall see in greater detail when dealing with patristic tradition, when Helvidius and Bonosus used these texts to disprove Mary's virginity, the Fathers of the Church denied unanimously that the brethren of Jesus were the children of Mary. Not a few, it is true, relying on the testimony of apocryphal writings, maintained that these brothers of the Lord were sons of St. Joseph by a previous marriage. But there is no need of recurring to this unsubstantiated hypothesis. In Scriptural usage the Hebrew word *a* (brother) has a very extensive meaning. Its primary and native meaning is the literal sense of brother in English, i.e., the son of the same father and mother. But it also is used to designate a half brother; Benjamin is called the youngest brother of the other sons of Jacob, though he was born from another mother (cf. Gen. 42:15; 43:5).

No Catholic exegete affirms that the word *a* (brother) etymologically means cousin. But on the other hand no Protestant or rationalist exegete can deny that this word is actually used to denote varying and even remote degrees of relationship. Thus, for example, Abraham speaks to Lot: "Let there not be, I beg, any quarrel between you and me or between your shepherds and mine: for we are *brothers*" (Gen. 13:8). But Lot was the son of Aran, Abraham's brother, and therefore was actually Abraham's nephew (Gen. 11:27). Similarly, Laban said to Jacob: "Should

---

1995.

[70] Lk. 8:20; Jn. 2:12, 7:3, 4, 5; Mt. 13:55; Mk. 3:22, 6:3; Acts 1:14; Gal. 1:19; 1 Cor. 9:5.

you serve me for nothing, because you are my *brother?* Tell me what recompense you would receive" (Gen. 29:15); but Laban was the son of Nachor who was Abraham's brother, whereas Jacob, the son of Isaac, was Abraham's grandson; Laban and Jacob, therefore, were nothing more than distant cousins. An even more striking example of distant relatives being called brothers is contained in 1 Paralipomenon 15:5-10; here, quite evidently, the 120 brothers of Uriel, the 220 brothers of Asaiah, the 130 brothers of Joel, and the 112 brothers of Aminadab are at the most cousins, and not sons of the same father and mother.

Furthermore, since neither the Hebrew nor the Aramaic languages had a single word to express the technical relationship of cousins, they frequently had to resort to the word *a* (brother); they could, of course, use the circumlocutions: "son of the father's brother," "son of the mother's sister," etc., but in daily and colloquial usage such phrases become too awkward and cumbersome. Even in our modern languages, unless there is some reason (legal or technical) for being more precise, we use the word "cousin" to denote any degree of consanguinity from the second; the Semites did the same thing with the word *a*, but from the first degree to the most remote relationships.

Moreover, the Septuagint version of the Old Testament invariably translated the Hebrew *aḥ* by the Greek *adelphos*, "brother." Did the same thing happen in the New Testament? We pass over the numerous examples of the New Testament in which the word "brother" is used metaphorically to designate, as brothers of Christ, the Apostles,[71] all those who do the will of Christ,[72] and even all Christians.[73] We know that the New Testament writings, though written mostly in Greek, flowed from a primitive Aramaic catechesis. *A priori*, then, it would be quite likely that the Aramaic *aḥ* (brother) would be rendered by the New Testament writers *brother* invariably (as occurred in the Greek Septuagint version of the Old Testament), to express varying degrees of relationship: brothers, uncles, cousins, etc. Since the rationalist argument from the brethren of the Lord is completely aprioristic, and is based on

---

[71] Mt. 28:10; Jn. 20:17.

[72] Mt. 12:50; Mk. 3:35.

[73] Rom. 1:13; 1 Cor. 1:10; James 1:2; 2 Pet. 1:10; cf. also Mt. 18:21; Lk. 6:42; Acts 9:17; 1 Cor. 8:13; James 2:15.

the native and etymological meaning, instead of on Scriptural usage, it loses its specious solidity and weight. If we had no other arguments than the usage of the Old Testament, the fact of a primitive Aramaic catechesis later developed into the Greek of the New Testament, and the quite probable inference that the New Testament writers followed the example of the Septuagint by translating *ah* of the Aramaic invariably into *adelphos* of the Greek, the Catholic dogma of Mary's perpetual virginity would be amply defended apologetically.

However, unlike the critics, we have overwhelming and cumulative reasons from Scripture itself, which would convince anyone not blinded by prejudice that Mary had no children besides Jesus. First of all, Christ in His dying moments entrusted and commended His mother to His disciple John (Jn. 19:26, 27); therefore, Mary had no other sons to receive her into their home; nor can it be objected with Zahn,[74] that Jesus preferred His faithful disciple to His brethren who were without faith in Him (Jn. 7:5: "Nor did his brethren believe in him"); for, whatever their attitude during His public life, we know that they believed after His death: (1) from the scene in the upper room described in Acts of the Apostles 1:14: "All these were persevering in prayer with one mind, with the women, and Mary the mother of Jesus, and with *his brethren,*" and (2) from the subsequent history of James "a brother of the Lord" (Gal. 1:9), and of his successor as Bishop of Jerusalem, Simeon, likewise "a brother of the Lord" (Mt. 13:55). It would have been scandalous in the infant community of the Church which was eminent for its lofty ideals and warm charity, if Mary had been separated from her own children and confided to the care of an outsider; nor would this scandal have been diminished in the baseless hypothesis of Mayor,[75] who supposes that the sons and daughters of Mary were all dispersed by marriage from her home.

In the infancy Gospels of Matthew and Luke, since they both teach unmistakably that Mary was a virgin at the time of Christ's conception, they likewise teach that she had no children older than Christ; furthermore, their manner of speaking not only does not attribute any

---

[74] Th. Zahn, Brüder und Vettern Jesu, in Forschungen zur Geschichte des N. T. Kanons, Vol. 6, 1900, p. 336 f.

[75] Cf. Hastings, Dictionary of the Bible, *under* Brethren of the Lord, *Vol. 1, p. 323* f.

children to Joseph, but rather excludes his having had any: "... they [the Magi] found the child with Mary his mother" (Mt. 2:11), "Arise [Joseph] and take the child and his mother and flee into Egypt" (Mt. 2:13), "... and they [the shepherds] found Mary and Joseph and the babe lying in a manger" (Lk. 2:16, cf. vv. 17, 21-22, 27, 33, 39-41). It is always a question solely of Mary and Joseph and the Child, never of other children either of Mary or Joseph; this silence is the more singular and proves even more certainly that there were no other children, if we compare Matthew and Luke with the apocryphal gospel of St. James which frequently mentions children of Joseph.

That the so-called brethren of the Lord were older than Christ is also apparent from the fact that they gave Him advice and reprehended Him (Jn. 7:3 ff.), and even on one occasion sought to lay hold of Him (Mk. 3:21); such actions according to Semitic customs would be proper only for older brothers or relatives. In addition in Mark 6:3 Jesus is designated so emphatically *the* son of Mary (*ho huios tes Marias*) that any other son besides Him cannot be legitimately supposed. Hence Renan, despite his denial of Christ's virginal conception, felt compelled to write: "Jesus ... was in his youth at Nazareth designated by the name of the son of Mary (Mk. 6:3). ... This supposes that he was recognized for a long period as the only son of the widow."[76]

Furthermore, the Evangelists expressly name the mother of at least some of the brethren of Jesus, and she is not Mary, the Mother of Jesus. St. Matthew records among those present at the crucifixion a Mary who is the mother of James and Joseph (Mt. 27:56); James and Joseph are called the brothers of Jesus by St. Mark (6:31). This same Mary (i.e., the mother of James and Joseph) is called Mary, wife of Clopas, by St. John (19:25). According to Hegesippus,[77] Clopas was the brother of St. Joseph; hence Mary, the wife of Clopas, was the Blessed Virgin's sister-in-law,

---

[76] Renan, *Les Évangiles et la seconde génération chrétienne* (Paris, 1877), *Appendice: Les frères et les cousins de Jésus*, p. 542: "Jesus ... fut ... désigné à Nazareth par le nom de fils de Marie (Mc. 6:3). ... Cela suppose qu'il fut longtemps connu comme fils unique de veuve."

[77] Cf. citation of Hegesippus in Eusebius, *Historia Ecclesiastica*, Vol. 3, 11, 20, and also Lagrange, *Évangile selon saint Jean* (Paris, 1947), p. 493: "On ne conçoit pas pourquoi Zahn rejette l'identité de Maria de Clopas avec Marie mère de Jacques le petit et José, Mc. 15:40; 16:1; Mt. 27:56, 28:1, l'autre Marie.'"

and her children were paternal cousins of Our Saviour.

Similarly, the sons of a certain Alpheus are also called brothers of Jesus. St. Matthew (13:55) places, among the brothers of the Lord, Jude who, St. Luke tells us (Lk. 6:16), was a brother of James; this James, however, is not the brother of St. John, the son of Zebedee, but is rather the other James distinguished by St. Mark (15:40) with the title James "the Less," and also called the "brother of the Lord" by St. Paul (Gal. 1:19). This James is frequently designated as the son of Alpheus (Mt. 10:3; Mk. 3:18; Lk. 6:15; Acts 1:13). The "brothers" of Jesus, then, are clearly relatives and not blood brothers, and at least some of them are specified as being the son of Mary the wife of Clopas, and others as being the sons of Alpheus.

One of the most scholarly and thorough treatises on this question is contained in M. J. Lagrange's commentary on the Gospel of St. Mark.[78] With his usual impartial objectivity the author examines all the texts separately, and then comparatively, and concludes finally:

> We have questioned each one of the sacred writers first without combining them. Paul (1 Cor. 9:5; Gal. 1:19), The Acts of the Apostles (1:14), and John (2:2; 7:3-10) speak about the brothers of the Lord only vaguely and without any determination. Matthew and Luke exclude expressly any blood brothers older than Christ; Luke excludes even younger blood brothers;[79] Mark and Matthew clearly indicate that James and Joseph are not the sons of the Blessed Virgin, but of "another Mary." No writer in the New Testament speaks of any other son of Mary except Jesus. An attentive examination of all the texts of the New Testament, whether they be taken in isolation, or in combination leads to this final conclusion: within His family circle we always find Jesus alone with Mary His mother and Joseph, until His twelfth year; thereafter there is silence. Only when He had entered His public life, do His "brethren" appear. This word could mean the brothers of His father or His mother or of both or any other relative; hence the exact meaning is not given, but it is clear that those of the "brothers" who are mentioned are only cousins. However, Catholic theologians have

---

[78] Note sur les Frères du Seigneur, pp. 79-93.

[79] Op. cit., p. 84; it is interesting to note that Lagrange bases this strong assertion on his conviction (shared by Loisy: *Les Évangiles synoptiques*, Vol. 1, p. 290), that Lk. 1:34 is unintelligible, unless it be understood of a firm resolve of Mary to preserve her virginity perpetually. Cf. *ibid.*, p. 82.

never exaggerated these indications. The perpetual virginity of Mary is a dogma, which they generally recognize to be derived from tradition rather than from Scripture.[80]

Further difficulties have been raised against the virginal conception, on the grounds that it was unknown to the first generation of Christians.[81] In proof of this statement, appeals are made to the silence of St. Paul and of St. Mark.

First of all, it is quite possible and probable that for some time the virginal conception of Christ could have been unknown to the first Christians; that it should not be revealed immediately was certainly a part of God's providential plan; one of the traditional motives assigned for Mary's marriage to Joseph was to conceal from the world the mystery of God made man, and hence also, the mystery of His virginal conception.[82] Jesus Himself guarded closely the intimate details of His human origin; He knew well that He was called the son of Joseph, but never explained that Joseph was merely His foster father. The precise manner of His human origin was one of those truths whose revelation would have hindered rather than helped the foundation of the Kingdom: "During the earthly life of Jesus the virgin birth ... would naturally remain a secret. To have spoken of it would have only given rise to slander and misunderstanding."[83] Therefore, it would be quite understandable if the first Christians generally were unaware of the virginal conception. Consequently, the Catholic dogma would not suffer

---

[80] *Op. cit.,* p. 80: "Cependant les théologiens n'ont jamais exagéré la portée de ces indications Scripturaires. La perpétuelle virginité de Marie est un dogme qu'ils reconnaissent généralement tenir de la tradition, plutot que de l'Écriture."

[81] Not a few independent critics have argued from the different genealogies of Jesus given by Mt. 1:1-7 and Lk. 3:23-28, on the grounds that the primitive catechesis was unaware of the virgin birth, and that Matthew and Luke, each in a different way, tampered with the primitive genealogy, to make allowance for the virginal conception of Christ. The most probable explanation of this discrepancy seems to be that Matthew describes St. Joseph's forebears according to the natural line of descent, whereas Luke follows the legal line according to the Levirate law; cf. Lagrange, *opera citata, in haec loca;* and J. Vosté, *De conceptione virginali Iesu Christi* (Romae, 1933), pp. 83-109.

[82] Cf. St. Ignatius of Antioch, in F. X. Funk, *Patres Apostolici,* Vol. 1 (ed. 2, 1901), p. 228 f.: "Et principem huius mundi latuit Mariae virginitas et partus ipsius. ..."

[83] J. Gresham Machen, *op. cit.,* p. 201.

in the least if it could be proved that the doctrine was not generally known until the year 80 (the date assigned by many critics for doctrinaire reasons to the infancy Gospels of Matthew and Luke). What is actually untenable is the insinuation that the first Christians were taught anything positive in the slightest way contrary to the virginity of Mary by any inspired writer of the New Testament; on this point the dogma itself is unassailable.

Independent critics generally do not openly maintain that St. Paul opposed Our Lady's virginity, but rather only that he was completely ignorant of it; nevertheless, beneath the urbanity of their language, the sinister impression is conveyed that his ignorance in some way undermines or impairs the Catholic dogma of Mary's virginity. It may well be doubted, however, that St. Paul was unaware of Mary's virginity. The argument that he demonstrated the divinity of Christ from His resurrection and not from His virginal conception and birth, has no probative force; clearly there is a marked difference between the two truths apologetically. The virginal conception of Christ, by its very nature, was reserved exclusively to the immediate and direct knowledge of the Blessed Virgin; on the other hand, the resurrection of Christ was a public fact, testified to by many witnesses, many of whom were alive when Paul wrote; hence the resurrection, with its concrete circumstances capable of proof, constituted a striking apologetic argument even for those who might be opposed to Christianity; one could hardly hope to impress a hostile mentality favorably by proposing the virginal conception as an argument for Christ's divinity.

Furthermore it is difficult to see how St. Paul could have been unaware of this truth because of his intimate relationship with St. Luke, who may properly be called a disciple of Paul.[84] Even though it be supposed that St. Luke himself only became aware of the virginal conception about the time that he wrote his gospel — an arbitrary supposition, impossible to prove — how can it be shown that the sources of St. Luke's narrative were completely unavailable and completely unknown to St. Paul? The critics cannot have it both ways; one of their

---

[84] Cf. Lagrange, *op. cit..* *Introduction*, p. VIII; A. Plummer, *Saint Luke,* in *The International Critical Commentary,* ed. 2 (London, 1898), p. XLIII ff.; A. von Harnack, *Lukas der Arzt* (Leipzig, 1906), pp. 1-19.

major accusations against St. Paul is that he corrupted the purity of primitive Christian doctrine by imposing on subsequent generations the fruits of his personal theological speculations; at least they cannot maintain that the doctrine of the virginal conception of Christ (which they detest just as heartily as Pauline teachings) was foisted on the Church by Paul, or that it was the fruit of his theological speculation.[85] We may further note that A. Resch, in a scholarly piece of research, has shown positive indications of a true literary and linguistic relationship between the Lucan catechesis of Christ's infancy and the Pauline epistles.[86]

There is nothing in the Pauline corpus which excludes the virginal conception. On the other hand, there is a probable allusion to it in Galatians 4:4, "But when the fulness of time came, God sent his son, born of a woman, born under the Law, that he might redeem those who were under the Law, that we might receive the adoption of sons." In this text Paul without any doubt presupposes the preexistence of Jesus, the Son of God. The expression "born of a woman" cannot be alleged against the virginal conception; for *gune* (woman) merely indicates the sex, and does not deny virginal status: "... here, as in other Scriptural texts dealing with Christ's human origin, only his Mother is designated and the very notion of an human father is studiously avoided."[87]

That Paul should not have mentioned explicitly or developed the virginity of Mary offers no difficulty whatsoever. He was primarily the theologian of the Redemption, of Christ's saving work on the cross; he was not an historian or a biographer like the evangelists. Consequently he speaks rarely of the events of Christ's life, and then, only of the Eucharistic institution, of His death on the cross, of His resurrection often, and of His glorious ascension; he never does more than allude to

---

[85] Cf. Lagrange, *La conception surnaturelle du Christ d'après saint Luc*, in Revue Biblique, Vol. 11, 1914, p. 207: "Le fait que saint Paul ne parle pas de la conception surnaturelle est un indice très significatif qu'elle n'est pas née de la spéculation théologique. Mais si les Apôtres n'ont pas protesté, c'est qu'eux-mêmes étaient éclairés."

[86] A. Resch, *Das Kindheitsevangelium nach Lukas und Matthäus*, in Texte und Untersuchungen, Vol. 10, 1897, pp. 264-276.

[87] Cornely, *Commentarius in Epistolas II ad Corinthios et ad Galatas* (Paris, 1907), p. 256. However, Lagrange, Steinmann, and others hold that the virginal conception, which was indeed known by Paul's readers, is not even insinuated here.

the preaching and miracles of Christ. What is surprising, therefore, in the fact that St. Paul does not mention the infancy or the baptism of Christ? However, not only in his epistles, but also in his preaching, as recorded at least in the Acts of the Apostles, we find no mention of Christ's supernatural origin; but the same is true of the early preaching of Peter and of the other Apostles. It by no means follows, however, from this silence that they were unaware of or denied what Matthew and Luke affirm so clearly in the infancy Gospels; rather the reason is to be sought in a prudent accommodation of their doctrine to the capacity of their unbelieving audience. It must be remembered, too, that the epistles of St. Paul, from the very fact of their literary genre, are necessarily occasional writings, which should not be expected to contain the entirety of his doctrine.[88]

Finally, the virginal conception of Christ is a necessary, though admittedly tacit, postulate of St. Paul's doctrine on original sin and Redemption. His entire Christology is founded on the divine preexistence of Christ as the Son of God, and on the reality of His Incarnation in order to effect our Redemption by the wiping out of sin, and especially original sin. In view of this doctrine, St. Paul simply could not have looked upon the Holy One of God as sharing through natural generation the sinful heritage bequeathed by the first Adam to the human race: "Therefore as through one man sin entered into this world and through sin death, and thus death has passed into all men, because all have sinned ..." (Rom. 5:12). Otherwise how would Christ have conquered sin? How, if He were born in a completely natural way, through human generation by the union of man and woman, would He have avoided the common inheritance of such generation? Mary, His Mother, it is true, was without stain of sin in her conception, but only in view of Christ and by His foreseen merits. But according to Paul, Jesus by His own nature, by His very origin, "knew nothing of sin, so that in him we might become the justice of God" (2 Cor. 5:21). If the first Adam in his innocence was of God (Gen. 2:7), the second Adam *a fortiori* must be of God, directly and immediately: "For since by a man came death, by a man also comes resurrection from the dead. For as in Adam all die, so

---

[88] Cf. Jean Levie, *Les limites de la preuve d'Écriture Sainte en théologie*, in *Nouvelle Revue Théologique*, Vol. 76, 1949, pp. 1009-1029.

in Christ all will be made to live" (1 Cor. 15:21-22).

According to rationalist critics, St. Mark was the first evangelist, and his Gospel was the genuine form of the primitive catechesis, which was Ebionitic. But Mark is silent on the supernatural origin of Christ, for these sole reasons, they maintain, either that the legend of his virginal conception was not invented when Mark wrote, or because he rejected it as a fiction. Here again, the conclusion is not only excessive but altogether arbitrary. It is true that Mark narrates the primitive catechesis, and by the unanimous voice of tradition, according to the preaching of St. Peter, whose disciple he was.[89] The primitive catechesis began with the baptism of Christ by St. John Baptist, and concerned itself only with His public life, as St. Peter himself testified in the Acts of the Apostles (1:22: "... beginning from the baptism of John until the day that he [Jesus] was taken up from us ..."). Peter in his preaching confined himself to those events of which he was a witness, but no one was a witness of Christ's supernatural origin, which by its very nature was hidden from human observation.

But granted that the virginal conception is never mentioned explicitly in the Gospel of Mark, it is never denied; rather it is implied throughout.[90] Compare the following texts from the three Synoptic Gospels relating the same event.

Mark 6:13	Matthew 13:55	Luke 6:23
"Is this not the carpenter, the son of Mary (*ho huios tes Marias*) the brother of James and Joseph and Jude and Simon?"	"Is not this the carpenter's son? Is not his mother called Mary and his brethren James and Joseph and Simon and Jude?"	"Is not this the son of Joseph?"

Nowhere in Mark's entire Gospel is Jesus called the son of Joseph, not even when, in relating the same incident, He is so called by the other

---

[89] Cf. Lagrange, *Évangile selon saint Marc* (Paris, 1947), pp. XIX-XXVI; H. B. Swete, *The Gospel of Mark*, ed. 3 (London, 1913), pp. XXIII-XXVI.

[90] Cf. V. McNabb, *The New Testament Witness to our Blessed Lady* (London, 1930), Ch. II, "The Witness of Mark," pp. 24-30.

Synoptic Gospels. This is brought out strikingly in the texts quoted above. Mark had no prologue, unlike Matthew and Luke who teach explicitly the virginal conception and the merely foster fatherhood of St. Joseph, and who can, therefore, call him the father of Jesus without any fear of being misunderstood.

Hence, if St. Mark were to set down simply, as Matthew and Luke did, that Jesus was considered by His fellow townsmen, the Nazarenes, to be the son of Joseph, it could be misleading to his readers who might well be unfamiliar with the other two Gospels and with the fact of Christ's virginal conception, and hence might be prejudiced against accepting this truth in the future. Lest this should happen, Mark gives a slight nuance to the question of the Nazarenes, which, without in any way altering or falsifying their thought, places it in harmony with the truth of Christ's virginal conception. Small in itself, this striking divergence of Mark from the expression of Matthew and Luke is a strong and almost inescapable indication that St. Mark was fully aware of the virginal conception.

We may add to this that according to an unbroken Semitic usage, perduring even to our day, a son is always designated by the name of his father; for example in Mark 10:46, the blind man is named "the son of Timeaus" (*Bar* [son of] *-timaeus*). But St. Joseph in the entire Gospel of St. Mark is never named in his own right, much less as the father of Jesus, as happens frequently in Matthew, Luke, and John. On the contrary, though never called the son of Joseph, in Mark Jesus is called the Son of God seven times,[91] the Son of Man (a Messianic title) fourteen times,[92] and the Son of David (also Messianic) four times.[93] In view of all these facts, Father V. McNabb poses the following dilemma to rationalist critics. Either St. Mark, following the doctrine of Peter, believed that Jesus was the true son of Joseph, or he did not. If he did, then, because of Semitic usage manifest otherwise in St. Mark's own Gospel, it would be almost unintelligible that he should never designate Jesus as the son of Joseph and never even mention the name of Joseph. But if he believed that Jesus was not the son of Joseph but was virginally conceived, all is

---

[91] Son of God, 1:1, 11; 3:11; 5:7; 9:7; 14:61; 15:39.

[92] Son of Man, 2:10, 28; 8:31, 38; 9:9, 12, 31; 10:33, 45; 13:26; 14:21 (twi ce), 41, 62.

[93] Son of David, 10:47 f.; 12:35, 37.

clear, and it is then manifest that St. Mark is an implicit witness to the supernatural origin of Jesus Christ, the Son of God.[94]

In the minds of critics, however, none of the preceding indications have any weight in the face of what they consider to be a denial of Mary's virginity in Mark 3:21. In the previous context, we have the narrative of the varied miracles of Christ in Capharnaum, of the crowd following after Him from Galilee, Judaea, Jerusalem and even from the confines of Tyre and Sidon, and finally the description of the choice of the Apostles; then in verse 20: "And they came to the house, and again a crowd gathered so that they could not so much as take their food [v. 21]. But when his own [*hoi par' autou*] had heard of it, they went out to lay hold of him, for they said 'He is beside himself' [v. 22]. And the scribes who had come down from Jerusalem said 'He has Beelzebub,' and, 'By the prince of devils, he casts out devils.' " The subsequent verses, 23-30, contain the long reply of Jesus against these accusations, and finally, we read in verse 31: "And his mother and his brethren came, and standing outside, they sent to him calling him [v. 32]. Now a crowd was sitting about him, and they said to him, 'Behold thy mother and thy brethren are outside, seeking thee' [v. 33]. And he answered and said, 'Who are my mother and my brethren?' [v. 34.] And looking around on those who were sitting about him, he said, 'Behold my mother and my brethren [v. 35]. For whoever does the will of God, he is my brother and sister and mother.' "

The argument from this passage against Mary's virginity is evolved, somewhat tortuously, on the supposition, *first*, that the friends of Jesus (the *hoi par' autou* of verse 21) are identical with His mother and brethren in verse 31; *second*, that, in verse 21, they wished to lead Jesus away because they thought He was demented; hence the conclusion: if Mary had conceived Christ supernaturally, she could never have shared such a belief.

But the suppositions and conclusion of the argument are not all well founded. There are probable grounds for doubting whether the friends of verse 21 are identical with "his mother and brethren" of verse 31. Not

---

[94] Cf. Vacandard, *Saint Marc et la conception virginale*, in Revue Pratique d'Apologétique, Vol. 4, 1907, pp. 412-418.

a few, including Knabenbauer,[95] think that they are by no means the same. However, Father Lagrange inclines strongly to the view that they are identical,[96] but rejects the other suppositions. He interprets the motivation of Christ's relatives in verse 21 as affection and concern for His well-being; they set forth from Nazareth, or possibly from Capharnaum, to urge and to constrain Him, with a sort of affectionate violence, to take care of Himself, and to allow Himself at least time to eat, according to the indication of verse 20: "... so that they could not so much as take their food." Furthermore, Lagrange shows that, in accord with St. Mark's style in other passages, the phrase: "For they said, 'He is beside himself,' " can be taken impersonally, namely: "It was said"; i.e., His relatives heard rumors of Christ's unceasing labors and unsparing zeal;[97] in other words, his family came because they were disturbed by what they had heard. Moreover, the Vulgate rendition of *exeste* by "in furorem versus est" ("He has become mad") is altogether too strong; in St. Mark, this verb, *existemi*, means a sort of exaltation or keyed-up state due to surprise, enthusiasm, or zeal (cf. 2:2; 5:42; 6:51); similarly St. Paul was not describing himself as demented when he wrote: "... *eite gar exestemen, Theo,*" "if we were transported in mind, it was unto God" (2 Cor. 5:13); the meaning is, quite clearly: to be transported, to go beyond ordinary bounds, to exaggerate, to be beside oneself, and, in the present case, to neglect the ordinary rules of health because of zeal. Finally, if we grant with Lagrange the identity of the persons in verses 21 and 31, and

---

[95] Cf. Knabenbauer, *Commentarius in Marcum* (Paris, 1907); his arguments are: (1) that in Mark 9:44; 11:73; 12:27; 13:52; 15:15; 16:16, and in 2 Maccabees 11:20, the phrase *hoi par' autou* means simply partisans, friends, or companions in war; (2) the relatives of Jesus, living at Nazareth, could not have found out so soon what had happened in verse 20, which is given as the reason for the interruption by the *hoi par' autou*; (3) when the mother and brothers are presented in verse 31, Mark uses a different designation; he therefore did not have the same persons in mind.

[96] Lagrange, *Évangile selon saint Marc*, p. 69 f.: "*Hoi par' autou* can also mean relatives (Prov. 31:21; Susanne, v. 33; Jos., *Antiq.* I, x, 5. 2); (2) the situation in verse 20 could have been prolonged or renewed, thus explaining the intervention of people from a distance; (3) Mark had in view the same persons, but designates them more precisely on their arrival; in verse 21, they had merely set forth, and by a literary device, Mark gives them time to arrive, by interposing the scene with the Scribes."

[97] Cf. Turner, in *Journal of Theological Studies*, Vol. 25 (1923), p. 383 f., quoted by Lagrange, loc. cit.

follow the rest of his interpretation, there is no difficulty whatsoever; Jesus does not in any way reprehend those who sought Him out; He does not prove to them that He is sane, as He did to the Scribes; he merely refuses to acknowledge their right to be occupied with Him when He is in the midst of His apostolic labors.[98]

With a thoroughness and singleness of purpose that admits no rest, rationalist critics, having convinced themselves that the virginal conception of Christ has no foundation historically, and having thereby justified themselves in rejecting the genuinity of Luke 1:34, 35, which they admit teaches this doctrine, turn their attention toward showing the origins of the doctrine. This process is almost as old as Christianity, and has turned up the most varying conjectures.

We have the testimony of Celsus, whom Origen opposed so vigorously,[99] that in the early days of Christianity the Jews spread a rumor that Christ was born of an adulterous union; Mary, though betrothed to Joseph, is supposed to have entered into a union with a certain Roman soldier named Panthera, because of whom Jesus was called *ben-Panthera,* "sons of Panthera."[100] This legend was revamped by the biologist Haeckel at the turn of the century.[101] In his *Life of Christ,* the Jewish author, Joseph Klausner, after a thorough investigation, concludes: "That there is no historical foundation for the tradition of Jesus' illegitimate birth and that the tradition arises from opposition to the Christian view that Jesus was born without a natural father, all this we have repeatedly seen."[102]

More respectfully, but with as little foundation, the virginal conception has been attributed to Jewish sources. Only a few rationalist exegetes have held this opinion,[103] and it has been thoroughly examined

---

[98] Cf. St. Ambrose, *Expositio Evangelii secundum Lucam; PL,* 15, 1678.

[99] Origen, *Contra Celsum,* 1, 32; *PG,* 11, 722 ff.

[100] Cf. Strack-Billerbeck, *Kommentar z. N. T. aus Talmud und Midrasch,* Vol. 1 (München, 1922), p. 36 f.

[101] Haeckel, *Die Welträtsel* (Berlin, 1899), pp. 377-380.

[102] J. Klausner, *Jesus of Nazareth* (tr. from the Hebrew by H. Danby, New York, 1925), pp. 23 f., 36, 232 f.

[103] Notably, A. von Harnack, *Lehrbuch der Dogmengeschichte,* Vol. 1, ed. 5 (Tübingen, 1931), p. 113.

and rejected by competent scholars such as J. Gresham Machen: "A Jew could accept the virgin birth when it actually occurred, but that is very different from evolving the notion of it from existing ideas. Very hostile to such an evolution of the notion was the whole tendency of the Jews' thought about God."[104] G. Dalman: "For never did the Jewish people expect that the Messias would be born without a human father, and not a single indication exists of a Messianic interpretation, in Jewish writings, of Isaiah 7:14, from which passage the entire narrative of a miraculous birth of Jesus could have had its origin, ready made."[105] And Th. Zahn writes categorically: "The supposition that the Christian narratives of the infancy Gospels (Mt. 1:18-25; Lk. 1:25-56) arose from rabbinical exegesis is altogether fantastic."[106]

There is no pagan religion, no mythological legend to which one or another critic has not attributed the supernatural origin of Christ. As Harnack relates,[107] some have appealed to Buddhism, others to Egyptian or Babylonian religions, others to Phrygian or Mithraic cults, or to the doctrines of the Persians; others have invoked Greek mythology, Eleusynian mysteries or others unknown, and finally some have spoken of a spontaneous and fraudulent evolution of the doctrine. Because of the absurdity of this multiplication of mutually contradictory theories,[108] there is greater unanimity among more recent rationalists in following the paths first indicated, it would seem, by H. Usener,[109] and then taken up by Soltau, E. Petersen, P. W. Schmiedel, Hillmann, and Loisy

---

[104] *Op. cit.*, p. 284.

[105] G. Dalman, *Die Worte Jesu*, Vol. 1 (Leipzig, 1898), p. 226.

[106] Th. Zahn, *Das Evangelium des Matthäus*, ed. 3 (Leipzig, 1910), p. 86: "Vollends phantastisch ist die Annahme, dass die christlichen Erzählungen ... aus der rabbinischen Exegese vom Jes. 7:14 erwachen seien." Cf. also Strack-Billerbeck, *op. cit.*, p. 49: "Darum hat das alte Judentum auch niemals erwartet, dass etwa der verheissene Messias auf dem Wege übernatürlicher Zeugung das Licht der Welt erblicken werde."

[107] A. von Harnack, *op. cit.*, Vol. 1, p. 113, note.

[108] Cf. Loisy, *op. cit.*, Vol. 1, p. 339: "L'hypothèse d'un emprunt direct à la mythologie ne semble pas à discuter."

[109] H. Usener, *Religionsgeschichtliche Untersuchungen, Vol. 1,* Das Weihnachtsfest (Bonn, 1899), p. 69 ff.

himself.[110]

The salient points of this trend, despite individual nuances, have been well summarized in general by pseudo-Herzog (Turmel): "To sum up, the dogma of the virginal conception first appeared toward the end of the first century, in Christian communities of Hellenic origin. Two factors concurred in its formation: the title *Son of God*, a favorite salutation given to the Savior, and the prophecy of Isaiah (7:14). The title itself gave rise to the notion of a miracle, and the prophecy was at hand to elevate this initial impression to the dignity of a dogma."[111]

Father Lagrange has reviewed thoroughly the notion of "Sons of God" among pagans. In some mythological legends, the gods were pictured as having intercourse with mortal women; from these unions were born heroes, semidivine beings. These unions between gods and men were effected in various ways. In the Homeric cycle, the gods united themselves to women with brutal lust, and thus were born giants, intermediaries between men and gods; in these instances, obviously there is no question of virginal motherhood. Second, conception also was pictured as having occurred, to the exclusion of all sexual intercourse, v.g., through the wind, flowers, air, etc., as in the golden rain sent down by Jove whereby Danaë conceived and bore Perseus. Finally there are other instances which concern historic men; thus Plato, Alexander the Great, Scipio, and Augustus were all considered to be sons of the gods, frequently only in the sense of adulatory praise.[112]

It is the contention of the more recent critics, then, that newly converted Christians from pagan origins, having heard Christ preached as the Son of God, recalled their native legends; if the pagan sons of God

---

[110] W. Soltau, *Die Geburtsgeschichte Jesu Christi* (Leipzig, 1902); E. Petersen, *Die wunderbare Geburt des Heilandes*, in *Religionsgeschichtliche Volksbücher*, Vol. 3, 1909; P. W. Schmiedel, *Mary*, in Cheyne's *Encycl. Bibl.*, Vol. 3, p. 2963 f.; J. Hillmann, *op. cit.* (*supra*, note 21), p. 245: "Es ist also die Idee der übernatürlichen Geburt auf heidenchristlichen Boden enstanden und später durch Jesaiah 7:14 beglaubigt"; Loisy, *op. cit.*, Vol. 1, p. 339.

[111] Herzog (Turmel), *La conception virginale du Christ*, in *Revue d'Histoire et de Littérature Religieuse*, Vol. 12, 1907, p. 126; cf. *ibid.*, p. 121: "Les récits qui nous expliquent si clairement que Joseph n'eut aucune part à la naissance de Jésus sont de la fin du première siècle. Le dogme de la conception virginale fit donc son apparition dans la conscience chrétienne aux environs de l'année 80."

[112] Cf. Lagrange, *art. cit.*, in *Revue Biblique*, Vol. 11, 1914, p. 63 f.

were such by the direct intervention of the gods, why not attribute the same honor to Jesus? The critics appeal to the first Christian apologetes in confirmation; St. Justin and Tertullian referred the divine origin of Christ to analogous mythological legends. For example, St. Justin writes: "When we proclaim that the Word, who first is the Son of God, was born without the intermediary of man, Jesus Christ our Master, we do not affirm anything new, or different from those who among you are called sons of Jupiter."[113] What is to be thought of this theory?

First, it is quite understandable that pagans, on hearing the Gospel, should have such thoughts about Jesus, the Son of God. Thus the Lystrians, on witnessing the miracle of Paul, cried out: "The gods have come down to us in the form of men" (Acts 14:10), and wished to offer sacrifice to him and Barnabas, through the priest of Jupiter. But we should note the vehemence of Paul's protest, that he and Barnabas were only mortal men (cf. Acts 14:13 ff.).

Furthermore, we see everywhere in the early preaching the sedulous care of the Apostles to make sure that their hearers grasp the truth of a transcendental, eternal, absolutely unique God, to whom all men owe the complete dedication of spiritual adoration; for example, St. Paul's powerful sermon to the Athenian philosophers and pagans in the Areopagus (Acts 17:22 ff.). Therefore it is not merely *a priori*, but also psychologically impossible that those who had renounced polytheism with its false worship and licentiousness, and, in the words of St. Paul, had "turned to God from idols, to serve the living and true God" (1 Thess. 1:9), would, as neophytes, return to their former base and immoral legends concerning the lascivious actions of pagan gods, and apply them to Christ's birth.[114]

Let us suppose, but not concede (simply because there are no historical grounds for doing so), that one or another small group of converted pagans should have so relapsed; is it not preposterous to suppose that a singular error of a few could have invaded the whole Church throughout its length and breadth, without leaving any historical trace of the slightest reaction?[115] The very hypothesis is

---

[113] Apologia; PG, 6, 359 ff.; cf. Tertullian, *Apologia adversus Gentes*; PL, 1, 449 ff.

[114] Cf. Lagrange, *art. cit.*, p. 66.

[115] *Ibid.*, p. 67.

fantastic, especially in view of the apostolic doctrine enjoining absolute separation from pagan infidels: "Do not bear the yoke with unbelievers. For what has justice in common with iniquity? Or what fellowship has light with darkness? What harmony is there between Christ and Belial? Or what part has the believer with the unbeliever? And what agreement has the temple of God with idols? For you are the temple of the living God ..." (2 Cor. 6:14-17).

The baselessness of this theory is further evidenced by the fact that the account of the virginal conception is written by Matthew and Luke, whose narratives, on the testimony of experts, have a unique and distinctive Semitic character, not only in language, but in thought, inasmuch as the annunciation and birth of Jesus are described as the fulfillment of the Messianic hope, which was exclusively Jewish. Is it not then absurd to picture Judaeo-Christians, such as Luke and Matthew, as having received the source of their doctrine on the virginal conception from pagan views which would so clearly contradict their strict monotheism?[116]

Regarding St. Justin, it is true, of course, that he compares the Christian dogma of the virginal conception with analogical legends of pagan mythology; but from the context it is evident that he does so with an apologetic end in view, by an argument *ad hominem,* without in the slightest way compromising or leaving doubtful his true, innermost, and completely orthodox conviction: "It is perfectly evident ... that the argument from analogy with the pagan stories, which he [Justin] uses ... is an *argumentum ad hominem* merely, and does not touch the real centre of his conviction."[117] Obviously, also the comparison limps, for the analogy is purely exterior and only apparent. Jesus is not the Son of God *because* He is born in time through the power of the Most High, as pagan heroes and demigods are supposedly sons of the pagan gods; but rather He who from eternity *is* the only-begotten Son of God, is born in time, becomes man and Messias and Our Saviour. That this was the deep faith of St. Justin, no one can deny sincerely.

---

[116] Cf. J. Gresham Machen, *op. cit.,* p. 62: "... Luke 1:5-2:52 is a strikingly Jewish and indeed Palestinian narrative...."; *ibid.,* p. 174: "... the essentially Jewish and Palestinian character of Matthew cc. 1 and 2 is scarcely less plain than that of Luke cc. 1 and 2."

[117] *Op. cit.,* p. 335.

The whole theory as described by Turmel above, and advocated in its essentials by so many other rationalists, is truly nebulous, indeterminate, intangible. Its proponents never descend to the practical and decisive issue of telling us who, concretely and historically, these newly converted pagans were, who foisted their legendary myths on the original Judaeo-Christian community. We are not told where they lived, by whom they were evangelized, or by what specific contrivings they managed to graft their paganism on the whole Church. On the other hand, the fact of the virginal conception is told by the evangelists, Luke and Matthew, simply, as real and historical, with no apologetic embellishment as if they were proposing something novel or unknown; nor is there a single historical indication in any contemporary document of the slightest reaction against such a marvelous fact as the virginal origin of Christ. Why? Because it was handed down and believed as a fact. Therefore, the infancy Gospels of Matthew and Luke are far from being the product of the idle dreams of the early Christians; rather the elaborate and pseudo-scientific postulate of pagan origins is an idle and nebulous dream of the critics themselves. We may conclude fittingly by quoting two authors, one a Protestant, the other a Catholic, who have both made serious and prolonged investigations of rationalist theories and of Christian tradition: "The impulse toward this belief must have been given from without ...it must have grown out of a conviction, cherished within a limited Palestinian circle of believers, that the traditional belief among them was based upon facts, of which some members of this community had been the original depositories and witnesses."[118] "The doctrine of the Virgin Birth, like the doctrine of the Resurrection of our Blessed Lord, created so many difficulties that the only reason for preaching it was its truth! ... The teaching of the Virgin Birth, if it were not true, would have been the death of Christianity."[119]

We have seen at some length the testimony of Scripture concerning Mary's perpetual virginity, and all of the outstanding objections raised against it by those who lack the gift of faith. We may summarize briefly:

---

[118] G. H. Box, *The Gospel Narratives of the Nativity and the Alleged Influence of Heathen Ideas, in* Zeitschrift für neutestamentliche Wissenschaft und die Kunde der älteren Kirche, Vol. 6, 1905, p. 100.

[119] V. McNabb, *op. cit.,* p. 17.

(1) the virginal conception of Christ is taught so clearly and unmistakably that it is to be believed as a revealed truth from Scripture alone; (2) the Virgin Birth is so strongly implied that any Catholic who is aware of the long dogmatic tradition of the Church and the solemn definitions of this dogma by the Vicar of Christ on earth cannot fail to hold that God, the primary Author of Scripture, intended to convey this truth, implicitly and obscurely it is true, in the texts of Isaiah, Matthew, and Luke; however, our faith in this dogma rests ultimately, not on the resources of historico-exegetical proof,[120] but rather on the teaching authority of the Church, which is the unique authentic interpreter of Scripture; (3) Mary's virginity after the birth of Christ is not contained explicitly in Scripture; however, the Sacred Writings not only contain nothing against it, but provide us with those revealed and dogmatic elements which constitute the analogy of faith; from this analogy of faith, from the need of synthesizing and harmonizing concrete revelation concerning God's existential plan of salvation, the Church under the guidance of the Holy Spirit grew in its vital awareness that all the elements of Mary's perpetual virginity were revealed truths and, therefore, were capable of solemn dogmatic definition. This full awareness required a long process of maturation concerning the virgin birth and Mary's virginity after Christ's birth. We shall now follow the details of this development in the Patristic Tradition.

II. THE PATRISTIC TRADITION CONCERNING MARY'S VIRGINITY

It is a recognized fact that the Fathers and ecclesiastical writers of the Apostolic age followed closely the plan and development of the Gospels and of the New Testament in their pastoral doctrine. It is equally true that the person of Our Lady does not play a leading role, even in the so-called infancy Gospels; neither Matthew nor Luke had any design of championing the Mother of the Saviour for her own sake. If they spoke of her more than did Mark or John, it was with the obvious and primary intention of focusing attention on Jesus, on His origins, on His first actions in this world. Mary's function in the infancy Gospels is

---

[120] Cf. *supra*, footnote 68.

to point to Christ; she is not delineated for herself, nor are there any traces of a piety which would derive satisfaction in circumstantial details concerning the Blessed Virgin apart from her relationship to Christ.[121]

The writings of the early Fathers corroborate this impression. Mary seldom enters into their perspective, except with regard to the virginal conception of Jesus, which was affirmed explicitly from the earliest documents,[122] for example, in St. Ignatius of Antioch. Even at this early period, belief in the virginal conception of Christ was proposed as an article of faith by St. Irenaeus,[123] and, most probably, before him by St. Justin[124] and Aristides.[125] Justin and Irenaeus even undertake the justification of this belief by speculative considerations, notably by the Eve-Mary parallel.[126] It is true that Justin's development of this parallel is not extremely well fashioned. Irenaeus, on the contrary, handles it with a much more highly developed theological sense, as the following example shows:

It was because of the disobedience of a virgin that man was struck down, and after his fall became subject to death. Similarly, due to the obedience of a virgin to the command of God, man was reborn unto the warmth of life. Man is the lost sheep whom the Lord came to search out here below; and this is the precise reason why He became man only through her who was a descendant of Adam, and He thus preserved the resemblance with the race of Adam. It was then just and necessary that Adam should be restored in Christ, in order that what was mortal might

---

[121] Cf. G. Jouassard, *Marie à travers la patristique*, in *Maria. Études sur la Sainte Vierge*, ed. H. du Manoir, S.J., Vol. 1 (Paris, 1949), p. 72. As W. J. Burghardt, S.J., in the first volume of this MARIOLOGY, *Mary in Western Patristic Thought*, pp. 121-174, so the present writer is deeply indebted to Canon Jouassard, whose article is not only the latest serious study on Mary's virginity and sanctity in the Fathers, but surpasses anything previously written, in the depth, extent, and critical acumen of his truly scholarly and scientific research.

[122] Cf. P. R. Botz, *Die Jungfrauschaft Mariens im N. T. und in der nachapostolischen Zeit: Eine dogmatisch-biblische Studie* (Bottrop, Westphalia, 1935).

[123] *Adversus haereses*, ed. Massuet, 1, 10, 1-2; *PG, 7, 549-553*; Massuet, 3, 21, 3-4; *PG, 7, 949-951*.

[124] *Dialogus cum Tryphone*, ed. Archambault, Vol. 2, 1909, pp. 144-146; cf. *ibid.*, Vol. 1, pp. 214-216.

[125] *Apologia*, 2, ed. Hennecke, *Texte und Untersuchungen*, Vol. 4, Part 3, p. 9.

[126] St. Justin, *Dial. cum Tryphone*, ed. Archambault, Vol. 2, pp. 122-124; *PG, 6, 709-712*.

be absorbed and grafted onto immortality, and that Eve should be restored in Mary, that a Virgin might become the advocate of a virgin, the disobedience of the one being blotted out and destroyed by the obedience of another.[127]

Two other developments of the Eve-Mary parallel may be found in St. Irenaeus' *Adversus haereses*.[128] He grasped the theological implications of the dogma of Christ's conception from a virgin, and stressed not merely the material fact, but also that Mary must be granted a certain role in the mystery of our salvation.[129]

Did St. Irenaeus' marvelous penetration into the virginal conception of Christ carry him on to further precisions concerning Our Lady's virginity? Unfortunately, no, at least according to those authentic writings of his which have come down to us for the most part only in translations; there is nothing in these translated passages to show that Irenaeus held the permanence of Mary's virginity, i.e., after the Annunciation, in the birth of Christ, and thereafter to the end of her life on earth. Certain critics[130] have believed themselves justified in holding that Irenaeus denied Mary's perpetual virginity, but without any decisive proof;[131] on the other hand, we must confess that there are no decisive texts to show the opposite.

---

[127] *Epideixis*, in *Patrologia Orientalis* (Graffin-Nau, Paris), 12-5, pp. 772-773; cf. the French translation by J. Barthoulot, in *Recherches de Sciences Religieuses*, Vol. 6, 1919, p. 391.

[128] *Adversus haereses*, 3, 22, 3-4 and 5, 19, 1; *PG*, 7, 958-960, 1175 f.

[129] Cf. G. Joussard, "Le premier-né de la Vierge" chez saint Irénée et saint Hippolyte, in *Revue des Sciences Religieuses*, Vol. 12, 1932, pp. 509-532; cf. Paul Galtier, S.J., *La Vierge qui nous régénère: Irénée, Adversus haereses, IV, 33*, in *Recherches de Sciences Religieuses*, Vol. 5, 1914, pp. 136-145. We possess St. Irenaeus' *Epideixis* only in Armenian, and his complete *Adversus haereses* only in Latin; though large parts of the latter are extant in Greek, there is very little in them that adds to our knowledge of St. Irenaeus' personal views on Mary's virginity.

[130] Notably H. Koch in his two successive works of which the second is a development of the first, and an answer to critics, *Adhuc Virgo: Mariensjungfrauschaft und Ehe* in *der altchristlichen Überlieferung bis zum Ende des IV Jahrunderts* (Tübingen, 1929); *Virgo-Eva, Virgo-Maria: Neue Untersuchungen über die Lehre von der Jungfrauschaft und der Ehe Mariens* in *der ältesten Kirche* (Berlin-Leipzig, 1937).

[131] See the reviews of Koch by J. Lebon, in *Revue d'Histoire Ecclésiastique*, Vol. 39, 1938, pp. 338-340, and by P. Simonin, in *Revue des Sciences Philosophiques et Théologiques*, Vol. 28, 1939, p. 299 f.

In these conditions of incertitude, one would naturally like to have the witness of contemporaries to complete and control the views of St. Irenaeus. At the present time there are scarcely any testimonies of this kind,[132] except within the range of the apocryphal writings; but the Apocrypha are peculiarly difficult to interpret and to evaluate.[133] They have undergone continuous recasting, and, as we now possess them, they can hardly be said to be the same as the original. This is particularly true of the well-known *Protoevangelium of Saint James*.[134] In the text we now possess, a firm and explicit belief is evident for Our Lady's virginity, not only before the birth of Christ, but also during and after His birth. This by no means proves that similar beliefs were, necessarily and in the same manner, expressed in the original works, whose compilation into one, according to modern textual criticism, took place in the third century, to form the *Protoevangelium.* Nevertheless, the belief in Mary's perpetual virginity must have been current in at least some of the circles that were partial to apocryphal narratives. We have an indication of this in a certain "Gospel" described by Origen,[135] as "according to Saint Peter," in which the paternity of the so-called brothers of the Lord, mentioned in the canonical Gospels, is ascribed to St. Joseph in a previous marriage. Likewise, the *Ascension of Isaiah*[136] and perhaps the *Apocryphal Gospel of Ezechiel*[137] tend to present the actual birth of Christ as miraculous. We thus have reason to assert a belief in the virgin birth from the second century. Other narratives also could well have propagated these ideas on the same popular level in which the

---

[132] We might appeal to Hegesippus, if his statements were more precise; cf. Th. Zahn, *Forschungen zur Geschichte des N. T. Kanons,* in *Theologische Literaturzeitung,* Vol. 6 (Leipzig, 1900), pp. 228-273.

[133] P. Jugie, *La Mort et l'Assomption de la Sainte Vierge* (Vatican City, 1944), p. 103 ff.

[134] Edited by E. Amann (Paris, 1930).

[135] *Comment. in S. Matt.,* 10, 17; PG, 13, 876 f.

[136] Ed. É. Tissérant, 11, 1-18.

[137] This is an apocryphal narrative whose source is disputed. It is not known whether its provenance is Christian or Jewish. We possess only detached and, usually, very brief fragments. In one of these, there is mention of one "who should give birth," and "not give birth" to a child. This fragment was soon interpreted as meaning the virginity of Mary *in partu;* cf. K. Koll, *Gesammelte Aufsätze zur Kirchengeschichte,* Vol. 3 (Tübingen, 1928), pp. 36, 41 f.

Apocrypha flourished and multiplied; the apocryphal writings were probably compiled among the simple populace who were within the Church, and not among sects tainted with heresy, as not a few have thought. Whatever their origins, we have no grounds for concluding that the Apocrypha contained and transmitted an authentic apostolic tradition concerning the dogma of Mary's perpetual virginity; in each instance such a tradition would have to be established — an impossible task with our present documentary sources. Moreover, in themselves, the apocryphal narratives scarcely measure up to the quality of sober objectivity characteristic of the transmission of a doctrine that is authentically apostolic in origin. Rather, they seem to bear witness to certain naïve and more or less spontaneous tendencies whose exact origin can hardly be evaluated critically today.

Up to the end of the second century, therefore, we have only fragmentary indications concerning Our Lady's perpetual virginity; at the most, they reveal that a certain number of interesting views were in circulation concerning Mary's virginity in the actual birth of Christ and thereafter; on the other hand, they reveal unmistakably, as we have seen, that the virginal conception of Christ was beyond all doubt or discussion in the apostolic Church; it was accepted as a revealed dogma of faith.[138]

THE THIRD CENTURY AND THE FIRST QUARTER OF THE FOURTH CENTURY

In the next period, although the writings of the Fathers became numerous and of extreme importance on other subjects, nevertheless there are very few which deal explicitly with Mary and the question of her perpetual virginity. The two most outstanding writers at the beginning of this period were the African Tertullian, and the Egyptian, who became a Palestinian by adoption, Origen. They furnish us with a basis of inquiry which can be enlarged by consulting some of their contemporaries, notably Clement of Alexandria.

---

[138] Cf. Schwartz, *Acta Conciliorum Oecumenicorum*, Tom. 1, Vol. 5, p. 82; St. Athanasius, Epistolae, n. 2-3; PG, 26, 1088; J. Lebon, *Sur quelques fragments de lettres attribuées à saint Epiphane de Salamine*, in *Miscellanea Giovanni Mercati*, Vol. 1, p. 25 f.

Tertullian is unmistakably clear — and radical. He accepts the virginal conception of Christ as a dogmatic truth.[139] But once launched into his polemic with the Docetists, Marcionites, and Valentinians, he is unsparing in advocating the birth of Christ as entirely normal, and in describing Mary as the mother of several children after Christ.[140] Tertullian in his forthrightness never claims to be traditional and never appeals to any dogmatic authority; on the other hand, he manifests not the slightest awareness that his denials of Our Lady's perpetual virginity contradict any ecclesiastical tradition, at least, known to him. Hence we cannot avoid inquiring whether there existed any such tradition in the Africa of Tertullian's era concerning the virgin birth, and Mary's subsequent virginity. At once, St. Cyprian, Arnobius, and Lactantius occur as likely witnesses, but their testimonies are entirely negative; St. Cyprian, for example, says absolutely nothing which would affirm or deny Tertullian's views; the same is true of anonymous writers of the period, whose works have been at times ascribed to Cyprian, and to Tertullian himself.

We are by no means justified, however, in thinking that Tertullian's opinions involved the sentiment of the African Church. It is quite possible, and perhaps probable that the fiery temperament of Tertullian could be solely responsible for wholly singular views, in this, as certainly in other matters. It is equally possible, as far as our present control of contemporary writings is concerned, that he could have publicized such opinions without ever suspecting that they might appear scandalous, and without their actually having been so; at least, we find absolutely no evidence that his statements during this period caused any offense. The African Church, as far as we know, seems to have been extremely reserved in its official declarations concerning the Blessed Virgin.

There exists a quite different perspective between Tertullian's and Origen's doctrine on Mary's perpetual virginity. After examining closely

---

[139] *De praescriptione haereticorum*, 13; PL, 2, 26; cf. ibid., 27, 49 ff., 44, 60.

[140] Concerning Christ's birth, cf. *Adversus Marcionem*, 3, 11; 4, 21; PL, 2, 336, 411 ff.; *De carne Christi*, 4, 20-23; PL, 2, 758-760, 785-790. Concerning Mary's virginity *post partum*, cf. *Adversus Marcionem*, 3, 11; 4, 19, 26, 36; PL, 2, 335, 404-406, 427, 450; *De carne Christi*, 7; PL, 2, 939; *De virginibus velandis*, 5; PL, 2, 898; *De monogamia*, 8; PL, 2, 939; *De pudicitia*, 6; PL, 2, 990 f.

these divergences and their foundations, one can scarcely avoid the impression that the answer is to be found in Christian ascetical practices and in the degree that they influenced these two authors. Tertullian himself was undoubtedly an ascetic, but as in all other things, according to his own lights and singular temperament.

With his ever increasing tendency toward Montanism, he was likewise an ever more passionate controversialist, particularly in his writings which deal with Mary's perpetual virginity. In these works his major preoccupation was to search out telling *ad hoc* arguments against concrete adversaries; hence the violent tones and attitudes adopted by him in speaking of Mary, for the sole purpose of bolstering his polemic.[141]

When Origen dealt with the question of Mary's perpetual virginity after Christ's birth, unlike Tertullian, he had no further polemical considerations, but faced the problem squarely, objectively, and for its own sake. Nevertheless, in his solution he was inspired, on his own admission, by the views of certain contemporary ascetics, devoted to a life of consecrated virginity; in their view, it was impossible and inconceivable that Mary should have submitted herself to any man after she had been overshadowed by the power of the Most High. Origen concurred fully with this conviction, and added that Mary, among all women, contained the firstfruits and perfect flowering of virginity, as her divine Son did among all men.[142] In addition, Origen held not only that Mary remained a virgin throughout her days on earth, but that she was motivated by the highest virtue, manifested by her very real and exalted sanctity, even though marred by certain deficiencies and imperfections. It is true that Origen never used the expression "ever Virgin," at least in the texts that we now possess, but he most certainly had the idea — an idea that he borrowed, not from a properly so-called tradition of the *Magisterium*, but rather from the conviction of apostles

---

[141] For the drastic change of Tertullian's perspective after he became a Montanist, see H. Rahner, *Die Marienkunde in der lateinischen Patristik*, in *Katholische Marienkunde*, ed. Sträter, Vol. 1 (Paderborn, 1947), pp. 154-161. One might also note the irenic passages dealing with Mary as the Mother of the Saviour, when there was no immediate controversial issue at stake, v.g., *De praescriptione haereticorum*, 22; *PL*, 2, 34.

[142] Comment. in Matth., 10, 17; PG, 13, 877.

and adepts of virginity.

Did Origen and the ascetics of his era consider that Mary's perpetual virginity excluded the loss of the signs of virginal integrity in her body at the moment of giving birth to Christ? This question cannot be answered with absolute certainty. It would seem, however, that Origen himself did not recognize the connection between what we now call virginity *in partu* and virginity *post partum*. The first was not unknown to him. He faced the problem in his commentary on the Epistle to Titus, and rejects the virginal birth.[143] Furthermore, we find no contrary indication in any texts of Origen which are certainly authentic; thus, he expressed himself in terms incompatible with Mary's virginity *in partu* in his Homilies on St. Luke,[144] translated by St. Jerome. From the contrary view expressed in Rufinus' translation of Origen's Homilies on Leviticus,[145] may we conclude that Origen vacillated on this matter, or that he changed his opinion definitively? G. Jouassard[146] is of the opinion that Rufinus very probably rewrote the original text of Origen to make it conform to his personal view that Mary remained a virgin *in partu;* on the other hand, J. Huhn has recently opposed Jouassard's conjecture.[147]

However, apart from this translation of Rufinus, there is nothing in the original writings of Origen positively in favor of the virgin birth, but rather, at the most, vague expressions.[148]

Whatever be the final decision of scholars on Origen, he certainly did not attain the clarity and precision of his predecessor, Clement of Alexandria, who had taken a stand on Mary's virginity *in partu* and *post partum*, a fact which shows that the issue was discussed in Egypt, at

---

[143] Cf. the text preserved in the *Apologia Origenis* by Pamphylus and Eusebius; *PG*, 17, 554, and reproduced in *PG*, 12, 493 f.

[144] *Hom. in Lucam*, 14; *PG*, 13, 1834, 1836 f.

[145] *In Lev.*, 8, 2; *PG*, 12, 493 f.

[146] Cf. G. Jouassard, *art. cit.* (*supra*, note 121), p. 81, who believes that this probably happened.

[147] See J. Huhn, *Das Geheimnis der Jungfrau-Mutter Maria nach dem kirchenvater Ambrosius* (Würzburg, 1954), p. 113 f.; cf. also Lehner, Die Marienverehrung in den ersten Jahrhunderten (Stuttgart, 1886), p. 124; and Neubert, Marie dans l'église anténicéenne (Paris, 1908), p. 182.

[148] Cf. *Comment. in Ioannem*, 2, 30; *PG*, 14, 181; *Comment. in Matt., Serm.* 26; *PG*, 13, 1631; Contra Celsum, 6, 73; *PG*, 11, 1408.

least, at the end of the second century. Clement's remarks on Our Lady are brief. If the Latin adaptation of Clement, *Adumbrationes in epistolas catholicas*, expresses his personal views accurately, he certainly held Mary's virginity *post partum*,[149] and thus may very well have been one of those ascetics, mentioned by Origen, who refused absolutely to admit the possibility of Mary's having had other children after Christ's birth. There can be no doubt about the virginal birth; Clement held it explicitly;[150] he realized that it was not held by a great number, who wished to maintain that Christ's birth in relation to His mother was perfectly normal and natural;[151] he protests vigorously against these views. Clement's uncompromising doctrine on the virginal birth has been attributed by some[152] to a Docetist tendency. Certainly, this claim is due to a gross exaggeration; Clement never denied that Christ was fully human or that He submitted Himself to the same lowly conditions of human life as ours, but rather stressed, altogether legitimately, that, since Christ was equally true God as well as true man, there was no physical necessity of His submitting to these humiliating conditions; in each case there was an act of voluntary condescension on His part. Much less is there any evidence that Docetism was responsible for Clement's doctrine on the virginal birth, which was probably greatly influenced by those different apocryphal sources which served as the bases for the compilation now known as *The Gospel of Saint James*.[153]

---

[149] *Adumbrationes in epistolas catholicas; PG,* 9, 731. These *Adumbrationes* are only a Latin adaptation of Clement's *Hypotypses*. We cannot rely absolutely on this text, since it is a translated adaptation, with the expressed intention of expurgating anything that might be offensive, cf. *PG,* 70, 1120. On the other hand, there is no indication that in the matter of Mary's virginity there was any emendation of Clement's own words. We may note that the texts of Clement cited by Eusebius (*Historia Ecclesiastica,* II, 1, 3-4 f., 9, 2 ff.) are unfortunately too vague to be decisive and to dissipate any hesitation.

[150] *Stromata,* 7, 16; *PG,* 9, 529-532.

[151] *Loc. cit.*

[152] Thus, L. Coulange (pseudonym for Turmel), *La Vierge Marie* (Paris, 1925), pp. 30-32, and A. von Harnack, *Lehrbuch der Dogmengeschichte,* Vol. 1, ed. 4 (Tübingen, 1909), p. 286, footnote 1.

[153] Cf. Ortiz de Urbina, *Die Marienkunde in der Patristik des Ostens,* in Sträter, *op. cit.,* pp. 94, 98. Note particularly the beginning of Chapter XVIII, 2 of our actual text of this apocryphal gospel in E. Amann, *Le Protoévangile et ses remaniemants latins* (Paris, 1910), p. 248 f.

The contrast between Clement's uncompromising stand and Origen's subsequent wavering position shows (and Clement's own statements corroborate this) that Catholics in Egypt felt that the matter of Mary's virginity *in partu* was quite open to discussion and by no means settled definitively. Was the same true of Mary's virginity *post partum*? Undoubtedly, for although Origen rallied to Clement's opinion here, he never asserts, or even implies, that there was any obligation for a Catholic to do so. He rather expresses his clear understanding that the virginity of Mary *post partum* was the particular view of those ascetics devoted to the practice of virginity and was based on their concept of her complete and perpetual virginity.

Thus we have the following picture of a considerable portion of the Catholic world at the end of the second century, and the first part of the third, namely, complete liberty to represent Mary's virginity as one wished, with the exception of her virginal conception, which was clearly regarded as a dogma beyond all dispute. Certainly, the concordant testimony of Tertullian, Clement, and Origen in itself, and apart from other considerations, would not constitute them as witnesses to the contemporary belief of the entire Christian world. But in these three we find the views of the outstanding leaders of thought in Africa, Egypt, and Palestine; at least indirectly they reflect the thought of Asia Minor, if not of the entire East. Rome itself is not excluded; for Tertullian was quite conversant with Roman views. Origen had not only been in Rome but had traveled widely from Italy through Greece to Arabia. Clement also was an experienced traveler and remained so even to the last years of his life.

It is unfortunate that we have no clear testimony from their contemporaries, such as St. Hippolytus.[154] In the West, Cyprian, Novatian, Arnobius, and Lactantius, as we have mentioned, contribute

---

[154] The most pertinent texts that we know of from Hippolytus concerning the virginity of Mary are an extract on "The Ark of the Alliance" (preserved by Theodoret); cf. the edition in *Griechische christliche Schriftsteller,* published by the *Kirchenväter Kommission* of the Prussian Academy, Vol. 1, Part 2 (Leipzig), p. 146 f.; also *PG,* 1, 83, 85-88. There is also a passage from the *Benedictiones Moysis,* if one can rely on the Georgian version which we have in *Texte und Untersuchungen,* Vol. 26, Part 1, p. 75. Neither text is definitive, either for or against Mary's virginity. Cf. also G. Jouassard, *art. cit.* (*supra,* note 129), Vol. 12, 1932, pp. 509-532, and Vol. 13, 1933, pp. 25-37.

PERPETUAL VIRGINITY 311

nothing positive; the same is true of Gregory the Wonder-Worker[155] and Denis of Alexandria in the East. Although an advocate of the ascetical practices of virginity, Methodius[156] is as vague as Hippolytus regarding Mary's virginity. Similarly the *Didascalia Apostolorum*, without being any more explicit, at least places Our Lady in a very exalted rank of sanctity, apparently above St. John the Baptist.[157]

To discover a more precise indication, we have to turn to the *De recta in Deum fide* at the beginning of the fourth century. Here we find the doctrine of the virginal birth viewed with a certain disquietude in Catholic circles, because of the fear of Docetism and Manichaeism.[158] This fact should not be surprising, for about the same time, Eusebius of Caesarea manifests the same sentiments,[159] although he explicitly denies that the "brothers of the Lord" are children of Mary.[160]

In the course of the third century, we must note an increased influence of the Apocrypha in favor of Mary's virginity *post partum*, and particularly, the new influence of a certain apocryphal writing attributed to Zacharias, and mentioned by Origen in his commentary on St. Matthew.[161] This latter work could well have exercised a favorable influence toward accepting Mary's virginity *in partu*, though it probably did not influence Origen himself. The increased influence of the

---

[155] It would be otherwise, if one could appeal legitimately to the homilies attributed to Gregory, but this is impossible; cf. M. Jugie, *Les homélies mariales attribuées à saint Grégoire le Thaumaturge*, in *Analecta Bollandiana*, Vol. 48, 1925, pp. 86-95.

[156] Methodius in his *Symposium* (*PG*, 18, 212) praises Mary's purity, but together with many other persons, several of whom are married, and without asserting any special preeminence for Mary.

[157] Cf. *Didascalia Apostolorum*, ed. R. H. Connolly (Oxford, 1929), Ch. 15, p. 142, and Ch. 19, p. 164.

[158] *De recta in Deum fide*, 4, 14, *Griechische christliche Schriftsteller*, Vol. 4, pp. 170-173.

[159] Cf. the text of Origen cited with approval in the *Apologia* re-edited in collaboration with Pamphilus, *PG*, 17, 554, and especially, *Demonstr. Evangel.*, 10; *PG*, 22, 773-776.

[160] The only text that seems to be decisive for this denial is in his *Comment. in Psalmos*, 68, 9; *PG*, 23, 737-740. Eusebius is prodigal with sonorous epithets applied to Mary. He is probably the first to call her "the Holy Virgin," and uses the title frequently; perhaps he also called her "the all-Holy Virgin." Jouassard, however, *op. cit.* (*supra*, note 121), p. 84, observes cautiously: "Mais que signifient au vrai ces expressions, surtout dans la bouche d'un homme de cour tel qu'Eusèbe?"

[161] *Serm.* 25; *PG*, 13, 1631 f.

Apocrypha in general was probably quite gradual and almost imperceptible, and yet for this very reason perhaps more efficacious.

FROM THE COUNCIL OF NICAEA TO THE PRELIMINARIES OF THE COUNCIL OF EPHESUS

Here we are in the golden age of patristic writings, so important and yet so widely scattered in their sources, that it is wise to distinguish clearly the West from the East, except to stress any possible influence of one on the other.

Naturally, the speculations of Arius on the person of Christ aroused interest in Marian theology; if Christ is not consubstantial with the Father, Mary obviously could not be truly the Mother of God. It is interesting to note one of the first documents concerning the Arian heresy before the Council of Nicaea, the encyclical letter of Alexander of Alexandria, in which he announces to his colleagues the deposition of Arius, and honors Mary formally with the title *Theotokos*.[162] From a source which is almost certainly St. Athanasius, we learn that Alexander thought so highly of Mary as the Mother of God, that he proposed her to the consecrated virgins of his diocese as the type and very image of the life of heaven.[163] He seems to have made this a theme of predilection, running through his various sermons and instructions — an important indication, since his successor in the See of Alexandria, St. Athanasius, was to follow his example so closely.

St. Athanasius was thoroughly convinced of the views of his master and predecessor concerning the life of virginity, not however to the extent that he spoke much of Mary in his writings that have come down to us in Greek; rather, he manifested such reserve with regard to Mary that it is difficult to determine whether he held the virginal birth.[164] On the other hand, in a work transmitted to us in Coptic, and most probably genuine, he is much less reserved.[165] The manuscript of this essay is

---

[162] PG, 18, 568.

[163] Cf. *Le Muséon*, Vol. 42, 1929, p. 259; note also *ibid.*, p. 256; cf. note 164, infra.

[164] Cf. *De Incarnatione Verbi, 17;* PG, *25, 125;* Ep. ad Epictetum, *7;* PG, 26, 1061 f.

[165] This work was discovered and edited by L. Th. Lefort, *Saint Athanase: sur la virginité*, in *Le Muséon*, Vol. 42, 1929, pp. 197-275. Several critics have favored the authenticity of this work, and their view seems certain because of St. Ambrose's obvious dependence on

incomplete and is also textually imperfect; nevertheless, enough can be read to understand that Athanasius defends vigorously against opponents that Our Lady had no children except Jesus. He also describes the life of Mary, especially as a young girl, in most flattering terms; the object of this essay is obviously to inspire and exhort Christian virgins to imitate and reproduce in their lives the example of Mary, the unique model of virginity.

In Egypt, then, we find St. Athanasius clearly teaching Mary's virginity *post partum;* however, he is well aware that his view is not universally accepted, but is even attacked. He betrays no surprise at this opposition, and by no means proposes his own views as an article of Catholic faith. Nothing stronger can be found in his contemporary, St. Cyril of Jerusalem; as a matter of record, not one word is to be found on Our Lady's virginity *post partum* in his famous *Catacheses.* Eusebius of Caesarea was equally reserved. If the *Acta Archelai* are a product of this same Palestinian milieu, they confirm the attitude of reserve toward Mary's virginity *post partum,* and show rather hostility toward the virginal birth.[166]

St. Ephraem of Syria is much less explicit than he is sometimes represented, if we restrict ourselves to those works which up to the present have been duly authenticated.[167] The *corpus* attributed to Ephraem is truly immense, but has never been assembled in a single edition, nor has it ever been studied as a whole in a truly critical manner. It is not difficult, however, to disengage a certain number of writings from this mass, especially poetic series and commentaries, which all modern critics admit to be authentic. Restricting our attention to these writings alone, we cannot avoid the conclusion that he, too, is quite reserved, and that what he writes about Mary is far from always being

---

it; cf. A. Spann, *Essai sur la théologie Mariale de saint Ambrose* (Lyon, 1931).

[166] *Acta Archelai,* 47-50; *PG,* 10, 1508-1516.

[167] For this reason, L. Hammersberger's, *Die Mariologie der ephremischen Schriften* (Innsbruck, 1938), should not be taken as an objective exposé of St. Ephraem's personal and genuine views on Mary, as Jouassard, *op. cit.,* p. 88, notes: "Dans ces conditions, l'exposé ne peut être qu'une sorte de mixture, dont un critique averti peut seul tirer quelque chose, et à grand peine, touchant Ephrem personnellement."

to her honor.[168] We find positive witness to Mary's virginity *post partum* only in his commentary on the Diatessaron,[169] and this through the medium of an Armenian translation. Even here, there is no question of proposing Mary's virginity *post partum* as an object of dogmatic belief; a fact which should make us less surprised to find in the East, even in the middle of the fourth century, persons, sometimes of considerable authority and prestige, who attributed to Jesus a veritable *cortège* of brothers and sisters.

For such is the undeniable fact; not perhaps in the case of Apollinaris, despite the rather common rumor that he denied Our Lady's virginity *post partum*. St. Epiphanius, who was aware of the rumor, found it difficult to believe.[170] Whatever be the truth concerning Apollinaris' views, there can be absolutely no doubt about the famous Bishop Eunomius of Cyzicum, who had no hesitation in airing his denial of Mary's virginity *post partum*, in a Christian cathedral, most probably at Constantinople, and in the presence of the Patriarch Eudoxius.[171] These men were Arians, it is true, and this fact probably explains their self-assurance in part, but only in part, since the Arians as well as Catholics called Mary "the Virgin," even "the Holy Virgin."[172]

The reply provoked by Eunomius' discourse is typical of the temper and attitude of the times. The answer came from a Catholic source,

---

[168] Cf. Jouassard, *op. cit.*, p. 84, note 9.

[169] Cf. the Latin translation by Aucher-Mösinger (Venice, 1876), pp. 23-26; cf. *ibid.*, pp. 54, 122 f., 245. The formulas in the Armenian are not any more coherent regarding the virgin birth. There are further grounds for hesitation, since St. Ephraem's *Madrascha IV*, which is certainly authentic and is handed down to us in Syriac, has certain passages which are scarcely compatible with the virgin birth. In his translation of this poem, *Ausgewählte Schriften des hl. Ephrem von Syrien*, in *Bibliothek der Kirchenväter*, Vol. 2 (Kempten, 1873), p. 61 f., P. Zingerle has softened the expressions, but his note 1, p. 62 (*ibid.*) allows us to capture the original idea. The Latin translation of this same *Madrascha* should not be used as rendering faithfully St. Ephraem; it is only a paraphrase, often far removed from the original Syriac.

[170] Cf. *Ankurôtos*, 13; *PG*, 43, 40 f.; *Panarion, haer.* 77, 36, and *haer.* 78, 1 f.; *PG*, 43, 696, 700.

[171] The scene of the event is known to us through the résumé by Photius of the *Historia Ecclesiastica* of Philostorgius: cf. Book 6, in *Griechische christliche Schriftsteller*, Vol. 21, p. 71; it is confirmed by the commentary, with its marked Arian nuance, called *Opus imperfectum in Matthaeum*, *PG*, 56, 635 f.

[172] Cf. Eunomius himself, *Liber apologeticus*, 17; *PG*, 30, 864.

which we have strong grounds to believe was St. Basil, in the form of a discourse on the feast of the Theophany.[173] In this sermon, after brief remarks on the eternal generation of the Word, the author takes up his main point, which is to comment on the account of the temporal birth of Christ given by St. Matthew. The author also focuses his attention on the possibility of conjugal relations between Mary and St. Joseph after the birth of Christ; he rejects this possibility, but not by appealing to dogmatic belief; he has no consciousness of any obligation from this angle, and even generously admits that there is no such obligation; faith, he candidly admits, demands only that we believe in the permanence of Mary's virginity up to (and including) the Incarnation; after the virginal conception there is no obligation imposed by faith.[174] Despite this openly acknowledged freedom of opinion, the author goes on to stress that many excellent Christians — he calls them "Philochristoi" — refuse to admit that Our Lady ever had conjugal relations with St. Joseph; he accepts and espouses their view, and adds as a reason the narrative of a certain Zachary who died in defense of Mary's honor.[175] We may pass over this confirmatory reason, which is certainly ill-suited to prove

---

[173] This discourse has been published by the Maurists under the title *Homilia in sanctam Christi generationem; PG,* 31, 1457-1476. The first editor, Dom Garnier, for reasons which seem quite trivial, relegated it to the *opera spuria.* The second editor, Dom Maran, on the other hand, was inclined to admit its authenticity; see *PG,* 29, 174. The majority of modern critics are still more favorable toward its authenticity; even if the author is not St. Basil, he certainly is one for whom the archenemy is Arianism, as the beginning of the discourse proves conclusively.

[174] *Loc cit.:* "[The opinion that Mary bore several children after Christ] ... does not run counter to faith; for, virginity was imposed on Mary as a necessity, only up to the time that she served as an instrument for the Incarnation, while, on the other hand, her subsequent virginity had no great importance with regard to the mystery of the Incarnation."

[175] A reference to the apocryphal source concerning a certain Zachary, mentioned by Origen, cf. his *Comment. in Matt., Serm.* 25; *PG,* 13, 1631 f. From these indications in Origen and Basil, it seems clear that this story was first given to the public to conciliate favor for Zachary, as an authorized witness and moreover a Jew, in support of Mary's virginity *post partum.* Zachary, so the story goes, was put to death for holding that Jesus was not born of an earthly father. Subsequently the story was used to insinuate something more, namely, that Mary never had conjugal relations with her husband; the same incident and use of it is found in a discourse which may come from Gregory of Nyssa; cf. *PG,* 46, 1136 f.

Mary's virginity *post partum,* but we should not gloss over lightly the situation revealed by such a tale being used as a proof. For, it is evident from this discourse that in a region of the Greek world, apparently Asia Minor,[176] an important Churchman, without any doubt the Archbishop of Caesarea, St. Basil, did not hold the perpetual virginity of Mary as a dogmatic truth, nor did his metropolitan Churches. Nevertheless, there was a strong movement toward advocating and accepting Mary's perpetual virginity — a movement gladly promoted by St. Basil himself, because of the "Philochristoi" who espoused it. Who were these cryptic *Philochristoi?* We are not told in the discourse, but they could well have been Origen and the ascetics of whom he speaks;[177] they might have been St. Athanasius and the ascetics formed under his guidance, or finally St. Epiphanius, if at that time he had adopted the views on ascetical life which were so characteristic of him and exercised such influence on Marian theology.

St. Epiphanius enters the picture at least while St. Basil was still Bishop, for Epiphanius alluded to Basil in his *Panarion* (written in 377), and even in his *Ankurôtos* (written in 374).[178] In the *Panarion,* St. Epiphanius repeats almost word for word a certain letter, addressed by him some years previously to the Christians of Arabia, in which he attacks an opinion current there, that Mary after the birth of Christ had conjugal relations with St. Joseph. Was this opinion very widespread? St. Epiphanius does not claim that it was. However, advocates of the same opinion were censured in a fragment, probably written by a predecessor of St. Epiphanius, Titus the Bishop of Bostra, who nevertheless admitted, as Epiphanius did later, that Joseph had children by a previous marriage and that these were the "brethren of the Lord."[179] In his writings, St. Epiphanius sustained with great forcefulness Our Lady's virginity after

---

[176] The exact place where this discourse was given is not certain.

[177] Possibly also Clement of Alexandria and his adherents.

[178] Cf. *Ankurôtos,* 13; *PG,* 43, 40 f.; in the *Panarion,* several times, cf. *PG,* 41, 164 f., 385-388, 908; *PG,* 42, 640, 696.

[179] This statement of Titus is contained in a fragment of the *Comment. in Lucam,* ed. Sickenberger, in *Texte und Untersuchungen,* Vol. 21, Part 1, p. 174 f. A similar view that Mary had several children is found in another fragment of different authorship; cf. *ibid.,* p. 257 f.

Christ's birth; he made use of all sorts of arguments, not only from Scripture, but also from supposedly historical sources, and stressed the previous marriage of St. Joseph to explain the "brethren of the Lord."[180]

The views of St. Epiphanius were destined to have ever increasing influence in the East, and finally to be accepted without question. The great authority enjoyed by him as Bishop of Constantia is well known. He placed in his catalogue of heresies the view that denied Our Lady's virginity *post partum*, without however citing any ecclesiastical precedent; his word was sufficient. Although the term "heresy" at that time was not too precise and by no means had the strict technical meaning of our day, it is quite clear that, although not everywhere nor immediately,[181] the doctrine attacked by Epiphanius was generally considered to be opposed to orthodoxy. His influence therefore concerning Mary's virginity *post partum* was paramount.

At this same period, the Church in Syria began to be pre-eminent in the quantity and quality of its ecclesiastical writings; not only those who wrote in Syriac contributed to this development, but also those whose native language was Greek. Unfortunately, it is difficult to determine with resources now available the views of Diodorus of Tarsus or of Theodore of Mopsuestia. Only in St. John Chrysostom do we find sufficiently abundant documentation to gain some idea of the views prevalent in Syria concerning Our Lady's virginity. Although Chrysostom never personally used the term "Mother of God," he was well aware of the fact and accepted it completely. It was this concept which seems to be the foundation of his assured doctrine on Mary's virginity; for he was absolutely convinced of her perpetual virginity,[182]

---

[180] The so-called historical sources of St. Epiphanius are certain ancient historians, but particularly the *Apocrypha*, and concern principally a previous marriage of St. Joseph together with an account of his sons and daughters; cf. *PG*, 42, 708, and *PG*, 41, 394. Scriptural arguments are used throughout, with *argumenta convenientiae;* as Jouassard (*op. cit.*, p. 91) notes: "... le tout présenté parfois dans un beau pêle-mêle."

[181] Cf. the case of St. Nilus; *PG*, 79, 181. Under the name of Amphilochius of Iconium (*PG*, 39, 48 f.), we read of an analogous situation with regard to Mary's virginity *in partu*.

[182] *In Matt., Hom.* 5, 2-3; *PG*, 57, 56-59. In this text, where we find St. John Chrysostom's most apodictic assertion, he presents Mary's virginity *in partu* and *post partum* only as deductions, whereas he considers her virginity *ante partum* to be contained formally and explicitly in Scripture, and hence to be *de fide*; cf. *PG*, 57, 58.

and specified particularly the virgin birth[183] — a conviction not to be found, as we have seen, in Epiphanius, nor in St. Gregory Nazianzen,[184] and only vaguely proposed by Amphilochius.[185]

Chrysostom's doctrine, preached first in Antioch where he was already renowned as an orator, and later in Constantinople with the added prestige of his office as Patriarch, exerted wide influence, not only in his immediate congregations, but in the court, and in the whole Christian world. One of his successors in the See of Constantinople, Atticus, preached a sermon in the capitol which had wide reverberations; in it he set Mary on a pinnacle above all creatures and developed extensively the antithesis between her and Eve; he expressed clearly her perpetual virginity, and also paid her the honor of having made an explicit vow, or at least intention, of preserving her virginity.[186]

Are we justified in asserting that Our Lady's perpetual virginity was universally accepted at this time in the East? We have every reason to ask the question, because toward the end of this period, St. Nilus wrote against certain persons who claimed the opposite. His position is set forth in three letters addressed to an exalted Churchman named Cyril, most probably Cyril of Alexandria.[187] Naturally the question arises as to Cyril's own views on the matter, but we must be content to say that there is nothing in Cyril's writings before 428 against Mary's perpetual

---

[183] *In Genesim*, Hom. 49, 2; *PG*, 54, 446. We may now add his discourse *De nativitate Domini*, 1; *PG*, 56, 387 ff., since J. P. Martin has shown its authenticity; cf. *Le Muséon*, Vol. 54, 1941, pp. 30-33.

[184] Certain expressions of Gregory could be interpreted for the virgin birth, but they are not formal and explicit; see his *Serm.* 50: *De baptismate Domini*, 45; *PG*, 36, 424.

[185] *De nativitate*, 1, 2, 4; *PG*, 39, 37-41; *De Hypapante*, 1; *PG*, 39, 44-48; however in following pages of the latter work (*PG*, 39, 45-48), he is much more precise, and comes close to an explicit affirmation of Mary's virginity in partu.

[186] This sermon, discovered only recently in Syriac, was published simultaneously, by J. Lebon, *Discours d'Atticus de Constantinople sur la sainte Mère de Dieu*, in *Le Muséon*, Vol. 46, 1933, pp. 167-202, and by M. Brière, *Une homélie inédite d'Atticus patriarche de Constantinople (406-425)*, in *Revue de l'Orient Chrétien*, Vol. 29, 1933, pp. 160-186. There is, however, legitimate doubt as to whether this discourse was preached by Atticus himself; some conjectures have named the orator variously, as Gregory of Nazianzen, or Proclus who at the time, it seems, was Atticus' secretary, and later was Bishop of Constantinople.

[187] St. Nilus, *Epistolae*, lib. 1, 269-271; *PG*, 79, 181 f.

virginity, nor, it must be confessed, in favor. In St. Nilus' three letters, the first and third deal with Mary's virginity *post partum*, and the second with her virginity *in partu;* he sharply rebukes his adversaries and borrows his arguments from Epiphanius, but does not imitate Epiphanius' *Panarion* by calling them heretics. Without any doubt, St. Nilus marks the close of an era, for at this period we have no knowledge of a single bishop who opposed Mary's perpetual virginity; the last member of the hierarchy in opposition was Bonosus, whose diocese was at least partially in Illyricum. He was condemned finally as a heretic by his colleagues in 392 and was deposed from his See. Perhaps his deposition took place in Thessalonica, but the formal decision was not taken without the intervention of the Western episcopate, to such an extent, as we shall see, that without their encouragement and inspiration, it probably would not have occurred.

Christian literature in the West flowered much more slowly after the year 325 than in the East. The first notable author was St. Hilary of Poitiers who flourished toward the middle of the fourth century. The next fifty years unfolded the first phase of Marian theology, Our Lady's perpetual virginity, and toward the year 400, this question was settled for all time in the West. The *Commentary on Saint Matthew,* written before the year 356, is the first work of St. Hilary that we possess. The saint takes a decided position in favor of Mary's virginity *post partum.*[188] This attitude proves, as does also the anonymous *Laudes Domini,*[189] that the doctrine was accepted widely in the West. Hilary, however, is aware of some adversaries; he files impressive charges against them, accusing them particularly of being irreligious and ignorant of spiritual doctrine. If they were inveterate heretics, recognized as such, would he have used stronger language? There is no doubt that the terms actually employed by Hilary tended to classify them as unorthodox. He gives us no clue as to their identity. His Scriptural arguments against them are not too strong, but at least the conviction of the exegete could not be stronger, and seems to have been founded principally on Hilary's esteem of

---

[188] *Commentary on Saint Matthew,* 1, 3-4; *PL,* 9, 921 f.; it is worthy of note that neither here nor elsewhere does the Bishop of Poitiers concern himself with Mary's virginity *in partu;* he ignores it completely.

[189] The *Laudes Domini* were written by an unknown rhetorician of Autun; cf. *PL,* 19, 384.

Mary's exalted privileges as Mother of the Saviour.

The author of the anonymous *Consultationes Zachaei*[190] equals, if he does not surpass, Hilary in his esteem for Mary. He is singular among his contemporaries in the fact that he holds as *de fide* not only Mary's virginity *post partum*, but also *in partu.*[191] This unknown author was also an adherent of the ascetical movement already favored by St. Hilary[192] — a movement which almost literally mushroomed in the second half of the fourth century, particularly in the West, and, most of all, in northern Italy. St. Zeno of Verona was an ardent champion of this movement,[193] and also of Mary's privileges; he was aware that some held that she had children after Jesus, but protested that Mary was always a virgin — a virgin in her conception of Christ, a virgin in giving birth, and a virgin after His birth.[194]

In this milieu, about the year 373 or 374, St. Ambrose became Bishop of Milan and successor to Auxentius, an Oriental by birth, and also a militant Arian. May not this fact explain, at least in part, how, by way of reaction, Ambrose became such an ardent champion of Mary? Scarcely three years had passed after his election when he published the fruits of his sermons and meditations on Mary in a small work entitled *De virginibus ad Marcellianam*,[195] dedicated to his sister. Here we find a portrait of Mary which is astonishing for this period; he does not hesitate to call her the Mother of God; he insists on her absolute and perpetual virginity. This early presentation of Ambrose's Marian

---

[190] Cf. the edition of Dom Morin in *Florilegium Patristicum* (Bonn, 1934). Dom Morin (*ibid.*, pp. 1-3) wishes to identify the author with Firmicius Maternus and to place him in a Roman *milieu;* he also feels that the author was in direct and favorable contact with the highest Roman ecclesiastical authorities. Scarcely a single critic has followed Morin in these conjectures.

[191] *Consultationes Zachaei*, 1, 9-11; *PL*, 20, 1078 f.; in Morin's edition, pp. 13-15. It is noteworthy that there is not even a single allusion whereby we can judge the author's views on Mary's virginity post partum.

[192] *Op. cit.; PL*, 20, 1151; in Morin's edition, p. 100 f.

[193] *Tractatus* 5, lib. 1; *PL*, 11, 301-311.

[194] *Tractatus* 8, lib. 2; *PL*, 11, 414 f., where we read the remarkable formula: "O Magnum sacramentum! Maria Virgo incorrupta concepit, post conceptionem virgo peperit, post partum virgo permansit."

[195] *PL*, 16, 187-232. For St. Ambrose's portrait of Mary, see *ibid.*, 208-211.

doctrine is without any doubt based on a small work of St. Athanasius,[196] but far surpasses Athanasius, especially in its uncompromising doctrine on Our Lady's perfect sanctity, without the slightest shadow of moral imperfection or blemish.

Also, from the beginning of his episcopacy, Ambrose was an ardent champion of virginity and of the ascetical practices of Egyptian monasticism, made known to the West by St. Athanasius, who spent several periods of exile in Treves, Rome, and northern Italy.[197] These ideals and practices were by no means received with universal favor. In the year 380, a certain Carterius entered the lists in Rome to espouse the cause of virginity and monastic practices; he drew his main argument from his contention of Mary's absolute and perpetual virginity. At the time there was marked hostility in some Roman circles against these ascetical practices, due probably to a reaction against Priscillianism and Manichaeism. Priscillian himself visited Rome and Milan in the years 381-382, in an attempt to stabilize his doctrinal views; among a certain group there seems to have been a strong temptation to identify and lump together all advocates of the ascetical life and of the practice of virginity with the Priscillianist faction.

Carterius soon found an open opponent in Helvidius. Despite St. Jerome's attempts to discredit him completely, Helvidius was a man of intelligence, and by no means devoid of all theological and literary formation. He wrote a well-constructed essay with the intent of proving that Mary had other children besides Jesus, but without any malicious design of denigrating the Mother of Christ. On the contrary, his intent was to extol what he considered her twofold greatness — her admirable

---

[196] Cf. *supra*, note 165. St. Ambrose's knowledge and utilization of this work is an accepted fact among critics; see A. Janssens, *Een Marialeven vermeld bij S. Athanasius (373) en S. Ambrosius (397)*, in *De Standaard van Maria*, Vol. 11, 1931, pp. 9-12; M. Lefort, in *Le Muséon*, Vol. 48, 1935, pp. 55-73; Dom Capelle, in *Recherches de Théologie Ancienne et Mediévale*, Vol. 4, 1932, p. 270; P. Halkin, in *Analecta Bollandiana*, Vol. 55, 1937, p. 117.

[197] Cf. E. Schwartz, *Zur Kirchengeschichte des vierten Jahrhunderts*, in *Zeitschrift für neutestamentliche Wissenschaft und die Kunde der älteren Kirche*, Vol. 14, 1935, p. 131 ff. It is quite probable that St. Athanasius re-edited his famous *Life of St. Anthony*, at the request of his Latin friends, because of their consuming interest in ascetical practices and the life of virginity; cf. G. Garitte, *Un témoin important du texte de la vie de s. Antoine par s. Athanase* (Rome, 1939).

and miraculous virginity until the birth of Christ, and her exemplary motherhood thereafter in giving birth to the brothers and sisters of the Lord mentioned in the Gospels. His final purpose was to prove against Carterius that virginity is not superior to marriage, but rather perfectly equal in perfection; the two states of life were lived with equal perfection by the Mother of the Saviour.[198]

This treatise of Helvidius impressed the Roman milieu profoundly, and so effectively that it even converted to his views some of the leading promoters of asceticism and the practice of virginity. Among those who remained firm in their conviction of the superiority of virginity there was great anxiety, but the hierarchy took no part in the conflict. At this juncture, St. Jerome took up the cudgels against Helvidius. Still young, but rich in experience and in his knowledge of Scripture, Jerome had only recently arrived at Rome from Constantinople, after his formation under the instruction of St. Gregory of Nazianzen and after his apprenticeship in Hebrew and exegesis in Syria. Recently, too, he had had a brief meeting with St. Epiphanius, who had come to Rome with Paulinus of Antioch to discuss the schism which was so troublesome to the Catholics of Syria and of the entire East. St. Epiphanius had just returned to the East, so it fell to the lot of Jerome, instead of Epiphanius, to repel the attack of Helvidius against Our Lady's virginity *post partum*. He could do it the more easily and authoritatively because of his close friendship with the reigning Pope Damasus, at the instigation of his friends who urged him to intervene. There were many among the ascetics whom he had encouraged in their arduous way of life.

St. Jerome's *Adversus Helvidium* is really not much more than a pamphlet.[199] It was, however, sufficiently long to permit him to tear his adversary to pieces. The essential theme is the superiority of virginity over marriage, which he wishes to prove by establishing that Mary never admitted conjugal relations with St. Joseph; he is certain that Scripture furnishes a solid proof, and founds the tradition of Mary's absolute virginity. His work enjoyed remarkable success; it quickly won back in Roman circles whatever ground had been lost to Helvidius. But above all, it succeeded so well in implanting the doctrine of Mary's

---

[198] Cf. Jouassard, *La personnalité d'Helvidius*, in *Mélanges* J. Saunier (Lyon, 1944).

[199] *PL*, 23, 183-206.

PERPETUAL VIRGINITY 323

virginity *post partum*, that it never again was seriously doubted in Roman circles.

Nevertheless, the opponents were by no means silenced; a little later, 389-390, they renewed the attack, again in Rome. Pope St. Damasus had died in the meantime and had been succeeded by Pope Siricius who was far from being numbered among Jerome's friends; in fact, before the election they had been rivals. Hence the situation of Jerome in Rome was entirely different from the days of Damasus, and he was obliged to flee to the Orient, fulminating dire prophecies against Babylon.[200] The new attack was launched by Jovinian who had himself for a time followed the ascetical life, but had grown weary and had relaxed his efforts. From this time he began to scoff furtively at his former associates, in words and in writing. Now, however, the Holy See intervened promptly.

Through information received from laymen, Pope Siricius submitted to his clergy for censure a tract in which the following scandalous statement was made: "It is a culpable abuse to exalt virginity as superior to the marriage state." This and other similar propositions were condemned as unorthodox, and Jovinian with eight of his followers was excommunicated.[201] Condemned by the highest ecclesiastical authority, Jovinian turned to the civil power for aid; he made an effort to delate his adversaries as Manichaeans; hence his journey to Milan where in 390 Emperor Theodosius was sojourning.

Discussions and interventions concerning Priscillianism had become so heated that, in view of Jovinian's charges of Manichaeism (associated popularly with Priscillianism), Pope Siricius became quite chary and timid about renewing the initiative against Jovinian. Hence he sent an embassy with full entourage to apprise the Bishop of Milan, St. Ambrose, of the whole matter, with the intent of conciliating his favor for the Roman ecclesiastical view, and of urging him to intercede for this viewpoint with the Emperor.[202]

---

[200] Cf. F. Cavallera, *Saint Jérome: sa vie et son oeuvre*, Vol. 1 (Louvain-Paris, 1922), pp. 113-120.

[201] Cf. St. Augustine, *Retractationes*, lib. 2, c. 22, n. 1; *PL*, 32, 639.

[202] Cf. W. Haller, *Jovinianus*, in *Texte und Untersuchungen*, Vol. 17, Part 2, p. 124 ff., and also the letter *Optarem* of Pope Siricius, placed by Migne among tne letters of St. Ambrose; *PL*, 16, 1121-1123.

St. Ambrose was by no means surprised at this turn of events. Since the publication of his *De virginibus ad Marcellianam* he had never wearied in his struggles in favor of virginity and of ascetical practices. On the other hand, whether or not he had yet adopted a definite stand on Priscillianism, he was utterly opposed to Manichaeism and to anything that might resemble it. He took up the request of Siricius gladly, and by a curious *tour de force* succeeded in prevailing on the civil power to expel Jovinian, on the score that he, who had initiated charges of Manichaeism against the advocates of virginity, was himself a Manichaean.[203]

Immediately on receiving the Pope's request, then, St. Ambrose brought the whole matter up before a synod composed of the bishops of northern Italy. This synod not only made its own the Roman condemnation, but even surpassed it, by signalizing as erroneous Jovinian's denial of Mary's virginity *in partu*, which had been passed over in silence by the Roman condemnation. This denial was considered by the bishops of northern Italy to be just as serious as Jovinian's denial of Our Lady's virginity *post partum*. Ambrose himself took the lead in advocating the virgin birth. He preached it publicly as did St. Zeno of Verona.[204] In its reply to the Pope,[205] the Synod presented a brief dissertation on Mary's virginity *in partu*, with the twofold aim of showing, first, how well founded was this doctrine, and consequently, of pointing out the obligation for all Catholics to accept it. Through the universal acceptance of the virgin birth, it was thought that the

---

[203] Cf. the synodal letter, *Recognovimus*, in reply to the *Optarem* of Siricius, *PL*, 16, 1128. This letter does not state openly, but implies that there was an exchange of identical accusations by both parties to the controversy. Jovinian had attacked the ascetical view as being Manichaean; the bishops of northern Italy hurled the accusation back at him with the argument that he, Jovinian, by denying the virginal birth, denied equivalently the birth itself of Christ, and was therefore convicted of Manichaean propensities; the insinuation is fallacious, but this mode of dialectic is not unique in polemical writings of this period.

[204] Cf. his *Comment. in Lucam*, derived from his sermons, lib. 2, nn. 43, 56; *PL*, 15, 1568 f., and 1572. The second of these texts leaves one a bit hesitant about the author's meaning, perhaps due to the fact that Ambrose was influenced by Origen, who in his commentary on Luke, used terms incompatible with Our Lady's virginity in partu.

[205] *Recognovimus; PL*, 16, 1123-1129.

superiority of virginity over marriage would be definitively assured and Mary's lofty eminence above all other creatures would be emphasized.

The charge of unorthodoxy leveled against Jovinian for his denial of the virginal birth was to have important repercussions. It is difficult to ascertain what precisely had been the Roman view up to this time; however, we do know that, shortly before, St. Jerome, with his undoubted authority and prestige, had taken up Mary's defense against Helvidius without admitting unqualifiedly that she was a virgin in the birth of Christ; in fact his description of Christ's birth equaled the realism of Tertullian's description.[206] Undoubtedly Jerome was motivated by his horror of the Apocrypha and by his revulsion from accepting their doctrine on the virgin birth.[207]

Jerome's previous attitude in his *Contra Helvidium* quite understandably gave rise to a delicate situation, when Rome was asked to advocate the views of Ambrose and of his fellow bishops in northern Italy on the virgin birth. Certainly by the very fact that the Milanese synod condemned Jovinian on this precise point, St. Jerome's apparent view became, to say the least, singular, and might even seem to have been included in the condemnation. The situation, embarrassingly delicate though it was, could not be passed over in silence, because Jovinian stepped up the tempo of his attacks and multiplied his tracts against the virgin birth. One of these was sent to St. Jerome; in it, St. Ambrose was made the object of recrimination on the ground that he was a Manichaean. Jerome was asked to state his views and clarify his position.

All this must have been acutely embarrassing for St. Jerome. Undoubtedly he would have preferred to decline, but circumstances would not permit him to remain silent. He finally wrote his *Adversus Iovinianum*,[208] an extensive work in which he spends most of his effort in defending the advocates of virginity and of ascetical practices. On the other hand he speaks very little of the Blessed Virgin; in fact, her role is so slight that a reader who knew nothing of the historical circumstances might never suspect that the question of her virginity *in partu* was the

---

[206] *PL*, 23, 191 f., 202 f.
[207] *PL*, 23, 192.
[208] *PL*, 23, 211-338.

sole occasion of the work.[209] The only indication of this is contained in a few lines blended into an exegetical development.[210]

These clandestine tactics could not satisfy the majority of his readers. In fact it shocked them; the more so because of Jerome's open and violent terms in describing the place of married persons in the Church; he pictured them boldly as second-class Christians. In Rome the protest was so strong that a former fellow student of Jerome, the Senator Pammachius, wrote to him to demand that his work be suppressed. Jerome was not one to accede to such a demand; he turned a deaf ear to this request, but at least had the grace to send a reply to Pammachius, in which he attempted an apology.[211] He tried to make his position more precise, explained his formulas, argued from tradition for his views, and above all praised St. Ambrose in extraordinary terms, comparing him, as an equal, with Cyprian, Tertullian, and many others, both Latin and Greek; in dealing with the Blessed Virgin he repeated the allusions of his *Adversus Iovinianum,* but without the slightest additional clarification. Thus Pammachius, or any other reader of this letter, was left free to find in Jerome's doctrine what he might, perhaps even the doctrine of Ambrose, who is so highly praised.

The question of St. Jerome's real view on the virgin birth, and of his agreement or disagreement with St. Ambrose and the Synod of Milan, never was elucidated beyond this point. St. Ambrose had the charity as well as tact to realize and appreciate St. Jerome's embarrassing position, and not to insist on further clarification; he was quite content to have his own views acclaimed by public acceptance, and to see particularly his thesis of Mary's virginity *in partu* more and more widely accredited in the West.

---

[209] Cf. F. von Lehner, *Die Marienverehrung in den ersten Jahrhunderten* (Stuttgart, 1886), p. 136 f.

[210] These lines occur in lib. 1, n. 31; *PL*, 23, 254. To grasp their meaning and import, they must be compared with St. Jerome's letter to Pammachius, *Ep. 48*, n. 20 f.; *PL*, 22, 510. Jouassard states, *op. cit.*, p. 110, note 39: "La correspondance entre les deux passages est indubitable. Elle permet d'entrevoir ce que le premier d'entre eux dissimule soigneusement, savoir que Jérome cherche à rétablir la situation en sa faveur pour ce qui concerne la virginité *in partu*. Il cherche justement à la rétablir, en laissant au lecteur le soin de deviner ce qu'il pense."

[211] This letter is entitled *Liber apologeticus ad Pammachium, PL,* 22, 493-511.

In the meantime, St. Ambrose was about to enter upon a new polemic involving Bonosus, the Bishop of Sardica in Illyria, who belonged to the twilight zone where the Latin and Greek languages and cultures intermingled. About the year 390, Bonosus took up and spread the view that Our Lady did not remain a virgin after Christ's birth. We have already seen that, during this period in the East, this view could be presented without provoking any scandal, even among the Catholics of Constantinople. It is not, therefore, surprising that the same doctrine should have reached the hinterland of Illyria, and have found a champion. But the influence of Jerome and Ambrose, and of the Roman and Milanese synods were too powerful and widespread to allow such views to go unchallenged in this frontier of the East. Bonosus' claim provoked the hostile reaction of neighboring bishops, who referred the matter to a synod convened in Capua during the winter of 391-392. Rather than give a decision, this synod preferred to send the case back to the Bishops of Illyria, who a little later turned to Milan for guidance, as Bonosus himself had done just previously. St. Ambrose refused to adjudicate the matter, since Bonosus was not under his jurisdiction. Nevertheless, he furnished the bishops of Illyria with directives and arguments for a solution of the crisis.[212]

St. Ambrose's major argument is derived from the divine maternity and its exigencies. Thus supplied with well-documented advice, the bishops of Illyria were not slow in solemnly excommunicating Bonosus and in classifying his doctrine as heretical. We thus have a new intervention of ecclesiastical authority on the question of Mary's virginity *post partum;* it occurred in a section of the Catholic world which had natural liaisons between the East and the West, and thus could not help exercising an influence far exceeding what one might expect from a purely local synod. From what we have seen, its influence was perhaps not completely decisive for the Eastern Church; as to the West, it merely added emphasis to a doctrine which was already fully accepted.

The fourth century's dying years found Ambrose's doctrine on Our Lady's absolute and perpetual virginity completely triumphant. During his later years, his chief preoccupation had been to assure this triumph,

---

[212] Cf. *De Bonoso; PL,* 16, 1172-1174.

and his chief contribution toward his ardently desired goal was his *De institutione virginis*.[213] In this treatise he cannot say enough in praise of virginity in general, and particularly of the Virgin of Virgins, Mary the Mother of God. He defends her privileges, especially against Bonosus, with the same arguments used in the letter to the bishops of Illyria,[214] plus others borrowed from St. Jerome's *Adversus Helvidium*.[215] He turns lovingly to the scene of Calvary to show Mary's heroic courage and spotless sanctity.[216]

St. Ambrose's lofty doctrine on the Blessed Virgin and her spotless sanctity far surpassed the doctrine then being preached by St. John Chrysostom, and also the doctrine of St. Cyril of Alexandria thirty years later.[217] In this work *De institutione virginis*, while the whole matter of Jovinian and St. Jerome is not forgotten, it is treated with discretion. In brief, this work, compiled of short, detached observations, so often typical of St. Ambrose's style, is a masterpiece of its kind, not in a literary sense, but in its theological penetration; it far surpassed anything previously written on Our Lady's virginity. It was to be the swan song of St. Ambrose who died in 397, but his spirit lived on in the great St. Augustine.

In the year 400, St. Augustine began to publish his works on Marian theology *De bono coniugali* and *De sancta virginitate*,[218] in which he sets forth Catholic doctrine on virginity and marriage. Mary, he establishes, is even greater by reason of her exalted sanctity than for her role as the Mother of God; for, her sanctity was due not only to the grace of God but also to her co-operation, which moved her to vow her virginity to God, before she knew His designs on her as the future Mother of the Son of God. Brought to its summit by Augustine under the direct influence

---

[213] *PL*, 16, 305-334.

[214] Compare in this work nn. 44 f.; *PL*, 16, 317, with the letter *De Bonoso*, n. 3; *PL*, 16, 1133. We may note here that according to J. Palanque, Bonosus was Bishop of Nisch; cf. *Revue d'Histoire Ecclésiastique*, Vol. 26, 1930, p. 130, note.

[215] N. 35 f.; *PL*, 16, 314 f.

[216] *Ibid.*, 317 f.

[217] Cf. Ph. Friedrich, *S. Ambrosius von Mailand über die Jungfräulichkeit Mariens*, in *Der Katholik*, Vol. 20, 1917, p. 248 f.

[218] *PL*, 40, 373-396; 397-428. Cf. Ph. Friedrich, *Die Mariologie des hl. Augustins* (Köln, 1907).

and inspiration of St. Ambrose, Latin Catholicism had nothing more to learn about Mary's absolute and perpetual virginity. St. Augustine, without hesitation, named both Helvidius and Jovinian as heretics, and Mary's perpetual virginity was placed beyond all discussion or doubt in the West.

In this development, we have noted constantly the slow but profound influence of the ascetics on the doctrine of Mary's virginity. This influence began very early, largely due to Origen. Its effect cannot be properly evaluated, unless we remember that the question of Mary's virginity was never dissociated from the question of her personal sanctity in the view of the ascetics; one implied the other necessarily and they were thus inseparable.[219] The ascetical movement increased immeasurably in the fourth century. Both the advocates and enemies of ascetical practices tended to focus their attention on Mary; her life, her actual state, her privileges were the central point of inquiry; diametrically opposed views on her virginity were the foundation for favoring or attacking ascetical practices.

Gradually, and with the ever increasing support of the hierarchy, the views of the ascetics began to prevail. Without being infallible, and despite certain mistakes, they saw more clearly and profoundly than their opponents. What is the explanation? Non-Catholic circles seize eagerly on the spontaneous attraction derived from representing and imagining Mary to have lived and fulfilled perfectly the ideals set for themselves by the ascetics;[220] as if this were the only possible explanation. It may well have had its importance, but only as a subsidiary point of view. The Church itself, and especially the supreme Magisterium, was never taken into tow by the ascetics; it was the function of the Church to judge them and their doctrine, particularly in view of the fact that their opinions were contested by men who were by

---

[219] Cf. St. Ambrose, *De institutione virginis*; *PL*, 16, 317: "An vero Dominus Iesus eam sibi eligeret matrem, quae virili semine aulam posset incestare coelestem, quasi eam cui impossibile esset virginalis pudoris servare custodiam? Cuius exemplo ceterae ad integritatis studium provocantur, ipsa ab huiusmodi quod per se ceteris propositum foret munere deviaret?"

[220] Thus Turmel, especially in his *Histoire des dogmes*, Vol. 2 (Paris, 1932), p. 430 ff.; cf. also his previous work, *La Vierge Marie* (Paris, 1925), p. 52 (under the pseudonym Louis Coulange).

no means devoid of all prestige and authority. Under the infallible guidance of the Holy Spirit, the Magisterium was finally to give its irrevocable decision in essential conformity with the views first clearly exposed and developed by the ascetical school. This decision would never have been made, if the Church had not recognized in their doctrine a true expression of faith. On the other hand, the Church carefully avoided the canonization of anything exaggerated or superfluous in their views. The ascetics, then, were primary instruments in this whole process. Over a long period of years, they labored effectively to place at the disposal of the Church a formulation which would adequately express the true doctrine on Our Lady's virginity; but they were only instruments. The sole ultimately responsible authority was, as it remains to this day and always will be in matters of faith, the *Ecclesia docens.*

It was quite natural, then, for the advocates of virginity and of ascetical practices to identify the perpetual virginity of Mary with their cause, as its model and exemplar. It is a trait of human nature to discern with much more ease what interests us than to penetrate something that is entirely foreign or even hostile to our interests. But there was something more. In addition to the action of the Holy Spirit, the practice of asceticism extending even to virginity gave enlightenment and insights necessary for the true understanding of Mary's privileges. Beyond the mere statements of Scripture, there were the harmonies and dynamic syntheses of various dogmas to be considered. If by the example of Christ's years on this earth, He revealed that the true happiness of living for God alone and for the fulfillment of His salvific will could only be attained and maintained by despising the base pleasures of this world and of the senses, how could His Mother, the Mother of God, be conceived as not following His example perfectly? Naturally, these and similar perspectives, for example, the exigencies springing from Mary's divine motherhood, were more open and available to men and women who strove with all their powers to reproduce in their own lives the example of Christ. Thus they constituted the *avant-garde* in the development of the doctrine of Mary's virginity. It was the radiation of their insights and passionately held convictions which brought to the forefront of Christian consciousness the full development of those germinal intuitions which were fertile in the minds of some from the very beginnings of Christianity.

This full consciousness did not develop consistently or evenly in all parts of the Catholic world; the period which we have just traced betrayed this unevenness, particularly between the East and the West. The West, just before the Council of Ephesus (431), had advanced far beyond the East; it had reached a settled and unshakeable conviction concerning Mary's personal sanctity and her perpetual virginity. In the East, nothing absolutely decisive had been accepted universally on these two fundamental points of Marian theology; there were still opponents of her virginity, who were not, for this reason alone, considered to be heretics. The primary reason for the superiority of the West was the remarkable initiative of St. Ambrose, of his great disciple St. Augustine, and of St. Jerome. But these three great leaders of Catholic thought were the beneficiaries of the extraordinary spiritual ferment of their time, and also of certain Greek Fathers spurred on by the same spirit. It may be reasonably doubted, for instance, that, without the inspiration of St. Athanasius, St. Ambrose would have penetrated so deeply into the truth of Mary's perpetual virginity; similarly, without the support of St. Epiphanius, St. Jerome undoubtedly would not have written so convincingly against Helvidius.

In the development of Marian doctrine during this period, there was, then, a clearly discernible and beneficent influence of certain Greek Fathers on Latin thought. But unfortunately, as far as we know, the influence did not work both ways, at least in the same proportion. Except for the frontier of Greek thought in Illyria, we search in vain for any instance of the East learning from the Latins, who by the end of this period had much to communicate. The absence of documentary evidence, however, does not by any means exclude such an influence, either by oral communication, or by written documents that have not come down to us.

At any rate, it was the work of the Council of Ephesus which, by defining the truth of Mary's divine maternity against Nestorius, thereby also settled, at least implicitly, for the Eastern Church the question of her perpetual virginity. For neither point was ever again questioned within Catholicism. The protestations of St. Nilus against opponents of Our

Lady's virginity were the last to be heard in the East, and these denials were made most probably before the Council of Ephesus. During the Council there was not the slightest evidence of uncertainty or dissent on this point; even before the Council convened, one of the future heads of the Nestorian sect, Theodoret, asserted openly and firmly Our Lady's virginity, not only in the conception of Christ, but also *in partu*.[221]

Furthermore, we have good grounds for thinking that unanimity on Our Lady's perpetual virginity had been reached generally before the Council of Ephesus; for, after the Council we find the same belief as deeply rooted in the minds of the dissidents as it was in the conviction of the Catholics.[222] As examples we might cite Timothy of Elyria[223] in the fifth century, and Severus of Antioch[224] at the beginning of the sixth. One can scarcely imagine either Timothy or Severus having undergone an influence from the Council of Chalcedon (451), which they both despised; Chalcedon, as we know, recognized explicitly Mary's perpetual virginity.[225]

Actually, after Ephesus, heretics, schismatics, and Catholics throughout the East were in unanimous accord on Our Lady's perpetual virginity, even though, as Anastasius the Sinaite remarked, there was no explicit statement of Scripture to justify their belief with regard to the virgin birth and Our Lady's subsequent virginity.[226] This unanimous accord explains why the entire East, whether dissident or Catholic, had no difficulty in accepting the third canon of the Lateran Council under Pope St. Martin I, in the year 649:

> If anyone, in conformity with the Holy Fathers, does not confess that Mary Immaculate, actually and truthfully is the holy Mother of God and ever

---

[221] *De Incarnatione Domini; PG*, 75, 1420-1477; cf. especially 1460 f.

[222] Cf. M. Jugie, *Theologia Dogmatica christianorum orientalium ab Ecclesia Catholica dissidentium*, Vol. 5 (Paris, 1935), pp. 272, 567 f.

[223] Cf. a text cited by J. Lebon, *La Christologie de Timothée d'Elure*, in *Revue d'Histoire Ecclésiastique*, Vol. 9, 1908, p. 695; see also p. 699 f.

[224] Homiliae 66, *Patrologia Orientalis* (Graffin-Nau, Paris), 8-2, pp. 331-333; *Hom.* 68, *P. O.*, 8-2, p. 350 f.; *Hom.* 77, *P. O.*, 16-5, pp. 846-849; *Hom.* 108, *P. O.*, 25-4, p. 721 f.; *Hom.* 109, *P. O.*, 25-4, pp. 762, 770 f.; *Ep.* 29, *P. O.*, 12-2, pp. 260-262.

[225] Cf. Schwartz, *Acta conciliorum oecumenicorum*, Tom. 2, Vol. 1, Part 3, p. 112.

[226] *Hodegos*, 1; *PG*, 89, 40.

virgin, inasmuch as she conceived Him, who is uniquely and truly God, — the Word born of God the Father from all eternity, in these latter times of the Holy Spirit without seed, and bore Him without any corruption, her virginity remaining also intact after His birth, let him be condemned.[227]

One could multiply texts to prove the complete assent of the West to Mary's perpetual virginity during the last centuries of the patristic era. It would serve no purpose, since this wholehearted belief was ingrained before the death of St. Augustine. Thus, when the Fathers of the Lateran Council drew up the third canon for solemn definition, there was not the slightest discussion or doubt about its acceptance; actually they did no more than to ratify solemnly, in a formula by no means more explicit, the doctrine proposed by St. Leo (d. 461), in his dogmatic letter to Flavian.[228]

Therefore, from the time of Augustine in the West, and from the era of the Council of Ephesus in the East, the dogma of Our Lady's perpetual virginity, *ante partum, in partu,* and *post partum* was recognized as such universally, and has never since been questioned by Catholics. It is true that there have been discussions about details of the virgin birth, in the eleventh century between Ratramnus and Paschasius Radbertus, and in the fourteenth concerning the views of Durandus of Saint Pourçain, but these discussions quite clearly did not touch the dogma in its essentials and hence need not be reviewed here in detail.[229]

However, one should not have a concept of dogmatic belief which precludes deeper penetration into revealed truths or greater precision concerning the exact object believed. For example, modern biology has shown the complete falsity and inadequacy of the medieval concept of generation; not to accept these scientifically established facts would give a false notion of Our Lady's part in the virginal conception of Christ, as Amandus Breitung, S.J., showed conclusively some years ago.[230]

Similarly, A. Mitterer has recently proposed some interesting

---

[227] DB, 256.

[228] PL, 54, 759: "Conceptus est Christus de Spiritu Sancto intra uterum Virginis Matris, quae illum ita salva virginitate edidit, quemadmodum salva virginitate concepit."

[229] Cf. E. Dublanchy, art. *Marie,* in *DTC,* Vol. 9, coll. 2382 f., 2385.

[230] Cf. A. Breitung, S.J., *De conceptione Christi inquisitio physiologico-theologica,* in *Gregorianum,* Vol. 5, 1924, pp. 391-423, 531-568.

questions concerning the virgin birth from a biological viewpoint.[231] Briefly, Mitterer holds that any birth would be essentially virginal if it were not caused by previous sexual intercourse or through impregnation by the sperm of a man; the integrity of the hymen, in itself, would by no means pertain to the essence of a virgin birth, as St. Thomas and many others have held insistently, nor would the perforation of the hymen in the act of birth prevent the birth itself from being virginal. Virginity itself, Mitterer claims, includes essentially only the following elements: (1) spiritually, the firm proposal of the will to exclude all deliberate sexual passion, and the actual exclusion itself; (2) corporally, the exclusion of all sexual intercourse and the exclusion of all possibility of contact between the ovum and sperm.

With regard to the birth of Our Lord, then, Mitterer holds that His Mother would have preserved her virginity completely, both in soul and body, even though the hymen were perforated in the act of giving birth; this contingency, moreover, would place more emphasis on the reality of Mary's true motherhood, i.e., the fact that she actively bore her Son, and was not a mere passive channel through which Christ passed. To the obvious objection that all this seems to run counter to Tradition, Mitterer answers disarmingly that he leaves this to the solution of exegetes and dogmatic theologians.

In the opinion of the present writer, Mitterer is correct when he claims that the nonperforation of the hymen at the time of birth does not pertain to the *essence* of virginity, generally speaking.[232]

---

[231] A. Mitterer, Dogma und Biologie der heiligen Familie nach dem Weltbild des hl. Thomas von Aquin und dem Gegenwart (Vienna, 1952); see especially, Ch. 3, No. 2, *Die hl. Mutterschaft Mariä* in *der Geburt,* pp. 98-129.

[232] Cf. the following reviews of Mitterer, *op. cit.,* by V. Andérez, in *Pensamiento,* Vol. 9, 1953, p. 387 f.; by P. Paniker, in *Revue Franciscaine,* Vol. 11, 1952, p. 676; by C. Robert, in *Revue des Sciences Religieuses,* Vol. 27, 1952, p. 162; by H. Doms, in *Theologische Revue,* Vol. 48, 1952, pp. 200-212; by K. Rahner, in *Zeitschrift für katholische Theologie,* Vol. 75, 1953, pp. 500-502: "Hinsichtlich der Frage der *virginitas in partu,* zeigt Mitterer begrifflich mit Recht dass der von einer heutigen Biologie her erarbeitete Begriff einer vollen Jungfrauschaft die Unverletztheit des Hymens, das Fehlen der Geburtsschmerzen nicht fordert"; by O. Semmelroth, in *Scholastik,* Vol. 28, 1953, p. 310: "Und was Mitterer sagt, scheint mir eine annehmbare Klärung zu sein. Da hk. Thomas von Aquin die virginitas in ihrem körperlichen Elemente zu sehr in die Unverletztheit des Hymens verlegte, konnte er die Jungfräulichkeit Mariens eigentlich nur auf Kosten ihrer wahren

However, in the concrete case now under discussion, it pertains at least to its *integral* concept. Such would seem to be, at any rate, the traditional view among Catholics. Furthermore, the teaching of the Church, extending back to Ambrose and Augustine, unequivocally refers to the birth of the Saviour as "miraculous" and "supernatural." Does this constitute merely an historical tradition based on faulty scientific notions, as Mitterer is inclined to believe? Is it not rather a dogmatic tradition transmitting to us a revealed truth which must be accepted with divine faith? In any event, while evaluating the various phases of Mitterer's thesis, the Catholic theologian must make sure that he does not lose sight of the genuine mind of the Magisterium on these matters, and that he adheres to it scrupulously.

We may conclude this chapter with the following observations.[233] The development of the dogma of Our Lady's perpetual virginity brings out strikingly the fact that no single prerogative of Mary can be understood in its full dogmatic richness unless it is comprehended, not in the abstract or in an isolated fashion, but synthetically, as an aspect of the unique endowments of the most favored creature of God. Notionally, the virginity of Mary in the conception of Christ can be separated from the virginal birth and from her perpetual virginity thereafter; in the divine plan of Mary's place in the economy of Redemption, however, these three aspects of her virginity are

---

Mutterschaft festhalten.... Gegen den Einwand aus den Aussagen der Väterüberlieferung stellt Mitterer mit Recht die Frage, ob in diesen Aussagen die Väter als Zeugen der Offenbarungslieferung sprechen, oder als solche, — unter falschen biologischen Voraussetzungen — die Offenbarungsgegebenheiten zu erklären suchen"; by P. Nober, in *Verbum Domini*, Vol. 31, 1953, pp. 49-51. For an exhaustive (mostly unfavorable) appraisal of Mitterer's book, cf. J. Alonso, C.M.F., *Mariología y biología. Reflexiones críticas a un libro interesante*, in *Ephemerides Mariologicae*, Vol. 6, 1956, pp. 197-221.

[233] Sometime after this chapter had been submitted to the publisher, there appeared the scholarly article, *L'Annonce à Marie*, in *Revue Biblique*, Vol. 63, 1956, pp. 346-375, by J.-P. Audet, O.P. In view of the research undertaken by this author, we are forced to state that the traditional arguments for Mary's vow of virginity were probably over-emphasized in our own presentation of the matter. Our conclusions, therefore, should be considered and weighed in the light of Audet's very convincing arguments against the traditional view. Cf. likewise in this regard N. M. Flanagan, O.S.M., *Our Lady's Vow of Virginity*, in *Marian Studies*, Vol. 7, 1956, pp. 103-133.

inseparable and follow necessarily from her divine motherhood, her Immaculate Conception and spotless sanctity, her unique share in Christ's passion and death, and her glorious maternal privilege of dispensing the fruits of her Son's Redemption. But Marian theology itself, however perfectly synthesized, must not be isolated or separated from the higher synthesis of Christology and the life of the Blessed Trinity, communicated to us through Christ and Mary. God in Himself, in His Trinitarian being, is not only the beginning, but the end of all theology, of all life, of all creation.

MARY'S FULLNESS OF GRACE

By FRANK P. CALKINS, O.S.M., S.T.D.

THE soul of the Blessed Virgin Mary was adorned with sanctifying grace in a most exceptional manner. We know this, first of all, from the words addressed to her by the Archangel Gabriel, "Hail, full of grace."[1] Commenting on this salutation of the angel, Pius IX, in the Bull *Ineffabilis Deus*, writes, "This solemn and unparalleled salutation, heard at no other time, shows the Mother of God as the seat of all divine graces, and as adorned with all the gifts of the Divine Spirit. It also shows her as the almost infinite repository and inexhaustible abyss of these gifts to such a degree, that being at no time guilty of sin and together with her Son partaking of a perpetual blessing, she deserved to hear Elizabeth, under the inspiration of the Holy Spirit say, 'Blessed art thou ...' "[2] What was expressed so well by Pius IX had been taught by the Fathers from the earliest times in their commentaries on the Angelic Salutation. Thus St. Ambrose says, "Truly, she alone is said to be full of grace, who alone received the grace which no other merited, that of being filled by the Author of grace."[3] St. Peter Chrysologus in one of his sermons eulogizes Our Lady, "Hail, full of grace. For grace is bestowed on individuals by portions, but on Mary it was bestowed in all its plenitude."[4] In assigning the basic reason for Mary's fullness of grace, St. Thomas points to the Divine Maternity and the intimate union which it postulated with Christ, the principle of all grace. "The nearer one approaches to a principle (of truth and life) the more one participates in its effects. ... But Christ is the principle of the life of grace; as God He is the principal cause, and as Man, His humanity is, as it were, an instrument always united to His Divinity. The Blessed Virgin Mary

---

[1] Lk. 1:28.

[2] Pius IX, *Ineffabilis Deus*, in Tondini, *Le Encicliche Mariane*, ed. 2 (Roma, 1954), p. 44.

[3] St. Ambrose, *Expositio in Evang. sec. Lucam*, lib. 2, n. 1285; *PL*, 15, 1556.

[4] St. Peter Chrysologus, *Serm. 143, de Annunt.*; *PL*, 52, 583.

being nearer to Christ than any other human being, since it is from her that He received His humanity, receives from Him, therefore, a fullness of grace surpassing that of all other creatures."[5]

The prerogative of the Immaculate Conception implies the same truth, because preservation from original sin could not possibly take place without the infusion of grace into the soul. Since in the present order of creation man has been elevated to the supernatural order, it follows that he must exist either in the state of grace or in the state of sin. There is no middle state. To be without sin, therefore, is to have grace; and conversely, to he without grace is to be in the state of sin. For this reason the Immaculate Conception of Mary is the same thing as her first sanctification; and we must believe that she was filled with grace from the first moment of her existence. For the sake of clearness, the question of Mary's fullness of grace may be divided into three parts: (1) Mary's *initial* fullness of grace; (2) her *growth* in this grace; (3) her *final* fullness of grace. We shall treat these points separately, indicating the various opinions expressed by Catholic theologians on the matter.

I. INITIAL FULLNESS

In regard to this first point, a preliminary question is raised by theologians, namely: How did it take place? Was it accomplished with full consent on the part of the Blessed Virgin, or did it take place unperceived by her, in the same manner in which a child is sanctified at Baptism? If Our Lady was sanctified in the first manner, we must necessarily conclude that she had the use of reason, at least temporarily, at the moment of her conception. Theologians for the most part hold this view.[6] They base their affirmation principally upon the sublime dignity of Mary's divine Motherhood. Because of her high dignity as Mother of God, it was fitting that she should be sanctified in the most perfect manner. It is obvious, however, that a reception of grace which is accompanied by voluntary consent on the part of the subject is certainly more perfect than that which is accomplished without any co-operation

---

[5] St. Thomas, III, q. 27, a. 5

[6] Cf. A. Martinelli, O.F.M., *De primo instanti Conceptionis B.V. Mariae.* Disquisitio de usu rationis (Romae, 1950), *passim*, but especially pp. 56-58. Cf. also G. M. Roschini, O.S.M., *Mariologia*, ed. 2, Vol. 2, pars 2 (Romae, 1948), p. 123.

of the subject; the former mode of reception should therefore be attributed to the Immaculate Virgin. That Mary continued to enjoy the use of reason in her infancy is not generally admitted by theologians, although some eminent writers, such as Suárez, and more recently, Father Hugon, are of this opinion.[7]

A. Mary's Fullness Compared With Christ's Fullness

From the words of the angel to Mary, "Hail, full of grace," we gather that Mary's soul was adorned, not with just a great amount, or a high degree of grace, but with a *fullness* of this supernatural quality. Elsewhere in Sacred Scripture, a fullness of grace is predicated of Christ (*Jn.* 1:14-16) and even of certain saints (*Acts* 6:3). Theologians, therefore, distinguish between fullness of grace as it is found in Christ, in Mary, and in the saints. In Christ the fullness is absolute, i.e., Christ possessed grace in the absolute maximum degree in which it can be possessed, "et quantum ad essentiam et quantum ad virtutem."[8] In Mary, the fullness is relative, i.e., she possessed grace in the fullness that was fitting and necessary for her office as Mother of the Saviour. In the saints, too, this fullness is relative, but since the office and dignity to which they are destined cannot possibly approach the dignity of Mary's sublime Maternity, their fullness of grace is necessarily inferior to Mary's both in excellence and in degree.

The fullness of grace in Christ was unique both in its intensity (it had the greatest degree of excellence grace can have) and in its extension (it was capable of producing all the possible effects of grace). The first was due to the fact that Christ's soul was united to the divinity not only by knowledge and love and the beatific vision, but more intimately still, by the Hypostatic Union. Now, if it is true that the closer a recipient is to the source of a perfection, the more fully it receives that perfection, then Christ's soul, which was so intimately united with God, must have received grace in its most excellent degree of perfection. The other part of the statement is true because Christ received grace not only for Himself, but also as Head of the Mystical Body, that He might be the

---

[7] E. Hugon, O.P., *Tractatus Dogmatici*, ed. 10, Vol. 2 (Parisiis, 1935), pp. 371-372; *id., Marie pleine de grace*, 5e ed. (Paris, 1926), pp. 24-32.

[8] St. Thomas, III, q. 7, a. 10.

source and principle of grace in others.[9]

Applying these two reasons for the fullness of grace in Christ to Mary's case, it is apparent at once that her fullness of grace must have been different from, and inferior to, that of Christ. Her union with God was intimate and marvelous, but in no sense could it be considered equal to a hypostatic union. Likewise, her fullness of grace was such that it enabled her to co-operate effectively in the distribution of grace to others, but never could Mary be called the Head of the Mystical Body and the principal source of grace in its members. We must conclude, therefore, that the fullness of grace attributed to Mary by the angel was a relative fullness, similar to that of Christ, but inferior. In other words, while the grace of Christ was supreme both in excellence and power, that of Mary had only that degree of excellence and power which was necessary for her to be the worthy Mother of the Saviour.

B. Mary's Fullness Compared With the Saints' Fullness

St. Thomas tells us more in particular how the grace of Mary compared with the fullness of grace given to some saints.[10] He calls their fullness a "plenitude of sufficiency." He calls Mary's a "plenitude of redundance," by which he means an overflowing fullness. By the plenitude of sufficiency granted to them, the saints were able to perform salutary acts of high merit and excellence, and achieve that degree of sanctity to which God called them. By the plenitude of redundance granted to her, Mary surpassed all the saints in the excellence and abundance of her merits. Her grace overflowed upon others, not in the sense that she was the *"auctrix gratiae"* for them, but in this sense, that from her soul grace overflowed into her body sanctifying her womb and making it the worthy dwelling place of the Redeemer. And as the Angelic Doctor says elsewhere,[11] "by bringing Christ forth, Mary in a manner dispensed grace to all." Among the Fathers, Basil of Seleucia writes: "Who does not marvel over the measure in which Mary surpasses all those whom we venerate as saints? If God bestowed so

---

[9] *Ibid.*, a. 9.

[10] *Comment. in Joannem*, cap. 1, l. 9; *In III Sent.*, d. 13, q. 1, a. 2.

[11] III, q. 27, a. 5, ad 1.

much grace on His servants, what kind of virtue do we think His Mother has? Must it not be a greater virtue than the virtue of those who are subject to her? Be it known to anyone that, if Peter was called blessed and had the keys of the kingdom consigned to him, she before all others should be called blessed to whom it was given to bring forth Him whom Peter orally avowed; if Paul was called a vessel of election because he carried forth and divulged the August name of Christ everywhere in the world, what kind of vessel will the Mother of God be?"[12]

It would nevertheless be a mistake to think that the grace given to Mary was specifically different from the grace given to other saints.[13] The specific nature of grace is determined by its object. But the object of grace, both in the case of Mary and in the case of all the saints, is one and the same, namely, union with God through knowledge and love. Consequently, the grace which sanctified the Immaculate Virgin and the grace which sanctifies an infant in baptism, or justifies a repentant sinner in confession, is specifically the same.[14]

C. THE QUANTITY OF MARY'S GRACE

Theologians measure the quantity[15] of initial grace bestowed on the Blessed Virgin by means of comparisons. They compare, for instance, Mary's initial grace with the initial grace of any one particular saint or angel. Then they compare her initial grace with the consummated grace of any particular saint or angel. By consummated grace, theologians do not mean the final and consummated grace of heaven, but rather the final grace which immediately precedes entry into heaven. It must be understood this way because the grace of heaven, i.e., *in statu termini*, although it is of the same specific nature as the grace of this life, is nevertheless of a different and higher order. Its object is "Deus visus."

---

[12] *Orat.* 39 in Deiparae Annuntiationem; PG, 85, 426-451.

[13] Father J. Alonso, C.M.F., defends this unusual opinion in his article *Naturaleza y fundamentos de la gracia de María*, in *Estudios Marianos*, Vol. 5 (Madrid, 1946), pp. 11-110.

[14] Cf. B. Ravagnan, *De Mariae plenitudine gratiae*, in *Marianum*, Vol. 3, 1941, pp. 102-123.

[15] Quantity here means "quantitas virtualis, non dimensiva." Cf. St. Thomas, II-II, q. 24, a. 4, ad 1. Roschini, *op. cit.*, Vol. 2, p. 132.

The object of grace in this life is "Deus non visus."[16] In both instances mentioned here, the common opinion of theologians proclaims the superiority of Mary's initial grace.

But now, a further and more daring comparison is made. Is the initial grace of Mary greater than the consummated grace of all the angels and saints in heaven collectively? Theologians are not of one accord in answering this question. Some eminent Mariologists, such as Terrien and Cardinal Lépicier, admit this only in regard to Mary's *final* grace.[17] However, the great majority of theologians accept it as very probable. It is the opinion of St. Alphonsus, Vega, Velázquez, Billot, Hugon, Campana, Merkelbach, Garrigou-Lagrange, and Roschini.[18] The authority of the Bull *Ineffabilis Deus* is offered as a proof of the doctrine. As a matter of fact, there are expressions in the papal document which seem to support this contention.[19] Although it may seem an exaggeration to say that Our Lady as a tiny infant was holier than the angels and all the martyrs, confessors, virgins, and apostles after long lives of labor and sacrifice, nevertheless, this will not seem so improbable if it is kept in mind that the Divine Maternity was the goal toward which Mary's grace was ordained. We must look at it this way: the initial infusion of grace was meant to prepare Mary to become the *worthy* Mother of God. Hence, there had to be some proportion between it and the sublime dignity of that Motherhood. On the other hand, the final consummated grace of all the angels and saints together does not have any proportion to the Divine Maternity. Their grace, after all, belongs to a completely

---

[16] Card. A. H. M. Lépicier, O.S.M., *Tractatus de Beatissima V. Maria Matre Dei*, ed. 5 (Romae, 1926), p. 250.

[17] J. B. Terrien, S.J., *La Mère de Dieu*, 7e ed., Vol. 1 (Paris, 1900), pp. 384-392. Card. Lépicier, *op. cit.*, pp. 230-233. For the lively controversy on this issue between F. X. Godts, C.Ss.R., and Card. Lépicier, see the former's *La sainteté initiale de l'Immaculée* (Bruxelles, 1904), and the latter's *De Maria numquam satis* (Romae, 1905).

[18] Cf. Roschini, *op. cit.*, Vol. 2, pp. 129-133, where many more authors are referred to. Note also the more recent controversy over this point between L. Baudiment, *De quelques outrances de la théologie mariale contemporaine*, in *L'Année Théologique*, Vol. 6, 1943, pp. 105-115, and P.-E. Vadeboncoeur, C.Ss.R., in *Quelle est cette outrance?* in *Revue de l'Université d'Ottawa*, Vol. 16, 1946, pp. 209-226.

[19] R. Garrigou-Lagrange, O.P., *The Mother of the Savior and Our Interior Life*, trans. Kelly (Dublin, 1949), pp. 82-83.

different and inferior order. Therefore, it is not surprising that even in its accumulated perfection, it is still not equal to the first grace received by the Mother of God.

II. MARY'S GROWTH IN GRACE

Even though Mary was "full of grace" from the beginning, nevertheless, this grace grew and increased all during her life. To understand, first of all, how growth is compatible with fullness we must hark back to the distinction between absolute fullness and relative fullness. It has been pointed out that Mary possessed grace not as Christ possessed it, in the absolute maximum degree in which it can be possessed, but in a relative fullness, i.e., in the fullness fitting and necessary to exercise her office as Mother of God. Now, such a fullness is finite, and capable of increase. Therefore, Mary's fullness of grace was compatible with growth and increase. At the moment of her conception, Mary had the fullness of grace which was befitting her as the future Mother of the Saviour. At the moment of the Incarnation, she possessed a greater fullness, one befitting the actual Mother of God. Finally, at the last moment of her earthly existence, she had an even greater fullness of grace, one namely, which was befitting her as the Mother of God and the Queen of Heaven.

Another point which we must keep in mind when we speak of the growth of grace is that this growth is not quantitative — as is that of a heap of stones which grows by having more added to it — but qualitative, as is the growth of knowledge which even if no new truths are added, can become more penetrating, more profound, more unified, more certain.[20]

A. THE FACT OF GROWTH

Some ancient theologians were of the opinion that Our Lady increased in grace only until the moment of the Incarnation.[21] At that moment, they maintained, she was so completely filled with grace that

---

[20] Garrigou-Lagrange, *op. cit.*, p. 91.
[21] Cf. for example, Venerable Bede, *Epist.* 7, l. 3; *PL*, 189, 287; Scotus, *In IV Sent.*, dist. 4, 2. 6, ad 1um; *op. omn.*, Vol. 16, pp. 454-459.

any further increase became impossible. However, the almost universal teaching of theologians is that the Blessed Virgin grew in grace both before and after the Incarnation. It is easy to see that the initial grace of Our Lady must have been unspeakably augmented at the moment when she conceived Christ in her virginal womb. The nearer one approaches to the source of any perfection, the more one participates in its effects. Now, when Mary actually and physically became the Mother of God, she was indubitably closer to the source of all grace, than when she was only being prepared for the Divine Motherhood. Her grace, therefore, must have reached new and wonderful heights at the moment of Christ's conception.

On the other hand, the process of growth in grace must have continued after the Incarnation too, because it is a doctrine of faith that, as long as a soul is *in statu viae* (as Mary's soul was), it is capable of such growth.[22] When one considers the exceptionally high degree of Mary's first grace, the abundance of the actual graces she received during her life, and her unfailing, ever zealous cooperation with them, one can understand how her growth in grace must have continued until the very hour of her death. "Who," asks St. Peter Canisius, "could doubt that she who was so intimately joined with the Emmanuel would not thereby grow from day to day, more pure, more holy, and in a certain sense, more divine?"[23] And St. Thomas says, "There was a threefold perfection of grace in the Blessed Virgin: the first consisted in a preparatory perfection, by which she was made worthy to be the Mother of Christ; and this was the perfection of her sanctification. The second perfection of grace came from the actual presence of the Son of God Incarnate in her womb. The third is the final perfection which she has in heaven."[24]

B. THE MANNER: "EX OPERE OPERANTIS"

The increase of grace in a soul is brought about either *ex opere operantis*, i.e., by way of good works and merit, or *ex opere operato*, i.e.,

---

[22] Council of Trent, sess. 6, can. 32. *D.B.*, 842.

[23] St. Peter Canisius, *De Maria Virgine incomparabili et Dei Genitrice libri quinque*, l. 4, c. 24 in ed. J. Bourassé, *Summa aurea de laudibus B.V. Mariae*, Vol. 8 (Parisiis, 1862), col. 1407.

[24] III, q. 27, a. 5, ad 2.

independently of the merit of the person, provided there is no obex. This twofold manner of increase was realized in the case of the Blessed Virgin. That she grew wonderfully in grace by reason of the meritorious acts which she performed in her life, hardly needs any proof. Our Lady was lavishly adorned with sanctifying grace; she received innumerable actual graces with which she co-operated in the most perfect manner possible; all her human acts were prompted by pure love of God, with absolutely no mixture of self-love; there could be nothing inordinate in any action which she performed because her soul was immaculate and utterly exempt from any motion of concupiscence. Now, the Council of Trent teaches that the good acts of a person in the state of grace merit an increase of grace.[25] Certainly, therefore, the countless good acts of Our Lady, performed from the most perfect of motives and in the most perfect manner possible, must have heaped merit and grace upon her spotless soul in a degree difficult to comprehend.

In this respect too, it is important to remember that the good works of Our Lady were different from those of any other saint, first, because they were more numerous, and second, because they were of a superior quality. A saint begins to make meritorious acts when he arrives at the age of reason. But if the opinion of some highly regarded theologians is true, that Our Lady had the use of her reason and free will even as an infant in her mother's womb, then she must have performed many more good works than any saint, on this score alone. Furthermore, even a great saint is not continually occupied in performing acts of virtue. Distractions, inculpable negligence, all the sad consequences of original sin make this impossible. But Mary never inherited original sin. Hers was not a fallen nature, prone to evil and experiencing difficulty in doing good. Therefore, nothing could impede her progress, and the result was an immeasurably greater number of good works than any saint could perform. Lastly, if it is true, as some theologians teach, that the Blessed Virgin had the use of reason and free will during the hours of sleep (because of her infused knowledge),[26] then an even greater number of

---

[25] Sess. 6, cap. 10. *D.B.*, 803.

[26] According to G. Alastruey, *Mariologia*, Vol. 1 (Vallisoleti, 1934), p. 349, this view is held by St. Bernardine of Siena, St. Peter Canisius, St. Francis de Sales, Contenson, Suárez, C. de Vega, Terrien, and Hugon.

good acts was possible for her. We must conclude, therefore, that by reason of sheer number alone, the good acts of Our Lady surpassed those of any saint or saints, and they brought about in her a continual progress in grace which almost defies description or measurement.

However, in good works, as in most things, it is quality that counts more than quantity. Good works increase our merit, and consequently our grace also, but they do this only when they are performed well. Daily Communion is a splendid good work, but if it be done mechanically, with no effort to be fervent, it would certainly not increase a person's holiness. If we examine the good works of Mary from this angle, we find that they were without even the tiniest flaw. She was simply incapable of doing a good act badly, because she was sinless, and a good act done badly is a moral imperfection. In her prayers, therefore, in her performance of her household duties, in all the actions of her life, there was no contaminating element of self-love, no vanity, no lack of fervor, no letdown from absolute perfection. She did all things well, solely to please God and to give Him honor and glory. And so we see, both in the number of her good works, and in the unspeakable perfection of them, Mary surpassed all the saints, and merited for herself an ever increasing growth in grace and holiness.

C. "Ex Opere Operato"

The other way by which grace increases in a soul is *ex opere operato*. The expression, "ex opere operato," was used by the Council of Trent in reference to the sacraments, and since then its use has been confined almost exclusively to them. However, long before the Council of Trent, the expression had its place in Scholastic usage.[27] It was taken in general to signify an act, considered independently of any merit of the person doing the act. Understanding the expression in this sense, theologians teach that the Blessed Virgin increased in grace, *ex opere operato*: (1) on the occasion of the great mysteries of religion which occurred during her life, and (2) by reason of the reception of certain sacraments.

At the time of the conception of Christ, at His birth, on the occasion of His resurrection and His ascension, on Pentecost Sunday, and

---

[27] Cf. Parente, *Dictionary of Dogmatic Theology* (Milwaukee, 1951), p. 97.

especially at the foot of the cross on Calvary, God flooded Mary's soul with new and enormous quantities of grace. Let us single out three of these mysteries: the Incarnation, the Cross Annunciation, Pentecost. An obvious reason for Mary's increase in grace at the Incarnation is the one mentioned before: actual motherhood brought Mary in closer contact with God than preparatory motherhood. But besides that reason, we find another one in this, that the proximate preparation for any perfection is always proportionate to that perfection. Now, the Divine Maternity is superior to every other dignity of nature or of grace. Hence, Mary must have received, as proximate preparation for it, a special increase of her fullness of grace.[28] Incidentally, what is said here about Mary's growth in grace, at the moment of Christ's conception in her womb, must be applied to the whole period of His infancy, when He lived on such intimate and familiar terms with the Blessed Mother. During all this time, Mary's charity and maternal love continued to develop and grow.

Another outstanding occasion when Mary's grace reached new heights was at the foot of the cross on Calvary. It was there she was proclaimed the Mother of the human race, when Christ spoke to her the words, "Woman, behold thy son." Just as the divine motherhood had annexed to it a wondrous grace of its own, so also this new spiritual motherhood called for a new and special grace to be added to the wealth of grace she already possessed.[29]

Last, the day of Pentecost marked a great increase in Mary's boundless treasury of grace. If the Apostles, on that occasion, were elevated by grace from fearful and timid disciples to courageous preachers of the Gospel, ready to suffer and die for the cause of Christ, how marvelous must have been Mary's progress in grace — she who was to be on earth, the maternal support of the infant Church.

D. MARY'S RECEPTION OF THE SACRAMENTS

Theologians are unanimous in stating that Mary advanced in grace also by means of the reception of the sacraments. However, there is not unanimity among them when they endeavor to establish what

---

[28] Garrigou-Lagrange, *op. cit.*, p. 101. Also B. Ravagnan, *De augmento gratiae initialis in B. Maria Virgine*, in *Marianum*, Vol. 3, 1941, p. 277.

[29] Cf. B. Ravagnan, *art. cit.*, in *Marianum*, Vol. 4, 1942, p. 42 ff.

sacraments were received by Our Lady. The Gospels make only the vaguest references to this matter, and the same is true of the early Fathers of the Church. The result is that later theologians, trying to solve the question with *a priori* reasoning, have proposed a variety of opinions.

In general, they all agree that the Blessed Virgin received the sacraments of Baptism and the Holy Eucharist. It is very reasonable to presume that she received Baptism, because, according to the ordinary plan of Divine Providence, this sacrament was meant to be the means of acquiring membership in the Church. Undoubtedly, God could have dispensed Mary from the obligation of this law, but since it is difficult to see any serious reason for such a dispensation, we may rightly conclude that none was given. If it is objected that Mary had no need for Baptism, being free from sin, it must be remembered that this sacrament was instituted not only for the remission of sin, but also for the reason mentioned above. Theologians, therefore, with one accord, teach that Mary was baptized.[30] They even go further and conjecture on the time and the minister of her Baptism. It is generally held that she was baptized by Christ Himself, sometime before His death and ascension. It is true that Baptism was not necessary for salvation before the death of Christ. Nevertheless, the Apostles were ordained priests and received the Holy Eucharist at the Last Supper. Baptism being the first of the sacraments, it is very likely, therefore, that they were baptized sometime previous to the Last Supper. If they were baptized, we can presume that the Blessed Mother, who preceded all others in holiness and conformity to Christ's will, was baptized also, and by Our Lord Himself, *honoris causa*.[31]

The Holy Eucharist was certainly received by the Blessed Virgin and, probably, with great frequency. The basic reason for believing this is the custom of frequent Communion which prevailed in the early Christian

---

[30] Cf. E. Campana, *Maria nel dogma cattolico*, ed. 4 (Torino-Roma, 1936), pp. 633-634; G. M. Roschini, *op. cit.*, p. 141; Alastruey, *op. cit.*, pp. 352-353; Card. Lépicier, *op. cit.*, pp. 239-240.

[31] Cf. Suárez, *In III*, disp. 19, sect. 1.

Church.[32] If other Christians, impelled by their love for Jesus, received Him every day in the Holy Sacrament, certainly Mary, who loved Him more than all others, would do this. St. Peter Canisius writes, "Who will deny or hesitate to believe that during this time, she [Mary] received greater merits, new gifts, and an increase in holiness, by reason of the Holy Eucharist, which she received daily, as was the custom among all the members of the newly-born Church."[33] After Christ had said, "Unless you eat my flesh and drink my blood, you shall not have life in you," is there any likelihood that His own Mother would abstain from Holy Communion? What rapturous joys Mary experienced in those intimate moments with Jesus each day it would be impossible for any human mind to fathom. But of this we can be certain, during those moments of union, Our Lady's soul must have been inundated with fresh torrents of grace, and must have advanced ever more and more in the ways of holiness.

Mariologists, for the most part, agree also as to the sacraments which Our Lady did not receive. They are the sacraments of Penance, Holy Orders, and Matrimony. Since the very essence of Penance consists in the absolution from sin, this sacrament certainly does not belong in the category of those received by the Immaculate Mother of God. Our Lady was in the enviable position of one who simply could not submit any subject matter for the absolution of the priest. This being the case, she was incapable of receiving this sacrament.

The sacrament of Holy Orders was never received by Our Lady for the simple reason that the reception of this sacrament is reserved to men only.[34] However, in a higher and more noble sense, she fulfilled the office of a priest. This office consists, more than anything else, in the offering of sacrifice to God. By bringing Christ, the supreme High Priest, into the world, and by sharing in His immolation on Calvary through her voluntary offering of Him to God, Mary acted as a priest in a very sublime manner. Hence, the eminent theologian Gerson says, "Although

---

[32] Cf. *Acts* 1:14; 2:46. A. Bea, S.J., "Erant 'perseverantes ... cum Maria Matre Jesu ... in communicatione fractionis panis," in *Alma Socia Christi*, Vol. 6 (I), De B.V. Maria et SSma. Eucharistia (Romae, 1952), pp. 21-37.

[33] St. Peter Canisius, *op. cit.*, lib. 1, sect. 2, cap. 9.

[34] *1 Cor.* 14:34.

Mary was never adorned with the sacramental character of Holy Orders, she was anointed above all others with the *dignity* of the priesthood, not in order that she might consecrate, but in order that she might offer to God, on the altar of her own heart, the pure and perfect Host."[35]

Matrimony, considered as a sacrament of the New Law, was never received by the Blessed Virgin. It is true she contracted a real marriage with St. Joseph, but this was done during the regime of the Old Law, when Matrimony had not as yet been raised to the dignity of a sacrament. When that elevation did take place, St. Joseph, it is commonly believed, was no longer among the living, and consequently, the marriage could not have become automatically a sacrament, as it did in other cases.

The sacrament of Confirmation presents a special difficulty for Mariologists. On the one hand, it is obvious that Our Lady was present with the Apostles on Pentecost, and received abundantly of the graces of the Holy Spirit.[36] On the other hand, the descent of the Holy Spirit on that occasion can hardly be called the sacrament of Confirmation in the strict sense, because the *signum sensibile* of the sacrament, as we find it in the Church today, was certainly lacking. For this reason, it is perhaps better to distinguish, as many theologians do, and attribute to Mary, the reception, not of the *sacramentum,* but of the *res sacramenti* only, i.e., the reception of the grace of the sacrament, but not the outward sign. Pope Eugene IV attributed this same kind of reception of Confirmation to the Apostles, when he wrote: "The effect of the sacrament consists in this that through it, the Holy Spirit is given for our strength, as He was given to the Apostles on the day of Pentecost."[37]

Did the Blessed Virgin receive the sacrament of Extreme Unction? Several eminent theologians hold the opinion that she did.[38] They see nothing in the reception of this sacrament which would be contrary to Mary's sinlessness. Vega, for instance, tells us that the primary effect of

---

[35] Gerson, *Super Cant. Magnificat,* tract. 9; quoted by Alastruey, *op. cit.,* p. 358.

[36] Acts 1:14.

[37] *Decretum pro armenis; D.B.,* 697.

[38] Pseudo-Albert the Great, *Mariale,* q. 43; *op. omn.,* Vol. 37, ed. Borgnet (Parisiis, 1890-1899), p. 84; Suárez, *In III,* disp. 18, sect. 3, n. 7; *op. omn.,* Vol. 19, ed. Vivès (Parisiis, 1860); C. de Vega, S.J., *Theologia Mariana,* Vol. 2 (ed. Neapoli, 1866), pp. 210-213.

Extreme Unction is not the remission of the remains of sin, but rather, the strengthening of the soul to face the difficulties which beset a soul at the hour of death. He adds, if Our Lady received Baptism, which is a sacrament instituted for the remission of original sin, why should we hesitate to say that she received the sacrament of Extreme Unction? In both cases, besides the remission of sin, which obviously does not apply to the Blessed Virgin, there are other effects which in no way detract from her sanctity, but rather increase it. He concludes by saying that if Mary was capable of receiving this sacrament, she certainly did so, in order to obtain the grace it contained, and in order to set an example of humility to the faithful.[39]

Notwithstanding the reasoning of these theologians, the common opinion, endorsed by most modern Mariologists, denies that Mary ever received Extreme Unction. The sacrament implies certain elements which are unworthy of her great holiness. First of all, the sacrament is reserved for the sick who are in danger of death; but Our Lady was never subject to sickness. Second, the words used in the administration of this sacrament are utterly incompatible with everything we believe about Mary; "Indulgeat tibi Deus quidquid per visum ... *deliquisti* ..." Last, granting that the primary purpose of this sacrament is the strengthening of the soul, who would say that Mary needed any such aid at the hour of death? No temptation of Satan assailed her at that hour; no fear of death and judgment entered her soul. On the contrary she welcomed death which was for her the gateway to an ecstatic reunion with Jesus in heaven.

In conclusion, we may say that the whole question about Mary's reception of the sacraments, although a very intriguing one, is nevertheless one surrounded with a certain amount of obscurity and uncertainty. In the absence of scriptural and patristic proofs, theologians can only conjecture about what sacraments she received. There will always be some discrepancy of opinion, therefore, among theologians, and a completely satisfying exposition of this phase of Mary's sanctification will probably never be found in this life.

---

[39] *Op. cit.*, p. 212.

III. FINAL FULLNESS OF GRACE IN MARY

Before explaining this final stage of the Blessed Virgin's glorious sanctification, a word should be said about what theologians call the accelerated rapidity of Mary's growth in grace. St. Thomas tells us that a natural movement always becomes more rapid, the nearer it approaches its term, while an unnatural movement tends to do just the opposite. For instance, a stone falling to earth gathers speed uniformly as it approaches the earth; while one thrown in the air is uniformly slowed down. Applying this to growth in grace, Aquinas says: "Grace perfects the soul and makes it tend towards the good in a natural way, like a second nature. It follows then that those who are in the state of grace should grow more in charity according as they come nearer the final goal, and are more strongly attracted by it."[40] We observe this accelerated progress in the saints. As they grow older and increase in holiness, they move more promptly and generously toward God. They advance in holiness not with a regular, but with an ever hastening step. What, then, must have been the rapid growth of Mary as she drew closer and closer to God! It must have been the greatest of all, because the rate at which it commenced was determined by her fullness of grace, and therefore surpassed that of all the saints. Besides that, her progress was continuous. Nothing held her back, neither the consequences of original sin, nor any venial sin, neither negligence nor distraction. And if, as is probable, her infused knowledge gave her the use of reason and will during the hours of sleep, there was in Mary an accelerated increase in grace all through her life, compared to which the accelerated motion of falling bodies under the force of gravitation is only a distant image.[41]

The Blessed Virgin's final fullness of grace refers to the perfection of her grace at the end of her life on earth. There was in Mary an initial fullness of grace (*prima sanctificatio*) and a subsequent growth in grace (*secunda sanctificatio*). There came therefore, a moment when the growth of grace in Mary reached its final apex, before it became heavenly glory. This we call her final or consummated fullness of grace.

---

[40] St. Thomas, *Comment. in Epist. ad Hebraeos*, 10, 25; I-II, q. 35, a. 6.
[41] Cf. Garrigou-Lagrange, *op. cit.*, pp. 87-90.

Although this final grace of Mary was something beyond words to describe, we must never think of it as something infinite. It is evident that, no matter what incomprehensible heights it reached, it always remained a created, accidental entity and, consequently, a finite thing. Moreover, as we remarked before, Mary's grace did not possess all the excellence of which grace is capable, nor did it extend to all the possible effects of grace. This was the reason for maintaining that her grace was inferior to that of her divine Son. Wherefore, in describing the wonderful final grace of the Blessed Virgin, authors use expressions like, *"pene infinita"* or *"pene immensa."* These expressions declare in some way the staggering proportions of Mary's grace, but at the same time, they do not offend.

The Bull *Ineffabilis Deus* describes Mary's unparalleled fullness of grace with their words: "God filled her above all creatures with such a wealth of heavenly grace, that, free from all taint of sin, beautiful and pure as she was, she possessed a fullness of innocence and sanctity greater than any conceivable in anyone outside of God Himself."[42] In a similar vein, Denis the Carthusian writes: "Outside of the holiness of Jesus, there is no greater holiness possible than that of His Mother, for her holiness cannot be comprehended in this life, and only the Incarnation surpasses the privilege she had of being the Mother of God."[43]

If such expressions of praise seem exaggerated and unwarranted, let it be recalled that the initial grace of Mary was probably greater than the accumulated final grace of all the angels and saints. Starting from that almost incomprehensible degree of perfection, Mary increased her holiness throughout the whole course of her life. She did this by means of uninterrupted and highly excellent meritorious acts, by means of the reception of sacraments, by reason of unusual infusions of grace at certain important moments of her life. What must we conclude, therefore, but that her final plenitude of grace was something almost infinite?[44]

No tongue or pen will ever adequately express the sublime holiness

---

[42] *Ineffabilis Deus*, ed. Tondini (Roma, 1954), p. 30.

[43] *De praeconio et dignitate Mariae*, lib. 1, a. 14; quoted by Alastruey, *op. cit.*, p. 362.

[44] Suarez, *In III*, disp. 18, sect. 4; in Alastruey, *op. cit.*, p. 363.

of the Mother of God. No mind will ever fully penetrate the significance of the truth we have been considering. Even the golden-tongued Chrysostom faltered when he tried to sum up the praises of this Masterpiece of God's grace. With unwonted plainness of language, he simply exclaimed: "Magnum revera miraculum, fratres dilectissimi, fuit Beata semper Virgo Maria. Quid namque illa majus aut illustrius ullo unquam tempore inventum est, seu aliquando inveniri poterit? Haec sola coelum ac terram amplitudine superavit."[45]

---

[45] *Serm. apud Metaphrasten;* in *Brev. Rom.*, Commune B.V.M., lect. 4.

OUR LADY'S KNOWLEDGE

By VERY REV. FRANCIS J. CONNELL, C.SS.R., S.T.D., LL.D.

HE nature and the extent of the knowledge possessed by the Blessed Virgin Mary while she was still on earth have never been decided by any official decree of the Church; but the problem has been studied extensively by theologians, particularly in their treatises on Mariology.[1] They agree that very little explicit information on this subject is provided in the deposit of divine faith, contained in Sacred Scripture and Divine Tradition. Nevertheless, from the privileges granted to Mary, especially the Divine Maternity and the Immaculate Conception, theologians attempt to discover, at least with a measure of probability, the kind of knowledge Mary possessed and the extent of this knowledge.

In discussing this question two extremes must be avoided. On the one hand, a person should not be so enthusiastic to ascribe to Our Lady every possible honor as to attribute to her a manner and measure of knowledge well-nigh equal to that of her divine Son in His human intellect. Mary's state in life and the task assigned to her did not call for so extensive an intellectual perfection. Christ was the God-Man and the Redeemer of the entire human race; consequently, the fullness of knowledge compatible with a created intellect was due to Him. For this reason it has been the commonly accepted teaching of Catholic theology, confirmed by a decree of the Holy Office,[2] that the Word Incarnate

---

[1] It would be impossible to cite even a small portion of the numerous theological books and articles which treat of Mary's knowledge. Hence, we shall mention only a few: F. Suárez, *De mysteriis vitae Christi*, disp. 4, sect. 7 and 8; *op. omn.*, Vivès, Vol. 19 (Parisiis, 1860), pp. 70*a*-73*b*; C. de Vega, *Theologia Mariana*, Vol. 1 (ed. Neapoli, 1866), nn. 957-959; G. M. Roschini, *Mariologia*, ed. 2, Vol. 2, pars 2 (Romae, 1948), pp. 184-194; A. Martinelli, *De primo instanti conceptionis B. V. Mariae. Disquisitio de usu rationis* (Romae, 1950); F. Girerd, *Science de Marie*, in *Nouvelle Revue Théologique*, Vol. 49, 1922, pp. 351-363; A. Michel, *Le mystère de Jésus et la science de la Sainte Vierge*, in *L'Ami du Clergé*, Vol. 61, 1951, pp. 769-772.

[2] D.B., 2184.

through the beatific vision knew all things actual — past, present, and future. But such a degree of knowledge was not necessary or congruous for Mary. She was a mere creature; and her share in the Redemption, though real and efficacious, was immeasurably inferior to the redemptive activity of her divine Son.

On the other hand, in view of Mary's dignity, as Mother of God, surpassing that of every other mere creature that has ever lived, and of her participation in the Redemption, it is surely unjustifiable to deny her an extraordinary measure of knowledge, particularly of a supernatural character. Moreover, in view of the statements of numerous saints and scholars, imbued with the sense of Catholic tradition, it is surely contrary to the mind of the Church to ascribe to Our Lady merely that degree of knowledge which would be suitable to a good woman preserved by God from the taint of original sin. Her Divine Maternity and her participation in the work of the Redemption, giving her a most important part in the eternal plan for the restoration of mankind to the adoptive sonship of God, call for a special privilege bestowed on her in the form of intellectual perfection.

There are three types of knowledge which Our Lady could have possessed during her earthly life — beatific, infused, and acquired. We shall consider each of these separately, and add another section concerning the knowledge which Mary now possesses in heaven.

I. BEATIFIC KNOWLEDGE

By beatific knowledge we mean that understanding which the intellect receives from the direct perception of the divine nature in the Trinity of Persons. Every human being is destined to enjoy the beatific vision for all eternity; but normally this is granted only when the soul has left the body.[3] To elevate its natural power so that the divine essence can be thus directly perceived, the intellect is granted the supernatural habit known as the light of glory.[4] No species, or intellectual similitudes, of the divine nature intervene; the divinity itself is the immediate object of the act of intellectual cognition.

---

[3] *D.B.*, 530.

[4] *D.B.*, 475.

It is the common teaching of theologians that Jesus Christ possessed the beatific vision in His human intellect throughout His entire lifetime; and the Church has approved this view by censuring the opposite opinion.[5] However, theologians also commonly teach that the privilege of the beatific vision was not granted to Mary habitually during her earthly life.[6] She possessed the virtues of faith and hope; she advanced in grace throughout her entire lifetime. But if she had possessed the beatific vision, faith and hope would have been excluded; and she could not have increased in grace and merit because her soul would have been *in statu termini*, as was the soul of Christ from the first instant of His conception.

However, it does not follow from this that Mary did not receive the privilege of the beatific vision *transiently* on certain occasions in the course of her lifetime; and there are many good theologians who believe it probable that she was thus favored. Among these are Suárez,[7] Vázquez,[8] St. Bernardine of Siena[9]— to mention a few of the old writers — and, among more recent writers, Roschini[10] and Martinelli.[11]

The main argument is the Mariological principle that whatever has been granted to any creature by God was not denied to Mary. But the privilege of a transitory enjoyment of the beatific vision was probably granted to Moses and St. Paul; for of Moses the Scripture says: "The Lord

---

[5] D.B., 2183-2185.

[6] F. de Guerra, in *Majestas gratiarum ac virtutum omnium Deiparae Virginis*, Vol. 1 (Segoviae, 1659), p. 67, and Th. F. Urrutigoyti, in *Certamen scholasticum expositivum argumentum pro Deipara ...* (Lugduni, 1660), nn. 1248-1422, held that Mary possessed the beatific vision during her entire lifetime. But they also held the unusual position that the soul in permanent possession of the beatific vision can possess the virtue of faith and can increase in merit. Cf. also R. Rábanos, *La gracia carismática de María*, in *Estudios Marianos*, Vol. 5, 1946, pp. 261-262. An excellent history of the various opinions on this point is given by J. de Aldama in his erudite article *¿Gozó de la visión beatífica la Santísima Virgen alguna vez en su vida mortal?*, in *Archivo Teológico Granadino*, Vol. 6, 1943, pp. 121-140.

[7] *De mysteriis vitae Christi*, disp. 19, sect. 4, n. 4; *op. omn.*, Vol. 19, p. 305a.

[8] *In S. Theol.*, disp. 56, c. 2, n. 5; *op. omn.*, Vol. 7 (Lugduni, 1631), p. 211b.

[9] *De conceptione B. M. Virginis*, sermo 4, a. 1, c. 2; *op. omn.*, Vol. 4 (Venetiis, 1745), p. 83b.

[10] *Op. cit., pp. 185-187.*

[11] *Op. cit., pp. 81-83.*

spoke to Moses, face to face, as a man is wont to speak to his friend,"[12] and St. Paul asserts that he was "caught up into paradise and heard secret words that man can not repeat."[13] The majority of commentators understand these expressions as indicating that these two saints were favored for a brief time with the beatific vision.[14] Consequently, it is argued, God would not deny this privilege to Mary, the Queen of Saints.

Of course, if one held that the scriptural statements regarding Moses and St. Paul are to be understood of a high measure of infused knowledge of God, without the direct vision of the divine essence, the argument given above would lose its value. Thus, Merkelbach states: "Since present-day interpreters of Scripture do not consider the opinion about the vision of God by Paul and Moses well founded, the probability of the vision by the Blessed Virgin deduced therefrom disappears."[15] However, Suárez, though he does not admit that Moses and Paul actually saw God "face to face," believes that it can be piously believed that Mary did see God sometimes in her lifetime.[16]

Even independently of the argument from comparison with Moses and Paul, we can give arguments of some value to render it at least probable that Mary enjoyed the beatific vision sometimes in her mortal life. Since she had a share in the work of the Redemption, it seems that from time to time she should have beheld immediately the goal to which redeemed mankind was destined, since it was because of His redemptive office that Christ as Man enjoyed the beatific vision, according to St. Thomas.[17] Roschini adds that, as she suffered so much in her mortal life, it was fitting that she should be consoled in the most sublime manner, by gazing from time to time on the rapturous beauty of the divine essence.[18]

Theologians have also attempted to determine with some degree of probability the particular occasions in Mary's life when this privilege

---

[12] *Exod. 33:11.*

[13] *2 Cor. 12:4.*

[14] Cf. Martinelli, *op. cit.*, p. 69 ff.

[15] B.-H. Merkelbach, *Mariologia* (Parisiis, 1939), p. 198.

[16] Suárez, loc. cit.

[17] *Summa Theologica*, P. 3, q. 9, a. 2.

[18] *Op. cit.*, p. 186.

would have been granted her. The most suitable occasion was doubtless the moment when the "Word was made flesh" in the chaste womb of Mary; and some add the time of Christ's birth, and the day of His resurrection. The question has been discussed by theologians whether Our Lady was granted a transitory vision of the divinity at the very moment of her conception. Martinelli, who discusses this question very thoroughly, concludes that it can be stated with probability that this favor was granted her on that occasion. He says: "If it is believed that Mary's intellect was at any time favored with such a clear vision of the divine essence, it is easily concluded that with great probability this took place on the occasion of the Blessed Virgin's own immaculate conception, since apart from the Incarnation no other moment of her mortal existence can be found which was so solemn, so happy and so excellent."[19]

It is impossible to determine the extent of the knowledge possessed by the Blessed Virgin from the intuitive vision of God, since this was dependent on the free choice of the Almighty. We can safely assert, however, that this knowledge was immeasurably inferior to that which her divine Son enjoyed throughout His entire lifetime; for all things actual — past, present, and future — were made known to Him in the vision of the divine nature.[20] Yet, in view of the ineffable measure of sanctity that adorned the soul of Mary even from the first instant of her earthly existence, it seems evident that she enjoyed a more intensive and extensive perception of the divine nature in the Trinity of Persons than any other created intellect, save that of the Word Incarnate, ever enjoyed or will enjoy in heaven. It should be noted, however, that this knowledge was not necessarily surpassing with reference to created objects. Its pre-eminence consisted principally in a profound understanding of God Himself, especially the sublime mystery of the Holy Trinity. With far more reason than St. Paul, Mary could exclaim: "Eye has not seen nor ear heard, nor has it entered into the heart of man, what things God has prepared for those who love Him."[21]

---

[19] *Op. cit.*, p. 82.

[20] D.B., 2183.

[21] *1 Cor.* 2:9.

II. INFUSED KNOWLEDGE

In general, infused knowledge is that which is obtained by direct infusion by God, not by human effort. Theologians distinguish two kinds of infused knowledge — that which is infused *per se,* and that which is infused *per accidens.* The former is that type of knowledge which, in its acquisition and use, is independent of the sensitive faculties, such as the imagination; the latter is dependent for its use on the sensitive faculties, although it has been directly infused by God.[22]

According to the more common theological view, Mary received *per se* infused knowledge in the course of her lifetime. For, such knowledge was granted to the angels; hence, by virtue of the principle that she was granted any privileges accorded to other creatures (as long as these privileges were compatible with her state and office), Our Lady must have enjoyed this divinely granted favor. It would seem, moreover, that she possessed this type of knowledge in the first instant of her life, so that she could accompany the privilege of her sanctification with an act of love. At the very moment when the Almighty manifested His special love for Mary by preserving her from original sin and by flooding her soul with an immense degree of sanctifying grace, Mary turned her heart to God with a most fervent act of divine charity. Since her perception of the infinite goodness of God on which this act of love was based came through *per se* infused knowledge, which could be exercised without the need of any sensitive faculties, we have no need of presuming that any miraculous development was granted to the body of Mary in her conception.

Father Martinelli argues to the opinion that Mary received *per se* infused knowledge in her conception, in these words: "Among those who pursue the study of Mariology it is the more probable and more common opinion that the Blessed Virgin Mary, at the time of her immaculate conception, received the actual use of reason from knowledge *per se* infused. For this type of knowledge granted to her by a singular privilege of God manifests those qualities which undoubtedly demonstrate it as probable: first, not only was this knowledge possible, but it was easy and did not exceed the state of a person on earth;

---

[22] Cf. A. Michel, *Jésus-Christ et la théologie,* in *D.T.C.,* Vol. 8, coll. 1273-1274.

moreover, it contributes toward the increase of grace, and, once its existence is granted, the many privileges which were given to the Mother of God are more readily understood and proved."[23]

Admitting that Mary received infused knowledge in the first instant of her existence, the question can be asked whether this was a transitory privilege, or was permanently possessed by Our Lady. The more probable opinion is that the privilege in question was permanent. In other words, from the very first moment of her mortal life Mary possessed and retained the use of reason. Through the infused (*per se*) knowledge which her intellect enjoyed she could understand the infinite goodness of the divine nature, the marvelous operations of divine providence, and especially the wonders of the plan of salvation which God had decreed, with Mary herself as one of the principal agents. And this knowledge was Mary's privilege throughout her entire lifetime. Not even sleep interrupted her contemplation of the divinity conferred through this infused knowledge; for she could employ these divinely granted intellectual species without the concomitant use of any sensitive faculties. Hence, through ardent acts of love of God based on this infused knowledge, Mary could constantly increase in grace and merit.

The chief object of this infused knowledge was supernatural truth. Some authors have ascribed to Mary an extensive knowledge of human affairs, as well as of divine things. According to this theory, Our Lady was fully conversant with philosophy, geography, physics, chemistry, etc., even from the first moment of her existence. Such was the view upheld by Christopher de Vega.[24] But it seems immoderate to ascribe such knowledge to Mary, because her office did not call for it. She was to be the Mother of God; hence, her miraculously granted knowledge was concerned chiefly with God. It would seem that this infused knowledge embraced a recognition of the doctrine of the Holy Trinity, although a fuller explanation of this sublime mystery was to come only later through the teaching of Mary's Son. Those who hold that Mary received the privilege of the beatific vision transiently in the first moment of her conception could hold that she also then possessed infused knowledge. For the soul enjoying the immediate vision of God

---

[23] *Op. cit.*, p. 86.
[24] *Op. cit.*, nn. 1056-1103.

through the beatific vision of God cannot merit by an act of divine charity based on this knowledge of the divine goodness, inasmuch as the will is necessarily drawn to love God perceived in Himself. But an act of love for God based on infused knowledge of His goodness can be meritorious, because this type of knowledge does not *necessarily* draw the will to love. Hence, it was through the medium of this infused knowledge that Our Lady co-operated in her own sanctification, making an act of divine love in the very moment when God bestowed on her the immeasurable blessing of supernatural sanctification.[25] By this same act of love she also merited *de condigno* heavenly glory, according to the teaching of Suárez.[26] The transitory possession of the beatific vision would not put Mary *in statu termini* and render her incapable of meriting.

With the passing of time the infused knowledge of Mary was doubtless increased through the bestowal of new species by the Almighty. Thus, while we can hold that she did not recognize from the beginning of her existence the full plan of God for the salvation of the human race, including the part she was to take in the fulfillment of this marvelous design, it is certain that at least from the time of the Incarnation she was aware that she was to be the Mother of the Redeemer. In the words of Roschini: "As regards the knowledge of the future, and especially with relation to the divine decree bearing on the sanctification and the salvation of mankind, the Blessed Virgin had to know this, as the Coredemptrix, at least in general, if not in reference to all particular points, from the time of the Annunciation."[27]

In connection with Mary's infused knowledge the question arises: "Did she know that her Son was true God, and if so, from what precise period?" To this we answer that it would surely be unreasonable and out of harmony with the Church's attitude toward Mary to hold that she was ignorant of this fundamental doctrine, at least after Our Lord had begun His public life and had declared that He was truly the Son of God. But was she cognizant of this doctrine even from the time of the

---

[25] Martinelli, *op. cit.*, p. 114.

[26] *De mysteriis vitae Christi*, disp. 4, sect. 8, n. 3; *op. omn.*, Vol. 19, p. 73b. For the opinion of other theologians on this point cf. Martinelli, *op. cit.*, pp. 118-121.

[27] *Op. cit.*, p. 190.

Incarnation, when the angel brought her the divine message that her Son should be called the Son of the Most High, and should possess a kingdom that would never end?[28] Some Catholic scholars have held that even after the Annunciation Mary was not aware that her Son was truly God. One of the arguments they use in support of this position is that the incident of the loss of the Child Jesus in the temple indicates that Mary and Joseph did not understand His statement that He must be about His Father's business[29] — something they would have understood had they been aware of His divine personality.[30] Others, however, argue that this lack of understanding on Mary's part merely indicates that she was not enlightened as to all the circumstances of the Redemption, although she knew that her Son was the Redeemer and that He was true God. Thus, she was unaware that the plan of God called for a stay of several days by her Son in Jerusalem when He was only twelve years old. This explains her surprise when He remained behind after she and Joseph had started back to Nazareth.[31] At any rate, the more common theological opinion holds that Mary was certain (through *per se* infused knowledge) from the time of the Annunciation that Jesus was a divine Person, and that she herself was truly the Mother of God. Similarly, she realized that the work of Redemption demanded the suffering and death of her Son, and the prevision of His future agony made her truly the Mother of Sorrows all her lifetime.

It is likewise possible that God infused into the soul of Mary at some

---

[28] Lk. 1:32.

[29] Lk. 2:49.

[30] Cf. E. Sutcliffe, *Our Lady and the Divinity of Christ*, in The Month, Vol. 180, 1944, pp. 347-350; id., *Our Lady's Knowledge of the Divinity of Christ*, in *The Irish Ecclesiastical Record*, Vol. 66, 1945, pp. 427-432; id., *Again Our Lady's Knowledge of Christ's Divinity*, The Irish Ecclesiastical Record, Vol. 68, 1946, pp. 123-128.

[31] Cf. Roschini, *op. cit.* pp. 193-194; H. Pope, *Our Lady and the Divinity of Christ*, in *The Irish Ecclesiastical Record*, Vol. 66, 1945, pp. 100-105; J. A. Kleist, The Annunciation, in The American Ecclesiastical Review, Vol. 114, 1946, pp. 161-169; Father Peter, *When Did Our Lady Know She Was Mother of God?* in *The Irish Ecclesiastical Record*, Vol. 67, 1946, pp. 145-163; D. Unger, *When Did Mary First Know of Her Divine Maternity?* in *The American Ecclesiastical Review*, Vol. 114, 1946, pp. 360-366; Father Peter, *Mariology and Exegesis*, in *The Irish Ecclesiastical Record*, Vol. 69, 1947, pp. 113-124; Sutcliffe, *Scripture, Tradition and Mariology*, in *The Irish Ecclesiastical Record*, Vol. 69, 1947, pp. 807-814; E. May, *The Scriptural Basis for Mary's Spiritual Maternity*, in Marian Studies, Vol. 3, 1952, pp. 122-123.

occasions in the course of her life knowledge which in itself was natural. Such knowledge would thus have been *per accidens* infused. Cardinal Lépicier believes that Mary received this type of knowledge in the first instant of her conception, for he does not allow the possibility of her receiving knowledge *per se* infused.[32] This view, however, has few supporters. As regards the divine bestowal of *per accidens* infused knowledge on Mary at other times, after she had come to the use of reason, while it is possible that it took place, there is no positive argument that it actually occurred.

III. ACQUIRED KNOWLEDGE

By acquired knowledge is meant that which is arrived at by means of our own natural powers. It may be experimental, that is to say, based on the data furnished by the senses, or deductive, namely, acquired by means of intellectual abstraction or by way of a reasoning process. It is obvious that Our Lady possessed both types of acquired knowledge, since she was subject to empirical reactions, and was endowed with an operative *intellectus agens* and with an *intellectus patiens* capable of functioning normally. As to the principal sources of Mary's information, we may safely state that, in addition to the natural experiences of daily life, they were the assiduous reading of Sacred Scripture[33] and, of course, the frequent discourses with her divine Son.

Regarding the perfection and extent of Mary's acquired knowledge, we surmise that they must have been exceedingly great, considering that she possessed the gift of integrity and that, therefore, her intellect retained all its native brilliancy. However, as in the case of her infused knowledge, this acquired knowledge must not be conceived as extending to human affairs not connected with her office as Mother of God and co-operator with her Son in the work of Redemption. Thus, it would be frivolous to imagine her devoting herself to the study of the many languages spoken in the civilized world of her time, although, during her

---

[32] *Institutiones Theologiae Speculativae*, Vol. 2 (Romae, 1932), pp. 335-337.

[33] Every verse of the *Magnificat* reveals that Mary was quite familiar with the Old Testament prophecies. Cf. on this point T. Gallus, Ad *"principium materiale" Redemptionis objectivae*, in *Divus Thomas* (Pl.), Vol. 57, 1954, pp. 246-250.

sojourn in Egypt, she doubtless acquired a good knowledge of the language of that country. Certainly, she must have been an excellent cook and a skillful seamstress. And with her natural knowledge guided and elevated by divine grace and faith, she must have been recognized as a woman of extraordinary wisdom and prudence. We can easily surmise that in the little village of Nazareth the simple folk must have often presented their daily problems to Joseph's wife in order to obtain advice and inspiration.

The ancient tradition that Mary was presented to the service of God as a little child, commemorated by the Church on November 21, is quite conformable to the view stated above, that her intellect was keen and brilliant. A mind such as that given to the child chosen to be the Mother of God must have attained the natural power of reasoning much sooner than that of the ordinary child.[34]

MARY'S KNOWLEDGE IN HEAVEN

Since the moment of the departure of her soul from earth (whether through death or in conjunction with a bodily assumption without death), Mary has been in possession of the beatific vision in the kingdom of heaven. Since the intensity and extent of this act of intelligence are in proportion to the measure of sanctity with which a soul leaves this world, and the holiness of Mary was so great that, in the words of Pope Pius IX, "under God, no greater can be conceived,"[35] Our Lady beholds the majesty and the beauty of the Triune God more clearly and more profoundly than all other creatures, both angels and men, being surpassed only by her divine Son.

In the light of the beatific vision the soul beholds also many created objects, including those happenings on earth which have a special interest for this particular soul. Thus, a saint who has established a religious order during his period on earth will behold in the vision of

---

[34] For a more detailed treatment of Mary's acquired knowledge, cf. Roschini, *op. cit.,* pp. 190-193; Rábanos, *art. cit.,* pp. 266-268. On Mary's immunity from all error, cf. Lépicier, *Tractatus de Beatissima Virgine Maria* (Romae, 1926), pp. 298-299, and G. Alastruey, *Tratado de la Virgen Santísima,* ed. 3 (Madrid, 1952), pp. 368-371.

[35] *Ineffabilis Deus, in* Acta et decreta Sacrorum Conciliorum recentiorum, Col. Lac., Vol. 6 (Friburgi Brisgoviae, 1882), p. 836.

God the successes and failures of his institute, and will thus be enabled to direct his prayers for his spiritual children in a definite form to the Almighty. Applying this norm to Our Lady, we conclude that her knowledge in the beatific vision of earthly events surpasses by far that of any other blessed soul (save the soul of Christ) because, as Coredemptrix and Dispenser of all grace and the spiritual Mother of all mankind, she has an interest in every human being and in all the events that take place or will take place on earth. The Redemptorist theologian, Father Herrmann, states: "The Blessed Virgin clearly beholds all men, especially the elect, and also all their thoughts and the secrets of their hearts, and all the prosperous and unfortunate events of the world."[36] The predictions of the Blessed Virgin in the apparitions at Fatima confirm this opinion as to the extent of her knowledge of the future.

However, it would not necessarily follow from this fact that Mary knows the ultimate fate of every human being — who will be saved, who will be lost. On this question we can have only conjectural knowledge. Yet, the great theologian Suárez did not hesitate to express the opinion that Mary's perception of created objects in the beatific vision embraces all things actual — past, present, and future — except those that are proper to her divine Son.[37] Such extensive knowledge might include the discernment of the saved and the lost, past, present, and future.

To some it might seem unsuitable to inquire in so detailed a fashion about the nature and extent of Mary's knowledge, particularly since we have so little explicit information on this point in the Bible.

But it must not be forgotten that in the tradition of the Church there are definite indications that the woman whom God chose to be the Mother of His Son was the recipient of many extraordinary privileges; and these would naturally include great perfection of the intellect, the noblest human faculty. And so, it is not unprofitable to seek some definite ideas on Mary's knowledge, since a study of this kind helps us to understand the sublime dignity of the Mother of God, and inspires us to be more ready to seek through her intercession the wisdom and the understanding that we need in the journey of life.

---

[36] *Institutiones Theologiae Dogmaticae*, Vol. 2 (Parisiis, 1926), n. 1087.
[37] *Op. cit.*, disp. 22, sect. 3, n. 5.

Mary's Spiritual Maternity

by WENCESLAUS SEBASTIAN, .O.F.M., S.T.D.

ARY'S Spiritual Maternity is one of the most certain and most universally accepted doctrines of Mariology. Not only do the faithful all over the world believe this truth, but they feel it deeply engraved in their hearts. The beautiful saying of St. Stanislaus Kostka, "The Mother of God is my mother," is an exact expression of the general consensus of the Church. To deny the fact of Mary's Spiritual Motherhood would be an act of grave temerity in the Faith.

Yet, if the existence of Mary's Spiritual Maternity is clearly attested to by the faith of the Church, its intimate nature still holds many a mystery for us. It is our purpose in this chapter to summarize the teachings of theologians on the nature of Mary's universal Motherhood, and to show that their doctrine is well founded on Holy Scripture, Tradition, and the Church's official Magisterium.

I

THE NATURE OF MARY'S SPIRITUAL MATERNITY

The analysis of the nature of Mary's Spiritual Maternity would not be complete if we did not clearly define its true concept, nor accurately ascertain its basis. In other words, we shall try to explain what the Spiritual Maternity really means, and from what Mariological prerogative it basically derives.

SECTION I. THE CONCEPT

Our knowledge of the supernatural order can be expressed only in terms of the natural order. The invisible world of God is mirrored in the created world around us, "being understood by the things that are made."[1] In creating the universe God intended it to be a reflection of His own perfections. Hence it is that the supernatural order is not an

---

[1] *Rom.* 1:9.

imitation of the natural order, but rather the reverse; the natural order is fashioned on the model of the supernatural order. Such concepts, therefore, as fatherhood and parenthood, in the order of nature are but images of the supernatural Fatherhood of God. In like manner, natural motherhood is merely a reflection of the Motherhood of Mary.[2] Therefore, to understand Mary's Spiritual Motherhood, we may legitimately study the nature of human motherhood and by a process of analogy conclude to the nature of Mary's supernatural Maternity.

1. Essence of Natural Motherhood

What is the essence of motherhood in the natural order? St. Thomas in his customary conciseness defines a mother as a woman who conceives and begets a child: "ex hoc dicitur aliqua mulier alicuius mater quod eum concepit et genuit."[3] The essence of motherhood resides in the process of generation which is traditionally defined as "Origo viventis a principio vivente coniuncto in similitudinem eiusdem naturae."[4] Generation among animate creatures is a physical action in virtue of which a living being produces out of its own substance another living being of the same physical species as itself.

The secondary functions of motherhood, the rearing and education of a child, can be regarded as truly maternal only if the person performing them has really conceived and engendered the child. To call mother anyone who rears and educates a child which she did not beget would be an improper use of the name. Legal language includes such terminology as motherhood of donation, of adoption, and of federation. A stepmother exercises a motherhood of donation by performing the secondary duties of motherhood in place of the deceased mother. A mother by adoption is one who has legally accepted an orphan or an abandoned child as her own. A mother-in-law becomes, by federation, mother of her daughter's husband or of her son's wife. In all these instances the person called "mother" does fulfill some of the duties and

---

[2] J. Beumer, S.J., *Maria Mutter der Christenheit*, in *Katholische Marienkunde*, ed. P. Sträter, S.J., Vol. 2 (Paderborn, 1947), p. 230. C. Vollert, S.J., *The Place of Our Lady in the Mystical Body*, in *Marian Studies*, Vol. 3, 1952, pp. 174-175.

[3] St. Thomas, *Summa Theologica*, P. 3, q. 35, a. 4.

[4] *Ibid.*, P. 1, q. 27, a. 2.

assume some of the attitudes of true motherhood, but everyone knows that she is not the real mother of the child. True motherhood is essentially based on the fact of physical generation.

The concept of natural, human motherhood is the key to our understanding of Mary's Spiritual Motherhood. If Mary is, in a true sense, the "Immaculate Mother of Jesus and our Mother," she must have conceived and engendered us spiritually and she must continue her maternal solicitude by rearing, nourishing, and educating us supernaturally. Can there really be question of generation in the supernatural order?

2. Existence of Supernatural Regeneration

Holy Scripture clearly speaks of a spiritual rebirth: "Amen, amen, I say to thee, unless a man be born again of water and the Spirit, he cannot enter the kingdom of heaven."[5] The context of these words of Our Lord leaves no doubt as to the spiritual nature of this rebirth. In answer to Nicodemus' query, "How can a man be born when he is old? Can he enter a second time into his mother's womb and be born again?" Our Lord explains that He is speaking of a spiritual birth: "that which is born of the flesh is flesh; and that which is born of the Spirit is spirit."[6] And He goes on to show how this rebirth is realized: "For God so loved the world that He gave His only-begotten Son, that those who believe in Him may not perish, but may have life everlasting."[7] Man must be reborn in a spiritual manner in order to have a share in eternal life, and this life is imparted to him because God has given His divine Son, through whom all are saved.

Theologically, our spiritual regeneration must be envisaged on two different planes, that of the objective and that of the subjective Redemption. On the former level Christ acquired through His condign merits the sum total of graces for all mankind, opening the gates of heaven and making it possible for all to be saved. On the latter He continues His causality by applying to individual souls the graces of

---

[5] Jn. 3:5.
[6] Jn. 3:6-7.
[7] Jn. 3:16.

Redemption. Though the production of grace in souls must be attributed to the efficient causality of the divine nature, Christ's humanity nevertheless acts as an instrumental cause in the process of justification.

By His Hypostatic Union Christ united His divine and human natures in one divine Person, and as a consequence His human soul was replenished with the fullness of sanctifying grace. Though this fullness of grace enabled Christ's human faculties to act supernaturally, it was destined moreover to flow out to men, making them participants in the divine nature and endowing them with supernatural life. This overflow of divine grace is commonly known as Christ's grace of Headship, in as far as it mystically unites us to Him, the Head of the Mystical Body. Thus it was that Christ's humanity was to become an instrumental cause of our revivification or spiritual rebirth. Yet by an express decree of God the causality of our Lord's human nature would not actually be exercised, and supernatural life would not *de facto* be imparted to mankind until Christ had suffered and died upon the cross. The Passion of Our Lord must consequently be considered, along with the Incarnation, as the adequate cause of our objective Redemption, or of our supernatural rebirth to the life of grace.

In this supernatural rebirth we find a proper analogy of proportionality with carnal birth in the natural order.[8] There is, first of all, a production of a new being, not as regards its natural, but as regards its moral and supernatural entity: a new creature, as St. Paul calls it, produced through Christ's intervention: "If then any man is in Christ, he is a new creature: the former things have passed away; behold, they are made new! But all things are from God, who has reconciled us to Himself through Christ."[9] Furthermore, we may speak of an "origo viventis" since grace, which is imparted to us through the merits of Christ's Passion, is a true life and makes us capable of a new activity in the supernatural order. The words "a principio vivente coniuncto" are also realized in the supernatural rebirth, for grace, which is granted us by God, derives from Christ's grace of Headship ("gratia capitalis") and

---

[8] E. Théorêt, *La Médiation mariale dans l'école française* (Paris, 1940), p. 47. Gregorio de Jesús Crucificado, O.C.D., *Naturaleza de la maternidad espiritual de María*, in *Estudios Marianos*, Vol. 7, 1948, p. 127.

[9] 2 Cor. 5:17-18.

is merely a redundance of His plenitude: "Of His fullness we have all received."[10] And this overflow of Christ's plenitude of grace into our souls makes them like unto the divinity: "In similitudinem naturae." Indeed, the grace imparted to us is the very grace of Christ, which makes us share *accidentaliter* in His divine nature in such a way that we are made His brothers by adoption. How truly then is our spiritual adoption a regeneration, a rebirth to a new life.

3. In What Does Mary's Spiritual Maternity Consist?

Since motherhood in the natural order can be regarded as an image of Mary's Spiritual Motherhood, the various meanings of the former can now be applied to the latter. That Mary is our Mother *at least* in a broader sense cannot be denied without disregarding the consensus of the Church; but the question is: must her Spiritual Motherhood be regarded as merely juridical; or are the conditions of a real motherhood, implying our supernatural regeneration, fulfilled in her? If we give a looser meaning to her Spiritual Motherhood, then we may rightly say of Mary, as is often said of an adopted mother: "She is not our mother."

A relatively small number of authors[11] attempt to limit Mary's Spiritual Motherhood to her intercession in heaven. Her share in the economy of grace would thus be restricted to the subjective Redemption. Their opinion is tantamount to saying that Mary is merely our Mother by donation or adoption; her Spiritual Motherhood would have to be understood in a merely juridical sense. For legal motherhood presupposes that the person called mother does not intervene directly in the production of the life of her son. In the order of grace we would have to suppose that Mary's direct intervention began only after the objective Redemption of mankind when human nature was reborn to the life of grace. Even in the application of the graces of Redemption to our

---

[10] *Jn.* 1:16.

[11] H. Lennerz, *Ex Mariologia*, in *Gregorianum*, Vol. 33, 1952, pp. 305-306; H. M. Köster, *Die Magd des Herrn* (Limburg an der Lahn, 1947), pp. 117-126; O. Semmelroth, *Urbild der Kirche* (Würzburg, 1950), pp. 60, 68-69; R. E. Kekeisen, *Dangerous Marian Year Reefs*, in *The Homiletic and Pastoral Review*, Vol. 55, January, 1955, pp. 287-289. Kekeisen's article has been refuted by J. B. Carol, *On "Dangerous Marian Year Reefs,"* in *The Homiletic and Pastoral Review*, Vol. 55, May, 1955, pp. 698-699.

souls, Mary would give us nothing of her own, and would merely apply Christ's merits to our spiritual regeneration.

Akin to their opinion is the interpretation which some authors give to Christ's supreme testament on the cross, formulated in the words "Behold thy Mother."[12] Christ, they say, gave us Mary at that moment to be our Spiritual Mother; His words made her what up to then she had not been; He *appointed* her to *act* as our mother by her intercession and the distribution of graces. Mary would, consequently, be our Mother not through any activity of hers, but merely through Christ's donation. She would have no share in the production of our spiritual life, and we would not bear in our souls the mark of our Mother; nor would her plenitude of grace have overflowed into us to impart supernatural life to us. With Father Dillenschneider we may answer these authors that Christ's supreme testament merely proclaimed a Spiritual Motherhood which already existed in a strict sense in Mary: "les paroles de Jésus mourant ne furent pas créatrices, mais révélatrices de la Mère des hommes."[13]

It might also be said that Mary's Spiritual Maternity is one of federation, or of affinity, arising from the relationship both Mary and we have to the Author of our spiritual life. It could follow from the fact that we are brothers of Christ, since we are adoptive sons and Christ is the true Son of the Father. Christ being the Son of Mary, and we in some way the brothers of Christ, Mary is our Mother. Again Christ proclaims in Holy Scripture that He is our Life and He is called such more than once by St. Paul. Since Mary is the Mother of Our Lord, the Life of our souls, she is our Spiritual Mother. Furthermore, in the doctrine of the Mystical Body we are the members of Christ. Since Mary is the Mother of the Head of the Mystical Body, she must have at least some relationship of motherhood to the members.

Though all these statements are true, they nevertheless give Mary's Spiritual Motherhood a restricted, juridical meaning. They leave our hearts unsatisfied, and like adopted, orphan children we could still exclaim: "Yes, Mary is our Mother, but she is not our *true* Mother!"

---

[12] Jn. 19:26-27.

[13] C. Dillenschneider, C.SS.R., *La Mariologie de S. Alphonse de Liguori; Sources et synthèse doctrinale* (Fribourg, 1934), p. 159.

Would it not be possible to admit a Spiritual Motherhood in the strict sense, based on a real and immediate causality by Mary in the act of our spiritual regeneration?

Just as in the natural order she only is a mother who really engenders her son, imparting natural life to him in co-operation with a man; so in like manner can Mary really be considered our Spiritual Mother only if she engenders us to the supernatural life, namely, if she intervenes with her personal influence in the origin of that life, imparting it to us in union with Christ who is its source and principle. Indeed, despite a substantial difference between the natural and the supernatural orders, the two are similar by an analogy of proper proportionality which warrants our comparing the conditions of Motherhood in both.

To become a mother both in the natural and supernatural order a person must have an aptitude for motherhood. In the natural order this aptitude consists in puberty whereby nature, perfected in the individual, tends to overflow into a new being; in the supernatural order the corresponding aptitude would be a plenitude of grace perfecting Mary's own spiritual life and overflowing into the lives of her spiritual children.

In a woman, the plenitude of life, despite its tendency to transmit itself to others, does not become maternal until she has been associated with a man and receives from him a principle of life which fecundates her, and to which she imparts of her superabundance of life. In a similar manner, Mary's plenitude of grace, even though it is given her in view of her Spiritual Motherhood, does not become maternal until, associated with Christ, she receives from Him the impulse to transmit the superabundance of her plenitude of grace. And she must associate herself with Christ precisely in the act or acts which produce life. Since, however, our supernatural life depends for its existence on both Christ's Incarnation and His sacrifice on Calvary, Mary, to be our Mother, must be associated with Christ in these all-important events: in the Incarnation by her Divine Maternity; in Christ's sacrifice by her Coredemption. The Incarnation may be considered as the Redemption in potency or "in actu primo," and the sacrifice on Calvary, as the Redemption in act, or in "actu secundo." Mary's co-operation in the production of the supernatural life follows a similar pattern. At the

Incarnation, in virtue of her Divine Maternity, she conceives us to the supernatural life, whereas on Calvary she begets us.

4. Does Mary Give Us Something of Her Own?

A qualification is called for at this point. The act of generation in the natural order is of a physical nature. A mother transmits something of her own physical life to her offspring, thus imprinting on him the mark of her motherhood. The new germ of life from which the child develops results from a union of the female with the male cell. The mother definitely puts something of her own into the production of a new life.

Generation in the supernatural life is also something physical. Grace, insofar as it perfects nature and raises it to a supernatural level, is a physical entity, produced in the souls of the just by God through the instrumentality of Christ's human nature. Whether Our Lord's humanity is a physical or moral instrumental cause is controverted; but theologians agree that through it Christ's grace of Headship flows out to us, in accordance with Scripture which says, "Of his fullness we have all received."[14] If Mary is to be our Spiritual Mother in the true sense she must, like Christ, give of her fullness of grace to engender us supernaturally. Just as the supernatural life flows to us through Christ's humanity, in a similar manner must it come to us through Mary. Father Llamera[15] has in recent years brought out the connection that exists between Christ's grace of Headship and Mary's plenitude of graces. Christ was predestined not only to be the Son of God, but also the Head of the human race; consequently, He was to regenerate men in God by communicating to them the divine sonship. For this reason He had to unite human nature to Himself and by it to incorporate in Himself the human race. And she who made it possible for the Word to become Man and to incorporate mankind was Mary. Her maternal action is, therefore, specified not merely by the human generation of the Word, but also by His Headship, namely by His vivifying union with the human race.

---

[14] *Jn.* 1:16.

[15] M. Llamera, O.P., *El mérito maternal conedentivo de María*, in *Estudios Marianos*, Vol. 11, 1951, pp. 108-112. W. Sebastian, O.F.M., *De B. Virgine Maria universali gratiarum Mediatrice* (Romae, 1952), pp. 184-186. M. Bignoni, O.F.M.Cap., *Encyclopaediae seu scientiae universalis concionatorium* (Coloniae Agrippinae, 1665), p. 246b.

Mary's generative action is thus an act of both Divine and Spiritual Motherhood: Divine through the Hypostatic Union, Spiritual through the Headship of her divine Son.

Mary received her fullness of grace through the Incarnation by her union with her divine Son, who made His grace of Headship overflow into her and fecundate her with its entire vivifying virtuality. Hence it is that our Blessed Mother's Spiritual Maternity is essentially related to Christ's grace of Headship, participating in its nature and making of her a living image of Christ. The finality of her Spiritual Maternity is the same as that of Christ's Headship: the generation of mankind in Christ, or the formation of the Mystical Body. Christ's Headship and Mary's Spiritual Maternity together form a single universal principle of supernatural vivification.

Naturally, the Spiritual Maternity is subordinated to, and totally dependent on, Christ's Headship, so that without the latter the former would be nonexistent. As Mary's Divine Maternity depends in its existence, nature, and transcendence on the Hypostatic Union, so does her Spiritual Maternity depend on Christ's grace of Headship. Yet, despite this essential dependence there exists a beautiful parallel between Christ and His Blessed Mother: what the Hypostatic Union and the grace of Headship are in Christ, the Divine and Spiritual Maternity are in Mary; and just as the Hypostatic Union includes or postulates the grace of Headship, in the same manner does the grace of the Divine Maternity include or postulate that of the Spiritual Maternity.

From the above reasoning we may conclude that Mary by her Spiritual Maternity really gives us something of her own. Our supernatural life is truly generated in our souls by her maternal influence as well as by virtue of Christ's Headship. But we can still ask ourselves what the precise nature of her influence or causality really is. Christ's humanity, as we have seen, exercises a role of instrumental causality in the production of grace, and a very representative group of theologians[16] say that this causality is not merely of a moral nature, but also of a physical nature. Christ's divine nature, hypostatically united with His human nature, produces grace, according to these authors, through the physical instrumentality of the latter. Can we go so far as

---

[16] Cf. A. Michel, *Jésus-Christ*, in *D.T.C.*, Vol. 8, part 1, col. 1314-1324.

to attribute a similar causality to Mary's Spiritual Motherhood?

Several authors have recently answered the question affirmatively. Taking as a starting point the fact that a number of mystics have described a mystical presence of the Blessed Virgin in the soul, these authors have tried to find a theological justification of such statements.[17] The only plausible explanation, they said, was to admit that Mary with Christ exercised a physical instrumental causality in the production of grace. Their arguments, however, are far from convincing. If theologians have had to resort to all sort of divergent opinions in their efforts to explain and prove that Christ's humanity was a physical instrumental cause of grace, *a fortiori* do they experience difficulties in demonstrating such a causality in Mary. At least Christ's humanity is substantially and intrinsically joined with His divinity through the Hypostatic Union; whereas Mary through the Divine Maternity is only extrinsically related to the Hypostatic Order.[18] Hence it is with good reason that Father Garrigou-Lagrange writes: "It must be admitted that it does not seem possible to prove with certainty that Mary did exercise physical causality. Theology will hardly advance beyond serious probability in this matter. ...."[19]

5. Spiritual Maternity and Coredemption

If Mary's Spiritual Maternity means that she spiritually regenerates us by transmitting to us her plenitude of grace which she receives from Christ's grace of Headship, is it exact to say with Father Llamera that her Spiritual Maternity consists formally in her plenitude of grace?[20] If

---

[17] Gregorio de Jesús Crucificado, O.C.D., *La acción de María en las almas*, in *Estudios Marianos*, Vol. 11, 1951, pp. 271-278. A. Plessis, S.M.M., *Manuel de Mariologie Dogmatique* (Montfort-sur-Meu, 1947), pp. 302-306.

[18] Gregorio de Jesús Crucificado, *art. cit.*, p. 272.

[19] *The Mother of the Saviour and Our Interior Life*, trans. B. J. Kelly (Dublin, 1949), p. 237.

[20] M. Llamera, *art. cit.*, p. 109: "la maternidad espiritual es considerada formalmente como gracia llena de María actuante en su función deigenerativa." M. Llamera, O.P., *La maternidad espiritual de María*, in *Estudios Marianos*, Vol. 3, 1944, p. no: "La fuerza demonstrativa de este argumento supone la verdad de las proposiciones siguientes: (1a) María fué llena de gracia en razón de su maternidad divina. (2a) La plenitud de gracia de María derivada de la divina maternidad, la habilita y la constituye formalmente en madre de los hombres."

that were so, Mary's Coredemption would not be part of the essence of her Spiritual Motherhood.

Father Llamera argues that just as the Incarnation constitutes Christ as Head of the human race and makes men His members, incorporated in and regenerated by Him, so does Mary's Divine Maternity constitute her as Spiritual Mother of us all and as an efficacious and *immediate* cause of our incorporation in and regeneration by Christ.[21]

We do not take exception to the fact that Mary's plenitude of grace is included in the essence of her Spiritual Maternity, but we do object to the teaching that this plenitude is the *immediate and complete cause* of our regeneration. Father Llamera bases his argument on the parallel he draws between Mary and Christ: Mary's plenitude of grace, derived from her Divine Maternity, is the immediate cause of our supernatural regeneration, because Christ's grace of Headship, derived from the Hypostatic Union, is the immediate cause of that same regeneration. Llamera's conclusion is inaccurate because the first part of the parallel is inexact.

We agree that from the Hypostatic Union derives the plenitude of the grace of Christ, and from this plenitude Christ's grace of Headship, as St. Thomas affirms.[22] Yet, we must remember that the grace of Headship is included merely *in actu primo* in the Incarnation, insofar as it denotes a capacity to influence us supernaturally; but in order that its influence be exercised *de facto* on the members of Christ's Mystical Body, it is necessary that an additional element intervene, namely, the Redemption. Without the latter, Christ's merits are neither applied to us, nor is the influence of His grace of Headship extended to us. Christ's Headship should be considered from a double point of view, namely, *in actu primo*, when it could be called "gratia capitalis *in potentia*," and *in actu secundo*, when it could be called "gratia capitalis *in actu.*" Prior to the Redemption Christ's Headship existed as an aptitude to regenerate us supernaturally. By it Our Lord possessed the *right* to represent

---

[21] *Ibid.*, p. 91: "Primera proposición: La Encarnación constituye a Cristo en Cabeza de los hombres y a éstos en miembros suyos, incorporándolos y regenerándolos en El. Segunda proposición: María por su maternidad divina, es causa eficaz e inmediata de nuestra incorporatión y regeneratión en Cristo."

[22] S. Thomas, *Summa Theologica*, P. 3, q. 8, a. 1.

humanity in such a way that, through a divine acceptance of the soteriological finality of the Incarnation, His satisfaction *could* become valid for us all. But He represented us *de facto* only through the application of His passion. Christ's Headship *in actu secundo,* or fully and effectively considered, supposes the Redemption accomplished and the doors of the fullness of His grace opened, allowing it to flow freely to mankind.

In our Blessed Mother there are also two phases of the plenitude of grace: an initial phase which begins at the Incarnation, when she becomes the Mother of God; and a final phase which is complete when she becomes our Coredemptrix. The act of Divine Motherhood is related to Christ as the Man-God and to Christ as Head of the Mystical Body. By engendering the Man-God she became the Mother of God; by begetting the Head of the Mystical Body she became the Spiritual Mother of mankind, receiving from the grace of Headship her fullness of grace to be transmitted to men. Yet, her Spiritual Motherhood and her plenitude of grace at the Incarnation are such only *in actu primo.* They are not realized completely and effectively *in actu secundo* until Mary has cooperated with her divine Son in the Redemption. We may therefore conclude that the Spiritual Maternity consists *formally* in Mary's plenitude of grace *and* in her Coredemption. That is why theologians commonly say that she conceived us at Nazareth and bore us on Calvary.

Section 2. The Divine Maternity, Source of Mary's Spiritual Maternity

The nature of the Spiritual Maternity, as we have described it, supposes a really superior and sublime supernatural power in Mary, and we naturally wonder what the source of this extraordinary virtuality actually is. Since the activity of an agent draws its excellence from the nature that gives rise to it — "operatio sequitur esse" — a complete understanding of Mary's maternal activity can only be obtained from a knowledge of the nature of her supernatural being. What is the Blessed Virgin? Is she a mother just like every other mother, but endowed with a far superior degree of sanctifying grace, or has her very being been raised to a different order of supernatural excellence? In other words, must we admit with some theologians[23] that in the supernatural order there are three distinct degrees of grace or three specific supernatural entities: the grace of union in Christ, the grace of the Divine Maternity in Mary, and sanctifying grace in the whole Mystical Body, including Christ and the Blessed Virgin? If so, we would have to conceive the supernatural world as made up of three levels: the level of the grace of union, that of the grace of the Divine Maternity, and that of sanctifying grace. The grace of union and of the Divine Maternity would be distinct from each other and also from sanctifying grace, but they would both postulate sanctifying grace as a supernatural principle of operation for the personal activities of Christ and His Blessed Mother. Since Mary's Spiritual Motherhood, like all her other prerogatives, is rooted in the Divine Maternity, the discussion is pertinent to our topic.

The question of the nature of Mary's supernatural being arose when theologians tried to explain *how* she was the Mother of God. The Council of Ephesus declared expressly that Christ was not "first born of the holy Virgin as an ordinary man, in such a way that the Word only afterwards descended upon Him; rather was He (the Word) united in the Womb itself, and thus is said to have undergone birth according to the flesh, inasmuch as He makes His own the birth of His own flesh. ... For this reason [the holy Fathers] have boldly proclaimed the holy Virgin the Mother of God (Theotokos)."[24]

From this official document it is evident that the "terminus qui" of the Divine Maternity is not the human nature of Christ, but rather the divine Person of Christ which unites the human and divine natures. Thus Mary's generation of Christ, like every generation, terminates in the person or suppositum. Since, however, biologically a mother is an active and not merely a passive principle in the generation of her offspring, we must attribute to Mary an active causality in the generation of the Man-God. In what manner does she exercise this

---

[23] L. Colomer, O.F.M., *Relaciones trinitarias engastadas en la maternidad divina*, in *Estudios Marianos*, Vol. 8, 1949, p. 103: "Tenemos, pues, tres gracias diferentes escalonadas de mayor a menor eminencia engarzadas entre sí: la de la Unión hipostática, la de la divina Maternidad y la de la gracia santificante. Las dos primeras exigen necesariamente la tercera."

[24] D.B., 111a. P. Palmer, S.J., *Mary in the Documents of the Church* (Westminster, Md., 1952), pp. 10-11.

causality?

In their efforts to explain Mary's maternal role in the generation of Christ, theologians have followed two distinct trends of thought. One school holds that Mary actively generated the human flesh of Christ, while God simultaneously infused His human soul and hypostatically united it with the Person of the Word and the divine nature. This is sufficient, according to these theologians, to explain Mary's Divine Motherhood, because of the communication of idioms between the divine and human natures. Since the human nature of Christ derived from Mary has at every instant of its existence been personally united with the Word, Mary, by producing what belonged to the Word, is said to have engendered God.[25] And since Mary needs nothing more than the human generative powers, common to all human mothers, to engender Christ's humanity, there is no need of a supernatural elevation of Our Lady's generative powers nor of her being.

A second group of theologians[26] follows an opposite trend. The theory of a simultaneous production of Christ's human nature by Mary, and of the unifying action by God is not sufficient, they say, to explain Mary's *active* role as the Mother of God. We must not lose sight of the analogy that exists between Mary's Divine Maternity and ordinary human motherhood. In the case of human generation theologians agree that parents are principal causes in the formation of the body of their child, and instrumental causes in the union of body and soul, inasmuch as by their generative action, they produce in the child's body dispositions which postulate the infusion of the soul by God. Thus, and

---

[25] J. A. de Aldama, S.J., *El tema de la Divina Maternidad de María en la investigación de los últimos decenios*, in *Estudios Marianos*, Vol. 11, 1951, p. 65, footnote: "La comunicación de idiomas se refiere aquí no a María, sino a Cristo mismo. Porque la naturaleza humana procedente de María ha sido siempre personalmente del Verbo, María, al producir por generación esa naturaleza, se dice que engendra a Dios. Podrá parecer necesario exigir más; pero es cierto que en esto no hay ningún 'nominalismo mariológico', ni ningún 'verbalismo agnóstico.' "

[26] J. M. Bover, S.J., *La gracia de la Divina Maternidad*, in *Estudios Marianos*, Vol. 5, 1946, pp. 146-164; Salmanticenses, *Cursus theologicus, De Incarnatione*, disp. 11, n. 17, Vol. 19 (Lugduni, 1686), p. 706; Crisóstomo de Pamplona, O.F.M.Cap., *Naturaleza de la maternidad divina y elevación de la Virgen Santísima al orden hipostático*, in Estudios Marianos, Vol. 8, 1949, pp. 65-92.

thus only, do they merit the name of parents. By analogy, a similar reasoning must be applied to the Mother of God. If Mary is the Mother of the Man-God, she is so inasmuch as she produces in His body dispositions which postulate the infusion of Christ's human soul and the union of His human nature with the Person of the Word. Or we might conceive Christ's soul as subsisting in the Word and being infused into the human flesh engendered by Mary. In that case Mary would by her generative action produce in Christ's body dispositions which postulate the infusion of Christ's soul already subsisting in the Person of the Word. Whatever theory we accept, we must still admit in Mary an instrumental causality in reference to the infusion of the human soul of Christ and of the union of His human nature with the Person of the Word.

Such an instrumental causality, terminating in the Person of the Word, would by far surpass Mary's human powers, and would postulate an elevation of Mary's generative powers to the supernatural order. This elevation alone, considered even independently of all the fullness of the grace of Mary and of her other supernatural gifts and privileges, would invest her with a dignity bordering on the Divinity, to use an expression of Cajetan.[27] It would warrant our affirming with a considerable number of theologians of recent and past years that Mary belongs to the Hypostatic Order. Several theologians go even further and say that not only does the grace of the Divine Maternity refer to her physical elevation and the moral dignity that irradiates therefrom, but also to her whole being. Her soul as well as her body was divinely prepared or consecrated for the functions of the Divine Motherhood.

The doctrine that the Blessed Virgin was in her very being elevated to the supernatural order has had a number of adherents and seems to be gaining popularity in our day. As far as we know, it was first taught by the Mercedarian Saavedra,[28] and almost contemporaneously by the

---

[27] Cf. on this M. J. Scheeben, *Mariology,* Vol. 1 (St. Louis, 1948), p. 159.

[28] S. de Saavedra, O.Merc., *Sacra Deipara, seu de eminentissima dignitate Deigenitricis Immaculatissimae* (Lugduni, 1655), disp. 26, sect. 3, n. 1097.

Jesuit Ripalda.[29] Their opinion was later adopted by Carlos Del Moral, a Franciscan.[30] In recent years numerous authors with various and often rather divergent arguments have arrived at a similar conclusion: the Divine Maternity is a supernatural entity distinct from, and superior to, sanctifying grace. Among authors to be mentioned particularly are: Crisóstomo de Pamplona,[31] Alonso,[32] Colomer,[33] Bover,[34] Rozo,[35] Van Biessen,[36] Ragazzini,[37] Basilio de San Pablo,[38] and Delgado Varela.[39]

According to these theologians, one can conceive of the Motherhood of God as a divine elevation of Mary's entire personal subsistent being in view of the temporal generation of the Man-God.[40] The Divine Maternity gave Mary a mysterious participation in the paternity of God the Father, since she engendered in time the same Son as the Father engendered in eternity.[41] But that is not all. Jesus, the Masterpiece of God's creation, came into this world to fulfill a soteriological mission. He is really God, the Son of God; but He is also the Saviour of men. Could

---

[29] J. M. de Ripalda, S.J., *De Ente supernaturali*, Vol. 2 (Parisiis, 1870), lib. 4, disp. 79, sect. 11, n. 82. Cf. G. Van Ackeren, SJ., *Does the Divine Maternity Formally Sanctify Mary's Soul?* in *Marian Studies*, Vol. 6, 1955, pp. 76-78.

[30] C. del Moral, O.F.M., *Fons illimis theologiae scoticae marianae ...*, Vol. 1 (Matriti, 1730), p. 130. Cf. I. de Guerra Lazpiur, O.F.M., *Integralis conceptus Maternitatis divinae juxta Carolum del Moral* (Romae, 1953), pp. 124-135.

[31] Crisóstomo de Pamplona, O.F.M.Cap., *art. cit.*

[32] J. Alonso, C.M.F., *Naturaleza y fundamentos de la gracia de la Virgen*, in *Estudios Marianos*, Vol. 5, Madrid, 1946, pp. 11-110.

[33] L. Colomer, O.F.M., *art. cit.*

[34] J. M. Bover, S J., *art. cit.*

[35] G. Rozo, C.M.F., *Sancta Maria, Mater Dei* (Mediolani, 1943).

[36] See J. A. de Aldama, S.J., *art. cit.*, p. 72.

[37] S. M. Ragazzini, O.F.M.Conv., *La divina maternità di Maria* (Roma, 1948).

[38] Basilio de San Pablo, C.P., *La divina Maternidad es intrínsecamente soteriológica*, in *Estudios Marianos*, Vol. 8, pp. 256-297.

[39] J. M. Delgado Varela, O.Merc., *Maternidad formalmente santificante*, in *Estudios Marianos*, Vol. 8, pp. 133-184.

[40] L. Colomer, O.F.M., *art. cit.*, p. 107: "... una elevación divina de todo el ser personal subsistente de la Virgen a traer al mundo al Hijo de Dios en naturaleza humana."

[41] *Ibid.*, p. 123: "La Virgen, para ser realmente Madre del Hijo de Dios, ha debido ser elevada a la prodigiosa participación de la paternidad divina del Padre."

the Blessed Virgin remain foreign to this second phase of Jesus' existence? By no means.

Mary's Divine Motherhood, as we have seen, is specified both by the human generation of God and by the birth of the Saviour of men. In the present order of Providence Christ's Incarnation is inseparably linked with His function as Redeemer. Christ came as the High Priest, Mediator, and Mystical Head of the human race. His human nature, the essence and operations of which are intrinsically destined to regenerate mankind, is derived from Mary alone. It seems only reasonable to conclude, therefore, that Mary's Motherhood is linked both with the Person of her divine Son and with His soteriological activity. In this way her supernatural dignity was the source not only of her Divine, but also her Spiritual, Maternity. Absolutely speaking, we could conceive of someone other than the Mother of God as the associate of Jesus in His redemptive mission, but the dignity of such a Co-redemptrix would have been greatly inferior. Our Lord could not have chosen a more apt subject than His Mother to share with her the spiritual fecundity that flows from the Redemption.

The relationship that arises between Jesus and Mary as a result of their association in the work of the Redemption takes on a new aspect. It differs from the relationship of Mother and Son in the Incarnation. The Redemption takes place on a soteriological plane, whereas the Incarnation is on the plane of the Hypostatic Union. In the Incarnation it was the Son who received His human nature from His Mother; in the Redemption it is the Mother who receives from her Son the overflow of saving grace to transmit it to mankind. Mary's relationship to Christ in the Incarnation is one of Motherhood; in the Redemption it is a relationship of Espousal. Nothing resembles matrimony more than this admirable union of Mother and Son in view of transmitting life to all of God's children. The grace of Divine Motherhood confers on Our Lady a sublime dignity which makes her the worthy Mother of the Word Incarnate and the fecund Spouse of the Saviour of Mankind.[42]

---

[42] *Ibid.*, pp. 109, 122.

II
THEOLOGICAL EVIDENCE

The preceding chapter was a discussion of the nature of Mary's Spiritual Maternity in the light of theological and dogmatic principles. Though the conclusions we arrived at are based on sound dogmatic reasoning, they are not sufficient by themselves to compel an acceptance of the doctrine of Mary's Spiritual Motherhood as a truth of faith, revealed by God for our belief. We must now go to the sources of divine Revelation to assure ourselves that the teaching we have thus far propounded is really of divine origin. Is the doctrine of Mary's Spiritual Motherhood truly founded: (1) on the faith of the Church as expressed by the documents of the Magisterium or teaching authority of the Church; (2) on the pages of Holy Scripture; (3) on the Tradition of the Fathers of the Church and of theologians and spiritual writers? Through the sections which follow we shall attempt to answer this question as concisely as possible.

SECTION 1. DOCUMENTS OF THE ORDINARY MAGISTERIUM

Since the doctrine of Our Lady's Spiritual Maternity has not as yet been defined *ex cathedra* as a dogma of faith, our inquiry is necessarily confined to the documents of the Ordinary Magisterium. Yet even these are far too numerous to be included in their totality in a study of so limited a scope as ours. The Ordinary Magisterium, taken in its entirety, comprises the pronouncements and statements of both Sovereign Pontiffs and bishops through the centuries of the Church's history. Giving a comprehensive analysis of such a mass of official evidence would lead us far beyond the space allotted to us in this symposium. Wherefore, we are limiting our investigation chiefly to the papal documents addressed to the Universal Church, having recourse only occasionally and rarely to lesser documents or to liturgical data approved by the Supreme Pontiffs. For the sake of brevity, we shall furthermore group our conclusions under four headings: (1) proof of the existence of the Spiritual Maternity; (2) delineation of the arguments adduced by the Pontiffs in support of their teaching; (3) the extent of Mary's maternal influence; (4) the degree of certitude attributed by the Popes to the doctrine in question.

1. The Existence of the Spiritual Maternity

When we inquire whether the Sovereign Pontiffs teach that Mary is our Spiritual Mother, we understand the term "Mother" in its full and proper connotation; namely, of a person who has engendered us to the supernatural life. "Strictly speaking, she is the spiritual mother of men who has really and universally engendered them to the life of grace."[43] Consequently, we shall not adduce texts in which the Popes merely call Mary our Mother, without giving any evidence of the meaning of the term. Even such titles as "Mother of Mercy" or "Mother of Grace," attributed to Mary in papal documents prior to Benedict XIV[44] cannot be used as arguments, since they could be interpreted as applying only to the distribution of graces by the Blessed Virgin. We must find at least some plausible evidence of the Pontiff's intention of presenting Mary as our Mother in the strict sense of the word.

Such evidence seems to exist in the fact that the Popes call Mary our *Genetrix*, or one who gave birth to us. Thus, for instance, in a prayer book seemingly composed by Pius VI we read these words: "Thou art a universal Mother of the faithful ... There on Calvary didst thou, so to speak, in anguish give birth to us in a moral wise and accept us as children."[45] Pius VII, in turn, styles Mary "our most loving Parent (parens),"[46] thus intimating that she was our Mother in the strict sense, since *Parens* in Latin has the same connotation as *Genetrix*. Even more explicitly Leo XIII writes: "Just as the most holy Virgin is the Mother (*Genetrix*) of Jesus Christ, so she is the Mother of all Christians, whom indeed she bore (*generavit*) on Mt. Calvary amid the supreme throes of

---

[43] C. Dillenschneider, C.Ss.R., *Marie au service de notre Rédemption* (Haguenau, Bas Rhin, 1947), p. 30.

[44] G. W. Shea, *The Teaching of the Magisterium on Mary's Spiritual Maternity*, in *Marian Studies*, Vol. 3, 1952, pp. 41-44.

[45] *Die allerbesten Gebethe von Pius VI* (Münster i. W., 1805), p. 5. This rare booklet, translated from the original Italian, is kept in the library of the Collegio Germanico-Ungarico in Rome. Reference taken from A. Baumann, *Maria Mater nostra spiritualis. Eine theologische Untersuchung über die geistige Mutterschaft Mariens in den Aeusserungen der Päpste vom Tridentinum bis heute* (Brixen, 1948), p. 33. Baumann confesses that he has been unable to locate the original.

[46] *Quod divino afflata*, January 24, 1806; in J. Bourassé, *Summa Aurea de laudibus B. V. Mariae*, Vol. 7 (Parisiis, 1862), col. 546.

the Redeemer."[47] In our own day Pope Pius XII, in the Marian pericope of the Encyclical *Mystici Corporis*, likewise affirms that Mary generated us spiritually when he says that "through the added title of pain and glory she became spiritually the Mother (*Genetrix*) of all His [Christ's] members."[48]

A further argument to prove that the Sovereign Pontiffs understood the term Spiritual Mother in the strict sense lies in the fact that they very frequently mention it in juxtaposition with the Divine Maternity. Surely they would not juxtapose, so repeatedly, Mary's Spiritual Maternity with her Divine Maternity, "if the former were not, in its own way, as real a maternity as the latter. It would be prejudicial to the true character of the Divine Maternity, to mention it on even terms with another maternity which is such only in an improper sense of the word."[49] The obvious conclusion to draw from these texts seems to be that just as Mary's Divine Maternity is a Motherhood in the true sense of the word, her Spiritual Maternity must also be a Motherhood in the strict sense.

We shall not attempt to give a complete enumeration of the papal texts which exemplify the above argument. However, a few must be quoted:

Benedict XIV:

> The Catholic Church, schooled by the Holy Spirit, has always most diligently professed, not only to venerate Mary most devoutly as *the Mother of the Lord and Redeemer* ... but also to honor her ... as *the most loving Mother* who was left her by the last words of her dying Spouse.[50]

Pius VI:

> While I already venerate thee as a Mother of the Most High, thou art

---

[47] *Quamquam pluries*, August 15, 1889; in A. Tondini, *Le Encicliche Mariane* (Roma, 1950), p. 116.

[48] *A.A.S.*, Vol. 35, 1943, pp. 247-248.

[49] Shea, *art. cit.*, p. 52.

[50] *Benedicti XIV opera omnia*, Vol. 16 (Prati, 1846), p. 428: "... Catholica Ecclesia, Sancti Spiritus magisterio edocta, eamdem (Mariam), et tamquam Domini ac Redemptoris sui Parentem, Coelique ac Terrae Reginam impensissimis obsequiis colere, et tamquam amantissimam Matrem extrema Sponsi sui morientis voce sibi relictam, filialis pietatis affectu prosequi studiosissime semper professa est."

also a universal Mother of the faithful.[51]

Gregory XVI:

... the Virgin Mother of God and the most loving Mother of us all.[52]

Pius IX:

... the most holy Mother of God, and the most loving Mother of us all, the Immaculate Virgin Mary.[53]

... the most holy Mother of God, the Immaculate Virgin Mary, who is the most dear Mother of us all.[54]

... the most holy Immaculate Virgin Mary, who is God's Mother and our own (*Dei Mater et nostra*).[55]

Leo XIII:

... the Mother of God and of men (*Dei et hominum Mater*).[56]

... Mary, Christ's Mother and our own (*Matrem Christi et nostram*).[57]

... at one and the same time God's Mother and our Mother (*simul Mater Dei, simul Mater nostra*).[58]

... just as the most holy Virgin is the Mother of Jesus Christ, so she is the Mother of all Christians.[59]

Benedict XV:

Let us all turn with confidence to the afflicted and Immaculate Heart of Mary, the most gentle Mother of Jesus and our Mother.[60]

... she who gave birth to the "Prince of Peace," and who is the benign

---

[51] Pius VI, *op. cit.*, p. 16. From Baumann, *op. cit.*, p. 12. Cf. pp. 33, 100.

[52] *Libenti sane*, addressed to the Bishop of Acqui on May 11, 1844; in *Pareri dell'Episcopato Cattolico ... sulla definizione dogmatica dell'Immacolato Concepimento della Beata Vergine Maria*, Vol. 6 (Roma, 1852), p. 639. Other references in Shea, *art. cit.*, p. 48.

[53] *Ubi primum*. Tondini, *op. cit.*, p. 2.

[54] Shea, *art. cit.*, p. 51.

[55] *Codicis Juris Canonici Fontes*, ed. P. Gasparri, Vol. 2 (Romae, 1928), p. 837.

[56] *Laetitiae Sanctae*, September 8, 1893. Tondini, *op. cit.*, p. 186.

[57] *Octobri mense*, September 22, 1891. Tondini, *op. cit.*, p. 138.

[58] *Adjutricem populi*, September 5, 1895. Tondini, *op. cit.*, p. 230.

[59] *Quamquam pluries*, August 15, **1889**. Tondini, *op. cit.*, p. 116.

[60] *A.A.S.*, Vol. 7, 1915, p. 254.

Mother of the human race.[61]

Pius XI:

... the Virgin Mother of God and the most benign Mother of us all.[62]
... the great Mother of God and of men.[63]

Pius XII:

... God's Mother and our most loving Mother too.[64]
... the Mother of Jesus and our Mother.[65]
O Immaculate Virgin, Mother of God and Mother of men.[66]

Though the passages we have quoted are but a few of a large number of similar examples, they show plainly that the Popes constantly associate Mary's Divine and Spiritual Maternity, using the one word *"Mater"* to express Mary's Motherhood of God and of men. Such an association argues that Mary is our Mother in some real sense of the word. Yet the reality of her Spiritual Motherhood is brought out even more forcibly when we consider the grounds the Sovereign Pontiffs advance for Mary's maternal functions in our regard, or the arguments they adduce to prove the existence of this Marian prerogative.

2. The Basis of Mary's Spiritual Maternity

An argument used by nearly all the Popes since Benedict XIV to prove the existence of the Spiritual Maternity is the supreme testament of Christ dying on the Cross: "Woman, behold thy son. ... Behold thy Mother."[67] Benedict XIV exhorts the faithful "to honor her with filial affection as the most loving Mother who was left to her [the Church] by the last words of her dying Spouse."[68] Pius VI, in the prayer book of

---

[61] *Cum annus*, addressed to the Bishop of Tarbes and Lourdes, 1919. Tondini, *op. cit.*, p. 354.

[62] *A.A.S.*, Vol. 14, 1922, p. 675.

[63] *A.A.S.*, Vol. 22, 1930, p. 453.

[64] *A.A.S.*, Vol. 42, 1950, p. 758.

[65] *A.A.S.*, p. 780.

[66] *A.A.S.*, p. 781.

[67] *Jn.* 19:26-27.

[68] *Benedicti XIV opera omnia*, Vol. 16 (Prati, 1846), p. 428.

which we made mention previously, entreats the Blessed Virgin in these words: "O Mary ... I commend myself to thee for today and for always, just as my crucified Jesus gave me, in St. John, unto thy charge under the cross."[69] In documents of the same name Pius VIII and Gregory XVI write of Mary as "our Mother, the Mother of piety and of grace, the Mother of mercy, to whom Jesus on the Cross committed us, as He was about to die."[70]

Pius IX and Leo XIII allude to the words of Christ's supreme testament on several occasions. Suffice it to quote here one passage from each of these Pontiffs. "Jesus Christ in Person," writes Pius IX, "made the choice, when of St. John He said to His Mother: 'Behold thy son.' We are, therefore, all sons of Mary most holy. Oh! read these words which are found in the divine testament made by Jesus Christ on Golgotha. ... Yes, in the midst of His torments Jesus by His testament left us Mary."[71] In *Octobri mense* of Leo XIII we read: "Such Jesus Christ ... proclaimed (*praedicavit*) her from the Cross, when He entrusted to her care and protection the whole human race in the person of His disciple John."[72]

Pius X and Benedict XV also adduce Christ's testament as an argument. Though Pius X does not seem to make any direct reference to Jn. 19:26-27 in his major documents, he is known personally to have granted an indulgence for the recitation of a prayer addressed to Mary in heaven: "Woman, behold in place of me thy Son." And the prayer goes on to say that "on that mount and with those words you were appointed as Mother of the faithful."[73] Benedict XV, in turn, writes: "It is likewise clear that she, having been constituted by Jesus Christ as the Mother of all men, received them as bequeathed to her by a testament of infinite charity."[74]

In the documents of Pope Pius XI allusions to the Saviour's testamentary utterance are very frequent. Typical of such allusions is a

---

[69] Baumann, *op. cit.*, pp. 12, 33, 100. Shea, *art. cit.*, p. 46.
[70] Pius VIII, Bull *Praestantissimum sane*, March 30, 1830, and Gregory XVI, Bull *Praestantissimum sane*, May 18, 1932; in J. Bourassé, *op. cit.*, Vol. 7, coll. 579, 589.
[71] *Allocution*, October 21, 1877; quoted from Baumann, *op. cit.*, p. 2. Shea, *art. cit.*, p. 54.
[72] Tondini, *op. cit.*, p. 136.
[73] A.S.S., Vol. 37, 1904, pp. 724-725.
[74] A.A.S., Vol. 10, 1918, p. 181.

passage in the Apostolic Letter *Explorata res,* of February 2, 1923. Speaking of Mary as the Patroness of a happy death, Pius explains that this doctrine rests, above all, on the fact "that the Sorrowful Virgin participated with Jesus in the work of the Redemption, and, having been constituted the Mother of men, has taken them to her heart as children commended to her by the testament of Divine Charity."[75]

Our present Holy Father does not refer to Christ's dying words quite so frequently, though he does so on occasion. Thus, in a letter to Cardinal Maglione, *Dum saeculum,* April 15, 1942, he writes: "Her only begotten Son, as He neared death while hanging on the Cross, bequeathed to us the dearest possession still left to Him on earth, by giving us His Mother to be our own."[76]

What is remarkable in these passages, and others of a similar tenor that we have left unquoted, is that the Supreme Pontiffs give no indication that they are using the Johannine text in an accommodated sense; rather they constantly leave us with the impression that the words apply to Mary's Spiritual Maternity in a genuinely scriptural sense. Indeed Leo XIII quite clearly points to such an interpretation when he writes: "Now in John, according to the constant mind of the Church (*quod perpetuo sensit Ecclesia*), Christ designated the whole human race (*in Joanne ... Christus designavit personam humani generis*)."[77]

Furthermore, the context and commentaries of the majority of the Pontiffs who use the Johannine text as an argument make it clear that Mary's Spiritual Motherhood did not commence with, or stem solely from, the Saviour's testamentary words. Our Lord on Calvary proclaimed and confirmed Mary for what she already was, truly our Mother; His words did not create that relationship. Were it otherwise, Mary would be our Mother, not in any real and proper sense of the word, but only because she had been invested by Christ with the rights and duties of a mother in our regard.[78] In proof of this statement let us

---

[75] *A.A.S.,* Vol. 15, 1923, pp. 104-105.

[76] Tondini, *op. cit.,* p. 450.

[77] *Ibid.,* p. 222.

[78] Shea, *art. cit.,* p. 45. R. Rábanos, C.M., *La Maternidad espiritual de María en el Protoevangelio y San Juan,* in *Estudios Marianos,* Vol. 7, 1949, pp. 49-50.

refer to the papal documents.

Pius VI, after stating that Mary is the universal Mother of the faithful because Christ on the cross proclaimed her as such, immediately adds: "There on Calvary didst thou, so to speak, in anguish give birth to us in a moral wise and accept us as children."[79] What gave Mary her dignity of Motherhood was her giving birth to us by her compassionating suffering beneath the cross. Pope Leo XIII explicitly associates Mary's Spiritual Motherhood with her compassion and the voluntary oblation she makes of her divine Son on Calvary. She "is the Mother of all Christians," he writes in *Quamquam pluries,* "whom indeed (*quippe quos*) she bore on Mt. Calvary amid the supreme throes of the Redeemer."[80] And in *Jucunda semper:* "... 'there stood by the cross of Jesus Mary, His Mother,' who animated by a desire of immense charity to receive us as her sons (*tacta in nos caritate immensa ut susciperet filios*), herself voluntarily offered up to Divine Justice her own Son, dying with Him in her heart, pierced by the sword of sorrow."[81] According to Leo XIII, Mary became our Mother by her compassion and the voluntary offering of her Son dying on the cross.

The same doctrine stands out in a homily of Benedict XV, delivered in St. Peter's, May 13, 1920, at the solemn canonization of St. Gabriel of the Sorrowful Mother and of St. Margaret Mary Alacoque. "For, as the first Adam had a woman as his associate in the Fall," says the Pontiff, "so the second Adam willed that there participate in the reparation of our salvation she whom, by styling her 'Woman' from the Cross, He declared to be the second Eve, that is, the ineffable sorrowing Mother of all men, for whom He was dying, to win life for them."[82]

On first reading, several of Pius XI's numerous references to Christ's testamentary utterance leave one with the impression that, in the Pope's mind, Christ's words created and not merely proclaimed Mary our Spiritual Mother. Thus he speaks of "Mary, under the Cross, *constituted* the Mother of men,"[83] and observes "that from His Cross, just when His

---

[79] Pius VI, *op. cit.*, p. 26. Baumann, *op. cit.*, p. 33.

[80] Tondini, *op. cit.*, p. 116.

[81] *Ibid.*, pp. 204-206.

[82] *A.A.S.*, Vol. 12, 1920, p. 224.

[83] *Actes de S. S. Pie XI,* Vol. 8 (Paris, La Bonne Presse), p. 147; Shea, *art. cit.*, p. 92.

death agonies were most acute and terrible, the Saviour *gave* to us all His very Mother to be our own: 'Behold thy son; behold thy Mother.' "[84] However, on other occasions he says that Our Lord "proclaimed"[85] Mary our Mother. Furthermore, two utterances of Pius XI remove all doubts as to what grounds we should attribute to Mary's Spiritual Motherhood.

In the Apostolic Letter *Explorata res,* he affirms "that the Sorrowful Virgin participated with Jesus in the work of the Redemption, and, having been constituted the Mother of men, has taken them to her heart as children commended to her by the testament of divine charity, and protects them with ineffable love."[86] The meaning of these words is obviously that Mary was constituted Mother of men because of her participation in the Redemption, and that she was consequently entrusted by Christ with the children she had spiritually begotten. This is brought out even more strikingly in Pius XI's consistorial allocution on December 24, 1934, in which he calls Mary "the Mother of mercy, the Mother of the Redeemer, the *Mother of the Redemption.*"[87] As Seiler fittingly remarks, to be a mother means to impart life, to transmit life from one's own life. When Pius XI calls her not merely the Mother of the Redeemer, but also of the Redemption, he implies that together with the Saviour, she brings us forth to the life of grace.[88]

That our present Holy Father does not attach a creative virtue to the Saviour's testamentary words is evident from the following excerpt of the Marian pericope of his *Mystici Corporis:*

> Always most intimately united with her Son, as another Eve, she offered Him on Golgotha to the Eternal Father for all the children of Adam sin-stained by his fall, and her mother's rights and mother's love were included in the holocaust. Thus, she who corporally was the mother of our Head, through the added title of pain and glory became spiritually the

---

[84] G. Roschini, *La Madonna nel pensiero e nell'insegnamento di Pio XI,* in *Marianum,* Vol. 1, 1939, p. 149.

[85] Tondini, *op. cit.,* p. 400. Roschini, *art. cit.,* pp. 148, 149.

[86] *A.A.S.,* Vol. 15, 1923, pp. 104-105.

[87] *L'Osservatore Romano,* December 26-27, 1934, n. 299.

[88] H. Seiler, S.J., *Corredemptrix. Theologische Studie zur Lehre der letzten Päpste über die Miterlöserschaft Mariens* (Rom, 1939), pp. 94-95.

mother of all His members.[89]

In the mind of the Sovereign Pontiffs the supreme testament of Christ dying on the cross is a basis for the doctrine of Mary's Spiritual Maternity only inasmuch as it *proclaims* that she is Our Mother; but what ontologically constitutes her as the Spiritual Mother of mankind in the full sense is her begetting us on Calvary through her compassion with the Redeemer and her voluntary oblation of her divine Son.

Yet, if the fact that Mary spiritually gave birth to us on Calvary is the fulfillment of her maternal status according to the Sovereign Pontiffs, nevertheless it must not be considered as its inauguration. Mary bore us beneath the cross, but she conceived us when, by her consent to the words of the Angel at Nazareth, she received into her chaste womb the Son of God and the Saviour of men. Her Spiritual Maternity began with her Divine Maternity. She became the Mother of mankind because and at the same time that she became the Mother of God. This truth, stressed particularly by Leo XIII and Pius X, has been taught likewise by Pius XI and Pius XII.

The Sovereign Pontiffs prior to Leo XIII had frequently paired the Divine and Spiritual Maternities, speaking of Mary as "Mother of God and Mother of men." Leo is the first to show the grounds of such a juxtaposition. He implies that there is an intrinsic connection between the two maternities: Mary is the Mother of men, because she is the Mother of the Redeemer. By the very fact that she became Christ's Mother, she became our Mother as well.

> As such (gentle, most tender, of a limitless loving kindness), [he writes], God gave her to us, Mary, in whom, by the very fact that He chose her for the Mother of His only-begotten Son (*cui, hoc ipso quod Unigenae sui Matrem elegit*), He infused without stint those maternal feelings which breathe nothing but love and pardon.[90]

But it was Pope Pius X who still further than Leo XIII defined the intrinsic connection between Mary's Divine and Spiritual Maternity.

At the Incarnation the Blessed Virgin conceived not only the God-Man, but also the Redeemer of mankind; not only the physical Body of

---

[89] *A.A.S.*, Vol. 35, 1943, p. 247.
[90] Tondini, *op. cit.*, p. 136.

Christ, but His Mystical Body as well. Hence the act of begetting Christ was the origin of both her Divine and Spiritual Maternity. Pius X's doctrine is so clear and expressive that it merits to be quoted at some length.

> For is not Mary the Mother of Christ? [he writes]. She is, therefore, our Mother also. Indeed everyone must believe that Jesus, the Word made Flesh, is also the Saviour of the human race. Now, as the God-Man He acquired a body composed like that of other men, but as the Saviour of our race He had a kind of spiritual and mystical Body, which is the society of those who believe in Christ. "We, the many, are one body in Christ" (*Romans* 12:5). But the Virgin conceived the Eternal Son not only that He might be made man by taking His human nature from her, but also that by means of the nature assumed from her He might be the Saviour of men. For this reason the angel said to the shepherds, "Today in the town of David a Saviour has been born to you, Who is Christ the Lord" (*Luke* 2:11). So in one and the same bosom of His most chaste Mother, Christ took to Himself human flesh and at the same time united to Himself the spiritual body built up of those "who are to believe in Him" (*John* 17:20). Consequently Mary, bearing in her womb the Saviour, may be said to have borne also all those whose life was contained in the life of the Saviour. All of us, therefore, who are united with Christ and are, as the Apostle says, "Members of His body, made from His flesh and from His bones" (*Ephesians* 5:30), have come forth from the womb of Mary as a body united to its head. Hence, in a spiritual and mystical sense, we are called children of Mary, and she is the Mother of us all. "The Mother in spirit ... but truly the Mother of the members of Christ, which we are" (St. Augustine, *De sancta virginitate*, ch. 6). If then the Most Blessed Virgin is at once the Mother of God and of men, who can doubt that she makes every effort to bring it about that Christ, "head of His body, the Church" (*Colossians* 1:18), infuses His gifts into His members, and above all that we might know Him and "live through Him" (*1 John* 4:9)?[91]

The doctrine contained in the above passage is henceforth considered as definitive and solidly established. Pius XI and Pius XII merely recall it and suppose it as the decisive teaching of the Magisterium. In *Lux Veritatis* the former says: "She, by the very fact that she brought forth the Redeemer of the human race, is also in a manner the most tender Mother of us all, whom Christ Our Lord deigned to have

---

[91] Enc. *Ad diem illum*, February 2, 1904. Tondini, *op. cit.*, pp. 310-312.

as His brothers."[92] Pius XII, in turn, writes in *Mystici Corporis:* "... 'in the name of the whole human race,' she gave her consent for a 'spiritual marriage between the Son of God and human nature.' Within her virginal womb Christ Our Lord already bore the exalted title of Head of the Church; in a marvelous birth she brought Him forth as source of all supernatural life."[93]

In conclusion we may say that the Sovereign Pontiffs present three arguments to prove Mary's Spiritual Maternity: (1) the testamentary utterance of the Saviour, which proclaims Mary as our Mother; (2) Mary's consent at Nazareth by which she conceived the Man-God and His Mystical Body; (3) Our Lady's compassion on Calvary and her voluntary offering of her divine Son, whereby she gave birth to us, her spiritual children.

3. The Extent of Mary's Spiritual Maternity

Once we have established what grounds the Sovereign Pontiffs advance for Mary's Spiritual Maternity, it is fairly easy to affirm to whom her maternal influence is extended. Mary's Spiritual Motherhood consists basically in her begetting us to the supernatural life; and, as a consequence of or a sequel to this essential function of motherhood, she further exercises her motherhood in caring for us; namely, in distributing to us the fruits of the Redemption. Thus the whole picture of her Spiritual Maternity comprises three distinct facets: (1) Nazareth, where she conceives us; (2) Calvary, where she begets us; (3) Heaven, where she intercedes for us and distributes the graces of the Redemption to us. Or again we may envisage Mary's influence from the two points of view of the objective and the subjective Redemption. Mary's share in the former consists in her conceiving and begetting us, and in the latter in her caring for us by distributing the graces of the Redemption to us.

Who were the ones who benefited by Our Lady's share in the objective Redemption? Obviously all those for whom Our Lord died upon the cross. That is why Benedict XV in a letter to the Archbishop of Vercelli, November 14, 1921, calls Mary "the most loving and most dear

---

[92] Tondini, *op. cit.,* p. 400.
[93] *A.A.S.,* Vol. 35, 1943, p. 247.

Mother of the whole human race."[94] Pope Pius XI, in turn, expressed belief in the same teaching, when for Mother's Day, 1934, he authorized the Servites, at their Shrine of the Sorrowful Mother in Portland, Oregon, to celebrate a Mass in honor of "Mary, Mother of the Human Race."[95] The universality of Mary's Spiritual Motherhood is furthermore contained, implicitly at least, in two of Pope Pius XI's pronouncements. In *Lux veritatis*, he writes: "She, by the very fact that she brought forth the Redeemer of the human race, is also in a manner the most tender Mother of us all, whom Christ our Lord deigned to have as His Brothers."[96] And in *Rerum Ecclesiae* he states that, "since on Calvary all men were commended to her motherly affection, she loves and cherishes no less those who do not know of their Redemption by Jesus Christ than those who happily enjoy the benefits of the Redemption."[97]

If we envisage Mary's maternal influence from the standpoint of her share in the subjective Redemption, it is evidently restricted to those who *de facto* receive the fruits of the Redemption, or who come under the influence of grace in one form or another. Primarily, they are the faithful, the members of Christ's Mystical Body. For this reason Pius VII, Pius VIII, and Gregory XVI call her Mother of the Church — of the Chief Shepherd and of the flock, the Mother of the whole Christian people.[98]

Pope Pius XII, in an allocution to the Genoese pilgrims, April 21, 1940, summarily includes both points of view, when he says: "To her ... Jesus committed in the person of John, under the world-redeeming Cross, all men as her children, the sheep and the lambs of a collected and dispersed flock, thus constituting her Divine Shepherdess, the common and universal Mother of the faithful, and likening her to Peter, who is their common and universal Father and earthly Shepherd."[99]

---

[94] *A.A.S.*, Vol. 14, 1922, p. 38.
[95] Cf. *The American Ecclesiastical Review*, Vol. 90, 1934, p. 510.
[96] Tondini, *op. cit.*, p. 400.
[97] *A.A.S.*, Vol. 19, 1926, p. 83.
[98] Baumann, *op. cit.*, p. 97.
[99] *Marianum*, Vol. 2, 1940, p. 407.

4. Dogmatic Certitude of the Spiritual Maternity

Though the Sovereign Pontiffs have not professedly spoken of the dogmatic certitude of the doctrine of Mary's Spiritual Maternity, nevertheless, several of their statements would seem to imply that this teaching is a revealed truth. Pius VI, for instance, in 1775 approved a decree of the Sacred Congregation of Indulgences which stated that "God willed Mary to be proposed to all the faithful as their common Mother."[100] Since God's will to that effect could be known only from Revelation, such language argues to the revealed character of the truth that Mary is our Spiritual Mother.

Furthermore, the fact that the Popes frequently mention Mary's Spiritual Maternity in the same breath as her Divine Maternity, which is an indubitable dogma of faith based on Revelation, would seem to imply that just as the latter is a divinely revealed teaching, so also should the former be considered as a truth of faith. Indeed, Pius XI not merely juxtaposes Mary's Spiritual Maternity with her Divine Maternity, but with a number of other dogmas of our faith. In the consistorial allocution of December 24, 1932, wherein the Holy Father made known his intention of proclaiming the Holy Year, he described the Redemption as an ensemble of divine works rather than a single work. Some of these divine works, he said, were "the last Supper and institution of the Eucharist, the First Communion and sacerdotal initiation of the Apostles; the Passion, Crucifixion, and Death of Jesus; Mary under the Cross, constituted the Mother of men; the Resurrection of Jesus, condition and pledge of our own. ..."[101] The mention of Mary's Spiritual Motherhood in the midst of important dogmas of our faith and of "divine works" pertaining to the objective Redemption, points significantly to the revealed character of the Spiritual Maternity.

The same inference results from the passage we already quoted from *Gloriosae Dominae* of Benedict XIV, in which the Pontiff presents the doctrine of Mary's Spiritual Maternity as a tenet of the constant Tradition of the Church: "The Catholic Church, schooled by the Holy Spirit, has always most diligently professed, not only to venerate Mary

---

[100] Baumann, *op. cit.*, p. 12.
[101] *Actes de S.S. Pie XI*, Vol. 8 (Paris, La Bonne Presse), p. 147.

most devoutly as the Mother of the Lord and Redeemer ... but also to honor her with filial affection as the most loving Mother who was left to her with the last words of her dying Spouse."[102] A constant tradition of the Church, under the guidance of the Holy Spirit, is one of the surest signs of the revealed character of a doctrine.

Section 2. Proofs From Holy Scripture

If the statements of the Supreme Pontiffs seem to point to the revealed character of Mary's Spiritual Maternity, we may well look into Holy Scripture and Tradition for valid proofs of this doctrine. Marian texts in Holy Writ are comparatively few. We shall limit our investigation to the four major texts commonly adduced in proof of Mary's prerogatives; namely, the Protogospel,[103] the Annunciation pericope,[104] Christ's supreme testament,[105] and the vision of the woman clothed with the sun.[106]

a) The Protogospel (Gen. 3:15)

> I will put enmity between you and the woman, between your seed and her seed; he shall crush your head, and you shall lie in wait for his heel.

Concerning these words addressed by God to Satan, after the latter had seduced Eve and Adam into committing the original sin in paradise, we may ask: (1) Is this a Marian text? (2) Does it prove Mary's Spiritual Maternity?

In answer to the first of these questions a whole gamut of opinions has been given by various commentators. A few Catholic authors hold that "the woman" in *Gen.* 3:15 does not in any real scriptural sense refer to Mary, but rather to Eve, and Eve alone.[107] Any attempt to find a

---

[102] *Benedicti XIV opera omnia*, Vol. 16 (Prati, 1846), p. 428.
[103] *Gen.* 3:15.
[104] *Lk.* 1:26-38.
[105] *Jn.* 19:26-27.
[106] *Apoc.* 12.
[107] H. Lesêtre, *Marie, Mère de Dieu*, in *Dictionnaire de la Bible*, Vol. 4, 1 (Paris, 1928), col. 779. W. Goossens, *De cooperatione immediata Matris Redemptoris ad redemptionem obiectivam* (Paris, 1939), p. 96. Heinisch-Heidt, *The Theology of the Old Testament* (Collegeville, Minn., 1950), pp. 304, 318-319, 328.

Marian connotation in the text is merely the fruit of pious accommodation. The vast majority of modern exegetes, however, see in the text some kind of scriptural reference to Mary. Some quote the text in relation to Mary without specifying the exact biblical sense underlying their interpretation.[108] Others teach that Mary is signified as an antitype of Eve.[109] A third group says that Mary is contained in the verse in its fuller sense. An increasing number of modern writers goes still further and affirms that the woman of *Gen.* 3:15, is to be understood of Mary alone, and that in the strict literal sense.[110]

This last opinion seems acceptable on several grounds. For one thing, it does not violate any rules of textual criticism. Though the Hebrew article in *ha' isscha* (the woman) can have an anaphoric meaning, thus making Eve the term of reference, it can also signify "a certain woman," different from Eve. Furthermore, the passage in question is a Messianic prophecy, and for that reason does not require the word "woman" to have an identical meaning here and in the context. Besides, as Father Peirce remarks, the fact that the speaker in verse 15 is God, whereas in the context he is the inspired author, also permits a difference of signification. Above all, the meaning of the passage seems entirely to exclude Eve. The verse prophesies perfect enmity between this woman and Satan, her seed and his. This perfect enmity could not have been

---

[108] F. H. Schüth, S.J., *Mediatrix; eine mariologische Frage* (Innsbruck, 1925), p. 96. J. E. Steinmueller, *Some Problems of the Old Testament* (Milwaukee, 1936), p. 67. E. Gallagher, S.J., *Evaluation of the Arguments in Favor of Mary's Co-Redemption*, in *Marian Studies*, Vol. 2, 1951, p. 109. For further bibliography see E. May, O.F.M.Cap., *The Scriptural Basis for Mary's Spiritual Maternity*, in *Marian Studies*, Vol. 3, 1952, p. 115.

[109] B. H. Merkelbach, O.P., *Mariologia* (Parisiis, 1939), p. 82. J. Bittremieux, *De Mediatione universali B. M. Virginis quoad gratias* (Brugis, 1926), p. 184. E. F. Sutcliffe, S.J., *Protoevangelium*, in *The Clergy Review*, Vol. 2, 1931, pp. 155-159. Further references in E. May, *art. cit.*, p. 115.

[110] B. Mariani, O.F.M., *L'Assunzione di Maria SS. nella Sacra Scrittura*, in *Atti del Congresso Nazionale Mariano dei Frati Minori d'Italia* (Roma, 1948), pp. 468-483. F. X. Peirce, S.J., *Mary Alone Is "the Woman" of Genesis 3:15*, in *The Catholic Biblical Quarterly*, Vol. 13, 1951, pp. 239-252. J. B. Carol, O.F.M., *De Corredemptione B. V. Mariae* (Civitas Vaticana, 1950), pp. 86-91. Cf. also E. May, *Mary in the Old Testament*, in MARIOLOGY, ed. J. B. Carol, Vol. 1 (Milwaukee, 1955), pp. 65-69.

verified in Eve who everywhere in Holy Scripture[111] and Tradition appears as the cause of ruin, never as one who opposed Satan. On the other hand, it was clearly verified in Mary, who was all pure, and never for a moment under Satan's power.

If we accept this interpretation of the Protogospel, we may lawfully use it as an argument to prove Mary's Spiritual Maternity. For the text prophesies that Mary, with her divine Son, will crush Satan's head; and this crushing, as we know, took place through the objective Redemption. Since the objective Redemption marks the rebirth of mankind to the supernatural life, Mary by her share in the work of the Redemption can aptly be called our Spiritual Mother. *Gen.* 3:15 can, therefore, be quoted as a valid scriptural proof of the Spiritual Maternity.

b) The Annunciation Pericope (Lk. 1:26-38)

... and when the angel had come to her, he said, "Hail, full of grace, the Lord is with thee. Blessed art thou among women. ..."

And the angel said to her, "Do not be afraid, Mary, for thou hast found grace with God. Behold, thou shalt conceive in thy womb and shalt bring forth a son; and thou shalt call his name Jesus. He shall be great, and shall be called the Son of the Most High; and the Lord God will give him the throne of David his father, and he shall be king over the house of Jacob forever; and of his kingdom there shall be no end."

But Mary said to the angel, "How shall this happen since I do not know man?"

And the angel answered and said to her, "The Holy Spirit shall come upon thee and the power of the Most High shall overshadow thee; and therefore the Holy One to be born shall be called the Son of God. ..."

But Mary said, "Behold the handmaid of the Lord; be it done to me according to thy word." And the angel departed from her.

The argument drawn from this Gospel passage hinges entirely on the status of Mary's knowledge at the moment of the Annunciation. Did she know, first of all, that her Son was God? And second, did her knowledge

---

[111] D. Unger, O.F.M.Cap., *Mary Immaculate, The Bull Ineffabilis Deus of Pope Pius IX* (Paterson, N. J., 1946), pp. 10-11, and note p. 30. J. B. Carol, O.F.M., *The Apostolic Constitution "Munificentissimus Deus" and Our Lady's Co-Redemption*, in *Marianum*, Vol. 13, 1951, p. 248 ff. Cf. E. May, *loc. cit.* More recently Father Unger has written an extensive book on the subject, entitled: *The First Gospel: Genesis 3:15* (St. Bonaventure, N. Y., Franciscan Institute, 1954).

include Christ's soteriological and redemptive mission? That Mary was aware of Christ's divinity from the very beginning has ever been the common view of the Church. This opinion has never been seriously questioned except by isolated individuals, who met with vigorous opposition from their contemporaries.[112] As regards Mary's knowledge of Christ's redemptive role, more and more writers are expressing the opinion that in consenting to the Incarnation, "the Virgin knowingly consented likewise to the moral regeneration of all mankind and to her part in it, and hence to her position as our spiritual Mother."[113]

c) Christ's Supreme Testament (Jn. 19:26-27)

Jesus, therefore, seeing his Mother and the disciple whom he loved standing by, said to his Mother, "Woman, behold thy Son!" Then he said to the disciple. "Behold thy Mother!" And from that hour the disciple took her into his own care.

As we have seen previously, this passage has frequently been used by the Supreme Pontiffs in support of Mary's Spiritual Maternity. The tenor of the pontifical texts would seem to indicate that the popes did not attribute a merely accommodative but rather a strictly biblical sense to the text. Can the existence of a truly biblical reference to Mary's Spiritual Maternity be defended on exegetical grounds?

There are still not a few exegetes who maintain that the words of Christ are applicable to Mary's Spiritual Motherhood only by accommodation.[114] An ever growing number of Mariologists and

---

[112] Concerning the controversy between E. F. Sutcliffe, S.J. (who asserted that Mary was ignorant of Christ's divinity) and several exponents of the traditional opinion, see E. May, *art. cit.*, in *Marian Studies*, pp. 122-123.

[113] E. May, *art. cit.*, p. 124. S. Tromp, S.J., *Corpus Christi quod est ecclesia* (Romae, 1946), Vol. 1, p. 13. A. Rivera, C.M.F., *La maternidad espiritual de María en San Lucas 1:26-38 y en el Apocalipsis XII*, in *Estudios Marianos*, Vol. 7, 1948, pp. 51-83. Further references can be found in E. May, *art. cit.*

[114] W. Newton, *A Commentary on the New Testament* (Catholic Biblical Association of America, 1942), p. 357. A. J. Maas, *The Life of Jesus Christ*, 5th ed. (St. Louis, 1909), p. 541. A. Durand, S.J., *Evangile selon Saint Jean* (Paris, 1938), p. 493. A. E. Breen, *A Harmonized Exposition of the Four Gospels*, Vol. 4, 3rd. ed. (Milwaukee, 1930), p. 130. J. Knabenbauer, S.J., *Evangelium secundum Ioannem* (Paris, 1898), pp. 546-547. A. Brassac, S.S., *The Student's Handbook to the Study of the New Testament* (St. Louis, 1913), pp. 386-387. Cf. M.

exegetes, however, see in the text a valid biblical proof. Possibly the majority affirm that the words of Christ have a literal reference to John and Mary, and a typical reference to Mary's Spiritual Motherhood.[115] Roschini maintains that Christ's words refer directly and literally to the Spiritual Maternity.[116] Perhaps the most logical interpretation would be to say that the Spiritual Motherhood is contained in the text in the fuller sense. John's filiation and Mary's Motherhood are both material and spiritual, particular and universal: material and particular in the obvious sense; spiritual and universal in the profound and fuller sense; and both in a truly literal sense.

In support of our statement there are arguments based both on the text itself and on the proximate and remote context.[117]

If we consider the passage itself we must admit that Christ's words could textually have a universal and spiritual meaning as well as a particular and material meaning. There is nothing to prove that a restricted interpretation must be adopted. On the contrary, there are indications of a more extensive sense. Why did Our Lord call Mary "Woman"? Why did He make a double recommendation when "Son, behold your mother" would have sufficed? What help could Mary have given John other than a spiritual help? Furthermore, why does the Evangelist speak of John as of the "disciple"? Did he not wish to present him as the representative of Christians, who are the "disciples" of Christ? Why did St. John give such a detailed account of this scene, when ordinarily he is so reticent on matters that concern him? Most

---

Gruenthaner, S.J., *Mary in the New Testament*, in MARIOLOGY, ed. J. B. Carol, Vol. I (Milwaukee, 1955), pp. 114-116. Incidentally, Gruenthaner's views are not at all shared by his editor, Father Carol. In his *Fundamentals of Mariology* (New York, 1956), p. 51, the latter writes: "In the light of the above papal declarations we do not quite understand how it is possible for so many Catholic scholars to hold that Christ's words from the cross refer to Mary's spiritual Motherhood only by accommodation."

[115] J. Bittremieux, *op. cit.*, pp. 188-191. J. Keuppens, *Mariologiae Compendium*, 2a edit. (1947), p. 139. G. Alastruey, *Tratado de la Virgen Santísima*, 2nd ed. (Madrid, 1947), pp. 750-753. Merkelbach, *op. cit.*, pp. 302-304. N. García Garcés, C.M.F., *Mater Corredemptrix* (Taurini-Romae, 1939), pp. 40-45. For further bibliography see E. May, *art. cit.*, p. 126.

[116] G. M. Roschini, O.S.M., *Compendium Mariologiae* (Romae, 1946), p. 277.

[117] R. Rábanos, C.M., *La maternidad espiritual de María en el Protoevangelio y San Juan*, in *Estudios Marianos*, Vol. 7, 1948, pp. 43-50

probably he considered the event as of extraordinary significance.

The immediate context likewise points to a spiritual and universal interpretation of the words of Christ's supreme testament. Christ's words on the cross and the actions accompanying His sufferings and death on Calvary are presented by St. John as a fulfillment of messianic prophecies. Thus the words "I thirst" are spoken in fulfillment of Ps. 21:16, "My tongue hath cleaved to my jaws." The utterance "It is consummated" refers to the concluding words of the same Psalm: "Which the Lord hath made."[118] The dividing of the garments, the bones left unbroken, the piercing with the lance were all in accomplishment of messianic prophecies. If the meaning of Christ's testament were restricted to John and Mary, the text would be the only one in the entire chapter without a more extensive and spiritual meaning. Furthermore, it is hardly conceivable that Christ should have chosen this most solemn occasion, when the Redemption of mankind was being enacted, to express anxiety about temporalities for which He could have provided before His Passion.[119]

That Christ's words have reference to Mary's Spiritual Maternity can furthermore be argued if we examine the remote context of the passage under discussion. An attentive study of St. John's Gospel will bring to light its eminently symbolical character. All its narrations have an underlying spiritual meaning. Our Lord speaks of water to the Samaritan woman, or He stands before the waters of Siloe, and He has in mind the waters of grace and the Holy Spirit. He multiplies the loaves to prepare the minds of the people for the multiplication of the Eucharistic bread. He draws the attention of His disciples to the ripening wheat fields, to remind them of the spiritual harvest of God's fields. He contemplates the candelabrum in the temple, and affirms that He is the Light of the world. He raises Lazarus from the dead to prove that He is the Resurrection and the Life. In the framework of Johannine symbolism a spiritual interpretation of Christ's testamentary utterance seems only logical.[120] The Saviour's words clearly affirm that Mary is our Spiritual Mother. Whether they create her or merely proclaim her as such cannot be

---

[118] *Ps.* 21:32.

[119] E. May, *art. cit.*, p. 127.

[120] R. Rábanos, *art. cit.*, p. 48.

inferred from the passage in question. Yet we have already seen from other scriptural passages that her Spiritual Maternity began with the Incarnation.

d) Vision of the Woman Clothed With the Sun (Apoc., Chap. 12)

Near the end of Chapter 11 the author of the Apocalypse announces the establishment of "Our Lord's and his [Christ's] kingdom."[121] Apparently, this is in anticipation of what takes place in Chapter 12. There St. John describes the marvelous sign which appears in the heavens. On the one hand appears a woman, clothed with the sun, the moon under her feet, and a crown of twelve stars on her head; she cries out, laboring in childbirth. On the other hand stands a mighty dragon, likewise crowned, waiting to devour the child that is about to be born. The woman brings forth a man child, who is to rule all the nations with an iron rod. Before the dragon has any power over them, the child is taken up to God and His throne, and the woman likewise is freed from his wrath. A struggle then ensues, the dragon and his angels fighting against Michael and his angels; with the result that the dragon, who is the devil or Satan, is routed, and the kingdom of God and Christ is established. The dragon then tries to persecute the woman, but when he fails, he turns against "the rest of her seed who keep the commandments of God and have the testimony of Jesus Christ."[122]

In the passage there are three principal figures: the Woman, the Son, and the Dragon. The text itself identifies the dragon as Satan. The Son is clearly the Messias, the Lamb who overcame the dragon with His Blood[123] and whose reign was established by the downfall of the dragon. To the Son St. John applies the messianic words of Ps. 2:9: "Thou shalt rule them [the nations] with a rod of iron." The Messias alone could be "taken up to God and to His throne," and He alone could be contrasted with "the rest of the seed"[124] of the woman.

The question still to be solved — a question of interest here — is: who

---

[121] *Apoc.* 12:15.
[122] *Apoc.* 12:17.
[123] *Apoc.* 12:11.
[124] *Apoc.* 12:17.

is the woman? If we take into account the general structure of the Apocalypse we feel compelled to identify the woman with the Church. This is the view of most exegetes today and of the Fathers of the Church.[125] Indeed the general theme of the Apocalypse is the struggle between good and evil considered on a universal plane. The principal adversaries in this struggle are God, Christ the Redeemer, and the Church militant and triumphant on the one hand; Lucifer, his wicked angels, and the hoard of men subject to their power and influence on the other. The Church is here considered as the early Church, or as the pre-Church of the Old Testament, or as both together. She is represented as a woman, in keeping with the allegorical method of the prophets, who frequently represented Israel under the symbolical figures of Spouse or Mother. Furthermore, the description of the woman, clothed in the sun of the divinity, with the moon under her feet (a sign of domination) and a crown of twelve stars on her brow (a reference to the twelve patriarchs, or the twelve tribes, or the twelve Apostles), makes the ecclesiological interpretation all the more credible. The Church brought forth Christ in the pains of childbirth through her age-long expectation of His advent, and through the persecutions she suffered to engender her other descendants to the supernatural life.

Yet if the passage in question undoubtedly has an ecclesiological meaning, is it entirely devoid of any Mariological connotation? What is surprising is that St. John here describes the Church with the allegory of a woman whose traits are those of the Blessed Virgin as described elsewhere in Scripture. The very use of the word "sign" recalls that other "sign," a Marian sign, spoken of in *Isa.* 7:14 — the sign of the Virgin begetting a Son. Of even greater significance is the parallelism that exists between this prophecy and that of the Protogospel. In both instances the figures and persons are the same: the woman and her progeny, the serpent and his in the Protogospel; the woman, her male child, and the rest of her seed; the dragon and his followers in the

---

[125] J. Bonsirven, S.J., *L'Apocalypse de Saint Jean,* in Verbum Salutis, Vol. 16, 1951, pp. 209-221. A. Rivera, C.M.F., *La maternidad espiritual de María en San Lucas 1, 26-38 y en el Apocalypsis XII,* in *Estudios Marianos,* Vol. 7, 1948, pp. 84-90. L. Poirier, O.F.M., *Le chapitre XII de l'Apocalypse fait-il allusion à l'Assomption?* in Vers le Dogme de l'Assomption (Montréal, 1948), pp. 93-102.

Apocalypse. In both cases the first group triumphs over the second. Could it be that St. John, to whom Our Lord entrusted His Blessed Mother, described the woman of the Apocalypse without at once thinking of Mary? It seems logical to conclude that in the mind of the Apostle the picture of Mary was to serve as a prototype for the Church whom he wished to describe. The Child to whom she gives birth is Christ both in His personal and in His Mystical Body. She is pictured as suffering the pains of childbirth, because she brought forth the Mystical Body amid the sorrows of her compassion on Calvary. If this interpretation is valid, the passage of the Apocalypse may be used as a scriptural proof of Mary's Spiritual Maternity.[126]

Section 3. Proofs From Tradition

There are two methods of presenting the argument from Tradition: the chronological method which deals with the Fathers of the Church individually, stating what each one taught on Mary's Spiritual Motherhood; and the theological method which attempts to offer a synthesis of the opinions expressed throughout the patristic age, and logically works the ideas of the individual Fathers into a complete thought-structure. We have chosen the latter method, mainly for brevity's sake. After carefully perusing the data available, it seemed best to group our texts under three headings: (1) Mary our Spiritual Mother by her role in the Incarnation; (2) Mary our Spiritual Mother by her compassion with Christ on Calvary; (3) Mary our Spiritual Mother by her mediation in heaven. Since, however, Our Lady's Spiritual Motherhood consists principally and essentially in regenerating mankind to the supernatural life, it will suffice that we develop the first two titles, taking the last for granted as a consequence of the other two.

1. Mary Our Spiritual Mother Through the Incarnation

The doctrine that Mary's Spiritual Maternity was inaugurated at the Incarnation dates back to St. Irenaeus and runs through the entire

---

[126] Cf. J. J. Weber, *La Vierge Marie dans le Nouveau Testament* (Paris, 1951), pp. 113-122; Rivera, *art. cit.*, p. 89; Gruenthaner, *art. cit.*, pp. 106-107; and especially the recent exhaustive volume by B. Le Frois, S.V.D., *The Woman Clothed With the Sun (Ap. 12), Individual or Collective?* (Rome, 1954).

patristic age. In fact it is supported by a much firmer tradition than the doctrine of the Spiritual Maternity as based on the Blessed Virgin's compassion with Our Lord on the cross.

St. Irenaeus

St. Irenaeus (d. c. 200) in two important passages mentions a spiritual regeneration by a virgin. In each case scholars have tried to determine who the virgin is, and what is meant by regeneration. They have been divided in their interpretation, some identifying the virgin with Our Lady, others affirming that she is a metaphorical prototype of the Church.

In the first text Irenaeus says:

> And those who proclaimed Him Emmanuel born of the Virgin[127] showed the union of the Word of God to His handiwork, because the Word will become flesh, and the Son of God the son of man — the Pure One opening purely that pure womb, which regenerates men unto God, which [womb] He made pure, and He became the same as we are.[128]

The essential clause is 'which [womb] regenerates men unto God." We can ask ourselves: Which is the womb that regenerates men unto God? That of Mary, or that of the Church? There never was question of any other. To resolve our dilemma the only proper and secure procedure is to leave aside all prejudice and to examine carefully the grammatical structure of the sentence as well as the context and parallel passages; in other words, to apply the normal principles and criteria of textual criticism.

The difficulty of grammatical interpretation lies mainly in the following lines, the parts of which form an integral unit:

---

[127] Isa. 7:14.

[128] Irenaeus, *Adversus haereses*, 4, 33, 12; ed. Harvey, 2, 266 (*PG*, 7, 1180): "Et qui eum ex Virgine Emmanuel praedicabant, adunitionem Verbi Dei ad plasma ejus manifestabant: quoniam Verbum caro erit, et Filius Dei Filius hominis; (purus pure puram aperiens vulvam eam quae regenerat homines in Deum, quam ipse puram fecit) et hoc factus, quod et nos." Cf. P. Galtier, S.J., *La Vierge qui nous régénère*, in *Recherches de Science Religieuse*, Vol. 5, 1914, pp. 136-145; *id., La maternité de grâce dans S. Irénée*, in *Mémoires et Rapports du Congrès Marial tenu à Bruxelles* 1921, Vol. 1 (Bruxelles, 1922), pp. 41-45; M.-A. Genevois, O.P., *La maternité universelle de Marie selon saint Irénée*, in *Revue Thomiste*, Vol. 41, 1936, pp. 26-51; W. R. O'Connor, *The Spiritual Maternity of Our Lady in Tradition*, in *Marian Studies*, Vol. 3, 1952, pp. 143-145.

The Son of God will become the son of man — the Pure One opening purely that pure womb, which regenerates men unto God.

The first of the three parts contains the principal clause, in which the author affirms that the Son of God will become incarnate. The second part is a phrase in apposition, in which the virginal conception of the incarnate Son of God is asserted. The third part is a relative clause, depending on the second part, and in it the author declares that the womb mentioned previously is the same which regenerates men unto God. Therefore, Irenaeus says of the same womb that it was opened purely by the Son of God, and that it regenerates men unto God. Now, it is evident that the womb opened purely by the Son of God is the virginal womb of Mary and in nowise the metaphorical womb of the Church. That same womb regenerates men unto God; Mary by the act of Divine Motherhood becomes the Spiritual Mother of men.

This interpretation is confirmed by the context of which the three parts just quoted are an essential element, not just a parenthesis. The fundamental theme of the whole passage is contained in the expression, "Emmanuel born of the Virgin." The expression consists of the two elements: (1) "Emmanuel" or *God-with-us*, that is, the Incarnation of the Son of God; (2) "born of the Virgin," namely, the conception and birth of the Son of God made man. These two thoughts are the only ones developed in the entire passage. The first thought, "Emmanuel," is expressed in four equivalent phrases: (1) "the union of the Word of God to His handiwork"; (2) "the Word will become flesh"; (3) "the Son of God will become the son of Man"; (4) "He became the same as we are." The second thought, "born of the Virgin," recurs three times in phrases referring to the virginal womb. The virgin in question can only be the Virgin Mary, Mother of the Emmanuel, as is evident from the very meaning of the words and from the double reference Irenaeus makes to *Isa.* 7:14 and *Mt.* 1:22-23.

But one might object that the regeneration of men seems to have no relation with the virginal generation of the Son of God. How can Irenaeus bring them together and almost identify them in the same sentence? The difficulty is only apparent, for in the mind of the holy Bishop of Lyons the Incarnation comprises not merely the individual Humanity of Christ, but universal humanity recapitulated in Christ. This recapitulation is the key to the entire soteriology of St. Irenaeus, just as it is the key to the theology of St. Paul. Statements like the following are frequent in the writing of the holy Doctor: "He it is [Jesus Christ] who recapitulated in Himself all the nations dispersed since Adam, and all tongues, and the generation of men with Adam Himself."[129] Or again: "[Christ] would not have blood and flesh, by which He redeemed us if He did not recapitulate in Himself the ancient formation of Adam."[130] It is not surprising, therefore, that the same pure womb should at once generate the Son of God and regenerate men unto God; for the Son of God recapitulated in Himself all mankind, even Adam himself, so that we might be born again to the life of God. For "how," asks St. Irenaeus, "could we be associated with incorruption and immortality, if previously incorruption and immortality had not become what we ourselves are?"[131] St. Irenaeus summarizes what we have thus far said. "Recapitulating in Himself Adam," he writes, "He, who was the Word, legitimately received from the Virgin Mary the generation of the recapitulation of Adam."[132]

The conclusions from the above are not hard to draw. Mary's Spiritual Maternity derives from and prolongs her Divine Maternity. If the Son of God became the son of man by purely opening the pure womb which regenerates men unto God, it is also true that the pure womb of the Virgin Mary generated purely the Son of God become man, and with Him regenerated men unto God. Second, the basis of the Spiritual Maternity is the recapitulation of mankind in Christ, the principle of solidarity between Christ and men, the organic and vital union of the Mystical Body. Third, the Spiritual Maternity consists in the

---

[129] *Adversus haereses*, 3, 22, 3; Harvey, 2, 123 (*PG*, 7, 957-958): "Ipse est qui omnes gentes exinde ab Adam dispersas, et universas linguas, et generationem hominum cum ipso Adam in semetipso recapitulatus est."

[130] *Adversus haereses*, 5, 1, 2: Harvey, 2, 316 (*PG*, 7, 1122): "Neque enim esset vere sanguinem et carnem habens, per quam nos redemit, nisi antiquam plasmationem Adae in semetipsum recapitulasset."

[131] *Adversus haereses*, 3, 19, 1; Harvey, 2, 103 (*PG*, 7, 939-940): "Quemadmodum autem adunari possemus incorruptelae et immortalitati, nisi prius incorruptela et immortalitas facta fuisset id quod et nos?"

[132] *Adversus haereses*, 3, 21, 10; Harvey, 2, 120 (*PG*, 7, 955): "Ita recapitulans in se Adam ipsum Verbum existens, ex Maria quae adhuc erat Virgo, recte accipiebat generationem Adae recapitulationis."

regeneration of men unto God. Therefore, it is a motherhood in the true sense and not a motherhood in a legal or metaphorical sense.

The second important text from St. Irenaeus reads as follows:

> How will a man go to God, if God does not go to man? And how shall a man leave his mortal birth unless he comes to the new birth wondrously and unexpectedly given by God as a sign of salvation, and which is from the Virgin, and by faith, a regeneration? Or what adoption will they receive from God by remaining in that birth which is according to man in this world? ... The Son of God became man re- ceiving in Himself the ancient formation.[133]

The whole problem, analogous to that of the preceding passage, lies in the interpretation of the phrases: "the new birth ... which is from the Virgin." Is this Virgin the Virgin Mary or the Virgin Church? The words which immediately follow it, "and by faith, a regeneration," would seem to suggest that the Virgin is the Church. However, the suggestion is merely apparent since both the context and parallel passages point to a Mariological interpretation; namely, that the Virgin is Mary.

In the context we see that Irenaeus expresses two main thoughts: (1) the Son of God becomes man and receives a new birth; (2) man by means of faith shares in or appropriates this new birth of the Son of God. Irenaeus writes: "How will man go to God, if God does not go to man?" Man's going to God expresses the subjective element of our spiritual rebirth; God's going to man refers to the objective element. Does the Virgin in question fit into the framework of the objective or the subjective birth? Let us again analyze what St. Irenaeus says of the new birth. According to him it is:

> ... the new birth wondrously and unexpectedly given by God as a sign of salvation, [a generation] which is from the Virgin, which is by faith, a regeneration.

---

[133] *Adversus haereses*, 4, 33, 4; Harvey, 2, 259-260 (*PG*, 7, 1074-1075): "Et quemadmodum homo transiet in Deum, si non Deus in hominem? Quemadmodum autem relinquet mortis generationem, si non in novam generationem mire et inopinate a Deo, in signum autem salutis [*Isa.* 7:13] datam, quae est ex Virgine per fidem regenerationem? Vel quam adoptionem accipient a Deo, permanentis in ac genesi, quae est secundum hominem in hoc mundo? ... Filius Dei factus est homo, antiquam plasmationem in semetipsum suscipiens."

The last clause, "which is by faith, a regeneration," expresses the subjective condition of our salvation, namely, the appropriation of, or participation in, the new generation by means of faith. The two lines which precede this clause are in apposition to "the new birth" and belong to the objective element. Therefore, the words "which is from the Virgin" must be interpreted objectively, its antecedent being "the new birth." The "faith" referred to in the passage has consequently no reference to the "Virgin" but rather to the individual soul to whom the Redemption is subjectively applied. The Virgin in question is the Mother of the Son of God, signified by Isaias. That she is also our Mother is implied in the last sentence of the passage quoted above: "The Son of God became man receiving in Himself the ancient formation [*plasmationem*]." From what we said in our commentary on the first passage, the "ancient formation" refers to the recapitulation or the incorporation of all humanity in Christ.

The Mariological interpretation provided by the context is further corroborated by several parallel passages of which we shall quote only two. "The Son of God," says St. Irenaeus, "... became the son of man. For this reason also the Lord Himself gave us a sign ... which man did not ask for, inasmuch as he did not even expect that she could become a pregnant Virgin who was a Virgin."[134] Do we not see a repetition here of the ideas expressed in the passage upon which we are commenting: the Son of God becoming man; a wondrous and unexpected birth; a sign of salvation; a begetting by the Virgin? Still more significant is the second passage, in which all the characteristic ideas seen above are repeated. "The Holy Spirit," writes Irenaeus, "signified ... His *birth which derives from the Virgin*. ... The saying of Isaias: '*the Lord* Himself *will give* you a *sign'* indicates the *unexpectedness of His birth*. ... But because an *unexpected salvation* began to appear for men ... *unexpected* also was the *Virgin's* begetting, it being *God* who *gave* this sign, and not man who

---

[134] *Adversus haereses*, 3, 19, 3; Harvey, 2, 104-105 (*PG*, 7, 941): "Filius Dei ... factus est Filius hominis. Propter hoc et ipse Dominus dedit nobis signum ... quod non postulavit homo, quia nec speravit virginem praegnantem fieri posse quae erat virgo."

caused it."¹³⁵ In the light of these two texts there is no room for doubt concerning the identity of the Virgin spoken of by Irenaeus and the Virgin prophesied by Isaias. She is the Virginal Mother of the Incarnate Son of God.

In conclusion we may affirm that St. Irenaeus very clearly teaches the Spiritual Maternity of Mary. His thought has been crystallized in three concise formulas, of which two are explicit and one implicit, which together form a complete structure. The explicit statements are: "The Son of God became a son of man, by opening purely the pure womb, which regenerates men to God"; "The new birth of the Son of God, which derives from the Virgin, is a birth of men." The implicit statement, of no less importance than the others, is: "The Word received legitimately from Mary the generation of the recapitulation of Adam." Three essential points characterize St. Irenaeus' doctrine on the Spiritual Maternity: (1) its basis is the recapitulation of mankind in Christ; (2) its origin is the Divine Maternity of which it is a prolongation; (3) its nature is the modality of a true spiritual generation.¹³⁶

Later Fathers

The idea of Christ recapitulating mankind in the womb of Mary can be traced through the writings of the later Fathers of the Church. St. Gregory the Wonder-Worker (d. 270) writes: "From on high came the divine Word, and in thy [Mary's] holy womb reformed Adam."¹³⁷ In order that Adam be reformed in the womb of Mary, he and his descendants had to be incorporated in Christ. Consequently, as Mary conceived Christ, she also conceived mankind with Christ and in Christ.

Still more significant is the testimony of the Ephesian Fathers. St.

---

¹³⁵ *Adversus haereses*, 3, 21, 5; Harvey, 2, 116-118 (*PG*, 7, 951-953): "Significavit Spiritus sanctus ... generationem ejus quae est ex Virgine. ... Quod autem dixerit Isaias ... Ipse Dominus dabit signum, id quod erat inopinatum generationis ejus significavit. ... Sed quoniam inopinata salus hominibus inciperet fieri ... inopinatus et partus Virginis fiebat, Deo dante signum hoc, sed non homine operante illud."

¹³⁶ J. M. Bover, S.J., *La maternidad espiritual de María en los Padres Griegos*, in *Estudios Marianos*, Vol. 7, 1948, pp. 91-104. Cf. the sober conclusion of W. J. Burghardt, S.J., *Mary in Western Patristic Thought*, in MARIOLOGY, ed. J. B. Carol, Vol. 1 (Milwaukee, 1955), pp. 128-130.

¹³⁷ *PG*, 10, 1151.

Cyril of Alexandria (d. 444) writes: "As Christ appropriated a body taken from a woman and was engendered by her according to the flesh, he recapitulated in himself the generation of man."[138] Elsewhere he comes back to the same idea when he says: "He made Himself our Head by His relationship to the flesh which he assumed."[139] Yet nowhere does he express the same thought more forcefully than in a rather extended passage, of which we can quote only the essentials. "We affirm," he tells us, "... that the Only-begotten ... became man *economically* ... and that with us and like us He submitted Himself to generation ... so that, born of a woman according to the flesh, He might recapitulate in Himself the human race ... and by the flesh united to Him, He might incorporate all in Himself."[140]

To express the doctrine of the recapitulation and of the inclusion of mankind in Christ, St. Cyril makes use of the Pauline term *oikonomia*. This and the term *mysterion* are used by St. Paul to denote the divine plan of the redemption and the incorporation of mankind in Christ, as is evident from the following excerpt (*Eph.* 1:7-10):

In whom we have redemption through his blood, the remission of sins, according to the riches of his grace, which hath superabounded in us, in all wisdom and prudence, that he might make known to us the *mystery* of his will according to his good pleasure, which he hath purposed in him, in the *dispensation* [*oikonomia*] of the fulness of times, to re-establish [recapitulate] all things in Christ, that are in heaven and on earth.

A little further on (3:2-9) he adds: "You have heard of the dispensation (*oikonomia*) of the grace of God, which is given me towards you: how that, according to revelation, the *mystery* has been made known to me ... that the Gentiles should be fellow heirs and of the same body: and co-partners of his promise in Christ Jesus. ... To me ... is given this grace, to preach among the Gentiles the unsearchable riches of Christ, and to enlighten all men, that they may see what is the dispensation (*oikonomia*) of the *mystery*. ..." In the light of these Pauline texts, we can understand the full meaning of St. Cyril's statements.

---

[138] *PG*, 76, 23-24.
[139] *PG*, 76, 1341-1342.
[140] *PG*, 76, 15-18.

The other Ephesian Fathers write in the same vein as St. Cyril. Theodotus of Ancyra (d. c. 446) writes: "God ... chose the virginal birth as the inauguration of the dispensation (*oikonomia*)";[141] and he even goes so far as to call Mary "the Mother of the dispensation (*oikonomia*)."[142] St. Proclus of Constantinople (d. 446) is no exception to the Tradition we are discussing. "The virginal womb," he observes, "bore this *mystery* of the divine dispensation (*oikonomia*)";[143] and with a daring equal to that of Theodotus, he calls Mary "the Mother of the mystery."[144] This beautiful theology of the Ephesian Fathers is an evolution of the theology of St. Irenaeus. Equally conversant with Pauline terminology, St. Irenaeus calls Mary the *Mother of the recapitulation,* St. Theodotus gives her the title of *Mother of the dispensation* (*oikonomia*), and St. Proclus greets her as the *Mother of the Mystery.* Mary is at once the Mother of God and the Mother of men in Christ Jesus; such is the message of the Ephesian Fathers.[145]

The intimate link between Mary's Divine and Spiritual Motherhood was also brought out by St. Augustine (d. 430), though perhaps not so clearly. In his treatise *On Holy Virginity*[146] he writes: "On this account that one woman [Mary] not only in spirit but also in body is a mother and a virgin. She is mother indeed in spirit, not of our head, which is the Saviour Himself, from whom rather she was spiritually born, since all who believe in Him, among whom is she herself, are rightly called the children of the bridegroom;[147] but clearly she is the mother of His members, which we are, because she co-operated by her charity that faithful ones should be born in the Church, and the faithful are members of that head. In body, however, she is the mother of the head." Although Augustine attributes our spiritual birth to Mary, it is not too clear whether that birth is involved in the birth of Christ.

St. Leo the Great (d. 461), however, very explicitly affirms that we

---

[141] *PG*, 77, 1351-1352.

[142] *PG*, 77, 1393-1394.

[143] *PG*, 65, 707-708.

[144] *PG*, 65, 791-792.

[145] J. M. Bover, *art. cit.,* p. 101.

[146] *PL*, 40, 398.

[147] *Mt.* 9:15.

were born to the spiritual life when Christ became incarnate. In one of his Christmas sermons he says: "While we adore the birth of our Saviour, we celebrate our own beginning. The generation of Christ is the origin of the Christian people, and the birthday of the head is the birthday of the body. ... The children of the Church, born in the waters of baptism, as they were crucified with Christ in His passion, and risen with Him in His resurrection, and placed on the right hand of the Father in His ascension, so were they engendered with Him in His Nativity."[148]

In the seventh century, pseudo-Modestus of Jerusalem (d. 634) expresses a thought very much in line with the reasoning of St. Irenaeus and the Ephesian Fathers when they refer to our recapitulation in Christ. He speaks of our mystical re-creation through Mary, the Mother of God. Writing of Mary's Assumption, he exclaims: "O most blessed dormition of the most glorious Mother of God, through whom we are mystically re-created and made the temple of the Holy Spirit."[149] At the end of the eleventh century St. Anselm (d. 1109) resumed and elaborated this idea of re-creation through Mary. "Every nature has been created by God," writes Anselm, "and God was born of Mary. God created all things, and Mary gave birth to God. God, Who made all things, made Himself from Mary; and so, all things which He had made, He remade. He who was able to make all things from nothing was not willing to remake them, when they were violated, without Mary. God then is the father of created things, and Mary the mother of re-created things. God is the father of the constitution of all, and Mary is the mother of the restitution of all. God generated Him through Whom all things are made, and Mary bore Him through Whom all things are saved. God generated Him without Whom there is nothing at all; and Mary bore Him without Whom nothing is well off at all."[150]

After St. Anselm the teaching that Mary's Divine Motherhood included her Spiritual Motherhood continued uninterrupted. St. Bernard (d. 1153), pseudo-Albert the Great (c. 1280), St. Bonaventure (d. 1274), St. Bernardine of Siena (d. 1444), St. Antoninus of Florence (d. 1459), all repeat it as in a refrain. "All generations will call you blessed," writes St.

---

[148] *Sermo 26, in nativ.*, PL, 54, 213.

[149] *Encomium in dormitionem B. Virginis*, 7; PG, 86 (2), 3294.

[150] *Oratio 52*; PL, 158, 956.

Bernard, "because you have generated life and glory for all generations. ... Rightly do the eyes of every creature look up to you because *in you, and by you, and of you* the benign hand of the Almighty has re-created whatever it had created."[151] Elsewhere he repeats the same thought: "In the eternal Word of God we were all made, and behold we die; in your brief reply [to the angel at the Annunciation] we are to be remade, in order that we may be called back to life."[152] A friend of Bernard's, the Premonstratensian Philip of Harveng (d. 1183), develops the thought that the Son of God in the Incarnation became the spouse and son of His mother. He became the spouse "by joining a virgin to Himself in a kind of conjugal union ... generating in her, or through her, spiritual sons by a spiritual efficacy, so that both He and she enjoy fruit and filial posterity."[153] The author of the *Mariale,* until recently attributed to St. Albert the Great, expresses the same thought when he writes: "The Blessed Virgin is the mother of all the good ... she was predestined before the ages to be the principle from which every created thing was to be re-created."[154]

St. Bonaventure reminds one of St. Augustine when he says: "Because the Virgin Mary conceived Him who is the head of all the elect and Whose members are the rest of the saved, she must have had an immense charity and benevolence to love all the elect with a maternal affection."[155] Two centuries later St. Bernardine of Siena, as a good Franciscan, continues in the Augustinian tradition: "She [Mary] had in her womb, that is in her intimate, maternal affection, the Son of God and the whole mystical Christ; that is, the head with the whole body of the elect."[156] By giving her consent to the Incarnation, she sought and procured the salvation of all the elect, "so that from that moment she bore them all in her womb, as a mother in the truest sense bears her

---

[151] *In festo Pentecostes,* 2; PL, 183, 328.

[152] *De laudibus Virginis Mariae, Homilia 4;* PL, 183, 83.

[153] *In Cantica Canticorum,* 1,1; PL, 203, 192.

[154] *Mariale,* in *Opera omnia Sti. Alberti,* ed. Borgnet, Vol. 37 (Parisiis, 1898), q. 145. Text in Keuppens, *op. cit.,* n. 233, p. 195.

[155] *Sermo 26, In nativitate Domini; Opera omnia,* Vol. 9 (Ad Claras Aquas, 1901), p. 125.

[156] Text in L. Di Fonzo, O.F.M.Conv., *La mariologia di S. Bernardino da Siena* (Roma, 1947), p. 40.

children."[157] St. Antoninus of Florence says that Mary is the sole mother of all men "because she has borne corporally a man, Christ, and in this man she has borne spiritually all the rest."[158]

The Eve-Mary Contrast

The idea of the spiritual recapitulation of mankind in Christ through Mary's Motherhood is implicitly contained in the Eve-Mary contrast so frequently found in the writings of the Fathers. Eve is presented as the author of natural life by natural generation; Mary, in contrast, appears as the author of supernatural life for men through her generation of Christ, the second Adam. As the Eve-Mary contrast in the Fathers is well known, there is little point in our dwelling on it at any length. It usually follows the same pattern: both Eve and Mary were virgins when they brought forth offspring; Eve, by her disobedience, brought forth death, while Mary, by her obedience, brought forth life. Such is the reasoning of St. Justin Martyr and St. Irenaeus of Lyons.[159]

A passage from Tertullian implicitly contains the idea of a recapitulation, a "going over again" of the work of creation by Almighty God. To fulfill His designs, namely, to bring life and salvation, the Creator makes use of the same sex which had brought ruin. "While Eve was yet a virgin, the ensnaring word had crept into her ear which was to build the edifice of death. Into a virgin soul, in like manner, must be introduced that word of God which was to raise the fabric of life; so that what had been reduced to ruin by this sex might, by the self-same sex, be recovered to salvation. As Eve had believed the serpent, so Mary believed Gabriel. The delinquency which the one occasioned by believing, the other effaced by believing."[160]

The early Church Fathers set the pace. Their successors all through Tradition, even to our latest Sovereign Pontiffs, keep repeating the Eve-Mary parallel to illustrate the doctrine of the Spiritual Maternity.

---

[157] *Ibid.*

[158] *Summa Theologica*, p. 4, tit. 15, c. 14, n. 3; cf. Terrien, *La Mère des hommes*, Vol. 2 (Paris, 1900), p. 100.

[159] S. Justinus, *Dialogus cum Tryphone*, 100; PG, 6, 710. S. Irenaeus, *Adversus haereses*, 3, 22, 4; *PG*, 7, 958. Also *Adversus haereses*, 5, 19, 1; *PG*, 7, 1175.

[160] *De carne Christi*, 17; *PL*, 2, 827-828.

Remarkable examples can be found in St. Ephraem,[161] St. Ambrose,[162] St. John Chrysostom,[163] St. Augustine,[164] St. Epiphanius,[165] St. Peter Chrysologus,[166] St. Bernard,[167] pseudo-Albert the Great,[168] and St. Bernardine of Siena.[169]

2. Mary Our Spiritual Mother by Her Compassion with Christ on Calvary

If the Incarnation as a basis of Mary's Spiritual Maternity is supported by an ancient and consistent patristic Tradition, as much cannot fully be said of Our Lady's compassion as an argument for her Motherhood of men. It is true that Origen's commentary on the words of Christ's supreme testament can be adduced in support of Mary's maternal dignity, but after him, until the ninth century, no Father that we know of links the Spiritual Maternity with Calvary. From the twelfth century, however, the Tradition is constant to our own day.

Origen (d. 254), in the preface of his commentary on St. John's Gospel, calls the Gospels the first fruits of Scripture, and the fourth Gospel the first fruits of the Gospels. He remarks, moreover, that no one can grasp the meaning of St. John's Gospel "who has not reclined upon the breast of Jesus and has not received from Jesus Mary, who has become his mother also." Origen then goes on to explain the meaning of the words "Behold thy son." "Whoever is perfect," he says, "no longer

---

[161] *S. Ephraem Syri hymni et sermones,* 4 vols., ed. T. J. Lamy (Mechlinae, 1882-1902); Vol. 2, p. 526. See also Keuppens, *op. cit.,* n. 59, p. 168.

[162] *Exhortatio virginitatis,* 4, 26; *PL,* 16, 359. *De obitu Theodosii oratio,* 44-77; *PL,* 16, 1463-1465. *Epistola* 63, 33; *PL,* 16, 1249-1250. *De institutione virginis,* 13, 82; *PL,* 16, 340. Cf. A. Pagnamenta, *La Mariologia di S. Ambrogio* (Milano, 1932), pp. 307-372; E. Vismara, S.S., *Il testamento del Signore nel pensiero di S. Ambrogio e la maternità di Maria SS. verso gli uomini,* in *Salesianum,* Vol. 7, 1945, pp. 7-38, 97-143.

[163] *Expositione in Psalmum* 44:7; *PG,* 55, 193.

[164] *De Agone Christiano,* 22, 24; *PL,* 40, 303. *Sermo 21,* c. 2; *PL,* 38, 335.

[165] *Adversus haereses,* 3, 2; *PG,* 43, 728-729.

[166] *Sermo 140; PL,* 52, 576.

[167] *De laudibus Virginis Mariae, Homilia 2; PL,* 183, 63. *Hom. 2 Super missus est; PL,* 183, 62.

[168] *Mariale,* q. 29; Keuppens, *op. cit.,* n. 258, p. 199.

[169] L. Di Fonzo, *op. cit.,* pp. 42-43.

lives Himself but Christ lives in him. Since Christ lives in him, it is said to Mary of him: 'Behold thy Son, Christ.' "[170]

Origen here identifies the true and perfect Christian with Christ. Though it is true that Mary has but one Son, Our Lord Jesus Christ, St. John is nevertheless identified with Christ, as is also every perfect Christian. In the mind of Origen, St. John does not seem to represent every Christian, but rather every perfect Christian, who has reached the full manhood of Christ in the spiritual life. It is not too clear whether Mary is the Mother of such perfect Christians through their spiritual generation or through adoption. If it were the former, we could extend her Motherhood to all Christians, since even the most lowly possesses inchoatively the life which has reached its fullness in the perfect Christian. As Origen's text stands, however, we cannot definitely say that it proves the universality of Mary's Spiritual Motherhood.

In the ninth century George of Nicomedia (fl. 880) introduces Christ as saying to Mary: "I wish the rest of the disciples likewise to be commended to you through him [John]." To John, Christ says in turn: "Now I constitute her [Mary] as a parent and guide not only of yourself but of the rest of the disciples, and I absolutely wish her to be honored with the prerogative of mother. ... Although I forbade you to call anyone your father on earth, still I wish this mother to be honored and called such by you. ..."[171] There is no indication in this passage as to the basis of Mary's Spiritual Maternity, although it is a testimony of its existence.

Eadmer of Canterbury (d. 1124) follows a line of thought similar to Origen's, only that he extends Mary's Motherhood to all. "O Lady," he writes, "if your Son has become our brother through you, have you not become our Mother through Him? This is what He said to John when He was about to die for us on the cross; to John, I say, who had nothing else than ourselves in the nature of His condition: 'Behold,' he said 'your mother.' O sinful man, rejoice and exult, for there is no reason to despair or to fear; whatever your judgment will be depends entirely upon the sentence of your brother and of your mother. ... Your judge, that is, your brother, has taught you to fly to the aid of His mother, and the same one, your mother, has admonished you to cling faithfully to the protection of

---

[170] *In Evangelium Joannis,* I, Praefatio, 6; *PG*, 14, 32.

[171] *Oratio 8, in sanctissimam Mariam assistentem cruci; PG,* 100, 1476-1477.

the wings of her Son. ..."[172] The significant words in the passage are: "To John ... who had nothing else than ourselves in the nature of His condition." They reflect Origen's identification of Christ and John by reason of the latter's spiritual conformity to the Former. We are Mary's sons because we have in us the image of Christ through the divine life of grace.

With Rupert of Deutz (d. 1135) we are taught that Mary's Spiritual Maternity is linked with Mary's suffering on Calvary as well as with Christ's testamentary utterance. Christ proclaimed Mary John's Mother and ours because she had given birth to us amid the pains of Calvary. "By what right," asks Rupert, "is the disciple whom Jesus loved the son of the mother of the Lord, or she his mother? It is by the fact that she then bore without pain the cause of the salvation of all when she gave birth to God made man from her flesh; and now with great pain she was in labour when, as we have just been told, she stood by His cross. ... Accordingly, because there the Blessed Virgin truly bore pains as of a woman in labour and in the passion of her only-begotten Son gave birth to the salvation of us all, she is clearly the mother of us all. Because then it was said by Him [Christ] of this disciple: 'Woman, behold your son,' most justly did he [John] have the care of his mother. Likewise the words to the disciple, 'Behold your mother,' could rightly be said of any other disciple, if he were present. Although, as we have said, she is the mother of us all, yet more fittingly was she, as a virgin, commended to this virgin."[173]

Gerhoh of Reichersberg (d. 1169) continues in the tradition of Rupert of Deutz. According to him Mary bore us amid the tortures of Calvary. After calling our Lady the "mother of the apostles, to one of whom it was said, 'Behold your mother,'" he continues: "What was said to one could have been said to all the holy apostles, the Fathers of the new Church. Because Christ prayed that all may be one who were to believe through their word, what was said to the one beloved disciple who loved Christ, belongs to all the faithful who love Christ with all their heart. That blessed mother standing by the Cross bore them all when, knowing

---

[172] *De conceptione Beatae Mariae Virginis; PL,* 159, 315.

[173] *Comm. in Evang. Joannis, lib. 12; PL,* 169, 789-790. Cf. C. Audisio, S.D.B., *La missione di Maria Santissima verso gli uomini secondo Ruperto di Deutz* (Torino, 1949).

that her only Son was suffering to liberate and save them, she was in torture, with the sword of compassion piercing her soul, in order to bring them forth. It is not then with a vain hope that we cry to her, not only *Ave Maris stella, Dei mater alma,* but also that which follows: *Monstra te esse matrem;* because of her twofold maternity; one, whereby she bore her only Son without pain; the other, whereby she bore to herself and to the same only Son many sons with great pain and sorrow."[174]

Perhaps no one more fittingly associates Mary's Spiritual Motherhood with her Coredemption than pseudo-Albert the Great. "Inasmuch as she was the cooperator [*adjutrix*] of the redemption by compassion," he writes, "Mary became in this way the mother of all by re-creation." She "bore her firstborn Son without pain in His Nativity; afterwards she bore the whole race simultaneously in the passion of her Son, where she became a helpmate to Him like unto Himself, where as the very mother of mercy she helped the Father of mercies in the highest work of mercy, and together with Him regenerated all men."[175]

We shall not follow the Tradition any further. The testimonies we have quoted represent a long enough period to make us realize that the mind of the Fathers and of the Church during the centuries in which they lived was definitely that Mary is our Spiritual Mother, that she engendered us to the life of grace, both by her consent at Nazareth and by the sorrows she suffered on Calvary. Thus the voice of Tradition, as well as that of Holy Scripture, re-echoes what the Sovereign Pontiffs have taught through the ages in their ordinary Magisterium. All together the documents we have consulted, even though they are but a cross section of a far more voluminous mass of written evidence, are

---

[174] *De gloria et honore Filii hominis,* 10, 1-2; *PL*, 194, 1105.

[175] *Mariale,* q. 148; from Keuppens, n. 257, p. 198. For the translation of most of the patristic texts we are indebted to W. R. O'Connor, *art. cit.,* in *Marian Studies,* Vol. 3, 1952, pp. 142-173. A more detailed treatment of Mary's Spiritual Maternity may be found in Hilarius a S. Agatha, O.C.D., *BB. Virginis Mariae maternitas universalis gratiae in verbis Jesu morientis ...,* in *Teresianum,* December, 1933, pp. 105-151; December, 1934, pp. 194-249; and especially in T. M. Bartolomei, O.S.M., *La maternità spirituale di Maria. Sua realtà e sviluppo, sua natura ed estensione,* in *Divus Thomas* (Pl.), Vol. 55, 1952, pp. 289-357. Cf. also J. M. Canal, C.M.F., *De definibilitate spiritualis Maternitatis B. M. Virginis,* in *Ephemerides Mariologicae,* Vol. 2, 1952, pp. 377-400.

nevertheless an assurance of the validity of the speculation we have presented in our first chapter. May our brief investigation stimulate Mariologists to go ever more deeply into the various phases of this consoling truth.

OUR LADY'S COREDEMPTION

by JUNIPER B. CAROL, O.F.M., S.T.D.

THOSE who are fairly abreast of current Catholic thought scarcely need to be apprised of the importance attached to the problem of Our Lady's Coredemption in contemporary theological literature. They are aware of the fact that during the past twenty-five years particularly, few questions in the vast field of the sacred sciences have engaged the attention of theologians more frequently and absorbingly than the one we are about to discuss. Even the Protestant theologian Giovanni Miegge recognizes this truth when he maintains that Mary's Coredemption is the central and fundamental issue in twentieth-century Mariology.[1] Indeed, considering "the pressure of public opinion," it is easy to foresee that this Marian prerogative will soon be solemnly defined by the Roman Pontiff.[2] If we believe Pierre Maury, another Protestant writer, the Coredemption is not only one of the primary principles of Mariology;[3] in the mind of the Popes and Catholic theologians, it is the very synthesis of the Marian tract.[4]

Despite their exaggerated appraisal, it is obvious that these non-Catholic authors reflect the current doctrinal preoccupations of their Catholic brethren. Be that as it may, it remains true that many dogmatic questions will not be satisfactorily solved nor properly understood until they are solved and understood through a well-focused prism of the fundamental doctrine relative to Our Lady's position in the economy of salvation.

Perhaps it is well to remark at the outset that, in writing this chapter, we make no pretense of either originality or thoroughness. Both are impossible under the circumstances. Our aim is simply to acquaint

---

[1] G. Miegge, *La Vergine Maria; saggio di storia del dogma* (Torre Pellice, 1950), p. 178.
[2] *Ibid.*, p. 194.
[3] P. Maury, *La Vierge Marie dans le catholicisme contemporain*, in *Le Protestantisme et la Vierge Marie*, ed. by Bosc-Bourguet-Maury-Roux (Paris, 1950), pp. 39-40.
[4] *Art. cit.*, p. 57.

English-speaking readers with the result of the many years of study which modern Mariologists have devoted to this complex yet enthralling doctrine. Considering the vastness of the field, our presentation will be, of necessity, somewhat sketchy and superficial.[5] It will follow the usual pattern adopted in similar dissertations, namely: preliminary notions and state of the question; the argument from the Magisterium (Section I); the teaching of Sacred Scripture (Section II); the data of Tradition (Section III); the nature and modalities of the Coredemption (Section IV); difficulties and solutions (Section V).

Preliminary Notions and State of the Question. Since the word "Coredemptrix," by its very definition, designates Our Lady's share in the work of man's supernatural rehabilitation as brought about by Christ, it is obvious that in order to have an accurate understanding of the doctrine expressed by that word, we must first have exact notions concerning the essence of Christ's redemptive work and likewise of the various ways in which Mary may be said to have co-operated therein.

We take the term "Redemption" to mean exclusively the restoring of the human race to the divine friendship lost by sin, in virtue of the meritorious and satisfactory acts which the Saviour performed while still on earth, and which He offered to the Eternal Father with and through His sacrificial death on the cross. The "price" which Christ paid for our ransom from the slavery of Satan was actually the sum total of His merits and satisfactions from the time of the Incarnation until His self-immolation on Calvary. The Eternal Father was so pleased with this price offered by His beloved Son, that He canceled our debt, was reconciled to the human race, and showed Himself ready to grant us again the graces necessary for our salvation. The Redemption just described is called by some *objective* Redemption,[6] by others, Redemption *in actu primo,* and again by others, Redemption *sensu proprio.* The actual

---

[5] For a more detailed treatment, cf. J. B. Carol, O.F.M., *De Corredemptione B. V. Mariae disquisitio positiva* (Civitas Vaticana, 1950).

[6] On this terminology cf. G. M. Roschini, O.S.M., *Equivoci sulla Corredenzione,* in *Marianum,* Vol. 10, 1948, pp. 277-282; J. M. Bover, S.J., *Cooperatio remota in ordine physico ad objectivam Redemptionem,* in *Analecta Sacra Tarraconensia,* Vol. 13, 1940, pp. 5-45; J. B. Carol, *Pater H. Lennerz et problema de Corredemptione mariana,* in *Marianum,* Vol. 2, 1940, pp. 194-200.

application of this Redemption to individual souls is referred to by some modern authors as the *subjective* Redemption (Redemption *in actu secundo;* Redemption *sensu lato*). In this chapter we are directly concerned with the Redemption itself (Redemption in the proper sense) and not with the application of its fruits to individuals.

Speaking in general, there are two ways in which Our Lady may be said to have co-operated in Christ's redemptive work: mediately (indirectly, remotely) and immediately (directly, proximately). Mary co-operated mediately, for example, by meriting some of the circumstances of the Incarnation, and chiefly by giving birth to the world's Saviour. Since Mary knowingly and willingly consented to the coming of Christ with a view to man's Redemption, it is clear that this co-operation of hers was moral and formal, notwithstanding its being mediate.[7] She co-operated immediately if her merits and satisfactions were accepted by Almighty God together with the merits and satisfactions of Christ to bring about the selfsame effect, namely, the restoration of the human race to God's former friendship. Another type of immediate co-operation would be had, for example, if Our Lady had determined Christ (by request, command, counsel, etc.) to perform the work of Redemption, thus directly influencing the Saviour's redemptive acts in themselves. This particular point will call for further observations when we discuss the nature of the Coredemption, under Section IV to follow.

Let us now cast a rapid glance at the various opinions expressed by Catholic[8] theologians in this connection. It is, of course, admitted by all that Our Lady had a *mediate* share in our Redemption inasmuch as she freely consented to become the conscious instrument of the Redeemer's coming by consenting to be His Mother. Furthermore, it is generally granted that Our Lady participated in our Redemption in the sense that, throughout her life, she united her sentiments, prayers, and sufferings

---

[7] Cf. the somewhat different views of J. M. Bover, *Virginis consensus fuitne vera Corredemptio?*, in *Alma Socia Christi,* Vol. 2 (Romae, 1952), pp. 164-176. In this writing we follow the more common practice of using the terms "immediate" and "proximate" interchangeably, although, strictly speaking, they do not mean exactly the same thing. Cf. *Marianum,* Vol. 14, 1952, pp. 62-63; R. M. Gagnebet, O.P., *Questions mariales,* in *Angelicum,* Vol. 22, 1945, p. 169.

[8] Non-Catholics, in general, deny all co-operation, except in the very broad sense that Our Lady gave birth to the world's Redeemer.

to those of her divine Son, desiring to be associated with His saving mission out of love for the human race. But the agreement ceases as soon as theologians endeavor to determine the precise value, efficacy, and extent of that co-operation. A first group, representing the minority, contends that Our Lady's association with the Redeemer, as just described, had no value or efficacy whatever for the Redemption itself (objective Redemption, as they call it), but only for the application of its fruits to individual souls (subjective Redemption, as they say). In other words, the human race was reinstated into the friendship of God in view of the merits and satisfactions of Christ *alone.* Mary, too, had merits and satisfactions of her own, but these merely won for her the right, or quasi right, to become the dispenser of all the graces which flow from the Saviour's redeeming sacrifice. Such is, in its barest outline, the opinion of H. Lennerz, S.J., W. Goossens, G. D. Smith, and several other distinguished theologians and Catholic writers.[9]

A second group, no less distinguished than the first, believes that Our Lady co-operated proximately, directly and immediately, in the Redemption itself (*objective* Redemption) inasmuch as Almighty God was pleased to accept her merits and satisfactions together with those of Christ (although subordinately to them) as having redemptive value for the liberation of mankind from the slavery of Satan and its supernatural rehabilitation. Hence, just as the world was redeemed by Christ, it was also coredeemed by Mary. The difference between the two causalities lies in this, that while Christ's merits and satisfactions were infinite, self-sufficient, and *de condigno ex toto rigore justitiae,* Our Lady's merits and satisfactions were finite, totally dependent upon those of Christ whence they drew all their value, and *de congruo.*[10] Such is the view which we ourselves have consistently upheld and which has the endorsement of the vast majority of Catholic theologians at the present time. Outstanding for their contributions in this connection are Msgr. J. Lebon,

---

[9] H. Lennerz, S.J., *De cooperatione B. Virginis in ipso opere redemptionis,* in Gregorianum, Vol. 28, 1947, pp. 576-597; Vol. 29, 1948, pp. 118-141; W. Goossens, *De cooperatione immediata Matris Redemptoris ad Redemptionem objectivam* (Parisiis, 1939), *passim;* G. D. Smith, *Mary's Part in Our Redemption,* 2nd ed. (New York, 1954), pp. 92-99.

[10] As we shall see later, some say that Mary merited our Redemption not merely *de congruo,* but de condigno ex mera condignitate.

J. M. Bover, S.J., the late Canon J. Bittremieux, C. Dillenschneider, C.Ss.R., C. Friethoff, O.P., P. Sträter, S.J., H. Seiler, S.J., G. M. Roschini, O.S.M., E. Druwé, S.J., and D. Bertetto, S.D.B.[11] In Section IV below we shall have occasion to discuss in greater detail the various ways in which these theologians explain the nature of Mary's Coredemption *sensu proprio*.

Within the past decade a small group of German theologians have undertaken to champion what many consider a "middle-course theory" between the two schools of thought just referred to. Summarized in a few words, their position may be stated as follows: Our Blessed Lord *alone* brought about our reconciliation with God *in actu primo*. This presupposed, Our Lady may be said to have proximately cooperated in the objective Redemption in the sense that she "accepted" the fruits of the Saviour's redemptive sacrifice and made them available to the members of the Church whom she officially represented on Calvary.[12] As the alert reader will observe, this theory does not adopt a true "middle course." While their advocates frequently use the terminology of the

---

[11] J. Lebon, *Comment je conçois, j'établis et je défends la doctrine de la médiation mariale*, in *Ephemerides Theologicae Lovanienses*, Vol. 16, 1939, pp. 655-744; J. M. Bover, *María Mediadora universal, o Soteriología Mariana* (Madrid, 1946), pp. 242-385; J. Bittremieux, *Adnotationes circa doctrinam B. Mariae Virginis Corredemptricis in documentis Romanorum Pontificum*, in *Ephemerides Theologicae Lovanienses*, Vol. 16, 1939, pp. 745-778; C. Dillenschneider, C.SS.R., *Marie au service de notre Rédemption* (Haguenau, 1947), passim; C. Friethoff, O.P., *De alma Socia Christi Mediatoris* (Romae, 1936), p. 53 ff.; P. Sträter, S.J., *Sententia de immediata cooperatione B. M. Virginis ad redemptionem cum aliis doctrinis marianis comparatur*, in *Gregorianum*, Vol. 15, 1944, pp. 9-37; H. Seiler, S.J., *Corredemptrix, Theologische Studie zur Lehre der letzten Päpste über die Miterlöserschaft Mariens* (Rom, 1939), passim; G. M. Roschini, *Mariologia*, 2nd ed., Vol. 2 (Romae, 1947), pp. 251-393; E. Druwé, S.J., *La Médiation universelle de Marie*, in *Maria. Études sur la Sainte Vierge*, ed. by H. du Manoir, S.J., Vol. 1 (Paris, 1949), pp. 410-572; D. Bertetto, S.D.B., *Maria Corredentrice* (Alba, 1951), passim.

[12] Cf. H. M. Köster, S.A.C., *Die Magd der Herrn* (Limburg an der Lahn, 1947), pp. 117-126; id., *Unus Mediator. Gedanken zur marianischen Frage* (Limburg an der Lahn, 1950), *passim*; id., *Die Stellvertretung der Menschheit durch Maria. Ein Systemversuch*, in a symposium of the German Mariological Society, entitled *Die heilsgeschichtliche Stellvertretung der Menschheit durch Maria*, ed. by C. Feckes (Paderborn, 1954), pp. 323-259. Also O. Semmelroth, S.J., *Urbild der Kirche. Organischer Aufbau des Mariengeheimnisses* (Würzburg, 1950), pp. 40-47, 50-51. A new edition of this work, and also of Köster's *Die Magd des Herrn*, has just come off the press (1954).

second group (a clever camouflage), actually their explanation (or destruction?) of Our Lady's Coredemption coincides substantially with that of Professors Lennerz and Goossens.[13]

With the above preliminary remarks in mind, we shall now proceed to give a resume of the arguments which would seem to establish the thesis championed by the theologians of the second group.

I. THE ORDINARY MAGISTERIUM ON MARY'S COREDEMPTION

Under the term "magisterium" we designate the teaching of the Supreme Pontiffs and of the body of bishops in communion with Rome. We refer to it as "ordinary" in contradistinction to the solemn and extraordinary teaching contained in *ex cathedra* pronouncements or conciliar definitions. We are dealing here with less important documents such as encyclical letters, papal allocutions, and the like.[14] As far as doctrinal questions are concerned, the Pope and the bishops, *and they alone*, constitute the authentic and divinely appointed teaching authority here on earth. While God's revelation is objectively preserved in Sacred Scripture and divine Tradition, nevertheless the data found in these sources must always be interpreted according to the mind of the living magisterium. It is only by following the guidance of this "proximate rule of faith" that the faithful can be sure of grasping the genuine sense of the *depositum fidei*. And by "the faithful" we mean, not only the simple, unlettered, ordinary Catholic, but the professional theologians as well, regardless of their learning and official status.

It is only within the past one hundred years that the Popes have turned their attention to the specific phase of Mariology being discussed here. Nevertheless, their repeated statements in this connection are

---

[13] For further details on this point cf. Father Vollert's excellent chapter on *Mary and the Church* in this same volume. Cf. likewise K. Rahner, S.J., *Probleme heutiger Mariologie, in Aus der Theologie der Zeit*, ed. by G. Söhngen (Regensburg, 1948), pp. 85-113, esp. pp. 106-107; C. Dillenschneider, *Le mystère de la Corédemption mariale. Théories nouvelles* (Paris, 1951), pp. 27-90, an extensive refutation of this theory.

[14] Due to space limitation we shall restrict this section to the teaching of the Supreme Pontiffs. Elsewhere we have treated the teaching of the bishops at length. Cf. *De Corredemptione ...*, pp. 539-619.

sufficiently clear and important to deserve separate treatment in this chapter.[15] The series of noteworthy testimonies fittingly opens with Leo XIII (1878-1903) whose numerous Marian encyclicals contributed so much to the recent Mariological movement. In his *Jucunda semper* (1894) Pope Leo states that "when Mary offered herself completely to God together with her Son in the temple, she was already sharing with Him the painful atonement on behalf of the human race ... (at the foot of the cross) she willingly offered Him up to the divine justice, dying with Him in her heart, pierced by the sword of sorrow."[16] A year later he wrote that "she who had been the cooperatrix in the sacrament of man's Redemption, would be likewise the cooperatrix in the dispensation of graces deriving from it."[17] The passage is worth noting because it clearly distinguishes the Redemption itself from its actual application, and points out that Our Lady co-operates in both.

A similar distinction is alluded to in the much-discussed text of the encyclical *Ad diem illum* (1904) of St. Pius X (1903-1914). Here we read: "Owing to the union of suffering and purpose existing between Christ and Mary, she merited to become most worthily the reparatrix of the lost world, and for this reason, the dispenser of all the favors which Jesus acquired for us by His death and His blood." The Pontiff then mentions that Christ is the source of grace, and Mary its channel; hence, far from him to ascribe to her the efficient causality of grace. Then he continues: "Nevertheless, because she surpasses all in holiness and in union with Christ, and because she was chosen by Christ to be His partner in the work of human salvation, she merits for us *de congruo*, as they say, that which Christ merited for us *de condigno*, and she is the principal dispenser of the graces to be distributed."[18] Some theologians, it is true, understand these words as referring exclusively to Our Lady's cooperation in the so-called subjective Redemption; but in all probability those who interpret them in the sense of a true and proper

---

[15] On this subject cf. Crisóstomo de Pamplona, O.F.M.Cap., *La Corredención mariana en el Magisterio de la Iglesia*, in *Estudios Marianos*, Vol. 2, 1943, pp. 89-110; Seiler, *op. cit.*; Bover, *op. cit.*, pp. 445-494; Bittremieux, *art. cit.*; Dillenschneider, *op. cit.*, pp. 45-71.

[16] In *A.S.S.*, Vol. 27, 1894-1895, p. 178.

[17] In *ibid.*, Vol. 28, 1895-1896, pp. 130-131.

[18] In *ibid.*, Vol. 36, 1903-1904, p. 453.

Coredemption (and they are the majority) have captured the genuine meaning of the papal passage.[19]

If some hesitation is conceivable as regards the teaching of Popes Leo and St. Pius, the stand of their successor, Benedict XV (1914-1922), leaves no room for doubt. He was the first Pope to formulate the doctrine of Mary's Coredemption in trenchant and unequivocal terms. His classical text is found in the Apostolic Letter *Inter sodalicia* (1918) and reads in part: "To such extent did (Mary) suffer and almost die with her suffering and dying Son; to such extent did she surrender her maternal rights over her Son for man's salvation, and immolated Him — insofar as she could — in order to appease the justice of God, that we may rightly say she redeemed the human race together with Christ."[20] It is to be noted that the Pope is not reviewing here the various aspects of Our Lady's remote connection with the redemptive work of her Son; the specific manner in which she is said to have redeemed the world with Christ is her direct participation in the Passion, in the sacrificial immolation itself, in order to make satisfaction for the sins of the world.[21]

Remarkable though it is, the above text lacks one thing: the word *Coredemptrix* itself. Benedict's immediate successor, Pius XI (1922-1939), was the first Pope explicitly to apply this title to Our Lady. Perhaps his most important testimony is that found in the prayer with which he solemnly closed the jubilee of our Redemption on April 28, 1935: "O Mother of love and mercy who, when thy sweetest Son was consummating the Redemption of the human race on the altar of the cross, didst stand next to Him, suffering with Him as a Coredemptrix ... preserve in us, we beseech thee, and increase day by day the precious fruit of His redemption and thy compassion."[22] Here Our Lady is styled Coredemptrix, not because she gave birth to the Saviour, but because of her proximate share in the Redemption itself; and the graces which flow

---

[19] Cf. L. Pillet, S.D.B., *La Corredenzione mariana nel magistero del Beato Pio X* (Torino, 1951). L. Di Fonzo, O.F.M.Conv., *B. Virgo "de congruo, ut aiunt, promeret nobis quae Christus de condigno promeruit,"* in *Marianum*, Vol. 1, 1939, pp. 418-459; the author holds that the doctrine is *implicitly* contained in the papal text.

[20] In *A.A.S.*, Vol. 10, 1918, pp. 181-182.

[21] Cf. Lebon, *art. cit.*, pp. 693-702; Seiler, *op. cit.*, pp. 81-86.

[22] In *L'Osservatore Romano*, April 29-30, 1935, p. 1.

from that Redemption are said to be the fruit of a joint causality: the Passion of Christ *and* the compassion of His Mother.[23]

While the present Holy Father, Pius XII, has not as yet employed the term "Coredemptrix" in any of his official documents,[24] nevertheless, his mind on this Marian prerogative is quite clear from several utterances in this connection. For example, in his encyclical *Mystici Corporis* (1943) he writes: "It was she (Mary) who, always most intimately united with her Son, like a New Eve, offered Him up on Golgotha to the Eternal Father, together with the sacrifice of her maternal rights and love, on behalf of all the children of Adam, stained by the latter's shameful fall."[25] In a detailed analysis of this passage, published elsewhere,[26] we have endeavored to establish that it contains a direct reference to Our Lady's Coredemption *sensu proprio*. We see no valid reason for a more restricted interpretation. Again, in his radio broadcast to the pilgrims gathered at Fatima on May 13, 1946, the same Pontiff stated:

> He, the Son of God, reflects on His heavenly Mother the glory, the majesty and the dominion of His kingship; for, having been associated with the King of Martyrs in the ineffable work of human Redemption as Mother and cooperatrix, she remains forever associated with Him, with an almost unlimited power, in the distribution of graces which flow from the Redemption. Jesus is King throughout all eternity by nature and by right of conquest; through Him, with Him and subordinate to Him, Mary is Queen by grace, by divine relationship, by right of conquest and by singular election.[27]

---

[23] For other pertinent statements of this Pope, cf. *L'Osservatore Romano*, November 1, 1933; *A.A.S.*, Vol. 15, 1923, p. 105; Vol. 20, 1928, p. 178. Cf. likewise Roschini, *De Corredemptrice* (Romae, 1939), pp. 34-36.

[24] Cf., however, the words of the Holy Father to A. Carrillo de Albornoz, S J., as reported in the latter's article *La pensée du Pape*, in *Marie*, Vol. 3, March-April, 1950, p. 59.

[25] *A.A.S.*, Vol. 35, 1943, p. 247.

[26] Cf. *Mary's Coredemption in the Teaching of Pius XII*, in *The American Ecclesiastical Review*, Vol. 121, 1949, pp. 353-361.

[27] *A.A.S.*, Vol. 38, 1946, p. 266. Cf. also his recent encyclical *Ad coeli Reginam*, October 11, 1954, N.C.W.C. trans., nn. 36-39. On this point see the remarkable article by W. G. Most, *Coredemption and Queenship* in the *"Ad caeli Reginam,"* in *The American Ecclesiastical Review*, Vol. 133, September, 1955, pp. 171-182. Cf. likewise *Marianum*, Vol. 17, 1955, pp. 334-368.

If, as the Pope points out, Mary's co-operation in the Redemption is the basis for her role in the application of its fruits, the former function cannot possibly be identified with her share in the subjective Redemption; it must refer to the very acquisition of graces, to the Redemption itself. Note also that Our Lady is Queen by right of conquest, which, in the teaching commonly received, means that she is our Queen because she is our Coredemptrix in the proper sense of the word.

Another passage deserving of mention is the one found in the Apostolic Constitution *Munificentissimus Deus* (1950) among the most cogent arguments in favor of the Assumption. It reads: "We must remember especially that, since the second century, the Virgin Mary has been designated by the holy Fathers as the new Eve, who, although subject to the new Adam, is most intimately associated with Him in that struggle against the infernal foe which, as foretold in the Protoevangelium (Gen. 3:15), finally resulted in that most complete victory over sin and death. ..."[28] Since the struggle and victory foretold in *Gen.* 3:15 refer to the work of Redemption,[29] it follows that Our Lady had an intimate share in the latter. Indeed, the purpose of that close association between Christ and His Mother had been specified by the same Pope on another occasion in these significant words: "Are not Jesus and Mary the two sublime loves of the Christian people? Are they not the new Adam and the new Eve whom the tree of the cross unites in sorrow and in love *in order to make satisfaction for the guilt of our first parents in Eden?*"[30]

In view of the above papal testimonies we feel that the thesis of Mary's Coredemption, as understood by the majority of theologians, may well claim the endorsement of the ordinary magisterium, especially as represented by Popes Benedict XV and Pius XII. In our evaluation of these and other papal utterances we must, of course, avoid the excesses of those who either minimize them or exaggerate them unduly. Both

---

[28] *A.A.S.*, Vol. 42, 1950, pp. 768-769.

[29] Cf. *Jn.* 12:31-33; *Col.* 2:14-15; *Hebr.* 2:14-15; *Ench. Bibl.*, n. 334.

[30] Cf. *L'Osservatore Romano,* April 22-23, 1940, p. 1. For various significant statements made by him as Cardinal Pacelli, cf. our article in *The American Ecclesiastical Review*, Vol. 121, 1949, pp. 360-361.

attitudes are reprehensible, particularly the former. While the passages quoted do not in any way constitute infallible pronouncements, nevertheless they should be received with humble respect and religious assent, coming, as they do, from the highest teaching authority in the Church. The Popes are undoubtedly well aware of the fact that their words are interpreted by a large number of theologians as favoring the doctrine of Mary's Coredemption *sensu proprio*. Had they felt that they were being misunderstood, they surely would have used the proper means to correct the error, considering the far-reaching implications of the thesis, and their duty to safeguard the purity of the faith. Yet, not only have they failed to sound a warning, but their statements in this connection have increased in number and emphasis in recent years.[31]

II. THE ARGUMENT FROM SACRED SCRIPTURE

It is common knowledge among Catholics and non-Catholics alike that Sacred Scripture contains no clear and explicit statement to the effect that Our Lady was destined to fulfill a coredemptive mission on behalf of the human race. However, Catholic writers in general agree that this mission is *implied* in the written word of God.[32] This suffices in order to consider any point of doctrine as revealed by God, as forming part of the original deposit of divine revelation.

The first, and indeed the most important, biblical passage generally advanced in support of our thesis is the well-known Protoevangelium, which embodies the promise of a future Redeemer. In striking simplicity the sacred text relates how, after the fall of our first parents in the garden of Eden, Almighty God addressed these words to the tempter disguised under the appearance of a serpent: "I will put enmities between thee and the woman, between thy seed and her seed; he shall crush thy head and thou shalt lie in wait for his heel" (*Gen.* 3:15). The Creator, therefore, is not only going to frustrate the evil designs of His enemy; in His infinite wisdom He plans a particularly humiliating device: to bring about the devil's utter defeat by using certain means

---

[31] Cf. D. Baier, O.F.M., in *Franciscan Studies,* Vol. 2, 1943, pp. 10-11.

[32] Cf. R. Rábanos, C.M., *La Corredención mariana en la Sagrada Escritura,* in *Estudios Marianos,* Vol. 2, 1943, pp. 9-59. Abundant bibliographical references may be found in our work *De Corredemptione...,* pp. 73-121.

which are similar (though in reverse) to those employed by the devil to perpetrate our spiritual ruin. Immediately the question arises: who is that mysterious woman chosen by God to wage a victorious battle against His enemy? The point has been widely discussed from time immemorial, but principally in recent years, in view of the obvious Mariological implications. It is well to bear in mind that the discussion does not center on the second part of the text (which the Vulgate renders: *"she* shall crush thy head ..."), for scholars agree that the original Hebrew read: *"He* (the seed of the woman) shall crush thy head," and hence no strictly biblical argument may be drawn from it in favor of Our Lady. The debate bears directly on the first part of the pericope, namely, on the identity of "the woman" who is at enmity with Satan. While a few interpreters still contend that the reference here is to Eve and Eve alone,[33] the vast majority of Catholic theologians and exegetes hold that "the woman" designates Our Blessed Lady, either in a typical sense[34] or even in a literal sense.[35] In our humble opinion, this latter view is the only one that can possibly be reconciled with the positive data of subsequent revelation, and with the various utterances of the magisterium as found in the *Ineffabilis Deus,*[36] *Munificentissimus Deus,*[37] and *Fulgens corona*[38] Indeed, there are very weighty reasons indicating

---

[33] Cf. A. De Guglielmo, O.F.M., *Mary in the Protoevangelium,* in *Catholic Biblical Quarterly,* Vol. 14, 1952, pp. 104-115; G. Calandra, O.F.M., *Nova Protoevangelii mariologica interpretatio,* in *Antonianum,* Vol. 26, 1951, pp. 343-366.

[34] Cf., among others, F. von Hummelauer, S J., *Commentarius in Genesim* (Parisiis, 1895), p. 161; J. Corluy, *Spicilegium dogmatico-biblicum,* Vol. 1 (Gandavi, 1884), p. 348; E. Mangenot, in *D.T.C.,* Vol. 6, coll. 1208-1212.

[35] Among many others, A. Bea, S.J., *Maria SS. nel Protovangelo (Gen. 3, 15),* in *Marianum,* Vol. 15, 1953, pp. 1-21; J. Prado, *Praelectiones Biblicae; Vetus Testamentum,* Vol. I (Taurini, 1934), pp. 53-54; J. Trinidad, *Quomodo praenuntietur Maria in Gen. 3, 15,* in *Verbum Domini,* Vol. 19, 1939, pp. 353-367.

[36] *Acta et decreta Sacrorum Conciliorum recentiorum. Collectio Lacensis,* Vol. 6 (Friburgi Brisgoviae, 1882), col. 839. Cf. our extensive commentary in *De Corredemptione ...,* pp. 100-121.

[37] *A.A.S.,* Vol. 42, 1950, pp. 768-769. Cf. our commentary *The Apostolic Constitution "Munificentissimus Deus" and Our Blessed Lady's Coredemption,* in *The American Ecclesiastical Review,* Vol. 125, October, 1951, pp. 255-273.

[38] *A.A.S.,* Vol. 45, 1953, p. 579.

that we are dealing here with an *exclusive*-literal Marian sense.[39]

Based on the above interpretation, the argument from the Protoevangelium may be formulated as follows: In the words of *Gen.* 3:15, Almighty God foretells a singular and absolute struggle between Christ and Satan, a struggle which will eventually culminate in the utter defeat of the latter. Since, on the one hand, this struggle-victory coincided with the redemptive work of the Saviour,[40] and on the other hand, Our Lady's struggle is identically the same as Christ's,[41] and she has an intimate share in His complete triumph,[42] it follows that her coredemptive mission is already foreshadowed in the sacred text. The passage itself does not, of course, elaborate on the various modalities of that mission, although the interpretation given by Pope Pius IX in *Ineffabilis Deus* would seem to point to a *direct* co-operation in the Redemption itself.[43]

This close association between the Redeemer and His Mother, foretold in the book of *Genesis*, is strikingly suggested also in several narratives of the New Testament. The Annunciation pericope, for example, with which we are all so familiar, has been discussed quite at

---

[39] Cf. the excellent articles by F. X. Peirce, S.J., *The Woman of Gen. 3, 15*, in *The Ecclesiastical Review*, Vol. 103, 1940, pp. 95-101; *id., Mary Alone is "The Woman" of Genesis 3, 15*, in *The Catholic Biblical Quarterly*, Vol. 2, 1940, pp. 245-252; also the exhaustive book by D. J. Unger, O.F.M.Cap., *The First-Gospel: Genesis 3, 15* (Franciscan Institute, St. Bonaventure, New York, 1954); and the masterly treatment by Eric May, O.F.M.Cap., in *Mary in the Old Testament*, in MARIOLOGY, ed. J. B. Carol, O.F.M., Vol. 1 (Milwaukee, 1954), pp. 63-69.

[40] Cf. above, footnote 29.

[41] Ineffabilis Deus, *in* Acta et Decreta ... ; Collectio Lacensis, *Vol. 6, col. 839.*

[42] *Munificentissimus Deus*, in *A.A.S.*, Vol. 42, 1950, p. 769.

[43] Cf. Carol, *De Corredemptione...*, pp. 112-116. We abstract here from the question as to how Catholic Tradition has interpreted the Protoevangelium. In general, we accept as valid the conclusions of T. Gallus, S.J., in his exhaustive and scholarly works: *Interpretatio mariologica Protoevangelii (Gen. 3, 15) tempore postpatristico usque ad Concilium Tridentinum*(Romae, 1949); *Interpretatio mariologica Protoevangelii posttridentina...*, pars prior: *a Conc. Trid. usque ad annum 1660* (Romae, 1953); pars posterior: *ab anno 1661 usque ad definitionem dogmaticam Immaculatae Conceptionis* (Romae, 1954). As to the patristic period specifically, we recommend the very penetrating study by R. Laurentin, *L'interpretation de Genèse 3, 15 dans la tradition jusqu'au debut du XIIIe siècle*, in Bulletin de la Société Française d'Études Mariales, Vol. 12 (Paris, 1955), pp. 79-156. However, we regret that we have to disagree with the *exegetical* interpretation which the learned author himself adopts on pp. 113-115.

length by Catholic writers in this connection. The scene introduces the Angel Gabriel informing Our Lady of God's economy relative to the coming of the promised Redeemer through her instrumentality. Since Mary has vowed perpetual virginity, she naturally questions the heavenly messenger as to the manner in which the divine decree is to be fulfilled. Being assured that the Incarnation of the Word will be accomplished through a supernatural overshadowing on the part of the Holy Spirit, she humbly surrenders to God's holy designs and answers: "Behold the handmaid of the Lord; be it done unto me according to thy word" (Lk. 1:38).

Interpreted in the light of Christian tradition, this sacred text leads us to the following conclusions: (*a*) that the angel was sent by God, not to impose a command which *had* to be obeyed by Mary regardless of her free choice,[44] but to request her consent to the divine plan; (*b*) that this plan concerned not merely the assumption of a human nature on the part of the Divine Word, but likewise the redemptive role with which the Incarnate Word would be charged; (*c*) that Our Lady gave her consent with adequate (not full) knowledge of what the Saviour's mission entailed;[45] and (*d*) that she gave it most willingly, namely, desiring and intending what God desired and intended to accomplish through the Incarnation. So much can be accepted — and is accepted — by Catholic theologians in general.

From the above we gather that Our Blessed Lady, by the very fact that she uttered her *fiat,* positively co-operated in the initial phase of the world's Redemption. Her *fiat* was not simply a gracious gesture by which she "accepted" the redemptive work of Christ. It was an act of formal participation in the soteriological mystery itself. It was such, not by an absolute necessity, but by a hypothetical necessity, since it was required by the divine Will disposing that Mary should represent

---

[44] On the perfect compatibility of Mary's act of *obedience* with her formal cooperation in the Redemption, cf. the pertinent observations made by Father Roschini, *Mariologia,* 2 ed., Vol. 2, pars prima (Romae, 1947), p. 295.

[45] From the very words of her *Magnificat* we gather that Our Lady must have been familiar with the prophecies concerning the redemptive mission of the future Messias. Cf. the detailed analysis of the text by T. Gallus, Ad *"principium materiale" Redemptionis objectivae,* in *Divus Thomas*(Pl.), Vol. 57, 1954, pp. 246-250. Cf. also Roschini, *La Madonna secondo la fede e la teologia,* Vol. 2 (Roma, 1953), pp. 339-340.

mankind in the supernatural alliance taking place between the Word and the human race.⁴⁶ As things stand, she was not merely a physical instrument, but a formal and official co-agent used by God to carry out His saving scheme.⁴⁷

May we advance a step further and say, with Prof. J. M. Bover and others,⁴⁸ that Mary's initial consent, taken by itself, implies an *immediate* co-operation in the *entire* redemptive work of her Son? Some theologians have raised difficulties against this view, and, obviously, for good reasons. Granted that a co-operation is usually considered remote or proximate, not by reason of its distance in time from the effect, but rather by reason of the amount of influence on the effect.⁴⁹ Nevertheless, this amount of influence may have varying degrees of "directness" and it is this specific circumstance that should be the deciding factor. For this reason we may conceive of a person knowingly and willingly giving his or her (hypothetically necessary) consent so that a certain action may be performed solely by a third party. In which case the effect will be ascribed to the person giving the consent as a moral, formal cause, yet not as an immediate coagent.

Be that as it may, the Annunciation scene is not the last word on our subject. In fact, the Evangelists do not fail to bring out the close association of Mary with her Son on the other two passages bearing directly on His redemptive mission, namely, the incident of the Purification and that of Calvary. In the former, Our Blessed Lady offers her Son to God (a public oblation corresponding to the private oblation she performed at the Incarnation) and hears the aged Simeon prophesy her future share in the Saviour's Passion: "Thine own soul a sword shall pierce."⁵⁰ In the latter, she is publicly proclaimed the spiritual Mother of

---

⁴⁶ Cf. *Summa Theologica*, P. 3, q. 30, a. 1; C. Dillenschneider, *Toute l'Eglise en Marie*, in *Bulletin de la Société Française d'Études Mariales* (Paris, 1953), pp. 111-113.

⁴⁷ H. Barré, C.S.Sp., *Le consentement à l'Incarnation rèdemptrice. La Vierge seule, ou le Christ d'abord?*, in *Marianum*, Vol. 14, 1952, pp. 233-266.

⁴⁸ Bover, *Virginis consensus fuitne vera Corredemptio?* in *Alma Socia Christi*, Vol. 2 (Romae, 1952), pp. 164-176: B. H. Merkelbach, O.P., *Tractatus de Beatissima Virgine Maria Matre Dei atque Deum inter et homines Mediatrice...* (Parisiis, 1939), p. 341.

⁴⁹ Merkelbach, loc. cit.

⁵⁰ Lk. 2:34-35. Cf. Gallus, *De sensu verborum Lc 2, 35 eorumque momento mariologico*, in *Biblica*, Vol. 29, 1948, pp. 220-239.

the human race as she regenerates everyone of us to the life of grace through her bitter compassion. "When Jesus, therefore, had seen his mother and the disciple standing whom he loved, he saith to his mother: Woman, behold thy son. After that, he saith to the disciple: Behold thy mother."[51]

The evangelist does not tell us that Mary was standing at the foot of the cross for the purpose of co-operating with her divine Son in the world's restoration. Nevertheless, his reference to her spiritual Motherhood is quite significant at this particular juncture. That the Saviour's words "Behold thy Mother" must be interpreted as signifying Mary's universal Maternity of grace in a scriptural sense, can scarcely be questioned any longer.[52] The mind of the magisterium on this point,[53] particularly as expressed by Pope Leo XIII,[54] is sufficiently clear to dispel all possible doubts. Now, in the present economy, the spiritual Maternity practically coincides with Our Lady's direct co-operation in the Redemption.[55] Therefore, if — as the Popes tell us — the former was publicly proclaimed by Christ's words on the cross, so was the latter, at least by implication. After all, it was then and there at the foot of the cross that Our Lady was bringing to its natural climax the initial oblation which took place at the Incarnation. It was then and there that she was surrendering her maternal rights on the divine Victim in order to satisfy

---

[51] Jn. 19:26-27. Cf. E. May, *The Scriptural Basis for Mary's Spiritual Maternity,* in *Marian Studies,* Vol. 3, 1952, pp. 125-130; T. Gallus, *art. cit.,* in *Divus Thomas* (Pl.), Vol. 57, 1954, p. 254 ff.

[52] It is still denied, however, by W. Newton, *A Commentary on the New Testament* (Catholic Biblical Association of America, 1942), p. 357; F. Ceuppens, O.P., *De Mariologia Biblica,* ed. 2 (Taurini, 1951), pp. 192-202, and several others. Cf. M. J. Gruenthaner, S.J., *Mary in the New Testament,* in Mariology, ed. J. B. Carol, O.F.M., Vol. 1 (Mediatrix Press), p. 116.

[53] Cf. especially Msgr. G. W. Shea, *The Teaching of the Magisterium on Mary's Spiritual Maternity,* in *Marian Studies,* Vol. 3, 1952, pp. 68-69, 92-93.

[54] Encyclical *Adjutricem populi* (September 5, 1895), in A. Tondini, *Le encicliche mariane,* ed. 2 (Roma, 1954), p. 222.

[55] Cf. W. Sebastian, O.F.M., *The Nature of Mary's Spiritual Maternity,* in *Marian Studies,* Vol. 3, 1952, pp. 14-34; M. Llamera, O.P., *La maternidad espiritual de María,* in *Estudios Marianos,* Vol. 3 (Madrid, 1944), pp. 67-162; Gregorio de Jesús Crucificado, O.C.D., *Naturaleza de la maternidad espiritual de María,* in *Estudios Marianos,* Vol. 7 (Madrid, 1948), pp. 124-144.

for the sins of mankind.[56] It was then and there that she was officially sharing the immolation of the Redeemer precisely in order to regenerate the human race to the life of grace together with Him and under Him.[57] Bearing this set of circumstances in mind, we are almost compelled to see in the brief but pregnant Johannine passage an implied reference to Our Blessed Lady's role as Coredemptrix of mankind.[58]

To sum up: all things considered, Sacred Scripture is far from being silent on the thesis of Mary's direct share in the Saviour's soteriological mission. Exegetes and theologians may continue to debate over the precise value of specific texts, but the content of all pertinent passages combined, especially when interpreted in the light of recent papal pronouncements, does lend considerable support to the doctrine in question.

III. THE TEACHING OF TRADITION

The doctrine of Our Lady's Coredemption is generally referred to as "traditional" in the Catholic Church. If by that is meant that this thesis, as we profess it today, has been taught in the Church from the beginning, the claim is hardly acceptable, for reasons to be indicated shortly. Nevertheless, since the teaching of contemporary theologians on this matter is but a further elaboration of what has been handed down from the beginning, under the guidance of the Holy Spirit, we are justified in considering that teaching as "traditional" or based on Tradition.

In order to follow the gradual development of the doctrine through the centuries, we shall divide this treatment in three sections corresponding to the three following periods: (*a*) the patristic period, that is, from the beginning to the eighth century; (*b*) the middle ages,

---

[56] Benedict XV, *Inter sodalicia*, in *A.A.S.*, Vol. 10, 1918, pp. 181-182; Pius XII, *Mystici Corporis*, in *A.A.S.*, Vol. 35, 1943, p. 247.

[57] Cf. Leo XIII, encyclical *Jucunda semper* (September 8, 1894), in *A.S.S.*, Vol. 27, 1894-1895, p. 178; Pius XII, in *L'Osservatore Romano*, April 22-23, 1940, p. 1.

[58] Cf. T. Gallus, "*Mulier, ecce filius tuus*" (*Jo. 19, 26*), in *Verbum Domini*, Vol. 21, 1941, pp. 289-297, esp. p. 296. Cf. also F.-M. Braun, O.P., *Eve et Marie dans les deux Testaments*, in *Bulletin de la Société Française d'Études Mariales*, Vol. 12 (Paris, 1955), pp. 9-34, esp. pp. 30-34.

from the ninth to the seventeenth centuries; and (c) the modern period, from the seventeenth century to the present time.

A. The Patristic Period

One of the most ancient doctrinal portraits of Our Blessed Lady is unquestionably that which represents her as the New Eve or Second Eve, next to the New or Second Adam. The implied doctrine has two phases, according to whether it is used as a parallel or as an antithesis. In the first case, Mary is compared with the first woman before the fall, and the comparison points to her sinlessness and especially her virginity. In the second case, Mary is set in contrast to Eve after the fall, and then the emphasis is placed on her unique position in the economy of salvation. The second aspect alone is of interest to us here. Briefly formulated, the antithesis amounts to this: Just as Eve shared Adam's responsibility in the process of original prevarication, so likewise Mary was instrumental with Christ in the reparation of the initial fall.

That this distinctive feature of Our Lady's mission was widely accepted throughout the patristic era is admitted by all Catholic theologians and historians at the present time. Hence, we may be dispensed from the burdensome task of offering here a more or less complete anthology of pertinent ancient texts.[59] The problem which divides modern scholars concerns rather the precise interpretation to be given to these numerous texts. The classical testimony of St. Irenaeus (d. c. 202), which we will now examine, may well serve as a typical example. Our discussion concerning him applies equally to all others, since the basic idea they express is substantially one and the same.[60]

The celebrated bishop of Lyons summarizes the antithetical parallelism as follows: "Just as she (Eve) ... having disobeyed, became the

---

[59] Abundant patristic quotations on this theme may be found in J. M. Bover, *La Mediación universal de la "Segunda Eva" en la tradición patrística*, in *Estudios Eclesiásticos*, Vol. 2, 1923, pp. 321-350; id., *B. V. Maria, hominum Corredemptrix*, in *Gregorianum*, Vol. 6, 1925, pp. 544-559; J. Bittremieux, *De Mediatione universali B. M. Virginis quoad gratias* (Brugis, 1926), lib. 1, *passim*.

[60] St. Irenaeus was not, of course, the first to use the "Eve-Mary" antithesis. Cf. St. Justin Martyr (d. c. 165), in *Dial. cum Tryphone*, c. 100; *PG*, 6, 709. The theory that the former actually depended on the latter has not as yet been proved.

cause of death to herself and to the entire human race, so Mary ... being obedient (to the angel's message), became the cause of salvation to herself and to the entire human race. ... Thus the knot of Eve's disobedience received (its) unloosing through the obedience of Mary. For what the virgin Eve bound by unbelief, that the virgin Mary unfastened by faith."[61]

Even a cursory analysis of the above passage will not fail to disclose that St. Irenaeus is therein comparing not only the virginity of Eve (something purely personal) with the virginity of Mary, but also, by way of contrast, the evil effect of Eve's action with the salutary effect of Mary's positive causality. Moreover, the manner in which Mary exercises her causality is not merely by being the Mother of the Redeemer, but by freely consenting, in humble obedience, to the designs of God as expressed by the angel. Hence we are dealing here, not with an exclusive causality of a physical nature, as Prof. Lennerz contends,[62] but with a formal co-operation in the moral order. Indeed, since the object of that obedient consent was the redemptive Incarnation itself, it follows that Our Lady's cooperation had a soteriological character and value. All this may be gathered from the words of the Saint without doing any violence to them.

Nevertheless, it should be borne in mind that, in the teaching of St. Irenaeus, the Incarnation was "redemptive" only in the sense that, by assuming a human nature, the God-Man was thereby "summing up" the human race in Himself, thus being capable of carrying out our reconciliation by theandric acts which actually followed the Incarnation itself. In other words, the Incarnation was the initial phase of the Redemption.[63] That Mary had a very definite role to play in that initial

---

[61] *Adv. haer.*, lib. 3, cap. 22, 4; *PG*, 7, 959. The same idea is repeated in lib. 5, cap. 19, 1; *PG*, 7, 1175; and in his *Demonstratio praedicationis apostolicae*, n. 33, in *Patrologia Orientalis*, ed. Graffin-Nau, Vol. 12 (Paris, 1919), pp. 772-773. Cf. the excellent study by N. Moholy, O.F.M., *St. Irenaeus: The Father of Mariology*, in *Studia Mariana*, Vol. 7 (Burlington, Wis., 1952), pp. 129-187, esp. pp. 151-172; also G. Jouassard, *La Nouvelle Eve chez les Pères anténicéens*, in *Bulletin de la Société Française d'Études Mariales*, Vol. 12 (Paris, 1955), pp. 35-54; *id.*, *La théologie mariale de saint Irénée*, in *Congrès Marial de Lyon* (Lyon, 1955), pp. 265-276.

[62] H. Lennerz, *De Beata Virgine*, ed. 3 (Romae, 1939), p. 132.

[63] Cf. *Adv. haer.*, lib. 5, cap. 17; *PG*, 7, 1169; lib. 3, cap. 21; *PG*, 7, 953.

phase is tersely declared by the author, and in this sense he styles her "the cause of salvation." Beyond that, the Bishop of Lyons does not specify; nor, for that matter, do the other Fathers who employ the Eve-Mary antithesis.[64] For this very reason we do not share the views of those who believe that the passage in question clearly points to Mary's *immediate* co-operation in the Redemption itself.[65]

The claim is sometimes made that, beyond comparing Mary with Eve, many Fathers and early Christian writers ascribe the various effects of the Redemption to Our Lady. Such an attribution, it is maintained, would hardly be justified if the Fathers had in mind only a remote causality on the part of Mary, just as one would not be justified in attributing the discovery of the American continent to Columbus' mother, simply because she had given birth to him.

We answer that if the testimonies of the Fathers are read in their proper context and in the light of parallel passages, they are found to ascribe the effects of the Redemption to Our Lady either because of her instrumentality in the Incarnation or because of her actual intercession in heaven, as we have shown elsewhere in detail.[66] As to the example of Columbus' mother, we fail to see the parity. The discovery of America can in no way be predicated of her because there was no internal nexus between the act of giving birth to Columbus and the future feat accomplished by him. The Incarnation, on the contrary, was the very beginning of our Redemption; it was redemptive in the sense explained above. Since Our Lady had formally co-operated therein, the early writers were amply justified in ascribing to her the work of Redemption *in globo*, regardless of what they thought concerning Mary's causality in the soteriological acts which followed the Incarnation and which, *per modum unius* with the sacrifice of Calvary, constituted our objective reconciliation with God.

---

[64] Cf. the excellent papers by B. Capelle, O.S.B., *Le thème de la Nouvelle Eve chez les anciens docteurs latins*, in *Bulletin de la Société Française d'Études Mariales*, Vol. 12 (Paris, 1955), pp. 55-76; and by Th. Camelot, O.P., *Marie, la Nouvelle Eve, dans la patristique grecque du Concile de Nicée à saint Jean Damascène*, ibid., pp. 157-172.

[65] Bover, *Concepto integral de la Maternidad divina según los Padres de Efeso*, in *Analecta Sacra Tarraconensia*, Vol. 7, 1931, p. 157; Lebon, art. cit., in *Ephemerides Theologicae Lovanienses*, Vol. 16, 1939, pp. 655-744, passim.

[66] Cf. Carol, *De Corredemptione ...*, pp. 140-142.

Perhaps the following example will serve to illustrate the point. Let us suppose that the coming of a certain doctor to a hospital is strictly necessary to save a patient who would certainly die unless an operation were performed on him. Let us suppose, furthermore, that the doctor refuses to go to the hospital without his wife's consent. The latter, ardently desiring the patient's health, gladly acquiesces. The operation is performed and the patient at once recover

It is evident that the wife formally and efficaciously contributed to the patient's recovery; he owes his subsequent health to her. And yet, she did not directly and immediately co-operate in the surgical operation itself, as performed by her husband. In our humble opinion, this is the type of co-operation which the Fathers and early writers ascribe to Our Lady in the process of man's rehabilitation. It is one thing to say that Mary's immediate co-operation in the Redemption itself is *implied* in, or *deduced* from, the teaching of the Fathers; it is another thing to assert that the Fathers themselves perceived this type of co-operation. The former is perfectly legitimate; the latter is quite unwarranted. The complex doctrine relative to Mary's role as the Second Eve contains, as in germ, many aspects to which the ancient writers simply did not advert. It was left to subsequent generations to arrive gradually at these aspects by way of analysis and/or deduction.[67]

B. THE MIDDLE AGES

The period which we designate here as the Middle Ages extends roughly from the ninth to the sixteenth century and may well be considered a transition period as regards our doctrine. It is during this time that theologians and Catholic writers in general, under the influence of SS. Bernard and Bonaventure, and particularly of pseudo-Albert the Great and Arnold of Chartres, begin to turn their attention to the properly soteriological character of Our Lady's association with the

---

[67] Cf. L. J. Riley, *Historical Conspectus of the Doctrine of Mary's Coredemption*, in *Marian Studies*, Vol. 2, 1951, pp. 46-47. The eminent patrologist Burghardt has recently endorsed the same sober conclusion (cf. *art. cit.*, pp. 128-129).

Saviour of mankind.[68]

As it was to be expected, we still find during this period (especially at the beginning) not a few authors who, at first sight, seem to be very explicit on the question of Mary's Coredemption, but who, upon closer examination, do nothing but repeat what their predecessors had taught. Among these we may mention St. Tarasius (fl. 807), St. George of Nicomedia (fl. 880), Alcuin (d. 904), and Eadmer of Canterbury (d. 1124) who, incidentally, seems to be the first to mention Mary's *merit* in connection with man's Redemption.[69]

With St. Bernard of Clairvaux (d. 1153) we take a definite step forward. It is in his writings that we hear, for the first time, of Our Lady's satisfaction for the damage caused by Eve,[70] although the context would indicate only a remote co-operation in our Redemption. His importance lies rather in the fact that he introduced the idea of Our Lady's offering the divine Victim in the temple for our reconciliation with God; an offering which, according to him, was accepted by the Eternal Father.[71] This idea was taken up and elaborated by his disciple, Arnold of Chartres (d. 1160), who may well be acknowledged as the first clear exponent of Our Lady's Coredemption. On Calvary, he writes, Christ and Mary "together accomplished the task of man's Redemption ... both offered up one and the same sacrifice to God: she in the blood of her heart (i.e., through her compassion), He in the blood of the flesh ... so that, together with Christ, she obtains a *common effect* in the salvation of the world."[72] The great influence of Arnold's remarkable

---

[68] For this period cf. particularly M. Müller, O.F.M., *Maria. Ihre geistige Gestalt und Persönlichkeit in der Theologie des Mittelalters,* in *Katholische Marienkunde,* ed. P. Sträter, S.J., Vol. 1 (Paderborn, 1947), pp. 282-295; C. Dillenschneider, *Marie au service de notre Rédemption* (Haguenau, 1947), pp. 201-267; E. Druwé, *art. cit.,* pp. 498-517; G. W. Shea, *Outline History of Mariology in the Middle Ages and Modern Times,* in MARIOLOGY, ed. Carol, Vol. 1 (Milwaukee, 1954), pp. 389-417.

[69] S. Tarasius, *PG,* 98, 1491-1492; George of Nicomedia, *PG,* 100, 1451; Alcuin, *PL,* 101, 1300 (this particular homily is not authentic); Eadmer, *PL,* 159, 573 and 578.

[70] St. Bernard, *Hom. 2 super Missus est; PL,* 183, 62.

[71] *Serm. 3 de Purificatione; PL,* 183, 370. On this point cf. R. Laurentin, *Maria, Ecclesia, Sacerdotium: Essai sur le développement d'une idée religieuse* (Paris, 1952), pp. 140-145.

[72] Arnold of Chartres, *De laudibus B. Mariae Virginis; PL,* 189, 1726-1727. Cf. Carol, *De Corredemptione ...,* pp. 156-159; Bertetto, *op. cit.,* pp. 51-55.

teaching is easily gathered from the innumerable authors of subsequent centuries who explicitly quote him approvingly on this matter.

Likewise deserving of mention in the history of this development are St. Albert the Great (d. 1280) and St. Bonaventure (d. 1274).[73] The noteworthy contribution of the Universal Doctor would seem to lie in his insistence that the *principium consortii* outlined by the Fathers be extended to the entire process of man's Redemption;[74] while it was left to the Seraphic Doctor to draw the only logical conclusion by pointing out that on Calvary Our Lady co-offered the divine Victim,[75] satisfied for our sins,[76] and paid the price of our Redemption.[77] The famous *Mariale*, until recently attributed to St. Albert, but written probably at the beginning of the following century,[78] frequently and forcibly echoes Bonaventure's far-reaching intuitions,[79] particularly as regards Our Lady's share in the redemptive merit of the passion.[80] In clearness of expression, however, all these authors were far surpassed by the great Dominican mystic-theologian, Blessed John Tauler (d. 1361). According to him, Mary offered herself, together with her Son, as a living victim for

---

[73] On St. Albert cf. M.-M. Desmarais, O.P., *St. Albert le Grand, docteur de la Médiation mariale* (Paris-Ottawa, 1935), bearing in mind the discovery to be mentioned below in footnote 78. On St. Bonaventure, cf. L. Di Fonzo, O.F.M.Conv., *Doctrina S. Bonaventurae de universali Mediatione B. V. Mariae* (Romae, 1935), and E. Chiettini, O.F.M., *Mariologia S. Bonaventurae* (Romae, 1942), pp. 44-75.

[74] *Comment. in Matth.*, 1, 18; *op. omn.*, ed. Borgnet, Vol. 20 (Parisiis, 1898), p. 36.

[75] St. Bonaventure, *Collatio 6 de donis Spiritus Sancti*, n. 17; *op. omn.* (Ad Claras Aquas, 1882-1902), Vol. 5, p. 486.

[76] *Ibid.*, n. 16.

[77] *Ibid.*, n. 15, also n. 5; *op. omn.*, Vol. 5, p. 484.

[78] The revolutionary discovery was made recently by Albert Fries, C.SS.R., whose extensive research on this question has been embodied in his book *Die unter dem Namen des Albertus Magnus überlieferten mariologischen Schriften* (Münster Westf., 1954). Bruno Korošak, O.F.M., who studied the problem independently of Fr. Fries, arrived at the same conclusion, but believes that the *Mariale* was written during the second half of the thirteenth century. Cf. his erudite book *Mariologia S. Alberti Magni ejusque coaequalium* (Romae, 1954), pp. 18 and 611, n. 4.

[79] Pseudo-Albert, *Mariale*, q. 42; *op. omn.*, Vol. 37, p. 80; q. 148; *op. omn.*, Vol. 37, p. 214.

[80] *Mariale*, q. 150; *op. omn.*, Vol. 37, p. 219. Cf. Laurentin, *Maria, Ecclesia, Sacerdotium ...*, pp. 183-194.

the salvation of all;[81] furthermore, "God accepted her oblation (on Calvary) as a pleasing sacrifice, for the utility and salvation of the whole human race ... so that, through the merit of her sorrows, she might change God's anger into mercy."[82] A little further he thus addresses Our Lady: "(At the foot of the cross), filled with sorrow, thou hast redeemed men together with thy Son."[83]

It is about this time that the ideas expressed above begin to be reflected with amazing limpidity in some liturgical hymns. And it is interesting to note that the term "Coredemptrix" is now making its appearance, perhaps for the first time in history.[84] The following excerpts will suffice:

> Pia, dulcis et benigna
> Nullo prorsus luctu digna,
> Si fletum hinc eligeres
> Ut compassa Redemptori
> Tu *Corredemptrix* fieres.[85]

> Laus Patri necnon Filio
> Sancto simul Paraclito
> Pro poenis matris et nati
> Quibus sumus reparati.[86]

---

[81] J. Tauler, *Sermo pro festo Purificat. B. M. Virginis; Oeuvres complètes*, ed. E.-P. Noël, Vol. 5 (Paris, 1911), p. 61.

[82] *Op. cit.*, Vol. 6, pp. 253-255.

[83] *Ibid.*, p. 256.

[84] In our work *De Corredemptione* ..., pp. 172-174, we stated that, to our knowledge, the two oldest witnesses to the term "Coredemptrix" were the anonymous *Tract. de praeservatione gloriosae V. Mariae* (written before 1323), and Alanus Varenius, who lived in the fourteenth century. The first attribution was actually an erroneous assumption on our part, based on Holzapfel's *Bibl. Franc. de Imm. Conc.* (Ad Claras Aquas, 1904); the second was based on a mistaken chronology furnished by Alva y Astorga's *Bibl. virg. Mariae*, Vol. 3 (Matriti, 1684), p. 505. We are most grateful to R. Laurentin who, in his characteristic scholarly fashion, has recently corrected our error. Cf. *Le titre de Corédemptrice. Etude historique*, in *Marianum*, Vol. 13, 1951, pp. 399-402.

[85] *Orationale of St. Peter's in Salzburg* (fourteenth-fifteenth century). In Dreves-Blume, *Analecta hymnica medii aevi*, Vol. 46, n. 79, pp. 126-127. Cf. Serapio de Iragui, O.F.M.Cap., *La Mediación de la Virgen en la himnografía latina de la Edad Media* (Buenos Aires, 1939), p. 173.

[86] *Orationale*; Dreves-Blume, *op. cit.*, Vol. 52, n. 51, p. 57; Serapio de Iragui, *op. cit.*, p. 166.

> Sit Trinitati gloria
> Pro redemptionis venia
> *Quam meruerunt miseris*
> *Filius et mater nobis.*[87]

As to the fifteenth century, its contribution to the evolution of our doctrine was virtually nonexistent. With the exception of St. Antonine of Florence, who repeats and somewhat elaborates the excellent ideas of pseudo-Albert,[88] the several Marian writers of this period, while emphasizing Mary's compassion on Calvary, are rather vague and ambiguous as to the nature and extent of that co-operation.[89] Something similar may be said, in general, concerning the authors of the sixteenth century. The two notable exceptions here would be Archbishop Ambrose Catarino, O.P. (d. 1553), and the eminent theologian of the Council of Trent, Alphonsus Salmerón, S.J. (d. 1585). The former trenchantly states that Our Blessed Lord and His Mother, taking upon themselves the sins of the world, merited our Redemption through their joint sufferings;[90] according to the latter, it was the will of the Saviour that His holy Mother, as a Coredemptrix, should have a share in His redeeming power; for this reason our Redemption proceeded actually from both: Christ and Mary.[91] As to Francis Suárez (d. 1617), who is sometimes styled "the father of modern Mariology," it is obvious that his stand on the Coredemption thesis does not approach, in perspicuity of expression, that of his illustrious confrère Salmerón. However, it must be noted in

---

[87] Cf. *Serapio de Iragui, op. cit.*, p. 165.

[88] St. Antonine, *Summa Theologica*, pars 4, tit. 15, cap. 20, paragr. 14 (ed. Veronae, 1740), p. 1064. Cf. also cap. 14, paragr. 2, p. 1002.

[89] Among these we may mention John Gerson (d. 1429), St. Bernardine of Siena (d. 1444), and Denis the Carthusian (d. 1471). On these authors cf. Bover, *Universalis B. M. Virginis mediatio in scriptis Johannis Gerson*, in *Gregorianum*, Vol. 9, 1928, pp. 254-259; L. Di Fonzo, *La Mariologia di S. Bernardino da Siena* (Romae, 1947), pp. 30-44; Dillenschneider, *op. cit.*, pp. 214-218.

[90] A. Catarino, *De Immaculata Conceptione Virginis Mariae opusculum*, disp. lib. 3, persuasio 14; ed. Alva y Astorga, *Bibliotheca virginalis Mariae ...*, Vol. 2 (Matriti, 1648), p. 56. Cf. also pp. 47-48.

[91] A. Salmerón, *Commentarii in evangelicam historiam et in Acta Apostolorum*, tract. 41; Vol. 10 (Coloniae Agrippinae, 1604), p. 339. Other texts may be found in M. Andreas, *La compasión de la Virgen al pie de la cruz, deducida de su triple gracia, según Salmerón*, in *Estudios Marianos*, Vol. 5, 1946, pp. 359-388.

all fairness that he was the first to discuss our subject *ex professo* in a strictly theological commentary.[92]

C. The Modern Period

If clear-cut and categorical statements like those of Tauler and Catarino were exceptional in the fourteenth and sixteenth centuries respectively, they became more and more common in the period immediately following. Indeed, the seventeenth century may well be considered the "Golden Age" of Mary's Coredemption. It is with the theologians of this epoch that the doctrine of Mary's direct co-operation in the Redemption reaches its fullest development; and this to such extent that subsequent generations can scarcely be said to have contributed any new element of importance in this connection.

Since the available data are so numerous and varied,[93] it seems preferable to group them under appropriate headings, giving their doctrinal content after the manner of a systematic synthesis. These headings will correspond to the various aspects under which Our Lady's prerogative is generally studied by theologians, namely: merit, satisfaction, sacrifice, and ransom or redemptive price.

a) Merit. From some of the testimonies previously recorded we gather that the explicit teaching regarding Our Lady's coredemptive merit dates back to at least the fourteenth century. By the middle of the seventeenth century the doctrine had become almost a theological axiom and was formulated as follows: the Blessed Virgin merited for us *de congruo* that which Christ merited for us *de condigno*.

Perhaps the first theologian to exploit the above axiom was the Jesuit

---

[92] F. Suárez, *De mysteriis vitae Christi*, disp. 23, sect. 1, n. 4; *op. omn.*, Vol. 19 (Parisiis, 1860), p. 331. Cf. Bover, *Suárez Mariólogo*, in *Estudios Eclesiásticos*, Vol. 22, 1948, pp. 311-337, esp. pp. 323-334; J. A. de Aldama, S.J., *Piété et système dans la Mariologie du "Doctor Eximius,"* in *Maria. Études sur la Sainte Vierge*, ed. H. du Manoir, Vol. 2 (Paris, 1952), pp. 977-990; id., *Un resumen de la primera Mariología del P. Francisco Suárez*, in *Archivo Teológico Granadino*, Vol. 15, 1952, pp. 293-337.

[93] In our book *De Corredemptione...*, pp. 198-480, we were able to gather well over three hundred testimonies from this period alone. The list may now be enhanced by the many texts recently discovered and published by René Laurentin in his remarkable work *Maria, Ecclesia, Sacerdotium* (Paris, 1952), and in his very erudite article *Le titre de Corédemptrice...*, in *Marianum*, Vol. 13, 1951, pp. 396-452.

Ferdinand de Salazar (d. 1646) in his *Expositio in Proverbia Salomonis*, published in Cologne in the year 1618.[94] He was soon followed by Roderick de Portillo, O.F.M., who, in 1630 tersely remarked: "... There is no doubt that (at the foot of the cross) the Blessed Virgin merited *the same thing* which her Son merited."[95] Only a few years later (1646) the controversial Angelus Vulpes, O.F.M.Conv., would echo Portillo with the declaration that it was through the merits of Christ *and* Mary that God had decreed to redeem mankind from the slavery of Satan.[96] By the year 1659 the Franciscan bishop of Acerno, Francis Guerra, could calmly refer to this doctrine as "the common opinion of theologians."[97] In partial support of this rather ambitious claim, we could quote here, among others, the Franciscans Van Hondeghem, Urrutigoyti, and Wadding;[98] the Augustinian Bartholomew de los Rios; the Dominican Dassier;[99] and the Jesuits Poiré, de Vega, de Rhodes, de Convelt, and Reichenberger.[100]

---

[94] F. Q. de Salazar, *Expositio in Prov. Salomonis*, cap. 8 (Coloniae Agrippinae, 1618). Text and commentary in Carol, *op. cit.*, pp. 232-234; cf. also the extensive and valuable treatment given in Laurentin, *op. cit.*, pp. 232-304. Cf. likewise De Salazar's *Pro Immaculata Deiparae Virginis Conceptione defensio*, cap. 21 (Compluti, 1618), pp. 132-133.

[95] R. de Portillo, *Libro de los tratados de Cristo Señor nuestro, y de su santísima Madre, y de los beneficios y mercedes que goza el mundo por su medio* (Tauri, 1630), p. 41.

[96] A. Vulpes (Volpe), *Sacrae Theologiae Summa Joannis D. Scoti, Doctoris Subtilissimi, et Commentaria*, Vol. 3, pars 4a (Neapoli, 1646), p. 450. Cf. Carol, *De Corredemptione ...*, pp. 205-207.

[97] F. de Guerra, *Majestas gratiarum ac virtutum omnium Deiparae Virginis Mariae*, Vol. 2 (Hispali, 1659), lib. 3, disc. 4, fragm. 10, n. 36.

[98] F. Van Hondeghem, *Domus propitiationis pauperis, sive Patrocinium Mariae Deiparae* (Bruxellis, 1655), pp. 320-321; Th. F. Urrutigoyti, *Certamen scholasticum, expositivum argumentum pro Deipara* (Lugduni, 1660), p. 544; L. Wadding, *De Redemptione Beatae Mariae Virginis* (Romae, 1656), p. 327.

[99] B. de los Rios, *De Hierarchia Mariana libri sex* (Antverpiae, 1641), p. 67; L. Dassier, *L'Evangile de la grâce, our Sermons sur les mystères et dévotions de la Sainte Vierge* (Lyon, 1685), p. 370.

[100] Francis Poiré, *La triple couronne de la bienheureuse Vierge Mère de Dieu*, ed. 4, Vol. 2 (Le Mans-Paris, 1849), pp. 264-265; Christopher de Vega, *Theologia Mariana*, Vol. 2 (ed. Neapoli, 1866), pp. 442-443, n. 1774; George de Rhodes, *Disputationes Theologiae Scholasticae ...*, Vol. 2: *De Deipara Virgine Maria* (Lugduni, 1676), pp. 265-266; Martin de Convelt, *Theatrum excellentiarum SS. Deiparae ex consociatione excellentiarum sui Filii*, Vol. 2 (Antverpiae, 1655), p. 491; cf. also pp. 528-530; Maximillian Reichenberger, *Mariani cultus vindiciae ...* (Pragae, 1677), p. 120.

450 Mariology

The last author mentioned, an erudite professor of the University of Prague, penned a lengthy and vigorous refutation of the unorthodox brochure *Monita salutaria B. V. Mariae ad devotos suos indiscretos*, in which the author, Adam Widenfeld, had questioned Mary's prerogative.[101]

Despite its Mariological deficiencies, the eighteenth century also yields some unequivocal testimonies in this connection, such as are found in the works of Van Ketwigh, the prolific Montalbanus, Nasi, Galiffet, del Moral, and Lossada.[102] With the exception of the last two, there is little originality in these authors. They seem to be satisfied with re-echoing the acquisitions of the past.

As to the nineteenth century, it would be comparatively easy to multiply the number of favorable witnesses. Perhaps the most influential are Castelplanio, Scheeben, Herrmann, R. de la Broise, Depoix, Faber, and Pradié.[103] All these authors, and many of their tributaries,

---

[101] A. Widenfeld, *Monita salutaria* ... (Gandavi, 1673), monita 9-10; English edition by J. Taylor, *Wholesome Advices from the Blessed Virgin to her Indiscreet Worshippers* (London, 1687), p. 8. On Widenfeld's teaching, and on the controversy aroused by his pamphlet, cf. Carol, *De Corredemptione* ..., pp. 302-318, E. Böminghaus, *Geschichte der Marienverehrung seit dem Tridentinum*, in *Katholische Marienkunde*, ed. P. Sträter, Vol. 2 (Paderborn, 1947), pp. 347-355, and esp. P. Hoffer, S.M., *La dévotion à Marie au déclin du XVIIe siècle, autour du Jansénisme et des "Avis salutaires de la B. V. Marie à ses dévots indiscrets"* (Paris, 1938).

[102] J. B. Van Ketwigh, O.P., *Panoplia Mariana* (Antverpiae, 1720), p. 106; S. Montalbanus, O.F.M.Cap., *Opus theologicum tribus distinctum tomis in quibus efficacissime ostenditur Immaculatam Dei Genitricem, utpote ex Christi meritis praeservative redemptam, fuisse prorsus immunem ab omni debito* ..., Vol. 2 (Panormi, 1723), p. 393, n. 603; G. A. Nasi, *Le grandezze di Maria Vergine* ... (Venezia, 1717), pp. 204, 229-250; J. de Galiffet, S.J., *L'excellence et la pratique de la dévotion à la Sainte Vierge*, ed. 2 (Lyon, 1767), pp. 41-42; C. del Moral, O.F.M., *Fons illimis theologiae scoticae marianae* ..., Vol. 2 (Matriti, 1730), p. 385, n. 20; D. Lossada, O.F.M., *Tractatus de Incarnatione (MS 12261 bibl. nat. matritensis)*, fol. 335r, nn. 322-323; cf. also fol. 335v, n. 324. On this rare work cf. Carol, *De Corredemptione* ..., pp. 342-344.

[103] L. di Castelplanio, O.F.M., *Maria nel consiglio dell'Eterno* ..., ed. 2, Vol. 1 (Napoli, 1902), p. 73; Vol. 2, p. 432; M. J. Scheeben, *Handbuch der katholischen Dogmatik*, Vol. 3 (Freiburg i. Br., 1927), pp. 608-609, nn. 1801-1802; J. Herrmann, C.Ss.R., *Institutiones Theologiae Dogmaticae*, Vol. 2 (Romae, 1897), pp. 335-339; R. M. de la Broise-J. V. Bainvel, *Marie Mère de grâce* (Paris, 1921), pp. 13, 22-23 (this article is substantially the same which Father de la Broise had published in *Etudes*, Vol. 68, 1896, pp. 5-31); H. Depoix, S.M.,

unhesitatingly uphold the coredemptive nature of Our Lady's merit. It is of interest to note here, in view of recent controversies, that, of all the writers mentioned thus far, only two (the Franciscans Charles del Moral and Dominic Lossada) defend the theory that Our Lady merited our Redemption *de condigno;* the others continue to adhere to a congruous merit.

b) Satisfaction. Christ's actions, eminently His Passion, offered to the Eternal Father in obedience and charity, constituted a superabundant compensation for the sins of the human race. That the Blessed Virgin also, particularly through her bitter compassion, offered some satisfaction for our sins is quite commonly held at the present time. Taught in the Middle Ages only occasionally, this phase of the doctrine begins to appear more and more boldly expressed in the Mariological treatises of the seventeenth century. We find it, for example, in Frangipane, Wadding, de Kreaytter, in the writings of Urrutigoyti and de Vega. The last two seem to be the first to defend the possibility of even a condign satisfaction on the part of Our Lady, without in the least detracting from the unique prerogative of the Saviour.[104]

The eighteenth century introduces no innovations in this respect; it simply holds fast to the Mariological legacy of the "Golden Age." Our Lady's share of Calvary's drama is clearly portrayed as having had a satisfactory value, *de congruo,* to placate the divine wrath and to restore men to the friendship of their Maker. This is the frank position taken by González Matheo, Peralta, Almeyda, Federici, Nasi, and others.[105] The Franciscans del Moral and Lossada, already known to us, go even further

---

Tractatus theologicus de Beata Virgine Maria, ed. 2 (Parisiis, 1866), pp. 212-213; F. W. Faber, *The Foot of the Cross* (London, 1857), pp. 381-389; H. Pradié, *La Vierge Marie, Mère de Dieu et chef-d'oeuvre de Dieu,* Vol. 2 (Tours, 1899), p. 64.

[104] P. M. Frangipane, *Blasones de la Virgen Madre de Dios y Señora nuestra* (Zaragoza, 1635), p. 66; L. Wadding, O.F.M., *De Redemptione Beatae Mariae Virginis* (Romae, 1656), p. 322; L. Kreaytter, O.S.B., *Fastus Mariales* (Venetiis, 1695), p. 177, n. 339; T. F. Urrutigoyti, *op. cit.,* p. 544; C. de Vega, *op. cit.,* Vol. 2, pp. 394-395, 418.

[105] D. González Matheo, O.F.M., *Mystica Civitas Dei vindicata...* (Matriti, 1747), p. 124, nn. 368-371; A. Peralta, S.J., *Dissertationes Scholasticae de Sacratissima Virgine Maria* (Mexici, 1726), p. 264; Th. de Almeyda, *La compassion aux douleurs de Marie* (ed. Braine-le-Comte, 1902), pp. 161-163; G. Federici, O.S.B., *Tractatus polemicus de Matre Dei,* Vol. 1 (Neapoli, 1777), p. 106; Nasi, *op. cit.,* p. 197.

and claim that Our Lady's compassion had a *condign* satisfactory value for our Redemption; not, of course, *ex rigore justitiae*, as in the singular case of Christ, but only *ex mera condignitate*.[106] Unfortunately, del Moral's penetrating presentation of this view does not seem to have allured any of the theologians of the nineteenth century; these, in ever growing numbers, continue to adhere to the common opinion, namely: Our Blessed Lady's atonement, while truly coredemptive, did not exceed the degree of "fittingness."[107]

c) Sacrifice. Our Blessed Lord redeemed the human race, not only by way of merit and satisfaction, but also by way of sacrifice. This means that He freely accepted the immolation of Himself and offered it to His Father in a truly sacerdotal action for the sins of mankind. That Our Blessed Mother shared also in this particular aspect of her Son's saving role, is quite generally admitted by theologians at the present time, although they are far from agreeing as to whether or not her oblation constituted a sacrifice *sensu proprio*. We shall have occasion to return to this point in the next section of this chapter.

Has Catholic tradition shown a sympathetic attitude to this phase of Mary's Coredemption? Unquestionably it has. Perhaps no other element of this complex doctrine has been so frequently stressed from the twelfth century to the present day. It is here precisely that the remarkable intuitions of Arnold of Chartres (d. 1163) exerted their greatest influence on virtually all subsequent writers. Echoing and elaborating Arnold's teaching, hosts of Marian theologians in the seventeenth century, such as Portillo, de Rojas, Tausch, Niquet, Reichenberger, and Crasset, while treating Mary's Coredemption, would seem to place the emphasis on her sacrificial oblation on Calvary.[108] Something similar may be said of those

---

[106] C. del Moral, *op. cit.*, Vol. 2, p. 240; D. Lossada, in his approbation of del Moral's work, p. IX.

[107] Cf., among others, Scheeben, *loc. cit.*; G. Ventura, *La Madre di Dio, Madre degli uomini* (ed. Torino, 1937), p. 291; F. M. Risi, *Sul motivo primario dell'Incarnazione del Verbo* (Brescia, 1898), lib. 4, p. 119. Cf. Carol, *op. cit.*, p. 491.

[108] R. Portillo, *op. cit.*, p. 40; F. de Rojas, O.F.M., *Elucidario de las grandezas de la Virgen María* (Madrid, 1643), pp. 192, 269, 275; C. Tausch, S.J., *De SS. Matre dolorosa libri tres* ... (Coloniae Agrippinae, 1645), p. 177; H. Niquet, S.J., *Nomenclator Marianus* ... (Rothomagi, 1664), cap. 7; cf. Dillenschneider, *Marie au service de notre Rédemption* (Haguenau, 1947), p. 160; M. Reichenberger, S.J., *op. cit.*, **p.** 116; J. Crasset, S.J., *La véritable dévotion envers*

OUR LADY'S COREDEMPTION 453

who touched on this subject during the eighteenth century, for example, Montalbanus, Van Ketwigh, and Martínez de Barrio.[109] None of these authors, of course, specify whether this oblation constituted a sacrificial action *sensu proprio* or not; but the point is that they regard it as having a soteriological character.

In the nineteenth century, particularly under the influence of Msgr. Van den Berghe and Father Giraud, M.S.,[110] we discover an even greater attention given by Catholic writers to this phase of Mary's coredemptive role. Not only devotional authors like Saintrain and Ambrosij,[111] but professional theologians of the caliber of Scheeben, Guéranger, Körber, and Risi[112] unmistakably point to Mary as Coredemptrix precisely inasmuch as she offered up the divine Victim on Calvary for our Redemption. Indeed, some authors so exaggerate the reality of this oblation that they speak of Our Lady's having a true priestly character;[113] a deformation which, unfortunately, is still countenanced by some even in our own twentieth century.

d) Redemptive price. The fourth aspect under which Our Lord's objective Redemption is generally considered in theology is that of "ransom" or the paying of a "price." To forestall unnecessary inaccuracies in this connection, it must be recalled that this new phase of the doctrine does not add anything positive to the Saviour's Passion.

---

la Sainte Vierge ... (Paris, 1679), pp. 13-14.

[109] S. Montalbanus, *op. cit.*, Vol. 2, p. 368, n. 521; Van Ketwigh, *op. cit.*, pp. 101-102; E. Martínez de Barrio, O.F.M., *Manualis mysticusque marianus liber ...* (Pampilonae, 1777), p. XVI.

[110] Oswald Van den Berghe, *Marie et le sacerdoce*, ed. 2 (Paris, 1875), *passim*, esp. pp. 49, 108-109; S. M. Giraud, M.S., *De la vie d'union avec Marie, Mère de Dieu*, ed. 14 (Paris, 1930), pp. 59-60. The first edition of this work appeared in 1864. On these two authors cf. Laurentin, *Maria, Ecclesia, Sacerdotium ...*, pp. 437-442, 463-467.

[111] H. Saintrain, C.Ss.R., *Marie, secours pérpetuel des hommes*, ed. 2 (Tournai, 1884), pp. 55-60; F. Ambrosij, *Discorsi teologico-morali in lode di Maria Vergine*, Vol. 1 (Ascoli, 1843), pp. 142-143.

[112] Cf. Scheeben, *op. cit.*, Vol. 3, pp. 608-609, nn. 1801-1802; P. Guéranger, O.S.B., *The Liturgical Year: Passiontiae and Holy Week*, ed. 3 (Worcester, 1901), pp. 172-174; J. Körber, *Maria im System des Heilsökonomie, auf thomistischer Basis dargestellt* (Regensburg, 1883), pp. 186-187, 192; F. M. Risi, *op. cit.*, lib. 4, p. 119, n. 186.

[113] Cf., for example, G. Guida, *Il sacerdozio di Maria; pensieri dommatici e morali* (Napoli, 1873), p. 12. On this author cf. Laurentin, *op. cit.*, pp. 417-421.

454   MARIOLOGY

The "payment of the price" is simply a metaphorical expression which does not indicate an operation specifically different from those described above. In point of fact, the merits and satisfactions of Christ constitute the "price" which He paid to the Eternal Father, and in virtue of which the human race was freed from the slavery of Satan. From this it logically follows that if Our Lady, together with Christ and under Him, satisfied for our sins and merited our supernatural restoration *in actu primo,* she had, by that very fact, a direct and proximate share in the actual paying of the price of our Redemption. In this respect, a twofold manner of co-operation is possible: (*a*) Mary paid the *same* price which her Son paid, that is to say, she offered to God the meritorious and satisfactory value of her Son's life; (*b*) she offered *her own* merits and satisfactions together with those of the Saviour for our Redemption. Either type of co-operation is sufficient to constitute her a Coredemptrix *sensu proprio.* Actually, both may claim a certain amount of "traditional" support. The Seraphic Doctor, St. Bonaventure, seems to be the first to clearly refer to this modality of Mary's Coredemption.[114] Strangely enough, we find no repercussions of his teaching in the literature of the period immediately following. The theme is quite frequently touched upon, although mostly *per transennam,* in the Marian treatises of the seventeenth century, among which we may recall those by the Jesuits de Guevara, de Convelt, Vieira,[115] and the Franciscans Vulpes and Urrutigoyti.[116] The latter categorically states that no other price was added to Christ's death, except the merits of our Coredemptrix; this, he says, is her exclusive privilege. More or less direct references to this subject are found in not a few subsequent writers such as Peralta,

---

[114] St. Bonaventure, *Collatio 6 de donis S. Sancti,* nn. 14-15; *op. omnia,* Vol. 5, p. 486. Cf. also p. 484, n. 5.

[115] H. de Guevara, *Commentarius in cap. primum Matthaei,* Vol. 2 (Matriti, 1634), fol. 77, col. 1; ref. taken from T. F. Urrutigoyti, *Certamen scholasticum, expositivum argumentum pro Deipara* (Lugduni, 1660), p. 509; M. de Convelt, *Theatrum excellentiarum SS. Deiparae ...,* Vol. 2 (Antverpiae, 1655), pp. 491, 528-530; A. de Vieira, *Sermones de Cristo, Señor Nuestro, y de Maria Santís-ima ...,* ed. 2, Vol. 2 (Barcelona, 1752), p. 193.

[116] A. Vulpes (Volpe), *Sacrae Theologiae Summa ...,* tomus tertius patris quartae (Neapoli, 1646), p. 450, col. 2; T. F. Urrutigoyti, *op. cit.,* p. 544.

Worpiz, and Nasi in the eighteenth century,[117] and Maynard, Stecher, Ventura de Ráulica, and Castelplanio in the nineteenth century.[118] The last author mentioned, a prolific writer whose Mariology exerted no little influence on Scheeben and others, expressly teaches that Our Lady's sorrows were offered up with the Passion of Christ to expiate our sins; the sufferings of the Son and of His Mother obtained one and the same effect.

Conclusion. In our extensive work *De Corredemptione B. V. Mariae*, so often referred to in this chapter, several hundred authors were quoted to substantiate the claim that the doctrine of Mary's Coredemption is fully endorsed by Catholic Tradition in the sense already explained. Not being able to reproduce that mass of testimony here, the only feasible substitute was a synthetic presentation of the available data. Nevertheless, we feel that the above survey, fragmentary and sketchy though it is, will be sufficiently adequate to establish that the thesis in question is far from being a novelty, an abrupt creation of the twentieth century.

The variety of nationalities and religious institutes represented by the authors mentioned in that survey is rather significant, for it clearly points to the fact that the doctrine professed is not peculiar to any one country or theological school. This important feature is quite noticeable particularly with regard to the testimony furnished by contemporary writers, whose names are legion. Thus, for example, Our Lady's Coredemption *sensu proprio* is openly proclaimed not only by the vast majority of theologians in so-called "Catholic" countries such as Spain, Italy, France, and Belgium, but also by not a few authors living in countries where Catholics are a minority, such as the United States of

---

[117] A. Peralta, *op. cit.*, pp. 251-252; G. Worpiz, *Cursus annuus, Praesidis Mariani* ... (Augustae Vindelicorum, 1706), p. 360; ref. taken from Dillenschneider, *op. cit.*, p. 140; G. A. Nasi, *op. cit.*, pp. 527-530.

[118] M. U. Maynard, *La Sainte Vierge* (Paris, 1877), pp. 252-253; Ch. Stecher, *Mater Admirabilis* (Innsbruck, 1885), p. 441; G. Ventura de Ráulica, *La Madre di Dio* ..., ed. cit., p. 330; L. de Castelplanio, *op. cit.*, Vol. 2, p. 432.

America,[119] Holland,[120] Germany, and Switzerland.[121] As to scholars from religious institutes representing the different theological traditions, it will suffice to recall such well-known names as Garrigou-Lagrange, Cuervo, Sauras, and Llamera among the Dominicans;[122] Bover, Druwé, de Aldama, and Boyer among the Jesuits;[123] and Balić, Di Fonzo, Crisóstomo de Pamplona, O'Brien, and W. Sebastian among the Franciscans.[124]

---

[119] Cf., among others, the various contributors to *Marian Studies* (published by The Mariological Society of America), particularly Vols. 2 and 3, and also the contributors to the first volume of this set of MARIOLOGY.

[120] Cf., for example, S. Tromp, S.J., in *Periodica de re morali*, Vol. 32, 1943, p. 401; *id., De zending van Maria en het geheimnis der Kerk*, in *Alma Socia Christi*, Vol. 11 (Romae, 1953), pp. 295-305; P. Ploumen, S.J., *Beoordeeling van enkele moeilijkheden aangaande die modaliteiten* [van het Medeverlossingswerk], in *Mariale Dagen* (Tongerloo, 1947), pp. 194-215; cf. likewise the collective Pastoral Letter of the Dutch hierarchy in 1943, excerpts of which are given in *Marianum*, Vol. 9, 1947, pp. 12-13, 31-32.

[121] Cf. P. Sträter, S.J., *Mariens Mitwirkung beim Erlösungsopfer*, in *Katholische Marienkunde* (ed. P. Sträter), Vol. 2 (Paderborn, 1947), pp. 272-313; M. Müller, O.F.M., *Maria; ihre geistige Gestalt und Persönlichkeit in der Theologie des Mittelalters, ibid.,* Vol. 1, pp. 268-316; C. Feckes, Das Mysterium der göttlichen Mutterschaft (Paderborn, 1937), pp. 125-153; H. Seiler, S.J., Corredemptrix. Theologische Studie zur Lehre der letzten Päpste über die Mitterlöserschaft Mariens (Rom, 1939).

[122] R. Garrigou-Lagrange, *De Christo Salvatore* (Taurini, 1945), pp. 513-521; M. Cuervo, *Sobre el mérito corredentivo de María*, in *Estudios Marianos*, Vol. 1, 1942, pp. 327-352; E. Sauras, *Causalidad de la cooperación de María en la obra redentora*, in *Estudios Marianos*, Vol. 2, 1943, pp. 319-358; M. Llamera, *María, Madre Corredentora...*, in *Estudios Marianos*, Vol. 7, 1948, pp. 145-196.

[123] For Bover and Druwé cf. footnote 11; J. A. de Aldama, *Cooperación de María a la Redención a modo de satisfacción por el pecado*, in *Estudios Marianos*, Vol. 2, 1943, pp. 179-193; C. Boyer, *Thoughts on Mary's Coredemption*, in *The American Ecclesiastical Review*, Vol. 122, 1950, pp. 401-415.

[124] C. Balić, *Die sekundäre Mittlerschaft der Gottesmutter (Hat Maria die Verdienste Christi de condigno für uns mitverdient?)*, in *Wissenschaft und Weisheit*, Vol. 4, 1937, pp. 1-22; also a letter to the author dated July 1, 1935; L. Di Fonzo, O.F.M.Conv., in a remarkably erudite study: *Dieci anni di studi mariani in Italia* (1939-1948), in *Miscellanea Francescana*, Vol. 50, 1950, pp. 53-96, esp. p. 64; Crisóstomo de Pamplona, O.F.M.Cap., *Solución de las dificultades contra la Corredención mariana propiamente dicha*, in *Estudios Marianos*, Vol. 3, 1944, pp. 235-254; S. O'Brien, O.F.M., *Recent Popes and the Doctrine of the Mediation of Mary*, in *The Clergy Review*, Vol. 22, 1942, pp. 97-106; W. Sebastian, O.F.M., *The Nature of Mary's Spiritual Maternity*, in *Marian Studies*, Vol. 3, 1952, pp. 14-34.

However, to those who follow the progressive line of testimonies scattered through the monuments of tradition, it will be equally evident that the complex doctrine of Mary's Coredemption, as we know it today, represents the result of many centuries of gradual development. The germ idea embodied in the concrete "New Eve" expression, found in the early days of the patristic period, underwent a long and, at times, imperceptible process of evolution before it attained to the stage of maturity. In the beginning, and up until about the eleventh century, the Fathers and ecclesiastical writers seem to have considered the doctrine in its more generic and fundamental concept, namely: Our Lady, by supplying her free consent to the redemptive Incarnation, was instrumental in bringing about our spiritual rehabilitation through Christ. The eleventh century ushers in the period of transition from the implicit to the explicit.[125] It is at this time that Mary's compassion and her oblation begin to receive more and more attention, and to be considered as having a soteriological value in behalf of the human race. The aspect of coredemptive merit, alluded to by pseudo-Albert the Great, found clear and definite expression in the writings of Blessed Tauler (d. 1361) and Archbishop Catarino (d. 1553). But the doctrine as a whole did not reach its peak until the seventeenth century. It was during this "Golden Age" of Mariology that Our Lady's prerogative, exactly as we profess it today, became the generally accepted teaching among

---

[125] If we believe Lennerz, the doctrine of Mary's Coredemption was *not even implicitly* contained in the teaching of the early Church. He claims that the testimonies of the Fathers and early writers relative to Our Lady's share in the Redemption *may* be understood in a sense other than the one we now attach to them. When Dillenschneider rightly pointed out that the same kind of reasoning considered legitimate in the case of the Immaculate Conception should be valid also in the case of her Coredemption, Lennerz promptly retorted with a *"nego paritatem."* The Immaculate Conception, he explained, was always believed in the Church as *implied* in the patristic teaching which portrays Our Lady as the most pure and innocent of God's creatures, as the woman who has always been full of God's grace, who had never been a friend of Satan, and the like (cf. *Gregorianum*, Vol. 28, 1947, pp. 579-581). In view of this, we are faced with the following dilemma: Either the patristic testimonies extolling Mary's singular innocence may be understood of her sanctification *after* conception, or they may not. If they *may*, then, according to Lennerz' own principle of exegesis, they have no value in favor of the Immaculate Conception. If they *may not*, then how does he explain the fact that the greatest medieval theologians (who, incidentally, were familiar with these patristic encomiums) did interpret them precisely in that sense?

theologians and Catholic writers. Scholars of subsequent centuries have not added any substantial element to the notion of Coredemption as expounded in that period; their work seems to be restricted to a theological elaboration and scientific systematization of the acquisitions of the past.

IV. NATURE AND MODALITIES OF MARY'S COREDEMPTION

In the preceding pages we have attempted to establish the *fact* of Our Lady's Coredemption understood in the proper sense. We have done this by appealing to the Magisterium, Sacred Scripture, and Tradition. Regardless of the shortcomings latent in our examination of these sources, one thing remains undeniable: the vast majority of theologians and Catholic writers at the present time unhesitatingly favor the doctrine under discussion. This fact alone sufficiently guarantees the legitimacy of our position, *donec contrarium probetur*. However, as St. Augustine so well expressed it: "Non aequaliter mente percipitur, etiam quod in fide pariter ab utrisque recipitur."[126] Which means that even among those who champion the thesis of Mary's proximate co-operation in the redemptive work of Christ, different opinions have been advanced with regard to the more intimate nature and extent of that co-operation. It may be helpful to summarize here the various points of contact and divergence in this matter.

The advocates of Mary's Coredemption *sensu proprio* are morally unanimous on the following phases of the doctrine: (*1*) Our Lady's free consent to become the Mother of the Redeemer as such constituted a true, formal co-operation in the Redemption; (*2*) Together with Christ and under Him, Mary *satisfied* (at least *de congruo*) for the sins of mankind, thus removing the obstacle to our reconciliation with God *in actu primo*; (*3*) Together with Christ and under Him, Our Lady *merited* (at least *de congruo*) the reinstatement of the human race in the friendship of God *in actu primo*; (*4*) Together with Christ and under Him, Our Lady offered up the divine Victim to the Eternal Father, particularly on Calvary, for the reconciliation of man with God *in actu primo*; (*5*) Our Lady's merits and satisfactions, pre-eminently those resulting from her

---

[126] *In Joan.*, tract. 98, 2.

bitter compassion, were accepted by the Eternal Father together with the merits and satisfactions of Christ as having the nature of a secondary ransom or redemptive price for our liberation from the slavery of Satan; (6) Any one of these functions, and *a fortiori* the combination of them, confers on Our Blessed Lady a strict right to be styled "Coredemptrix" of the human race *sensu vero et proprio*.

The area of disagreement is not as wide as it might appear on the surface. It may be reduced to the three following points: (1) the nature of Mary's coredemptive merit; (2) the nature of her sacrifice; and (3) the nature of her influence or causality with reference to the redemptive actions of Christ.

As regards the first point, it may be well to recall that merit (meaning "a right to a reward") is generally divided in condign and congruous. The former supposes an equality between the meritorious action and its reward; the latter is based on fittingness coupled with the generosity of the one granting the reward. Condign merit may be of two kinds: either *ex toto rigore justitiae*, if there is equality not only between the meritorious work and the reward, but also between the persons giving and meriting the reward; or *ex mera condignitate*, if the latter equality is wanting.[127]

While theologians are agreed that Christ alone merited our Redemption *de condigno ex toto rigore justitiae*, they are divided as to the nature of Our Lady's coredemptive merit. The majority still believes that hers was only a merit *de congruo*, inasmuch as it was fitting that God should reward her unique co-operation with the Redeemer in our behalf.[128] A second group proposes that it be designated by a new name, namely, merit *de digno* or *de super-congruo*.[129] This would differ from our

---

[127] We follow the subdivision of condign merit proposed by Father M. Llamera, O.P., in *Alma Socia Christi*, Vol. 1 (Romae, 1951), p. 245. Cf. also M. Cuervo, O.P., *La cooperación de María en el misterio de nuestra salud...*, in *Estudios Marianos*, Vol. 2, 1943, pp. 137-139.

[128] Cf., among others, C. Friethoff, O.P., *De alma Socia Christi Mediatoris* (Romae, 1936), pp. 75-77; R. Garrigou-Lagrange, *op. cit.*, pp. 516-519; M.-J. Nicolas, O.P., *La doctrine de la Corédemption dans le cadre de la doctrine thomiste de la Rédemption*, in *Revue Thomiste*, Vol. 46, 1947, pp. 26-27.

[129] Cf. C. Dillenschneider, *Pour une Corédemption bien comprise*, in *Marianum*, Vol. 11, 1949, pp. 242-245; D. Bertetto, S.D.B., *Maria Corredentrice* (Alba, 1951), p. 106; G. M. Roschini, O.S.M., *On the Nature of the Corredemptive Merit of the Blessed Virgin Mary*, in

merit, not in species, but in degree, and also insofar as the object of Mary's merit is the Redemption itself, while the object of our merit is only the application of the Redemption. Others, finally, uphold the theory that Our Lady merited our Redemption *de condigno;* not, of course, *ex toto rigore justitiae,* but only *ex mera condignitate,* in the sense explained above.

Condensed in a few words, the reasoning supporting this last theory is this: Our Lady was not a mere member of the Mystical Body; she cooperated in our Redemption in an official capacity, as a public person, as a representative of mankind. Specifically, since God had predestined her to regenerate the human race to the supernatural life of grace, her merit in the acquisition of that grace must have had an "ecumenical" character in behalf of the whole Mystical Body. In this sense we may speak of her merits having an intrinsic ordination to the salvation of all. Furthermore, dignified to an ineffable degree by her singular grace and the divine Maternity, her merit must have been likewise proportionate to the reward to be received. If this utterly unique function of Mary in the redemptive economy was the result of a positive divine decree, then surely God owed it to Himself to reward her merits not only out of fittingness, but in justice.

This opinion, which until a few decades ago was looked upon with considerable suspicion,[130] is now finding increasing support among contemporary theologians. True, the reasoning process varies according to authors,[131] but their conclusions coincide with the one indicated

---

Marianum, Vol. 15, 1953, pp. 278-287.

[130] Cf. for example, the recriminations of E. Amort, *Controversia de Revelationibus Agredanis ...* (Augustae Vindelicorum, 1749), pp. XXIX-XXX.

[131] Cf. J. Lebon, *Comment je conçois, j'établis et je défends la doctrine de la Médiation mariale,* in *Ephemerides Theologicae Lovanienses,* Vol. 16, 1939, pp. 674-678; A. Fernández, O.P., *De Mediatione B. Virginis secundum doctrinam D. Thomae,* in *La Ciencia Tomista,* Vol. 38, 1938, pp. 145-170; C. Balić, *art. cit.;* L. Colomer, O.F.M., *Cooperación meritoria de la Virgen a la Redención,* in *Estudios Marianos,* Vol. 2, 1943, pp. 155-177; M. Cuervo, *art. cit.;* J. A. de Aldama, S.J., *Cooperación de María a la Redención ...,* in *Estudios Marianos,* Vol. 2, 1943, pp. 179-193; E. Sauras, O.P., *Causalidad de la cooperación de María ...,* in *Estudios Marianos,* Vol. 2, 1943, pp. 319-358; F. Vacas, O.P., *María Corredentora pudo merecer de condigno ex condignitate,* in *Boletín Eclesiástico de Filipinas,* Vol. 18, 1940, pp. 719-729; M. Llamera, O.P., *El mérito maternal corredentivo de María,* in *Estudios Marianos,* Vol. 11, 1951, pp. 83-140. On the lively discussion conducted by Father Llamera on this point at

above, which, incidentally, expresses also our personal preference on the subject.

The second point of divergence concerns the nature of Mary's cooperation by way of sacrifice. That Our Lady had a positive share in our Redemption through her offering of the Victim on Calvary is clearly taught by recent Pontiffs[132] and, of course, admitted by all. The disagreement begins when theologians attempt to determine whether or not that offering constituted a sacrificial act *sensu proprio*. The question is particularly delicate because of the related discussion concerning the so-called priesthood of Mary. A good deal has been written in recent years in an effort to clarify the issues involved and to reconcile conflicting opinions; unfortunately, the noble endeavor has not been wholly successful.

In view of the multiplicity of terms employed by the various authors in this connection, it is difficult to group their views under clearly defined headings. In general, however, two currents of thought are easily discernible. The first, represented by such well-known writers as Seiler, Petazzi, Sauras, and Llamera, claims that Our Lady's oblation constituted a sacrificial and sacerdotal act in a true and proper sense.[133] They explain that, while Mary did not receive the sacramental character of Orders, nevertheless she was invested with a *true* priesthood, analogous to the substantial priesthood of Christ and far superior not only to the mystical priesthood shared by all Christians, but also to the ministerial priesthood of those properly ordained. If we believe Prof. Bover, Mary's elevation to the divine Motherhood was already an "ordination to the priesthood."[134] According to Sauras, her "ordination" was constituted by the unique grace of her spiritual maternity, analogously to the capital grace of the Saviour.[135]

---

the recent International Marian Congress in Rome, cf. *Alma Socia Christi*, Vol. 1 (Romae, 1951), pp. 243-255.

[132] Cf. above, footnotes 14, 18, 23.

[133] H. Seiler, *op. cit.*, pp. 14-32, 131, 138 ff.; G. M. Petazzi, S.J., *Teologia Mariana* (Venezia, s.a.), pp. 43-45; E. Sauras, ¿*Fué sacerdotal la gracia de María?* in *Estudios Marianos*, Vol. 7, 1948, pp. 387-424; M. Llamera, *María Madre Corredentora* ..., ibid., pp. 166-167.

[134] J. M. Bover, S.J., *María Mediadora universal* ... (Madrid, 1946), pp. 351-354.

[135] E. Sauras, O.P., *art. cit.*, p. 424.

The other current, diametrically opposed to the first, reflects the views of the majority. Among the more articulate representatives of this trend we may mention García Garcés, Roschini, and Friethoff.[136] They readily agree with their adversaries that Mary's oblation on Calvary, so often recalled in recent papal documents, constituted a true co-operation in the Saviour's redemptive sacrifice; but they emphatically deny — and rightly so — that this co-operation shared the formality of a true and proper sacrifice. The fundamental reason for this position would seem to be that, in order to offer a sacrifice *sensu proprio,* one must be a priest *sensu proprio,* and Our Lady was not. Her priesthood is of the same kind as that of all the baptized, although of a higher degree because of her singular grace and dignity. Perhaps it is for this very reason that the Holy See has repeatedly frowned on the use of the title "Virgin-Priest" as applied to the Blessed Virgin.[137] Incidentally, this controversial title, so tenaciously vindicated by some, does in no way help our proper understanding of Mary's share in the sacrifice of her Son. It adds nothing but confusion to an already difficult and thorny question. In our humble opinion it should be banished from our Catholic literature, both theological and devotional. The extremely cautious attitude of the Holy See in this respect should be a warning to all.[138]

As mentioned before, the third point of discrepancy concerns the

---

[136] N. García Garcés, C.M.F., *Cooperación de María a nuestra Redención a modo de sacrificio,* in *Estudios Marianos,* Vol. 2, 1943, pp. 195-247; *id., La Santísima Virgen y el Sacerdocio, ibid.,* Vol. 10, 1950, pp. 61-104 (an excellent refutation of Llamera's views); G. M. Roschini, *L'essenza del sacrificio eucaristico ...* (Roma, 1936); *id., Ancora sull'essenza del sacrificio eucaristico ...* (Rovigo, 1937); *id., La Madonna secondo la fede e la teologia,* Vol. 2 (Roma, 1953), p. 406; C. Friethoff, *op. cit.,* pp. 139-149.

[137] Cf. R. Laurentin, *Le problème du sacerdoce marial devant le Magistère,* in *Marianum,* Vol. 10, 1948, pp. 160-178. On the whole question of Mary's "priesthood," cf. the prodigious investigation undertaken by Laurentin in his *Maria, Ecclesia, Sacerdotium; essai sur le développement d'une idée religieuse* (Paris, 1952), and his *Marie, l'Eglise et la sacerdoce; étude théologique* (Paris, 1953).
For a sound and objective evaluation of Laurentin's views on the subject, cf. N. García Garcés, C.M.F., *María, la Iglesia y el sacerdocio,* in *Ephemerides Mariologicae,* Vol. 5, 1955, pp. 429-443.

[138] In *L'Ami du Clergé,* 1928, p. 49, the editors state that they have been requested "by orders from above" to make a public declaration to the effect that "the Holy Office has expressly forbidden the attribution of this title (Virgin-Priest) to the Blessed Virgin."

modality of Mary's immediate co-operation with Christ in the Redemption itself. A survey of contemporary theologians discloses at least three different approaches in this connection. According to some, Our Lady not only did not place any obstacles to prevent the redemptive mission of her Son, but she also encouraged, entreated, and urged Him to lay down His life for our salvation. This moral causality on her part exerted an immediate influence on the will of Christ and directly *determined* the positing of His redemptive acts. This seems to be the position of Merkelbach, Seiler, and Sträter.[139] Merkelbach, for example, writes that "as the Son was moved to obey the command of His Father (to suffer and die), so He could not help being influenced likewise by His Mother's consent. ... Through her consent and desire, Mary morally influenced her Son and disposed Him to accomplish the Redemption of the human race. ..."[140]

According to a second group of theologians,[141] Our Lady's immediate co-operation should be explained rather in the sense that her own merits and satisfactions were accepted by the Eternal Father together with (and subordinate to) the merits and satisfactions of Christ for the selfsame purpose: the reconciliation of the human race *in actu primo*. In other words, the total effect was produced by the joint causality of the Redeemer and the Coredemptrix; both acquired a right to the graces which would save all men; both constituted (though in a different way) the total principle of salvation. Hence, Our Lady's co-operation was redemptive, not because it directly influenced and determined Christ's redemptive will or His theandric actions, but rather because the actions of Christ conferred a redemptive value on Mary's co-operation, thus

---

[139] B.-H. Merkelbach, O.P., *Tractatus de Beatissima Virgine Maria* ... (Parisiis, 1939), p. 342; H. Seiler and P. Sträter, *De modalitate Corredemptionis B. Mariae Virginis, in Gregorianum,* Vol. 28, 1947, pp. 293-336, esp. pp. 320-323.

[140] Merkelbach, loc. cit.

[141] D. Bertetto, *Maria Corredentrice* (Alba, 1951), pp. 23-24, 94-95, 142; R. Gagnebet, O.P., *Questions mariales,* in *Angelicum,* Vol. 22, 1945, pp. 169-171; M.-J. Nicolas, O.P., *La doctrine de la Corédemption dans le cadre de la doctrine thomiste de la Rédemption,* in *Revue Thomiste,* Vol. 47, 1947, 20-42; C. Dillenschneider, *Le mystère de la Corédemption mariale* ... (Paris, 1951), pp. 159-160. On the somewhat fluctuating position of Dillenschneider, cf. the very pertinent observations of A. Rivera, in *Ephemerides Mariologicae,* Vol. 3, 1953, pp. 500-501.

enabling it to concur in the production of the same effect.[142]

A third theory, not necessarily incompatible with the second, was proposed a few years ago by the Hungarian Jesuit, Tiburtius Gallus. According to the distinguished theologian, the Blessed Virgin, being the true Mother of Christ, had a strict right to protect her Son's life from unjust aggressors. By surrendering this right, she removed an impediment to her Son's sacrificial immolation, and thus furnished the material principle for the redemptive act. The obedience of Christ to His Father's will decreeing His sacrifice has a twofold causality: first, by a priority of nature, it elevates and actuates Mary's obedience for the same purpose; second, it becomes, together with Mary's obedience, the efficient cause of the entire redemptive work. Hence, our Redemption depends on Christ's renunciation as a formal element, and on Mary's renunciation as a material element. The latter, Gallus explains, is not merely accessory; it is necessary inasmuch as it is required by divine disposition. The two elements constitute one single moral cause of the Redemption. Furthermore, since Christ's obedience imprints its soteriological character on Mary's co-operation, her merits in our behalf become coredemptive *de condigno*, and not merely *de congruo*.[143]

---

[142] In his article *De cooperatione qualificata in delictis officialibus*, in *Periodica de re morali, canonica, liturgica*, Vol. 38, 1949, pp. 321-342, the eminent canonist F. Hürth, S.J., suggests the following explanation: Christ *alone* was charged with the official function to bring about our Redemption through the sacrificial offering demanded by God. He alone (not Mary) wrought our salvation. Mary's will in no way "influenced" or "determined" the will of her Son to fulfill His redemptive mission. Nevertheless, the Saviour deigned to assume His Mother's will into His own, thus fusing it, as it were, with the internal element of His official function as Redeemer. In this sense we have a true coredemptive co-operation on the part of Mary, without in the least encroaching on the unique prerogative of her Son (cf. esp. p. 339). Father Dillenschneider (*op. cit.*, pp. 14-16) fears that in this theory Our Lady's Coredemption is diluted almost to the point of losing its very essence. He forgets that in some sections of his book (for example, pp. 17, 60, 88) he himself seems to reduce Mary's co-operation to the fact that she shared (though officially) in the redemptive *fiat* of her Son. In all fairness to him, however, we must note that elsewhere (pp. 148-152) Dillenschneider admits considerably more than the mere "co-operation by consent."

[143] T. Gallus, *Ad B. M. Virginis in Redemptione cooperationem*, in *Divus Thomas* (Pl.), Vol. 51, 1948, pp. 113-135; id., *Mater Dolorosa "principium materiale" Redemptionis objectivae*, in *Marianum*, Vol. 12, 1950, pp. 227-249. To the objections of Dillenschneider against this theory (op. cit., pp. 24-25), Father Gallus has replied recently in a lengthy and noteworthy article: *Ad "principium materiale" Redemptionis objectivae*, in *Divus Thomas* (Pl.), Vol. 57,

If we were to express our personal preference in this delicate question, we would say that, while the first and third theories are not devoid of appealing features, nevertheless, the second seems better calculated to safeguard the reality of Mary's Coredemption, without in the least compromising the intangible rights of the unique Redeemer.

V. DIFFICULTIES AND SOLUTIONS

In the course of the foregoing exposé we have had occasion to recall that, while the doctrine of Our Lady's Coredemption enjoys the support of most contemporary theologians, nevertheless there are some authors who still find it difficult, if not altogether impossible, to conciliate this teaching with other irrevocable data of divine revelation. Their difficulties and pointed observations deserve a fair and dispassionate hearing at this time. The formulation of adequate answers and solutions should furnish us with an additional opportunity to shed further light on some of the apparently nebulous issues involved.

The first objection is based on Sacred Scripture, particularly on the well-known text of St. Paul: "For there is one God, and one mediator of God and men, the man Christ Jesus, who gave himself a redemption for all."[144] That the Apostle is here openly proclaiming the oneness of the Redeemer to the exclusion of any other, acting even in a secondary capacity, is clear from the parallelism which he establishes with the oneness of God. Just as the oneness of God is incompatible with the existence of secondary gods, so is the oneness of the Mediator (Redeemer) incompatible with the existence of secondary mediators or redeemers. So argues Prof. Werner Goossens.[145]

The objection is not new. It has been raised — and answered — countless times, particularly since the sixteenth century. It may be observed, in general, that if the oneness of the Mediator were as absolute as Goossens contends, it would exclude likewise the mediatorial activity of all the saints in the sphere of the subjective Redemption. *Quod nimis probat, nihil probat.* Even in the light of the parallelism stressed by the

---

1954, pp. 230-261.

[144] *1 Tim.* 2:5. Cf. also *Acts* 4:12.

[145] W. Goossens, *De cooperatione immediata Matris Redemptoris ad redemptionem objectivam* (Parisiis, 1939), pp. 30-31.

author, one could perhaps point out that, just as the oneness of God does not exclude our sharing His divine nature through sanctifying grace, neither does the oneness of the Mediator exclude an analogous participation of Our Lady in His mediatorial role.[146] That St. Paul is here speaking only of the principal and self-sufficient Mediator is evident from the fact that he himself elsewhere bestows this very title on Moses.[147] Besides, if the Pauline passage had the exclusive sense claimed by Goossens, would the Magisterium of the Church, the sole official interpreter of Holy Scripture, allow the vast majority of theologians to continue teaching the doctrine of Mary's Coredemption? Surely, the Popes would have at least sounded a note of warning. Instead, they have repeatedly shown favor to the doctrine, as we indicated above.

A second difficulty springs from the undeniable theological axiom: *Principium meriti non cadit sub merito,* that is to say, the principle or cause of merit cannot be the result or effect of merit. The implications of this axiom, which have been fully exploited in recent years, particularly by Prof. Lennerz, may be summarized as follows: In order to co-operate in the Redemption, Mary must first be redeemed and in possession of grace which will render her co-operation acceptable to God. Now that redemption of Mary, that grace conferred on her, is, of course, the *effect* of Christ's redemptive work. Therefore, the latter must have been already completed *before* Mary received its effect. If so, how could she aid Christ in producing something which was already produced?[148]

The answer generally given to the above objection was that Our Lady had been redeemed in a very unique manner, namely, through a preservative grace which enabled her to co-operate with her Son at the time He was bringing about our Redemption. To which Father Lennerz promptly retorted that this was nothing but a subterfuge which left the original difficulty intact. The reason is simple. If Mary received a preservative grace at the time of her Immaculate Conception, it was in

---

[146] Cf. Bertetto, *op. cit.*, p. 77; Crisóstomo de Pamplona, O.F.M.Cap., *Solución de las dificultades contra la Corredención mariana propiamente dicha, in Estudios Marianos,* Vol. 3, 1944, pp. 237-240.

[147] Cf. *Gal.* 3, 19.

[148] Cf. H. Lennerz, *De Beata Virgine,* ed. 3 (Romae, 1939), p. 233.

view of the future merits of Christ; it was because the future merits of the Saviour were foreseen by God and applied to Mary by anticipation. Obviously, this presupposes that the Redemption was foreseen as having been already accomplished; now, since Mary had not as yet co-operated therein, the Redemption would still be incomplete, still unfinished. In which hypothesis the same Redemption would have to be considered as accomplished and unaccomplished at one and the same time, which is contradictory and absurd.[149]

Father Lennerz' reasoning, which, incidentally, has now been popularized for the benefit of English-speaking readers by Canon George D. Smith,[150] made a profound impression in some quarters. It constitutes, admittedly, the gravest speculative difficulty militating against Our Lady's Coredemption. Nevertheless, the advocates of this doctrine do not consider it insurmountable. An adequate solution may be formulated as follows:

The alleged contradiction indicated by Lennerz presupposes that we postulate one and the same Redemption as being complete and incomplete under one and the same respect. Now this supposition is false. In our theory, when the Redemption was applied to Mary it was already complete *as regards herself only;* it was still unaccomplished *as regards the rest of mankind.* Once Mary has received the effect of Christ's Redemption, she is able to co-operate with Him in the Redemption of all others. Is this perhaps equivalent to introducing *two* Redemptions, as Canon Smith fears? Not at all. There is only one Redemption for Mary and for the rest of men. But in that one Redemption we may distinguish two *signa rationis,* as the Scholastics would say, two modes of operation taking place at one and the same time, but made possible only by a priority of nature. In this hypothesis, Christ redeems Mary, and her alone, with a preservative Redemption; then, together with her, *in signo posteriori rationis,* He redeems the rest of mankind with a liberative Redemption. This, we repeat, does not correspond to two numerically distinct Redemptions, but rather to a *twofold intention* on the part of the Redeemer; and this twofold intention, in turn, corresponds to a twofold

---

[149] Lennerz, *Considerationes de doctrina B. Virginis Mediatricis, in* Gregorianum, Vol. 19, 1938, pp. 424-425.

[150] G. D. Smith, *Mary's Part in Our Redemption,* rev. ed. (New York, 1954), pp. 92-99.

acceptance of the Redemption on the part of the Eternal Father: first, with a logical priority, God deigns to accept Christ's Redemption for Mary alone; then, once Mary is redeemed, God accepts Christ's Redemption *with Mary's co-operation* for the rest of the human race.[151] Since the redemptive value of Christ's whole life was *eternally present* in the mind of God, there is no room for a chronological "before" and "after" which would, of course, compromise the absolute oneness of the objective Redemption.

At this juncture the adversaries point out that the above solution, while unassailable in itself, is nevertheless a gratuitous hypothesis without any basis in the sources of revelation. To which Father Dillenschneider rightly answers: "It is not at all necessary that this explanation find a formal support in Sacred Scripture and Tradition, provided that it be not opposed by either, and that it be justified by the belief, sufficiently accredited in the Church, concerning a direct cooperation of Mary in our objective Redemption. Now, such a belief does exist, and it would be vain to deny it. This being so, if the thesis of Mary's immediate Coredemption is sufficiently warranted, and we feel

---

[151] Cf. F. Tummers, *Het mede-verdienen van de h. Maagd in het verlossingswerk*, in Bijdragen van de philosophische en theologische Faculteiten der Nederlandsche Jesuiten, *Vol.* 1, 1938, *pp.* 81-103, *esp. p.* 93; ibid., pp. 99-101, the author endeavors to explain further how Our Lady could merit the Redemption which was actually the principle of her own merit. In his view, Christ's Redemption was the cause of Mary's merit only per *modum causae finalis,* while Mary's merits caused the Redemption per *modum causae efficientis.* Hence, he thinks, the famous objection based on the axiom "principium meriti non cadit sub merito" automatically vanishes. For a critique of this solution, cf. Lennerz, *art. cit.,* pp. 442-444. In his turn, the learned professor of Louvain, Msgr. J. Lebon, proposed a still more radical and novel solution, which may be summarized as follows: Our Lady was both a private and a public person. As a private person, the principle of her merit was indeed the *gratia Christi;* as a public person, however, the immediate principle of her merit was a *gratia Dei,* a special grace which did not flow from the Cross and which, therefore, enabled her to merit the Redemption itself. For Lebon the very fact that Mary was the Mother of the Redeemer *as such,* gave her a true right over the life of the Victim. Her free renunciation of these rights (joined with the renunciation by Christ of His rights over His own life) constituted, by divine disposition, a direct participation in the redemptive act itself. Cf. also the solutions advanced by J. M. Bover, in *Redempta et Corredemptrix* (*Marianum,* Vol. 2, 1940, pp. 39-58), and by R. Gagnebet, in *Difficultés sur la Corédemption: principes de solution?* (In *Alma Socia Christi,* Vol. 2, 1952, pp. 13-20, esp. pp. 16-18).

that it is, then the explanation which shows its harmony with the preredemption of the Immaculate Virgin is likewise warranted."[152] The same author further recalls that when the Franciscan Duns Scotus (d. 1308) had recourse to his "preredemption" theory in order to reconcile the doctrine of the Immaculate Conception with the dogma of the universality of Redemption, he could not claim any scriptural or traditional data in its favor. And yet, his explanation was accepted and definitively introduced in Catholic theology for the good reason that it alone solved the major difficulty of trying to harmonize the dogma of universal Redemption with the living tradition of the Church relative to Our Lady's original sanctity.[153]

Still reluctant to endorse the doctrine, the adversaries have recourse to a further objection. Granted, they say, that, theoretically, the thesis involves no contradiction. In point of fact, however, we are faced with the following serious dilemma: either Mary's co-operation adds something positive to the Redemption wrought by Christ, or it does not. If it does, it would enhance the value of Christ's merits and satisfactions, which is unthinkable. If it does not, then it is superfluous and useless. In either case it should be discarded.

We reply: Since the merits and satisfactions of the God-man possessed an infinite value and a superabundant efficacy, they could not possibly be enhanced by those of Our Blessed Lady. Nevertheless, her co-operation, without being an intrinsic "addition" to the work of her Son, constituted a *new title* in the eyes of God for the granting of pardon to the human race. Her merits and satisfactions are accepted by God as an integral part of the universal redemptive economy, as a positive contribution made by a purely human representative of mankind. As such they become a new reason moving God (humanly speaking) to cancel our debt *in actu primo*.

In this connection Father Dillenschneider borrows an example from Christology to illustrate the point. We know, he writes, that from the first moment of the Incarnation and in virtue of the Hypostatic Union, the God-Man had an initial exigency to the glorification of His body. On

---

[152] Dillenschneider, *Pour une Corédemption bien comprise,* in *Marianum,* Vol. 11, 1949, pp. 109-110. Cf. H. Seiler, *op. cit.,* pp. 123-131, esp. p. 129.

[153] Dillenschneider, *Le mystère de la Corédemption mariale ...,* p. 162.

the other hand, we know that this bodily glorification was also merited by His sacred Passion and death. Now, are we to suppose that this merit argues to a deficiency in the previous connatural right to glorification? Not at all. After the Passion, the bodily glorification is due to Christ by a twofold title: the Hypostatic Union *and* the infinite merit acquired through His sufferings.[154] Something similar may be said concerning the reconciliation of the world *in actu primo*. It is granted by God in view of a double title, without the implication that one of them (constituted by the Marian element) betrays any deficiency in the other.

We have an analogous situation in the sphere of the subjective Redemption. Whenever we co-operate with divine grace to perform some salutary act, our co-operation adds nothing to the intrinsic value of Christ's grace. On the contrary, the former is entirely dependent upon the latter. And yet, that share of ours is not at all superfluous and useless; indeed, it is necessary to produce the salutary act because God has decreed that the work of our sanctification should be not only divine but human as well. "*Qui ergo fecit te sine te, non te justificat sine te.*"[155] If this is possible in the realm of subjective Redemption, why not also in the order of objective Redemption? Is not the divine element in one case as incapable of being intrinsically enhanced as in the other?

It may be asked further: Why did God decree to grant our reconciliation in view of this twofold title? The answer would seem to lie in the very nature of the redemptive alliance between God and the human race. That alliance is frequendy described in Sacred Scripture as a mystical espousal. Since the Redeemer's bride is the community of the redeemed, it is fitting that the latter be actively represented on Calvary at the climax of this mystical marriage. Now, if we know from the living tradition of the Church that Our Blessed Lady is both the intimate associate of the Saviour in the entire process of salvation and also the prototype of the community to be redeemed, is it not reasonable to suppose that God wished her actively to represent that community at

---

[154] Dillenschneider, *Marie au service de notre Rédemption* ..., pp. 356-357.

[155] St. Augustine, *Sermo 169*, cap. 11, n. 13; *PL*, 38, 923. Cf. Ch. de Koninck, *La part de la personne humaine dans l'oeuvre de la Rédemption*, in *Laval Théologique et Philosophique*, Vol. 10, 1954, pp. 44-53.

the most solemn moment of the spiritual nuptials?[156] Is not Mary's official function as the New Eve to offer atonement for our sins together with the New Adam?[157] And if almighty God Himself freely appointed her to that official role, did He not owe it to Himself to accept her meritorious co-operation as a new title for our Redemption *in actu primo*?

A final attempt was recently made by Father Lennerz to weaken our position. If God — he wrote in substance — freely decreed not to accept Christ's Redemption without Mary's co-operation, the latter must be said to belong to the very essence of the redemptive work. In this event, the work of Christ alone, without Mary's co-operation, is not sufficient to redeem the human race.[158]

The above reasoning, based as it is on an obvious equivocation, is not at all conclusive. Its underlying weakness is the author's confusion of that which is *necessary* with that which is *essential*. Our Lady's co-operation is hypothetically necessary because it was decreed by God, but it remains nonessential. Hence, God accepts Christ's merits and satisfactions as an essential element of our Redemption, and at the same time He deigns to accept Our Lady's merits and satisfactions as a nonessential (though necessary), secondary, and totally subordinate element of the same Redemption. The point here is that God's acceptance does in no way alter the intrinsic nature of either element.

Having disposed of these speculative stumbling blocks, let us now turn our attention to a difficulty of a more practical character: the one sometimes raised against the title "Coredemptrix" itself. In the opinion of some, this title had better be banished from Catholic theology for the following reasons. First of all, it is a "novelty," unknown before the past century.[159] Then again, the very nature of the word is apt to mislead the

---

[156] Dillenschneider, *Le mystère de la Corédemption mariale* ..., p. 135. Cf. R. Laurentin, *Notre Dame et la Messe au service de la paix du Christ* (Tournai, 1954), pp. 44-45.

[157] Pius XII, cf. above, footnote 30.

[158] H. Lennerz, *De cooperatione B. Virginis in ipso opere Redemptionis*, in *Gregorianum*, Vol. 28, 1947, pp. 577-578; also Vol. 29, 1948, p. 141.

[159] Thus Pohle-Preuss, *Mariology*, 5th ed. (St. Louis, Mo., 1926), pp. 122-123, where we are informed that the term was "invented" by Castelplanio (died in 1872) and Faber (died in 1863).

uninitiated, to engender confusion in the minds of those who are less enlightened and even merely prejudiced. After all, the prefix "co" in the word Coredemptrix does seem to place Our Lady on an equal footing with her Son in the redemptive economy.[160] Finally, it has the disadvantage that it can only be explained by being explained away.[161]

Since we have on previous occasions, and indeed quite at length, vindicated the legitimacy of this Marian title, an answer *per summa capita* would seem to suffice at this time.

First of all, the fact that a word is new does not necessarily militate against its legitimacy, especially if it is used to convey an old idea. There was a time in history when words like *transubstantiation, omoousios, theotokos,* and others were new, and yet they were subsequently consecrated by ecclesiastical usage. Second, it is not correct to state that the title "Coredemptrix" was first introduced in Catholic theology during the nineteenth century. Actually, it can be traced back to at least the foureenth century in a liturgical book preserved with other manuscripts at St. Peter's in Salzburg.[162]

As regards the structure of the term "Coredemptrix" we may point out that the prefix "co" is the exact equivalent of the Latin *cum* which means "with," not "equal," as every grammarian knows. For this reason St. Paul could rightly say that we are God's "co-workers" in the process of our sanctification, without in the least equating the efficacy of God's grace with that of our own co-operation.[163] Besides, if the prefix "co" means "equal," what then does the word "co-equal" mean? Hence we see no justified fear that the title "Coredemptrix" will mislead and confuse the less enlightened and the prejudiced. A sensible way to prevent that confusion would seem to be to instruct such people so as to make them more enlightened and less prejudiced.

---

[160] Thus A. Michel, *Mary's Coredemption*, in *The American Ecclesiastical Review,* Vol. 122, March, 1950, p. 184.

[161] L. E. Bellanti, S.J., *Mary, Coredemptrix and Mediatrix,* in *Our Blessed Lady,* Cambridge Summer School Lectures for 1933 (London, 1934), p. 214.

[162] Cf. above, footnote 85. On the history and usage of the term "Coredemptrix" cf. Laurentin, *Le titre de Corédemptrice. Etude historique,* in *Marianum,* Vol. 13, 1951, pp. 396-452.

[163] 1 Cor. 3:6-9. Cf. Carol, *The Problem of Our Lady's Coredemption,* in *The American Ecclesiastical Review,* Vol. 123, July, 1950, pp. 32-51, esp. pp. 34-37.

OUR LADY'S COREDEMPTION

Last, the claim that the expression "Coredemptrix" can only be explained by being explained away does not correspond to actual facts. If by that term we meant only that Our Lady brought the Redeemer into the world and that she now intercedes for us in heaven, we surely would be explaining it away. But when we style Mary our Coredemptrix we mean exactly what we say, namely, that "she together with Christ redeemed the human race."[164] It is true, of course, that this apparently bold statement must be understood and explained in a sense which is compatible with other undeniable truths of our Catholic faith; that is to say, we must emphasize that Our Lady's share in the redemptive process was entirely secondary, nonessential, and subordinate to the unique causality of the Saviour, to whose merits she owed the very possibility of being His partner. But we ask: Is that "explaining it away"?

We have an analogous case in connection with the word "infallibility," to mention but one example. Etymologically, as it stands, this term means simply inability to err. When we apply it to the Holy Father we must, of necessity, narrow down its meaning to a highly restricted and specific area. Once the required limitations are clearly drawn, it is obvious that the Pope *can* err on a variety of subjects.

Now we ask: When a Catholic theologian thus explains Papal infallibility, is he merely "explaining it away"? Not at all. The Church has a perfect right to select any term she deems suitable to convey a given doctrine, and to attach to that term a specific and restricted meaning. Something similar may be said concerning the title "Coredemptrix" which has been widely used in the Church for several centuries, and has been repeatedly endorsed by the Holy See in recent years.[165] In our humble opinion, this fact alone more than sufficiently warrants its legitimacy.

CONCLUSION

The exposé undertaken in these pages has been an attempt to familiarize our readers with the very essence of the Catholic position

---

[164] Pope Benedict XV, Apostolic Letter *Inter sodalicia* (March 22, 1918), in *A.A.S.*, Vol. 10, 1918, pp. 181-182.

[165] Cf. *A.S.S.*, Vol. 41, 1908, p. 409; Vol. 5, 1913, p. 364; Vol. 6, 1914, p. 108. Cf. Carol, *The Holy See and the Title of "Coredemptrix,"* in *The Homiletic and Pastoral Review*, Vol. 37, April, 1937, pp. 746-748.

relative to Mary's role in the process of man's Redemption, and with the theological justification of that position. We have not only surveyed contemporary attitudes and opinions on this question; we have also inquired into the past, searching the written and spoken word of God. Such an investigation is necessary in order to ascertain whether and to what extent the Catholic teaching of today may be considered an authentic development of the original data furnished by the sources of revelation, or rather a deviation from, and a corruption of, that primitive deposit of divine truth. The final decision on this point must be left, not to the professional theologians (much less to the historian), but solely and exclusively to the living Magisterium of the Church. The theologian may, to be sure, evaluate the result of his investigation and formulate positive or negative conclusions accordingly; but these must always be of a tentative nature, always subject to the final judgment of the *Ecclesia docens*. In the absence of a definitive and infallible pronouncement of the Magisterium concerning Our Lady's Coredemption, we have endeavored to discover at least the "mind" of that teaching authority as represented by recent Pontiffs. If our interpretation of their repeated utterances on this vital problem is sound and objective, then it would seem safe to conclude that the current doctrine of Mary's direct co-operation in the objective Redemption bears the unmistakable mark of a genuinely Catholic truth authentically developed from the original deposit of revelation. Incidentally, this conclusion is quite generally accepted among contemporary theologians, although it is not always formulated in so many words.

May we now advance a step further and speak of the doctrine's definability? Several eminent scholars have declared themselves favorable in this respect.[166] We can think of no solid reason militating

---

[166] Cf., for example, E. Druwé, S.J., *La Médiation universelle de Marie*, in *Maria. Études sur le Sainte Vierge*, ed. H. du Manoir, Vol. 1 (Paris, 1949), p. 566; C. Friethoff, *op. cit.*, pp. 4-5, 226-227; J. Bittremieux, *De Mediatione universali B. M. Virginis quoad gratias* (Brugis, 1926), p. 229; J. Lebon, *art. cit.*, pp. 680-681; F. X. Godts, C.Ss.R., *De definibilitate Mediationis universalis Deiparae* (Bruxellis, 1904); P. Villada, S.J., *Por la definición dogmática de la Mediación universal de la Santísima Virgen* (Madrid, 1917), pp. 194-195; and countless other authors who teach the same thing, at least equivalently, by their endeavor to show that the thesis is implicitly contained in the sources of revelation, and taught by the Magisterium. In our work *De Corredemptione* ... (pp. 589-607) the reader will find

OUR LADY'S COREDEMPTION   475

against their stand. Indeed, if our appraisal of the copious testimonies gathered here and elsewhere is valid and cogent, then the extant data constitute an overwhelming array of evidence pointing to the revealed character of this doctrine. Theologians may and will, of course, debate the further question as to whether it was revealed formally or only virtually. While such discussions are undoubtedly legitimate and often fruitful, nevertheless, it is well to bear in mind that the solution of this question is not at all necessary in order to proceed to a dogmatic definition. The course adopted by the Supreme Pontiff with regard to the Immaculate Conception and Mary's Assumption is an evident proof of it. Whether or not the Vicar of Christ will some day consider our doctrine sufficiently well established to be proclaimed an article of Catholic faith remains, of course, pure conjecture; but it is our fervent hope and humble prayer that the decision will be made in a not too distant future.

---

numerous statements of bishops who think along the same lines. Particularly worthy of note is the *Votum dogmaticum* which Bishop J. Th. Laurent, Vicar Apostolic of Hamburg, submitted to the Vatican Council for a definition (cf. p. 593). More recently, on November 26, 1951, a formal *Postulatum* was presented to the Holy Father by His Eminence, Emmanuel Cardinal Arteaga, Archbishop of Havana, and the entire Cuban hierarchy, requesting the dogmatic definition of Our Lady's Coredemption, and of her universal Mediation. The document itself is dated October 6, 1951. Since we are privileged to possess a copy of the original (which has not been made public), we can vouch for the fact that the petition urges the Holy Father to define the doctrine of the Coredemption *in exactly the same sense* vindicated throughout this paper. This represents the first time in history that a step of this nature has been taken by the hierarchy of any country.

Mary, Dispensatrix of All Graces

By ARMAND J. ROBICHAUD, S.M.

HEN Our Blessed Lord uttered His *Consummatum est* on the cross, the bloody immolation of His mortal life drew to its dramatic close. It was then and there that His sacrificial act, embodying the infinite merits and satisfactions of His whole earthly career, definitively sealed what Catholic theologians are wont to call the "objective Redemption" of mankind. Yet the *Consummatum est* referred only to the first act of the divine drama representing the whole economy of the world's salvation. The second act would be the enduring process in which the treasury of graces, merited by the Saviour through His life and death, is made available and is actually communicated to individual souls to enable them to attain to their supernatural goal.

The prominent role which Our Blessed Lady played as Coredemptrix in the first phase of this redemptive work has been the subject of the preceding chapter. Our discussion at present centers exclusively on her active share in the second phase of Christ's salvific economy, namely, her unique prerogative as Dispensatrix of all graces.[1]

Before endeavoring to establish the fact of Mary's prerogative, it is well to explain briefly its exact meaning. When we assert that Our Lady is the *Dispensatrix* of all graces we mean that she actually *obtains* them for us, through some true causality on her part, the nature of which will be discussed later. By "all graces" we mean sanctifying grace, the infused theological and moral virtues, the gifts of the Holy Spirit, all actual graces, the charismatic gifts, and even temporal favors having a bearing on our supernatural end. In brief, everything which produces, conserves, increases, or perfects the supernatural life of man. This universally

---

[1] Very frequently Our Lady is called "Mediatrix" in the restricted sense that she *dispenses* all graces to all men. In itself, however, the word "Mediatrix" has a broader meaning and includes Our Lady's co-operation in both phases of the redemptive work. Cf. J. B. Carol, O.F.M., *The Theological Concept of Mediation and Coredemption*, in *Ephemerides Theologicae Lovanienses*, Vol. 14, 1937, pp. 642-650.

extends likewise to the beneficiaries of Mary's mission, for it affects *all* human beings of *all* times, including the souls in purgatory. Those who lived before Mary's time received their graces in view of her future merits; those living after her, particularly after her Assumption into heaven, receive all graces through her actual intercession, or even, according to some, through her physical instrumental causality. Moreover, the doctrine does not mean that Our Lady's intercession must be invoked as a prerequisite for the reception of graces. Whether we address our petitions to her, or directly to Christ or to some other saint, the favor will be granted in every instance through Mary's causality.

The doctrine of Mary's actual share in the dispensation of every single grace has met with unqualified support in Catholic quarters particularly since the seventeenth century. The exceptions to this remarkable consensus are relatively few and far between. To recall the most important: Theophilus Raynaud, S.J. († 1663), who claimed that our thesis was only a pious opinion lacking solid foundation in the sources. For him, Our Lady was the "channel of all graces" in the sense that she gave birth to Christ, the Author of all graces.[2] Again, in the eighteenth century, the otherwise learned L. A. Muratori († 1751) referred to this teaching as "a sheer exaggeration" and "an error."[3] When St. Alphonsus Liguori undertook to defend Mary's prerogative, he was answered by Muratori's nephew who, in turn, drew an excellent rebuttal from the Saint entitled *Risposta ad un anonimo ...*[4] More recently, Prof. John Ude,[5] Anton Fischer,[6] and Jean Guitton[7] have expressed similar views on the subject, provoking vigorous protests in certain quarters.

Our treatment of this question will be divided into two parts,

---

[2] *Marialia. Diptycha Mariana; op. omn.,* Vol. 7 (Lugduni, 1665), p. 223 f.

[3] *Della regolata devozione de' cristiani; opere ...,* Vol. 6 (Arezzo, 1768), 199-200. The book appeared under the pseudonym Lamindo Pritanio.

[4] Found in an appendix to *The Glories of Mary,* ed. E. Grimm (Brooklyn, 1931), pp. 684-694.

[5] Ude, I*st Maria die Mitlerin aller Gnaden?* (Bressanone, 1928).

[6] Fischer, in *Beilage zur Ausburger Postzeitung,* February 13, 1924. Cf. *L'Ami du Clergé,* Vol. 42, 1925, pp. 49-51.

[7] Guitton, *The Virgin Mary,* trans. by A. Gordon Smith (New York, 1952), p. 138. Cf. W. G. Most, *Jean Guitton and the Mediatrix of All Graces,* in *The Homiletic and Pastoral Review,* Vol. 53, 1953, pp. 698-701.

namely: (I) the *fact* of Our Lady's role as Dispensatrix of all graces; and (II) the *nature* of that office. Our conclusion will contain a brief discussion concerning the theological note to be attached to this thesis, and also its definability.

I. THE FACT OF MARY'S ROLE AS DISPENSATRIX OF ALL GRACES

Since the truth of our thesis rests completely on the free will of God, the first duty of the theologian is to inquire into the sources of revelation (both proximate and remote) in order to ascertain what God Himself has deigned to disclose to us in this connection. Once we have established the thesis by means of positive theology, we shall endeavor to corroborate it by means of speculative theology. Hence the subdivision of this first part into the following sections: (A) The Ecclesiastical Magisterium; (B) The Sacred Liturgy, reflecting the mind of the Magisterium; (C) Sacred Scripture; (D) Tradition; and (E) Theological Reasoning.

A. The Ecclesiastical Magisterium

By "ecclesiastical magisterium" we mean the teaching of the Supreme Pontiff and of the bishops under him and with him. Since this constitutes "the proximate and universal criterion of truth for all theologians,"[8] its paramount importance hardly calls for emphasis here. The solemn and extraordinary magisterium having made no decision as yet on our subject, we shall limit ourselves to the consideration of the ordinary magisterium as exercised by the Popes only.[9]

It is particularly within the past century that the Popes have made repeated and very explicit references to Our Lady's role as Dispensatrix of all graces. However, even in centuries past, we discover occasional indications of an implicit belief in this doctrine as conveyed by titles and expressions such as *Mother of grace, Mother of the Church, Mother of*

---

[8] Pius XII, *Humani generis*, in *A.A.S.*, Vol. 42, 1950, p. 567.

[9] The mind of the bishops is sufficiently disclosed in connection with the celebration of the Feast of Mary Mediatrix.

men, *our Mother*, and the like.[10] Thus, for example, Sixtus IV (1471-1484) speaks of Our Lady as the "Mother of grace ... sedulous and constant intercessor before the King," and of her "merits and intercession of divine grace."[11] Again, Benedict XIV (1740-1758) states that Mary is "like a celestial stream through which the flow of all graces and gifts reach the soul of all wretched mortals."[12] And Pius VII (1800-1823) condenses the whole truth in the significant expression "Dispensatrix of all graces."[13] With Pius IX (1846-1878) a new era begins in the field of Mariology. This is particularly so as regards the Marian prerogative we are now discussing. In his encyclical *Ubi primum* (1849) the Pope of the Immaculate Conception writes: "The foundation of all Our confidence, as you know well, Venerable Brethren, is found in the Blessed Virgin Mary. For God has committed to Mary the treasury of all good things, in order that everyone may know that through her are obtained every hope, every grace, and all salvation. For this is His will, that we obtain everything through Mary."[14] Again, in his *Ineffabilis Deus* (1854), Pius alludes to our doctrine in these words:

... since she has been appointed by God to be the Queen of heaven and earth, and is exalted above the choirs of angels and saints, and even stands at the right hand of her only-begotten Son, Jesus Christ, our Lord, she presents our petitions in a most efficacious manner. What she petitions, she obtains. Her pleas can never be unheard.[15]

In Leo XIII (1878-1903), whose contributions to Mariology in general are well known, we find a frequent and vigorous exponent of the thesis that Mary is the channel of absolutely every grace. Our references will

---

[10] Cf. numerous references in G. W. Shea, *The Teaching of the Magisterium on Mary's Spiritual Maternity*, in *Marian Studies*, Vol. 3, 1952, pp. 41-43.

[11] Sixtus IV, *Cum praecelsa*, in the appendix to Ch. Sericoli, O.F.M., *Immaculata B. M. Virginis Conceptio juxta Xysti IV Constitutiones* (Romae, 1945), pp. 153-154.

[12] Benedicti XIV, *op. omnia*, Vol. 16 (ed. Prati, 1846), p. 428.

[13] Pius VII, *Ampliatio privilegiorum ecclesiae B. M. Virginis ab angelo salutatae in coenobio Fratrum Ordinis Servorum B. M. V. Florentiae, A.D. 1806;* in J. Bourasse, *Summa aurea ...,* Vol. 7 (Parisiis, 1862), col. 546.

[14] Cf. *Papal Documents on Mary*, ed. by W. J. Doheny, C.S.C., and J. Kelly (Milwaukee, 1954), p. 3. Hereafter referred to as Doheny-Kelly.

[15] Doheny-Kelly, pp. 26-27.

be limited to only a few of his most outstanding utterances. In the very first of his memorable Rosary encyclicals, *Supremi apostolatus* (1883), he styles Our Lady "the guardian of our peace and the dispensatrix of heavenly graces."[16] A year later, in his *Superiore anno,* he speaks of the prayers presented to God "through her whom He has chosen to be the dispenser of *all* heavenly graces."[17] And a little further: "to her we must fly, to her whom the Church rightly and justly calls the dispenser of salvation, the helper and the deliverer. ..."[18]

But it is in his encyclical *Octobri mense* (1891) that Pope Leo has left us his most striking pronouncement of this subject. Having recalled that the eternal Son of God did not wish to accomplish the mystical union between Himself and mankind at the time of the Incarnation without first seeking the free consent of Our Lady as representative of the whole human race, the Pope adds:

> With equal truth can it be affirmed that, by the will of God, *nothing* of the immense treasure of every grace which the Lord has accumulated, *comes to us except through Mary.* ... How great are the wisdom and mercy revealed in *this design of God.* ... Mary is our glorious intermediary; she is the powerful Mother of the omnipotent God. ... This design of such dear mercy realized by God in Mary and confirmed by the testament of Christ (Jn. 19:26-27), was understood from the beginning and accepted with the utmost joy by the holy Apostles and the earliest believers. It was also the belief and teaching of the venerable Fathers of the Church. All the Christian peoples of every age accepted it unanimously. ... There is no other reason for this than a *divine faith.*[19]

In connection with this remarkable passage we would like to make the following observations:

1. The truth proposed by Pope Leo is: the will of God is that we obtain absolutely everything through Mary.
2. The encyclical is addressed to the whole Church.
3. The Pope appeals to the universal belief of the Church from the

---

[16] *Ibid.,* p. 29. In our translation of Leo XIII we follow Doheny-Kelly, although with slight modifications here and there.

[17] *Ibid.,* p. 41.

[18] *Ibid.,* p. 42.

[19] *Ibid.,* pp. 55-57. Cf. J. Bittremieux, *Doctrina Mariana Leonis XIII* (Brugis, 1928), pp. 83-84.

Apostles to our own day, thereby officially interpreting tradition. This unanimous consensus of the *Ecclesia docens* with the *Ecclesia discens* in a matter that could not be learned except through revelation is a guarantee that God did reveal it.
4. Pope Leo gives us to understand that God implied this truth in the Annunciation pericope (*Lk.* 1:26-38), and also in the proclamation of Christ from the cross, as narrated in St. John's Gospel (19:26-27). Therefore, the doctrine is based on the written word of God.

Inspired, no doubt, by the teaching of his predecessor, St. Pius X (1903-1914) found occasion to add the weight of his own authority to the same belief. It is well known that before writing his encyclical *Ad diem illum* (1904), to commemorate the golden jubilee of the proclamation of the Immaculate Conception, he desired to reread in its entirety the treatise on *The True Devotion* by St. Louis M. Grignion de Montfort. Little wonder, then, that his admirable encyclical is thoroughly impregnated with the doctrine of Mary's universal Mediation. For our specific purpose, the most important section of the encyclical reads as follows:

By this union of will and suffering between Christ and Mary, "she merited to become in a most worthy manner the Reparatrix of the lost world"[20] and, consequently, the *Dispensatrix of all the gifts* which Jesus acquired for us through His death and blood. Indeed, we do not deny that the distribution of these gifts belongs by strict and proper right to Christ. ... Yet ... it was granted to the august Virgin to be together with her Only-begotten Son the most powerful Mediatrix and Conciliatrix of the whole world. So Christ is the source ... Mary, however, as St. Bernard justly remarks, is the channel, or she is the neck by which the Body is united to the Head, and the Head sends power and strength through the Body. For she is the neck of our Head, through which all spiritual gifts are communicated to His Body.[21]

While the above passage with its complete context has occasioned endless discussions and a variety of opinions as to its bearing on Mary's

---

[20] Eadmerus, *Liber de excellentiis B. Virginis,* cap. 9; *PL,* 159, 573.

[21] *A.S.S.,* Vol. 36, 1903-1904, pp. 453-454. Cf. D. J. Unger, O.F.M.Cap., *Mary Immaculate. The Bull "Ineffabilis Deus" of Pope Pius IX, translated and annotated* (Paterson, N. J., 1948), pp. 8-10.

role as Coredemptrix, nevertheless, its clear enunciation of the dispensatrix thesis has been frankly admitted by all.[22]

Benedict XV (1914-1922) continued the trend of his predecessors, and also added contributions of his own to our doctrine. For example, he re-echoes Leo XIII in statements such as:

> ... since all the graces that the Author of all good deigns to bestow upon the poor descendants of Adam are, by favorable design of divine Providence, dispensed through the hands of the most holy Virgin. ...[23]

In his Apostolic Letter *Inter sodalicia* (1918) the Pope tells us that the reason we receive all graces through Mary is because she had previously redeemed the world together with Christ.[24]

Objections have at times been raised against the universality of Mary's mediation on the grounds that we receive many favors through the intercession of other saints too. Benedict XV made an important pronouncement on this point in an allocution after the solemn reading of the decree approving the two miracles for the canonization of Joan of Arc. The promoter of the faith had objected that one of the two miracles had been worked at Lourdes, and thus should be attributed to Mary, not to Joan of Arc. To which the Pope answers:

> If in every miracle we must recognize the mediation of Mary, through whom, according to God's will, every grace and blessing comes to us, it must be admitted that in the case of one of these miracles the mediation of the Blessed Virgin manifested itself in a very special way. We believe that God so disposed the matter in order to remind the faithful that the remembrance of Mary must never be excluded, even when it may seem that a miracle is to be attributed to the intercession or the mediation of one of the blessed or one of the saints.[25]

It is also worth mentioning here that it was Benedict XV who, upon request of Cardinal Mercier, granted to the dioceses of Belgium, and to all the Ordinaries who might petition it, permission to celebrate the

---

[22] Cf. L. Di Fonzo, O.F.M.Conv., B. Virgo "de congruo, ut aiunt, promeret nobis quae Christus de condigno promeruit," in Marianum, Vol. 1, 1939, pp. 418-459.

[23] Letter *Il 27 aprile,* to Card. Gasparri; *A.A.S.,* Vol. 9, 1917, p. 266. Cf. also *Cum Sanctissima Virgo,* in *A.A.S.,* Vol. 9, 1917, p. 324.

[24] *A.A.S.,* Vol. 10, 1918, p. 182.

[25] *Actes de Bénoît XV,* Vol. 2, 1926, p. 22; in E. Druwé, *art. cit.,* p. 514.

special feast of Mary *Mediatrix of All Graces* on May 31 of each year.[26]

We conclude our references to Pope Benedict with a quotation from a letter he addressed to the American hierarchy relative to the National Shrine of the Immaculate Conception in Washington:

> ... all the Catholics of the United States will have their eyes turned towards that holy church placed under the protection of the Immaculate Virgin, *Dispensatrix of all graces* ... and will come in great numbers to manifest their religion and their piety.[27]

Pope Pius XI (1922-1939) is in perfect harmony with his predecessors on this point. Since it would be repetitious to elaborate on his many pronouncements, we shall select only two passages in which our doctrine is very clearly stated:

> We have nothing more at heart than to promote more and more the piety of the Christian people toward the Virgin treasurer of all graces at the side of God (gratiarum omnium apud Deum sequestram).[28]

> Confiding in her intercession with Jesus, "the one Mediator of God and man" (1 Tim. 2:5), who wished to associate His own Mother with Himself as the advocate of sinners, as the dispenser and mediatrix of grace ...[29]

Our gloriously reigning Pontiff, Pope Pius XII, may rightly be hailed as the greatest Marian Pope in modern times. Indeed, he has done more than any of his predecessors to make the world more Mary-conscious. He is the Pope of the Assumption, of the first Marian Year in history; he has instituted the liturgical feast honoring Our Lady's Queenship; he has solemnly consecrated the human race to her Immaculate Heart. Hence

---

[26] Cf. *La Vie Diocésaine,* Vol. 10, 1921, pp. 96-106. The rescript of the Sacred Congregation of Rites is dated January 12, 1921. The document was not inserted in the *A.A.S.* On the suggestion of Cardinal Mercier, many archbishops of the world requested the Pope's permission to celebrate the feast in their own dioceses. Some of their letters appear in *Mémoires et Rapports du Congrès Marial tenu à Bruxelles 1921,* Vol. 2 (Bruxelles, 1922), pp. 655-679.

[27] *A.A.S.,* Vol. 11, 1919, p. 173.

[28] Pius XI, *Cognitum sane,* January 14, 1926, in *A.A.S.,* Vol. 18, 1926, p. 213. Cf. G. M. Roschini, O.S.M., *La Madonna nel pensiero e nell'insegnamento di Pio XI,* in *Marianum,* Vol. 1, 1939, pp. 121-172.

[29] Encyclical *Miserentissimus Redemptor,* May 8, 1928, in *A.A.S.,* Vol. 20, 1928, p. 178. Cf. J. Bittremieux, *Ex doctrina mariana Pii XI,* in *Ephemerides Theologicae Lovanienses,* Vol. 11, 1934, pp. 100-101.

we would naturally expect his teaching on Mary's mediation to be at least as eloquent as that of his predecessors.

In numerous documents the Pope gives evident proof of his belief when he urges the faithful to ask and expect various graces and blessings from the Mother of God.[30] In some of these, he is particularly explicit on this point. For example, in his letter *Superiore anno* (1940), he writes:

> And since, as St. Bernard declares, "it is the will of God that we obtain all favors through Mary," let everyone hasten to have recourse to Mary. ....[31]

And again, in *Mediator Dei* (1947):

> She teaches us all virtues; she gives us her Son and with Him all the help we need, for "God wished us to have everything through Mary."[32]

The same thought, expressed in the same words, occurs in the encyclical *Doctor Mellifluus* (1953), commemorating the eighth centenary of the death of St. Bernard.[33] And in an allocution on April 21, 1940, he reminds a group of pilgrims from Genoa that Our Lady is "the channel of graces which regenerate us to the spiritual life and help us regain the celestial country."[34] Similar references are found also in his encyclical *Mystici Corporis* (1943), where Mary's queenly prerogative is indicated as one of the foundations for her universal mediation.[35] Another basis, Mary's Coredemption, is clearly recalled in his memorable broadcast to Fatima in 1946, where he tells us that, because Mary "had been united as Mother and Minister, with the King of martyrs in the ineffable work of Redemption, she remains always associated with Him ... in the distribution of graces flowing from the Redemption."[36]

In closing the testimony of Pius XII we quote from a decree of the

---

[30] Pius XII, *Quamvis plane,* in *A.A.S.,* Vol. 33, 1941, pp. 110-112; *Carissimis Russiae populis,* in *A.A.S.,* Vol. 44, 1952, p. 505; *Fulgens corona,* in *A.A.S.,* Vol. 45, 1953, pp. 577-592.

[31] *A.A.S.,* Vol. 32, 1940, p. 145.

[32] English translation, Vatican edition (1948), p. 54.

[33] *A.A.S.,* Vol. 45, 1953, p. 382.

[34] Cf. *L'Osservatore Romano,* April 22-23, 1940, p. 1.

[35] *A.A.S.,* Vol. 35, 1943, pp. 247-248.

[36] *Ibid.,* Vol. 38, 1946, p. 266. Cf. also *Ad coeli Reginam,* October 11, 1954, in *A.A.S.,* Vol. 46, 1954, pp. 635-636.

Sacred Congregation of Rites by which the Pope recognizes the miracles proposed for the canonization of Louis M. Grignion de Montfort. It is important because of its reference to tradition and the teaching of theologians. The opening paragraph reads:

> Gathering together the tradition of the Fathers, the *Doctor Mellifluus* (St. Bernard) teaches that God wants us to have everything through Mary. This pious and salutary doctrine all theologians at the present time hold in common accord.[37]

Conclusion: Our consideration of the argument from the magisterium may close with the following observations of Canon Bittremieux, which we summarize and gladly make our own:

1. The doctrine that Our Lady is the Dispensatrix of absolutely every grace is inculcated not only by one Pope, but by a series of them; to be exact, by every Pope in the past one hundred years.
2. The magisterium exercised by the Popes in the present matter is thoroughly assertive and categorical.
3. The doctrine is taught not only in allocutions and private letters, but also in authentic public documents addressed to the whole Church; likewise through the institution of the liturgical feast of Mary *Mediatrix of All Graces.*
4. This stand engages the magisterium in a very grave matter which pertains to the domain of faith. Hence these pronouncements require our religious assent.
5. The Popes realize that their authority tends *per se* to strengthen the theologians' conviction that Mary's universal mediation is a revealed truth; nevertheless they encourage and promote this doctrine with ever increasing frequency and clearness.
6. Moreover, we must bear in mind the perpetual and permanent ordinary assistance of the Holy Spirit who overshadows the Popes in their work as pastors and teachers of the faithful in the exercise of their ordinary magisterium.[38]

To these sober conclusions of the renowned Belgian Mariologist, we

---

[37] *A.A.S.*, Vol. 34, 1942, p. 44.
[38] J. Bittremieux, *De mediatione universali B. M. Virginis quoad gratias* (Brugis, 1926), pp. 154-156.

would add one of our own: It is our considered opinion, *salvo meliori judicio*, that, even though we do not have as yet a solemn definition on the matter, the doctrine of Our Lady's universal mediation of graces should be classified as *de fide divina ex ordinario magisterio*.

This conclusion is based particularly on our previous observations concerning Pope Leo XIII's encyclical *Octobri mense*.

B. THE SACRED LITURGY

Having examined the pronouncements of the ordinary magisterium, we now direct our attention to the liturgy, which is rightly considered an authentic reflection of the mind of the *Ecclesia docens*. The liturgy is Catholic doctrine translated into action, and for this reason it becomes an excellent vehicle of education in the truths of our holy faith.[39] The sacred rites of the Church argue to a belief, not indeed in the sense that they gave rise to it, but rather in the sense that they presuppose its existence. Hence the Church's practice to search the liturgy prior to the dogmatic definition of certain doctrines.[40] During the discussion of controversial subjects, the Church and the Fathers "have never failed to look to the age-old and time-honored sacred rites for enlightenment,"[41] being well aware that "the law of prayer determines the law of belief." Bearing this in mind, let us now review briefly a few of the various liturgical testimonies relative to our doctrine both in the East and in the West.[42]

1. *The Latin Liturgy* — Particularly significant as revealing the mind of the Church is the special feast of Mary *Mediatrix of All Graces* approved and commended by Pope Benedict XV in the year 1921, and observed in numerous dioceses on May 31. The central theme of the

---

[39] Cf. Pius XI, *Quas primas*, December 11, 1925, in *A.A.S.*, Vol. 17, 1925, p. 603.

[40] For example, the dogmas of the Immaculate Conception and the Assumption.

[41] Pius XII, *Mediator Dei*, November 20, 1947, in *A.A.S.*, Vol. 39, 1947, p. 541.

[42] Cf. Serapio de Iragui, *art. cit.*, in *Alma Socia Christi*, Vol. 2, p. 222 ff.; G. Gumbinger, O.F.M.Cap., *Mary in the Eastern Liturgies*, in MARIOLOGY, ed. J. B. Carol, O.F.M., Vol. 1 (Milwaukee, 1954), pp. 281-344; S. Daly, O.S.B., *Mary in the Western Liturgy*, in MARIOLOGY, Vol. 1, pp. 245-280, esp. pp. 369-372; I. Van Houtryve, O.S.B., *Le méditation de Marie dans la liturgie*, in *La Vie Diocésaine*, Vol. 11, 1922, pp. 349-360.

feast is Our Lady's role in the actual dispensation of all graces.[43] Consequently, the Office and Mass abound in references to this doctrine. A few instances will suffice:

> Behold my Lord has entrusted everything to me, and there is nothing which is not in my power, or that he has not given to me. (Antiphon for the *Magnificat*, First Vespers.)

> O Lord Jesus Christ, our Mediator with the Father, who hast deigned to appoint thy most Blessed Virgin Mother to be our Mother also and our Mediatrix with thee, mercifully grant that all who shall approach thee seeking favors, may rejoice having obtained everything through her. *(Oration for Office and Mass.)*

> Let us come and adore Christ the Redeemer who has willed that we should have all good things through Mary. (*Invitatorium*.)

> Who will distribute this sacred flow (of grace) to the redeemed? This care is confided to Mary who, as arbiter, directs the course of salvation. Everything which the Redeemer merited for us is dispensed by Mary, His Mother, at whose request the Son willingly diffuses His blessings. *(Hymn at Matins.)*

The lessons for the second noctum are taken from the works of St. Ephraem, St. Germain, and St. Bernard, containing glowing descriptions of Our Lady's mediatorial office.

It may be of interest to note in this connection that long before the present feast of Mary Mediatrix was established, the Holy See had granted the various branches of the Franciscan Order a special Mass and Office for the feast of Our Lady of the Angels (August 2), the Oration of which opens with these significant words: "O God who hast wished to dispense *all* favors to men through thy most holy Mother ..."[44]

2. *The Eastern Liturgy* — The Orientals have no special feast honoring Our Lady as Dispensatrix of all graces. Nevertheless, their liturgical books contain many more allusions to this Marian prerogative than do those of the Western Church. We do not, of course, discover any attempts to convey the doctrine in dogmatic formulas, but the rich

---

[43] Cf. J. Lebon, *A propos des textes liturgiques de la fête de Marie Mediatrice*, in *Marianum*, Vol. 14, 1952, pp. 122-128.

[44] D. Baier, O.F.M., *The Franciscan Office of St. Mary of the Angels and the Mediation of Grace*, in *Orate Fratres*, Vol. 10, 1936, pp. 399-402.

imagery and the variety of ways in which Mary's universal intercession is constantly emphasized unequivocally points to their consciousness that she is the channel of all heavenly graces. The gathering together of the numerous texts reflecting this conviction would constitute sufficient material for a separate dissertation. For reasons of necessary brevity we shall select but a few pertinent passages.

For the *Byzantines,* for example, Our Lady is "the bridge that brings mortals from earth to heaven."[45] In their Divine Office she is addressed as the one "through whom the human race has found salvation" and through whom "we shall find Paradise."[46] During the Mass, before Mary's icon, the celebrant invokes her protection as "the fountain of mercy."[47]

The *Coptic* liturgy is even more explicit. In one of its tropars we read that our salvation is insured "because *every help* comes to the faithful through Mary, the Mother of God."[48] And in a certain *theotokia:* "We have no hope before the Lord Jesus Christ, except through thy prayers and intercession, O Queen of us all."[49] Even in the administration of the various sacraments the priest's prayer implies that the effects of the sacred rites are obtained somehow through the intercession of Mary.[50]

The *Syrians* are hardly less clear in conveying the same doctrine through their liturgy. Thus, in one of their many beautiful prayers they address Our Lady as follows: "How can I praise thee duly, O most chaste Virgin? For thou alone among men art all-holy; and thou givest to all the help and grace they need."[51]

From the *Armenian* liturgy, so rich in references to Mary's place in

---

[45] *Officio del Inno Akatistos in onore della SS. Madre di Dio* (Grottaferrata, 1949), p. 15. *Ibid.,* p. 32: "Hail, dispenser of divine goodness!"

[46] Gumbinger, *art. cit.,* p. 300.

[47] S. Salaville, *Marie dans la liturgie byzantine ou grec-slav,* in *Maria. Études sur la Sainte Vierge,* ed. H. du Manoir, S.J., Vol. 1 (Paris, 1949), p. 303.

[48] *Kitab al ebsallyati wa al Turwhat* (Cairo, 1913), p. 131. Cf. G. Giamberardini, O.F.M., *La mediazione di Maria nella chiesa egiziana* (Cairo, 1952), p. 75.

[49] *Al Khwlagy ...,* pp. 206-207; Giamberardini, p. 56.

[50] E. Denzinger, *Ritus Orientalium,* Vol. 1 (Wirceburgi, 1863), pp. 205, 238, 259, 437. Giamberardini, pp. 73-74.

[51] D. Attwater, *Prayers from the Eastern Liturgies* (London, 1931), p. 20.

the economy of salvation, these two passages will suffice. "Rejoice, O Mother of God, throne of salvation and hope of the human race, Mediatrix of law and grace."[52] "We take refuge in thee, O most holy one ... dispenser of graces; thou art a fountain for the thirsty, rest for the afflicted, thou who hast borne the Word Divine."[53]

Written on a somewhat similar vein, the following excerpts from the *Chaldean* liturgy on the feast of the Immaculate Conception are likewise significant. "O Queen of queens, all rich, enrich thy servants with benefits, O Mother of the Most High. For He has made thee the dispensatrix of His treasures and the universal Queen. ... It is in thy bosom that He has placed His treasures, and in thee He has gathered together graces as in a sea, and He has made thee the source of life for mortals. ..."[54]

From these testimonies, which could easily be multiplied, it is sufficiently clear that the sacred liturgy, both in the East and in the West, faithfully mirrors the mind of the Church relative to the doctrine of Mary's universal mediation in the dispensation of every grace.

C. SACRED SCRIPTURE

It may be safely stated that most Marian truths find their ultimate basis in the written word of God. The doctrine of Our Lady's universal mediation of graces is no exception. It is contained in the sacred pages, not formally and explicitly, of course, but rather by implication. And this implication is arrived at especially with the aid of the magisterium and the constant teaching of tradition.

Of the various biblical passages generally adduced in this connection, some make possible the formulation of a defensible argument in favor of the doctrine, while others constitute mere indications of a possible design on God's part to confer His favors through Our Blessed Lady. Let us examine briefly a few of those more frequently invoked by Mariologists.

---

[52] V. Tekeyan, *La Mère de Dieu dans la liturgie arménienne*, in *Maria. Études sur la Sainte Vierge*, ed. H. du Manoir, S.J., Vol. 1 (Paris, 1949), p. 359.

[53] Tekeyan, *art. cit.*, p. 360.

[54] A. M. Massonat, O.P., *Marie dans la liturgie chaldéenne*, in *Maria. Études sur la Sainte Vierge*, ed. H. du Manoir, S.J., Vol. 1 (Paris, 1949), pp. 348-350.

1. The Protoevangelium (Gen. 3:15)

I will put enmity between you and the woman, between your seed and her seed; he shall crush your head and you shall lie in wait for his heel.

These words, addressed by God Himself to the serpent-tempter after the fall of our first parents in the garden of paradise, constitute a messianic prophecy forecasting the future Redemption through Jesus Christ.[55] At the side of the victorious Saviour we find a woman sharing His enmity with the serpent (Satan) and His triumph over the infernal powers.

The magisterium of the Church unquestionably favors the opinion which identifies that "woman" with Our Blessed Lady.[56] Catholic tradition lends strong support to the same view,[57] which is now shared by the majority of theologians and a growing number of professional exegetes.[58] Presupposing, as we must, the Marian sense of the passage, we may argue thus: Our Lady is indissolubly associated with Christ both in the exercise of a perpetual struggle with the devil and in the complete victory over him.[59] This mission of Christ as Restorer of the supernatural order did not terminate with the cancellation of our debt on Calvary and with the acquisition of graces through His infinite merits, but continues with the communication of those graces to individual souls. It is only through the actual reception of the fruits of Christ's Redemption that individual souls are able to attain to their supernatural destiny in heaven

---

[55] Cf. *Enchir. Bibl.*, No. 334.

[56] *Ineffabilis Deus*, in *Acta et decreta Sacrorum Conciliorum recentiorum. Collectio Lacensis*, Vol. 6 (Friburgi Brisgoviae, 1882), col. 839; *Munificentissimus Deus*, in *A.A.S.*, Vol. 42, 1950, pp. 768-769; *Fulgens corona*, in *A.A.S.*, Vol. 45, 1953, p. 579. Cf. J. B. Carol, O.F.M., *De Corredemptione B. V. Mariae disquisitio positiva* (Civitas Vaticana, 1950), pp. 100-121.

[57] Cf. T. Gallus, S.J., *Interpretatio mariologica Protoevangelii (Gen. 3, 15) tempore postpatristico usque ad Conc. Tridentinum* (Romae, 1949); id., *Interpretatio mariologica Protoevangelii posttridentina ...*, pars prior: *a. Conc. Tridentino usque ad annum 1660* (Romae, 1953); pars posterior: *ab anno 1661 usque ad definitionem dogmaticam Immaculatae Conceptionis* (Romae, 1954); D. J. Unger, O.F.M.Cap., *The First-Gospel: Genesis 3:15* (St. Bonaventure, N. Y., 1954), pp. 90-235.

[58] Cf. Carol, *op. cit.*, pp. 84-87; and Unger, *op. cit.*, pp. 285-291, where numerous references will be found.

[59] *Ineffabilis Deus*, in *Collectio Lacensis*, Vol. 6, col. 839; *Munificentissimus Deus*, in *A.A.S.*, Vol. 42, 1950, p. 769.

and thus boast of a complete and perfect triumph over the infernal foe. From which we conclude: It is highly fitting that, since Mary was so closely associated with the Saviour in the initial phase of the victory, she should have an active share also in its ulterior and decisive phase. In this sense, the Protoevangelium may rightly be considered as a biblical basis for Mary's role as Dispensatrix of all graces.[60]

2. *Our Lord's Testament* (*Jn.* 19:26-27)

When Jesus therefore had seen his Mother and the disciple standing whom he loved, he said to his Mother: "Behold thy son." After that he said to the disciple: "Behold thy mother."

The value of the above text for our thesis hinges on whether or not it contains a truly biblical reference to Our Lady's spiritual motherhood. Catholic scholars are not agreed on this point. For example, a large number of exegetes still maintain that Our Lord's words can be used in this connection only in a purely accommodated sense.[61] On the other hand, the vast majority of theologians and not a few biblical interpreters recognize in them a proclamation of Our Lady's mystical motherhood of mankind, either in a literal or at least a spiritual sense.[62]

The undeniable advantage of this latter position is that it enjoys considerable traditional support,[63] and what is more important, it conforms perfectly with the repeated pronouncements of the ordinary magisterium. The most striking of these was made by Pope Leo XIII when he declared that "the Church has always felt" that Christ

---

[60] Cf. J. Bover, S.J., *Universalis B. Virginis mediatio ex Protoevangelio* (*Gen.* 3, 15) *demonstrata*, in *Gregorianum*, Vol. 5, 1924, pp. 569-583.

[61] F. Ceuppens, O.P., *De Mariologia Biblica*, ed. 2 (Taurini, 1951), pp. 199-202; M. Gruenthaner, S.J., *Mary in the New Testament*, in MARIOLOGY, ed. J. B. Carol, O.F.M., Vol. 1 (Milwaukee, 1954), pp. 115-116.

[62] See many references in E. May, *The Scriptural Basis for Mary's Spiritual Maternity*, in *Marian Studies*, Vol. 3, 1952, pp. 125-130.

[63] Cf. the numerous references given by T. M. Bartolomei, O.S.M., *La maternità spirituale di Maria ...*, in *Divus Thomas* (Plac.), Vol. 55, 1952, pp. 304-309, and by Hilary of St. Agatha, O.C.D., *BB. Virginis Mariae maternitas universalis gratiae in verbis Jesu morientis: "Ecce filius tuus ... Ecce mater tua,"* in *Teresianum*, December, 1933, pp. 134151.

designated the whole human race in the person of the beloved disciple.[64]

In view of the above, a reasoning along the following lines would seem to be amply justified: Our Blessed Lord, about to consummate His redemptive sacrifice, openly proclaims Mary as the Mother of the redeemed. Obviously, this motherhood of Mary pertains to the supernatural order, the order of divine grace by which we become the children of God. But this maternal function is inconceivable without the transmission of supernatural life; it presupposes or implies the communication of grace. Nor is the integral concept of spiritual motherhood sufficiently verified by our regeneration to the life of grace only *in actu primo*. Unlike human motherhood, which does not necessarily require a continuous vital influence from mother to offspring, a true spiritual motherhood cannot be properly exercised without an enduring personal communication of life, for the good reason that no advance is possible in the supernatural order without the actual aid of divine grace. As Father Plessis rightly observes, this maternal role involves "the Virgin's cooperation in the diffusion, conservation and increase of the supernatural life of souls. These things are not obtained except by grace, either by habitual grace procuring and developing the supernatural life, or by actual grace preserving and protecting this life, or again by arousing and preparing the sinner to receive it."[65] Therefore, we conclude that Mary's role as Dispensatrix of every single grace may be deduced from the Saviour's testament on the cross.

Two other biblical passages are sometimes mentioned in support of our doctrine, namely: the Visitation pericope (*Lk.* 1:39-45), and the wedding feast at Cana (*Jn.* 2:1-11). In the former we learn that, at the sound of Our Lady's greeting, St. John the Baptist leaped with joy and was sanctified in the womb of his mother Elizabeth; in the latter we witness the Saviour working His very first miracle at the request of His Mother.[66]

---

[64] Enc. *Adjutricem populi,* September, 1895, in *Actes de Léon* XIII, Vol. 4 (Paris, n.d.), p. 238. Cf. G. W. Shea, *The Teaching of the Magisterium on Mary's Spiritual Maternity,* in *Marian Studies,* Vol. 3, 1952, pp. 68-69, 92-93.

[65] A. Plessis, S.M.M., *Manuel de Mariologie dogmatique* (Montfort-sur-Meu, 1947), p. 293.

[66] Cf. Leo XIII, *Augustissimae Virginis,* September 12, 1897, in *Actes de Léon XIII,* Vol. 5, p. 168. Doheny-Kelly, p. 123.

It should be stated in this connection that neither of these texts is sufficient to establish the Catholic thesis that *all* graces are actually dispensed through Our Lady's intercession. However, while showing that God did use her instrumentality for the conferring of specific favors in specific circumstances, these passages may well contain a veiled indication of God's design with reference to all other cases. Beyond that we hesitate to go.

D. THE ARGUMENT FROM TRADITION

In this section of our study we understand tradition to mean that divine orally revealed doctrine consigned to writing or transmitted by word of mouth under the vigilance of the living magisterium of the Church. The organs of this tradition include preachers, teachers, doctors, writers, artists, and the faithful in general insofar as they treat of revealed religion or profess it. Its monuments are the extant works of the Fathers, theologians, and ecclesiastical writers which deal with things pertaining to revealed religion, and works of Christian art reflecting the faith of the Church.

As with other phases of Mariology, the teaching of tradition concerning the doctrine now under discussion has not always been universal or uniform. The positive data now available point rather to a gradual development which slowly progresses toward a period of maturation.[67] This evolution of the original germ ideas falls into the three following stages: (1) from the beginning until the eighth century; (2) from the eighth to the sixteenth century; and (3) from the sixteenth century to the present time. In view of the limited space at our disposal, we shall attempt to give here only a summary of the numerous testimonies available.

1. *From the Beginning to the Eighth Century* — This primitive period

---

[67] Bittremieux, *De mediatione* ..., pp. 194-226; Dublanchy, art. *Marie*, in *D.T.C.*, Vol. 9 (2), coll. 2398-2403; Druwé, *art. cit.*, pp. 539-552; Bover, *Maria Mediatrix*... (Brugis, 1929); W. J. Burghardt, S.J., *Mary in Western Patristic Thought*, in Mariology, ed. J. B. Carol, O.F.M., Vol. 1 (Milwaukee, 1954), pp. 122-130; G. Bardy, *La doctrine de l'intercession de Marie chez les Pères grecs*, in *La Vie Spirituelle*, Vol. 56, 1938, pp. [1]-[37]; P. Hoffer, *L'intercession de la Très-Sainte Vierge chez les maîtres de l'Ecole Française*, in *La Vie Spirituelle*, Vol. 56, 1938, pp. 65-101.

is characterized for the most part by general references to Our Lady's share with Christ in the economy of man's salvation. Mary is set forth as the Second Eve, co-operating with her divine Son, the Second Adam, in the process of our supernatural restoration. This corresponds to the share which the first Eve had with the first Adam in our fall. Eve and Mary are the first mothers of the entire race: Eve, mother of men according to the flesh; Mary, their spiritual mother in the supernatural order of grace. These testimonies, which, according to Cardinal Newman, constitute "the rudimentary teaching of antiquity,"[68] implicitly point to Mary's co-operation in the distribution of all graces.

St. Irenaeus of Lyons († c. 200) may well speak for his contemporaries when, after establishing the Eve-Mary antithesis, he concludes that Our Lady "became the cause of salvation both for herself and for the whole human race."[69] Elsewhere the holy Bishop writes:

Though the one (Eve) disobeyed God, yet the other (Mary) was drawn to obey Him, and thus the Virgin Mary became the virgin Eve's advocate. And just as the human race was bound to death by a virgin, so it was released by a Virgin, and the balance was maintained: a virgin's disobedience by a Virgin's obedience.[70]

Substantially the same ideas recur in such early and important writers as St. Justin († c. 165), St. Epiphanius († 403), St. Ambrose († 397), St. Jerome († 420), St. Augustine († 430), St. Peter Chrysologus († c. 450), and many others.[71]

The title "Mediatrix," so frequently applied to Our Lady in

---

[68] Newman, *The New Eve* (Oxford, 1952), p. 13.

[69] Irenaeus, *Adversus haereses*, lib. 3, cap. 22; *PG*, 7, 958.

[70] *Adversus haereses*, lib. 5, cap. 19; *PG*, 7, 1175. In another place (lib. 4, cap. 33; *PG*, 7, 1880), with reference to Our Lord's virginal birth, Irenaeus remarks parenthetically: "The Pure One opening purely that pure womb which regenerates men unto God." On the meaning of this disputed text cf. P. Galtier, S J., *La Vierge qui nous regénère*, in *Recherches de Science Religieuse*, Vol. 5, 1914, pp. 136-145; N. Moholy, O.F.M., *St. Irenaeus: Father of Mariology*, in *First Franciscan National Marian Congress...* held in Washington, D. C., 1950 (Burlington, Wis., 1952), pp. 159-163.

[71] Justin, *Dialogus cum Tryphone*, cap. 100; *PG*, 6, 709; Epiphanius, *Panarion*, haer. 78, n. 18; *PG*, 42, 728; Ambrose, *Epist.* 63, n. 33; *PL*, 16, 1249-1250; (ed. 1866); Jerome, *Epist.* 22, n. 21; *PL*, 22, 408; Augustine, *De agone christiano*, n. 22 (24); *PL*, 40, 303; Peter Chrysologus, *Sermo 99; PL*, 52, 479.

subsequent centuries, made its first appearance about this time. The first to use it seems to have been St. Ephraem († 373) who addresses Our Lady thus: "I call upon you, Mediatrix of the world; I invoke your prompt protection in my necessities."[72] Others employing the same title, or that of *Sequestra*, are: St. Epiphanius, Theodotus of Ancyra († 440), one of the more highly regarded Fathers of the Council of Ephesus, Antipater of Bostra († after 451), and Basil of Seleucia († 499).[73]

St. Cyril of Alexandria († 444), "the most noble defender of the Virgin Mother of God,"[74] has left us a significant testimony of his faith in Mary's intercession in a homily pronounced in the presence of the bishops assembled at Ephesus in 431. In it he hails Our Lady as the one

> through whom the devils are put to flight ... through whom the fallen creature is taken up to heaven; through whom all creation, held fast by the madness of idolatry, has come to the knowledge of truth; through whom holy baptism has come to believers ... through whom nations are brought to repentance ... through whom the only-begotten Son of God has shone forth ... through whom the dead are raised, and kings reign.[75]

We may close this period with the beautiful words of an *Encomium* attributed to St. Modestus of Jerusalem († 634), but probably written at the end of the seventh century: "The human race has been saved in thee (Mary), and through thee it has obtained favors and everlasting blessings from Him (God)."[76]

2. *From the Eighth to the Sixteenth Century* — It is during this period, particularly in the twelfth century, that the evolution of our doctrine

---

[72] *Sancti Ephraem Syri opera graece et latine*, ed. Assemani, Vol. 3 (Romae, 1746), p. 525. In his fourth sermon on the Mother of God (*ed. cit.*, Vol. 3, pp. 528-529) the Saint calls Mary "dispensatrix of all gifts ... Mediatrix of the whole world."

[73] Epiphanius, *Hom. 5 de laudibus S. Mariae Deiparae*; PG, 43, 491. R. Laurentin, *Court traité de théologie mariale* (Paris, 1953), p. 161, maintains that this homily was written about the eighth century; Theodotus of Ancyra, *Hom. 5 in die Nativit. Domini*; PG, 77, 1416 (uncertain authenticity, according to Laurentin, p. 167); Antipater, *Hom. in S. Joan Bapt.*; PG, 85, 1771; Basil of Seleucia, *Orat. 39, in SS. Deiparae annuntiationem*; PG, 85, 443. Cf. J. B. Carol, O.F.M., *The Theological Concept of Mediation and Coredemption*, in *Ephemerides Theologicae Lovanienses*, Vol. 14, 1937, pp. 649-650.

[74] Pius XII, *Orientalis Ecclesiae decus*, April 9, 1944, A.A.S., Vol. 36, 1944, p. 129.

[75] St. Cyril, *Homiliae diversae*, 4; PG, 77, 992.

[76] Pseudo-Modestus, PG, 86, 3306.

reaches the explicit stage. Thus we hear St. Germain of Constantinople (✝ 733) address the Mother of God: "No one obtains salvation except through thee, O most holy One! ... To no one is mercy granted except through thee!"[77] What St. Germain taught in the East, St. Peter Damian (✝ 1072) re-echoes in the West: "In thy hands" — he apostrophizes Our Lady — "are the treasures of the mercies of God."[78]

However, it was St. Bernard of Clairvaux (✝ 1153) who expressed this teaching in categorical and unmistakable language and who, for this reason, has been styled the "Doctor of Mary's Mediation." According to the Saint, "God has willed that we should have nothing which would not pass through the hands of Mary."[79] And again: "This is the will of Him Who wanted us to have everything through Mary."[80] These two generic statements, which have become classic in Marian literature, receive more precision when the holy Doctor tells us that "God has placed in Mary the plenitude of every good, in order to have us understand that if there is any trace of hope in us, any trace of grace, any trace of salvation, it flows from her."[81] Of course, he assures us elsewhere, "God could have dispensed His graces according to His good pleasure, without making use of this aqueduct (Mary); but it was His wish to provide this means whereby grace would reach you."[82] The tremendous influence of St. Bernard's teaching in this respect can best be gathered from the fact that numerous Marian writers of subsequent centuries unhesitatingly endorse his position as something already well established.

Thus, for example, the author of the *Mariale* heretofore attributed to St. Albert the Great, unequivocally states that "every single grace passes

---

[77] *Hom. in S.* Mariae zonam; PG, 98, 377.

[78] St. Peter Damian, *Sermo 44, in nativitatem B.V.M.;* PL, 144, 740.

[79] St. Bernard, *Hom. 3 in vig. nativit.,* n. 10; *PL,* 183, 100. For bibliography on the Saint's Mariology, cf. J. Keuppens, *Mariologiae compendium* (Antverpiae, 1938), p. 202; a whole issue of *Marie,* Vol. 7, March-April, 1954; and the entire Volume 14 of *Estudios Marianos* (Madrid, 1954), esp. pp. 249-270.

[80] *Hom. in nativit. B.V.M., n. 7;* PL, 183, 441.

[81] *Ibid.,* n. 6.

[82] *Ibid.,* nn. 3-4; PL, 183, 440. For other authors of this period cf. I. Ruidor, S.J., La mediación de María en la distribución de las gracias según los escritores eclesiásticos de la primer a mitad del siglo XII, *in* Estudios Marianos, Vol. 12, 1952, pp. 301-318.

through the hands of Mary."[83] And Richard of St. Lawrence († c. 1245), St. Bonaventure († 1274), James of Varagine († 1298), and John Gerson († 1429) do nothing but repeat the same ideas in a variety of ways.[84] St. Bernardine of Siena († 1444), who shares with the abbot of Clairvaux the title "Doctor of Mary's Universal Mediation," trenchantly sums up the matter in the following remarkable passage: "This is the process (in the distribution) of divine graces: from God they flow to Christ, from Christ to His Mother, and from her to the Church. ... I do not hesitate to say that she has received a certain jurisdiction over all graces. ... They are administered through her hands to whom she pleases, when she pleases, as she pleases, and as much as she pleases."[85]

3. *From the Sixteenth Century to the Present Time* — This third period might be characterized as one of theological progress.[86] In the preceding centuries the teaching concerning Mary's role as Dispensatrix of all graces had evolved from the implicit to the explicit stage. This prerogative of hers was generally accepted; it was considered part of the Christian thought and cult. The writers of the third era will direct their endeavors to demonstrating, explaining, and elaborating the various phases of the doctrine. They will base their demonstration on the testimonies of the ecclesiastical writers who had previously affirmed the truth, especially since the time of St. Bernard. They will now begin to discuss *ex professo* the nature of Mary's mediatorial office. A more

---

[83] *Mariale,* q. 164; *op. omn.,* ed. Borgnet, Vol. 37 (Parisiis, 1898), p. 241.

[84] Richard of St. Lawrence, *De laudibus M.M. Virginis,* lib. 2 cap. 3 n. 4 in St. Albert the Great's *op. omn.,* Vol. 36, p. 91; St. Bonaventure, *Sermo 6 de maternitate B.M. Virginis; op. omn.,* Vol. 9 (Quaracchi, 1901), pp. 720-721; cf. L. Di Fonzo, *Doctrina S. Bonaventurae de universali mediatione B.V. Mariae* (Romae, 1938), pp. 289-296; James of Varazze (Varagine), *Sermones aurei de Maria Virgine* ... (Venetiis, 1590), f. 8v-10; cf. P. Lorenzin, O.F.M., *Mariologia Jacobi a Varagine, O.P.* (Romae, 1951), pp. 74-87; Gerson, *Sermo de annuntiatione,* 4; *op. Omn.,* Vol. 4 (Parisiis, 1635), col. 1366; cf. Bover, *Universalis B.M. Virginis mediatio in scriptis Joannis Gerson,* in *Gregorianum,* Vol. 9, 1928, pp. 264-267.

[85] St. Bernardine, *Sermo 5 de nativitate B.M.V.,* cap. 8; op. omn., Vol. 4 (Lugduni, 1650), p. 96; cf. Ceslaus ab Haczow, O.F.M.Cap., *Mediatio B. V. Mariae juxta doctrinam S. Bernardini Senensis, in Collectanea Franciscana Slavica,* Vol. 2 (Sibenici, 1940), pp. 103-124.

[86] Cf. Godts, *op. cit.,* pp. 370-420; Roschini, *Mariologia,* ed. 2, Vol. 1 (Romae, 1947), pp. 276-305; G. W. Shea, *Outline History of Mariology in the Middle Ages and Modern Times,* in Mariology, ed. J. B. Carol, O.F.M., Vol. 1 (Milwaukee, 1954), p. 309 ff.; J. B. Terrien, S.J., *La Mère des hommes,* 6th ed., Vol. 1 (Paris, 1933), p. 580 ff.

profound study of the sources of revelation will also be undertaken so as to determine its theological note and even the possibility of its definition by the Church. The result of all these efforts will be greater precision in the formulation of the doctrine and likewise a more thorough grasp of Mary's place in the economy of salvation.

All this vitality manifested in the study of this aspect of Mariology was occasioned chiefly by three historical events: the pseudo-reformation, the rise of Jansenism, and the dogmatic definition of the Immaculate Conception. The first two can be grouped together as they both attacked accepted Catholic views concerning the Mother of God and her position in the divine plan, particularly her role as Mediatrix, and the consequent filial devotion manifested by Catholics. Their censures naturally compelled not a few Catholic apologists of the era to take up the arms of their profession in defense of their Tower of Ivory.

The pseudo-reformers, attacking from without, under the false plea of reinstating Christ in His rightful position as the center of Christianity, assailed the very legitimacy of devotion to His Mother. To them it was simply "Mariolatry."[87] The Jansenists, attackers from within, thought that Catholic devotion to Mary, while praiseworthy in itself, was then giving way to excesses and dangerous exaggerations. They accepted the defined dogmas of the Church, but reacted unfavorably toward the evolution of some Marian doctrines and to some manifestations of her cult. Their hypercritical views were codified in the notorious *Monita salutaria* of Adam Widenfeld.[88]

The third event was the promulgation of the Bull *Ineffabilis Deus* on December 8, 1854. It is well known that the dogmatic definition of Mary's absolute sinlessness in her conception focused theological attention on her intimate association with her Son in the all-out struggle against the forces of evil. This opened new vistas for the Mariologists and led them to a more profound and assiduous study of Mary's role in

---

[87] Cf. C. Dillenschneider, C.Ss.R., *La Mariologie de S. Alphonse...*(Fribourg, Suisse, 1930, pp. 4-32.

[88] Cf. Dillenschneider, *op. cit.*, pp. 33-67; P. Hoffer, *La dévotion à Marie au déclin du XVIIe autour du Jansénisme et des "Avis salutaires de la Vierge Marie à ses dévots indiscrets"*(Paris, 1938). Hoffer's judgment on the *Monita* and their author is much more lenient than that of Dillenschneider. Cf. Carol, *De Corredemptione...*, p. 303 ff.

the dispensation of graces.[89]

In the sixteenth century, when the Protestant pseudo-reform broke out, Mary had her champions. Chief among these was St. Peter Canisius († 1597).[90] One of his titles to glory is his Marian apology *De Maria Virgine incomparabili et Dei Genitrice sacrosancta*. Among other things, the holy Doctor stresses the point that St. Bernard did not place Mary on an equal footing with Christ, as the Protestants claimed. Christ, he explains, is the only source of life; Mary is the "aqueduct" which transmits to us the waters of grace. "Because of her compassion, she merited that the power and merits of Christ's Passion should be communicated to men through her."[91] The same teaching was proposed by his contemporaries St. Thomas of Villanova († 1555), John Maldonatus († 1583), and the renowned theologian of the Council of Trent, Alphonsus Salmerón († 1585).[92]

During the course of the seventeenth century the doctrine of Mary's universal mediation of graces was so generally taught and accepted that it would not be difficult to multiply explicit testimonies to that effect. The imposing list would include great Doctors of the Church like St. Robert Bellarmine († 1621) and St. Francis de Sales († 1622); eminent theologians of the caliber of Suárez († 1617), Petavius († 1652), and Contenson († 1674); preachers of stature like Bossuet († 1704) and Bourdalou († 1704); Scripture scholars like Cornelius a Lapide († 1637) and de Salazar († 1646).[93]

---

[89] Cf. J. Bellamy, *La théologie catholique au 19ieme siècle*, 3rd ed. (Paris, 1904), pp. xvi, 274-275.

[90] Cf. Dillenschneider, *op. cit.* pp. 109-113.

[91] St. Peter Canisius, *De Maria Virgine ...*, lib. 5, cap. 27 (Ingolstadii, 1577), p. 743.

[92] St. Thomas of Villanova, *Hom. in annuntiationem*, cap. 5; op. omn., Vol. 4 (Manilae, 1883), p. 464; cf. V. Capánaga, O.S.A.R., La mediación de la Virgen María según Santo Tomás de Villanueva, *in* Estudios Marianos, *Vol. 1, 1942, pp. 271-283; Maldonatus,* Commentarii in quatuor evang., *Vol. 2 (Moguntiae, 1863), p. 34; Salmerón,* Commentarii in evangelicam historiam et in Acta Apostolorum, *tract. 5, Vol. 3 (Coloniae Agrippinae, 1604), pp. 39-40.*

[93] Bellarmine, *Concio 42 de nativitate B. M. Virginis,* in *op. omn.,* Vol. 7 (Neapoli, 1872), p. 297 ff.; Francis de Sales, *Sermon 61, pour la fête de l'Assomption,* in *Oeuvres,* Vol. 9 (Annecy, 1898), pp. 459-462; Suárez, *In 3m,* q. 38, art. 4, disp. 24, sect. 1, n. 5; *op. omn.,* Vol. 19 (Parisiis, 1860), pp. 336-337; Petavius, *Dogmata Theologica,* Vol. 7: *De Incarnatione*

Outstanding likewise for their contributions to Mariology were the members of the so-called *French School*, which flourished at this time. Father Olier († 1657), St. John Eudes († 1680), and St. Louis Grignion de Montfort († 1716) are but a few of the leading masters of this School in whose writings we recognize Our Blessed Lady as the Treasurer and the Dispensatrix of all graces.[94] In their perspective, Mary's right to distribute the fruits of Christ's Redemption is that which differentiates her intercession from that of the other saints. It is a sequel to her spiritual motherhood and her queenship. The following passage from St. Louis de Montfort, re-echoing St. Bernardine of Siena, is remarkable for its lucidity:

> God the Son has communicated to His Mother all that He acquired by His life and His death, His infinite merits and His admirable virtues; and He has made her the treasurer of all that His Father gave Him for His inheritance. It is by her that He applies His merits to His members, and that He communicates His virtues and distributes His graces. She is His mysterious canal; she is His aqueduct, through which He makes His mercies flow gently and abundantly.
>
> To Mary, His faithful spouse, God the Holy Spirit has communicated His unspeakable gifts; and He has chosen her to be the dispensatrix of all He possesses, in such sort that she distributes to whom she wills, as much as she wills, as she wills and when she wills, all His gifts and graces. The Holy Spirit gives no heavenly gift to men which does not pass through her

---

(Parisiis, 1867), pp. 87-96; Contenson, *Theologia mentis et cordis*, lib. 10, d. 6, cap. 2, refl. 1; cf. Godts, *op. cit.*, p. 387; Bossuet, *Troisième sermon pour la conception de la B.V. Marie; Oeuvres*, Vol. 5 (Paris, 1926), pp. 603-604; Bourdalou, *Premier sermon sur l'Assomption de la Vierge; Oeuvres complètes*, Vol. 3 (Paris, 1880), pp. 234-246; Cornelius a Lapide, *Comment. in Prov.*, 31:25; *op. omn.*, Vol. 6 (Parisiis, 1860), p. 517; Salazar, *Pro Immaculata Deiparae Virginis Conceptione defensio* (1625), p. 269; cf. Godts, *op. cit.*, p. 383.

[94] J.-J. Olier, *La vie intérieure de la Très-Sainte Vierge* (Paris, 1875), pp. 189, 321; Eudes, *Le Coeur admirable de la Très Sacrée Mère de Dieu*, livre 6e, or. 3; *Oeuvres choisies*, Vol. 7 (Paris, 1935), p. 318; De Montfort, *True Devotion to the Blessed Virgin Mary*, nn. 140-142, trans. F. W. Faber, rev. ed. (Bay Shore, N. Y., 1946), pp. 102-104; cf. L. Ledoux, *The Acquisition and the Distribution of Grace in the Works of St. Louis-Mary de Montfort*, in Alma Socia Christi, Vol. 8 (Romae, 1953), pp. 59-65; H.-M. Guindon, S.M.M., *La coopération de la Très-Sainte Vierge à l'acquisition et à la distribution de la grâce selon Saint Louis-Marie de Montfort*, in Alma Socia Christi, Vol. 8, pp. 66-96.

virginal hands.[95]

In the eighteenth century our doctrine continued to make rapid progress. By this time it was certainly more than just a "pious opinion." The authors who questioned it or passed over it in silence became the very rare exceptions. Among its numerous supporters we might include St. Leonard of Port Maurice († 1751), Natalis Alexander, O.P. († 1724), Benedict Piazza, S.J. († 1761), and John B. Scaramelli, S.J. († 1752). However, towering above all others is the great figure of St. Alphonsus Liguori († 1787), whose popular *Glories of Mary* is rightly credited with giving the decisive blow to the few adversaries of Mary's prerogative.[96] His vigorous and masterful reply to the objections of the otherwise learned Muratori has become a classic in Marian literature. Summarized in his own words, the holy Doctor's thesis is this:

> God, who gave us Jesus Christ, wills that all graces that have been, that are and will be dispensed to men to the end of the world through the merits of Jesus Christ, should be dispensed by the hands and through the intercession of Mary.[97]

To establish his thesis, he marshals an imposing array of testimonies from the Fathers and Doctors of the Church, from the Sacred Liturgy, Sacred Scripture, and the Christian sense of the faithful. The doctrine, then, is not "a pious exaggeration," as Muratori contended. "I consider it as *indubitably true* that all graces are dispensed by Mary."[98]

The innumerable authors who have treated our topic during the period subsequent to St. Alphonsus are all tributaries of his. Suffice to

---

[95] De Montfort, *op. cit.*, nn. 24-25, pp. 15-16. Other propounders of our doctrine who deserve at least a passing mention are: J. B. Novati († 1648), F. Poiré, S.J. († 1637), C. de Vega, S.J. († 1672), J. Crasset, S.J. († 1692), G. de Rhodes, S.J. († 1661), J. Miechow, O.P. († 1698), J. Serrano, O.F.M. († 1637), F. Guerra, O.F.M. († 1658), J. de Carthagena, O.F.M. († 1617), L. d'Argentan, O.F.M.Cap. († 1680). Cf. Godts, *op. cit.*, pp. 377-391; W. Sebastian, O.F.M., *De B. Virgine Maria universali gratiarum Mediatrice doctrina Franciscanorum ab an. 1600 ad an. 1730* (Romae, 1952), esp. pp. 161-206, where numerous texts and references will be found.

[96] Cf. C. Dillenschneider, *La mariologie de S. Alphonse de Liguori* (Fribourg, Suisse, 1934), pp. 166-195; Godts, *op. cit.*, pp. 16-21.

[97] St. Alphonsus, *The Glories of Mary*, Ch. 5, ed. E. Grimm (Brooklyn, N. Y., 1931), p. 162.

[98] *Op. cit.*, introd., p. 32.

mention Ven. William Chaminade, founder of the Marianists, Cardinals Pie and Dechamps, M. J. Scheeben, P. Jeanjacquot, S.J., and H. Depoix, S.M.[99] Following the encyclicals of Leo XIII, not a few theologians considered that the time was ripe to create a favorable atmosphere with a view to obtaining a dogmatic definition of the doctrine. Among those who have contributed most to this laudable movement, especially within the past five or six decades, the following are particularly deserving of mention: R. de la Broise, S.J., J. V. Bainvel, S.J., Cardinal Mercier, F. X. Godts, C.Ss.R., Canon J. Bittremieux, Msgr. J. Lebon, and the indefatigable J. M. Bover, S.J.[100] At the present time we know of no Catholic theologian who seriously questions the truth of Mary's universal mediation in the sense already explained, and it is safe to say that the vast majority of them consider it sufficiently warranted by the sources to be defined by the Church.

E. THE ARGUMENT FROM THEOLOGICAL REASON

In the preceding pages we have endeavored to show that the data furnished by positive theology, particularly when viewed in the light of the living magisterium, substantially establishes the doctrine expounded in this chapter. The present section of our study is intended to corroborate our position by recurring to speculative theology. Specifically, we would like to emphasize the internal nexus between our thesis and other accepted doctrines of Catholic theology. It will appear that the dispensation of all graces through Mary is but a natural corollary demanded by several other truths. These are, principally, Our Lady's spiritual maternity, her Coredemption, and her universal queenship.

1. *The Spiritual Maternity* — Mary is really and truly the Mother of

---

[99] *cf. Esprit de notre fondation d'après les écrits de M. Chaminade et les documents primitifs de la Société,* Vol. 1 (Nivelles, 1910), p. 150; Card. E. Pie, *Discours* 24; *Oeuvres,* 5th ed., Vol. 3, p. 466; cf. Godts, *op. cit.,* p. 414; Card. Dechamps, *La Nouvelle Eve,* Ch. 13; *Oeuvres complètes,* Vol. 5, pp. 134, 152; Scheeben, *Mariology,* trans. T. L. M. J. Geukers, Vol. 2 (St. Louis, 1947), pp. 239-272; Jeanjacquot, *Simples explications sur la coopération de la Très-Sainte Vierge à l'oeuvre de la Rédemption,* 3rd. ed. (Paris, 1880), pp. 151-158, 207-221; Depoix, *Tractatus theologicus de Beata Maria Virgine,* ed. 2 (Parisiis, 1866), pp. 215-228.

[100] Their contributions have already been mentioned in the course of this chapter.

mankind in the supernatural order of grace. She conceived us at the time of the Annunciation and brought us forth through her bitter compassion on Calvary. Now, the integral concept and full import of this motherhood requires not only the transmission of supernatural life *in actu primo*, which took place at the foot of the cross, but also a continual fostering, conserving, and increasing of that life, and, if need be, of repairing it. All this incessant maternal activity is carried out through the actual communication of grace to her children. Thus, Mary's office as universal spiritual Mother cannot be properly exercised except through her enduring co-operation in the dispensation of all graces to all men.

2. *The Coredemption* — As Coredemptrix, Our Lady is Christ's associate in His entire redemptive work. But this redemptive work of the Saviour comprises two phases: the acquisition of all graces through His merits while still on earth, and the actual application of those graces to individual souls. Consequently, it is reasonable to suppose that Our Lady's association extends not only to the first, but also to the second phase of the redemptive process.

This reasoning was formulated with remarkable incisiveness by Cardinal Pacelli (now Pius XII, gloriously reigning) when, having distinguished between the objective and subjective Redemption, he stated: "After all, the application of the merits of Christ constitutes, together with their acquisition, a single, complete work: that of salvation. It was fitting that Mary should co-operate equally in the two phases of the same work. The unity of the divine plan demands it."[101] Popes Leo XIII, Pius X, and Benedict XV had previously called our attention to this nexus between the two Marian prerogatives.[102]

3. *Mary's Universal Queenship* — As queen, it is Our Lady's function, with and under Christ, to lead men to their final supernatural goal which is the beatific vision in heaven. The only proportionate means to attain that end is supernatural grace. Therefore, in order properly to fulfill her royal mission in our behalf, Mary must have a perennial share in the

---

[101] Card. Pacelli, in *L'Osservatore Romano*, December 6, 1937, p. 3.
[102] Leo XIII, *Adjutricem populi*, September 5, 1895, in *A.S.S.*, Vol. 28, 1895-1896, pp. 130-131; Pius X, *Ad diem illum*, February 2, 1904, in *A.S.S.*, Vol. 36, 1903-1904, pp. 453-454; Benedict XV, *Inter sodalicia*, March 22, 1918, in *A.A.S.*, Vol. 10, 1918, pp. 181-182.

distribution of graces to all her subjects.

Under another aspect (which partially coincides with the one from the Coredemption) this same argument was recently enunciated by Pius XII as follows:

> Jesus Christ alone, God and Man, is King in the full, proper, and absolute sense of the term. Yet Mary also, although in a restricted way and only by analogy, shares in the royal dignity as the Mother of Christ who is God, as His associate in the labors of the divine Redemption, and in His struggle against His enemies, and in the victory of heaven over them all. From this association with Christ comes the royal function by which she can dispense the treasures of the divine Redeemer s Kingdom. Finally, from this association with Christ comes the unfailing efficacy of her maternal intercession with the Son and with the Father.[103]

It may be well to note in this connection that the three theological arguments briefly outlined above do not carry the same weight in the opinion of modern theologians. For example, the fundamental argument, i.e., the one based on the Coredemption, is considered by some as *apodictic*,[104] by others as a reason from *fittingness*,[105] or as one which establishes the doctrine *with certitude*.[106] More recently, Father Roschini has written that he regards it as yielding a *true theological conclusion* of the highest value.[107] Be that as it may, we must bear in mind that theological reasoning need not always be apodictic. It suffices that it show the internal harmony of a given doctrine with others belonging to the deposit of faith, and thus corroborate a thesis which has previously been established from the data of positive theology.

---

[103] Pius XII, *Ad coeli Reginam*, in *A.A.S.*, Vol. 46, 1954, p. 635.

[104] For example, F. S. Müller, S.J., in *Zeitschrift für katholische Theologie*, Vol. 51, 1927, p. 420.

[105] Cf. L. Lercher, S.J., *Institutiones Theologiae Dogmaticae*, ed. 2, Vol. 3, (Oeniponte, 1934), p. 362, n. 384.

[106] For example, Bittremieux, *De mediatione ..., p. 164*.

[107] Roschini, *Mariologia*, ed. 2, Vol. 2, pars 1 (Romae, 1947), p. 407. Cf. Friethoff, *De alma Socia Christi Mediatoris* (Romae, 1936), pp. 183-185.

II. THE NATURE OF MARY'S ROLE AS DISPENSATRIX OF ALL GRACES

The *fact* of Mary's prerogative as channel of all graces is no longer the subject of discussion and controversy among Catholic theologians. The first part of our study has revealed the reason why. But theologians are not satisfied with that acquisition, important though it is. Besides answering the question *an sit*, they are instinctively curious as to the further question *quomodo sit*. Hence their attempts to probe into the very nature of Mary's unique prerogative. And it is within this area that their agreement ceases. Briefly, all admit that Our Lady exercises some true causality in the actual dispensation of every single grace; but there is divergence of thought as to the type of causality and the precise manner in which her role is exercised. In order to forestall misunderstandings in this matter, it may be helpful to recall summarily the various types of causes which come into play in the present discussion.

A physical cause is that which directly produces an effect. It is called principal, if it produces the effect of itself and by its own power; instrumental, if it produces the effect in virtue of a power received from the principal cause. For example, a saw is an instrumental cause used by a carpenter (the principal cause) in cutting wood.

A moral cause is that which by counsel, request, or command induces another agent to produce an effect. It is called principal if it moves the physical cause in virtue of its own dignity, merit, or some inherent quality. It is called instrumental if its dignity or meritorious quality is derived from the principal moral cause. Thus, if a king releases a prisoner in view of the queen's written request, the queen herself would be the principal moral cause of the royal amnesty, while her written request would be the instrumental moral cause of the prisoner's release.

With these preliminary notions in mind, let us now review briefly the position of theologians in this matter, including the points in which they are at variance.

All theologians are in accord that Mary is not the principal cause of grace, whether physical or moral. Only God can be the principal physical cause of either habitual or actual grace. He alone can elevate a creature to the supernatural order through a participation in the divine nature; He alone can act directly on a created intelligence and will.

Again, Mary is not the ultimate principal moral cause of grace because no creature can be the final motive of God's action. God is the uncaused Cause and, consequently, cannot be moved to action by any creature. The ultimate reason for His actions is Himself.

The expressions used to convey our Marian doctrine, to bring it within the grasp of our intelligence, are figures and metaphors, and hence not to be taken literally. The very nature of grace itself warns us. Habitual and actual graces are accidents that cannot be transferred from one subject to another. Over and above that, they are accidents of a spiritual order that cannot be conceived materially. It is true that the totality of these graces is often represented as a "treasure," but we must not imagine a coffer of precious things from which Mary draws with bountiful hands to distribute them to man. Rather, we must visualize them as existing in heaven *virtually*, i.e., they exist in their primary cause or in their origin, namely Christ; also in their cause of dispensation, i.e., in Mary's power as advocate. Therefore, the traditional expressions of "treasurer," "almoner," and others which are synonymous indicate in Mary a real charge or function. God has truly entrusted to her the administration of the treasury of His graces; He has constituted her Dispensatrix of all His goods.

In what precise way does Our Lady fulfill this role of hers? Theologians all agree that she enjoys the power of intercession. By divine disposition she possesses the right to act as a proximate moral cause in the conferring of every grace. This she has always in subordination to Christ "who lives always to make intercession for us."[108] In this mediatorial function three things are to be noted. First, she knows all our spiritual needs, for as Mother of all men she must be aware of everything which, directly or indirectly, bears on the supernatural life she has been commissioned to give us and to nourish in us. Second, she is impelled by her boundless maternal charity to plead our case. That she actually prays for us is a matter of faith, and is included in the general dogma of the intercession of the saints.[109] Third, her intercession is most

---

[108] *Hebr.* 7:25.
[109] Council of Trent, session 25; *D.B.*, 984.

powerful and efficacious. Her prayers are always answered, for God will not turn a deaf ear on her whom He honors and loves above all creatures. Rightly, then, has Catholic tradition honored her with the title *omnipotentia supplex*.

Mary's intercession is presented to God either expressly or interpretatively, according to the principle laid down by Aquinas concerning the manner of intercession of the saints.[110] At times she actually pleads our cause explicitly when she actually prays for us. At other times, she does this implicitly when she humbly but confidently advances her maternal rights, or her rights as Coredemptrix, by presenting to God her previous merits which congruously obtained the salvation of the world.

At this point ends the harmony and unanimity among theologians. The majority of theologians explain Mary's causality in the distribution of graces by way of intercession only (*moral* causality), as outlined in the preceding paragraphs.[111]

A second group, a very small minority, not satisfied with the above explanation, has transposed Billot's theory of the "intentional causality" of the sacraments, and applied it to our doctrine. According to the proponents of this view,[112] the terminus of Mary's intercession is not grace itself, but rather a *title* to its reception. In other words, Our Lady, by virtue of the power invested in her by God, efficaciously designates specific graces for specific persons, and this expression of her will entitles these persons to receive those graces. In the last analysis, this view seems to be reducible to moral causality.

---

[110] St. Thomas, *Summa Theol.*, 3a, suppl. q. 72, a. 3.

[111] It would seem that, until recently, every author championed this view. Among its modern adherents we may mention: Godts, *op. cit.*, pp. 89-90; de la Broise-Bainvel, *op. cit.*, 90-91; Bittremieux, *op. cit.*, pp. 291-301; Friethoff, *op. cit.*, pp. 203-204; Terrien, *op. cit.*, Vol. 1, p. 563; J. de Aldama, *Mariologia*, in *Sacrae Theologiae Summa*, ed. a Patribus S.J., Vol. 3 (Matriti, 1950), pp. 395-396; J. Van der Meersch, *Tractatus de divina gratia*, ed. 2 (Brugis, 1924), p. 372; J. B. Carol, O.F.M., *art. cit.*, in *Our Lady's Digest*, Vol. 6, March, 1952), p. 420; *id.*, *Fundamentals of Mariology* (New York, 1956), pp. 66-67.

[112] B.-H. Merkelbach, O.P., *Mater divinae gratiae*, in *Revue Ecclésiastique de Liège*, Vol. 10, 1914-1915, p. 34 ff. More recently, in his *Mariologia* (Parisiis, 1939), p. 367 ff., the author has given his allegiance to the moral causality theory. For a description of the intentional causality cf. Keuppens, *op. cit.*, pp. 148-149.

A last group maintains that neither of the above opinions expresses completely the doctrine contained in the teaching of tradition concerning the mode of Mary's mediation in the dispensation of graces. Her intercession, they say, may be a sufficient explanation of how Mary obtains the graces from God, but it does not seem to take into account the peculiar power of distribution attributed to her in traditional phrases such as "channel" or "aqueduct" of graces. No doubt we may be dealing here with metaphors; but, as Father Jennet points out, a metaphor demands a relation based on an analogy between the proper and the figurative sense.[113] To distribute something presupposes a possession, a dominion, which certainly is not included in the notion of intercession. Therefore, these men propose the theory of physical instrumental causality, according to which Mary serves as a separated *physical instrument* through which graces literally flow to us.

Although rather recent, the above theory has won some important adherents in the past few decades.[114] It does seem to give a more satisfactory meaning to Mary's role. It is with this view that the sympathies of the author of this chapter rest. However, while maintaining this particular viewpoint, he makes his own the words of Father Hugon: "We have here a delicate question which we approach with reserve and timidity.... We do not make any categorical assertions, we discuss only a hypothesis which others may reject at their pleasure."[115] Obviously, we are still in the realm of theory, of opinion, where certitude is lacking. Father Garrigou-Lagrange, himself a champion of this view, in his venerable wisdom states:

> It must be admitted that it does not seem possible to prove with certainty that Mary did exercise physical causality. Theology will hardly

---

[113] L. Jennet, *Extension et mode de la coopération de Marie à la distribution des grâces*, in *Le Premier Congrès Marial de Québec*, 12-16 juin, 1929 (Québec, 1931), p. 292.

[114] For example, Card. A. H. Lépicier, O.S.M., *Tractatus de B.M.V.*, ed. 5 (Romae, 1926), pp. 480-482; E. Hugon, O.P., *La causalité instrumental*, ed. 2 (Paris, 1924), pp. 194-204; Roschini, *op. cit.*, Vol. 2, pars 1, pp. 408-420; Plessis, *op. cit.*, pp. 302-306; E. Sauras, O.P., *Causalidad de la cooperación de María en la obra redentora*, in *Estudios Marianos*, Vol. 2, 1943, pp. 319-357; E. Mura, *Le Corps Mystique du Christ*, ed. 2, Vol. 2 (Paris, 1937), pp. 150-176; R. Garrigou-Lagrange, O.P., *The Mother of the Saviour and Our Interior Life*, trans. B. J. Kelly (Dublin, 1948), pp. 236-242.

[115] Hugon, *op. cit.*, p. 195.

advance beyond serious probability in this matter for the reason that it is very hard to see in the traditional texts quoted where precisely the literal sense ends and the metaphorical sense begins. ... Tradition ... uses metaphors which are, at very least, expressive, but we cannot affirm with certainty that they are more than metaphors. ... Mary's influence on our souls remains ... shrouded in mystery.[116]

In this matter, in which theologians can give rein to their speculations, and are free to advocate either of the opinions discussed above, the following admonition of our reigning Pontiff is particularly timely:

> In these and other questions about the Blessed Virgin let theologians and preachers of the word of God take care to avoid certain deviations lest they fall into a twofold error. Let them beware of teachings that lack foundation, and that, by misuse of words, exceed the bounds of truth. And let them beware of too great a narrowness of mind when they are considering that unique, completely exalted, indeed almost divine dignity of the Mother of God which the Angelic Doctor teaches we must attribute to her "by reason of the infinite good which is God."[117]

Before concluding this section of our study, an objection, which is sometimes raised, should be briefly touched upon. If Mary is the Dispensatrix of all graces, would this not encroach on the efficacy of the sacraments? The sacraments, if validly conferred, will infallibly and automatically produce grace in the souls of those who receive them, provided they have the proper dispositions. This being the case, it would seem that Mary's intervention does not extend to sacramental graces.

We must bear in mind that the grace which is conferred by a duly administered sacrament was condignly merited by the Redeemer and congruously merited by the Coredemptrix; hence, it is due to Mary in some way. But she has an even more proximate relation to the sacred rite. The minimum dispositions required for a fruitful reception of a properly administered sacrament, even the desire to receive it, are actual graces obtained through Our Lady's mediation. That a man on his deathbed be comforted by the last rites, that a pagan submit to the laver of regeneration, that a newborn babe, in preference to others, become a

---

[116] Garrigou-Lagrange, *op. cit.*, pp. 237, 239.

[117] Pius XII, *Ad coeli Reginam*, in *A.A.S.*, Vol. 46, 1954, p. 636.

child of God, all this is due without any doubt to Mary's actual intervention. So in like manner with reference to the other sacraments.

The explanation of how these actual graces are conferred will depend upon the particular opinion one adheres to. As to sacramental grace itself, some of the proponents of the physical instrumental causality would advance the following process: "Grace begins in the Divine Nature, passes through the Sacred Humanity of Christ (a physical instrument), passes through Mary (also a physical instrument), and finally passes through the sacrament (also a physical instrument)."[118]

CONCLUSION

At the end of this study on the Dispensatrix of all graces, it behooves us to evaluate our findings by reviewing, in a summary fashion, the evidence presented. This evaluation will set forth the relationship existing between this Marian truth and divine revelation. Consequent upon this, a basis will be had for an appraisal of the dogmatic value and definability of the doctrine.

Without any shadow of doubt this truth has been, and continues to be, frequently inculcated by the *Ecclesia docens*. The official teaching authority, particularly within the past one hundred years, has conveyed this truth not only in a large number of papal documents, but through the medium of the liturgy as well. Does it seem possible that the Popes would inculcate into the hearts and minds of the Christian people, with such insistence and continuity, a doctrine which is not the authentic expression of the living faith of the Church?[119]

As to Sacred Scripture, we believe we have shown that some of its passages, interpreted in the light of the magisterium and tradition, do contain implicit references to Mary's prerogative. This is particularly

---

[118] W. G. Most, *Mary in Our Life* (New York, 1954), p. 38.

[119] P. Aubron, *La médiation universelle de la Sainte Vierge*, in Nouvelle Revue Théologique, Vol. 65, 1938, p. 34. Although the episcopal magisterium was not discussed in this chapter, we might mention here a significant incident reported by Bittremieux (*op. cit.*, p. 153, n. 6) in this connection. It refers to a letter addressed by Cardinal Mercier to all his fellow bishops inviting them to state whether they favored a dogmatic definition of our doctrine. Over four hundred and fifty bishops replied in the affirmative, and only three in the negative. The latter did not deny Mary's prerogative, but felt that a solemn pronouncement by the Church would not be opportune at the time.

true of the Protoevangelium and Our Lord's testament on the cross.

The teaching of tradition is likewise a witness to our truth. Suffice to recall in this connection the words of Leo XIII in his encyclical *Octobri mense:* "It is the belief and teaching of the venerable Fathers of the Church," and also the words of the decree of the Sacred Congregation of Rites approved by Pius XII: "Gathering together the tradition of the Fathers, the *Doctor Mellifluus* teaches that God wants us to have everything through Mary. This pious and salutary doctrine all theologians at the present time hold in common accord." With but few exceptions, the Fathers of the Church did not, of course, convey these ideas explicitly and in so many words. Nevertheless, they may be said to have implied as much (perhaps being unaware of it) in their more general teaching concerning Mary's unique role as Christ's intimate partner in the economy of man's salvation. Theologians of subsequent centuries, particularly under the influence of St. Bernard and St. Alphonsus, gradually arrived at the conclusion (now almost unanimously accepted) that the doctrine does bear the characteristics of one belonging to the original *depositum fidei*.

In view of the above, what theological note should we attach to our thesis? In this matter, as in others not as yet defined by the Church, we can expect to find a difference of opinion among theologians. We note also that, objectively, the status of a doctrinal proposition remains the same, but in the process of dogmatic evolution our knowledge and appreciation of it will vary. What is considered as "probable" today may well be a "defined dogma" tomorrow.

With regard to the thesis that Mary is the Dispensatrix of every single grace, some theologians consider it *doctrina catholica,* that is, a doctrine which is taught in the whole Church, e.g., in papal encyclicals, but which is not always infallibly proposed.[120] The greater number of theologians, however, classify it as *fidei proxima,* that is to say, a truth which, in the almost unanimous consent of theologians, is contained in the written or orally transmitted word of God.

While admitting the validity of the above notes, we would like to advance a personal opinion, without prejudice to a better sentiment, and

---

[120] Definitions of theological notes used here are those given in *Sacrae Theologiae Summa,* edited by the Spanish Jesuits, Vol. 3 (Matriti, 1950), pp. 3-4.

always subject to a definitive judgment of the Church. From the evidence adduced throughout this chapter, we feel justified in qualifying our thesis as *de fide divina,* that is to say, a truth which is formally contained in divine revelation. The reason which warrants this qualification is not the unanimous consent of theologians (as in the case of *fidei proxima* mentioned above), but rather the authority of the Popes. As previously indicated, the way Leo XIII speaks in this connection, especially in his encyclical *Octobri mense,* leads us to believe that we are dealing with a truth *formally-implicitly* contained in the original deposit of faith.

In the light of all this, our doctrine is certainly definable by the Church. There seems to be only one possible step left in its evolution, and that is a dogmatic definition. As Father Garrigou-Lagrange says, it is *proximately definable.*[121] In all likelihood, an eventual dogmatic pronouncement by the Church would restrict itself to the fact that all graces come to us through Mary, and abstract from the further question of the nature and modality of her mediatorial function; just as the Council of Trent defined that the sacraments produce grace, without determining the particular type of their causality.

When we review the history of the dogma of the Immaculate Conception and witness the prolonged opposition it drew from so many and so prominent theologians (St. Bernard, St. Thomas Aquinas, etc.), and then compare it with the moral unanimity in favor of Mary's role as Dispensatrix of all graces, we cannot but marvel that the latter has not as yet been raised to the status of a dogma. Fortunately, we have sufficient reason to believe that the long-expected definition is approaching. May it be our lot to see that day, and even to assist at an event so glorious for Our Blessed Lady and so consoling for all her children.

---

[121] Garrigou-Lagrange, *De Christo Salvatore* (Taurini, 1945), p. 521.

SELECT BIBLIOGRAPHY

P. Aubron, S.J., La médiation universelle de la Sainte Vierge, *in* Nouvelle Revue Théologique, *Vol. 65, 1938, pp. 5-35; de la Broise-Bainvel, S.J.,* Marie, Mère de grâce *(Paris, 1921); J. Bittremieux,* De mediatione universali B. M. Virginis quoad gratias *(Brugis, 1926);* L *Bello, O.F.M.,* De B. Maria Virgine omnium gratiarum mediatrice *(Romae, 1938); J. M. Bover, S.J.,* Maria Mediatrix: Patrum veterumque scriptorum testimonia in quibus "Mediatricis" titulus adhibetur *(Brugis, 1929); J. B. Carol, O.F.M.,* Mary, Mediatrix of All Graces, *in* Our Lady's Digest, *Vol. 6, 1952, pp. 417-426; E. Dublanchy, S.M.,* Marie médiatrice, *in* La Vie Spirituelle, *Vol. 1, 1922, pp. 321-332; E. Druwé, S.J.,* La médiation universelle de Marie, *in* Maria. Études sur la Sainte Vierge, *ed. H. du Manoir, S.J., Vol. 1 (Paris, 1949), pp. 419-572; C. Friethoff, O.P.,* De Alma Socia Christi Mediatoris *(Romae, 1936); F. X. Godts, C.Ss.R.,* De definibilitate mediationis universalis Deiparae...*(Bruxellis, 1904);* L *Jennet, C.J.M.,* Extension et mode de la coopération de Maria à la distribution des grâces, *in* Le Premier Congrès Marial de Québec, 12-16 juin, *1929 (Québec, 1931), pp. 261-300;* L *Leloir,* La médiation mariale dans la théologie contemporaine *(Bruges, 1933); Serapio de Iragui, O.F.M.Cap.,* La mediacion de la Virgen en la himnografia latina de la Edad Media *(Buenos Aires, 1939);* id., La mediación de la Virgen en la liturgia, *in* Alma Socia Christi, *Vol. 2, p. 222 ff.; E. Théoret,* La médiation mariale dans l'Ecole Française *(Paris, 1940); R. Vilain, S.J.,* Notes sur Marie médiatrice, *in* Nouvelle Revue Théologique, Vol. 53, 1926, pp. 748-775.

Mary's Death and Bodily Assumption

by LAWRENCE P. EVERETT, C.SS.R., S.T.D.

N NOVEMBER 1, 1950, Pope Pius XII defined the Assumption of the Blessed Mother of God into heaven in the following words: "Wherefore, after we have poured forth prayers of supplication again and again to God, and have invoked the light of the Spirit of Truth, for the glory of Almighty God Who has lavished His special affection upon the Virgin Mary, for the honor of her Son, the immortal King of the Ages and the Victor over sin and death, for the increase of that same august Mother, and for the joy and exultation of the entire Church; by the authority of Our Lord Jesus Christ, and of the Blessed Apostles Peter and Paul, and by Our own authority, We pronounce, declare, and define it to be a divinely revealed dogma: that the Immaculate Mother of God, the ever Virgin Mary, having completed the course of her earthly life, was assumed body and soul into heavenly glory."[1]

MEANING AND SCOPE OF THE DEFINITION

1. *We define it to be a divinely revealed dogma:* In the definition of the Immaculate Conception of Our Blessed Mother, Pope Pius IX used a somewhat different formula.[2] The formula used by Pope Pius XII in the definition of the Assumption is, however, similar to that used by the Fathers of the Vatican Council in their definition of Papal Infallibility.[3] By the terms *revealed dogma* is meant that the Assumption of Mary body and soul into heavenly glory is a fact contained within the deposit of revelation given to us by God and is now solemnly proposed by the Pope to be believed as such by all the faithful.

2. *Having completed the course of her earthly life:* Due to the dispute over the fact of Our Blessed Lady's death, the question of the precise

---

[1] Constitution, *Munificentissimus Deus,* in *A.A.S.,* Vol. 42, 1950, p. 770.

[2] Cf. *Ineffabilis Deus,* in *Acta Pii IX,* pars 1, Vol. 1, p. 616.

[3] Cf. *D.B.,* 1839.

scope of the doctrine of the Assumption was likewise a matter of dispute among theologians prior to November 1, 1950. Some maintained that the object of this privilege is the *glorious resurrection* of the Blessed Virgin, presupposing, therefore, the fact of her death.[4] This opinion was based upon the reasoning that in theological investigation we must not separate those truths which are inseparable in Tradition, the Liturgy, and the pious belief of the faithful. This opinion took for granted that the death, glorious resurrection, and bodily Assumption of the Blessed Virgin were taught as inseparable truths in Tradition and were always believed to be such by the faithful. Other theologians, on the contrary, maintained that the doctrine of the Assumption has within its scope only the *glorious Assumption* of Mary, body and soul into heaven, whether she died or not.[5]

The fact of Mary's death and subsequent resurrection is uncertain. We cannot say, therefore, that they are included within the scope of the definition of Pope Pius XII.[6] For a Pope defines only what is certain. And should it be established later beyond shadow of doubt that Mary actually died and subsequently rose again before her sacred body saw corruption,

---

[4] Cf. Al. Janssens, De *glorificatione corporali B. Mariae Virginis*, in Ephemerides Theologicae Lovaniensis, Vol. 8, 1931, p. 437 ff.

[5] Cf. F. S. Mueller, S.J., *Origo divino-apostolica doctrinae evectionis Beatissimae Virginis ad gloriam coelestem quoad corpus* (Oeniponte, 1930). Cf. the critique of Father Mueller's work by J. Bittremieux in *Ephemerides Theologicae Lovaniensis*, Vol. 8, 1931, p. 465 ff., in which he attempts to harmonize the two opinions by distinguishing between the Assumption in the abstract and in the concrete. Abstractly considered, the essential object of the Assumption is the bodily glorification of the Blessed Virgin. Considered in the concrete, and as it actually took place, the object would include her death and subsequent resurrection. But, as Father Roschini points out, this opinion presupposes the fact of Mary's death and subsequent resurrection, as does that of Father Janssens. Cf. *Summula Mariologiae* (Romae, 1952), p. 174. Father C. Balić, O.F.M., distinguishes between the Assumption *in recto* and *ex obliquo*. Considering the Assumption *in recto* its object is the glorification of the living body; *ex obliquo*, it includes the death and resurrection. He designates the latter as the *terminus a quo* of the Assumption and the former the *terminus ad quem*. Cf. *De definibilitate Assumptionis B. V. Mariae* (Romae, 1945), p. 42 ff.

[6] We do, however, find commentaries on the Constitution in which it is maintained that the death and subsequent resurrection of the body of Mary are included within the scope of the definition. Cf., for example, B. García Rodríguez, C.M.F., *La razón teológica en la constitución 'Munificentissimus Deus,'* in *Ephemerides Mariologicae*, Vol. 1, 1951, p. 46 ff.

this new discovery would have no bearing whatever upon the scope of the definition in the *Munificentissimus Deus*. For that alone is within the scope of a definition which the Holy Father or an Ecumenical Council intends to define at the moment of definition. And, by the same reasoning, those who maintain that Mary did not die cannot say that Pope Pius XII defined that Mary was assumed into heavenly glory without having previously died and risen again. The fact alone of her Assumption, body and soul, into heaven is now of faith by virtue of this Constitution, and not her death, resurrection, *or* bodily immortality.

A brief glance at the history of the doctrine of the death and resurrection of Mary and at the theological arguments adduced in support of them should serve to justify the opinion just stated.

In the first three centuries there are absolutely no references in the authentic works of the Fathers or ecclesiastical writers to the death or bodily immortality of Mary. Nor is there any mention of a tomb of Mary in the first centuries of Christianity. The veneration of the tomb of the Blessed Virgin at Jerusalem began about the middle of the fifth century; and even here there is no agreement as to whether its locality was in the Garden of Olives or in the Valley of Josaphat. Nor is any mention made in the Acts of the Council of Ephesus (431) of the fact that the Council, convened to defend the Divine Maternity of the Mother of God, is being held in the very city selected by God for her final resting place. Only after the Council did the tradition begin which placed her tomb in that city.

The earliest known (non-Apocryphal) mention concerning the end of Mary's life appears in the writings of St. Epiphanius, Bishop of Constantia, the ancient Salamina, in the isle of Cyprus. Born in Palestine, we may assume that he was well aware of the traditions there. Yet we find these words in his *Panarion* or *Medicine Chest* (of remedies for all heresies), written in c. 377: "Whether she died or was buried we know not."[7] Speaking of the cautious language used by St. Epiphanius, Father Roschini says: "To understand his words fully we must remember that he was conscious, when writing, of two heresies which were then living and dangerous: that of the Antidicomarianites, and that of the Collyridians. The former denied the perpetual virginity of Mary, the

---

[7] *Haereses*, 78, 11, *PG*, 42, 716.

latter, erring in the opposite direction, maintained that divine worship should be given to her. To assert that Our Lady died was to give a handle to the one heresy (for it was to suggest that the body of Mary was subject to the corruption of the tomb, and thus minimize her prerogatives); to assert that she did not die was to encourage the other."[8] And with the exception of a so-called contemporary of Epiphanius, Timothy of Jerusalem, who said: "Wherefore the Virgin is immortal up to now, because He who dwelt in her took her to the regions of the Ascension,"[9] no early writer ever doubted the fact of her death. They did not, however, examine the question; they merely took the fact of her death for granted.

Apparently influenced by the apocryphal *Transitus* writings of the fifth to the seventh centuries, later Fathers and Church writers likewise spoke of the death of Mary as a fact taken for granted. For all men, including Christ, died: therefore, Mary, too. Like their predecessors, they did not consider *ex professo* the theological arguments for or against.

St. Isidore of Seville (d. 636) appears to be the first to cast some doubt upon the fact of Mary's death. Obviously ignoring the Apocrypha, he said of the death of Mary: "... nowhere does one read of her death. Although, as some say, her sepulchre may be found in the valley of Josaphat."[10] Tusaredo, a Bishop in the Asturias province of Spain in the eighth century, wrote: "Of the glorious Mary, no history teaches that she suffered martyrdom or any other kind of death."[11] Although St. Andrew of Crete (d. 720) generally introduced much theological argumentation into his writings, he states, with very little argumentation, that Mary died because her Son died.[12] The same is true of a similar teaching of St.

---

[8] G. M. Roschini, *Did Our Lady Die?* in The Irish Ecclesiastical Record, *Vol. 80, 1953*, pp. 75-76.

[9] For a critique of the teaching of Timothy of Jerusalem and the various manuscripts in which his doctrine may be found, cf. M. Jugie, *La mort et l'Assomption de la Sainte Vierge* (Città del Vaticano, 1944), p. 70 ff. Cf. B. Capelle, *Les homilies liturgiques du prétendu Timothée de Jérusalem*, in *Ephemerides Liturgicae*, Vol. 63, 1949, pp. 5-26. After a very thorough and scholarly investigation the author concludes that Timothy is an unknown author who lived between the sixth and seventh centuries (p. 23).

[10] *De ortu et obitu Patrum*, 67; PL, 83, 150.

[11] *Epistola ad Ascaricum*, 11; *PL*, 99, 1239-1240.

[12] *Oratio 12 in dormit. SS. Deiparae; PG*, 97, 1051-1054.

John Damascene (d. 749).[13] And about one hundred years later, Theodore Abou-Kurra (d. c. 820) likened the death of Mary to the sleep of Adam in the Garden when God formed Eve from one of his ribs.[14] This, obviously, was not a true death.

All the great Scholastics of the thirteenth century taught that Mary died. The principal reason for their so teaching was obviously the fact that they denied the Immaculate Conception in the sense in which it was defined by Pope Pius IX.[15] Thus we read in the writings of St. Bonaventure: "If the Blessed Virgin was free from original sin, she was also exempt from the necessity of dying; therefore, either her death was an injustice or she died for the salvation of the human race. But the former supposition is blasphemous, implying that God is not just; and the latter, too, is a blasphemy against Christ for it implies that His Redemption is insufficient. Both are therefore erroneous and impossible. Therefore Our Blessed Lady was subject to original sin."[16]

After the definition of the Immaculate Conception by Pope Pius IX in 1854 the question of whether or not Our Blessed Lady died gradually became a subject of wide theological discussion and is today one of the most widely disputed Mariological questions. The impetus to further study out of which arose the present state of dispute was given by the writings of Dominic Arnaldi of Genoa who died in the year 1895. Arnaldi defended the thesis that Our Blessed Lady's complete freedom from sin demanded her freedom from the penalty of death.[17]

---

[13] *Hom. 2 in dormit.*, n. 2; *PG*, 96, 726.

[14] *Opuscula*, op. 37; *PG*, 97, 1594.

[15] Cf. C. Piana, *La morte e l'Assunzione della B. Vergine nella letteratura medioevale, in* Atti del Congresso Nazionale Mariano dei Frati Minori d'Italia (Roma, 1948), pp. 283-308.

[16] *In III Sent.*, d. 3, q. 2, ad 4; *op. omnia*, Vol. 3 (Ad Claras Aquas, 1888), p. 66. T. Gallus, *Ad "immortalitatem" B. M. Virginis, in Marianum*, Vol. 12, 1950, pp. 44-45, contends that the teaching of the Middle Ages concerning Mary's death was based on the false premise that Mary had contracted original sin. This is perhaps true of the thirteenth century, but Father Piana has shown that many subsequent theologians who believed in the Immaculate Conception taught also Mary's death. Cf. *L'Assomption de la Vierge et l'école franciscaine du XVe siècle, in Congrès Marial du Puy-en-Velay, 1949* (Paris, 1950), esp. pp. 64, 72.

[17] Cf. *Super definibilitate dogmatica Asumptionis corporeae B. V. M. Deiparae Immaculatae* (Augustae Taurinorum, 1884), p. 32.

Today we have diametrically opposed views on the death of Mary supported by outstanding Mariologists. The most outspoken proponents of the thesis that Mary did not die are Roschini and Gallus.[18] Father Freithoff, O.P., expressed the view that "the death of Mary is not certain, either historically or from revelation."[19] On the other hand, Father C. Balić, O.F.M., maintains that "the *terminus a quo* of the Assumption is the death of Our Lady, the *terminus ad quem* is the glorification of her body in heaven. The object of the Assumption *in recto* is the glorification of the living body, and *ex obliquo* her death and resurrection."[20] Father J. F. Bonnefoy, O.F.M., goes so far as to state that "the death of the Most Holy Virgin may be considered as historically proved and explicitly revealed: as such (explicitly revealed) it may be the subject of a dogmatic definition: there is no reason why it should not be."[21] And the *Mariological Week* held at Salamanca (Spain) in 1949, which was devoted exclusively to the question of the death of Mary, sent a petition to the Holy See requesting the definition "... of the bodily Assumption of the B. V. Mary into heaven, *after death.* ..."[22] It is little wonder, then, that Cardinal Pizzardo, the Secretary of the Congregation of the Holy Office, in an address on the occasion of the First International Mariological Congress in Rome (1950) referred to the question of the end of the life of the Blessed Virgin as a very obscure problem, and one which demands further study and clarification by theologians.[23]

All theologians agree, of course, that Mary was not subject to death

---

[18] Roschini, *Il problema della morte di Maria SS. dopo la Costituzione Dogmatica "Munificentissimus Deus,"* in *Marianum*, Vol. 13, 1951, pp. 148-163; *id., Il problema della morte di Maria SS. Risposta alle contestazioni del P. Sauras,* in *Ephemerides Mariologicae*, Vol. 3, 1953, pp. 25-53. T. Gallus, *art. cit.*, and also *La Vergine Immortale* (Roma, 1949).

[19] *De doctrina Assumptionis corporalis B. M. V. rationibus theologicis demonstrata, in* Angelicum, *Vol. 16, 1938, p. 12. In the same sense M. Jugie,* op. cit., passim, esp. p. 539.

[20] Cf. footnote 5.

[21] *Définibilité de l'Assomption, in* Congrès Marial du Puy-en-Velay *(Paris, 1950), p. 241. Cf.* his more recent article La Bulle Dogmatique "Munificentissimus Deus" *(1 Nov. 1950), in* Ephemerides Mariologicae, Vol. 1, 1951, pp. 89-130, esp. 104-114.

[22] *Votum SS. Dno. Pio XII prolatum de corporea Asumptione B. M. Virginis in coelum, post mortem, definienda, in* Estudios Marianos, Vol. 9, 1950, p. 11 ff.

[23] Cf. *Alma Socia Christi. Acta Congressus Mariologici-Mariani Romae anno sancto* 1950 *celebrati,* Vol. 1: *Congressus ordo et summarium* (Romae, 1951), p. 104.

as a penalty for sin. However, God willed that "she die for higher reasons pertaining to her relationship with Christ and the part she was to play in the work of Redemption."[24] The reasons brought forth by those who maintain that Our Blessed Mother actually died may be reduced to the following two:

a) Conformity to Christ: The condition of the Mother should not be better than that of her divine Son. The Verbum willingly assumed passible and mortal flesh and came into the world "in the likeness of sinful flesh,"[25] in order that, through it, He might redeem us from our sins. As the Mother of the passible and mortal Redeemer from whom He took His mortal flesh, Mary, too, had to be passible and mortal. She did not, however, voluntarily assume mortal flesh as did her divine Son as something from which she was exempt. This was God's will for her although she died not as a penalty for sin but *pro conditione carnis.*

This argument, however, might justly be called a *post factum* argument, proposed to explain the fact of Mary's death after her death had been taken for granted. However, in its favor is the theological axiom: *lex orandi statuit legem credendi.* And until recently these words were in the Secret of the Mass for the Assumption. One may argue, however, that the Liturgy in this instance merely stated a popular belief, one which everyone took for granted in view of the fact of Christ's death. For, the Second Council of Orange is quite explicit in its teaching that those who hold that the penalty of death (*reatus poenae*) is transmitted to the body without the transmission of sin or the death of the soul (*reatus culpae*) to all the children of Adam, do an injustice to God.[26] Hence, where there is no sin there can be no *obligatory* death of the body in a child of Adam. Hence, it would appear that if we are to defend the fact of Mary's death we must look to another reason, one wherein the acceptance of death by Mary would be a *voluntary* act. Theologians see this in Mary's role of Coredeemer of the human race.

Mary's role of Coredeemer: Due to the teaching of the Second Council of Orange, many theologians who maintain that Mary died claim that

---

[24] E. A. Wuenschel, C.Ss.R., *The Definability of the Assumption,* in *Proceedings of the Second Annual Meeting of The Catholic Theological Society of America,* 1947, p. 99.

[25] *Rom.* 8:3.

[26] *D.B.,* 175.

she had a right to immortality but, like her Son, freely accepted death in order that she might coredeem the human race together with Him. Yet the objection is raised against this opinion that Mary should then have died on Calvary with Christ. For, with the death and resurrection of Christ the Redemption was completed *in actu primo* and, consequently, the Coredemption. This, too, goes counter to the traditionally accepted belief that Mary coredeemed us by a spiritual compassion, suffering in her soul the agony Christ suffered for us in His Body.

The Constitution *Munificentissimus Deus* leaves the question open. In the words of the definition death is not mentioned but only "having completed the course of her earthly life." The question of the death of Mary is not treated as a subject bearing upon the Assumption. True, the Holy Father frequently mentions the death of the Blessed Virgin in the body of the document, but in every instance he quotes someone else. He does not give his own views on the subject. Consequently, I believe we can say with Father Roschini that "the question of Mary's death is a matter for free discussion."[27]

Finally, we should note here that whether Mary died or not, she was not subject to the law of death, the corruption of the grave. If she died, then she was assumed into heaven before her sacred body saw corruption. For, so long as the bodies of the just remain in the dust of the earth, they are under the dominion of death, and they sigh for the ultimate redemption of their bodies.[28]

Was assumed body and soul into heavenly glory: The Assumption of Our Blessed Mother was a privilege granted not to her body alone nor to her soul alone but to the *person*, Mary. True, we speak of the *bodily* assumption of the Blessed Virgin but this is due to the fact that there never has been any dispute over the question of her soul enjoying the beatific vision once she completed the course of her earthly life. Thus, the Holy Father said: "... the ever Virgin *Mary* ... was assumed."

The precise degree of glory to which Our Blessed Mother was

---

[27] *Art. cit.*, p. 87 ff.

[28] Cf. *Rom.* 8:10, 23. On the question of Mary's death, cf. the recent study by J. B. Carol, O.F.M., *The Immaculate Conception and Mary's Death*, in *Our Lady's Digest*, Vol. 9, February, 1955, pp. 302-310, and also his *Fundamentals of Mariology* (New York, 1956), pp. 167-181.

assumed has never been defined by the Church. It is, however, *certain* theological teaching that her degree of grace at the first moment of her Immaculate Conception was greater than that possessed by any individual angel or man at the first moment of sanctification. This teaching is based on the law of filial piety whereby the Verbum loved His designated Mother more than any other creature. That the first influx of grace was greater than the consummated grace of any individual man is the *common teaching* of theologians and taught for the same reason as that given for the above opinion. And that Mary's first influx of grace was greater in degree than the consummated grace of all men and angels together is a *solidly probable opinion*.[29]

Add to this the fact that the degree of sanctifying grace received by Mary at the moment of her Immaculate Conception was increased *ex opere operato* through the great dignity of the divine maternity and her reception of some of the sacraments, as well as *ex opere operantis* during every moment of her life on earth, and we find that the degree of glory to which she was assumed is beyond human comprehension and second only to that of Christ as Man. For the degree of glory enjoyed in heaven is determined by the degree of sanctifying grace with which the soul is adorned at the moment of death.

We shall now outline and comment upon the reasons given in the Constitution *Munificentissimus Deus* which led the Holy Father to the definition of Mary's Assumption into heaven. The Constitution may be divided as follows:[30]

---

[29] St. Alphonsus bases this opinion (with relation to all *men*, not angels) on Mary's office of Coredeemer. Thus, he says: "If Mary, as the already destined Mother of our common Redeemer, received from the beginning the office of mediatress of all men, and consequently, even of the saints, it was also requisite that even from the beginning she should have a degree of grace exceeding that of all the saints for whom she was to intercede. ... If, by means of Mary, all men were to render themselves dear to God, necessarily Mary was more holy and more dear to Him than all men together. Otherwise, how could she have interceded for all others?" *The Glories of Mary* (Brooklyn, 1931), p. 158.

[30] This division is based on that of Father I. Filograssi, S.J., from *Constitutio Apostolica "Munificentissimus Deus" de Assumptione Beatae Mariae Virginis,* in *Gregorianum*, Vol. 31, 1950, pp. 483-484.

I. The Assumptionistic Movement (pp. 754-756);[31]
II. The teaching of the Ordinary and Universal Magisterium (pp. 756-757);
III. Indications of our present belief found in remote testimonies (pp. 757-767);
  a) The faithful have professed this faith under the leadership of their shepherds (pp. 757-758);
  b) This faith is shown in temples, images, various exercises of devotion to the Blessed Virgin assumed into heaven (p. 758);
  c) This faith is shown in the Solemn Liturgies (pp. 758-760);
  d) This faith is shown in the testimonies of the Fathers and Doctors of the Church (pp. 760-762);
  e) This faith is shown in the writings of the theologians of the Church (pp. 762-767).

I. THE ASSUMPTIONISTIC MOVEMENT

Toward the beginning of the *Munificentissimus Deus* our Holy Father speaks of the Assumptionistic Movement within the Church in these words:

> That privilege (the Assumption of Mary) has shone forth in new radiance since Our predecessor of immortal memory, Pius IX, solemnly proclaimed the dogma of the loving Mother of God's Immaculate Conception. These two privileges are most closely bound to one another.[32]

---

[31] The numbers in parentheses refer to the official text of the *Munificentissimus Deus*, in *A.A.S.*, Vol. 42, 1950, pp. 754-771.

[32] Although the Holy Father uses the expression "these two privileges are most *closely bound* to one another," he does not settle the disputed question of the manner in which they are so bound. Some theologians maintain that the Assumption does not follow necessarily from the Immaculate Conception but only as a *fitting consequence* (as, for example, P. Renaudin, O.S.B., *Assumptio B. Mariae Virginis Matris Dei* [Taurini-Romae, 1933], Ch. 10, 170). Others hold that these two truths are so connected that the Assumption is formally implicitly revealed in the Immaculate Conception. This opinion is held by Father Gabriel Roschini, *Compendium Mariologiae* (Romae, 1946), p. 469, and in *The Assumption and the Immaculate Conception*, in *The Thomist*, Vol. 14, 1951, p. 59 ff. Father Juniper Carol, O.F.M., raises the following objection against this opinion: "The Sacred Scriptures (e.g., *Gen.* 2:17; *Rom.* 5:12) do establish a positive nexus between sin and death. However, in order to show that our doctrine (the Assumption) is formally implicitly revealed in the revelation of Mary's absolute exemption from sin, it would have

Christ overcame sin and death by His own death, and one who through Baptism has been born again in a supernatural way has conquered sin and death through the same Christ. Yet, according to the general rule, God does not will to grant to the just the full effect of the victory over death until the end of time has come. And so it is that the bodies of even the just are corrupted after death, and only on the last day will they be joined, each to its own glorious soul.

Now God has willed that the Blessed Virgin Mary should be exempted from this general rule. She, by an entirely unique privilege, completely overcame sin by her Immaculate Conception, and as a result she was not subject to the law of remaining in the corruption of the grave, and she did not have to wait until the end of time for the redemption of her body.

Thus, when it was solemnly proclaimed that Mary, the Virgin Mother of God, was from the very beginning free from the taint of original sin, the minds of the faithful were filled with a stronger hope that the day might soon come when the dogma of the Virgin Mary's bodily Assumption into heaven would also be defined by the Church's supreme teaching authority.

Actually, it was seen that not only individual Catholics, but also those who could speak for nations or ecclesiastical provinces, and even a considerable number of the Fathers of the Vatican Council, urgently

---

to be proved that death, whether permanent or transitory, is *always and necessarily* a punishment due to sin, even after Christ paid our debt on the cross. And this is what some grave theologians will not admit. Besides, we have a decision of the Council of Trent according to which the sacrament of Baptism completely remits not only the guilt of original sin but also *all* punishment due to it (*DB*, 807). And yet many Christians, even while in possession of baptismal grace, not only die but are also subject to corruption until the day of the general resurrection. The Angelic Doctor ... gives us a cue to the possible solution of this difficulty by distinguishing between punishments due to the *person* and punishments due to the *nature* (*Summ. theol.* III, q. 69, a. 3, ad 3). According to this, the decision of the Council may well refer to the former, not to the latter. We say that this is a *possible* solution, for the Council speaks of *all* punishment without making any distinction. Hence the difficulty seems to remain. At any rate, we believe that the doctrine of Mary's Assumpion may be drawn from her Immaculate Conception by a somewhat different process which would give us a 'theological conclusion.' " *The Definability of Mary's Assumption*, in *The American Ecclesiastical Review*, Vol. 118, March, 1948, pp. 168-169. In the original article submitted to *The American Ecclesiastical Review*, Father Carol had written: "And yet *many* Christians, even while in possession of baptismal grace, not only die but ..." He now informs us that, for some unexplained reason, whoever prepared the manuscript for the printer took the liberty to substitute the word "most" for "many," thus rendering his statement utterly false.

petitioned the Apostolic See to this effect.[33]

The petitions of which the Holy Father speaks above were collected and evaluated at his command[34] in two volumes edited by W. Hentrich and R. de Moos and entitled: *Petitiones de Assumptione corporea B. V. Mariae in coelum definienda ad Sanctam Sedem delata*.[35] From the year 1869 to the year 1941, resident bishops, ruling 820 sees or 73 per cent of all the Catholic sees of the world, submitted 1789 of these petitions.[36] To these petitions were added 656 by titular bishops, 261 by vicars apostolic, 26 by abbots and prelates nullius, 61 by general superiors of clerical orders, 336 by minor prelates, 32,291 by priests and male religious, 50,975 by female religious, and 8,086,396 by the laity.[37]

The most significant petition was that submitted by nearly 200 bishops attending the Ecumenical Council of the Vatican in which they stated:

> Since, according to apostolic teaching (*Rom.* 5, 8; *1 Cor.* 15, 24, 26, 54, 57; *Hebr.* 2, 14-15 and other places), that triumph which Christ wrought over Satan, the serpent of antiquity, was constituted by the three-fold victory over sin and the fruits of sin, which are concupiscence and death, its integral parts; and since according to Genesis (3, 15) the Mother of God is shown as associated in a singular manner with her Son in this triumph; according to the unanimous vote of the Holy Fathers, we do not doubt that in the aforesaid oracle the same Blessed Virgin is shown as sharing in that threefold victory; and therefore in the same place it was foretold that she would be made victress over sin through her Immaculate Conception, over concupiscence through her virginal maternity, and also over death through her accelerated resurrection in the likeness of her Son.[38]

---

[33] *Op. cit.*, pp. 754-755.

[34] Cf. *op. cit.*, p. 755.

[35] Typis polyglottis Vaticanis, 1942.

[36] Cf. *Petitiones*, Vol. 2, pp. 832-842.

[37] *Op. cit.*, pp. 842-854.

[38] *Acta et decreta sacrorum conciliorum recentiorum. Collectio Lacensis*, Vol. 7 (Friburgi Brisgoviae, 1882), p. 869 ff.

II. THE TEACHING OF THE ORDINARY AND UNIVERSAL MAGISTERIUM

And, since we are dealing with a matter of such great moment and of such importance, we considered it opportune to ask all Our venerable brethren in the episcopate directly and authoritatively that each of them should make known to Us his mind in a formal statement.[39]

Urged on by the petitions submitted to the Holy See requesting the definition of the Assumption, Pope Pius XII issued on May 1, 1946, a letter to the bishops of the world entitled *Deiparae Virginis Mariae*. Following the method of Pope Pius IX before the definition of the Immaculate Conception,[40] the Holy Father requested that the bishops answer the following questions: "Do you, Venerable Brethren, in your outstanding wisdom and prudence, judge that the bodily Assumption of the Blessed Virgin can be proposed and defined as a dogma of faith? Do you, with your clergy and people, desire it?"[41] The following are the words of the Holy Father relative to the response of the bishops:[42]

> ... those whom "the Holy Spirit has placed as bishops to rule the Church of God"[43] gave an almost unanimous affirmative response to both these questions. This "outstanding agreement of the Catholic prelates and the faithful,"[44] affirming that the bodily Assumption of God's Mother into heaven can be defined as a dogma of faith, since it shows us the concordant faith of the Christian people which the same doctrinal authority sustains and directs, thus by itself and in an entirely certain and infallible way, manifests this privilege as a truth revealed by God and contained in that divine deposit which Christ has delivered to His Spouse to be guarded faithfully and to be taught infallibly.[45] Certainly this teaching authority of the Church, not by any merely human effort but under the protection of the Spirit of Truth,[46] and therefore absolutely without error, carried out the

---

[39] *Op. cit.*, p. 756.

[40] Cf. *Ubi primum*, in *Acta Pii IX*, pars 1, Vol. 1, p. 162 ff.

[41] *Op. cit.*, p. 756.

[42] *Op. cit.*, pp. 756-757.

[43] *Acts* 20:28.

[44] Pius IX, *Ineffabilis Deus*, in *Acta Pii IX*, pars 1, Vol. 1, p. 615.

[45] Cf. Vatican Council, *De fide catholica*, cap. 4.

[46] Cf. *Jn.* 14:26.

Commission entrusted to it, that of preserving the revealed truths pure and entire throughout every age, in such a way that it presents them undefiled, adding nothing to them and taking nothing away from them. For, as the Vatican Council teaches, "the Holy Spirit was not promised to the successors of Peter in such a way that, by His revelation, they might manifest new doctrine, but so that, by His assistance, they might guard as sacred and might faithfully propose the revelation delivered through the Apostles, or the deposit of faith."[47] Thus, from the universal agreement of the Church's ordinary teaching authority we have a certain and firm proof, demonstrating that the Blessed Virgin Mary's bodily Assumption into heaven — which surely no faculty of the human mind could know by its own natural powers, as far as the heavenly glorification of the virginal body of the loving Mother of God is concerned — is a truth that has been revealed by God and consequently something that must be firmly and faithfully believed by all the children of the Church. For, as the Vatican Council asserts, "all those things are to be believed by divine and Catholic faith which are contained in the written word of God or in tradition, and which are proposed by the Church, either in solemn judgment or in its ordinary and universal teaching office, as divinely revealed truths which must be believed."[48]

In the above statement of our Holy Father the following words are of the utmost importance: "This outstanding agreement of the Catholic prelates and the faithful ... shows us the concordant teaching of the Church's ordinary doctrinal authority and the concordant faith of the Christian people which the same doctrinal authority sustains and directs, thus by itself in an entirely certain and infallible way, manifests this privilege as a truth revealed by God ..."

There are two norms of Faith: the one proximate and the other remote. The proximate norm of Faith is the Magisterium of the Church and the remote norm is Sacred Scripture and the documents of Tradition. Thus, *by itself,* as the Holy Father says, that is, without the need of any investigation whatever into the pages of Sacred Scripture or the documents of Tradition, the almost unanimous affirmative response of the Catholic bishops of the world is certain proof that the Assumption of the Blessed Mother of God is a truth revealed to us. The living

---

[47] *De Ecclesia Christi,* cap. 4. D.B., 1836.

[48] *De fide catholica,* cap. 3. D.B., 1792.

Magisterium, i.e., the bishops of the world together with the Pope, is the authentic, divinely appointed interpreter of Sacred Scripture, and only in dependence upon the Magisterium do the Fathers of the Church have any authority as witnesses to the deposit of Faith.[49]

In the passage quoted above the Holy Father very significantly pointed out the fact that the bishops of the world in communion with the Holy See arrived at their conclusion as to the definability of the Assumption not as do theologians or Scripture scholars, through mere human industry, but "under the protection of the Spirit of Truth." For the efficient cause of their infallibility, when they teach as a group a doctrine of faith or morals in union with the Pope, is the Holy Spirit of Truth dwelling within the Church. Consequently, even before Pope Pius XII defined the Assumption, it was, objectively speaking, a truth of Divine and Catholic Faith and one to be believed as such by all the faithful.

Finally, we should note in the above-quoted words of the Holy Father relative to the response of the bishops the parenthetical remark of the Holy Father that "the Blessed Virgin Mary's bodily Assumption into heaven — which surely no faculty of the human mind could know by its own natural powers, as far as the glorification of the virginal body of the Mother of God is concerned — is a truth that has been revealed by God ..." Quite obviously, the *taking up* of the body of the Blessed Virgin Mary is *per se* an object of sense cognition and could be known, therefore, through natural powers. But the heavenly glorification of the Blessed Virgin, included within the notion of the Assumption, embraces the supernatural beatification of her soul with its secondary effects flowing into her body together with the preternatural transformation of her body. These gifts, being *super* and *preter*natural, are not the objects of our natural senses.

---

[49] Cf. St. Thomas, *Summ. Theol.*, II-II, q. 10, a. 12, c.

III. INDICATIONS OF OUR PRESENT BELIEF FOUND IN REMOTE TESTIMONIES

A. The Faithful Have Professed This Faith Under the Leadership of Their Pastors

Christ's faithful, through the teaching and the leadership of their pastors, have learned from the sacred books that the Virgin Mary ... led a life troubled by cares, hardships, and sorrows, and that ... a terribly sharp sword had pierced her heart as she stood under the cross of her divine Son, our Redeemer. In the same way, it was not difficult for them to admit that the great Mother of God, like her only begotten Son, had actually passed from this life. But this in no way prevented them from believing and from professing openly that her sacred body had never been subject to the corruption of the tomb, and that the august tabernacle of the Divine Word had never been reduced to dust and ashes. Actually, enlightened by divine grace and moved by affection for her, God's Mother and our own sweetest Mother, they have contemplated in an ever clearer light the wonderful harmony and order of those privileges which the most provident God has lavished upon this loving associate of our Redeemer, privileges which reach such an exalted plane that, except for her, nothing created by God other than the human nature of Jesus Christ has ever reached this level.[50]

Guided by the Spirit of Truth dwelling within her, the Church — the faithful, under the teaching and leadership of their bishops — has always seen the Assumption of Our Blessed Mother into heaven as her crowning privilege implicitly contained within the complete notion of the Divine Maternity. "The Church sees it there, not as the result of a logical deduction, still less as a mere *convenientia*, but as one element of that miracle of miracles which God willed His Mother to be. The Church sees it with a supernatural insight imparted by the Divine Spirit Who dwells within her. The Bishops of the Austrian Empire call it a simple intuition."[51] And it was this intuition which gave birth to such Mariological axioms as *"potuit, decuit, fecit"* of Scotus,[52] and the

---

[50] *Munificentissimus*, pp. 757-758.

[51] E. A. Wuenschel, *art. cit.*, p. 91.

[52] According to Angel Luis, C.Ss.R., Principio fundamental o primario, ¿Cómo enunciarlo si se da ese único principio?, in *Estudios Marianos*, Vol. 3, 1944, p. 190, this famous axiom was not formulated by Scotus but by one of his disciples, namely, F. Mayron, *In III Sent.*, d. 3, q. 2. The words which are the basis of this interpretation of his thought are: *"Deus*

following of St. Alphonsus: "... when an opinion tends in any way to honor the most Blessed Virgin, when it has some foundation and is not repugnant to the faith, nor to the decrees of the Church, nor to truth, the refusal to hold it, or to oppose it because the reverse may be true, shows little devotion to the Mother of God."[53]

The complete notion of the Divine Maternity contains within its connotation much more than the fact that Mary gave birth to the Son of God. For the Son of God is our Redeemer. She is, therefore, and has always been believed to be the Mother of God, the Redeemer, *as Redeemer*, making her His associate in the work of the Redemption and the Coredeemer of the human race. From these two offices, the Divine Maternity and the Coredemption, flow all the unspeakable prerogatives of soul and body with which God adorned His Mother and ours. She is the one foretold by God in the Protoevangelium who, together with her Son would crush the head of the serpent beneath her immaculate foot.[54] Immaculately pure from the first moment of her conception, she knew not the stings of concupiscence nor the slightest stain of personal moral imperfection. Virgin of Virgins, she was subject to no man nor to pain and the corruption of the flesh in conceiving and bringing forth Christ. Embellished with a degree of grace that far surpassed the combined holiness of all angels and saints together she was always believed to be the "Lily Among Thorns; Land Wholly Intact; Immaculate; Always Blessed; Free From All Contagion Of Sin; Unfading Tree; Fountain Ever Clear; The One And Only Daughter Not Of Death But Of Life; Offspring Not Of Wrath But Of Grace; Unimpaired And Ever Unimpaired; Holy And Stranger To All Stain Of Sin; More Comely Than Comeliness Itself; More Holy Than Sanctity; Alone Holy Who, Excepting God, Is Higher Than All; By Nature More Beautiful, More Graceful And More Holy Than The Cherubim And Seraphim Themselves And The Whole Hosts Of Angels."[55]

---

potuit facere quod ipsa numquam fuisset in peccato originali. ... Si auctoritati Ecclesiae, vel auctoritati Scripturae non repugnet, videtur probabile quod est excellentius attribuere Mariae" (Op. Oxon., III Sent., d. 3, q. 1, n. 4).

[53] *Glories of Mary* (ed. Brooklyn, 1931), p. 158.

[54] *Gen.* 3:15.

[55] Pope Pius XII, *Fulgens Corona*, in *A.A.S.*, Vol. 45, 1953, pp. 579, 580.

It is little wonder, then, that the faithful under the leadership of their bishops have always believed that this "august tabernacle of the Divine Word had never been reduced to dust and ashes." For, associated with Her Son in His complete victory over Satan, she shared with Him in His victory over the empire of Satan and, therefore, death.[56] Like Him, she did not have to wait until the end of time for the redemption of her sacred body as we do,[57] but through her anticipated resurrection in the likeness of her Son "she received the blessings of the Redemption first and in the fullest measure."[58]

B. This Faith Is Shown in Temples, Images, Various Exercises of Piety to the Blessed Virgin Assumed Into Heaven

The innumerable temples which have been dedicated to the Virgin Mary assumed into heaven clearly attest this faith. So do those sacred images, exposed therein for the veneration of the faithful, which bring this unique triumph of the Blessed Virgin before the eyes of all men. Moreover, cities, dioceses, and individual regions have been placed under the special patronage and guardianship of the Virgin Mother of God assumed into heaven. In the same way, religious institutes, with the approval of the Church, have been founded and have taken their name from this privilege. Nor can We pass over in silence the fact that in the Rosary of Mary, the recitation of which this Apostolic See so urgently recommends, there is one mystery proposed for pious meditation which, as all know, deals with the Blessed Virgin's Assumption into heaven.[59]

C. This Faith Is Shown in the Solemn Liturgies

This belief of the sacred Pastors and of Christ's faithful is universally manifested still more splendidly by the fact that, since ancient times, there have been both in the East and in the West solemn liturgical offices commemorating this privilege. The holy Fathers and Doctors of the Church have never failed to draw enlightenment from this fact since, as everyone knows, the sacred liturgy, "because it is the profession, subject to the supreme teaching authority within the Church, of heavenly truths, can

---

[56] *Rom.* 5:12; *Hebr.* 2:14; *Rom.* 8:10.
[57] *Rom.* 8:23; *1 Cor.* 15:52-56.
[58] E. A. Wuenschel, loc. cit.
[59] *Munificentissimus*, p. 758.

supply proofs and testimonies of no small value for deciding a particular point of Christian doctrine."[60]

The first remote testimony to which Pope Pius XII turns in order to indicate the fact that our present belief in the Assumption of the Blessed Mother was likewise the belief of the Church from the earliest times is the *Sacred Liturgy*. Again, by this procedure, our Holy Father followed the example set by his predecessors and especially that of Pope Pius IX in his argumentation relative to the definition of the Immaculate Conception.[61] For the Church prays according to her beliefs. And in the Sacred Liturgy we profess in a public and solemn manner the great truths of Faith contained within the deposit of revelation. Pope Pius XII very succinctly expressed this relationship between the Faith and the Sacred Liturgy in the words: *"Lex credendi legem statuat supplicandi"* — "Let the rule of belief determine the rule of prayer."[62]

The value of the existence of a feast in early times as an argument from Tradition is, therefore, obvious. The organ of divine Tradition is the living *Magisterium* of the Church, or the Pope and the Catholic bishops of the world in union with him. The principal means whereby that Tradition is preserved and handed down from generation to generation are the writings of the Fathers, the creeds, the practices of the Church, the monuments of Christian antiquity, and the Sacred Liturgy. And it is well to bear in mind with reference to the Liturgy that the institution of a feast in honor of one or the other prerogatives of the Blessed Mother does not mean that the belief of the Church began with its institution. The institution of the feast means that the belief of the Church has come to maturity. For the feast is but the solemn liturgical expression of a belief which has been *explicit* for many years, and *implicitly* contained in some other explicitly believed truth for centuries before that.

The feast of the Assumption began in the East as did many of the older Marian feasts. According to Father Martin Jugie, A.A., Our Blessed Mother was implicitly honored *in her Assumption* by the feast known as "The Memory of Mary," the celebration of which began in the East

---

[60] *Ibid.*

[61] *Ineffabilis Deus,* in *Acta Pii IX,* pars 1, Vol. 1, p. 600 ff.

[62] *Mediator Dei,* in *A.A.S.,* Vol. 39, 1947, p. 541.

around the fourth century. Honor was given to Mary's Assumption through this feast, according to Jugie, because the Church intended thereby to celebrate the "birthday" of Mary, or her entrance into heaven, as was her custom in celebrating the birthday, i.e., the day of a martyr's death and entrance into heaven. However, due to the fact that neither Sacred Scripture nor early Tradition speaks explicitly of the last days of our Blessed Mother on earth and of her Assumption into heaven, the liturgy of this feast did not mention them either. Later, when the apocryphal *Transitus Mariae* — in which the death and Assumption of Mary are described in detail — became popular among the faithful, the facts of her death and Assumption were inserted into the feast and the *Memoria S. Mariae* liturgy was changed and became the feast of the *Dormitio*, or the "Falling to Sleep" of the Blessed Mother.[63] Father Faller, S.J., maintains that the feast of the Assumption — or the feast of August 15 — was always the same feast as the *Memoria B. Virginis* and was celebrated in the East from the beginning of the fifth century.[64]

Whatever may be the merits of the opinions mentioned above, the dispute is relatively unimportant theologically. The feast of the *Dormitio* or *Koimesis* — the object of which was the death, resurrection, and Assumption of the Blessed Mother — was widely established in the East by the end of the sixth century. For Emperor Maurice (582-602) decreed that it be celebrated throughout the Byzantine Empire on August 15.[65] And it is important to note that the Emperor did not establish the feast but merely fixed the date. The feast was well established before the date was fixed.

Theodore Petrensis wrote a life of the Palestinian Abbot St. Theodosius (d. 529) a little after the death of the Saint. In this biography we read that St. Theodosius performed a miracle of multiplying bread to feed the multitude that had gathered from afar for the feast celebrated in honor of Mary *in die memoriae Deiparae*. Theodore was an eyewitness to the miracle. His most important contribution to the history of the feast of the Assumption, however, is the fact that he refers to the

---

[63] Cf. *La mort et l'Assomption de la Sainte Vierge* (Città del Vaticano, 1944), p. 174 ff.
[64] Cf. *De priorum saeculorum silentio circa Assumptionem B. Mariae Virginis* (Romae, 1946), pp. 18-26.
[65] Nicephorus Callistus, *Hist. Eccles.*, 18, 18, in *PG*, 147, 292.

Memoria Deiparae as an annual feast in the liturgical calendar of Palestine.[66] And to this testimony should be added that of St. Gregory of Tours who states that the feast was celebrated in Jerusalem in the latter part of the sixth century.[67]

There is, moreover, testimony to prove that the feast existed at an even earlier date in Syria. James of Sarug (c. 490), inspired by the occasion of the feast of August 15, wrote a poem in which he expresses the fact of the Assumption of Mary into heaven and speaks of her sacred body going forth to paradise.[68]

The earliest testimony for the existence of the feast in the West is of a later date. The reason for this may be found in the following words of Father Wuenschel, C.Ss.R.: "In the West the doctrinal development of the Assumption was retarded by several factors. The infrequent and difficult contacts with the East and a general ignorance of Greek caused the writings of the Eastern Fathers to remain a closed book to the Latins till rather late in the scholastic age, when Jacobus de Voragine (c. 1230-1298) had access to the works of the Greek witnesses, especially the homilies of St. Germanus and St. John Damascene.[69] Besides isolation from the East and ignorance of its literature, there was also a strong animus against the apocrypha in scholarly circles. These were about the only early literature on the subject known in the West, and their legendary character engendered doubts about the truth of the Assumption. The development of the doctrine in the West, therefore, was more or less independent of the East, so that the two trends of thought confirm each other."[70] Consequently, since the rule of belief determines the rule of prayer, one could not expect to find the feast at a time when the belief in the Assumption was not *explicit*.

---

[66] Cf. H. Usener, *Der heilige Theodosius* (Leipzig, 1890), pp. 38, 144; *Acta Sanctorum*, 11 Januarii, p. 690, n. 31; E. A. Wuenschel, *art. cit.*, p. 77.

[67] *De Gloria Martyrum*, lib. I, cap. 4, 9. *PL*, 71, 708, 713.

[68] *De transitu Dei Genitricis Mariae*, ed. A. Baumstark, in *Oriens Christianus*, Vol. 5, 1905, pp. 91-99. On this testimony, cf. Faller, *op. cit.*, p. 20.

[69] *In dormitionem B. V. Mariae*; *PG*, 96, 700-761; *Canon in dormitionem Dei Genetricis*; *PG*, 96, 1364-1368; Valentine A. Mitchel, *The Mariology of Saint John Damascene* (Kirkwood, Mo., 1931), pp. 138-169.

[70] *Art. cit.*, p. 87.

There are no certain references to the existence of the feast in the West earlier than the middle of the seventh century. The earliest witness appears to be the Gospel Lectionary of Wurzburg (c. 650) in which the feast for August 15 is found to be *Natale Sanctae Mariae*.[71] And in this century Pope Sergius I (687-701) decreed that on the feast of the Dormition (as well as on the Annunciation and the Nativity of our Blessed Mother) there should be a procession from the church of St. Adrian to the church of St. Mary Major.[72] Most probably it was this same Pope who introduced the feast of the Dormition into the Roman calendar since there are no traces of it there before 690. A Syrian by birth, Pope Sergius was well acquainted with the feast from his homeland. The name of the feast was changed from the Dormition to the Assumption of St. Mary at the beginning of the eighth century.[73] And Pope Leo IV (847-855) introduced the solemn vigil and octave.[74] From Rome the feast soon spread to England, France, and Spain.

In the *Munificentissimus Deus* the Holy Father cites the Gregorian Sacramentary which Pope Adrian I sent to the Emperor Charlemagne between the years 784-790. The following are the words quoted from the Sacramentary: "Venerable to us, O Lord, is the festivity of this day on which the holy Mother of God suffered temporal death, but still could not be kept down by the bonds of death, who has begotten Thy Son Our Lord incarnate from herself."[75] Although the words "could not be kept down by the bonds of death" express the idea of Assumption only implicitly, they are commonly understood in the sense of Resurrection and Assumption of Mary and not only bodily incorruption.

The Holy Father then quotes the Gallican Sacramentary which designates this privilege of Mary as "an ineffable mystery all the more worthy of praise as the Virgin's Assumption is something unique among

---

[71] Cf. Christopher Lee, *The Feast of the Assumption of the Blessed Virgin Mary*, in *The Irish Ecclesiastical Record*, Vol. 54, 1939, p. 177.

[72] Cf. *Liber Pontificalis*, Vol. I, p. 376.

[73] We know this from the Sacramentary sent by Pope Adrian I to Charles the Great between the years 784 and 791. Cf. Roschini, *Mariologia*, ed. 2, Vol. 2, pars 2 (Romae, 1948), p. 154.

[74] Cf. Liber Pontificalis, Vol. 2, p. 112.

[75] *Munificentissimus*, p. 759.

men." And of the Byzantine liturgy he says: "... in the Byzantine liturgy not only is the Virgin Mary's bodily Assumption connected, time and time again, with the dignity of the Mother of God, but also with the other privileges, and in particular with the virginal motherhood granted her by a singular decree of God's providence. 'God, the King of the universe, has granted thee favors that surpass nature. As He kept thee a virgin in childbirth, thus He kept thy body incorrupt in the tomb and has glorified it by His divine act of transferring it from the tomb.' "[76]

D. THIS FAITH IS SHOWN IN THE TESTIMONIES OF THE FATHERS OF THE CHURCH

However, since the liturgy of the Church does not engender the Catholic faith, but rather springs from it, in such a way that the practices of the sacred worship proceed from the Faith as the fruit comes from the tree, it follows that the holy Fathers and the great Doctors, in the homilies and sermons they gave to the people on this feast day, did not draw their teaching from the feast itself as from a primary source, but rather they spoke of this doctrine as something already known and accepted by Christ's faithful.[77]

In the *Munificentissimus Deus* Pope Pius XII quotes but three Fathers of the Church, all Orientals. St. John Damascene (d. 749), in one of his homilies compared the bodily Assumption of the Blessed Virgin with her other prerogatives and privileges: "It was fitting that she, who had kept her virginity intact in childbirth, should keep her own body free from all corruption even after death. It was fitting that she, who had carried the Creator as a child at her breast, should dwell in the divine tabernacles. It was fitting that the spouse, whom the Father had taken to Himself, should live in the divine mansions. It was fitting that she, who had seen her Son upon the cross and who had thereby received into her heart the sword of sorrow which she had escaped in the act of giving birth to Him, should look upon Him as He sits with the Father. It was fitting that

---

[76] *Ibid.* For further details cf. the well-documented paper by B. Capelle, *L'Assunzione e la liturgia,* in *Marianum,* Vol. 15, 1953, pp. 241-276, and the select literature mentioned in it. Cf. likewise J. B. Carol, O.F.M., *Fundamentals of Mariology* (New York, 1956), pp. 170-172, 190-193.

[77] *Munificentissimus,* p. 760.

Mary's Death and Bodily Assumption 537

God's Mother should possess what belongs to her Son, and that she should be honored by every creature as the Mother and the Handmaid of God."[78]

St. Germanus of Constantinople (d. 733) argued to the fact of the Assumption of Mary from the great dignity of the divine maternity and the holiness of her virginal body: "Thou art she who, as it is written, appearest in beauty, and thy virginal body is all holy, all chaste, entirely the dwelling place of God, so that it is henceforth completely exempt from all dissolution into dust. Though still human, it is changed into the heavenly life of incorruptibility, truly living and glorious, undamaged and sharing in perfect life."[79]

Finally, in the homily attributed to St. Modestus of Jerusalem (d. 634), we find these words: "As the most glorious Mother of Christ, our Saviour and our God and the giver of life and immortality, has been endowed with life by Him, she has received an eternal incorruptibility of the body together with Him Who has raised her up from the tomb and has taken her up to Himself in a way known only to Him."[80]

These three witnesses, St. John Damascene, St. Germanus of Constantinople, and St. Modestus of Jerusalem, are seventh- and eighth-century Patristic writers. The explicit belief in the Assumption of the Blessed Mother by the faithful is, of course, traceable to a much earlier date as the witness of the Sacred Liturgy shows. However, apart from the Apocrypha, there is no authentic witness to the Assumption among

---

[78] *Encomium in dormitionem Dei Genitricis semperque Virginis Mariae*, hom. 2, n. 14; *PG*, 96, 741.

[79] *In Sanctae Dei Genitricis dormitionem sermo 1; PG*, 98, 346.

[80] *Encomium in dormitionem Sanctissimae Dominae nostrae Deiparae semperque Virginis Mariae*, n. 14; *PG*, 86-II, 3306. Concerning the attributing of this testimony to St. Modestus of Jerusalem Father Faller says: "Concerning S. Modestus of Jerusalem (d. 17 December, 634) they (scholars) rightly doubt whether or not the homilies on the Assumption (*PG*, 86, 3277-3312) ascribed to him can be attributed to him with certitude. This is especially true since the Christological formula of the two wills in Christ (par. 10, col. 3304 B-C) was called into doubt only in the year of the death of Modestus through a letter of the Patriarch Sergius to Pope Honorius, so that it is very likely that Modestus of Jerusalem had no knowledge of this controversy before his death. Hence this testimony should be transferred to the end of the seventh or the beginning of the eighth century. But, even so, it very probably precedes the testimonies of St. Andrew of Crete, St. Germanus, and St. John Damascene" (*op. cit.*, p. 9).

the Fathers of either the East or the West prior to the end of the fifth century.

Doubtless the Holy Father made no mention of the Apocrypha due to the fact that many non-Catholic critics maintain that the later tradition of the Church expressing belief in the Assumption is an outgrowth of them.[81] Nothing could be further from the truth. The explicit belief of the Church in the Assumption is not based upon them, although the Apocrypha do have a positive value in that they witness a popular belief among the faithful in the Assumption of the Blessed Mother of God.

Failing to find in the sacred books of the Bible sufficient detail to satisfy their curiosity concerning certain phases of the lives of Christ and Mary, some of the faithful of the second and third centuries A.D. drew these details from other sources, frequently spurious, from their own imaginations, and from the popular beliefs of the time. And in the firm hope that their works would be accepted as canonical scripture, they attributed them to the Apostles and Evangelists. This apocryphal literature is divided into gospels, epistles, and apocalypses.[82]

Written originally in Latin, Greek, Syriac, and Coptic, the Apocrypha passed through many versions and the result is an overwhelming variety of subject matter and detail. In describing the death of Mary and its sequel, however, they all agree in stating that the death of Mary was an exception to that of the rest of mankind and, with but few exceptions, they state that her sacred body was preserved incorrupt and that it was

---

[81] As, for example, E. Renan, *L'Eglise Chrétienne*, in *Histoire des origines du Christianisme*, Vol. 6 (Paris, 1879), p. 513; C. Tischendorf, *Apocalypses Apocryphae* (Leipzig, 1866), p. 34; H. Zoeckler, "Maria," in *Realencyklopädie für protestantische Theologie und Kirche*, Vol. 13, p. 300; the article entitled: *Assumption* in the *Encyclopaedia Britannica*, 14th ed., Vol. 2, 1939, p. 567. Father T. Livius, C.Ss.R., in his work *The Blessed Virgin in the Fathers of the First Six Centuries* (London, 1839), p. 365, quotes the objective view of the Anglican Mozley on this question. Mozley writes: "The belief was never founded on that story (the apocryphal). The story was founded on the belief. The belief, which was universal, required a definite shape, and that shape at length it found" (*Reminiscences of Oriel College and the Oxford Movement*, Vol. 2, p. 368).

[82] For a complete treatment of the Assumption in the Apocrypha cf. A. C. Rush, C.Ss.R., *The Assumption in the Apocrypha*, in *The American Ecclesiastical Review*, Vol. 116, 1947, pp. 5-31; A. Vitti, S.J., *Libri apocryphi de Assumptione*, in *Verbum Domini*, Vol. 6, 1926, pp. 225-234; M. Jugie, *op. cit.*, pp. 103-171; E. A. Wuenschel, *art. cit.*, p. 73 ff.

assumed into heaven.

The absence of an uninterrupted chain of explicit testimonies linking our times with the Apostolic period was used by some Catholic theologians previous to the definition of Pope Pius XII as well as by non Catholic critics as an argument against the doctrine of the Assumption or its definability. Against these we quote the words of the eminent Mariologist, Father Juniper Carol, O.F.M., written previous to the definition: "In order to establish the continuity of a given doctrine throughout the ages it is not necessary that we possess an uninterrupted chain of explicit testimonies linking our times with the apostolic period. The reason for this is quite obvious. Since the custody and infallible interpretation of the deposit of faith has been entrusted by God to a *living* organism which is the Church, and since the Church of today is the same moral person it was in the first or second century, it follows logically that whatever the Church of today holds and teaches as pertaining to the original deposit of revelation was also held and taught (at least implicitly) by the Church of the first centuries. Either we accept this as an incontrovertible principle or we will be confronted with very serious difficulties trying to reconcile the fact that the deposit of revelation was closed at the death of the last Apostle with the fact that the Church has defined as divinely revealed certain truths which were not always explicitly believed, such as the Immaculate Conception, to cite but one example."[83] In our development of the doctrine of the Assumption according to the writings of the Doctors and theologians of the Church having their foundation in Sacred Scripture, we shall see in what manner the Assumption was implicitly taught and believed since Apostolic times.

Toward the end of the fourth century St. Epiphanius (d. 403), Bishop of Constantia, indicated, in his dispute with the Antidicomarianites and the Collyridians, his belief in the Assumption of the Blessed Virgin even though he was in doubt about the manner of her passing from this life. Proposing three possibilities concerning the manner in which the course of her earthly life came to an end, he definitely implies his belief in her glorious Assumption although he attempted no solution to the former

---

[83] *The Definability of Mary's Assumption,* in *The American Ecclesiastical Review,* Vol. 118, 1948, pp. 164-165.

mystery. Thus we read in his *Adversus haereses:* "Say she died a natural death. In that case she fell asleep in glory, and departed in purity, and received the crown of her virginity. Or say she was slain with the sword according to Simeon's prophecy. Then her glory is with the martyrs, and she through whom the divine light shone upon the world is in the place of bliss with her sacred body. Or say she left this world without dying, for God can do what He wills. Then she was simply transferred to eternal glory."[84] And around the beginning of the fifth century we find another witness in the East, Timothy of Jerusalem, who wrote: "The Virgin is immortal up to now, because He Who dwelt in her took her to the regions of the Ascension."[85]

The earliest known Patristic witness to the belief in the Assumption in the West appears to be St. Gregory of Tours (d. 593). However, due to the detail with which he describes the death of our Blessed Mother with the Apostles in attendance, and her Assumption at the command of Christ, some scholars believe that he was greatly influenced by the Apocrypha.[86] The Saint said: "When finally the Blessed Virgin had fulfilled the course of this life, and was now to be called out of this world, all the Apostles were gathered together from each region to her house ... and behold the Lord Jesus came with His angels and, receiving her soul, entrusted it to the Archangel Michael and departed. At the break of day the Apostles lifted the body with the couch and laid it in the sepulchre, and they guarded it awaiting the coming of the Lord. And behold the Lord again stood by them, and commanded that the holy body be taken up and borne on a cloud into Paradise, where now, reunited with (her) soul and rejoicing with the elect, it enjoys the good things of eternity which shall never come to an end."[87] Later on, in the same work, we read: "Mary, the glorious Mother of Christ, who, we believe, was a virgin before and after childbirth, was, as we have said before (c. 4), carried to Paradise preceded by the Lord amidst the singing

---

[84] *Adversus haereses*, 78:23; *PG*, 42, 737. Translation of E. A. Wuenschel, *art. cit.*, p. 79.
[85] Cf. note no. 9.
[86] For example, Father Michael Quinlan, S.J., *The Assumption of the Blessed Virgin Mary,* in *The Irish Ecclesiastical Record,* Vol. 68, 1946, p. 82.
[87] *De gloria beatorum martyrum* 4; *PL,* 71, 708.

of angelic choirs."[88]

Certainly, from the end of the sixth or the beginning of the seventh century on, with but few exceptions, the entire Christian Tradition is in favor of the doctrine of the Assumption of the Blessed Mother of God into heaven. And it was unanimously accepted by the great Scholastics of the twelfth and thirteenth centuries many of whom either doubted or explicitly denied the Immaculate Conception.[89]

E. This Faith Is Shown in the Writings of the Doctors and Theologians of the Church[90]

The above-mentioned arguments of the Fathers of the Church, as well as the reasons advanced by the Doctors and theologians, "are based upon the Sacred Writings as their ultimate foundation."[91]

"Often there are theologians and preachers who, following in the footsteps of the Holy Fathers, have been rather free in their use of events and expressions taken from Sacred Scripture to explain their belief in the Assumption."[92] The Holy Father mentions a few of the texts usually cited in this fashion. They are the words of the Psalmist: "Arise, O Lord, into Thy resting place: Thou and the ark, which Thou hast sanctified."[93] They also mention in this connection the Spouse in the Canticles "that goeth up by the desert, as a pillar of smoke of aromatical spices, of myrrh and

---

[88] *Op. cit.*, 9; *PL*, 71, 713.

[89] An exhaustive collection of references to the Scholastic exponents of the doctrine of the Assumption may be found in the article entitled *Marie* in the *Dictionnaire Apologétique de la Foi Catholique*, Vol. 3, coll. 277-280. Cf. likewise the monumental work of C. Balić, *Testimonia de Assumptione Beatae Virginis Mariae ex omnibus saeculis*, Vol. 1 (Romae, 1948), Vol. 2 (Romae, 1950).

[90] A complete treatment of the theological argumentation contained in the *Munificentissimus Deus* may be found in the excellent article by Father B. García Rodríguez, C.M.F., *La teología de la "Munificentissimus Deus,"* in *Ephemerides Mariologicae*, Vol. 1, 1951, p. 45 ff.

[91] *Munificentissimus*, p. 768. For a scholarly treatment of the scriptural arguments of the *Munificentissimus Deus* see Father M. Peinador's article, *De argumento scripturistico in Bulla dogmatica*, in *Ephemerides Mariologicae*, Vol. 1, 1951, p. 27 ff.

[92] *Munificentissimus*, p. 762.

[93] Ps. 138:8.

frankincense"[94] to be crowned. And in the Woman clothed with the Sun, whom St. John contemplated on the Isle of Patmos, they likewise saw the Assumption of the Virgin Mary.[95] Finally, in the words of the Angel Gabriel spoken at the moment of the Annunciation, "Hail, full of grace, the Lord is with thee, blessed art thou among women,"[96] they saw the Assumption of Our Lady into heaven as the "fulfillment of that most perfect grace granted to the Blessed Virgin and the special blessing that countered the curse of Eve."[97]

With the exception of the Angelic Salutation, which was also used by Pope Pius IX as a scriptural argument for the Immaculate Conception,[98] the other texts mentioned above are used in an accommodated sense only. The solid scriptural foundation upon which the proof of the Assumption of Mary into heaven rests, as advanced by the Fathers, Doctors, and theologians is threefold: (1) the most intimate union of the Blessed Virgin with her divine Son; (2) the Divine Maternity; and (3) the coredemptive role of Mary whereby she was the New Eve associated with Christ, the New Adam, in gaining a *complete* and *perfect* victory over Satan.

1. *The Most Intimate Union of the Blessed Virgin With Her Divine Son*

Of this union Pope Pius XII says: "These (the Sacred Scriptures) set the loving Mother of God as it were before our very eyes as most intimately joined to her Divine Son and as always sharing His lot. Consequently, it seems impossible to think of her, the one who conceived Christ, brought Him forth, nursed Him with her milk, held Him in her arms, and clasped Him to her breast, as being apart from Him in body, even though not in soul, after this earthly life."[99] And so close does this union between Christ and Mary appear to be in the Sacred Scriptures that Pope Pius IX tells us that Christ and Mary, from all eternity, were contained in "one and the same decree" of

---

[94] Cant. 3:6. Cf. also 4:8; 6:9.
[95] *Apoc.* 12:1.
[96] *Lk.* 1:28.
[97] *Munificentissimus*, p. 763.
[98] *Ineffabilis Deus*, in *Acta Pii IX*, pars 1, Vol. 1, p. 609.
[99] *Munificentissimus*, p. 768.

predestination.[100]

2. The Divine Maternity

Since our Redeemer is the Son of Mary, He could not do otherwise, as the perfect observer of God's law, than to honor, not only His eternal Father, but also His most beloved Mother. And, since it was within His power to grant her this great honor, to preserve her from the corruption of the tomb, we must believe that He really acted in this way.[101]

In the revealed notion of Mary's divine Motherhood the Church has always (though at times implicitly) seen her glorious Assumption into heaven by a supernatural intuition, one result of the Spirit of Truth dwelling within her.[102] Of this insight Father Wuenschel writes:

> The expositions of the Fathers and theologians and the language of the Liturgy vary in viewpoint and emphasis, but they all involve this fundamental principle: the Assumption is implicit in the revealed notion of the Divine Maternity taken in its concrete historical reality. This includes immeasurably more than the bare relationship of motherhood to the Person of the Word. It is the living notion with which the Church was born, which she has been contemplating, expounding, defending, sounding even more deeply, for nineteen centuries. It is the notion of Mary as Mother of the Divine Redeemer precisely as Redeemer, with Whom she was predestined from all eternity, and through Whom she was to receive the blessings of the Redemption first and in fullest measure. It is the notion of Mary as Queen of the created universe, Queen of the Kingdom ransomed with the Blood of the immaculate Lamb. It is the notion of Mary, therefore, as possessing a dignity that exalts her above the Cherubim and Seraphim, endowed with a personal holiness that is unique and supreme among creatures, immune to the slightest shadow of sin, exempt from all penalty for sin. It is the notion of Mary as a virgin in the highest and most perfect

---

[100] *Acta Pii IX*, p. 599. Cf. also *Munificentissimus*, p. 769.

[101] *Munificentissimus*, p. 768.

[102] It is disputed among theologians whether the Assumption is formally implicitly contained within the notion of the Divine Maternity or not. Father Juniper Carol, O.F.M., maintains that it is not, for there is a nexus of fitness only between these two prerogatives. With this opinion we agree. Cf. *The Definability of Mary's Assumption*, in *The American Ecclesiastical Review*, Vol. 118, 1948, p. 167. Father Crisóstomo de Pamplona holds the positive view in an article entitled, *La Asunción basada en los grandes privilegios marianos*, in *Estudios Marianos*, Vol. 6, 1947, p. 270 ff.

sense, because her virginity was confirmed and consecrated by her espousals with the Holy Spirit and her miraculous motherhood of the God-Man. Her very body became inconceivably sacred as the *caro deifera*, the living tabernacle of the Word, Who took flesh of her flesh and made her womb the paradise of the Second Adam.

In this revealed notion of Mary's immaculate, virginal motherhood the Church sees her bodily Assumption as her crowning privilege. The Church sees it there, not as the result of a logical deduction, still less as a mere *convenientia*, but as one element of that miracle of miracles which God willed His Mother to be.[103]

3. *The Coredemptive Role of Mary Whereby She Was the New Eve Associated With Christ, the New Adam, in Gaining a Complete and Perfect Victory Over Satan*[104]

We must remember especially that, since the second century, the Virgin Mary has been designated by the holy Fathers as the New Eve, who, although subject to the New Adam, is most intimately associated with Him in the struggle against the infernal foe which, as foretold in the *protoevangelium*,[105] would finally result in the most complete victory over sin and death which are always mentioned together in the writings of the Apostle of the Gentiles. Consequently, just as the glorious resurrection of Christ was an essential part and the final sign of this victory, so that struggle which was common to the Blessed Virgin and her divine Son should be brought to a close by the glorification of her virginal body, for the same Apostle says: "when this mortal thing hath put on immortality, then shall come to pass the saying that is written: Death is swallowed up in victory."[106]

Without doubt this is the principal argument for the Assumption of Mary taken from the Sacred Scripture by our Holy Father. And although

---

[103] *Art. cit.*, p. 91.

[104] It is not our purpose here to outline the theology of the Coredemption. We refer the reader to the exhaustive work by Father Juniper B. Carol, *De Corredemptione Beatae Virginis Mariae disquisitio positiva* (Civitas Vaticana, **1950**). On the specific point being discussed here cf. also his commentary, *The Apostolic Constitution "Munificentissimus Deus" and Our Lady's Coredemption*, in *The American Ecclesiastical Review*, Vol. 125, October, 1951, pp. 255-273.

[105] *Gen.* 3:15.

[106] *Munificentissimus*, p. 768.

the *Munificentissimus Deus* does not in this passage use the term "Coredemptrix"[107] the doctrine, nevertheless, is clearly put forth.

By the title "Coredemptrix" we do not mean that Mary co-operated in the Redemption of the human race only in the sense in which this title may be applied to all who pray and suffer for sinners and, thereby, share in the work of applying the fruits of the Redemption to the souls of men. Coredemption is here taken in the strict sense of a direct and formal co-operation of Mary with Christ in the very act whereby He redeemed the human race. Such a title is truly hers for she allowed the whole plan of Redemption to take place by her free consent to become the Mother of the Redeemer; by freely forfeiting her maternal rights over her divine Son in offering Him in death to atone for the sin of Adam and for the sins of the entire human race; and by uniting her sufferings with those of her Son. Thus did Mary co-operate with Christ in the very act of liberating the world from the power of Satan. She merited for herself the title "New Eve" and became in actuality the Woman foretold in the *Protoevangelium* who, with her Seed, would crush the head of the Serpent beneath her immaculate foot.

The work of Christ which effected the Redemption of the human race was accomplished through everlasting enmities with Satan culminating in a *complete* and *perfect* victory for Christ over the devil and his empire. Concerning the co-operation of Mary in gaining this complete and perfect victory over Satan, the teaching of the Church is quite explicit as is seen in the following quotation from the Bull *Ineffabilis Deus* of Pope Pius IX: "The Fathers and writers of the Church ... when quoting the words by which at the beginning of the world the Almighty announced His merciful remedies prepared for the renewal of mankind, and by which He crushed the audacity of the deceitful Serpent and wonderfully raised up the hope of our race saying, 'I will put enmities between thee and the woman, between thy seed and her seed' — when quoting these words, they taught that in this divine oracle the merciful Redeemer of the human race, the Only-begotten Son of God, Jesus Christ, was clearly and openly pointed out beforehand, and that

---

[107] The Holy Father, however, does speak of Our Blessed Mother as "the noble Associate of the divine Redeemer who has won a complete triumph over sin and its consequences" (*ibid*).

His Most Blessed Mother, the Virgin Mary, was designated, and that at the same time *the very same enmities of both towards the devil* were signally expressed. Hence, just as Christ, the Mediator between God and man, having assumed human nature, blotted out the handwriting of the decree that stood against us, and fastened it triumphantly to the cross,[108] so the Most Holy Virgin, united with Him by a most intimate and indissoluble bond, was, with Him and through Him, eternally at enmity with that poisonous Serpent, and most completely triumphed over him, and thus crushed his head with her immaculate foot."[109]

In this passage Pope Pius IX identifies the redemptive work of Christ with the crushing of the head of the Serpent.[110] And, according to the text of the Holy Father, this complete overthrow of Satan's empire was effected by Christ and Mary acting *as one principle;* Mary's activity, however, being subordinate to that of Christ (with *Him* and through *Him*). This same interpretation was given to the *Protoevangelium* by the Fathers of the Vatican Council in their petition (signed by 113 Bishops and Archbishops) requesting of the Holy See the definition of Mary's Assumption into heaven.[111]

Now, St. Paul is very explicit in his teaching that death came into the world and *rules over* mankind as a result of sin. Thus, he says, "Therefore, as through one man sin entered into the world and through sin death, and thus death has passed on to all men because all have sinned..."[112] Satan rules over the empire of death to which all are subject who have contracted sin, inasmuch as sin came into the world through

---

[108] Col. 2:14.

[109] *Acta Pii IX*, pars 1, Vol. 1, p. 607.

[110] This is also the teaching of St. Paul in Col. 2:14; *Hebr.* 2:4.

[111] Cf. *Acta et decreta Sacrorum Conciliorum recentiorum. Collectio Lacensis,* Vol. 7 (Friburgi Brisgoviae, 1882), p. 869 f. For further literature on the Assumption in the Protoevangelium, cf. A. Bea, *La Sacra Scrittura "ultimo fondamento" del domma dell'Assunzione,* in *La Civiltà Cattolica,* a. 101, Vol. 4, 1950, pp. 547-561; M. Peinador, *Más sobre el argumento escriturístico en la Bula "Munificentissimus Deus,"* in *Ephemerides Mariologicae,* Vol. 1, 1951, pp. 395-404. Cf. likewise the excellent study (written before the definition) by L. Di Fonzo, *De Immaculatae Deiparae Assumptione post praecipua recentiora studia critica disquisitio,* in *Miscellanea Francescana,* Vol. 46, 1946, pp. 45-104, esp. pp. 72-74.

[112] *Rom.* 5:12.

his instigation. As a result "we ourselves groan within ourselves waiting for the adoption of sons, *the redemption of our body.*"[113] This redemption shall take place only when "the trumpets shall sound, and the dead shall rise incorruptible and we shall be changed. For this incorruptible body must put on incorruption, and this mortal body must put on immortality. But when this mortal body puts on immortality, then shall come to pass the word that is written, 'Death is swallowed up in victory! O death, where is thy victory? O death, where is thy sting?'"[114]

Christ freely subjected Himself to death because this was the will of His heavenly Father. Satan gained not even a slight partial victory over Him. For, far from being conquered by death, He died "... that through death He might destroy him who had the empire of death, that is to say, the devil."[115] For the empire of death includes not just the separation of the soul from the body, but *death with its consequent bodily corruption* imposing thereby the obligation upon all, even the just, of waiting until the general resurrection for the liberation of the body and the full enjoyment, as a person, of the beatific vision. It was through Christ's *anticipated* resurrection that He destroyed the empire of death making His victory over Satan complete and perfect.

Mary's association with Christ in gaining *together with Him* as one principle a complete and perfect victory over Satan *demanded* her anticipated resurrection and bodily glorification (if she died) or her anticipated bodily glorification (if she did not die). This anticipated resurrection or bodily glorification effected the union of her sacred body with her already glorified soul and "since a glorified body must be where the soul is, and Mary's soul is certainly in heaven, *therefore Mary is in heaven with her glorified body and soul.*"[116]

---

[113] *Rom.* 8:23.

[114] *1 Cor.* 15:52-55.

[115] *Hebr.* 2:14.

[116] J. B. Carol, *The Definability of Mary's Assumption,* in *The American Ecclesiastical Review*, Vol. 118, 1948, p. 176.

The Universal Queenship of Mary

By FIRMIN M. SCHMIDT, O.F.M.Cap., S.T.D.

HE unique royal dignity of Mary flows spontaneously from her special position in God's redemptive plan for mankind. In prophecy as well as in fulfillment Mary is most intimately associated with man's redemption and sanctification. In the words of Pope Pius IX in the Bull *Ineffabilis Deus*: "Mary's origin was pre-ordained by one and the same decree with the Incarnation of Divine Wisdom."[1] And Pope Pius X in his encyclical letter *Ad diem illum* adds:

> ... almost every time that the Scriptures prophesy of the grace that was to appear among us (cf. Titus 2, 11), the Redeemer of mankind is associated with His Mother. The Lamb, the Ruler of the earth, will be sent — but from the root of Jesse. It was really Mary crushing the serpent's head that Adam was seeing and so he dried the tears that the malediction had brought to his eyes. ... After Christ we find in Mary the end of the Law and the fulfillment of the figures and oracles.[2]

Hence, with Christ, but subordinate to Him, Mary fulfills a decisive mission in God's plan for salvation. Christ is truly the Redeemer. But according to the will of God, Mary is in a true and proper sense the Coredemptrix.[3] Christ, the God-Man, is the only primary and self-sufficient Mediator between God and man. Under Christ, and in virtue of His power, Mary, too, is a unique Mediatrix between God and man. And similarly, just as Christ is King of the Universe, so also Mary is truly the Queen. It is simply according to the all-wise plan of God that Mary should be most intimately and uniquely associated with her Son — in

---

[1] *Mary Immaculate*, translation of the Bull *Ineffabilis Deus*, by Dominic J. Unger, O.F.M.Cap. (Paterson, N. J., 1946), p. 3.

[2] *Mary Mediatrix*, Encyclical Letter *Ad diem illum* ..., translated by Dominic J. Unger, O.F.M.Cap. (Paterson, N. J., 1948), p. 5.

[3] Juniper B. Carol, O.F.M., *De Corredemptione Beatae Virginis Mariae disquisitio positiva* (Civitas Vaticana, 1950), 643 pp.

predestination, in redemption, in mediation, in royal dignity, in glory.[4] This is what Pope Pius XII clearly had in mind when he wrote in his apostolic constitution *Munificentissimus Deus*, defining the dogma of Mary's bodily Assumption and glorification:

> Thus from all eternity and by "one and the same decree" of predestination the august Mother of God is united in a mysterious way with Jesus Christ; immaculate in her conception, a spotless virgin in her divine motherhood, the noble companion of the Divine Redeemer, who won a complete triumph over sin and its consequences, she finally obtained as the crowning glory of her privileges preservation from the corruption of the tomb, and like her Son before her, she conquered death and was raised body and soul to the glory of heaven, where as Queen she shines refulgent at the right hand of her Son, the Immortal King of ages.[5]

In view of this uniquely intimate association of Mary with Christ, it is imperative that the prerogatives of the one (Mary) be seen and understood in the light of the perfections of the other (Christ). Just as we cannot understand Mary as our Coredemptrix unless we have first of all a clear grasp of Christ as our Redeemer; so likewise we cannot fully appreciate Mary as Queen of the Universe, unless we first understand that Christ is the King of the Universe.

In the light of Christ our King we are able to appreciate the greatness of Mary our Queen; in the light of Mary our Queen, we are able to get some idea of the greatness of Christ our King. The two go hand in hand.[6]

THE NOTION OF "KING" AND "QUEEN"

The term "king" can be understood in a metaphorical sense as well as proper. In the metaphorical sense it simply refers to someone's supreme excellence in comparison with others in the same category. For example, when the lion is called the king of animals, or when Virgil is called the king of poets, the term king is used in a metaphorical sense. In the proper sense a king is a man who, in his own authority, rules the

---

[4] Cf. St. Lawrence of Brindisi, *Mariale* (Patavii, 1928), p. 454.

[5] *A.A.S.*, Vol. 42, 1950, p. 771; English translation for N.C.W.C. by Msgr. J. C. Fenton, *Assumpta est Maria*, pp. 18-19.

[6] Patrick J. Kelly, O.P., *The Reign of Our Lady with Christ the King* (Rome, 1940), p. 15. Cf. also F. W. Faber, *The Foot of the Cross* (London, 1932), pp. 388-389.

members of a perfect society and leads them to their common end. A king in the proper sense exercises his supreme authority over his subjects by means of the threefold power: legislative, judiciary, and executive.

Just as "king" can be understood in a metaphorical as well as proper sense, so also the term "queen." Hence, metaphorically taken, "queen" is indicative of a certain pre-eminence or excellence in comparison with others. Thus, when we speak of theology as the "queen" of the sciences, or of charity as the "queen" of the virtues, we are using "queen" in the metaphorical sense. In the proper sense, queen is related to actual ruling. And this ruling can be twofold — absolute or relative. A queen in the proper, absolute sense is a woman who, on her own authority, rules the members of a perfect, organized society and leads them to their common end. In her own name, she exercises the threefold power: legislative, judiciary, and executive. Such a woman is really nothing else than a "female king." A queen in the proper, relative sense is a woman who partakes of the dignity of a king in her capacity as the king's consort, or as the king's mother.

CHRIST THE KING

That Christ as Man is King in the metaphorical sense and in the proper sense is beyond all doubt. Christ as Man is first in all things. In the words of St. Paul: "He is ... the first-born of every creature. ... All things have been created through and unto him, and he is before all creatures ... that in all things he may have the first place."[7] Kingship in the metaphorical sense is also clearly attributed to Christ by Pope Pius XI, when he said:

> Christ has long been proclaimed King because of His pre-eminence over all creatures. Christ is said to reign in the minds of men because of the keenness of His intellect and the extent of His knowledge, and because He is Truth Itself and the source of all truth for all men. He reigns, too, in the wills of men, for His own human will was ever perfectly and completely obedient to the Will of the Father. ... He reigns, too, in our hearts by His love "which surpasses knowledge" (Eph. 3:19).[8]

---

[7] *Col.* 1:15-19.

[8] *A.A.S.*, Vol. 17, 1925, p. 595.

Besides enjoying a unique pre-eminence of perfection over all creatures, Christ is also King in the strict and proper sense. He has a true jurisdiction that is all-embracing. Pope Pius XI authentically vindicated this proper title for Christ in his encyclical *Quas primas*.[9] After he had spoken of the supreme excellence of Christ in comparison with the rest of creation, the Pope considers the title of King in the proper sense. He says: "To Christ as Man belong the title and power of King in strict reality ... and consequently to Him belong supreme and absolute dominion over all created things."[10]

MARY THE QUEEN

In union with Christ and subordinate to Him, Mary also enjoys the twofold royal title. By reason of her excellence and sanctity, she certainly is deserving of the title of Queen in the metaphorical sense. As the Messenger from God declared at the Annunciation, so have all devotees of Mary ever looked up to her as the most favored one of God: "Hail, full of grace, the Lord is with thee, blessed art thou among women" (Lk. 1:28). Pope Pius XI in the encyclical letter *Lux veritatis* speaks of the exalted dignity of Mary in the words of Cornelius a Lapide:

> The Blessed Virgin is Mother of God, and therefore by far excels all the angels, even the seraphim and cherubim. She is Mother of God, therefore most pure and holy, so much so that under God no greater purity can be imagined. She is Mother of God, and therefore whatever privilege has been granted to any of the saints (in the way of grace ingratiating, *gratum faciens*), that she has above all.[11]

The fact that Mary is invoked as Queen in the metaphorical sense does not detract in any way from her proper royal prerogatives. It merely tells us of the unique excellence of her who is Queen also in the proper sense.

It is primarily in the proper and strict sense that the title of Queen is applied to Mary. This does not, however, in any way derogate from

---

[9] *Ibid.*, p. 596 f.
[10] *Loc. cit.*
[11] *A.A.S.*, Vol. 23, 1931, p. 513; English translation from N.C.W.C. publication, *The Light of Truth*, p. 28.

Christ the King. For Mary is not Queen in the proper, absolute sense. She is not the supreme ruler, nor a substitute ruler. Rather, it is in the relative, though proper, sense that Mary is the Queen. She is Queen of the Kingdom of which Christ is King. Her royal prerogatives come from and are entirely dependent upon the King. Christ is the one and only supreme ruler, and source of sovereignty in this Kingdom.

An analysis of the status of a temporal queen will convey some idea of the queenly status of Mary. But such an analysis will never result in a complete understanding of Mary's royal dignity. Just as Christ surpasses earthly kings in dignity, power, and authority, so likewise Mary surpasses earthly queens in dignity, power, and authority. Mary is a unique Queen. There is no model by which we can measure her status, just as there is no model for measuring the status of Christ the King. As grace surpasses nature, as the supernatural order surpasses the natural order, so does the queenly status of Mary surpass temporal queens. Temporal queens, at their best, can only reflect partially the royal prerogatives of Mary. The comparison that Cornelius a Lapide made between the supernatural order and the natural order can be preserved in comparing the royal dignity of Mary with an earthly and temporal queen: "The order of nature was created and established for the order of grace. ... The order of grace, the heights of which are occupied by Christ and the Blessed Virgin, is the idea and exemplar according to which God created and arranged the order of nature and of the whole universe."[12]

THE KINGDOM OF CHRIST AND MARY

Ultimately, the precise royal dignity of Mary as Queen must be sought in her most intimate relationship with Christ the King. While a redemption without a coredeemer and a kingdom without a queen are conceivable, nevertheless it was God's will that there be an associate of Christ in His Kingdom. In the words of pseudo-Albert the Great: "The Blessed Virgin has not been called by the Lord to be a minister of His, but an associate and partner."[13]

---

[12] Cornelius a Lapide, S.J., *Commentarius in Ecclesiasticum*, cap. 24; in *Commentarii in Scripturam Sacram*, Vol. 9 (Parisiis, 1859), p. 618.

[13] *Mariale*, q. 42; in *Alberti Magni opera omnia*, ed. Borgnet, Vol. 37 (Parisiis, 1898), p. 81.

This mutual relationship between Christ and Mary is beautifully crystallized in the memorable radio broadcast by Pope Pius XII to the pilgrims at Fatima in Portugal, May 13, 1946. Part of the Holy Father's message is as follows:

> He, the Son of God, reflects on His heavenly Mother the glory, the majesty and the dominion of His Kingship; for, having been associated with the King of Martyrs in the ineffable work of human Redemption as Mother and cooperatrix, she remains forever associated with Him, by an almost unlimited power, in the distribution of the graces which flow from the Redemption. Jesus is King throughout all eternity by nature and by right of conquest; through Him, with Him and subordinate to Him, Mary is Queen by grace, by divine relationship, by right of conquest and by singular election. And her kingdom is as vast as that of her Son and God, since nothing is excluded from her dominion.[14]

In this significant statement of the Holy Father we see confirmed the wonderful parallel between Christ the King and Mary the Queen. Just as Christ is King by a natural right and by right of conquest,[15] so likewise, the Holy Father assures us, Mary is Queen "by divine relationship and by right of conquest." Obviously, the "divine relationship" has reference to the Incarnation. This relationship was actually contracted at the moment of Mary's *Fiat*. Christ as Man was King from the very first moment of the Incarnation. Mary, by consenting to be the Mother of this King, became a Queen in the proper sense of the word.[16]

Second, just as Christ is King by the title of conquest, so in a similar way, Pope Pius XII tells us, Mary is truly Queen by the title of conquest. Christ's conquest of His Kingdom was brought about by the work of Redemption.[17] Similarly, Mary's Queenship by the title of conquest

---

[14] *A.A.S.*, Vol. 38, 1946, p. 266. Translation from the Portuguese by Juniper B. Carol, O.F.M., *Mary's Coredemption in the Teaching of Pope Pius XII*, in *The American Ecclesiastical Review*, Vol. 121, November, 1949, p. 358.

[15] Pius XI, *A.A.S.*, Vol. 17, 1925, p. 599.

[16] Cf. P. Sträter, S.J., *Maria als Königin*, in *Katholische Marienkunde*, ed. P. Sträter, Vol. 2 (Paderborn, 1949), p. 320 f.

[17] Pius XI, *A.A.S.*, Vol. 17, 1925, p. 600.

comes from her co-operation with the work of Redemption.[18] Hence, it is legitimate to conclude that Christ's natural right to Kingship coincides with Mary's right to Queenship by reason of her divine relationship. Furthermore, Christ's title of King in virtue of His conquest coincides with Mary's right to Queenship in virtue of her co-operation with His conquest or Redemption. Through Christ the King, and subordinate to Him, Mary is Queen in the true sense of the word.

To really understand this exalted dignity of Mary it is not sufficient to see her only in the role of Queen, namely in her intimate association with the King. Rather it is important to see especially the nature of the Kingdom in which she is the Queen. This Kingdom is primarily a spiritual kingdom. As Christ Himself said, it is a "kingdom that is not of this world."[19] It is a Kingdom "that men prepare to enter by repentance, and which they cannot enter except through faith and Baptism."[20] Hence, Mary's Queenship, like Christ's Kingship, is primarily spiritual. However, it is not exclusively spiritual. For since Christ, even as Man, has authority over temporal and civil matters,[21] so, in keeping with the parallelism formulated by Pope Pius XII, Mary must also have a certain regal authority in temporal and civil matters.

Furthermore, the Kingdom of Christ is not limited in time or in extent. All men, taken individually and collectively, come under the sway of Christ's royal power. Pope Pius XI, in the encyclical *Quas primas*, describes the extent of this authority, by repeating the words of Pope Leo XIII:

> His (Christ's) empire includes not only the Catholic nations, not only the baptized persons, who though rightly belonging to the Church have been led astray by error or have been cut off by schism, but also those who are outside the Christian faith, so that truly the whole of mankind is subject to the power of Christ.[22]

---

[18] Cf. J. B. Carol, in *The American Ecclesiastical Review*, Vol. 121, November, 1949, p. 359. Cf. also his article *Mary's Universal Queenship*, in *Our Lady's Digest*, Vol. 8, May, 1953, pp. 5-10.

[19] *Jn.* 18:36.

[20] *Quas primas*, in *A.A.S.*, Vol. 17, 1925, p. 600.

[21] Pius XI, loc. cit.

[22] *Pius XI, loc. cit.*

Even the angels are subject to Christ, as Pope Pius XI further assures us.[23] Since "Mary's Kingdom is as vast as that of her Son's"[24] it follows logically that Mary's queenly authority extends to the entire human race, and even to angels. And therefore, "nations, as well as families, and individuals owe veneration and homage to the Queen of the Universe, no less than they owe adoration and homage to the King of the Universe. Therefore, Mary is rightly invoked in behalf of nations, as Queen of Peace."[25]

No Catholic today would dare to question the fact that Mary is Queen in the proper and strict sense. In fact, it can be safely asserted that Catholic life demands, or supposes, acknowledgment of Mary as Queen. In many prayers officially approved by the Church Mary is addressed and respected as a true Queen. Even when the title of Queen is not expressly used, Mary is frequently acknowledged as having genuine authority over us. Consecration to the Immaculate Heart of Mary is a typical example.[26] Besides, a prayerful attitude toward Mary is genuinely characterized by the mark of submissiveness as of a subject.

As Queen, Mary has exercised her royal prerogatives from the very foundation of the Kingdom. Furthermore, the doctrine of Mary's universal Queenship is part of the original deposit of faith. It is integrally interwoven with other truths contained and originally concealed in the Marian treasures. Like "pearls of great price," one after another of these truths about Mary is being singled out, clarified and polished so that it may be seen in all its sparkling beauty. It has taken centuries for many of the special privileges of Mary to emerge in all their supernatural beauty. The Queenship of Mary is a typical example of how a truth in the original deposit of revelation becomes constantly more clearly understood in the Church under the guidance of the Holy Spirit. In this wonderful process there is not a creation of a new truth or fact. Rather

---

[23] *Ibid.*, p. 598.

[24] *A.A.S.*, Vol. 38, 1946, p. 266.

[25] Cf. F. Schmidt, O.F.M.Cap., *Our Lady's Queenship in the Light of Quas primas*, in *Marian Studies*, Vol. 4, 1953, pp. 125-126.

[26] Cf. Kilian J. Healy, O.Carm., *The Theology of the Doctrine of the Immaculate Heart*, in *Proceedings of the Fourth Annual Meeting of the Catholic Theological Society of America*, 1949, p. 120 f.

it is an advance in understanding. It can be compared with a precious gem. Even without light the gem is precious. But as more light is cast on the gem, and that from different angles, the more its beauty and formation and structure can be appreciated. In a similar way this pearl of Marian doctrine, the Queenship, has begun to sparkle. With the passing of the centuries new lights have been cast on it, and the result is, not something new, but a new view of a fact and truth given to us by the infallible Truth itself. At the present day, it is safe to say the doctrine of the Queenship is approaching its final stage of clarification.

In order to understand more completely and to appreciate more fully the true significance of this doctrine, it is of some importance to consider it in its prime source and to see it in its historical development, or rather, its gradual clarification. For the sake of order and convenience, we shall view this Marian privilege successively: (1) in the *magisterium,* or authentic teaching power in the Church; (2) in its scriptural foundation; and (3) in its presentation by the Fathers and theologians of the Church. This threefold view of the Queenship of Mary will be followed by a specific analysis of the manner in which Mary exercises her royal prerogatives.

I

THE MAGISTERIUM AND THE QUEENSHIP

In endeavoring to ascertain whether or not a doctrine belongs to the deposit of faith, it is the *magisterium* of the Church that must be recognized as the "proximate and universal criterion of truth."[27] Even in the proper understanding and interpretation of Sacred Scripture the theologian must be guided by this authentic teaching authority.[28] It is for this reason especially that the data of the *magisterium* are here presented as of foremost importance. They have a theological priority over every other rule of faith in the Church.

Although there has never been a solemn declaration or definition of Mary's Queenship by a Pope or ecumenical council, nevertheless the

---

[27] *Humani generis,* in *A.A.S.,* Vol. 42, 1950, p. 567; English translation from N.C.W.C. publication, No. 18.
[28] *Ibid.,* No. 21.

Church in her ordinary teaching or *magisterium* has repeatedly stressed this doctrine. The ordinary teaching authority of the Church has a manifold expression. It includes encyclical letters, papal documents, and statements directed to the Universal Church, and also particular messages of the Popes that often explain general pronouncements.[29] In addition to these papal statements, the liturgy is also a genuine vehicle of the Church's ordinary teaching authority. And finally, the teaching of the bishops throughout the world is an authentic expression of the same *magisterium*.

Although the teaching of the bishops can be most informative and effective in the process of uncovering or determining true doctrine,[30] nevertheless for the present purpose, it will be sufficient to examine the significant papal statements to the Universal Church, since the bishops' teaching is necessarily in harmony with that of the Vicar of Christ on earth. As is acknowledged by all, the supreme teaching authority in the Church ultimately is vested in the Holy Father.

After a survey of papal teaching, the liturgy will be utilized as an expression of the Queenship of Mary.

A. Papal Statements[31]

During the very first years of the early Church express reference to Mary as Queen seems nonexistent. However, this is not surprising. For in those days the doctrine concerning Mary and her prerogatives was overshadowed by a consideration of the Person and the natures of the God-Man. It seems to have been the result of a special divine providence that there was an express consideration of Marian truths only after the doctrine about the God-Man had been sufficiently defended and clarified. Thus, for example, official pronouncement about the divine Maternity of Mary logically came after the authentic defense and definition of the divinity of Christ. So it was with other doctrines

---

[29] Cf. Eamon Carroll, O.Carm., *Our Lady's Queenship in the Magisterium of the Church*, in *Marian Studies*, Vol. 4, 1953, p. 36.

[30] See the excellent work along similar lines by J. B. Carol, *Episcoporum doctrina de Beata Virgine Corredemptrice*, in *Marianum*, Vol. 10, 1948, pp. 210-258.

[31] Cf. E. Carroll, *art. cit.,* pp. 29-81. We are deeply indebted to this author for his scholarly work on Mary's Queenship in the magisterium.

concerning Mary.

1. From the Beginning Until the Fifteenth Century

In spite of the fact that the Queenship of Mary did not come directly under consideration of the Popes, nevertheless occasionally they refer to Our Lady as Queen. Thus as early as the seventh century St. Martin I (d. 655) and St. Agatho (d. 681) in official statements apply this title to Mary in passing.[32]

Pope St. Gregory II (715-731), in a letter written about the year 728 to St. Germain, Patriarch of Constantinople, defending mainly the cult of images against the Iconoclasts, also spoke of Mary as true *ruler of all Christians* who will be victorious in the battle against the enemies.[33]

In the same century, during the pontificate of Pope Adrian I, the Seventh Ecumenical Council was convened at Nicea to condemn the heresy of Iconoclasm and to proclaim infallibly the legitimacy of the cult of images. This, the Second Council of Nicea, did not have as its direct object the prerogative of Mary's royal dignity. However, in the acts of the council, Mary is acknowledged as Queen.

> ... definimus in omni certitudine ac diligentia ... sanctas imagines proponendas ... tam videlicet imaginem Domini et Salvatoris nostri Jesu Christi, quam intermeratae *dominae* nostrae sanctae Dei genitricis ...[34]

The historical circumstances surrounding the council, and the fact that Gregory II's letter concerning Mary's Queenship was approvingly read at the council lead us to conclude that Mary was already at that time looked upon as Queen in the genuine sense of the word.

Other Popes of the eighth century implicitly acknowledge Mary as Queen by assuming the attitude of a servant toward Mary.[35]

Innocent III (1198-1216) composed a hymn in honor of Mary, and recommended it for public use by attaching an indulgence to it. The

---

[32] Cf. P. Aubron, S.J., *De la souveraineté de Marie*, in *Souveraineté de Marie. Congrès Marial de Boulogne s/M.*, 1938 (Paris, 1939), pp. 121-125.

[33] Cf. L. J. L. M. De Gruyter, *De Beata Maria Regina* (Buscoduci, 1934), p. 64.

[34] *D.B.*, 302.

[35] P. Aubron, *art. cit.*, p. 115; cf. G. M. Roschini, O.S.M., *I Papi e Maria*, in *Marianum*, Vol. 4, 1942, pp. 155-156.

introductory words of the hymn are "Empress of Angels — Consolation of sinners."[36]

Nicholas IV (1288-1292) honored Mary as Queen not only by an official document, but also by consecrating a church to Mary "Queen of the Angels."[37]

At the order of Gregory IX (1227-1241) in 1239 the *Salve Regina* (Hail, Holy Queen) was said in the churches of Rome every Friday after Compline in preparation for Saturday.[38]

In 1390 Boniface IX (1389-1404) confirmed the feast of the Visitation by the Bull *Superni benignitas Conditoris*, in which Mary is called the "perfect Queen," the "royal Virgin," and "Queen of the Heavens."[39]

2. From the Fifteenth to the Nineteenth Centuries

Concomitant with the discussions about the Immaculate Conception of Our Lady, especially during the fifteenth century and thereafter, there have been significant statements concerning Mary's other prerogatives, including the Queenship. This is not surprising in view of the fact that the privileges of Mary are so closely interrelated. Treating of the Immaculate Conception in the well-known constitution *Cum praecelsa*, addressed to the Universal Church in February, 1477, Pope Sixtus IV (1471-1484) spoke in these pertinent words:

When ... we search and discover the sublime proofs of those merits which cause the Queen of heaven, the glorious Virgin Mother of God, raised upon her heavenly throne, to outshine like the morning star all other constellations, and in the secrecy of our hearts ponder the fact that as the way of mercy, the Mother of grace, prone to compassion, the consoler of the human race, she intercedes as a sedulous and tireless suppliant with the King whom she bore, for the salvation of the faithful who are weighed down with their sins ...[40]

The same Pope also composed and indulgenced a prayer in praise of

---

[36] Cf. Angel Luis, C.Ss.R., *La Realeza de María* (Madrid, 1942), p. 80.

[37] *Ibid.*

[38] Cf. E. Flicoteau, O.S.B., *Le Salve Regina*, in *Marie*, Vol. 3, November-December, 1949, p. 105.

[39] *Bullarium magnum*, ed. C. Coquelines, Vol. 3 (Romae, 1741), p. 378.

[40] D.B., 734.

"Mary ... Queen of the World."[41]

The most significant papal pronouncement in the sixteenth century concerning our doctrine was the official approval of the Litany of Loreto by Sixtus V in the Bull *Reddituri* in 1587. This Litany has many queenly titles of Mary.[42]

In the seventeenth century Paul V (1605-1621) publicly acknowledged Our Lady's ruling power by placing his pontificate under the protection of Mary, "the most powerful Queen."[43] In that same century, Pope Gregory XV in his Apostolic Brief to the city of Seville (1622) styles Mary a "heavenly Queen."[44] And Urban VIII spoke of Mary as the "Empress of Heaven," and of the effectiveness of her sovereign power.[45]

The highlight of the eighteenth century was the issuing of the "Golden Bull" *Gloriosae Dominae* by Pope Benedict XIV on September 27, 1748.

It is particularly worthy of note that in this Bull, Pope Benedict not only attributes a proper royal dignity to Mary, but he says that under the Holy Spirit's guidance, the Catholic Church has *always* professed Mary to be the "Queen of heaven and earth."[46]

The early part of the nineteenth century was characterized by a continued recognition of the queenly status of Mary. Gregory XVI (1831-1846), for example, publicly expressed the thanksgiving of the citizens of Rome to "Mary, Queen of heaven," for having protected them from the cholera epidemic.[47]

3. From Pius IX to Pius XII

With the solemn definition of the Immaculate Conception of Our Lady by Pope Pius IX a new era dawned for Mariology. It marked the

---

[41] Luis, *op. cit.*, p. 79, note 1.

[42] Cf. J. C. Fenton, *Our Lady's Queenly Prerogatives*, in *The American Ecclesiastical Review*, Vol. 120, 1949, p. 425.

[43] E. Carroll, *art. cit.*, p. 42.

[44] *Bullarium magnum*, ed. cit., Vol. 3, p. 751.

[45] Luis, *op. cit.*, pp. 81-82.

[46] *Benedicti XIV opera omnia*, Vol. 16 (Prati, 1846), p. 428.

[47] *Acta Gregorii Papae XVI*, Vol. 2 (Romae, 1901), pp. 271-274.

beginning of an ever increasing awareness of Mary's true dignity and of her relation to Christ and to the human race. This inevitably led to a more careful consideration of Mary's genuinely royal status. *Ineffabilis Deus* itself, the Bull defining Mary's Immaculate Conception, set the pattern for further analysis and clarification of Mary's Queenship:

> She is the most excellent glory, ornament and impregnable stronghold of the Holy Church. For she has destroyed all heresies and snatched the faithful peoples and nations from all sorts of very great calamities. ... Nothing is to be feared, and nothing is to be despaired **of,** under her guidance, under her patronage, under her kindness and protection. Because, while bearing towards Us a truly motherly affection and taking care of the work of Our salvation, she is solicitous about the whole human race. And, since she has been appointed by God to be the Queen of heaven and earth, and is exalted above all the choirs of angels and classes of saints, and even stands at the right hand of her only-begotten Son, Jesus Christ Our Lord, she presents Our petitions in a most efficacious manner. She obtains what she asks for. She cannot be frustrated.[48]

Pope Pius IX's clear statement naturally effected a widespread interest in Mary's royal status. In 1864 a number of bishops approached the Pope and expressed the desire of the faithful that the Queenship of Mary be solemnly proclaimed. Although the request was received favorably, no direct action was taken.[49]

Pope Leo XIII, during his long reign of 25 years (1878-1903), issued many encyclicals and other official documents dealing with Mary.[50] Of those which refer directly to the Queenship of Mary, the most important are: *Supremi apostolatus* (1883), *Magnae Dei Matris* (1892), and *Adjutricem populi* (1895).

In *Supremi apostolatus,* Pope Leo speaks of Mary's great power with her Son. He further associates this power with the fact of her divine Maternity and co-operation in the work of Redemption.[51]

---

[48] Translation by D. J. Unger, *op. cit.,* pp. 22-23.

[49] Cf. Broussolle, *L'Assomption,* Vol. 3, 1918-1920, pp. 179-180.

[50] Cf. E. Carroll, *art. cit.,* p. 47 f. Cf. also J. Bittremieux, *Doctrina Mariana Leonis XIII* (Brugis, 1928); A. Tondini (ed.), *Le Encicliche Mariane* (Roma, 1950), pp. 29-57; William R. Lawler, O.P. (ed.), *The Rosary of Mary,* translation of encyclicals and apostolic letters of Leo XIII (Paterson, N. J., 1944).

[51] Cf. Lawler, *op. cit.,* pp. 2-3; Tondini, *op. cit.,* pp. 66-68.

Magnae Dei Matris not only confirms Mary's royal dignity, but attributes it to Mary because of her suffering with Christ, and her co-operation in the work of Redemption:

> ... The crown of the kingdoms of heaven and of earth will await her because she will be the invincible Queen of martyrs; it is thus that she will be seated in the heavenly city of God by the side of her Son, crowned for all eternity, because she will drink with Him the cup overflowing with sorrow, faithfully through all her life, most faithfully on Calvary.[52]

Adjutricem populi very beautifully associates Mary's exalted office in the early Church assembled in the Cenacle, with her queenly position in the Church today.[53] Her work for the Church then is continued by her now. "With wonderful care she nurtured the first Christians by her holy example, her authoritative counsel, her sweet consolation, her fruitful prayers."[54]

Besides the many encyclicals bearing on Mary's Queenship, there were also several lesser communications issued by Leo XIII which allude to this prerogative. For example, in a letter to the Mexican bishops, the Pope speaks of Our Lady of Guadalupe as "Your Queen."[55] In speaking of a Marian event at Lourdes, the same Holy Father expressed the hope "that the Queen of Heaven may ratify it."[56]

It is well to recall also that in addition to the many express statements about Mary's Queenship during the reign of Leo XIII there was issued also the important decree of the Sacred Congregation of Rites, defending the cult of hyperdulia for "the Queen and Sovereign of the angels."[57]

St. Pius X (1903-1914) in his encyclical *Ad diem illum* writes thus on our subject:

> ... Since she surpasses all creatures in sanctity and in union with Christ, and since she was chosen by Christ to be His associate in the work of

---

[52] Lawler, *op. cit.*, p. 88; E. Carroll, *art. cit.*, p. 49.
[53] Lawler, *op. cit.*, p. 129 f.
[54] De Gruyter, *op. cit.*, p. 150.
[55] Tondini, *op. cit.*, p. 196.
[56] Carroll, *art. cit.*, p. 52.
[57] Cf. J. Keuppens, *Mariologiae compendium*, 2nd ed. (Heverle-Louvain, 1947), p. 164.

human salvation, she merits for us congruously, as they say, what Christ has merited for us condignly, and she is the principal minister of the graces to be distributed. Christ "has taken His seat at the right hand of the Majesty on high" (Hebr. 1, 3), and Mary as Queen stands at His right hand; "she is the safest refuge and the most trustworthy helper of all who are in danger, so that nothing is to be feared and nothing is to be despaired of, under her guidance, under her patronage, under her kindness and protection."[58]

The importance of this passage is emphasized by the manner in which the Holy Father associates Mary with Christ the King in the work of salvation. Rightly, therefore, is she crowned as Queen, standing at His right hand. It is interesting to note also that in this passage the Holy Father tells us that Mary as Queen is the "safest refuge and most trustworthy helper of all who are in danger." This is really an explicit description of the traditional title of "Mary, Queen of Mercy."[59]

On the occasion of the fiftieth anniversary of his ordination to the priesthood, on August 4, 1908, St. Pius X in his letter *Haerent animo* recommends all the clergy to the "great Virgin Mother, Queen of the Apostles. For she it was who by her example taught those first fruits of the sacred order how they should persevere unanimously in prayer till they were clothed in virtue from above. ..."[60] He likewise approved the title "Regina Cleri," and attached an indulgence of 300 days to the ejaculation "Regina Cleri, ora pro nobis."[61] Benedict XV (1914-1922) spent the greater part of his pontificate in the atmosphere of World War I. In spite of adverse circumstances, he had utmost confidence in Mary, the Queen of Peace. It was he who in a letter to Cardinal Gasparri, May 5, 1917, ordered the invocation "Queen of Peace" added to the Litany of Loreto. The rest of the letter speaks of Mary as the dispenser of all graces, and as all powerful by grace.[62]

Pope Pius XI (1922-1939) issued many Marian documents. Father G.

---

[58] English translation from Unger's *Mary Mediatrix* (Paterson, N. J., 1948), pp. 9-10.

[59] Cf. Thomas U. Mullaney, O.P., *Queen of Mercy*, in *The American Ecclesiastical Review*, Vol. 126, June, 1952, pp. 412-419.

[60] Carroll, *art. cit.*, p. 54.

[61] *Actes de Pie X*, Vol. 4 (Paris, La Bonne Presse), p. 226.

[62] *Actes de S.S. Benoît XV*, Vol. 1 (Paris, 1924), p. 150.

Roschini lists forty-six distinct items written by this Pope between 1922 and 1938 that have direct reference to Mary.[63] While not all of these have a direct reference specifically to Mary's Queenship, nevertheless he frequently manifests his mind adequately as to this Marian prerogative. While expressing or clarifying other Marian truths, this Pope, as also many others, shed a new light on this point.

Among the many Marian documents of Pope Pius XI, *Lux veritatis* is particularly worthy of note. This encyclical letter was published on December 25, 1931, to commemorate the fifteenth centenary of the Council of Ephesus, honoring Mary in her divine Maternity. After speaking of the great dignity and power of Mary that come from the divine Maternity, the Holy Father explicitly appeals to Mary's royal power in behalf of the Church:

> Under the auspices of the heavenly Queen, We desire to beg for a very special favor of the greatest importance, that she who is loved and venerated with such ardent piety by the people of the East, may not permit that they should be unhappily wandering and still kept apart from the unity of the Church and thus from her Son, whose Vicar on earth We are.[64]

Another important Marian document of Pope Pius XI is the *Rerum Ecclesiae*, issued on February 28, 1926. It is significant not only because of its unmistakable references to Mary as Queen, but primarily because it speaks of the specific function of Mary's universal missionary interest:

> May Mary, the most Holy Queen of the Apostles, graciously second our common undertakings; Mary, who since as she holds in her mother's heart all men who were committed to her on Calvary, cherishes and loves, not only those who happily enjoy the fruits of the Redemption, but those likewise who still do not know that they have been redeemed by Jesus Christ.[65]

In other Marian documents, Pope Pius XI styles Our Lady "Queen

---

[63] G. M. Roschini, *La Madonna nel pensiero e nell'insegnamento di Pio XI*, in Marianum, Vol. 1, 1939, pp. 121-172.

[64] A.A.S., Vol. 23, 1931, p. 513; English translation from the N.C.W.C. publication, *The Light of Truth*, p. 31.

[65] A.A.S., Vol. 18, 1926, p. 83; English translation from *The Global War for Christ* (New York: America Press, 1944), No. 39.

Sovereign of heaven and earth, of men and angels."[66] "Mother of Divine Grace, the Conqueror of all heresies, the Help of Christians,"[67] "Queen of Italy,"[68] "Queen of Ireland,"[69] "Immaculate Queen of Peace,"[70] "Queen of the Kingdom of Poland."[71]

Many Marian documents and events have highlighted the pontificate of Pope Pius XII. Undoubtedly, the dogmatic definition of Our Lady's Assumption into heaven is of primary significance. However, other prerogatives of Mary also were given clear and authentic consideration by the Holy Father. Among these, the Queenship of Our Blessed Mother seems to have been of special concern to him.[72] After an extensive discussion of the Marian doctrine of Pope Pius XII, Father Bertetto concludes:

> If we should wish to determine, from the documents we have, what truth Pius XII has above all illuminated in Our Lady, it seems no mistake to say: the Queenship. To document this affirmation it would be sufficient to point to the solemn act of the consecration of the human race. ...
>
> The Queenship of Mary is particularly connected with her Assumption into heaven; and is above all recognized by Pius XII in the consecration of the world to the Immaculate Heart. The title of Queen, which Pius XII gives so frequently to Mary, is taken in the more precise sense of the word — always, however, subordinately to God who is by essence the unique and absolute Sovereign of all creatures — and it (the Queenship) is founded on solid theological reasons. ... On this point the teaching of Pius XII far surpasses in richness and development that of his predecessors.[73]

It is commonly acknowledged that the consecration of the world to the Immaculate Heart of Mary by Pope Pius XII on October 31, 1942, was

---

[66] George W. Shea, *The Teaching of the Magisterium on Mary's Spiritual Maternity*, in *Marian Studies*, Vol. 3, 1952, p. 91.

[67] A.A.S., Vol. 20, 1928, p. 16.

[68] *Ibid.*, p. 73.

[69] Cf. *The Catholic Bulletin*, Vol. 22, July, 1932, p. 528.

[70] Cf. *L'Osservatore Romano*, April 29-30, 1935, p. 1.

[71] A.A.S., Vol. 29, 1937, p. 380.

[72] Carroll, *art. cit.*, p. 62 f.

[73] D. Bertetto, S.D.B., *La dottrina mariana di Pio XII*, in *Salesianum*, Vol. 11, 1949, pp. 22-23; Carroll, *art. cit.*, pp. 61-62.

an epoch-making event. The formula of consecration is a very clear recognition of Mary's queenly office. In the preliminary prayer, she is addressed as "Queen of the most holy Rosary, Help of Christians, Refuge of Mankind, triumphant in all battles for God."[74]

The final words of the formula of consecration are as follows:

> Finally, just as the Church and the entire human race were consecrated to the Heart of your Jesus, because by placing in Him every hope, it may be for them a token and pledge of victory and salvation; so, in like manner, they are henceforth perpetually consecrated to you, to your Immaculate Heart, O our Mother, and Queen of the world: in order that your love and protection may hasten the triumph of the kingdom of God. And may all peoples at peace among themselves and with God proclaim you blessed, and intone with you throughout the entire world the eternal "Magnificat" of glory, love, and adoration of the Heart of Jesus in whom alone they can find truth, life, and peace.[75]

It is especially worthy of note that an obvious parallel is established between the consecration to the Sacred Heart by Leo XIII and this consecration by Pius XII to the Immaculate Heart. Consecration, by its very nature, is an expression of reverent submission and an acknowledgment of the dominion of him to whom the consecration is made.[76] In the consecration to the Sacred Heart there is the recognition of Our Lord's supreme dominion. In the consecration to the Immaculate Heart there is also a true dominion recognized in Our Blessed Mother. However, Mary's dominion is subordinate to that of Christ and dependent upon Him. Pope Pius XII himself in subsequent documents confirmed the significant parallel between the two consecrations.[77]

Perhaps his clearest statement on this point was his radio message *Bendito seja O Senhor* at Fatima, May 13, 1946, on the occasion of the solemn crowning of Our Lady by Cardinal Masella, the Papal Legate. An important paragraph of that address is quoted here:

---

[74] W. J. Doheny and J. P. Kelly (ed.), *Papal Documents on Mary* (Milwaukee, 1954), p. 202.

[75] *Ibid.*, pp. 203-204.

[76] Cf. K. Healy, *art. cit.*, p. 121; also St. Thomas, IIa, IIae, q. 81, a. 8.

[77] *A.A.S.*, Vol. 40, 1948, p. 107; Sr. Claudia Carlen, I.H.M., *Guide to the Documents of Pius XII, 1939-1949* (Westminster, Md., 1951), No. 1057. Cf. also *A.A.S.*, Vol. 40, 1948, p. 171; Sr. Claudia, *op. cit.*, No. 1116.

He, the Son of God, reflects on His heavenly Mother the glory, the majesty and the dominion of His Kingship; for, having been associated with the King of martyrs in the ineffable work of human Redemption as Mother and cooperatrix, she remains forever associated with Him, with an almost unlimited power in the distribution of graces which flow from the Redemption. Jesus is King throughout all eternity by nature and by right of conquest; through Him, with Him, and subordinate to Him, Mary is Queen by grace, by divine relationship, by right of conquest, and by singular election.[78]

In this statement the Holy Father not only says that Mary is truly and properly a Queen, but he also states the theological foundation of Mary's royal dignity, the extent of her rule, and in a general way the nature of her rule.

The encyclical *Mystici Corporis*[79] issued by Pope Pius XII on June 29, 1943, is acknowledged as a treasure of Catholic doctrine on the constitution and function of the Church, which is the Mystical Body of Christ. As an epilogue to the entire encyclical the Holy Father speaks of Mary's relation to the Mystical Body. This has been rightly called a "Mariology in miniature."[80] The Pope here summarizes Mary's part in God's plan of Redemption. He traces Mary's position in this divine plan from the Immaculate Conception to her crown of glory in heaven. Speaking of her co-operation with Christ in the Sacrifice of the Cross where "she offered Him ... to the Eternal Father," the Holy Father says: "Bearing with courage and confidence the tremendous burden of her sorrows and desolation, truly the Queen of Martyrs, she more than all the faithful 'filled up those things that are wanting of the suffering of Christ ... for His Body, which is the Church.' ..."[81]

The Holy Father concludes the epilogue of the encyclical with these significant words:

> May she, then, most holy Mother of all Christ's members, to whose Immaculate Heart We have trustingly consecrated all men, her body and

---

[78] *A.A.S.*, Vol. 38, 1946, p. 266. Translation from J. B. Carol, Mary's *Coredemption in the Teaching of Pope Pius XII*, in *The American Ecclesiastical Review*, Vol. 121, 1949, p. 359.

[79] *A.A.S.*, Vol. 35, 1943, pp. 193-248.

[80] E. Carroll, *art. cit.*, p. 69.

[81] *A.A.S.*, Vol. 35, 1943, p. 248. English translation from N.C.W.C. publication, No. 107.

soul refulgent with the glory of heaven where she reigns with her Son — may she never cease to beg from Him that a continuous, copious flow of graces may pass from its glorious Head into all the members of the Mystical Body. May she throw about the Church today, as in times gone by, the mantle of her protection and obtain from God that now at last the Church and all mankind may enjoy more peaceful days.[82]

It is to be noted that the Holy Father speaks very forcefully of Mary as a Queen who has a true dominion. "She *reigns* with her Son." Her actual royal dignity could hardly have been stated more clearly. It is obvious that the Holy Father has something more in mind than the mere title of Queen. She actually participates in the sovereignty of Christ the King.[83]

The particular importance of these quotations from the encyclical *Mystici Corporis* is to be found not merely in the analysis of the words and phrases which have a bearing on the Queenship, but in understanding them in their proper context. Viewed in this light, Mary is seen first of all as Mother of all the members of the Mystical Body. And in consequence of this position, which she freely accepted at the moment of the Incarnation, she became inseparably associated with her Son's work of Redemption and sanctification. Just as Christ in His death on Calvary was truly a victorious King, so Mary as "Queen of Martyrs," actively participated in the victory. And hence, since Christ as King reigns triumphantly in heaven, so likewise Mary as a true Queen "reigns in heaven with her Son." In summary, the epilogue of *Mystici Corporis* presupposes a perfect parallel between Christ the King and Mary the Queen, in battle and victory.

The definition of Mary's bodily Assumption into heaven naturally leads to the consideration of Mary in glory. Pope Pius XII himself set the pattern for this in the document wherein the definition was made. And the Holy Father tells us that it is *as Queen* that she has entered into glory: "... Like her Son before her, she conquered death and was raised body and soul to the glory of heaven, where as Queen she shines

---

[82] *Ibid.*, No. 107.

[83] Cf. E. Carroll, *art. cit.*, p. 71, an excellent analysis of the pertinent texts from Mystici Corporis.

refulgent at the right hand of her Son, the Immortal King of Ages."[84]

Other statements by the Holy Father in connection with the Assumption of Our Blessed Lady repeat the fact that it was as Queen that Mary received the crown of glory. Thus, on October 30, 1950, just two days before the definition, he addressed these words to the cardinals and bishops in Consistory: "On the first of November, the Feast of All Saints, the radiant brow of the Queen of Heaven and of the beloved Mother of God will be wreathed with new splendor, when, under divine inspiration and assistance, We shall solemnly define and decree her bodily Assumption into heaven."[85] Immediately after the Bull of the definition had been read on November 1, 1950, the Holy Father delivered a homily on the Assumption.[86] Several times in that homily he refers to the glorious "Queen of the Universe." It is his closing prayer, however, that is of special interest to us:

> We believe with all the fervor of our Faith in your triumphal Assumption, both in body and soul, into heaven, where you are acclaimed as Queen by all the choirs of Angels and all the legions of the Saints. ... We believe, finally, that in the glory where you reign, clothed with the sun and crowned with the stars, you are, after Jesus, the joy and gladness of all the Angels and of all the Saints.[87]

In addition to the Assumption documents, the Fatima statements, the epilogue of the encyclical on the Mystical Body, and the Consecration of the human race to the Immaculate Heart of Mary, Pope Pius XII has issued many other Marian declarations which manifest his mind on the Queenship of Mary. To newly-weds, he speaks of Mary as "Queen of the Family."[88] During the war, he invokes Mary as "Queen of Peace and Mercy."[89] To the pilgrims of Genoa, he speaks of Mary as "... the august sovereign of the Church militant, suffering and triumphant; as the

---

[84] A.A.S., Vol. 42, 1950, pp. 768-769. English translation from N.C.W.C. publication, No. 40.

[85] A.A.S., Vol. 42, 1950, pp. 774-777, English translation, *Homily on the Assumption*, in *The Catholic Mind*, Vol. 49, January, 1951, pp. 78-80.

[86] A.A.S., Vol. 42, 1950, pp. 779-782.

[87] *Ibid.*

[88] Cf. Sr. Claudia, *op. cit.*, No. 39.

[89] A.A.S., Vol. 32, 1940, p. 12; cf. E. Carroll, *art. cit.*, p. 77.

Queen of Saints ... the teacher of every virtue, of love, of fear, of knowledge, and of holy hope." The month of May, the Holy Father tells us, is to be celebrated in a way that will do just honor to Mary, our Queen. For "... just as Christ Jesus is King of all, the Lord of Lords ... so His dear Mother Mary is honored as Queen of the world by all the faithful and has obtained so great a power of intercession with God."[90] He further speaks of Mary as "Queen of Mothers,"[91] "Queen of the Clergy,"[92] and "August Queen of Heaven."[93] Father E. Carroll lists nineteen separate occasions on which Pope Pius XII refers to Mary as Queen from May 3, 1939, until May 4, 1952.[94] It may rightly be concluded that the doctrine of Mary's Queenship is very close to the heart of Pope Pius XII.

In declaring the year 1954 a Marian Year, and by honoring that year with special blessings, the Holy Father has given further evidence of Mary's supernatural sovereignty. The encyclical letter *Fulgens corona* which ushered in the Marian Year, presupposes that Mary is our Queen. It is as subjects that genuine Christians should dedicate themselves to Mary. And Mary is presented as "the most powerful Mother of God who is also our tender mother, and ... efficacious and ever-present patronage."[95]

The special prayer composed by Pope Pius XII for the Marian Year, calls upon Mary as our Queen,[96] "Conqueress of evil and death ... to bend tenderly over our aching wounds, to convert the wicked, dry the tears of the afflicted and oppressed, comfort the poor and humble, quench hatreds, sweeten harshness, safeguard the flower of purity in youth, protect the Holy Church, make all men feel the attraction of Christian goodness. ..."

With the declaration and celebration of the Marian Year, the "radiant

---

[90] *A.A.S.*, Vol. 34, 1942, p. 125; cf. E. Carroll, *art. cit.*, p. 78.

[91] *A.A.S.*, Vol. 37, 1945, pp. 284-295; cf. Sr. Claudia, *op. cit.*, No. 718.

[92] *A.A.S.*, Vol. 40, 1948, pp. 108-110; cf. Sr. Claudia, *op. cit.*, No. 1076.

[93] *A.A.S.*, Vol. 31, 1939, pp. 706-708; cf. Sr. Claudia, *op. cit.*, No. 158.

[94] Cf. E. Carroll, *art. cit.*, p. 76 f.

[95] *A.A.S.*, Vol. 45, 1953, p. 590.

[96] Cf. Doheny-Kelly, *op. cit.*, p. 269 f. Concerning further utterances of Pius XII on this matter, see the appendix at the end of this chapter.

crown of glory" of Mary our Queen truly sparkles with greater brilliance.

B. Liturgy's Testimony to Mary's Queenship

The liturgy is the Church's official form of public worship. And since worship must be grounded on doctrine, the liturgy is a reliable guide to Catholic doctrine. In the words of Pope Pius XII, "... the liturgy of the Church does not engender the Catholic faith, but rather springs from it, in such a way that the practices of the sacred worship proceed from the faith as the fruit comes from the tree. ..."[97]

The Pope has often stressed the forcefulness of an argument that is based on the liturgy of the Church. For example, in his encyclical *Mediator Dei*, he says that in defining truths revealed by God, the Holy Fathers and Councils "have not seldom drawn many an argument from this sacred science of the liturgy."[98]

This is pointedly illustrated in the Bull *Ineffabilis Deus* of Pope Pius IX, where he defines the dogma of the Immaculate Conception. After summarizing the public prayer life of the Church whereby the Immaculate Conception of Mary was proclaimed or implied, the Holy Father concluded: "Thus the law of faith was confirmed by the law of prayer."[99]

What is true of the doctrine of the Immaculate Conception should likewise be true of the Queenship of Mary. It is with this happy assurance that the liturgies of both East and West are looked upon as a rich source of solid doctrine. For the sake of order, these two liturgies will be reviewed separately.

A. Western Liturgy

It will be unnecessary to investigate every individual word or phrase of the official prayers of the Church. It will be sufficient to point out the theme or doctrine contained or implied in the main Marian feasts as found in the Breviary and Missal.

---

[97] *A.A.S.*, Vol. 42, 1950, p. 760.

[98] *Ibid.*, Vol. 39, 1947, p. 540. Cf. K. B. Moore, O.Carm., The Queenship of the Blessed Virgin in the Liturgy of the Church, in Marian Studies, Vol. 3, 1952, p. 220, note 7.

[99] English translation by Unger, *Mary Immaculate...*, p. 5.

1. Breviary

Mary's royal dignity is proclaimed or acknowledged in several of her feasts.[100] In fact, recognition of Mary as Queen is made in the recitation of the Divine Office almost every day of the year. The final antiphons address Mary as Queen: *Ave, Regina Caelorum, Ave, Domina Angelorum* — Hail Queen of Heaven, Sovereign Lady of the Angels (said from February 2 until Wednesday in Holy Week); *Regina Caeli, laetare* — Queen of Heaven, rejoice (said during Easter season); *Salve Regine* — Hail holy Queen (during the rest of the year).

On February 11, the feast of the Apparition of the Blessed Virgin Mary, the antiphon for the *Magnificat* of second Vespers has: "Today, the glorious Queen of heaven appeared on earth."

The new office for the feast of the Assumption has several pertinent references. The hymn for the first Vespers reads:

> Gleaming as you are in resplendent glory,
> All nature extols thee,
> You who have been called to scale
> the heights of every dignity.
> Queen in thy triumph we beseech thee,
> Turn thine eyes on us poor exiles,
> That through thy gracious help
> We may attain our home in Paradise.[101]

The concluding verse in the hymns at Matins and Lauds speaks of Mary as having received a crown, and as having been appointed our Queen. The lessons of the third Nocturn, taken from the homilies of St. Peter Canisius (*De Maria Deipara*, lib. 5, cap. 6), recall the "most renowned Queen of heaven, and sovereign lady of the world." The antiphon for the *Magnificat* of second Vespers clearly states Mary's ruling power: "Today the Virgin Mary ascended into heaven: rejoice, because she reigns with Christ forever."

The feast of the Immaculate Heart of Mary, celebrated on the octave day of the Assumption (August 22), may rightly be classified as a feast honoring Mary's Queenship. The versicle and response, following the

---

[100] See the appendix at the end of this chapter.

[101] Moore, *art. cit.*, p. 223.

sixth lesson, refer explicitly to this prerogative.

The feast of the Nativity of the Blessed Virgin (September 8) in its hymn at Lauds describes Mary as "the glorious Sovereign Lady." On the feast of the Seven Dolors of Mary on September 15, Mary is invoked as the "Queen of Martyrs," because she stood at the cross of Jesus.

On the feast of the Most Holy Rosary, October 7, Mary is invoked several times under her title of Queen. The hymn for Lauds has a verse that expresses Mary's ruling authority beautifully: "... because she is near the throne of her Son, she is in command of all creatures." The hymn at second Vespers portrays Mary as partaking in the triumph of her Son, a "Queen refulgent with glory." The antiphon for the *Magnificat* speaks of the "most glorious Queen of the world." In recent years some religious orders have been granted a feast in honor of Mary's Queenship. Thus, on the octave day of the Immaculate Conception (December 15), the various Franciscan branches celebrate the feast of "Mary, Queen of the Friars Minor" as a second-class feast. The Office itself abounds with prayers and antiphons expressive of Mary's true royal dignity. For example, in second Vespers, the antiphon for the *Magnificat* addresses Mary in the following manner: "O most worthy Mary, perpetual Virgin, Queen of the world, you who brought forth Christ the Lord, the Savior of all, intercede for our peace and salvation."

Similar encomia and recognitions of Mary's queenly dignity are found throughout the Office. She is revered as a true Queen. She is invoked as "Queen of Mercy."

On the Saturday before the second Sunday after Easter, in some places there is celebrated the feast of "The Blessed Virgin Mary, Mother of the Good Shepherd." The entire Office associates Mary intimately with the care of the flock (faithful). The oration speaks of Mary "taking care of our needs by her vigilant protection." The second Nocturn refers to Mary as the "Sovereign Lady (*domina*) who feeds the poor."

On May 31, in some dioceses and religious congregations and orders, there is celebrated the feast of "Mary, Mediatrix of All Graces." The antiphon for the *Magnificat* of the first Vespers recalls that "all power" has been given to Mary. The second Nocturn has one lesson from St. Ephraem, another from St. Germain, Bishop of Constantinople, and the third from St. Bernard. All three speak of Mary's queenly position.

Among other significant statements, in St. Ephraem's lessons is found the following: "My Sovereign Lady ... after the Trinity, her royal dignity is over everything."

2. Missal

The feast of the Sorrowful Mother on the Friday of Passion Week refers to Mary Our Queen in these words of the Tract: "The holy Mary, the Queen of heaven and the sorrowful Sovereign Lady of the world was standing near the cross of our Lord Jesus Christ."

The Communion verse of the Mass of Our Lady of Mount Carmel (July 16) is an appeal to the "Virgin Mary, the most worthy Queen of the world."

The Introit of the new Mass for the feast of the Assumption quotes Apocalypse 12:1, which could have reference to Mary's Queenship.

The Introit of the Mass of the Immaculate Heart of Mary (August 22) repeats a popular expression about Mary's queenly dignity: "Let us go with confidence to the throne of grace, that we may obtain mercy."

The Communion verse of the Mass of Our Lady of Good Counsel (April 26), said in some dioceses and religious orders, calls upon Our Queen in these words: "O Mary, perpetual Virgin, most worthy Queen of the world, who hast brought forth Christ our Lord, the Savior of all, intercede for our peace and salvation."

On Saturday within the octave of the Ascension there is a special Mass allowed in some places in honor of Mary, Queen of the Apostles.

On December 15 the various branches of Franciscans celebrate the Mass in honor of the "Blessed Virgin, Queen of the Friars Minor." Mary is proclaimed and invoked as a true Queen practically throughout the Mass.

Besides these testimonies to Mary's Queenship from the Breviary and Missal, there are not a few officially approved prayers and blessings which have a direct reference to Mary Our Queen.[102] The Litany of Loreto is an outstanding example.

---

[102] Cf. L. de Gruyter, *op. cit.*, p. 69. For the new Mass of Mary's Queenship, see the appendix at the end of this chapter.

B. Eastern Liturgy

The Oriental Church just as well as the Western Church forcefully testifies to Mary's Queenship in her liturgy.

In the *Liturgy of St. James*, at the beginning of Mass, the deacon expresses the intentions to the people in these words: "Let us call to mind the most holy Immaculate, most glorious Mother of God, the Virgin Mary, our Blessed Queen ... so that through her prayers and intercessions, all of us may obtain mercy."[103] After the Consecration and again after Communion, the deacon repeats practically the same expression.

In the *Liturgy of St. Basil*, the celebrant calls upon Mary as "Our Sovereign Lady" after the consecration of the Mass.

In the preparation for Mass in the *Liturgy of St. John Chrysostom* the priest offers the first of the breads "in honor and in memory of our glorious blessed Queen. ..."[104] In addition to these, the expression "Our Glorious Queen" is repeated three times in the Litany.

In the Syrian-Maronite rite Mary is addressed as "Our Blessed Sovereign Lady."

In the anaphora of the ancient *Coptic Liturgy*, there is found a threefold incensation of the image of the Blessed Virgin, while the priest makes a threefold invocation of Mary. At the second he addresses Mary, "Hail Virgin, true Queen." And at the third she is called upon as our "Advocate ... that our sins may be taken away."[105]

In the *Ethiopic Liturgy* Mary is called "Sovereign Lady" quite frequently.

In the administration of the Sacraments in the *Liturgy of St. John Chrysostom*, Mary is invoked again as "Our Glorious Queen."

In the profession of faith demanded of Jewish converts to the faith we find the following significant words: "I firmly and truly believe and declare that ... since (Mary) is truly the Mother of the God-Man, she for that reason was made the *Leader* (Princeps) and Sovereign Lady

---

[103] Maximilianus, Princeps Saxoniae, *Praelectiones de liturgiis orientalibus*, Vol. 2 (Friburgi Brisgoviae, 1913), pp. 23-24. From L. de Gruyter, *op. cit.*, p. 70.

[104] Cf. L. de Gruyter, *op. cit.*, p. 70.

[105] Assemanus, *Codex liturgicus Ecclesiae universae*, Vol. 7 (Parisiis-Lipsiae, 1902), pp. 20-21. Cf. L. de Gruyter, *op. cit.*, p. 71.

(*Domina-Kyrian*) of all creatures."[106]

In the administration of Extreme Unction Mary is also addressed as follows: "Come, O Sovereign Lady, deliver us from dangers, you who alone art our unfailing help."[107]

In the *Coptic Liturgy*, the power of a true queen is ascribed to Mary in the administration of Extreme Unction. There she is called Leader (*Prostates*) of the human race.[108] She is also referred to as a "true Queen" in the same context.[109]

C. ANCIENT LITURGIES

In addition to the Liturgy in use at the present day, ancient prayers of public worship, which are no longer in existence, also recognized Mary as a true Queen. For example, in a Litany which was in use during the middle of the eighth century the following invocations are found:

> O great Mary ...
> Mary greatest of Marys ...
> Most great of women ...
> Queen of the angels ...
> Mistress of the heavens ...
> Mistress of the tribes ...
> Destruction of Eve's disgrace ...
> Regeneration of life ...
> Chief of the virgins ...
> Queen of life.[110]

A hymn from an old Germanic missal refers to Mary as "Glorious and Powerful Empress."[111]

---

[106] Εὐχολόγιον τὸ μέγα (Romae, 1873); in app. p. 95; cf. L. de Gruyter, *op. cit.*, p. 72.

[107] Εὐχολόγιον ..., p. 188; cf. L. de Gruyter, *op. cit.*, p. 72.

[108] H. Denzinger, *Ritus orientalium coptorum, syrorum et armenorum in administrandis sacramentis*, Vol. 2 (Wirceburgi, 1864), pp. 499-500; cf. L. de Gruyter, op. cit., pp. 72-73.

[109] *Ibid.*

[110] From the *Leabhar-Breac*, i.e., *The Miraculous Book*, the text of which was published in *De Standaard van Maria*, 1931, pp. **278-281**. **Cf.** L. de Gruyter, *op. cit.*, p. 73.

[111] Cf. L. de Gruyter, *op. cit.*, p. 74. Cf. also the recent article by Robert V. Callen, **S.J.**, *Selected Signs of Mary's Universal Queenship in Medieval Liturgy*, in *Marianum*, **Vol. 16, 1954,** pp. 441-464.

UNIVERSAL QUEENSHIP OF MARY

This brief conspectus of the official prayer of the Church reveals beyond all doubt that Mary is a real Queen. She is presented not only as the most perfect creature but also as someone having real authority. In both East and West, the liturgy tells of Mary's true dominion over everything under Christ. There is not a place under the sun where Mary is not honored daily in the official prayer of the Church as Queen of heaven and earth.

II
SACRED SCRIPTURE AND MARY'S QUEENSHIP

Nowhere in Sacred Scripture is Mary expressly and directly called a Queen. Neither in the Old Testament nor in the New Testament do we find a proper, royal title ascribed to Mary. Despite the absence of explicit biblical data, it can nevertheless be truly asserted that this doctrine has a valid basis in Sacred Scripture. The texts that have been utilized are: *Genesis* 3:15, the Annunciation pericope, and *Apocalypse* 12:1. In addition to these, there are other secondary passages that seem to corroborate Mary's prerogative by reason of their figurative or spiritual significance.[112] These are: *Psalm* 44; *3 Kings* 2:19; and *Esther* 2:17 and 5:3.

GENESIS 3:15

Before the Protoevangelium can be proposed as a true scriptural argument for any specific Marian prerogative, it must first be vindicated as a true Marian text. On this point, however, there can hardly be any serious doubt any longer. In the various Marian documents issued by the authentic teaching authority in the Church since the Bull *Ineffabilis Deus* in 1854, a truly Marian sense for Genesis 3:15 has been continually and ever more clearly supported. While it is true that there has never been an official and definitive interpretation by the *magisterium*, still the mind of recent Popes is clearly in favor of a true Marian sense.[113] Guided by

---

[112] Eustace J. Smith, O.F.M., *The Scriptural Basis for Mary's Queenship*, in Marian Studies, Vol. 4, 1953, p. 114.

[113] Smith, *art. cit.*, p. 111. Cf. also J. B. Carol, *De Corredemptione B.V.M.* (Civitas Vaticana, 1950), pp. 100-121; id., *The Apostolic Constitution "Munificentissimus Deus" and Our Blessed Lady's Coredemption*, in *The American Ecclesiastical Review*, Vol. 125, October, 1951, pp. 255-273; D. J. Unger, *The First-Gospel: Genesis 3, 15* (St. Bonaventure, N. Y., Franciscan

the authentic teaching authority, Catholic exegetes in ever greater numbers have come to recognize the Protoevangelium as the first genuine scriptural reference to Mary.[114] The passage reads: "I will put enmities between thee and the woman, between thy seed and her seed. He shall crush thy head and thou shalt lie in wait for his heel."

In this text Christ's complete triumph over Satan is clearly foretold. In view of the fact that "the woman" is inseparably associated with "the seed" in the battle against Satan, she will partake in the victory of the seed, namely the Redeemer. It was as Redeemer that Christ became King by the title of conquest.[115] Consequently, "the woman" (Mary), by reason of her close association with Christ in the conquest, is foretold as having also a true dominative power over those freed from the slavery of Satan. Hence, Mary is here foreshadowed as Queen in the proper sense.

It is quite true that the argument for Mary's Queenship from Genesis 3:15 is recognized only: (1) after the redemptive message of this passage is understood; and (2) after the relationship between the Redemption and Kingship of Christ is grasped.

With these notions clearly in mind we can aptly summarize the argument of the Protoevangelium as follows:

> In Genesis 3:15 Our Blessed Lady is formally introduced as Christ's intimate associate in the work of Redemption. Since it was precisely the redemptive task that won for Christ the title of King by right of conquest, it follows that Mary, too, in her capacity as Coredemptrix, shares Christ's Kingship also by right of conquest.[116]

LUKE 1:26-38

While Mary is not expressly referred to as a Queen in the circumstances that surround the Annunciation and Incarnation, nevertheless an analysis of these circumstances reveals her in that role. Mary is presented as playing a vital part in establishing God's Kingdom on earth. She is not a passive instrument. Rather, she is asked to become the Mother of Him who "shall be king over the house of Jacob forever ...

Institute, 1954), pp. 43-90.

[114] Cf. Unger, *op. cit.*, pp. 281-294.

[115] *A.A.S.*, Vol. 17, p. 599.

[116] Cf. Smith, *art. cit.*, p. 112; cf. also L. de Gruyter, *op. cit.*, p. 55 f.

and whose kingdom shall be without end."[117] Her free consent was needed for inaugurating that Kingdom, and hence because of her intimate co-operation in the very foundation of the Kingdom, she is rightly recognized as a true Queen with a genuine, participated sovereignty in this Kingdom.

Christ as Man is properly a King basically by reason of the hypostatic union.[118] It is in the divine relationship[119] that was established in consequence of Mary's deliberate consent to become the Mother of this King, that we find the fundamental reason for her royal prerogative.

It was as Redeemer and King that the Word of God assumed human nature. When Mary pronounced her *fiat*, she freely consented not only to become a mother, but to become the Mother of this Person who is God and Man, Redeemer and King. Mary's *fiat*, consequently, was a consent to the entire series of events that associated her with the redeeming and sanctifying mission of her Son. In view of the perpetual and intimate association between the Redeemer and His Mother, inaugurated by Mary's *fiat*, the Annunciation is properly recognized as the beginning of Mary's Queenship.[120]

APOCALYPSE 12:1

The apocalyptic style of the last book of the Bible presents some difficulty in grasping the exact notion intended by the divine Author. Hence, here also before this passage can be vindicated for Mary's Queenship, it must first of all be established as a true Marian text. In recent years Marian scholars have successfully proved its Marian sense against those who questioned it.[121] While the woman in this passage is

---

[117] *Lk.* 1:32-33.

[118] *A.A.S.*, Vol. 17, p. 599.

[119] F. Schmidt, *Our Lady's Queenship in the Light of "Quas primas,"* in Marian Studies, Vol. 4, 1953, p. 123.

[120] Cf. Smith, *art. cit.*, p. 113. Cf. also P. Sträter, *Maria als Königin*, in *Katholische Marienkunde*, ed. P. Sträter, Vol. 2 (Paderborn, 1949), p. 320 f.

[121] Cf. D. Unger, O.F.M.Cap., *Did St. John See the Virgin Mary in Glory?* in *Catholic Biblical Quarterly*, Vol. 11, 1949, pp. 248-262, 392-405; Vol. 12, 1950, pp. 75-83, 155-161, 292-300, 405-415. For a summary of the argument, cf. E. May, O.F.M.Cap., *The Scriptural Basis for Mary's Spiritual Maternity*, in *Marian Studies*, Vol. 3, 1952, p. 131 f.

shown to be Mary by means of genuinely scriptural arguments,[122] it may be well to indicate that here, as well as in other Marian passages of Scripture, the *magisterium* of the Church has been a reliable guide. Although the text was never formally defined as to its exact meaning, nevertheless, the Popes have frequently used it in such a way as to indicate a true Marian sense. The words of Pope Pius X in his encyclical letter *Ad diem illum* are significant. After quoting *Apocalypse* 12:1, he adds: "No one is ignorant that this woman signified the Virgin Mary."[123]

A careful analysis of Apocalypse 12:1 reveals a close parallel to *Genesis* 3:15. In fact, John seems to describe here the final outcome of the war between Satan and the woman along with her Seed, foretold in the Protoevangelium.[124] It is a full victory that is ascribed to the woman: "... a great sign appeared in heaven: a woman clothed with the sun, and the moon was under her feet, and upon her head a crown of twelve stars." These figures are readily accepted as indicative of a true Queen in royal glory.[125]

Secondary Texts

Psalm 44:10: "The Queen stood on the right hand in gilded clothing, surrounded with variety." The psalm is clearly Messianic. And even though the word "Queen" would readily lend itself to direct application to Mary, nevertheless, the context argues directly in favor of the Church.[126] Tradition has utilized this passage to express the glorious dignity of Mary.

There are other passages from the Old Testament that seem to present figures or types of Mary as Queen. Chief among these are *3 Kings* 2:19 and *Esther* 2:17 and 5:3. At best, the queens spoken of in these sections are only imperfect figures of the true Queen of heaven and earth.

In the New Testament, several narratives justify us in recognizing

---

[122] Cf. May, *art. cit.*, p. 133.
[123] Translation from Unger, *Mary Mediatrix* ..., p. 16.
[124] Cf. May, *art. cit.*, p. 134.
[125] Cf. Smith, *art. cit.*, p. 112.
[126] Smith, *art. cit.*, p. 114.

Mary as Queen. The first of these is the account of the Visitation (*Lk.* 1:39-56). Mary, already bearing the Incarnate Word, was instrumental in the sanctification of John in the womb of Elizabeth. Elizabeth's greeting is one of deep respect, as if she perceived Mary's royalty: "And how have I deserved that the mother of my Lord should come to me?"[127] The response of Mary to this greeting seems to be indicative of her royal status. "Magnificat," she says, "My soul magnifies the Lord ... Because he who is mighty has done great things for me. ..."[128]

Another episode of the New Testament in which we may see Mary as Queen is the visit of the Magi (*Mt.* 2:1-12). In this account by Matthew the Magi are presented as showing homage to royalty. While it was Christ the King who was primarily honored by their visit and gifts, nevertheless Mary is not a mere host in this visit. She and the Child are inseparable in this entire episode.

While Scripture does serve as a basis for the doctrine of Mary's Queenship, nevertheless it must be admitted that it is rather meager. It is quite true to say that only after the doctrine of the Queenship is known, does a person really grasp its true biblical basis. It may be concluded that if the argument from Scripture would be properly formulated in this connection, it would involve several other prerogatives that are formally contained in the sacred text. Mary's Queenship is directly connected with her Divine Maternity, her office of Coredemptrix, her intimate association with her Son in the work of Redemption, her office of Mediatrix. The Queenship of Mary is a position or status that cannot be separated from her other prerogatives, even though it is distinct. Hence, where Scripture testifies to Mary's divine Maternity, her Coredemption, her Mediation, it indirectly testifies to her Queenship. What Pope Pius XII said about Mary's glorious Assumption can be re-echoed here in reference to our doctrine: "... the proofs and considerations of the Holy Fathers and the theologians are based upon the Sacred Writings as their ultimate foundation."[129]

---

[127] *Lk.* 1:43.

[128] *Lk.* 1:46-55.

[129] Pius XII, *Munificentissimus Deus*, in *A.A.S.*, Vol. 42, 1950, p. 770.

III
TRADITION AND MARY'S QUEENSHIP

The deposit of Catholic doctrine was complete by the time of the death of the last Apostle. Since that time nothing new has been added to the deposit of public revelation. However, during the course of centuries, the wealth of doctrine of the original deposit has emerged in ever greater clarity. Under the influence of the Holy Spirit what was once concealed deeply in the prime deposit was gradually brought up to the surface in explicit expression of truth. Like a gem, there was nothing added in its composition. There was only the polishing of something that was there all along. This is true of the doctrine of the Queenship of Mary. It was contained in the original treasure of revelation. But it took time for this doctrine to issue forth into the broad daylight of explicit clarity. And thus it is correct to say that the doctrine of Mary's Queenship is as old as the deposit of faith. The grasp of the doctrine is the only thing that may be called new.

It is the function of Tradition to tell us the extent of the grasp or the understanding of the doctrine in any particular age of history. It should be borne in mind that tradition is not to be identified with history. Tradition, as a proximate rule of faith, is nothing else than the teaching of the ecclesiastical *magisterium* at any given time in history.[130] From this it is clear that the Fathers of the Church, or, for that matter, the theological writers at any period of the Church's history, are not to be identified with Tradition. Nor are they to be looked upon as a constitutive part of Tradition. Rather they are to be looked upon as reflectors of Tradition. The purpose, therefore, of studying the writings of the Fathers of the Church and other ecclesiastical writers is to discern, at least indirectly, the teaching of the Church at any given age. By considering the outstanding representatives of each era from the first centuries of the Church down to our own day, we should be able to observe not only that there has been a true progress in the understanding of a specific doctrine, but also that the particular doctrine under observation has never undergone any change, as far as its intimate

---

[130] See the excellent treatise on this point by Walter J. Burghardt, S.J., *The Catholic Concept of Tradition* in *the Light of Modern Theological Thought*, in *Proceedings of the Sixth Annual Convention of the Catholic Theological Society of America* (1951), pp. 42-75.

truth is concerned. The only change noticeable is in its advance in clarity. That this is the case concerning Mary's Queenship will be clear from a careful analysis of representative writings of the various ages of the Church to the present day.

For the sake of order and convenience, the entire history of the Church will be considered under the following divisions:

1. From the Beginning to the Sixth Century
2. From the Seventh to the Twelfth Century
3. From the Thirteenth to the Sixteenth Century
4. From the Seventeenth to the Nineteenth Century
5. From the Nineteenth Century to the Present Time.

Before looking into the first period, it may be well to recall that there is an obvious parallel to be expected between the ecclesiastical *magisterium* and the ecclesiastical writers in the development of a doctrine. As a rule, the ecclesiastical writers reflect quite accurately the belief of the faithful. And the faithful, in turn, believe what they are taught by the *magisterium*. It is by divine Providence, at least in a broad sense, that the unbroken thread of a specific doctrine can be traced in the works of ecclesiastical writings from the implicit to the explicit.

A. FROM THE BEGINNING TO THE SIXTH CENTURY

It is commonly admitted that during the first centuries of Christianity the Fathers did not deal directly with the doctrine of Mary's Queenship. They were primarily concerned with Mary as the Second Eve. This is particularly true of St. Irenaeus (d. c. 200) and those who were dependent upon him.[131] During the course of the third and fourth centuries, the Fathers of the Church treated of Mary chiefly in their commentaries on Scripture. Thus they repeated and explained the Evangelists' accounts of the Annunciation, Visitation, the visit of the Magi, and the Marriage Feast at Cana. Special emphasis was placed on Mary as the *Mother of the Lord*. The Visitation scene naturally led to this distinctive title of Mary. It was at the Visitation that Elizabeth spoke of

---

[131] *Adversus haereses*, lib. 5, cap. 19; *PG*, 11, 1175.

Mary as "the Mother of my Lord."[132] Scholars have seen in this technical title the first step in the development of the doctrine of the Queenship, historically speaking.[133] "Lord," in the New Testament language, implies dominion and, consequently, has the connotation of kingship. Hence, it was natural that once the full import of "Mother of the Lord" was grasped, further development of the (*dominus* to *domina*) royal implication would follow.

In the fourth century, St. Ephraem of Syria (d. 373) spoke of Mary as "the Most Holy Sovereign Lady (*Domina*), Mother of God."[134] During the following century, Peter Chrysologus (d. 451) also used the word "Domina" as a royal title of Mary.[135] Although this does not as yet express the fact that Mary is a true Queen, nevertheless it was an important step in the right direction.

Parallel with the title "Mother of the Lord," we find the title "Mother of Christ who is King," or "Mother of the King."[136] Many times in the New Testament we see the title of King applied to Christ. It was natural, then, for the early Fathers to speak of the Mother of Christ as the Mother of the King. While this title did not speak explicitly of Mary as Queen, it nevertheless set the stage for investigating that title.[137]

By the beginning of the fifth century new interest was directed toward our Blessed Mother. The definition of the divine Motherhood at the Council of Ephesus in 431 was the providential impetus needed for careful consideration of other privileges of Mary. As scholars rightly observe, the divine Maternity from that time on became the center around which all other titles of Mary were crystallized.[138] Titles like "Sovereign Lady," "Immaculate Sovereign Lady," became more

---

[132] *Lk.* 1:43.

[133] Malachi J. Donnelly, S.J., *The Queenship of Mary During the Patristic Period*, in Marian Studies, Vol. 4, 1953, p. 86. *Cf.* H. Barré, La Royauté de Marie pendant les neuf premiers siècles, in Recherches de Science Religieuse, Vol. 29, 1939, pp. 129-162.

[134] *Opera omnia*, ed. Assemani, **Vol.** 3, p. 524.

[135] *Sermo 142, de Annuntiatione B.M.V.; PL*, 52, 579.

[136] Cf. Donnelly, *art. cit.*, p. 89.

[137] *Loc. cit.*

[138] Cf. Donnelly, *art. cit.*, p. 92; L. de Gruyter, *op. cit.*, p. 105.

common.[139] By the end of the sixth century the term "Queen" is occasionally applied to Mary.[140]

B. FROM THE SEVENTH TO THE TWELFTH CENTURY

In the first decades of the seventh century, interest in the Assumption of our Blessed Mother spread rapidly throughout the Christian world. In speaking of Mary in her glory, the Fathers of this period inevitably refer to her as a gloriously reigning Queen. Thus, for example, St. Modestus of Jerusalem (d. 634) applies verse 10 of Psalm 44 to Mary: "The Queen stood on the right hand in gilded clothing."[141]

Perhaps the outstanding representative of this early period concerning Mary's Queenship is St. Ildephonse of Toledo (d. 669). He sees Mary's royal dignity as intimately associated with that of Christ the King.[142] His attitude toward Mary is one of subjection and respect. He prays to Mary: "I am your servant, for your Son is my Lord. You are my Queen because you have become the handmaid of my King."[143]

By the eighth century the fact of Mary's Queenship was firmly established. From its implicit stage it had emerged to the explicit. From now on the writers of the Church will reflect in their writings primarily the meaning of Queen as applied to Mary. St. Andrew of Crete (d. 740) speaks of Mary as a Queen in prophecy, a Queen during her life, a Queen in glory.[144] He applies the title of Queen as completely proper to Mary.[145]

In St. Germain of Constantinople (d. 733) we find an echo of St. Andrew of Crete. Addressing Our Lady, he says: "You, who enjoy maternal authority over God, obtain for those also who have fallen into serious sin the powerful grace of forgiveness. For you are necessarily heard, since God will fulfill the desires of his true and undefiled Mother

---

[139] Cf. Donnelly, *loc. cit.*, footnote 43.

[140] For example, Byzantium, *Oratio in Simeonem et in B.V.M.*; PG, 86, 250.

[141] Encomium in dormitionem sanctissimae Dominae nostrae Deiparae semperque Virginis Mariae, n. 10; PG, 86, 3289-3290. The authenticity of this *sermon* is disputed.

[142] *De virginitate perpetua sanctae Mariae adversus tres infideles*, c. 12; PL, 96, 106.

[143] *Ibid.*

[144] *Hom. 4 in nativ. B.V.M.*; PG, 97, 872. *Hom. 3 in nativ.*; PG, 97, 833. *Hom. 1 in nativ.*; PG, 97, 820. *Hom. in dormit.*; PG, 97, 1045.

[145] PG, 97, 1072, 1088, 894; cf. Luis, *op. cit.*, p. 46.

with regard to everything, and in everything for everyone."[146]

St. John Damascene (d. 749) with his penetrating theological mind not only speaks of Mary as the Queen and Sovereign Mistress of every creature and powerful Queen,[147] but also tells us of the theological foundation for this prerogative. According to him, Mary is Queen because she is the Mother of her Creator.[148]

At this time in the West, St. Bede, the Venerable (d. 735), sees the Queenship of Mary implied in her name. In this he was not original, but simply summarized the analyses of the name "Mary" made by St. Jerome, St. Peter Chrysologus, Eucher of Lyons, and St. Isidore of Seville before him.[149] These Fathers recognized Mary's Queenship and used the name of Mary as a fitting expression of it. A similar usage is found also among ninth-century writers. Wallafrid Strabo (d. 849),[150] Alcuin (d. 804),[151] and Rabanus Maurus (d. 856),[152] are outstanding examples.

That the title of Queen was recognized as the proper title of Mary is clearly indicated at this time by an author known as Joseph "the Hymn Writer" (d. 883). In at least 239 passages he speaks of Mary as the sovereign of heaven and earth.[153]

In the twelfth century, among the many devotees of Mary who were eloquent in extolling her Queenship, St. Anselm of Canterbury (d. 1109), Eadmer (d. 1124), St. Bernard (d. 1153), and Nicholas of Clairvaux (d. c. 1176) are deserving of mention. While these men were capable of theological treatises, nevertheless it is only in their sermons, prayers, and hymns that we find their doctrine on Mary's Queenship. Their

---

[146] *Oratio 2 in dormit. Deiparae; PG*, 98, 351; cf. Luis, *op. cit.,* pp. 46-48. Other pertinent references in Donnelly, *art. cit.,* p. 98.

[147] *Hom. 2 in dormit.; PG*, 96, 721.

[148] *Ibid.* Cf. Donnelly, *art. cit.,* p. 99.

[149] Donnelly, *art. cit.,* p. 100.

[150] *PL*, 114, 859. On the true author of this piece, cf. R. Laurentin, *Court traité de théologie mariale* (Paris, 1954), p. 143.

[151] *Carmen 86; PL*, 101, 749.

[152] *Comment. in Matthaeum,* I, 1; *PL*, 107, 744.

[153] *Mariale, passim; PG,* 105, 991, 1002, 1005, 1007, 1010, 1019, 1022, 1026, 1027, 1030. Cf. Luis, *op. cit.,* p. 52. On the doubtful authenticity of the *Mariale,* cf. Laurentin, *op. cit.,* p. 173.

reputation as theologians, however, is a guarantee of the solidity of the doctrine contained in their sermons and prayers.[154]

St. Anselm of Canterbury glories in such phrases as "Queen of Angels, Queen of heaven." He is fond of appealing to Mary as Queen of Mercy, because of her closeness to Christ the King.[155]

Eadmer, a worthy disciple of Anselm, faithfully adhered to the doctrine of his master. It is particularly when dealing with the Assumption that he speaks of Mary as the gloriously reigning Queen by her Son's side.[156] The following is a classical passage:

> Just as God, by preparing all things with His own power, is the Father and Lord of all, so the Blessed Mary, by repairing all things with her merits is the Mother and Sovereign Lady of all things. For God is the Lord of all, because He created all things in their proper nature. And Mary is the Sovereign Lady of things because she restored them to their pristine dignity.[157]

Even though Eadmer does not use our present terminology in speaking of the foundation of Mary's Queenship, it is obvious that he considers the Maternity and Coredemption of Mary as the ultimate explanation of that dignity. Because of these clear expressions, Eadmer is rightly considered by some Mariologists as having exerted tremendous influence on subsequent writers.[158]

St. Bernard of Clairvaux, who never tired of proclaiming the praises of Mary, speaks of Mary's Queenship as something commonly known. The passages in which he uses such titles as "Queen," "Sovereign," and the like are innumerable.[159] Just as his contemporaries, so also Bernard sees Mary's Queenship grounded in, and associated with, her divine

---

[154] Cf. William F. Hill, S.S., *Our Lady's Queenship in the Middle Ages and Modern Times*, in *Marian Studies*, Vol. 4, 1953, pp. 136-143. This writer is greatly indebted to Father Hill for his excellent article.

[155] *Orat. 52*; PL, 158, 952.

[156] *De excellentia B.V.M.*; PL, 159, 572.

[157] *Op. cit.*; PL, 159, 578.

[158] Hill, *art. cit.*, pp. 138-140.

[159] Cf. for example, PL, 183, 61, 62, 83, 415, 416, 428, 431, 432, 433, 436. Cf. Luis, *op. cit.*, p. 57.

Maternity, and her coredemptive activity.[160]

In addition to St. Anselm, Eadmer, and St. Bernard, there are a number of other ecclesiastical writers at this time who pay tribute to Mary as Queen. We may mention, for example, Rupert of Deutz (d. 1153),[161] Peter the Venerable (d. 1156),[162] and Peter of Blois (d. 1200).[163]

The particular contribution of this period to the doctrine under discussion is the clear expression of the foundation of Mary's royal dignity. They see Mary as a true Queen because she is the Mother of God, and because she co-operated in the Redemption of man. However, these writers say very little about the nature of Mary's Queenship or the extent of her power.

C. From the Thirteenth to the Sixteenth Century

During this period of Scholasticism, the theologians treated of Mary and her prerogatives primarily in their tracts on the Incarnation. With them Mariology was not a separate treatise of theology. Nevertheless, the great theological minds of these centuries shed their bright light on many obscure points of Mariology, including some aspects of Mary's Queenship. St. Bonaventure, Conrad of Saxony, St. Anthony of Padua, and Pseudo-Albert the Great were the most renowned witnesses to Mary's royal dignity during the thirteenth century. St. Thomas, too, spoke of Mary as Queen when he applied to her the text of Psalm 44:10.[164]

St. Bonaventure (d. 1274) refers to Mary as Queen particularly in his Assumption sermons, in which he attributes tremendous power to Mary, the Sovereign Lady of Heaven. He speaks of her as the Queen of heaven as well as of earth,[165] the "glorious empress of all creatures."[166] In another sermon the Seraphic Doctor writes: "After she was assumed into heaven,

---

[160] *PL*, 183, 415-416. For the testimony of Nicholas of Clairvaux, St. Bernard's secretary, cf. *Serm. 44 in nativ. B.V.M.* (among the works of St. Peter Damian); *PL*, 144, 739.

[161] *Comment. in Cant.* lib. 3, cap. 4; *PL*, 168, 891.

[162] *Prosa in honorem Matris Domini*; *PL*, 189, 1018.

[163] *Serm. 33 de Assumptione B.V.M.*; *PL*, 208, 660.

[164] *Comment. in ps. 44*, cap. 7.

[165] *Serm. 4 de Assumptione; op. omnia*, Vol. 9 (Ad Claras Aquas, 1901), p. 673.

[166] *Serm. 2 de Assumptione*; Vol. 9, p. 691.

she was seated at the right hand of the eternal King, and crowned with the glorious crown by which she was conformed to the majesty of the eternal King. ... Hence it is as Queen that she is seated at the right hand of the eternal King."[167] While the Seraphic Doctor speaks in glowing terms about Mary's dignity and power, he is nevertheless careful not to make her equal to her Son, the Eternal King. He affirms that God's supreme and absolute power over creatures cannot be communicated to creatures. However, the Seraphic Doctor tells us, God gave to Mary the highest place possible for,

> She presides and immediately assists in subordination to the King ... and that for a threefold reason: 1. because of the closeness of her heart to the heart of the King ... ; 2. because of her frequent intercession in behalf of sinners ... ; and 3. because just as Christ with His Mother saved the human race, so also they are the rulers of the human race.[168]

St. Bonaventure further clarifies Mary's office as Queen by designating it as an office of mercy. According to him, Mary has been given all grace and supreme power of impetration. For these reasons she is truly Queen of Mercy.[169]

Conrad of Saxony (d. 1279), disciple of St. Bonaventure, was also a faithful imitator of his master's style and doctrine. He, too, speaks of Mary as "Sovereign Lady of angels ... of men ... and of demons."[170] Conrad describes how Mary's queenly power is exercised over angels, men, and demons. *Over angels:* insofar as they obey Mary's precepts in protecting and guarding men; *over men:* insofar as all graces come to them through the hands of Mary; *over demons:* insofar as by her mediation she has overcome the infernal enemies.[171]

St. Anthony (d. 1231) in his sermons on the Assumption of the Blessed Mother calls her "Queen of Heaven." To illustrate the royal dignity of Mary, he has recourse to figures of the Old Testament. For example, he finds in Sarah a figure of Mary, "for Sarah means princess.

---

[167] *Serm. 5 de Assumptione;* Vol. 9, pp. 699-700.

[168] *Serm. 3 de Assumptione;* Vol. 9, p. 695.

[169] *Serm. 2 de Assumptione;* Vol. 9, p. 692.

[170] *Speculum B. M. Virginis* (ed. Ad Claras Aquas, 1904), p. 38.

[171] *Op. cit.*, pp. 38-42.

... Mary is a glorious Virgin, Princess, and our Queen."[172] And then he adds: "Mary became our Princess and Queen at the time of the Annunciation."[173]

The famous *Mariale,* until recently attributed to St. Albert the Great (d. 1280), is one of the most important works in the history of the development of Mariology.[174] It is a veritable encyclopedia of Mariology. The author (who wrote at the close of the thirteenth century or the beginning of the fourteenth) does not merely summarize the doctrine of those who preceded him, or were his contemporaries. Rather, he stamps it with his own erudition and either develops various theological implications, or else points the way for further theological development. His contribution to the doctrine of Mary's Queenship can hardly be overestimated. As his predecessors, he saw that Mary's queenly dignity was rooted in her Maternity and coredemptive activity. However, with his orderly mind, he investigated very thoroughly the exact relationship between Mary's cooperation in the Redemption and her Queenship. Mary was the associate of Christ in acquiring the Kingdom. Therefore, he concludes, she is associated with Him as Queen in triumph.[175]

In his analysis he thus associates Mary with Christ the King: "From the same dominion and rule from which her Son received the name of King, she received the name of Queen ... for she truly became the Sovereign Lady of all, seeing that she is the Mother of the Creator of all."[176] Hence, "she is Queen of the same Kingdom of which He is King."[177]

The author effectively shows the extent of the power of Mary as Queen by a comparison with the power of Holy Orders in the Church. Even the greatest power in the bishops of the Church, he says, is weaker

---

[172] *In Assumpt. B. V. Mariae,* in *S. Antonii Patavini, thaumaturgi incliti, sermones dominicales et in solemnitatibus,* ed. Locatelli (Patavii, 1895), p. 730.

[173] *Ibid.* Cf. Louis Rohr, O.F.M., *The Use of Sacred Scripture in the Sermons of St. Anthony of Padua* (Washington, D. C., 1948), pp. 80-81.

[174] Preserved in *Alberti Magni opera omnia,* ed. P. **Jammy,** Vol. 20 (Lugduni, 1651), pp. 3-156.

[175] *Mariale,* q. 43; ed. cit., p. 42.

[176] *Mariale,* q. 168; *ed. cit.,* p. 123.

[177] *Mariale,* q. 165; ed. cit., p. 120.

than the power of the heavenly Queen. "The Pope himself," he writes, "is the servant of the servants of God, but Mary is the Empress of the whole world."[178]

That the author of the *Mariale* was speaking of queenship in the strict sense is clear from his own words. He said, "That woman would properly be called queen of France who would truly and rightly have dominion over all who are in France. But the most Blessed Virgin truly, rightly, and properly has dominion over all who are in God's mercy."[179]

The thirteenth century, which produced the great theological summas, rightly shed its light on Mariology. As far as the Queenship is concerned, St. Bonaventure, Conrad of Saxony, and Pseudo-Albert the Great reached a certain peak in presentation that was difficult to surpass in subsequent centuries.[180]

The ecclesiastical writers of the fourteenth and fifteenth centuries quite frequently treat of Mary's Queenship, but they hardly contribute anything substantially to the development attained by the immortal trio of the thirteenth century. These writers (of the fourteenth and fifteenth centuries) are of some importance insofar as they form a link between the thirteenth and sixteenth centuries, by accepting and repeating the teaching of their predecessors.

One writer who is especially worthy of mention at this time is St. Bernardine of Siena (d. 1444). One statement of his has become a standard expression in speaking of the extent of Mary's queenly power. He said: "All creatures who serve the Trinity serve also the glorious Virgin Mary."[181]

During the sixteenth century St. Peter Canisius (d. 1597) was the outstanding champion of Mary's prerogatives in the face of Protestant attacks. As to the Queenship, his defense was forceful and categorical.

> Cur ... illam Reginae nomine, Damascenum et Athanasium sequuti, non compellemus, cujus et pater David Rex inclytus et filius Rex regum

---

[178] *Mariale*, q. 42; ed. cit., pp. 42-43.

[179] *Mariale*, q. 162; ed. cit., p. 113.

[180] Cf. Luis, *op. cit.*, pp. 63-67.

[181] *Serm. 5 de B. V. Maria*, cap. 6; *opera omnia*, Vol. 4 (Venetiis, 1745), p. 92: "Tot creaturae serviunt gloriosae Virgini Mariae quot serviunt Trinitati." Cf. also Ch. 8. Cf. G. Folgorait, S.M., *La Vergine bella in San Bernardino da Siena* (Milano, 1939), p. 524.

Dominusque dominantium, sine fine imperans, laudem in Scripturis praestantissimam tenent? Regina est insuper, si cum illis conferatur quibus, veluti regibus, coeleste regnum cum Christo Rege sommo contigit, utpote illius cohaeredibus et in eodem veluti throno, ut Scriptura loquitur, cum illo collocatis. Regina est etiam nulli electorum secunda, sed simul angelis et hominibus tanto praelata dignius, quo nihil illa sublimius ac sanctius esse potest, quae sola cum Deo Filium habet communem et quae supra se Deum et Christum tantum, infra se reliqua videt omnia.[182]

This doctrine, the holy Doctor insists elsewhere, is fully warranted by the constant tradition of both the Latin and the Greek Church.[183]

The fact that relatively few authors wrote on this subject in the fourteenth, fifteenth, and sixteenth centuries is not at all surprising. During the first part of this era, the ecclesiastical writers contented themselves mostly with commentaries on the *Sentences* of Peter Lombard and on the *Summa* of St. Thomas, in which our doctrine was not discussed. During the sixteenth century theological endeavor centered mainly on answering Protestant attacks; and Mary's Queenship was not one of the principal points of controversy.[184]

D. From the Seventeenth to the Nineteenth Century

The seventeenth century again brought back a revival of interest in the Queenship of Mary. It is especially during this century that this Marian prerogative and its implications are discussed with theological precision. While in former times the doctrine was obviously accepted in the strict sense, nevertheless, it is at this period that we find methodical investigation into such things as the precise meaning of queen, dominion, and rule.

Among the many outstanding writers who devoted their talents to proclaim the glory of Mary as Queen, we note Francis Suárez (d. 1617), St. Lawrence of Brindisi (d. 1619), Ferdinand de Salazar (d. 1646), Justin

---

[182] *De Maria Virgine incomparabili ...*, lib. 5, cap. 13; in *Summa aurea de B.V.M.*, ed. Bourassé, Vol. 9, col. 150.

[183] *Ed. cit.*, col. 151: "Et, quod multo est amplius, Ecclesia non modo latina sed etiam graeca et syriaca Reginam illam coeli solemni epitheto publice multis jam saeculis salutat ac praedicat."

[184] Cf. Hill, *art. cit.*, p. 154.

of Miechow (d. 1689), Christopher de Vega (d. 1672), and particularly Bartholomew de los Rios (d. 1652). The Marian writings of these theologians not only contain a treasury of Marian doctrine in general, but they may be said to represent a golden age in the history of the specific doctrine of Mary's Queenship.

The Spanish Jesuit, Francis Suárez, known for his methodical approach to theological questions, applied his scientific method also to Mariology. Although he does not have a formal treatise devoted to Mary's Queenship, nevertheless he does treat it adequately while on the subject of the Immaculate Conception.[185] His orderly procedure left its mark on subsequent approaches to this question. Suárez draws a significant parallel between Christ's Kingship and Mary's Queenship. Christ as Man is King because of the hypostatic union. Mary is Queen because she is the Mother of the King.[186] Christ is King by conquest because of the Redemption. Mary, too, is Queen by a title of conquest, by reason of her co-operation in the Redemption.[187]

While Suárez sees the striking parallel between Christ the King and Mary the Queen, he is careful not to make Mary a "Lady-King," with full, independent power. Her Queenship is to be explained in union with Christ's Kingship, but according to her own sex and her relationship with Christ.[188]

The Capuchin St. Lawrence of Brindisi, one of the most popular and vigorous preachers of his time, contributed his share to the glorification of Mary's Queenship in the form of sermons. Although he is referred to as a *popular* preacher, nevertheless his sermons are grounded firmly in theology. Mariology, in its every aspect, was a favorite subject of his. The well-known Mariologist, G. Roschini, pays the following tribute to the Saint: "... He was the greatest Mariologist of his time. He has all the

---

[185] *De mysteriis vitae Christi,* q. 27, disp. 3, art. 2, sect. 5; *opera omnia,* Vol. 19 (Parisiis, 1856), pp. 44-46.

[186] *De mysteriis vitae Christi,* disp. 22, sect. 2, n. 2; *ed. cit.,* Vol. 19, p. 326.

[187] *Ibid.:* "Sicut enim Christus eo quod nos redemit, speciali titulo Dominus est ac Rex noster, ita et B. Virgo propter singularem modum quo ad nostram redemptionem concurrit. ...."

[188] *Ibid.:* "Et infra (Athanasius) quasi explicans vel limitans hoc dominium, dicit '*esse secundum sexum femineum,*' ac si diceret esse tale quale esse solet in uxore vel matre propter conjunctionem ad regem."

polemic power of a Canisius or Bellarmine, all the theological solidity of a Suárez, and all the ascetical fascination of a St. Francis de Sales."[189]

There is no doubt that St. Lawrence accurately reflects the teaching of true tradition. In his thoroughness, he first of all establishes the fact that there is a true scriptural basis for this Marian prerogative.

He makes a careful analysis of Genesis 3:15[190] and Apocalypse 12:1.[191] In both he sees the basis for Mary's royal prerogative. His particular analysis of these texts have hardly been improved since his time.

St. Lawrence presents a very forceful treatise of Mary's Queenship in his commentary on the Annunciation text.[192] It was at the Incarnation, he says, that Christ became King. By describing Mary's part in this crowning of Christ the King, he clearly sees Mary in a role of a true and genuine Queen. Along with the Incarnation text of Scripture, St. Lawrence develops masterfully the true significance of Mary as the "spouse of God." This very fact that she co-operated with God in the Incarnation is for St. Lawrence a valid argument for her Queenship.[193]

The Saint is aware of the force of tradition as a rule of faith. For him, the fact that the Church teaches this doctrine is a conclusive proof in its favor.[194]

In his theological presentation of this matter, St. Lawrence dwells on the similarity between Christ and Mary. The two are alike, he says, in nature, grace, and glory.[195] It is in connection with this similarity that he develops the implications of the expression *Socia Christi*.[196]

Concerning the extent of Mary's Queenship, the author's words bear a striking resemblance to the clear statement of Pope Pius XII in his radio address in 1946 to the people of Fatima.[197] St. Lawrence said: "The Virgin Mother of God is a Queen of such a type and nature that her

---

[189] G. M. Roschini, O.S.M., *La Mariologia di S. Lorenzo da Brindisi (Padua*, 1951), p. 13.
[190] 190 *Mariale; opera omnia,* Vol. 1 (Patavii, 1928), p. 164.
[191] *Op. cit.*, p. 386.
[192] *Op. cit.*, p. 391.
[193] *Op. cit.*, pp. 50, 178-179.
[194] *Op. cit.*, p. 454.
[195] *Op. cit.*, p. 231.
[196] *Op. cit.*, pp. 254, 288.
[197] *A.A.S.*, Vol. 38, 1946, p. 266.

Kingdom is no less than that of God, nor her sovereignty less than that of Christ."[198]

Practical preacher that he was, St. Lawrence treated also of the purpose of Mary's Queenship. As he summarized it: "For the salvation of the Christian people Mary was exalted in heaven and crowned Queen and Empress of the Universe."[199] She is really the Queen of Mercy;[200] and hence he logically concludes: "What can there be lacking to the man who has Mary as his omnipotent advocate with the omnipotent God?"[201]

Notable progress in this field was made about this time by the well-known biblical scholar, Ferdinand de Salazar, S.J. Perhaps his most significant contribution to our doctrine was his careful examination of the intimate reasons why the Mother should share in the royal dignity of her Son. Ordinarily, he says, it is the other way around: the son receives his dignity from his parents. After some technical analysis and argumentation, he concludes to the fact that parents can partake in rights that belong to their child, if a natural right is involved or a right by conquest, but not in case of a right derived from a vote. In both of these ways Mary partakes in the royal rights of her Son (by natural right and by right of conquest).[202]

Of no less value is the contribution of the Polish Dominican, Justin Miechow, known for his valiant defense of Mary's Queenship against Protestant attacks. According to him Mary's Queenship is grounded in a natural right, divine right, and human right. By *natural right,* because she is of the family of David. Of *divine right,* because she is the Mother of Christ. By *human right:* (1) through the title of heredity received through her Son; (2) through the title of conquest, by her Coredemption; (3) by right of purchase, and (4) through the title of gift or donation.[203]

---

[198] *Mariale,* p. 23.

[199] *Op. cit.,* p. 587.

[200] *Op. cit.,* p. 389.

[201] *Op. cit.,* p. 58.

[202] *Expositio in Proverbia Salomonis* (Lugduni, 1637), pp. 233-235.

[203] *Discursus praedicabiles super litanias lauretanas,* disc. 371, Vol. 2 (Lugduni, 1660), pp. 459-460. In disc. 214, Vol. 2, p. 18, n. 2, he writes: "Quod quidem dominium in duobus fundatum esse docent theologi. Primo, in conjunctione et affinitate quadam inter Deum et Virginem. Secundo, in singulari quadam ad nostram redemptionem cooperatione."

As to Christopher de Vega, one of the most prolific Mariologists of the seventeenth century, his treatment of the Queenship bears some resemblance to that of de Salazar, although the latter's approach is considerably more scientific. For de Vega, Mary is Queen, not merely in a metaphorical sense, but also in a true and proper sense: "Hinc pronum erit praecipuum nostrum intentum aggredi, videlicet B. Virginem Dei Genitricem vere et proprie Reginam esse ac Dominam universi."[204]

According to him, Mary's universal dominion is based on the fact that she is the Mother of God, the Coredemptrix of mankind, the Spouse of the Holy Spirit; also on the gift of original justice.[205]

If de Vega was "the first theologian who studied directly and formally, in a scientific manner, the Queenship of Mary,"[206] it remains true that the most elaborate treatise on the subject during this period was the one written by the Spanish Augustinian, Bartholomew de los Rios. His work *De Hierarchia Mariana* is a serious, *ex professo* investigation of the theological basis for Mary's royal dignity.[207] After establishing the fact of Mary's Queenship with scholastic precision, the author undertakes a lengthy investigation of its threefold theological foundation in this order: (1) The Immaculate Conception and the fullness of grace placed Mary at the summit of the hierarchy of order and dignity. (2) The divine Maternity gives Mary the closest possible relationship with God, and makes her the heiress of the Kingdom of her Son. (3) Her Coredemption wins her the share of the kingdom lost by Eve, for she helped to liberate those enslaved by Satan.[208]

After a very thorough study of the doctrine as presented by his illustrious confrere, Father A. Musters, himself an authority on the subject, draws the following conclusions: (*a*) Bartholomew de los Rios gave the doctrine of Mary's sovereignty a "solid ontological or

---

[204] *Theologia Mariana*, palaestra 27, cert. 1, Vol. 2 (ed. Neapoli, 1866), p. 349. *Ibid.*: "Hic nos reginae nomen non translatitie et improprie, sed vere et proprie, quatenus adsignificat jus regni, dominium ac potestatem in res ac subditos, desumimus."

[205] *Ibid.*

[206] *Luis, op. cit.*, p. 70.

[207] *De hierarchia mariana libri sex, in quibus imperium, virtus et nomen B.V.M. declaratus, et mancipiorum ejus dignitas ostenditur* (Antverpiae, 1641).

[208] *Op. cit.*, pp. 91 ff., 54-73.

metaphysical basis founded on her supreme grace and the divine Maternity." (*b*) "He gave great precision and logical clarity to the nature of her absolute dominion over all creation, second only to that of God Himself."[209]

To the above judicious comment we may add that Father de los Rios' scholarly work exerted considerable influence on virtually every author who wrote on this point in subsequent centuries.[210] Among these we shall single out as worthy of mention: St. Alphonsus Liguori (d. 1787) and St. Louis M. Grignion de Montfort (d. 1716).

Although St. Alphonsus did not write a special treatise on Mary's Queenship, nevertheless, his epoch-making *The Glories of Mary* abounds in references to this doctrine. Indeed, the very first chapter of the book is largely devoted to this specific question. The opening paragraph clearly states that Mary deserves the title of Queen because she is the Mother of the King of Kings.[211] This, then, is the foundation of her prerogative. How does she exercise her royal power? The Saint goes to great lengths to stress that the characteristic note here is, of course, "mercy." He points out that in the Kingdom of God, justice is exercised by God, while mercy is assigned to His Mother.[212] From the context it is evident that the holy Doctor does not deny that the all-just God is also merciful. He merely wishes to emphasize the distinctive feature of Mary's queenly power. As to the extent of her dominion, his opinion coincides with that of St. Bernardine of Siena, whom he quotes approvingly: "... all things that are in heaven and on earth, are subject to the empire of God; so are they also under the dominion of Mary."[213]

Sharing the immense popularity of *The Glories of Mary*, the remarkable *Treatise on the True Devotion*, by St. Louis Grignion de Montfort, has had a tremendous influence on modern spiritual writers.

---

[209] A. Musters, O.E.S.A., *La souveraineté de la Vierge d'après les écrits mariologiques de Barthélemy de los Rios* (Bruges, 1946), pp. 176-177.

[210] Cf. Hill's excellent analysis of our author's teaching, *art. cit.*, pp. 164-167.

[211] *The Glories of* Mary, ed. by E. Grimm, third reprint revised (Brooklyn, N. Y., 1931), p. 35. On this matter, cf. Francis J. Connell, C.Ss.R., *St. Alphonsus and the Queenship of Mary*, in *Alma Socia Christi*, Vol. 3 (Romae, 1952), pp. 122-126.

[212] *Op. cit.*, pp. 36-39.

[213] Op. cit., *p. 36.*

The basic truth pervading the whole treatise is Mary's over-all position in the divine plan.[214] With this as a foundation, the author draws a perfect parallel between Christ and Mary. Her influence in the supernatural order is as extensive as that of Christ. Her association with Him is inevitably universal. This universal association is hypothetically necessary, but relative. If she forms one principle of salvation and intercession with Christ, it is with Christ as the only principal and all-sufficient cause; Mary's role remains entirely secondary, dependent, relative.[215]

It should be borne in mind that, by taking the attitude of a "slave" in his consecration to Mary, St. Louis does not substitute slave for child; the former is simply added to the latter. As he understands it, there is nothing degrading in being a "slave" of Mary. The idea merely emphasizes our recognition of her unique dominion over souls. Theoretically and practically, it is "a slavery of love which accentuates, rather than diminishes, the filial character of our love for Mary."[216]

E. FROM THE NINETEENTH CENTURY TO THE PRESENT TIME

With the solemn definition of the Immaculate Conception in 1854 there arose a very articulate interest in the perfections of Our Blessed Lady, in her privileges and prerogatives. The Queenship was by no means neglected. Indeed, few topics have received a more serious attention during the period now under discussion. And the inspiration was furnished, to be sure, by the repeated statements of the Roman Pontiffs, from Pius IX to Pius XII, gloriously reigning.

The theologians and Catholic writers who have devoted their talents to Our Lady's royal dignity within the past one hundred years are, of course, too numerous to be discussed here. Restricting ourselves to our contemporaries, the names of de Gruyter, Luis, Barré, Roschini, and

---

[214] Cf. Frank Setzer, S.M.M., *The Spiritual Maternity and St. Louis M. De Montfort*, in *Marian Studies*, Vol. 3, 1953, p. 199. Cf. also Maurice-M. Cadieux, S.M.M., *La royauté universelle de Marie dans l'oeuvre de saint Louis-Marie de Montfort*, in *Alma Socia Christi*, Vol. 8 (Romae, 1953), pp. 97-132.

[215] *True Devotion to the Blessed Virgin Mary* (ed. Bay Shore, N. Y., 1947), p. 74.

[216] R. Garrigou-Lagrange, O.P., *The Mother of the Saviour and Our Interior Life* (Dublin, 1948), p. 307.

Santonicola are certainly deserving of special mention.[217] They have become the great champions of the doctrine in the twentieth century, and have worked tirelessly to formulate it in its proper theological perspective.

Among the various factors which have contributed to the promotion of Mary's Queenship we must recall the many Marian Congresses held throughout the world during the past few decades. It is mostly through them that theologians and the Catholic laity have urged the Holy See solemnly to proclaim Our Lady's royal prerogative. A partial list would include the Congresses of Lyons (1900), Fribourg (1902), Rome (1904), Einsiedeln (1906), Zaragoza (1908), Salzburg (1910), Trier (1912), Boulogne-sur-Mer (1938), Casalmonferrato (1939), Zaragoza (1940), and Agrigento (1941).[218] To these we may add the fourth National Convention of The Mariological Society of America (Cleveland, 1953), entirely devoted to the theological discussion of the same theme.[219]

Finally, a word must be said in this connection concerning the *Pious Movement "Pro Regalitate Mariae."* Much of what has been accomplished as regards the promotion of Mary's Queenship is due, undoubtedly, to the tireless efforts of this organization. Officially established in Rome after World War II, the movement soon extended its manifold activities throughout the world and has been the inspiring force behind the countless manifestations of the Marian apostolate "pro regalitate."[220]

IV
THE NATURE AND EXTENT OF MARY'S QUEENSHIP

Mary is Queen of the Kingdom of which Christ is King. In order to appreciate more completely Mary's actual status as Queen it will be of some importance to analyze the nature of the Kingdom of Christ and

---

[217] Besides the already cited works of de Gruyter, Luis, and Barré, cf. Roschini, *Royauté de Marie*, in *Maria. Études sur la Ste. Vierge*, ed. H. du Manoir, Vol. 1 (Paris, 1949), pp. 603-618; A. Santonicola, C.Ss.R., *La Regalità di Maria*, 2nd ed. (Milano, 1942). Further bibliography in E. Carroll's article, *Marian Studies*, Vol. 4, 1953, pp. 29-30.

[218] Cf. A. Santonicola, *La Regalità di Maria*, in Alma Socia Christi, *Vol.* 3 (Romae, 1952), pp. 151-153.

[219] These papers and discussions were published in *Marian Studies*, Vol. 4, 1953.

[220] Cf. Santonicola, *art. cit.*, pp. 153-156.

how that Kingdom is ruled. In the words of Pope Pius XII:

> He, the Son of God, reflects on His heavenly Mother the glory, the majesty and dominion of His Kingship ... Jesus is King throughout all eternity by nature and by right of conquest; through Him, with Him, and subordinate to Him, Mary is Queen by grace, by divine relationship, by right of conquest and by singular election.[221]

The Kingdom of Christ is primarily a *spiritual* Kingdom. As our Lord Himself said, His "Kingdom is not of this world." It is a Kingdom "that men prepare to enter by repentance, and which they cannot enter except through faith and Baptism."[222] Since Mary is Queen of this Kingdom, her royal power must deal primarily with things spiritual. Besides, the very fact that Mary is presented to us as co-conqueror of Satan identifies her power as being primarily of a spiritual nature.

While Christ's Kingdom is primarily spiritual, it is not exclusively so. Pope Pius XI assures us in his encyclical letter *Quas primas* that Christ the King has authority also over temporal and civil matters.[223] Since Mary is Queen for the entire Kingdom of Christ, it follows logically that under the King she has queenly authority also over temporal matters.

MARY, QUEEN OF THE UNIVERSE

Pope Pius XI in his encyclical letter *Quas primas* further emphasizes the fact that the Kingdom of Christ is not bounded either in time or in extent. Repeating the words of Leo XIII, he says:

> His (Christ's) empire includes not only the Catholic nations, not only the baptized persons, who though rightly belonging to the Church have been led astray by error or have been cut off from her by schism, but also those who are outside the Christian faith, so that truly the whole of mankind is subject to the power of Christ.[224]

In his well-known address to the pilgrims at Fatima on May 13, 1946, Pope Pius XII states emphatically that "Her (Mary's) kingdom is as vast as that of her Son and God, since nothing is excluded from her

---

[221] *A.A.S.*, Vol. 38, 1946, p. 266.
[222] *Ibid.*, Vol. 17, 1925, p. 600.
[223] *Ibid.*, Vol. 17, 1925, pp. 600-601.
[224] *Ibid.*, Vol. 17, 1925, p. 598.

dominion."[225]

Hence, combining the two authentic statements of Pope Pius XI and Pope Pius XII, we arrive at the inevitable conclusion that Mary's queenly authority extends to the entire human race, and even to the angels.[226] Nations, as well as families and individuals owe veneration and homage to Mary, because she is the Queen of the universe; just as they owe adoration and homage to Christ, because He is the King of the universe.

EXTENT OF AUTHORITY OF MARY OUR QUEEN

The supreme authority in the Kingdom belongs to Christ. The Kingdom itself belongs to Christ and to no one else. He is the source of all genuine authority. As Pope Pius XI clearly stated: "The Word of God, who is of the same substance with the Father, necessarily has all the things in common with the Father; and for that reason He has the supreme and absolute authority over all creatures."[227] From this clear statement it is obvious that whatever authority, power, or title we apply to Mary, we may not imply that she has it in the absolute sense. Her authority and dominative power come from, and are dependent upon Christ, the source of all authority. "She is neither an substitute ruler, nor the source of sovereignty within the realm."[228] On the other hand, Mary does not enjoy merely a *delegated* authority of Christ. She is not His vicar, nor merely His minister, or legate.[229] "Her ineffable dignity and glory proceed precisely from her union with our Lord."[230] She is really one with Christ in the exercise of authority in the Kingdom. In the Kingdom of Christ, the governing is characterized by perfect unity. For it is of the essence of royal power that it be one. Hence, whatever or wherever Mary's authority may be, it must be characterized by its union

---

[225] *Ibid.*, Vol. 38, 1946, p. 266.

[226] *Ibid.*, Vol. 17, 1925, p. 598. Cf. J. B. Carol, O.F.M., *Fundamentals of Mariology* (New York, 1956), p. 80.

[227] *Ibid.*, Vol. 17, 1925, p. 596.

[228] Cf. J. C. Fenton, *Our Lady's Queenly Prerogatives*, in The American Ecclesiastical Review, Vol. 120, November, 1949, p. 428.

[229] Ferdinand Vandry, *The Nature of Mary's Universal Queenship*, in *Marian Studies*, Vol. 4, 1953, p. 24.

[230] Fenton, *art. cit.*, p. 428.

with that of the King. And this union is realized precisely by Mary's close and unique association with Christ in the governing of the Kingdom.

Christ as King rules the Kingdom by a threefold power: legislative, judicial, and executive.[231] Since Mary as Queen is intimately associated with Christ the King in governing the Kingdom, the question naturally arises: Does Mary exercise her authority by partaking formally in these powers? Is she formally a legislator? Is she formally a judge? Is she formally an executive? These questions could perhaps be reformulated and simplified in this manner: Does Mary exercise her authority *in the same way* that Christ exercises His?

Before considering the specific functions of government, it is well to bear in mind that Christ the King and Mary the Queen agree wholeheartedly in absolutely everything. The will of one is the will of the other. What Mary wills, Christ accomplishes. What Christ accomplishes, Mary wills. There cannot be even the least disagreement between the two. Christ is the perfect King. Mary is the perfect Queen. For example, we cannot say there is any disagreement between Christ's justice and Mary's mercy. For even though Christ is most just, He is never lacking in mercy. Neither the King nor the Queen of this Kingdom is ever lacking in either mercy or justice.

But abstracting from this perfect harmony of mind and will between Christ and Mary, does Mary participate *formally* as lawgiver, as judge, as executive in the government of Christ's Kingdom?

The answer to the question whether Mary as Queen participates in the *legislative* function of Christ's Kingdom is to be found in the analysis of the unique nature of this Kingdom. It is a Kingdom that is primarily spiritual. The ultimate goal of the Kingdom is eternal salvation. Whatever is conducive to that end must be regarded as a means to the end. Hence the law in this spiritual kingdom is grace primarily, precepts only secondarily. It is grace that prompts the subjects of this Kingdom to conform to the Ruler's will. St. Thomas expressed it this way: "Now, that which is preponderant in the law of the New Testament and on which its whole efficacy is based is the grace of the Holy Spirit, which is given to those who believe in Christ" (Ia-IIae, q. 106, a. 1). Hence the

---

[231] *A.A.S.,* Vol. 17, 1925, p. 599.

governing of the Kingdom of Christ is carried out primarily by the distribution of grace.[232]

In view of this unique manner in which the legislative power of Christ is exercised, it can readily be understood that Mary does participate in it. Since the law of Christ's Kingdom is grace, it can be truly asserted that Mary as Queen participates directly in the legislative power of the King insofar as she participates in acquiring and in distributing that grace. This is authentically confirmed by Popes Pius X and Pius XII. In his encyclical *Ad diem illum* Pope Pius X speaks of Mary's relation to grace in this way: "... Since she (Mary) was chosen by Christ to be His associate in the work of human salvation, she merits for us congruously, as they say, what Christ merited for us condignly, and she is the principal minister of the graces to be distributed."[233]

In his address to the pilgrims at Fatima Pope Pius XII stated: "for having been associated with the King of Martyrs in the ineffable work of human Redemption as Mother and cooperatrix, she remains forever associated with Him by an almost unlimited power, in the distribution of graces which flow from the Redemption."[234]

Hence, since the law in the Kingdom of Christ is primarily grace, and since Mary participates in the procuring of that grace for individuals, it follows logically that Mary participates in the legislative power of Christ.

In the Kingdom of Christ precepts are secondary and subsidiary to grace. They exist for the sake of grace, either to prepare the way for grace, or to insure the permanence of grace.[235] Because of this, we may conclude that Mary participates also in these secondary functions of Christ's legislative authority, whether it be as teacher (*magistra*) or simply as mediatrix.[236] Concerning this secondary function of Christ's legislative authority it may be further observed: "Mary helped to enlighten the Apostles and continues to enlighten us (concerning the

---

[232] Cf. Thomas U. Mullaney, O.P., *Queen of Mercy*, in *The American Ecclesiastical Review*, Vol. 126, June, 1952, p. 418.

[233] English translation by Unger, *Mary Mediatrix...*, pp. 9-10.

[234] *A.A.S.*, Vol. 38, 1946, p. 266.

[235] *Ibid.*, Vol. 17, 1925, p. 595 f.

[236] Cf. L. de Gruyter, *op. cit.*, p. 160; Mullaney, *art. cit.*, pp. 117-122.

teaching of the New Law) when, for instance, she manifests herself exteriorly in sanctuaries such as Lourdes, La Salette, and Fátima."[237]

To what extent Mary participates also in the judicial and executive functions of Christ's government is not so easily determined. Some theologians deny that Mary has any part in the royal judicial and executive power.[238] They claim that there is simply no basis for it in either Scripture or Tradition, since Mary is usually called Queen of Mercy.[239] Other theologians[240] have no objection to Mary's participation in Christ's judicial and executive power, in an analogous manner, or indirectly, through consent and prayer. Further discussions on these points must bear in mind the following principles: (1) Christ the King must always retain *supreme* judicial and executive powers. There may not be two Judges with the same or equal powers in this Kingdom. (2) Mary must retain her characteristics as a true Queen. She may not become a miniature King. (3) The Kingdom of which Christ is King and Mary is Queen must be recognized as having a government *par excellence*. Genuinely temporal kings and queens have, and exercise, royal power in an imperfect manner. Temporal power enjoyed by kings and queens of this world is only an imperfect reflection of the excellence of the royal dignity of Christ and Mary. (4) The law of this Kingdom is grace primarily, precepts only secondarily.

CONCLUSION

In view of these principles it seems legitimate to conclude that in some way Mary does partake of Christ's judicial and executive powers. Because of her status as Queen (which must be preserved) she cannot be formally a judge or executive. However, by her very power of intercession with the King, her influence must be genuine in every function of the King. This power could be called indirect or analogous. Since Mary really co-operated in Christ's work of Redemption, and since she is now the dispenser of all grace, her queenly influence necessarily

---

[237] Garrigou-Lagrange, *op. cit.*, p. 273.

[238] Luis, *op. cit.*, pp. 123-127; Carroll, *art. cit.*, pp. 30-32.

[239] Garrigou-Lagrange, *op. cit.*, p. 273.

[240] Roschini, *Mariologia*, Vol. 2, pars prima (Romae, 1947), p. 426.

(even though indirectly) has its effect on the manner in which the law (of grace) of this Kingdom is applied and is fruitful. Hence, Mary's complete power as Queen is based on her co-operation in the acquisition of grace, and on her role as dispenser of all grace. And it is in this capacity that her influence is felt in all the activities of the government of this Kingdom. In this manner we can understand why Mary is traditionally invoked as "Queen of Mercy."

APPENDIX

This chapter was already in the hands of the Editor when the Holy Father issued the new encyclical *Ad caeli Reginam* (October 11, 1954), establishing a liturgical feast to honor Our Blessed Lady as Universal Queen. This papal document, which satisfies an old and ardent desire on the part of the faithful, brings to a fitting climax the many previous utterances of the Holy Father bearing on this consoling truth. The official text of the encyclical appears in the *A.A.S.*, Vol. 46, 1954, pp. 625-640, and an English translation has already been made available through the N.C.W.C. services. Besides the general introduction and the closing exhortation, the Apostolic Letter is divided into three main sections: (I) The traditional basis for the Queenship (the testimony of the Fathers and of the various liturgies); (II) The theological reasons in support of the doctrine (divine Maternity and Coredemption); (III) The nature of the prerogative (Mary's unique primacy and her powerful intercession). The day selected for the new feast is May 31 of each year, and the Holy Father urges all to renew on that day their total consecration to Mary's Immaculate Heart. Cf. G. M. Roschini *Breve commento all'enciclica "Ad caeli Reginam,"* in *Marianum*, Vol. 16, 1954, pp. 409-432. The same issue of *Marianum* (pp. 481-507) has an interesting article by E. Lamirande, O.M.I., on *The Universal Queenship of Mary and her Maternity*.

The official text of the Office and Mass for the new feast was approved by the Sacred Congregation of Rites on May 31, 1955, and appears in the *A.A.S.*, Vol. 47, 1955, pp. 470-480. We shall summarize here the contents of both, the references being to that particular issue of the *Acta*.

DIVINE OFFICE

A marked characteristic of the Office is the association of Mary the Queen with Christ the King. This is particularly noticeable in the versicles and responses. Note the following:

I. Vespers and I Nocturn: V. Hail, Queen of mercy.
R. From whom Christ our King was born.[241]

II Nocturn: V. Near the cross of Jesus stood His Mother.
R. An associate in suffering, the Queen of the world.[242]

III Nocturn: V. All generations shall call me blessed.
R. Because he who is mighty has done great things for me.[243]

Lauds and II Vespers: V. The Virgin Mary ascended into the heavens.
R. She reigns with Christ forever.[244]

In the small hours the identical expressions are utilized as the short responses and as versicles and responses. It may be observed also that the responses at the end of the lessons of the nocturns repeat the theme of association and dependence of the Queen upon the King.

The *invitatorium* of Matins, also in keeping with this theme, is as follows: "Come, let us adore Christ the King who crowned his Mother."[245]

It is interesting to note not only the association but also the dependence of Mary the Queen upon Christ the King. Throughout the Office it is clearly expressed or supposed that Christ is the source and reason for Mary's royal dignity.

As far as Sacred Scripture is concerned, Ecclesiasticus 24:5, 7 is used as the *Capitulum* of both Vespers, Lauds, and Tierce: "I came out of the mouth of the most High, the firstborn before all creatures: I dwelt in the

---

[241] *A.A.S.*, Vol. 47, 1955, p. 470 f.
[242] *Ibid.*, p. 472.
[243] *Ibid.*, p. 474.
[244] *Ibid.*, pp. 475, 478.
[245] *Ibid.*, p. 470.

highest places, and my throne is in a pillar of a cloud."[246]

Sections of the same twenty-fourth chapter of Ecclesiasticus are used also for the three lessons of the first nocturn.

A number of the responses following the lessons of the three nocturns are significant scriptural phrases used in connection with time-honored royal titles of Mary. For example, after the first lesson of the first nocturn there is the following tribute to Mary:

> R. Blessed are you, O Mary, who hast believed the Lord: the things that have been spoken to you have been accomplished. Behold you have been raised above the choirs of angels to the heavenly sovereignty.
> V. Hail Mary, full of grace, the Lord is with thee.[247]

After the fourth lesson we find the following:

> R. Receive the word, O Virgin Mary, which has been delivered to you by the Lord: Behold you will conceive and bring forth Him who is God as well as Man.
> V. And you will be called Queen over all nations.[248]

Following the sixth lesson there is the well-known passage of Apocalypse 12:1:

> R. And a great sign appeared in heaven: a woman clothed with the sun, and the moon was under her feet, and upon her head a crown of twelve stars.
> V. Whose Son reigns forever.[249]

The fourth and fifth lessons are taken from a well-known work of St. Peter Canisius: *De Maria Deipara Virgine incomparabili*.

The sixth lesson is a quotation from the encyclical *Ad caeli Reginam* on Mary's Queenship.[250]

The lessons of the third nocturn are introduced by the Annunciation text of St. Luke (1:26-33), and are taken from St. Bonaventure's sermon

---

[246] *Ibid.*, pp. 470, 475, 478.
[247] *Ibid.*, p. 471.
[248] *Ibid.*, p. 473.
[249] *Ibid.*, p. 474.
[250] *Ibid.*, p. 472 f.

on the royal dignity of the Blessed Virgin Mary. The theme of this homily is expressed in the leading statement: "The Blessed Virgin Mary is the Mother of the most high King through the noble conception, according to the word spoken to her by the angel: 'Behold you will conceive. ...' "[251]

MASS

The Mass of the feast repeats the theme of the Office and besides puts an emphasis on the beneficial effect of Mary's royal status. This is expressed especially in the Oration, Secrets, and Postcommunion prayers. The Offertory and Communion prayers likewise stress Mary's beneficial ministration as Queen. Thus, the Offertory prayer tells us: "Mary is resplendent through her descent from the royal line; in mind and spirit we most faithfully request to be helped by her prayers."[252]

The Communion prayer says: "Most worthy Queen of the world, Mary, perpetual Virgin, intercede for our peace and salvation, you who have brought forth Christ the Lord, the Savior of all."[253]

The Epistle of the Mass is taken from Ecclesiasticus 24:5-7, 9-11, 30-31.

The Gospel is taken from the Annunciation text of Luke 1:26-33. The final words of this text are as follows:

> Do not be afraid, Mary, for thou hast found grace with God. And behold, thou shalt conceive in thy womb and shalt bring forth a son: and thou shalt call his name Jesus. He shall be great, and shall be called the Son of the Most High; and the Lord God will give him the throne of David his father, and he shall be king over the house of Jacob forever; and of his kingdom there shall be no end.[254]

Since the "Sacred Liturgy is a faultless mirror of doctrine,"[255] the new feast in honor of Mary our Queen should teach the faithful not only the truth of Mary's royal dignity, but also the way to Christ the King.

---

[251] *Ibid.*, p. 474.
[252] *Ibid.*, p. 479.
[253] *Ibid.*, p. 479.
[254] *Ibid.*, p. 479.
[255] *A.A.S.*, Vol. 46, 1954, p. 631.

Mary and the Church

by CYRIL VOLLERT, S.J., S.T.D.

N MARIOLOGY, as in all theology, success achieved in the development of one question fosters progress in other questions that are closely connected with it. In this way the definition of the Blessed Virgin's Assumption, pledge of the glorification of the Church which it prefigures, has promoted interest and understanding about the relations uniting the mystery of Mary and the mystery of the Church. At the present time, theological attention is concentrating more and more on these relations.

The problem is far from a definitive solution. Tradition has been intensively examined, but hoped-for results have not been fully realized. From the first centuries of the Christian era the Fathers did, indeed, contemplate similarities existing between Mary and the Church;[1] their thought can be summarized in a few propositions. The Virgin Mary is the Mother of Christ; the Church is also a virgin and our mother; Mary is the mother of all the faithful; Mary is the ideal model of the Church. Reflections of the Fathers about these topics are deeply influenced by their perception of the close likeness which both Mary and the Church have with Eve, mother of all the living. A convenient compendium of early tradition on the relations between Mary and the Church is exhibited in the conclusion that Mary is the type and mother of the Church.[2]

Although the parallelism between Mary and the Church was soon apprehended, it was not a prominent theme of the patristic era and was never the object of a synthesis. The interest of the Fathers was centered on the economy of salvation, which is inaugurated in Christ's Mother and is carried out in the Church. In this connection, they have much

---

[1] Cf. O. Semmelroth, S J., *Urbild der Kirche* (Würzburg, 1950), pp. 25-36; H. Rahner, S.J., *Maria und die Kirche* (Innsbruck, 1951); A. Müller, *Ecclesia-Maria. Die Einheit Marias und der Kirche* (Freiburg in der Schweiz, 1951).

[2] Thus I. Vodopivec, B. *V. Maria typus et mater ecclesiae*, in *Alma Socia Christi*, Vol. II, 1953, pp. 269, 272.

more to say about the Church than about Mary.[3]

After the famous definition pronounced by the Council of Ephesus, interest in the relations between Mary and the Church waned and turned to the divine maternity, which has continued to dominate Mariology to our own day. Some of the writers and doctors of the Middle Ages cultivated the parallelism, repeated the teaching of the Fathers, developed old analogies, discerned some new ones, and sought to unify the doctrine under the concept of the mystical body. The Blessed Virgin is presented as image and type of the Church, its most eminent member, and its loving mother.[4] Many medieval authors have nothing whatever to say about the relations between Mary and the Church, and those who do consider the question assign much more importance to other aspects of Marian theology. The notion that the Mother of God is the prototype of the Church is far from prominent in medieval Mariology; in fact, the study of relations between Mary and the Church was never, at that epoch, a major preoccupation.[5] Subsequent to Albert the Great, the parallel between Mary and the Church was almost completely neglected.

Our own age has returned to the subject. Scheeben initiated the movement, although at first he had few followers. The past thirty years have produced many rich studies, both positive and speculative.[6] Resurgence of interest in the question has its explanation in the progress that has been made in Mariology and ecclesiology. Declarations of the magisterium have imparted new vigor for research and have stimulated further advance. In Mariology, the definitions of the Immaculate Conception and the Assumption have focused attention on the principles of Marian theology, illustrated the correct methods to employ, and thrown light on Mary's functions in the economy of salvation. In

---

[3] Y. M. J. Congar, *Marie et l'Église dans la pensée patristique*, in *Revue des Sciences Philosophiques et Théologiques*, Vol. 38, 1954, pp. 5, 22.

[4] The best of the medieval studies is that of H. Barré, C.S.Sp., *Marie et l'Église du vénérable Bède à saint Albert le Grand*, in *Bulletin de la Société Française d'Études Mariales*, Vol. 11, 1951, pp. 59-143. This series will hereafter be referred to as *BSFEM*.

[5] *Ibid.*, p. 125.

[6] Vodopivec, *art. cit.*, p. 256, note 4, gives a good skeletal bibliography. Cf. also the excellent *Bibliographie critique sur Marie et l'Église*, prepared by R. Laurentin, in *BSFEM*, Vol. 9, 1951, pp. 145-152. Other studies will be mentioned in the course of the present chapter.

ecclesiology, the dogmatic constitutions of the Vatican Council on the Church of Christ and the encyclical of Pius XII on the mystical body have provided similar incentives. The ecclesiological movement has sought clarification from the Blessed Virgin's place in the divine plan, while Mariology has more accurately ascertained her position and offices in the Church. Such studies have increased our knowledge of the mutual relations between Mary and the Church, and have furnished insights into the importance and activity of each in God's design for our eternal welfare.

Progress in dogmatic and theological development is not rapid. Yet there is a forward march. Our own century has witnessed the culmination of slow ascent in the case of the Assumption; a similar phenomenon is observable in the Coredemption question. In the investigation of the parallel between Mary and the Church, the moderate success thus far obtained need cause no astonishment; we are dealing here not with a dogma, but with a theological idea, a comparison rich in power to aid in the construction of valuable syntheses and to exhibit new facets of ancient problems.

The inquiry into the relations between Mary and the Church has become one of the dominant concerns of current Mariology. It is drawing more closely together the two treatises notably developed in modern times, ecclesiology and Mariology. Both Mary and the Church are mothers of men; they should be united. If we wish to penetrate more deeply into the mystery of Mary, we must contemplate it in its connections with other basic mysteries, especially those of the Blessed Trinity, Christ, and the Church. The parallel between Mary and the Church is not a secondary theme that is situated merely on the periphery of Catholic teaching; it is necessary for comprehending the redemptive Incarnation. Although the comparison was a minor object of patristic and scholastic thought, it is a part of the reserves of Christian wealth, and we of today are beholding its entrance into theology.

Before a comparative study of Mary and the Church can be undertaken, a preliminary question must be settled; we must define the terms of the comparison, Mary and the Church. In speaking of the Blessed Virgin, the risk of equivocation is slight; but the notion of the Church is complex and admits of diverse senses. Therefore we must determine the precise sense of the word, and this sense must remain constant throughout.

Ordinarily, when we speak of the Church, we invest it with a personality of its own. Though it is a society composed of individuals, we think of it as an organism that lives its own life. As such, it can be understood in two ways; the name "Church" may designate the totality made up of Christ the head and all the members that are joined to the head; or it may designate only the body that is united to Christ the head.[7] The second sense emphasizes the distinction between the person of the Saviour and the persons who have been saved by Him and respond to His love. Clearly, Mary is comparable to the Church understood in the second sense, as designating the body that is united to Christ the head.

Sacred Scripture presents the Church, as thus distinct from Christ, under various images and figures. St. Peter calls the Church "a holy nation, a purchased people" and "the people of God" (*1 Pet.* 2:9 f.). Hence the Church is the new people of God, the new Israel, in continuity with the ancient Israel but surpassing it. This new people of God is the posterity of Abraham, not according to the flesh, but according to the spirit; the true descendants of the father of believers are the followers of Christ, who is the seed of Abraham (*Gal.* 3:16, 29). Mary is comparable to the Church regarded as the new people of God, for she is the ideal personification of the Church and the perfect realization of what God wishes to accomplish with the coming of His Son.

The Christian community is the people of God in Christ the head, whose life circulates in it. From the idea of the people of God united to Christ, we pass naturally to the concept of the Church as the body of Christ. Under this figure, the Blessed Virgin is the first and most important member of the body, the one closest to the head, surpassing the rest in excellence and eminence, because her position as Mother and associate of the Saviour is superior to that of all the other members.

A third symbol, the image of conjugal union between Christ and His Church, eliminates the danger of misunderstanding our connection with Christ. The title "spouse of Christ" reminds us that, notwithstanding our insertion into Christ the head, we retain our separate personalities and

---

[7] Thus S. Thomas, *In IV Sent.*, dist. 49, q. 4, a. 3 ad 4.

our individual consciences. The Church, bride of Christ, preserves an attitude of submission, receptivity, and love toward Him. Under this figure, which emphasizes the distinction between Christ and the Church, the Blessed Virgin is again the first member, in whom the union of the redeemed with the Redeemer reaches a perfection unattainable by anyone else.

Accordingly, in comparing Mary with the Church, we are considering the Church as the mystical body of Christ and the spouse of Christ, an extension of the image under which the prophets designated the chosen people in anticipation of the Church. These figures are complemented by another one, likewise ancient, that depicts the Church as the mother of the faithful.

In pondering the relationship between Mary and the Church, we are not thinking of the Church in a wide sense, as including those who have been saved before the advent of Christ in virtue of their faith in the coming Redeemer. We mean rather the community of the baptized that was founded by Christ, the Catholic Church on earth and in its culmination in heaven. As is evident, to carry out the comparison, we must set the Blessed Virgin apart from the rest of the Church. That is, the Church is here understood, not as a whole composed of Mary and all other Christians, but only as that part of the Church which is made up of the latter. The comparison is between two parts of the same whole, the Blessed Virgin on one side and all the rest of the members on the other.

I. FOUNDATION OF THE ANALOGY

Development of the parallel between Mary and the Church, a theme that is capable of contributing clarification to Mariology, is in the domain of speculative theology. The structure must rest on a solid foundation, which has its deepest base in the designs of God for man's salvation.

A. Mary and the Church in the Divine Plan

The key to the mystery is offered by St. Thomas: "It belongs to the essence of goodness to communicate itself to others.... Hence it pertains to the supreme Good to communicate Himself to creatures *summo modo*, in the highest possible manner."[8] The world created by God adds nothing whatever to Him and profits Him not at all. We can assign no reason for God's creative activity other than the inclination of the Supreme Good to communicate Himself. Creation is the beginning of His self-communication. Participation in God's goodness, reflection and representation of the divine perfections, are the aim of all creatures. Since no individual thing can be a sufficient image of the infinite Good, a universe of beings, a hierarchy with the spirit world at its summit, was called into existence.[9]

God can give Himself in a more perfect way than by producing feeble vestiges of Himself. He can make Himself known and loved by admitting intellectual beings into a supernatural participation of His own nature and His own acts of knowledge and love. In this case, besides mere resemblance, there is union between Creator and creature. Such union leaves the created person at an infinite distance from the Creator. But God has the power to give Himself wholly, to associate a created nature substantially in His own existence, to be one with such a nature by communicating Himself *summo modo*.

This is what God has done by becoming incarnate. He has communicated Himself *summo modo* to a created nature issuing from the Virgin Mary. But His intention in thus communicating Himself envisioned the universe. Through the one created nature assumed by the divine Word in hypostatic union, all other beings are offered a participation in divinity. In particular, all men are summoned to receive from Jesus Christ a share in the divine nature.

The Church, in the eternal plan, is the prolongation of Christ; it is His body, in which every member has a definite place, an individual way of resembling the God-man, a spiritual vocation and a supernatural activity. Complete self-communication would be lacking, if the power of action were not conferred. Christ makes His members His co-operators, by granting them the redemptive energy of charity and the ability to merit, pray, and act for mankind's salvation. Human nature is social; and the grace of Christ that is given to human nature is social. The community of the redeemed is socially organized into a body that is the

---

[8] *Summa theol.*, IIIa, q. 1, a. 1.
[9] *Ibid.*, Ia, q. 47, a. 1.

complement of Christ and His fullness. The multitude of persons composing it form a unity, which the Son of God has taken to Himself and espoused.

In the divine plan Mary has a place and function analogous, though vastly superior, to those of the Church. The Second Person of the Trinity became incarnate, not in a nature created for this purpose, but in the womb of the Blessed Virgin. Her union with the Word is not hypostatic, as is the union between the assumed human nature and the Son of God; it is a union of person with person, the intimate relationship of motherhood. God utilized the woman in the Incarnation, not because He needed an instrument, but rather because He wished to exploit to the utmost, *summo modo*, the possibilities of union with the Incarnate Word which the maternal powers of woman presented to Him.[10]

Christ admits all His members to a share in His activity. To His Mother He gave a greater and a higher power of acting than to any other member. As she participated in the hypostatic union at the very instant of the Incarnation, so she co-operated with her Son at the very moment of the Redemption.

Thus the theology of the Blessed Virgin is closely connected with the theology of the Church. The underlying principle is the same in both cases: God's intention to communicate Himself supernaturally to the world, in a self-communication that enables mankind to collaborate with Him for its own salvation.

B. RELATION OF MARY AND THE CHURCH TO CHRIST

In Sacred Scripture, tradition, and the liturgy, the Church is often personified in feminine imagery. This femininity characterizes the relationship which St. Paul, following the lead of the Old Testament, discerned between Christ and mankind. Femininity is receptivity of being; it is an attribute that well describes the creature in its sincerest attitude toward the Creator. The receptivity that is common to every creature is especially typified by woman in relation to man, who is the head of the woman as Christ is the head of man (*Eph.* 5:23). Quite naturally, then, the creature who is loved by God appears under the

---

[10] M. J. Nicolas, O.P., *Marie et l'Église dans le plan divin*, in BSFEM, Vol. 11, 1953, p. 165.

symbol of woman. Any particular creature is too imperfect to be, by itself alone, the well-beloved spouse of God. Only the universe of creatures, by the concert of their many complementary perfections, can suitably be called an image of God; and only mankind in its entirety can be regarded adequately as the spouse of Christ.

The fullness of grace, which overflows to the Church, abounds in the soul of Christ, head of the Church and supreme principle in the order of grace, of whose plenitude all receive. Therefore the Church is completely dependent on the Incarnate Word.

Mary's relationship to Christ essentially transcends that of the Church. She is not an ordinary member who simply participates, even in a uniquely privileged way, in the common relationship which all the other members have with Christ. She is united to the Incarnate Word in a way that is exclusive to her and that surpasses the relations which the rest of the Church has with Christ by grace. Her personality and her life are dominated by her divine maternity; every grace that is given to her is gauged by her state as Mother of God, and is not imparted to her through the agency of the Church. Her relations with Christ are defined by her divine motherhood which, in the order of the divine decrees, is prior to the establishment of the economy of grace and the founding of the Church.

Yet Mary is related to the Church through the relations which both she and the Church have with Christ. The kinship between Christ and Mary is comparable with the kinship between the Church and Christ's members. Mary is the Mother of Christ, and the Church, through grace, generates Christ in the souls of the baptized; as Mary cared for and nourished the infant Christ, so the Church cares for, nourishes, and cherishes Christ in souls. Mary is the new Eve, and the Church also is the new Eve; each is mother of all the supernaturally living. Furthermore, because of the mystic oneness of the Church with Christ, Mary's relationship with the physical Christ is extended to His members; the mother of the head is also the mother of the body. The underlying cause of the likeness is the fact that the Church, along with its head, is the mystic Christ, according to the Saviour's own words: "I am Jesus whom thou persecutest" (*Acts* 9:5). Consequently, the Mother's relationship to her Son necessarily flows over to the Church. Christ stands in the middle between them, uniting both. Thus all comparison between the two terms arises from the relationship of each term to Christ: Mary is the Mother of Christ, the Church is the body of Christ and indeed is the mystic Christ Himself.

C. Mary Considered Apart From The Church

Although Mary is a member of the Church, she may be considered apart from the Church. First of all, she is prior to the Church. Because of her, Christ was never without His Church; in her, who belongs to the era of Christ's grace and of explicit faith in Him, the Church was a concrete person before it was a mystical person or an organized institution.

Her predestination, too, differs from that of all other persons. Like all the others, she was redeemed. The grace that was given to her came from the foreseen merits of Him who was to be her Son. But she was redeemed quite otherwise than the rest of men; she was preserved from contracting the sin of nature. She was redeemed apart, and therefore placed apart. Her fullness of grace, which grew in her all her life, was not dependent on the Church, but has its explanation in her divine maternity, its rule and measure. Thus she constitutes an order apart, so that she alone can enter into comparison with the rest of the Church. This fact makes possible an analogy between her, a particular person, and the collectivity which is the Church.

The Blessed Virgin's association with the Church in the divine plan draws them together, yet at the same time shows how unique Mary's situation is in the universe. The bond linking her to Christ is unattainable by other Christians. However, although all supernatural graces have in her their most eminent perfection, the hierarchical and sacramental powers that essentially constitute the Church were never conferred on her. Hence the Church adds something to Mary. The divine maternity is greater than all the functions and offices exercised by the Church, but is radically different from them. Among the countless members of the Church, therefore, the Blessed Virgin can be considered apart from all the others, and then be compared with them.

Ultimately, the foundation of the parallelism between Mary and the Church is perceived in the Incarnation, which is God's effort to communicate Himself to all mankind. Except for the hypostatic union, this communication reaches its highest point in the Blessed Virgin, Mother of God. Her divine maternity, with all the consequences that flow from it, places her apart, so that she alone is comparable and superior to all the rest of the Church. Yet the Church, too, has closest ties of relationship with the Incarnate Word; through Him, Mary and the Church are related to each other. What the Church is collectively, Mary is first individually.[11]

II. THE ANALOGY PRESENTED

In the problem about Mary and the Church, the inquiry concerns the relations, similarities, and analogies discoverable between both, along with the mutual influences they exert. The comparison is between Mary and all the rest of the Church. Understood in this way, Mary and the Church can be brought together for study, and analogies between them can be perceived. From early times, in fact, Mary, Mother and Virgin, has been likened to the Church, mother and virgin. Such resemblances, however, involve great and essential differences, which must not be overlooked. Thus Mary is the Mother of the divine Word, whom she generated according to His human nature; the Church is mother, not of the divine Word, but of Christians, whom it regenerates, not according to human nature, but for participation in the divine nature. Mary is literally a virgin; the Church is a virgin in the sense that it has never adulterated the faith but has always remained true to Christ's teaching. The Church is mother of the faithful, and Mary is also mother of the faithful.

Doctrines such as these are the ancient and common patrimony of the Christian people. But they do not exhaust the possibilities of our knowledge about Mary and the Church. Further investigation can be undertaken and is being vigorously carried on, with the hope of imparting greater intelligibility to both Mariology and ecclesiology.

In tracing the parallel between Mary and the Church, a simple and at the same time systematic method may be followed. It consists in pondering one by one the main attributes, perfections, activities, and

---

[11] Cf. Nicolas, *art. cit.*, p. 169.

mysteries of the Blessed Virgin, and then inquiring whether their analogies are discernible in the Church.

A. Maternity of Mary and the Church

In the supernatural order, the Mother of Christ is also the mother of the Church and therefore our mother. The Church, too, is our mother. What are the meaning and value of this twofold maternity? That is the initial problem confronting us. The present inquiry proposes to put in order and synthesize the data acquired from Scripture and tradition, with the aim of bringing out several conclusions. In particular, does any conclusion derived from this twofold maternity possess any power to promote clarification of the relations between Mary and the Church?

1. The Divine Motherhood

Mary is the true Mother of the divine Word. She brought Him forth into the world, and sustained Him in His vocation up to the sacrifice of His life for the redemption of mankind. The divine maternity is absolutely unique; only the Incarnation could make it possible. The assertion that Mary is the Mother of God involves no metaphor; she is God's Mother in the same sense as other women are mothers of their children, by literal generation. No application of the term, Mother of Christ, can be made except in reference to her. Hence her maternity offers to Mariology an unshakable and sharply delineated substructure. The theology of the Blessed Virgin could not but suffer if it lost sight of this unique point of departure, or if attempts were made to construct it on other, less stable foundations. Intelligibility in the study of Mariology comes ultimately from it, and we must start with it if we wish to illuminate all other aspects of her position in the plan of salvation and to clarify her function in the career of her Son and in the Church.

2. Mary, Mother of the Church

Tradition exhibits the relationship between Mary and the Church in various ways. According to St. Augustine, "Mary is a part of the Church, a holy member, an excellent member, the most eminent member, but still a member of the whole body."[12] St. Ambrose asserts that she is "a type of the Church."[13] St. Bernard saw the Blessed Virgin as intermediary between Christ and the Church: "Mary is placed between Christ and the Church."[14] Titles of this kind express some aspects of Mary's relationship to the Church. Of them all, which is the most basic, central, illuminating? A few modern authors, such as O. Semmelroth and A. Müller, select the view that Mary is the prototype of the Church. But this idea is not primary, and is not wholly valid, since Mary is not the prototype of the ecclesiastical hierarchy which is essential to the Church. None of the formulas proposed completely satisfies the Catholic mind; they all fail to explain why Mary is the foundation or model of the Church, or why she stands between Christ and the Church. The truth that is most securely anchored in the sources of revelation and most clearly defines the relations between Mary and the Church is the simple fact stated by Leo XIII, that the Blessed Virgin is the mother of the Church.[15]

Mary had been prepared for the divine maternity by her Immaculate Conception and all the graces flowing from it. When the angel announced God's proposal, Mary offered to God her free acquiescence and in return received the Son of God into her womb. In consequence of her consent to be the Mother of the Messias, she entered into a relationship with all the subjects of the messianic King. Mary became the Mother of Christ; beyond that, her maternity extended to the entire Christian populace, to the whole Church founded by Jesus Christ.

That the Blessed Virgin is mother of the head and body, hence of the Church, is completely certain from tradition, and no Catholic would think otherwise. The only question is how and in what way Mary is mother of the Church: is she our mother only morally or juridically, or in some deeper, more ontologically real sense?

The moral and juridical maternity is clear; Mary embraces all the faithful with motherly love and helps them from heaven with her

---

[12] *Sermo 25 de verbis evangelii Matth.*, 12, 41-50, in *PL*, 46, 938.

[13] *In Lucam*, 2, 7, in *PL*, 15, 1555.

[14] *In dom. infra oct. Assumpt.*, 5, in *PL*, 183, 432.

[15] Encycl. *Adiutricem populi*, in *A.S.S.*, Vol. 28, 1895-1896, p. 130: "verissime quidem mater Ecclesiae."

prayers. But tradition asserts more than this. She is our mother because she generates us, causing in us a real origin of supernatural life. When did she give birth to us? Three main alternatives occur: the Incarnation, association in the Redemption, and heavenly intercession. The latter is an aspect of her moral maternity, and the Incarnation is only a remote origin of our supernatural life. Hence Mary's spiritual maternity depends mostly on her coredemptive activity. The more closely she was associated in the work of redemption, cause of our regeneration and birth of the Church, the more truly she is our mother.

The Incarnation establishes a direct continuity between Mary and the Church, for the faithful are the body of Christ, who is generated and formed in them. By consenting to become the Mother of Jesus, Mary had also to take under her maternal charge His mystical body. The birth of the Redeemer from a daughter of our race inaugurated solidarity between Him and all mankind. From the moment of the Incarnation, Christ contained in mysterious fashion all the members of the mystical body He came to redeem. Mary gave Him the power to make our nature His own; in her and from her virginal flesh Christ took to Himself the humanity that constitutes Him our kinsman.

Therefore the womb of Mary is the womb of the Church. Such is the authoritative doctrine of St. Pius X:

> In one and the same womb of His most chaste Mother, Christ took to Himself human flesh and at the same time added to it a spiritual body made up of all those who were to believe in Him. Therefore Mary, while carrying the Savior in her womb, may be said to have carried likewise all those whose life was contained in the Savior's life. All of us, consequently, who are united to Christ ... have come forth from Mary's womb, like a body attached to its head.[16]

As the Pope here teaches, we were all contained in the womb of Mary from the moment she conceived her Son; by the very fact that she became the Mother of Jesus, she also became our mother. Her spiritual maternity is rooted in the mystery of the Incarnation.

This is a true maternity. When Mary consented to the Incarnation, she represented all mankind and spoke in the name of the whole human

---

[16] Encycl. *Ad diem illum*, in *A.S.S.*, Vol. 36, 1903-1904, p. 452 f.

race.[17] When she conceived Christ, she spiritually conceived all the faithful. Because she is mother of Christ the head, she is mother of the whole body. This is not a mere moral maternity, but is a supernatural reality, for Christ's members form one mystical person with the individual Christ, Son of Mary,[18] a situation which has no counterpart in the relationship between a natural society and its founder. Accordingly, the Incarnation establishes a vital union between us and Christ, and consequently between Mary and the Church.

The maternity which thus has its inception in the Incarnation is the ontological reason why Mary's co-operation with the Redeemer on Calvary could be elevated by God to a true generation of members of the mystical body. Although she was already the mother of the faithful because she was mother of Christ, she did not become our mother in the fullest sense except from the moment when she was present on Calvary. At that solemn hour Jesus made her the mother of John, type of all the disciples whom Christ and His Father love. At a stroke, her maternity acquired a new dimension. United to her Son in the sacrifice, she received from Him her maternal mission with regard to the Christian community. This is the proper understanding of the words, "Woman, behold thy son." For the Beloved Disciple represented all those who, like him, lovingly adhere to the Saviour.[19] From then on, Mary is fully mother of the whole Church. Briefly, the Blessed Virgin spiritually conceived the Body of Christ along with the head at the conception of Jesus and, as associate of the Redeemer, gave birth to it under the cross when the Church itself was born.

Thus, on the basis of her divine maternity, Mary is the spiritual mother of the Church; her spiritual maternity is the prolongation of her maternity over Christ. The two maternities are analogous, for her

---

[17] Cf. St. Thomas, *Summa theol.*, IIIa, q. 30, a. 1: "Per annuntiationem expectabatur consensus Virginis loco totius humanae naturae."

[18] Pius XII, Encycl. *Mystici Corporis*, in *A.A.S.*, Vol. 35, 1943, p. 226: "The divine Redeemer and the society which is His body form a single mystical person, that is, in Augustine's words, the whole Christ."

[19] F. M. Braun, O.P., *La Mère des fidèles* (Paris, 1953), pp. 113, 181. Cf. Leo XIII, Encycl. *Adiutricem populi*, in *A.S.S.*, Vol. 28, 1895-1896, p. 130: "In John, as the Church has always perceived, Christ designated the person of the human race, especially of those who would cleave to Him by faith."

spiritual maternity refers, not to the God-man, but to His members, and is not according to the flesh but is exercised on a higher, more spiritual level.

To perceive the relations between Mary and the Church in their proper perspective, we must always come back to the basic idea that she is the mother of the Church.[20] Maternal foundation of the Church, she is the very womb of the mystical body.

3. The Church, Mother of Christians

The Blessed Virgin is our mother, for her maternity with respect to Christ is continued in her relations toward the Church. Yet the Church, too, is our mother, for from her we receive our supernatural life and education. This maternity, exercised by the Church, is founded on the divine maternity of Mary. The expression "Mother of Christ" has no meaning apart from the Incarnation of the Son of God in Mary. But the Incarnation is prolonged in the Church, for grace is a participation in the divine life that is fully possessed by Christ in His humanity. Therefore, to be born to the life of grace is to be born to the life of Christ.

Consequently, every Christian who receives sanctifying grace gives birth to Christ in himself; he becomes the "mother of Christ" in a limited sense, that is, with reference to the mystical body of Christ. Jesus Himself said: "Whosoever shall do the will of God, he is my brother and my sister and mother" (*Mk.* 3:35; cf. *Mt.* 12:50). No paternal title is here mentioned; the reason is that the soul which gives birth to Christ in itself acts in complete dependence on the initiative of the eternal Father, and so contributes a cooperation that bears some resemblance to the feminine role of mother.

Furthermore, if birth to the life of grace is a new birth of Christ, everyone who collaborates in the birth of Christ in others is also a "mother of Christ." St. Paul told the Galatians that he was suffering the pains of childbirth until Christ would be formed in them (*Gal.* 4:19). The same idea is applied by St. Augustine to all who bring about the birth of

---

[20] F. M. Braun, O.P., *Marie et l'Église, d'après l'Écriture,* in *BSFEM,* Vol. 10, 1952, p. 7.

Christ in others.[21] With much greater reason the maternal function attributed to anyone who collaborates in the work of salvation is attributed to the Church itself, the very organism of salvation; in a more profound sense than any individual, the Church is Christ's mother. "The mother of Christ is the whole Church, because by God's grace it gives birth to His members, that is, His faithful."[22]

Christ's own words, "Whosoever shall do the will of God, he is my brother and my sister and mother," guard us against an erroneous understanding of this maternity. The three titles of brother, sister, and mother cannot be taken in their proper sense. Literal motherhood is excluded; the three terms are metaphors, expressing the close union existing between Jesus and those who carry out His Father's will. Such persons have sanctifying grace and consequently share in Christ's sonship; they become united to Him by a tie that resembles the union between brothers and sisters. And since their birth to the life of grace is not brought about without their own free co-operation, each of them acquires a kind of maternal relationship to Him.

Thus the title, brother or sister of Christ, must be understood in an analogical sense: as brothers and sisters are related in a particular way because of their reception of life from the same parents, so Christ and we have the same life of grace, and we are all children of the same Father. As for the term, mother of Christ, it is verified literally in Mary; when applied to us, it is only a metaphor indicating a certain likeness between our collaboration with God and maternal collaboration; it is not a true exercise of the functions of motherhood. And the Church itself, in its entirety, is the mother of Jesus in the sense that in it and through it God continues to give His Son to the world by forming for Him a body, the mystical body of Christ.[23]

Therefore Mary's motherhood with regard to Christ incomparably transcends the metaphorical maternity that is ascribed to each of the

---

[21] *De sancta virginitate*, 5, in *PL*, 40, 399: "Mater eius est omnis anima pia faciens voluntatem Patris eius fecundissima caritate in iis quos parturit, donec in eis ipse formetur."

[22] *Ibid.*; cf. *Serm. 192*, 2, in *PL*, 38, 1012: "Caput vestrum peperit Maria, vos ecclesia."

[23] On this point see J. Lécuyer, C.S.Sp., *Marie et l'Église comme Mère et Épouse du Christ*, in BSFEM, Vol. 10, 1952, p. 33 f.

faithful and to the Church. Alois Müller's theory that the two maternities occupy the same ontological level and that Mary is literally the mother of Christ only because she, unlike us, possesses grace in plenitude, is completely inadmissible.[24] According to this opinion, grace of itself requires divine maternity, conformably with the text from Mark quoted above; hence Mary's maternity is an effect of her fullness of grace. If this line of reasoning were correct, we should also have to conclude that Mary is literally the sister of Christ, which is indeed nonsense. The argument from analogy requires a delicate touch in theology, especially when the question concerns metaphor rather than proper analogy. In the present case, the maternity of the Church does not clarify the Incarnation or Mary's maternity; in fact, it is not even intelligible except in dependence on the maternity exercised by the Blessed Virgin. We can be regarded as Christ's brothers and sisters only in the sense that we are admitted by grace into the divine life that is fully possessed by Him in the sacred humanity He derived from Mary; and we do our part to bring about His birth in ourselves and others, thus imitating Mary's maternity in a remote fashion and on an essentially lower level, only in the sense that we freely collaborate in the reception of His grace. But Mary's grace was not the cause of her maternity; it was the cause of the faith and love which produced in her the disposition that enabled the power of the Holy Spirit to act on her for the conception of Christ. Hence her maternity, far from being a privileged instance of the maternity common to all believers, is forever first and unique and belongs to a totally different order.[25]

When we compare Mary's spiritual maternity with that of the Church, we easily perceive that the former is the nobler and is the

---

[24] For an exposition of Müller's ideas, consult his articles, Um die Grundlagen der Mariologie, in Divus Thomas (Freiburg), Vol. 29, 1951, pp. 389 f., 393-401; L'unité de l'Église et de la Sainte Vierge chez les Pères des IVe et Ve siècles, in BSFEM, Vol. 9, 1951, p. 36 f.

[25] Cf. Lécuyer, art. cit., p. 34. Müller's speculative development goes far beyond the patristic evidence he gathered in his book, Ecclesia-Maria, and owes more to Scheeben than to the Fathers. Among the many criticisms and correctives of his notions about the maternity of Mary and the Church, see H. Lennerz, S.J., Maria-Ecclesia, in Gregorianum, Vol. 35, 1954, pp. 91-94, and Y. M. J. Congar, Marie et l'Église dans la pensée patristique, in Revue des Sciences Philosophiques et Théologiques, Vol. 38, 1954, pp. 31-35.

source of the latter. Mary's maternity acts and is actuated in the maternity of the Church. But these two mothers do not have two separate families or give birth to different children; they exist in the same Christian family; they have the same sons and daughters whom they cherish with a common love. The same kind of maternity is realized in Mary and the Church; yet the first is the foundation of the second.[26] One never operates without the other. Mary's maternity brings forth the whole body of Christ, the Church, which is also the mother of Christ's members; for Mary, by Christ's will, gave birth to the Church, so that it too might be the mother of Christians.[27]

The maternity of the Church, which receives its power of generating from the Blessed Virgin in subordination to Christ,[28] visibly and strikingly manifests Mary's maternity. Both maternities coalesce into a single, continual communication of life to the faithful, so that they are two aspects or functions of one spiritual maternity rather than two adequately distinct maternities. As Christ is socially prolonged in His mystical body, so Mary's maternity is prolonged in the Church.

The Church is our mother mainly as minister of the sacraments, without which no supernatural life is given. Mary is our mother because grace, without which the sacraments do not cause life in us, is deposited in the treasury of the Church through her co-operation in Christ's redeeming sacrifice. Mary's spiritual maternity more directly influences the internal, spiritual nature of the Church, but thereby also reaches the social, hierarchical structure of the body. For, as St. Augustine points out, the Blessed Virgin co-operated by charity, not by authority, that Christ's members might be born.[29] Authority belongs to Christ, who committed it to the apostles and their successors. But the hierarchy continually receives supernatural power from the source of the Cross, whose saving grace Christ confers on the Church through His Mother.

---

[26] Cf. Congar, *art. cit.*, p. 37.

[27] I. Vodopivec, *B. V. Maria typus et mater ecclesiae*, in *Alma Socia Christi*, Vol. 11, 1953, p. 290 f.

[28] See below, section F, 2, on the coredemptive activity of Mary and the Church.

[29] *De sancta virginitate*, 6, in *PL*, 40, 399: "[Maria est] plane mater membrorum eius, quod nos sumus, quia cooperata est caritate ut fideles in ecclesia nascerentur."

B. The Spouse of Christ

Occasionally in past centuries, and more frequently in recent times, the title "Spouse of Christ" has been applied both to Mary and to the Church. What is the meaning of this appellation, and what value does it have for throwing light on the relations between Mary and the Church?

The notion of God's espousals with His people is very ancient, and Christian usage of the idea owes much to the Old Testament, in which it is a favorite theme. God's alliance with Israel is likened to the matrimonial bond that unites man and woman and that requires an unswerving fidelity from both parties. If the chosen race is unfaithful to God and slips into idolatry, it commits adultery.[30] Thus the vocation of the people of Israel has a feminine trait. God chose the race of Abraham, formed it into a nation, and took it to Himself as His spouse.

But the chosen race of the Old Covenant prefigures the chosen race of the New Testament. God wishes to take all mankind into His love. The true spouse is not Israel according to the flesh, but the spiritual posterity of Abraham, the Church.

This transition involves an important change, resulting from the unique event that ushered in the new era. God became man in Christ, the Word was made flesh. Since human nature and divine nature are united in Him, we may speak of the espousals of humanity and divinity on the day of the Incarnation. And since the Church is His body, we are led to the further metaphor that the Church is His bride. This union is the great mystery or sacrament: "They shall be two in one flesh" (*Eph.* 5:31); St. Paul adds expressly that he is referring to Christ and the Church.

Transfer of this metaphor from the Church, regarded collectively as a moral person, to each individual belonging to the society, is quite justified. Titles that are proper to the Church, such as spouse or temple of God, can be attributed to every member of the body. For Christ loves each member of His body and calls each of them to be His bride.

If every member of the Church can be called the spouse of Christ because of the love to which each soul is invited to respond, can the

---

[30] The main texts are given by C. Dillenschneider, *Le mystère de la corédemption mariale* (Paris, 1951), pp. 111-114.

same title be applied to Mary? Of all the members of the Church, she is the one most richly endowed with divine grace, the one most closely united in love to Christ, the one who has most perfectly responded to God's advances. Although she is the Mother of Christ, her maternity differs from that of other mothers in this respect, that her Son is a preexisting Person who chose her and asked her consent, somewhat as a man asks a woman to become his bride.

Yet the tradition of the Church is unfavorable to this suggestion. Nowhere in Sacred Scripture do we read that Mary is the bride of the Lamb or the spouse of the Word.[31] The Fathers, too, are silent on the subject. Although they established between Eve and Mary a relation analogous to that which St. Paul discerns between Adam and Christ, they know nothing of the bridal relationship exploited by some contemporary Mariologists, implying that Mary is to Christ what Eve is to Adam. For the Fathers, the new Eve associated with the new Adam *as His spouse* is not Mary, but the Church.[32] They never join the two expressions, Mother of God and spouse of the Word; the spouse is not the Blessed Virgin, but human nature assumed in Mary's womb.

To tell the truth, the idea that the Blessed Virgin is the spouse of Christ hardly occurs prior to the Middle Ages. St. Ephraem has a hymn in which he calls Mary "Thy mother, Thy sister, Thy spouse, Thy handmaiden"; but the condition of the text is not good and the meaning is not clear. In the eighth century, an obscure passage of a sermon by Pseudo-Augustine refers to Mary as "bride of Christ." Apparently Rupert of Deutz, that "untidy thinker," is the chief innovator in this matter, and passed his fancy on to French divines of the seventeenth century and to Scheeben two centuries later.[33]

Clearly, the voice of tradition is far from decisive and is by no means loud concerning the notion of bride or spouse of Christ as applicable to the Blessed Virgin. Other souls are readily regarded as "spouses of

---

[31] F. M. Braun, O.P., *Marie et l'Église, d'après l'Écriture,* in *BSFEM,* Vol. 10, 1952, p. 15.

[32] Y. M. J. Congar, *Marie et l'Église dans la pensée patristique,* in *Revue des Sciences Philosophiques et Théologiques,* Vol. 38, 1954, p. 3; in footnote 1, Congar gives a number of examples typical of patristic teaching.

[33] See the excellent review of the sparse evidence by J. H. Crehan, S.J., *Maria Paredros,* in *Theological Studies,* Vol. 16, 1955, pp. 414-423.

Christ"; but when we come to Mary we sense a certain reluctance and even embarrassment. In any case, the idea of "spouse of Christ" as attributed to Mary is but a facet of her maternity: she is mother of a preexisting person, the Word, who received from her His human nature. Her association with her Son in the work of redemption, source of our supernatural life, may be symbolized by calling her "spouse of the Word." This metaphor, difficult to understand and apply, adds nothing to the maternity of Mary and merely stresses one of its aspects.

An earlier and more trustworthy tradition represents the Incarnation as the nuptials between the Son of God and the human nature He assumed. Although the Fathers have no idea of a bridal relationship between Christ and Mary, they observe that the virginal womb of the Mother is the *thalamus* or bridal chamber in which the mystery of the nuptial union between divinity and humanity was accomplished. This theme is quite universal in patristic times.[34] Hence the Blessed Virgin is personally implicated in this mystic marriage, for the Word sought her free consent to the union and, as soon as it was given, formed a body for Himself from her flesh. Her place in the mystery has been signalized by St. Thomas in a celebrated passage that has influenced all subsequent thinking on the subject. One of the reasons he assigns for the message brought to Mary by the angel is "that there might be made known a sort of spiritual marriage between the Son of God and human nature. At the Annunciation, therefore, the consent of the Virgin was awaited in place of that of the whole human race."[35] Thus the Incarnation is like a marriage between divinity and humanity. But the humanity that is thereby joined to the Word embraces, in addition to the individual nature hypostatically united to Him, the whole of human nature that is mystically included in it, that is, the body of Christ, the Church.

Mary, however, did not contract the matrimonial union on her own behalf. She acted as a representative or proxy. "The true bride of Christ, the Church, was not yet of age at the date of the Annunciation and therefore someone had to act for her. God's prevision had provided such

---

[34] St. Augustine has many passages on the subject, e.g., *Enarr. in psalmos*, 90, in *PL*, 37, 1163: "Verbum sponsus, caro sponsa, et thalamus uterus virginis."

[35] *Summa theol.*, IIIa, q. 30, a. 1. Leo XIII quotes this passage several times in his encyclicals on the Rosary, and Pius XII uses it in the epilogue of Mystici Corporis Christi.

a proxy."[36] Mary herself is not the spouse; she represents the spouse, that is, the Church, whose consent is expressed by her *fiat*. "The eternal Son of God, when He wished to take man's nature to Himself and so contract a mystical marriage with the whole human race, did not do so before obtaining the perfectly free consent of the one chosen to be His Mother, who thus acted in the person of the human race itself."[37]

The bridal idea is, indeed, prominent in tradition. But it is applicable to Mary only in the sense that she was the representative of mankind at the moment of the Incarnation. In accepting the espousals of Christ with human nature, Mary personified the Church, bride of the Word Incarnate. She is the perfect realization of the Church, for all our acts of consent to God's proposals depend on her consent; by willing the Incarnation, Mary willed the entire Redemption, and also all our good acts of willing, all our responses to the grace of her Son.[38] As later on Calvary, the Church was present in Mary at the Incarnation, and has as its ideal model her lifelong attitude of acceptance, which was always that of a faithful spouse of Christ.

Moreover, because Mary's Son is God, the relationship between her and Christ goes much deeper than in other maternities. Her Son is a preexisting Person who, unlike other sons, could ask of His Mother her free consent, and could conclude with her an engagement for a common enterprise. From this point of view, the Blessed Virgin's maternity has traits of resemblance with the union which a woman agrees to contract with a man in marriage.

Her consent to become the Mother of the Redeemer was her personal way of responding to God's love and will concerning her. The union with God and the alliance of love to which the divine Spouse invites every soul, were fulfilled in her more perfectly than in any other creature. Since her answer to the invitation of divine love was given with a generosity that tolerated no reserves, she is the ideal of all responses made by faithful souls to God's proposals. Accordingly, she is

---

[36] J. H. Crehan, S.J., *Maria Paredros*, in *Theological Studies*, Vol. 16, 1955, p. 421.

[37] Leo XIII, Encycl. *Octobri mense*, in *A.S.S.*, Vol. 24, 1891-1892, p. 195. Immediately after these words, the Pope quotes the passage from St. Thomas, mentioned above.

[38] Cf. J. Lécuyer, C.S.Sp., *Marie et l'Église comme Mere et Épouse du Christ*, in BSFEM, Vol. 10, 1952, p. 29.

the flawless model of every person who surrenders to God and requites His love with a love which Scripture likens to the love of a bride toward her husband. In this respect, the bridal metaphors of the Old Testament are applied to her more fittingly than to anyone else;[39] but that is true because of her divine maternity, for by her *fiat* Mary consented to be the Redeemer's Mother.

The metaphor of spouse, rich in content though it may be, discloses only a partial aspect of Mary's vocation. Penetration of its meaning leads inevitably to her divine maternity. With reference to the Blessed Virgin, the term "spouse" is always equivocal and cannot correctly describe the union of Jesus with His Mother.

The relationship between this Son and this Mother is much stronger and more comprehensive than the relationship between spouses, although it contains all the perfection found in the union of a man and a woman who are linked in the same destiny. Mary is Christ's Mother associated with Him in His redemptive mission, and verifies eminently, but transcendently, all that the biblical imagery of spouse conveys.[40] Hence Mary is not aptly called the spouse of the Incarnate Word; she is His Mother and she is likewise the mother of His mystical body which is the Church, spouse of Christ. Maternal union and bridal union are here expressed; the first exists between Christ and Mary, the second between Christ and the Church. The two categories should not be intermingled.

Whatever is significant in the metaphor of spouse in connection with Mary, is not an attribute added to her maternity but is a perfection of her maternity. The Blessed Virgin is the *Socia Christi* and the Church is the *Sponsa Christi.* Although the two ideas ought to be kept distinct, they are very close and, through Christ, draw Mary and the Church closer to each other.

C. The New Eve

Some modern Mariologists endeavor to plumb a relationship between the Blessed Virgin and her Son that is expressed by the formula:

---

[39] *Ibid.,* p. 36.

[40] F. M. Braun, O.P., *Marie et l'Église, d'après l'Écriture,* in *BSFEM,* Vol. 10, 1952, p. 16.

what Eve is to Adam, Mary is to Christ. This is a relationship of bride to bridegroom, and would make Mary the spouse of Christ. Neither Sacred Scripture nor the Fathers know anything about such a parallel. Yet both Scripture and the Fathers recognize between Eve and Mary a relationship analogous to that which St. Paul establishes between Adam and Christ: as Christ is the new Adam, Mary is the new Eve. On the other hand, the Church is also celebrated as the new Eve. Can this line of thought contribute to the clarification of our knowledge about the connections between Mary and the Church?

Adam is the type of the One who was to come (*Rom.* 5:14), and the latter is identified in the same context as well as in 1 Corinthians, Chapter 15. He is Jesus Christ, the *novissimus Adam*. Although the Apostle does not speak of a new Eve, he places at the side of the new Adam a female figure, the Church that submits and unites herself to Christ in love; this is His spouse and our mother (*Eph.* 5:22-32). Here the idea of the new Eve is at least foreshadowed, if not implicitly indicated. Does the Bible also suggest that Mary is the new Eve? The prophecy of Simeon associates the Saviour and His Mother together is a way that recalls the woman and her seed in Genesis 3:15. Several passages in the Gospel according to St. John point to the same parallel.[41] In the opinion of good exegetes, the words uttered by Christ on the cross, "Woman, behold thy son," contain an illusion to the woman of Genesis.

Scholarly examination of the Apocalypse, Chapter 12, has demonstrated that the woman in that exalted passage is Mary.[42] Many proofs are brought forward to show this, such as the fact that the woman in question is the Mother of the Messias. One of the arguments is particularly pertinent here; it consists in a comparison between Apocalypse 12 and Genesis 3:15. In both texts the encounter of the woman with the adversary is emphasized, and in both the woman is mentioned first. The adversary-dragon is identified with the adversary-serpent of Genesis. Both passages identify the dragon's opponent as the offspring of the woman. In Genesis the offspring gains the final victory

---

[41] Cf. A. M. Dubarle, O.P., *Les fondements bibliques du titre marial de nouvelle Ève*, in Recherches de Science Religieuse, Vol. 39, 1951, pp. 49-64.

[42] For example, see the excellent work by B. J. Le Frois, S.V.D., *The Woman Clothed with the Sun* (Rome, 1954), especially the evidence presented, pp. 38-47.

over the serpent; the same is true in the Apocalypse, but with a clarification: the victory of the collective offspring is won by reason of the individual, the Lamb. The same closed unit of woman and offspring is discerned in both texts. "So many and such close points of contact between Ap. 12 and Gen. 3, 15 point to the same actors in the scene. Since the woman in Gen. 3, 15 is Mary, the mother of the Messias, so also here in Ap. 12."[43] And because the woman in Genesis is she who is known as the new Eve, the woman in the Apocalypse is likewise the new Eve.

Furthermore, although the woman of the Apocalypse designates a definite person, the Blessed Virgin, this person embodies in herself a collectivity. "Just as the male Child represents at the same time the historical Christ and the mystical Christ ... so the Woman signifies, first, the personal Mother of Jesus, and then the People of God, as realized in the Church."[44] Under the figure of the woman in the Apocalypse, St. John portrays Mary as the Church; the individual personifies a collectivity, and the collectivity is embodied in a concrete person. The great task of the Virgin-Mother is perpetuated in the gigantic task imposed on the Church, the regeneration of all mankind in Christ.[45] Consequently, as Mary is the new Eve, the Church is likewise the new Eve.

Under this aspect of the new Eve, Mary and the Church are identified with each other. The two unite in their opposition to the ancient serpent. Yet Mary and the Church are not the new Eve in the same way. Mary is the new Eve because Christ, her issue, crushes the head of the serpent, and hence because she is the Mother of Christ. The maternal function with which she is charged makes her, after victory over Satan has been won, the "mother of all the living," as Eve is (*Gen.* 3:20); these are "the rest of her seed, who keep the commandments of God and have the testimony of Jesus Christ" (*Apoc.* 12:17). The Church, on the contrary, is called the new Eve because it is the spouse of Christ

---

[43] *Ibid.*, p. 222.
[44] F. M. Braun, *La Mère des fidèles*, p. 143.
[45] B. J. Le Frois, *op. cit.*, p. 262.

(*Eph.* 5:31 f.), prefigured by the spouse of the first Adam.[46]

The theme of the new Eve is developed by the Fathers in their reflections on the idea of recapitulation (*recirculatio, recircumlatio*) that is so prominent in St. Irenaeus.[47] God's plan had been clear from the very outset: a man and a woman, Adam and Eve, were to transmit to all mankind a life of union with God. Restoration of the plan so tragically compromised soon after its inception was to be made by another man and another woman. The man is Jesus Christ, the new Adam. A woman had to have her place in the restoration, for the feminine sex was meant to co-operate in the Redemption. From an early period that was in continuity with the apostolic age, the Fathers recognized this woman. The new Eve is Mary and the Church.

Evil and death had been introduced into the world by the woman, in consequence of her gross disobedience. It was necessary that a woman should reintroduce life by obedience and faith. This woman, the second Eve, is the Church, divinely formed from the side of the second Adam sleeping the sleep of death on the cross, as the first Eve had been formed from the side of the slumbering Adam. Like the first Eve, wife of Adam, the second Eve is the bride of Christ, and hence mother of all the living.

But the new Eve as a definite woman, as the virgin repairing by her obedience what the first Eve had ruined by her disobedience, is Mary. This teaching is found in most of the Fathers, with the exception of those who do not think of Mary in this connection and apply the idea only to the Church. However, Mary is the new Eve, not because she is the spouse of the new Adam, but because she is the Mother of Christ and, in Him, of regenerated mankind. Thus St. Irenaeus, like his predecessor, St. Justin, and his imitator, Tertullian, compares Eve, virgin and spouse of Adam, to Mary, virgin and spouse of Joseph. The former was disobedient to God and so was the cause of death; the latter was obedient to God and so became the cause of salvation. But she caused

---

[46] Cf. C. Sträter, S.J., *Marie, Mère de l'Église, in* Ephemerides Mariologicae, Vol. 4, 1954, p. 442.

[47] For a summary of patristic teaching on the second Eve, see N. F. Moholy, O.F.M., *Saint Irenaeus: The Father of Mariology,* in *Studia Mariana*, Vol. 7: First Franciscan National Marian Congress in Acclamation of the Dogma of the Assumption, 1950 (Burlington, Wisconsin, 1952), pp. 151-172; W. J. Burghardt, S.J., *Mary in Western Patristic Thought,* in Mariology, ed. J. B. Carol, Vol. 1, pp. 110-117.

the regeneration of humanity by generating her Son.[48] Accordingly, the principle of *recirculatio* from Eve to Mary is based on the Blessed Virgin's divine maternity.

Not only the Church, therefore, but also Mary is celebrated in tradition as the new Eve, mother of all who live the new life brought by Christ.

Later ages made a further application. If Mary is mother of all the living, she is associated with her Son in His work of Redemption. The consent which she freely gave at the Annunciation to be the Mother of Christ and which was necessary for carrying out the recapitulation, was enlivened anew at the Crucifixion and was fully conscious of the mystery that was taking place. By co-operating in the redeeming sacrifice, she is the new Eve in a heightened sense, source of our life, mother of the body as she is mother of the head.

Thus the comparison between Eve and Mary leads to the idea of "mother of the Church." If the Blessed Virgin is mother of the body, she is mother of the Church which is Christ's body. It leads further to the concept of Mary's coredemptive function; for if she is truly mother, she had a part in the true birth of the Church that occurred on the cross. Indeed, in the growing conviction of theologians, the most important aspect of the spiritual maternity is that which took place on Calvary.

The parallel between Eve and Mary, which was studied early in Christian thought, has proved attractive to contemporary theology. As Eve contributed to our ruin, Mary and the Church co-operate for our redemption; the affinity between the mystery of Mary and the mystery of the Church is very close. Some authors go so far as to make the idea of Mary as new Eve and type of the Church the basic principle of Mariology. The proposal is quite untenable, because the title of "new Eve" is dependent on and included in the divine maternity. Mary is the new Eve because she is the mother of the Redeemer.[49]

Virginity of Mary and the Church

From ancient times Mary, mother and virgin, has been likened to the

---

[48] St. Irenaeus, *Adversus haereses*, 3, 22, 4; 4, 33, 4, in *PG*, 7, 959, 1074 f.

[49] See the Chapter, *The Fundamental Principle of Mariology*, sect. II, A. 2, in the present volume.

Church, which is also mother and virgin. This comparison involves great differences, which must not be disregarded. Mary is the Mother of Jesus Christ; the Church is the mother of Christians who are "other Christs." Mary is literally a virgin; the Church is a virgin in the sense that it has never adulterated the faith but has always been true to Christ's doctrine. Maternity and virginity are literal for Mary, but analogous and metaphorical for the Church.

In Judaeo-Christian writings, a virgin is a person or a community that is given to God and remains faithful to Him. Sexual connotations are nonexistent or unimportant. In the Old Testament, the matrimonial union with God, a common theme, consecrates and guarantees virginity and at the same time makes it maternally fruitful, so long as Israel does not abandon its divine Bridegroom for false gods. Virginity in this connection means fidelity; heresy and apostasy are a kind of adultery that destroys virginity.[50] Faith and nuptial fidelity are linked together; infidelity is disruptive of both. Union with God shelters virginity and hallows it by enriching it with a fecundity that is free from all corruption. Its fruit is an imperishable life of which the Holy Spirit is the transcendent cause.

Therefore the Church, spouse of Christ, is a virgin. "Christ is the Bridegroom, the Church is His bride: spouse in her love, a virgin in her integrity," as long as she does not let herself be seduced by committing adultery against truth; for "adulterers are all they who seek to adulterate the truth of faith and wisdom."[51] As applied to the Church, the notion of virginity is always linked to the purity of faith. The very maternity of the Church is virginal because, pure in faith and virginally undefiled by any heresy, she brings forth the children of God by the action of the Holy Spirit, without the intervention of any unchaste agent.

When the bibical idea of virginity refers to persons, it implies, indeed, bodily integrity, especially as a sign of spiritual fidelity, total consecration to God, and permanent union with Him. Mary, Mother of God and Virgin of virgins, is the ideal of virginity in every respect. Her divine maternity is entirely according to God, by reason of her

---

[50] Cf. G. Philips, *Perspectives mariologiques: Marie et l'Église*, in *Marianum*, Vol. 15, 1953, p. 455.

[51] St. Ambrose, *Expositio Evangelii sec. Lucam*, 8, 9, in C.S.E.L., Vol. 32.4, p. 395.

incorruptible reception of the Word in the complete yielding of faith. She conceived and bore her Son with unimpaired virginity, through the action of the Holy Spirit, to the exclusion of all power of this world. Her spiritual maternity, too, is wholly virginal; Christ is the Bridegroom of the Church, drawing it from the spiritual womb of Mary by the activity of His Spirit, and no influence of any impure causality has anything to do with the existence or life of the Church. Like Christ, the members of His body, which is the Church, are born of Mary as children of God solely by the power of the Holy Spirit.[52]

The virginity of the Church helps us to understand the virginity of Mary. The Church is not only one flesh, but one spirit, with Christ: "He who is joined to the Lord is one spirit" (*1 Cor.* 6:17). Though real, the union is spiritual and mystical. We should think of the virginity of the Blessed Virgin in the same way; it is not only the absence of carnal association with any man, but is also the absolutely spiritual and mystical union of her soul with God that preceded the actual Incarnation.

By the perfection of its virginity, therefore, the Church draws very near to the virginal Mother of God.

E. HOLINESS OF MARY AND THE CHURCH

As the virginity of the Church aids us to arrive at a deeper appreciation of Mary's virginity, so Mary's holiness assists us to understand better the holiness of the Church. The holiness of Mary is essentially the same as the holiness of the Church; it is a sanctity that comes from the same God, leads back to the same God, and is the formal effect of the same grace. The main difference lies in the respective receptivity of Mary and the Church.[53] Human liberty is a power of reception, but also of refusal. No refusal or even reluctance ever marred Mary's attitude of acceptance toward God's advances; but the Church is a collectivity made up of men and women who have never completely held their souls open to God's boundless generosity.

---

[52] Cf. C. Sträter, S.J., Marie, *Mère de l'Église*, in *Ephemerides Mariologicae*, Vol. 4, 1954, p. 443.

[53] R. Laurentin, *Sainteté de Marie et de l'Église*, in *BSFEM*, Vol. 11, 1953, p. 11. The first ten pages of this article present a good discussion of the notion of sanctity.

Like us, Mary was redeemed. All the graces given to her are owing to the foreseen merits of her Son's charity and His sacrifice on the cross. But unlike us, she never contracted the sin of nature from which the rest of men have to be liberated. The fullness of grace with which she was endowed surpasses the totality of the grace ever given or to be given to all mankind and the angels. Her grace recapitulates the whole order of grace, which achieves its highest perfection in her, for it was conferred on her by reason of her divine maternity.

All men are called to holiness in a collective vocation, that is, in the society which is known as the Church. This society is holier than the sum of the individuals composing it, for the individuals are united to the God-man, the divine head who divinizes the Church. Christ's Spirit, the Holy Spirit, dwells in the Church, which thus possesses within itself a divine principle of holiness.

The Church is holy because it has received from God means of holiness in great profusion, faith and the sacraments which are vitalized by Christ its head and by the Holy Spirit who animates it as its soul. These means of grace infallibly produce holiness in the members of the body. The Church, to be sure, is not without sinners; but it is without sins. The defects and faults which result from the weakness of the members, and of which the Church always disapproves, do not stain the Church; for the Church is *ex maculatis immaculata*.[54] "The mystic spouse of Christ has never been contaminated in the course of the centuries, nor can it ever be contaminated."[55] The fragility and infirmity of the members can never be attributed to the Church itself.[56] However, although the Church is completely holy and unsullied by stain, its members are subject to many defects and sins that interfere with and hamper the diffusion of its holiness.

Comparison between the holiness of Mary and the holiness of the Church discloses the differences that separate the two and brings out the superiority of Mary's sanctity over that of the Church. The Blessed Virgin's fullness of grace is measured by the deeper capacity for grace which God opened in her and by her higher destiny. Mary was called to

---

[54] St. Ambrose, *Expositio Evangelii sec. Lucam*, 1, 17, in C.S.E.L., Vol. 32.4, p. 21.

[55] Pius XI, Encycl. *Mortalium animos*, in *A.A.S.*, Vol. 20, 1928, p. 14.

[56] Pius XII, Encycl. *Mystici Corporis Christi*, in *A.A.S.*, Vol. 35, 1943, p. 225.

be literally the Mother of the Saviour; the Church is called to be metaphorically His spouse. Hence Mary was summoned to share in the mysteries of Christ's life; the Church begins its career with Christ's death. Mary was given the office of co-operating in the mysteries of the Incarnation and Redemption; the Church is limited to the task of dispensing the graces of these mysteries. Corresponding to the Blessed Virgin's incomparable vocation is a holiness that vastly surpasses the holiness of the Church.

Mary's entire life and each of her actions were always and undeviatingly directed toward God. No obstacle, no inordinate love of creatures, no weariness, hesitancy, or tepidity, ever slowed down the flight of her soul. But in the Church the flowering of grace varies according to persons, times, and places. Its ascent toward God is paralyzed by the infirmities of its members, so that the Church always remains below the level of holiness which the power of grace is able to bestow. Although the Church itself cannot be defiled, yet it is composed of sinful members, who must constantly purify themselves, do penance, and be converted. In Mary there is no sin, hence no room for purification; her holiness is beyond the virtue of penance. Reform and conversion have no place in her.

The cause of salutary activity in Mary and the Church is the same Holy Spirit and the same grace of Christ. But Mary's receptivity is incomparably more perfect; it erects no barrier, admits no reserve, sets no limits to the power of grace. All the resources of her mind and will and heart were fully responsive to God's initiative. The other members of the Church offer to grace a receptivity that is shrunk by sin and the results of sin. This contrast in receptivity deeply affects the beginning, the progress, and the consummation of the holiness of Mary and the Church.[57]

The beginning of Mary's existence is her Immaculate Conception. She was redeemed from sin by way of preservation, in prevision of Christ's sacrifice. Her Immaculate Conception forever kept all concupiscence away from her. The Church, born from the side of the Saviour on the cross, also begins by a spiritual conception that is stainless; yet it is formed of members who all (except Mary) contract

---

[57] See R. Laurentin, *Sainteté de Marie et de l'Église*, in *BSFEM*, Vol. 11, 1953, p. 23 f.

original sin. Consequently, although the members of the Church are purified from all guilt when they emerge from the regenerating waters of baptism, they are burdened with the grievous weight of concupiscence, which opposes and slows down the growth of grace.

Mary's progress in sanctity was constant, rapid, and uninterrupted. She mounted from holiness to holiness, always full of grace because each grace increased the capacity of her soul for further grace that promptly filled it to repletion, bearing her aloft, the perfect Mother of God, to the height of Calvary, there in the agonizing struggle to be the perfect associate of the Redeemer. The grace of the Church also grows, aspiring to the full measure of the stature of Christ (*Eph.* 4:13), and time is doled out to us on earth to permit this growth. But the Church is an assembly of sinners and penitents; in its members it must unceasingly reform itself, repent, and be converted anew. Its progress is menaced by the collectivity's sluggish response to grace.

Sanctity flowers into glory and resurrection. Glory is the refulgence of holiness, and the resurrection is its final triumph. The Church still awaits this consummation. Here below, the Church plods along in the order of earthly holiness, with all its humiliating setbacks; in heaven, it has not yet reached the glory of the resurrection, that incorruptibility and luminous splendor of body which is the ultimate radiation of holiness. But Mary is now in glory; prior to the Church, she was taken up to heaven, body and soul. She has realized in her personal destiny what the Church has yet to realize in its collective destiny. Yet her Assumption, coming at the climax of her last fullness of grace, prefigures and anticipates the assumption of the Church.

Thus the Blessed Virgin, who excels the Church by reason of her Immaculate Conception and outstrips it through her unimpeded progress in sanctity, also precedes it in the glorious triumph of her holiness. Like Mary, however, the Church is totally holy in the measure of its own capacity. Christ is all-holy and without sin; she whom the Father chose to be the Mother of His Son is completely holy; and the Church is the bride whom Christ has taken to Himself with Mary's collaboration, the spouse whom Christ sanctified by His death that she might be without spot or stain, holy and immaculate (*Eph.* 5:25-27). Both Mary and the Church are endowed with the fullness of grace, though in different degree. Both are holy because of their relation to the Saviour; the holiness of Mary is that of the Mother of Christ, the holiness of the Church is that of the spouse.

F. COREDEMPTIVE MISSION OF MARY AND THE CHURCH

The renewal of biblical and patristic studies, combined with a more adequate comprehension of ecclesiology, has led theologians during these latter years to desire a clearer perception of the part providentially assigned to the Blessed Virgin and the Church in the economy of salvation. Mary's maternal relation to the person of Christ has occupied the attention of theologians for many centuries; today their efforts are concentrated on her relation to her Son's work.

Investigation of the contributions made by Mary and the Church to man's redemption is not new. The study has a history, and in that history three phases are discernible.[58] The first period begins with St. Irenaeus and runs on for a thousand years. It produced no more than vague gleams of insight, seeds for future growth. Yet these rough outlines of doctrine concerning Mary's share in the Redemption were sketched against the background of the Church. Mary's faith at the time of the Incarnation, inception of Christ's redemptive life, was contrasted with Eve's infidelity at the time of the Fall, and was set in parallel with the faith of the Church.[59]

During the second period, from the twelfth to the end of the nineteenth century, the Blessed Virgin's co-operation in the sacrifice of the Cross was recognized more and more distinctly. However, as views about the Coredemption took firm shape, the connection between Mary and the Church was gradually obscured. The seventeenth century, which is so important for the development of ideas on the Coredemption, is also the century in which the ties linking Mary and the Church became so tenuous as almost to fall apart.

Scheeben inaugurates the third period, which comes to a climax in our own decade. Of the two forms the modern enterprise takes, one is

---

[58] R. Laurentin, *Rôle de Marie et de l'Église dans l'oeuvre salvifique du Christ*, in BSFEM, Vol. 10, 1952, p. 44 f.

[59] For some pertinent texts, see H. Holstein, S.J., *Marie et l'Église chez les Pères anténicéens*, in *BSFEM*, Vol. 9, 1951, pp. 13-19.

a reaction that has gone to excess. In opposition to an exaggerated assimilation of Mary to Christ, it advocates an exaggerated assimilation of Mary to the Church, depressing her co-operation in salvation to the level of the co-operation furnished by the Church. Our Lady's contribution has been reduced to pure receptivity; the Mother of the Saviour has been denied a productive collaboration in the redeeming work of her Son.

1. Theories of Receptive Coredemption

The impetus to the contemporary effort along this line was supplied by H. M. Köster.[60] Controversy on the coredemptive problem had revolved around two positions, the thesis that Mary cooperated productively in objective Redemption, and the antithesis that such co-operation undermines the transcendence of Christ, sole efficient cause of Redemption. Köster puts forward a synthesis: Mary did, indeed, co-operate actively in objective Redemption, but not by way of efficient-productive causality. Her co-operation was limited to receptivity; in the name of all mankind she accepted Redemption.

In reaction against an excessive likening of the Blessed Virgin to Christ, Köster argues that salvation is accomplished in an alliance or covenant which supposes two subjects or poles, God and man. God gives salvation, man receives it. Christ, the unique mediator, offers the grace of Redemption; the human race must accept it. Such reception is the function of the Church, and also of Mary, acting as the responsible representative of mankind. Since Christ is not a human person, He cannot receive and confirm the treaty of Redemption in the name of men. Christ is, indeed, the mediator between God and men; but only in His divinity, according to Köster. Although He is the absolute summit of humanity, He lacks a human personality and has no need of salvation; therefore, He cannot express mankind's solidarity, co-operation, and acceptance of God's gift. Someone is still required to represent the

---

[60] Of Köster's publications on the subject, the most important are *Die Magd des Herrn* (Limburg an der Lahn, 1947), and *Unus mediator, Gedanken zur marianischen Frage* (Limburg, 1950). The first proposes the new theory, the second undertakes to defend it against criticisms. In a second edition of his *Die Magd des Herrn* (1954) the author re-elaborates his thesis and again endeavors to answer his many adversaries.

human race in this attitude; some summit in the order of human persons having the need of salvation has to ratify the alliance in which salvation objectively consists. The desired summit is found in Mary, who thus is assigned a "free place" in the economy of Redemption that does not encroach on the place reserved for Christ. As a human person, Mary fills a lacuna which Christ's divine personality had to leave open. Mary is the only one who can give the response exacted of collective mankind. Hence Christ alone is the active principle of salvation; His Mother's office, like that of the Church, is purely receptive. The consent to salvation which each individual must pronounce in the order of subjective Redemption, Mary pronounces for us all in the order of objective Redemption. As Christ is wholly turned toward the Father, Mary is wholly turned toward the Son, so that to be incorporated into Mary is to be taken up into her momentum toward Christ.

This theory finds for Mary a place different from that of Christ, and assigns to her a role in objective Redemption without attributing to her a causality that belongs exclusively to Christ, the *unus mediator*. All objections against Mary's mediation melt away. Since her co-operation is completely "receptive" and implies no productive causality in the sacrifice of Calvary, she no longer infringes on Christ's transcendence; yet she retains an unequaled position in the history of man's restoration, and has a more manifest intervention in the distribution of graces.

Defects and weaknesses inherent in Köster's proposals called for immediate criticism and led to definite rejection. The very title of the book, *Unus mediator*, demands repudiation. Christ is, in all truth, the *unus mediator;* but this mediator is *"homo* Christus Iesus" (*1 Tim.* 2:5). A mediator is one who stands between extremes to unite them; but Christ in His divinity does not stand between God and man. He is mediator as He is priest, in His *human* nature. Köster erects his edifice on a foundation that is perilously shaky; he interprets the Greek *diatheke* as a bilateral contract in the strictest sense. While the word does have this meaning, especially in the Old Testament, it means primarily a testament in the New Law. Man's co-operation is needed, not to contract a bilateral treaty with God, but to apply the fruits of Redemption to himself.

Köster develops a theory of mediation between the Son and

mankind. But the alliance is between God, that is, the Father, and mankind in the incarnate Son, "through the redemption that is in Christ Jesus, whom God hath proposed to be a propitiation through faith in His blood" (*Rom.* 3:24 f.). Christ is on the side of man; although He is not a human person, He has a true human nature, a human will, and a human love. Instead of saving Christ's transcendence, which needs no saving, the author compromises the truth of the Saviour's Incarnation by slighting His human nature, and devaluates the sufficiency of His mediation. A "free place" is found for the Blessed Virgin by removing the sacred humanity from its rightful position; to make space for Mary, the theory tends to separate Christ from the rest of men.

Furthermore, according to all tradition, "the man Christ Jesus" is the first to receive the grace which He in turn communicates to the members of His mystical body; "of His fullness we have all received," for He alone is our head. But in Köster's theory Mary is our summit and our head; she, not Christ, stands on our side to transmit to us the grace she has received. Incorporated into her, we enter into her movement toward Christ. To be consistent, we should speak of the mystical body, not of Christ, but of Mary.[61] None of this has roots in tradition or support from the Fathers. "The idea of a personal summit of fallen mankind other than Christ is diametrically opposed to their teaching on redemption."[62]

Mariologists have in general concurred in the verdict with which Dillenschneider sums up his refutation of Köster. The theory simultaneously asserts too much and too little. It assigns too much to Mary, because it makes Mary, to the detriment of Christ the head, the personal summit of mankind in need of redemption; her representative role is needed to make up for Christ's insufficiency in this regard. It also gives Mary too little, because it reduces her salvific co-operation to a mere "acceptance," made in the name of us all, of the redemptive effects caused by Christ alone.[63] Mary's whole contribution is the "reception" of salvation for herself and for mankind. The current of tradition has carried the doctrine of Mary's Coredemption far beyond this stage,

---

[61] Cf. Congar, in *Revue des Sciences Philosophiques et Théologiques*, Vol. 34, 1951, p. 628 f.

[62] C. Dillenschneider, *Le mystère de la corédemption mariale* (Paris, 1951), p. 129.

[63] *Ibid.*, p. 61. Cf. likewise, in this same volume, J. B. Carol's chapter on *Our Lady's Coredemption*, p. 411.

which leaves her standing on the level of subjective Redemption.

Hardly any theologian has accepted the full theory proposed by Köster. However, several have followed the main lines of his thought concerning Mary's part in our Redemption. In particular O. Semmelroth owes much to Köster, although he recoils from the traces of monophysitism discernible in his predecessor's works. Semmelroth insists that Christ is the summit of mankind and the representative of collective humanity.[64] Apart from such corrections, however, Semmelroth's theory is hardly more than an improvement over that of Köster. Thus he writes:

> If Christ is to offer His representative sacrifice for mankind, and if this sacrifice of the God-man is to be truly the sacrifice of mankind, He must in a certain sense be established by mankind as its representative. Mankind must take its place behind Him and make His sacrifice its own. The God-man's solidarity with mankind must be perceived not only by God the Father, who accepts His sacrifice, but also by the men for whom He offers Himself in sacrifice.[65]

Here occurs Mary's opportunity to co-operate in our restoration. Christ alone, as representative of mankind, offers the sacrifice. But Mary is there at His side, representing the acceptance of men who are to be redeemed, and pronouncing the *fiat* by which they are to appropriate to themselves the alliance with God that is wrought in Christ. The Blessed Virgin is able to discharge this function because she is the *Urbild*, the archetype of the Church. To her is attributed a "coredemption," not of the same kind as that of Christ, but the same as that of the Church, the community of redeemed men, who co-operate in their redemption by "freely accepting" it. Each person must voluntarily receive redemption for himself; but reception of redemption by the whole Church, a "living totality," was made, at the time Jesus was accomplishing His work, in the person of Mary. Thus she has a place in the order of objective Redemption. But her contribution is not productive of the Redemption; hers is a "receptive" Coredemption. According to Semmelroth's own summation of his thesis, "Mary is the type of the mediating Church in

---

[64] O. Semmelroth, S.J., *Urbild der Kirche. Organischer Aufbau des Mariengeheimnisses* (Würzburg, 1950), p. 84 f. A second edition of this work appeared in 1954.
[65] *Ibid.*, p. 84.

the sense that, by appropriating for herself the work of Christ, she receives its fruits for herself and at the same time for the whole Church."[66] She stands on the side of mankind to receive salvation, not on the side of Christ to give salvation.

This theory makes little account of the tradition of many centuries and pays slight heed to the statements of modern popes about Mary's coredemptive activity. It also overlooks the fact that Christ Himself is on the side of man as well as on the side of God; for He is mediator between God and man. He is on the side of man even considered as redeemable, for He has taken upon Himself our sins. His divine personality does not prevent Him from being the supreme expression of man and his need of Redemption. Furthermore, mankind's acceptance of salvation, which is undeniably necessary, is not an integrating factor in the concept of Redemption, but a condition of its efficacy for man, and presupposes Redemption as already accomplished. Most important of all, man's response to the Redeemer's sacrifice of Himself implies much more than mere reception of salvation; it must be a will to contribute to the reparation of sin and reunion with God. Mary's *fiat* at the foot of the cross is far more than a simple reception of salvation wrought exclusively by Christ; it is a wholehearted will to co-operate in Redemption by a love like His, a love of complete conformity to the Father's will, and an oblation. Mary on Calvary indeed represents the Church; but precisely by this active co-operation.

The theory of Mary's receptive coredemption, advocated by Köster and further developed by Semmelroth, reaches a high point in the writings of Alois Müller. In a conclusion to his study of the Fathers on the unity between Mary and the Church, Müller distills what seems to him to be the essence of patristic theology about Mary and the Church: "Mary is the perfect (realization of the) Church, The essential mystery of the Church is the mystery of Mary."[67] The mystery is one of feminine, receptive collaboration in redemption. "The mystery of Eve is the mystery of Mary and the Church; the mystery of the Church is the mystery of Mary; and the mystery of Mary is the mystery of man's

---

[66] *Ibid.*, p. 60.

[67] A. Müller, *Ecclesia-Maria. Die Einheit Marias und der Kirche* (Freiburg in der Schweiz, 1951), p. 232. A second edition of this work appeared in 1955.

salvation, of the union with God that is given by God and received by the creature."⁶⁸ Mary stands on the side of mankind; as the Mother of the Saviour she is the most eminent member of the Church, the person most perfectly redeemed. She is rightly called our Coredemptrix, not in the sense that she, along with Christ, gives us salvation, but in the sense that she has "received" salvation from Christ in our name and for us.⁶⁹ The Blessed Virgin is placed at the head of receiving mankind because she is the summit of redeemed humanity; as such, she is the first and universal mediatress of salvation, the associate of the Saviour; but only in the way and in the measure in which the entire Church has this same function.⁷⁰

Müller's explanation places Mary on the side of men; it insists that her attitude in the presence of her Son is receptive like that of the Church, and that she distributes the graces of Redemption as the Church does. That is quite true; but we may not neglect other data that are well founded in revelation merely because they do not fit into a narrow framework. We are not justified in concluding that, because Mary is on the side of men, she cannot be the active associate of Christ. No such choice is imposed; we must retain both truths. We do not have to detach the Blessed Virgin from her Son in order to keep her close to us. She stands near Christ without letting us go; she is precisely the link that fetters us to Him. Her association with the Redeemer does not cut her off from us sinners.⁷¹

Undoubtedly, Christ alone is the origin and source of Redemption and of all grace. No theologian is tempted to duplicate the one Mediator. But this unique Mediator has willed to associate His Mother with Himself in effecting our Redemption. All she has, she has received from Him. Her attitude is receptive, certainly; but her co-operation is also productive. From Christ she has received a supernatural activity that cannot be reduced to a mere reception of the fruits of Redemption for subsequent distribution to the Church. This office has, of course, been

---

⁶⁸ *Ibid.*, p. 229.

⁶⁹ *Ibid.*, p. 218.

⁷⁰ A. Müller, *L'unité de l'Église et de la Sainte Vierge chez les Pères des IVe et Ve siècles*, in BSFEM, Vol. 9, 1951, p. 37.

⁷¹ Cf. G. Philips, *Perspectives mariologiques: Marie et l'Église*, in *Marianum*, Vol. 15, 1953, pp. 462-467.

given to her; but it flows from another that is more fundamental: she contributed actively to the acquisition of grace. Standing at the foot of the cross and having, like her Son, learned through painful experience what obedience is, she associated herself in the sacrifice and offered the Victim who belonged to her, His Mother. Yet it is true that she contributed to the sacrifice no element that did not have its source in this very immolation, and all her merits and her co-operation itself came to her from her Son. Thus she collaborated with the Saviour in a way that is both receptive and productive.

Accordingly, Müller's insistence about the place of Mary exclusively on the side of men is an incomplete expression of the truth; she also stands at the side of Christ. Extremist theories are easy to grasp, but the oversimplification involved in them exposes them to error. Depiction of the Saviour as a purely active principle, and of Mary or the Church as purely receptive, issues in an illusory clarity. Mary and the Church are, in their own order, active causes; and Christ is also receptive. He is Mediator in His humanity, and as man is indeed the active principle of salvation. But He began by consenting, accepting, and obeying; and so He continued to the end of His life.

2. Doctrine of Productive Coredemption

Theologians of the minimizing persuasion, with Köster, Semmelroth, and Müller at their head, share a common ambition. They seek to clarify the part played by Mary and the Church in our Redemption; particularly they desire to check a movement that has at times excessively assimilated the Blessed Virgin to Christ and that failed to relate her salvific role to the Church. In reaction against such deviations, they tend to detach Mary from Christ and to assimilate her excessively to the Church. This reaction has, in turn, stirred up a counterreaction; most contemporary Mariologists and ecclesiologists endeavor to eliminate all distortion, so as to leave intact Mary's active co-operation in the redemptive task of Christ. Victory over the champions of receptive Coredemption, though seemingly assured, is not yet completely won. Further studies directed to the solution of outstanding difficulties and the integration of all elements pertinent to the problem are needed. The future must provide them. Yet many contributions toward a solution have been offered. They bring into clearer light the truth that Mary, as representative and indeed as personification of the Church, collaborated with Christ in the three great steps of the mystery of Redemption: the Incarnation, the Cross, and the Resurrection. Both Mary and the Church have a mission in the economy of salvation; that of Mary was exercised on an *essentially* higher level, and is consequently far superior to that of the Church.

In the design of His wisdom, God has decreed that the eternal salvation of His intellectual creatures should involve their free cooperation. If He had so willed, He could have given His children all that they need without any concurrence on their part. But that is not His plan, either for the angels or for men. Even after man's fall, such collaboration is required. God, the source of grace, alone can reconcile sinful mankind with Himself; but He does not do so without man's free activity. This principle, strikingly formulated by St. Augustine,[72] is revealed in the scriptural imagery of a nuptial alliance proposed by God and accepted by man, the loving espousal between Christ and the Church,[73] foreshadowed by the marriage between Yahweh and Israel. In this matrimonial relationship, God is like the man, and humanity is like the woman; that is, the man symbolizes God's initiative and power, while the woman symbolizes mankind's receptivity and the fecundity which results from union with God.

The supreme realization of God's plan to save man by man is the redemptive Incarnation. God's own Son became man that the Redemption might be a human as well as a divine achievement; but from the outset He required the consent of the human race and the free donation of its flesh and blood. This consent and donation were given by Mary, who acted in the name of all mankind. Perfectly redeemed by preservation from every taint of sin, she cooperated in the Incarnation as Mother of the Saviour, and later, still as the divinely chosen representative of humanity, was taken into active association with the Redeemer in His sacrifice on the cross.

---

[72] *Serm.* 169, 11, 13, in *PL*, 38, 923: "Sine te fecit te Deus. Non enim adhibuisti aliquem consensum, ut te faceret Deus. ... Qui ergo fecit te sine te, non te iustificat sine te. Ergo fecit nescientem, iustificat volentem."

[73] Among many passages, cf. *Eph.* 5:22-32; *Apoc.* 19:7 f.; 21:2-9; 22:17; *Mt.* 9:15; 25:1-10.

During the first phase of her salvific activity (from the Incarnation to Pentecost), which is the foundation of all her subsequent offices on behalf of the human race, Mary preceded the Church, taking her place at the side of Christ to co-operate with Him in the accomplishment of our Redemption. The Son of God became man and in His person inaugurated the reunion of God with man; when the appointed hour arrived, the God-man saved the world by the sacrifice of His life. Mary collaborated actively, in both mysteries.[74]

In response to God's proposal, conveyed by the angel, Mary replied: "Behold the handmaid of the Lord." Her consent was given in the name of the whole human race: "loco totius humanae naturae," says St. Thomas,[75] and his many commentators have approved the formula as definitive. More important, the Angelic Doctor's insight has been consecrated by the teaching authority of the Church. "The eternal Son of God, when He wished to take man's nature to Himself and so contract a mystical marriage with the whole human race, did not do so before obtaining the perfectly free consent of the one chosen to be His Mother, who thus acted in the person of the human race itself."[76] "In the name of the entire human race, she gave her consent for a spiritual marriage between the Son of God and human nature."[77] Thus, in the mystery of the Incarnation, Christ the Redeemer, Bridegroom of the Church, and the Church personified in Mary, give themselves to each other out of obedience to the Father who decreed this salvific union.

According to all Catholic tradition, from the time of the early Fathers, Justin, Irenaeus, and Tertullian, the object of Mary's faith and consent was God's whole plan of salvation. Therefore, since Mary made her acts of faith and consent in the name of the entire Church, the Church, spouse of Christ, as personified in her, uttered its consent to its

---

[74] Cf. R. Laurentin, Rôle de Marie et de l'Église dans l'oeuvre salvifique du Christ, in BSFEM, Vol. 10, 1952, pp. 50-59.

[75] Summa theol., IIIa, q. 30, a. 1.

[76] Leo XIII, Encycl. Octobri mense, in A.S.S., Vol. 24, 1891-1892, p. 195.

[77] Pius XII, Encycl. Mystici Corporis Christi, in A.A.S., Vol. 35, 1953, p. 247. Mary's representative function has been studied extensively in a recent symposium published by the German Mariological Society, and edited by Prof. Carl Feckes under the title: Die heilsgeschichtliche Stellvertretung der Menschheit durch Maria (Paderborn, 1954).

own salvation and through her co-operated in its own Redemption.

Much more than mere receptivity is found in Mary's response to God. She was active spiritually, for she elicited an act of perfect faith. She was active in giving her consent, both interiorly and exteriorly, as evidenced by her words, "Behold the handmaid of the Lord," which expressed her active and definitive adherence to God's plan. Of necessity she was active physically, by conceiving her divine Son and continuing, for nine months, to form the Saviour's body that would be immolated on the cross and the blood that would be shed for our Redemption.

The activity exercised by the Blessed Virgin at the time of the conception and birth of Christ was carried on all during her life in faithful correspondence with divine grace, and achieved its climax on Calvary.

At the time of the Incarnation, Mary represented the Church, and in the name of mankind pronounced the words that express our desire for redemption. But we may not say that from then on Christ simply represents God and that the Blessed Virgin represents the human race. For Christ Himself perfectly represents mankind; though a divine Person, He is the perfect man. His redemptive actions and sufferings are human; in the crucified Christ all humanity, embraced by Him who is our head, offers to God a human reparation for human sin, although He who offers the sacrifice is God.

What, then, remains for Mary? Has her presence on Calvary any redemptive meaning? The Incarnate Word fully represents humanity; but by God's will, Mary represents aspects of humanity which Christ did not assume. She represents the mere creature, whereas Christ is the Creator; she is a human person, whereas Christ is a divine person; she represents the redeemed, for Christ is not redeemed.[78] On Calvary, therefore, by the will of God, Mary represents the co-operation of the redeemed in their own redemption, the union and fellowship of the faithful with their Saviour.

In His supreme hour of sacrifice, the Redeemer draws His Mother into His vast suffering to associate her in His redeeming act. He receives her dedication, love, and merits, and integrates her agony into His own passion, to offer them all to the Father, who accepts her co-operation

---

[78] Cf. R. Laurentin, *art. cit.*, p. 54.

along with the Son's operation to grant reconciliation to the world.

Although Mary acts in solidarity with Christ, her solidarity with our race is not in any way impaired but is immensely enhanced. She acts on our behalf; as the representative of us who need redemption, she unites us all to the redemptive act itself.

Her very maternity over us acquires a new perfectfon by reason of her suffering. Her first childbearing, which made her the Mother of God, was without pain; her second childbearing, by which she became fully the mother of us sinners, was painful in the extreme. Wounded in her divine maternity by the death of her only Son, she offered her grievous sufferings, along with her Son, for the salvation of mankind. While the Son offered Himself for the Redemption of us all, who are responsible for His death, His Mother made her oblation for the same purpose and, co-operating in our birth to supernatural life, became the mother of the Church that issued from the Saviour's side.

Mary's contribution to the work of Redemption far surpasses that of the Church. Not only did she precede the Church during the mortal life of Christ, but she was integrated into the very foundation of salvation, the very Passion that procured our reconciliation with God. She co-operated in the birth of the Church, not merely by giving human nature to the Saviour, but by suffering with Him. She who was one with Him at the Incarnation, was one with Him at the moment of Redemption. But the activity of the Church is exercised in the *application* of the merits and atonement of Calvary. Mary was associated with our Redemption at its beginning and achievement, whereas the Church is associated with it according to its successive realization in time and place. By her *fiat*, never recalled but rather growing in intensity as her understanding of God's redemptive plan matured in her mind, she united us all to the redemptive act of the one Mediator, for that *fiat* was uttered in our name. By her universal merit she shared, in subordinate fashion, in the Saviour's quality of universal cause of grace. At the Redemption, as at the Incarnation, the activity of the Mother of God unfolded in an order (the hypostatic order) and on a level (the level of objective Redemption) essentially higher than that of the Church. In itself, the Church does not enter this order and cannot rise to this level; but it does so in the person of Mary, who preceded it and represented it as she stood with Christ.

A second phase of Mary's salvific mission in the Church extended from Pentecost to the Assumption. During this period Mary lived in the Church and co-operated in the application of the Redemption by her prayers and merits. She had preceded the Church but was now in the Church, a woman effaced in the multitude, without official voice in its councils. Like all the other members of the Church, she was submissive to the authority of the apostolic hierarchy, as she had always been submissive to God.

However, although she possessed no office and occupied no position of authority, she was still the first and most important member of the Church. Her hand did not hold the keys of the Kingdom, but her prayers sustained the apostles' hands that had them, and her hidden activity induced many a person to come knocking at the door. She conferred no sacraments; but their power derives from the sacrifice of the Cross, in which she co-operated.

Finally, the third and last phase of her mediatorial activity, enduring from her Assumption to the assumption of the whole Church into heaven, put an end to her temporary obscurity. Now, as at the beginning, she again precedes the Church, assists it with supernatural aid, and awaits its eventual triumph.

The mystery of Christ's resurrection and ascension is the glorious culmination of the mystery of redemption. The entire Church is implicated in this mystery, and has inaugurated its own resurrection in its head. Mary has actually arisen and has attained her total glorification. Her assumption is full of meaning for all of us. At the end of the world the Church will arise in all its members at once. But this final resurrection of the collective Church is personified in Mary, whose resurrection is the prelude of the future bodily victory of the rest of us.

The Mother of God is now in heaven. The Church is also in heaven, in many of its members who are the saints. They all pray for us and our countless needs, thus continuing to carry out the divine plan of associating the creature with the Creator. Mary is not merely one intercessor among others. By the efficacy and universality of her activity she is first and above all others; her prayer is more powerful than the prayers of the whole Church.

Her activity in heaven is the prolongation of her function of representing and personifying the Church at the various stages of our Redemption. In the name of us all, she welcomed the Saviour who came on earth to save us; in the name of us all, she actively co-operated with the Redeemer in the mystery of Calvary. Rightfully now, in the name of the Church, she shares in the mystery of the risen Christ and obtains for her children, everyone of whom she knows personally, all the graces that sanctify them.

Her coredemptive activity, obviously, has no lacuna to cover up in the redemptive work of her Son. All she has, she has received from Christ; yet her mission was never one of mere receptivity, for she was and is intensely productive. What she received was power to act and co-operate with the Redeemer for the salvation of mankind. She stands next to the Redeemer, not as redemptress, but as Coredemptress subordinate to Him, and she can act only under His initiative and in dependence on Him. But dependence does not exclude productivity. Her redemptive office is wholly derived from Christ, for it is the collaboration of a subordinate associate, which supposes His activity as principal cause, with whom, however, she truly acts.

Accordingly, Mary's coredemptive mission was not simply passive, as Christ's own mission was not wholly active.[79] Christ, too, received and consented. He received from His Father His office, His doctrine, His work, and all the gifts He was to diffuse. If the Incarnation is a mystical marriage, consent is required not only from the bride (which is human nature, not Mary, even though Mary lent her voice to mankind), but also from the Bridegroom. According to St. Thomas, no grace, not even the grace in which the first man was created, is conferred without the free acceptance of the recipient.[80] Christ's capital grace, of whose fullness we have all received, is no exception. The Son's first words addressed to the Father on entering the world, "Behold I come ... it is written of me that I should do thy will, O God" (Hebr. 10:7), have their echo in Mary's reply to the angel: "Behold the handmaid of the Lord; be it done to me according to thy word." Both the Son and the Mother received, both

---

[79] Cf. G. Philips, *Sommes-nous entrés dans une phase mariologique?*, in Marianum, Vol. 14, 1952, p. 24.

[80] *Summa theol.*, Ia, q. 95, a. 1 ad 5.

consented, and both acted.[81]

CONCLUSION

In God's eternal plan, the salvation of fallen mankind is accomplished through His Church, which entered the world in His Son Jesus Christ, therefore through Mary. "God appeared in the form of a man to renew eternal life; then what had been decided by God began to be fulfilled."[82] But the mystery of mankind's union with God which is effected in the Church, is first and most perfectly realized in the Saviour's own Mother, who is at once a symbol and a cause of our supernatural regeneration.

The more a person allows himself to be occupied by God, the more that person, without relinquishing his individuality, is divinely transformed. By freely consenting to be the Mother of the Redeemer, Mary allowed herself to be totally taken over by God. Union with God, the alliance of love, was more perfectly achieved in her than in any other creature. God had His way with her completely and, meeting with no trace of resistance on her part, fully conformed her to the image of His Son.[83] And Christ, from whom Mary received her whole spiritual life that assimilated her to Him, is in turn the image of His Mother, from whom He received His human features along with the human nature she imparted to Him.

Furthermore, the Church is the body of Christ, His prolongation here on earth; hence the Church, too, reflects the image of the Incarnate Word, and in its salvific mission continues His redemptive career. Therefore the Church, through the humanity of Christ, is necessarily assimilated to Mary, who is spiritually one with the Church as she is one with her Son. Both Mary and the Church are conformed to Christ, and through Christ are assimilated to each other. All the divine life that abounds in the Church is present in Mary in superabundance, as the effect is present in its cause, for she, the Mother of Christ, is also mother

---

[81] Cf. H. Barré, C.S.Sp., *Le consentement à l'Incarnation rédemptrice. La Vierge seule, ou le Christ d'abord?*, in *Marianum*, Vol. 14, 1952, pp. 223-266.

[82] St. Ignatius of Antioch, *Epist. ad Ephesios*, 19, in *PG*, 5, 660.

[83] "Whom he foreknew, he also predestinated to be made conformable to the image of his Son" (*Rom.* 8:29).

of the Church.

Fittingly, then, Mary is celebrated as the prototype of the Church, its first and best realization. She is the ideal personification of the Church, the perfect model of the perfection to which the Church aspires. She is the Church in microcosm but is better than it; she represents the utmost limit to which the Church constantly tends but which it can never reach, the ideal and perfect figure in which the Church can see what Christ requires of it and what He desires it to be. She surpasses the Church more than in mere degree, because she pertains to a higher order, as is shown by her Immaculate Conception, her divine maternity, her active and productive cooperation with the Saviour in objective Redemption, and her Assumption. She is more than the type of the Church; she is its transcendent archetype, both as redeemed and as redeeming.

> The Blessed Mother of God who, like us, is descended from Adam, has no privilege or grace that does not come from her Son, Redeemer of the human race. ... The gifts which the Son has showered on His Mother are so great that they immeasurably surpass the gifts and graces of all men and angels, since there can never be a dignity that exceeds or equals the divine maternity. ... Although it is true that the Blessed Virgin is a member of the Church, as we also are, it is no less true that she is an absolutely unique member of the mystical body of Christ.[84]

Therefore the analogies between Mary and the Church which theology, drawing on Scripture and tradition, tries to apprehend, involve fundamental differences. The similarities never coincide but always suppose an excess in favor of the Blessed Virgin. Our Lady's superiority is summed up in her first and basic relation to the Church: she is the mother of the Church. And this maternity flows from her divine maternity. To penetrate into the depths of the mystery of Mary and the Church, we must, in the last analysis, come back to this truth. The fact that she is the Mother of God, associated with the Saviour in His mission of Redemption, accounts for the consequent fact that she is the mother of the Church, and is the foundation of all the analogies that enable us to draw Mary and the Church together in the same vision. When we bear in mind that the Blessed Virgin is the Mother of Christ and, by

---

[84] Pius XII, radio message to the International Marian Congress in Rome, October 24, 1954, in *A.A.S.*, Vol. 46, 1954, p. 679.

extension, the mother of His body which is the Church, we perceive without peril of error that her perfections elevate her to a height which the Church can never attain, and moreover that the Church, which has been confided to her by God, cannot mount up toward that height without her constant aid and maternal love.